A Terrible Thing to Waste

To Ellie—
Words don't do it.
You're the rock
of the history
department
and a
true
friend.
Thanks so much!

A Terrible Thing to Waste

Arthur Fletcher and the Conundrum

of the Black Republican

DAVID HAMILTON GOLLAND

UNIVERSITY PRESS OF KANSAS

G.S.U. 5.9.19

Zelda Rose Golland

David Gollands

son

Published by the University Press of Kansas (Lawrence, Kansas 66045), which was organized by the Kansas Board of Regents and is operated and funded by Emporia State University, Fort Hays State University, Kansas State University, Pittsburg State University, the University of Kansas, and Wichita State University

Library of Congress Cataloging-in-Publication Data is available.

ISBN 978-0-7006-2764-6 (cloth)
ISBN 978-0-7006-2765-3 (ebook)

British Library Cataloguing-in-Publication Data is available.

Printed in the United States of America
10 9 8 7 6 5 4 3 2 1

The paper used in this publication is recycled and contains 30 percent postconsumer waste. It is acid free and meets the minimum requirements of the American National Standard for Permanence of Paper for Printed Library Materials Z39.48–1992.

For my parents, stepparents, and parents-in-law
and
In memory of Steven A. Levine, Cindy R. Lobel, and
Paul D. Naish, brilliant historians we lost too soon

CONTENTS

INTRODUCTION

My . . . conservative friends know the cost of everything but the value of nothing. My . . . liberal friends know the privilege of freedom, but they think its cost is free, that it's yours for the taking. Not so.
—Arthur Fletcher, circa 1996

Until recently, Arthur Allen Fletcher, the self-styled "father of affirmative action enforcement" who helped coin the phrase "a mind is a terrible thing to waste," has been largely left out of treatments on the civil rights era. Most who know the broad outlines of his story have not known quite what to make of this civil rights politician who remained loyal to the Republican Party despite its gradual abandonment of the principles he espoused.

The life of Arthur Fletcher represents the triumph, tragedy, and conundrum of the postwar Black Republican. In 1946, when he returned home after World War II, the Republican Party was the party of Lincoln, a big tent, truly welcoming of African Americans. In 1960 its presidential platform was stronger on civil rights than that of the Democrats. But the New Right conservatism, epitomized by Barry Goldwater's 1964 presidential candidacy and President Richard M. Nixon's Southern Strategy, steadily alienated Black voters. Ronald Reagan appealed to unreconstructed white southerners and the northern white working class, for whom the achievements of the civil rights era represented a loss of privilege. Whereas Fletcher triumphantly implemented affirmative action during the early Nixon administration, his ability to promote civil rights policy tragically eroded in the years that followed despite his constant loyalty and continued presidential appointments. Since 1980, African Americans who are right of center on issues other than civil rights have faced a conundrum: support Democrats with whom they agree on civil rights but little else, or stick with a Republican Party from which they have been steadily alienated.

Arthur Fletcher was born in poverty to a single mother in Phoenix, Arizona, in 1924, and went on to advise four United States presidents—Richard

Nixon, Gerald Ford, Ronald Reagan, and George H. W. Bush. As assistant secretary of labor in the Nixon administration he implemented the Philadelphia Plan, the first major national affirmative action initiative. He later served as chairman of the Commission on Civil Rights in the first Bush administration. Along the way, he was wounded in Europe during World War II; advised the legal team for the *Brown v. Board* case; was the first Black player for the Baltimore Colts football team; endured the suicide of his first wife and the disintegration of his family; lost a close race for lieutenant governor of Washington State (while campaigning with former child actress Shirley Temple and employing as his driver the future serial killer Ted Bundy); stared down the Soviet representative to the United Nations on the issue of refuseniks; led the United Negro College Fund (UNCF) through a major transformation; took on Marion Barry in the first open election for mayor of Washington, DC; and ran for the 1996 Republican presidential nomination to protest the party's abandonment of his signature policy achievement, affirmative action.

Biographies of civil rights figures tend to follow a familiar narrative arc: early exposure to the scourge of Jim Crow; a youthful first protest; a gradual rise to influence demonstrating both intelligence and patriotic bona fides (to deflect the charge of communism); a climactic period in the spotlight; and then a long decline (or early tragedy). Although Fletcher had a number of experiences that would seem to fit this arc, his overall story is an exception.

Fletcher's early exposure to Jim Crow came from witnessing his mother's employment as a maid despite her training as a schoolteacher. His youthful first protest was a boycott of his high school yearbook; Black students refused to sit for portraits at their integrated school, which placed their photos after those of white students. His gradual rise to influence began with a GI Bill–funded college education and culminated in his appointment as assistant secretary of labor. His climactic period was his implementation and defense of the Philadelphia Plan, after which he called himself the father of affirmative action enforcement. His long decline followed his removal from the Nixon administration, which had deprioritized civil rights, and lasted until his death in 2005 at age eighty.

It is the deviations from the set story arc that make the Fletcher story compelling. He was raised in the segregated military in the Southwest, which provided a far more sheltered environment than life as the child of a Mississippi sharecropper or Atlanta preacher. He became a Republican when the most important civil rights leader of his generation—Martin Luther King Jr.—eschewed partisanship, and he remained so even as the leading light of the next—Jesse Jackson—became active in Democratic politics. His first political foray fell flat after he hitched his wagon to a corrupt politician—and flirted with similar venality himself. His rise to influence was further interrupted in 1960 after his wife's suicide. It was the many negative experiences he had in the first half of his life—both because of Jim Crow and coincidental to it—that made him the sort of civil rights leader who could work both inside and outside the system, combining political skills with organizational ones. He was as comfortable in the party meeting or corporate boardroom as he was in the ghetto street, church pulpit, backyard barbecue, or protest picket line. His climactic period took place during what was only the first of an eventual six presidential appointments; his supposed decline included dramatic achievements reported in the national press—especially when he became chairman of the United States Commission on Civil Rights—punctuated by long periods out of the spotlight. He was still starting new civil rights projects well into his seventies as he steadfastly fought the Republican Party's growing hostility to the causes he championed.

The story of Arthur Fletcher fills a gap in a growing body of historical and sociological research on Black Republicans. These include Leah Wright Rigueur's *Loneliness of the Black Republican* (Princeton University Press, 2015), which recounts the important but understudied role of liberal and moderate Black Republicans during the era of the New Deal order. She makes a decent case for Fletcher having led a Black cabinet in the Nixon administration, and an even more compelling one for his having remained an important and revered figure among Black Republicans through the 1970s. Her analysis concludes with the rise of Reaganism, which she depicts as triumphant for a new cadre of Black conservatives; I argue that these Black conservatives were a different group than Fletcher's ilk, and that Reagan's election, rather than a triumph for Black Republicanism, in fact represents a shift of power from leaders like Fletcher to the new order in which antipathy to affirmative action serves as a litmus test. Joshua D. Farrington, meanwhile, in *Black Republicans and the Transformation of the GOP* (University of Pennsylvania Press, 2016), depicts Black Republicans as a middle- and upper-class faction within state and local party organizations, siding with the eastern establishment wing and fighting to determine their direction in the postwar era. He sees the shift against civil rights within the party as beginning with the Nixon nomination in 1960, despite the pro–civil rights platform propounded by the party that year, but agrees that Reaganism and its triumphs provoked the party's eventual renunciation of civil rights issues. Timothy N. Thurber's *Republicans and Race* (University Press of Kansas, 2013) chronicles how the Republican Party moved from being the party of Lincoln to embracing Nixon's Southern Strategy in the three decades after World War II. For Thurber, New Deal–era Republican leaders were never quite as welcoming of Black voices so much as willing to exploit a northern Black electorate leery of a Democratic Party with such deep roots in the segregationist South; with the passage of the Civil Rights Act of 1964 and the eventual move of conservative white southerners into the Republican Party, fewer Black voters, let alone Black politicians, were comfortable in the GOP. *Black Elephants in the Room* (University of California Press, 2016), by sociologist Corey D. Fields, illuminates the current conundrum of the Black Republican: seen as traitors by fellow African Americans for their adherence to a party actively bent on voter suppression and other anti–civil rights activities, today's Black Republicans are likewise distrusted by their white counterparts and are quick to decry affirmative action to demonstrate party loyalty. The distance between Rigueur, Farrington, and Thurber on the one hand, who conclude their work with the rise of the Reaganites, and Fields, who picks up the story in the twenty-first century, is vast. The crucial shift among Black Republicans—the eclipse of those who fought for civil rights by conservatives who decried affirmative action—took place during that missing quarter century, the last third of Fletcher's life. In fact, Fletcher was the last prominent Black Republican to publicly support affirmative action, and recounting his vigorous activities after 1980 in politics and policy allows us to explore this shift.

The postwar rise of conservatism, and its subsequent takeover of the Republican Party, has been well chronicled. The field was pioneered by George Nash's *The Conservative Intellectual Movement in America since 1945* (Basic Books, 1976) and has continued lately with *Invisible Hands: The Making of the Conservative Movement from the New Deal to Reagan*, by Kim Phillips-Fein (Norton, 2009); *The Roots of Modern Conservatism: Dewey, Taft, and the Battle for the Soul of the Republican Party*, by Michael Bowen (University of North Carolina Press, 2011); *Creating Conservatism: Postwar Words That Made an American Movement*, by Michael J. Lee (Michigan State University Press, 2014); and *The World of the John Birch Society* by D. J. Mulloy (Vanderbilt University Press, 2014), among others. Journalist Rick Perlstein has popularized the topic in a trilogy of books: *Before the Storm: Barry Goldwater and the Unmaking of the American Consensus* (Hill & Wang, 2001); *Nixonland: The Rise of a President and the Fracturing of America* (Scribner, 2008); and *The Invisible Bridge: The Fall of Nixon and the Rise of Reagan*

(Simon & Schuster, 2014). Geoffrey Kabaservice, meanwhile, in *Rule and Ruin: The Downfall of Moderation and the Destruction of the Republican Party* (Oxford, 2012), has told the same story from the perspective of the moderates. Whereas for Thurber the southern segregationists who joined the GOP in the years after 1964 proved to be the tail that wagged the Republican dog, Kabaservice shows that the rise in conservative numbers in the party paralleled a simultaneous decline in moderates. With the Democratic Party freed from its southern segregationist roots, Republican moderates felt free to switch to a party that better represented their own interests, especially after the rise of Bill Clinton and the moderate Democratic Leadership Council.

There has also been scholarship on the new Black conservatives who replaced civil rights liberals like Arthur Fletcher. Peter Eisenstadt, seeking to demonstrate a big tent in *Black Conservatism: Essays in Intellectual and Political History* (Garland Publishing, 1999), tried to lump into the conservative camp every Black political thinker who saw value in the American republic, taking even the hint of agreement with Booker T. Washington as evidence of conservatism. One of that volume's essayists, Paula F. Pfeffer, even went so far as to include avowed leftists like Bayard Rustin and A. Philip Randolph because they didn't approve of the tactics of Stokely Carmichael and H. Rap Brown. New Right Black conservativism, on the other hand, has been discussed recently by Michael L. Ondaatje in *Black Conservative Intellectuals in Modern America* (University of Pennsylvania Press, 2010) and by Ralph A. Rossum in *Understanding Clarence Thomas: The Jurisprudence of Constitutional Restoration* (University Press of Kansas, 2014). While informative, however, they do not delve into the conundrum exemplified by otherwise right-of-center civil rights liberals.

I tell the story of Arthur Fletcher's life over seven chapters, which follow two major story lines of twentieth-century African American history. The first of these story lines is that of the civil rights era of the 1950s and 1960s. The traditional narrative is that Black veterans grew up under Jim Crow and, upon returning home from the war, refused to accept their continuing relegation to second-class status. Joining with sympathetic whites, they built a movement to overturn that system, starting with the *Brown v. Board* decision and continuing with the Montgomery bus boycott and Freedom Rides. The next generation came of age in the 1960s, took over organizations like the Congress of Racial Equality, and engaged in violent urban rebellions, forcing the federal government to pass revolutionary civil rights legislation. While there are significant problems with this narrative, as detailed by my own first book[1] and the recent work of a number of other scholars, the first half of Arthur Fletcher's life had several elements that fit the narrative, as I chronicle in the first three chapters.

The second major story line is the decline of African American influence in Fletcher's Republican Party during the 1970s and 1980s. Nixon's Southern Strategy and Reagan's New Right took advantage of the increasing association of the Democratic Party with the cause of civil rights, and built a new Republican coalition thanks to a white backlash in the South and among suburbanites and skilled workers (so-called Reagan Democrats). As liberal and moderate Blacks increasingly voted for Democratic candidates, Black Republicans lost influence. Scholars like Rigueur and Farrington use this transition narrative as a raison d'être for their work analyzing Black Republicans during the preceding period. The history is, of course, not as clean and clear as this narrative suggests, and the Fletcher story allows me to explore and problematize it in Chapters 5, 6, and 7.

Chapter 4, at the center of the book, serves as the linchpin between these two narratives, the turning point for both the civil rights movement and Black Republicanism. It chronicles Fletcher's service as assistant secretary of labor during the Nixon administration, during which he launched and promoted the Revised Philadelphia Plan, a comprehensive affirmative action program requiring federal government contractors and unions to make a good-faith effort to meet integration goals. Here we see not only the culmination of the first narrative, where Fletcher built on the successes of the civil rights era, but also the beginning of the second, when President Nixon and his closest advisors jettisoned Fletcher and his ideas in favor of a Northern version of the Southern Strategy. Nixon's decision to transfer Fletcher from the Department of Labor to an innocuous job at the United Nations was a microcosm for the eventual collective decision by Republican leaders to abandon civil rights initiatives altogether.

This project is the culmination of more than eight years of work. I was fortunate to have the advice of Professor Joshua Freeman of Queens College, who served on my dissertation committee at the City University of New York Graduate Center. In a conversation during that earlier project, he asked, "Why don't you write a biography of Arthur Fletcher?" My reply—half in jest because at that time I did not know even whether my dissertation would be published—was "maybe for my second book." And now here we are.

My dissertation advisor, Clarence Taylor of Baruch College, has likewise remained encouraging, as have Martin Burke of Lehman College, David Nasaw of the CUNY Graduate Center, and Brian Purnell of Bowdoin

College. I continue to cherish advice from members of my old dissertation study group, most of whom are now tenured historians: David Aliano of the College of Mount St. Vincent; Jacob Kramer of Borough of Manhattan Community College (BMCC); Alejandro Quintana of St. John's University; Vava Roczniak of Bronx Community College; Joseph Sramek of Southern Illinois University, Carbondale; and Alex Stavropoulos of Mercy College. Kris Burrell of Hostos Community College and Kevin McGruder of Antioch College read every chapter and gave insightful commentary, as did my father, Jeffrey Golland of New York's Mount Sinai Health System. Rachael Goldman of BMCC transcribed an early interview with Fletcher's surviving children. Thanks also to Hillel Swiller, Phil Luloff, and the reading group at the Mount Sinai Division of Psychotherapy for their insightful observations, especially pertaining to Fletcher's early years. Special thanks are also due to Margaret, Chris, and Rania Calas, who know why.

At Governors State University I have been fortunate to have an administration dedicated to fostering scholarship, coupled with the regular encouragement of colleagues. Provost Deborah Bordelon (now at Columbus State University in Georgia) authorized travel and research grants; Dean Reinhold Hill (now vice chancellor of Indiana University–Purdue University Columbus) authorized scholarly reassigned time every year and recommended my tenure. Benjamin Almassi, Sayoni Bose, Daniel Cortese, Donald Culverson, Jayne Goode, James Howley, Debbie James, Elizabeth Johnson (now at Indiana University Northwest), William Kresse, Kerri Morris, Lydia Morrow Ruetten, Rashidah Muhammad, Jelena Radovic-Fanta, Joshua Sopiarz, Elizabeth Todd-Breland (now at the University of Illinois at Chicago), Stephen Wagner, Ellen Walsh, Nicole Warmington-Granston, Barbara Winicki, and most importantly Andrae Marak have helped create an academic environment conducive to work of this sort. Lana and I leaned on family friend Giggy Wagner for childcare far more often than was reasonable to ask.

Outstanding archivists included Mary Finch at the George Bush Presidential Library in College Station; Morgan Davis and Sarah D'Antonio at the Robert J. Dole Institute of Politics in Lawrence; Christian Goos, Nancy E. Mirshah, and Jeremy P. Schmidt at the Gerald R. Ford Presidential Library in Ann Arbor; Eric Van Slander and Ross Phillips at the National Archives in College Park; Ryan Pettigrew at the Richard Nixon Presidential Library in Yorba Linda; Vanessa Williamson and David B. Snyder at the US Commission on Civil Rights Rankin Memorial Library; Steven Fisher at the University of Denver; Jenny Mandel at the Ronald Reagan Presidential Library in Simi Valley; and Virginia Butler, Brittany Grace, and Dana Simmons at the

William J. Clinton Presidential Library in Little Rock. Mary Frances Berry, George H. W. Bush (through his lawyer, Jim McGrath), Robert Dole, Daniel Evans, Nat Jackson, Samuel Reed, Eddie Rye Jr., and Charles Pei Wang kindly shared their recollections of Art Fletcher.

Mark Peterson, professor emeritus of political science at Art's alma mater, Washburn University, generously provided the primary source research for his 2011 *Kansas History* article on Art's early years, Art's funeral video, and the video and transcript of Art's exhaustive 2003 interview with the Washburn University political science department; arranged lodging for my visit to Kansas; gave me a tour of the *Brown v. Board* sites, Junction City, and Fort Riley; and read and commented on several chapters. Likewise, John C. Hughes, historian of the Washington Office of the Secretary of State and biographer of Fletcher's 1968 running mate, Slade Gorton, was a model of scholarly collaboration, sharing primary sources and personal recollections. Longtime Fletcher family friend Kathy Keolker, whom Art and his second wife, Bernyce, considered a daughter, graciously gave me an interview, a tour of Pasco, and copious additional documents, including her personal correspondence with Bernyce.

This book would have been very different (and a good deal shorter) without the support of the Fletcher family, who have made themselves unfailingly available without attempting to influence its tone or conclusions. Phyllis Fletcher, Arthur's granddaughter by his youngest son Phillip, is an NPR radio personality in Seattle. She provided me with her own research on her father, Phillip, and gave me an early introduction to Art's personal life. Sylvia Fletcher, Art's only surviving daughter, sat for an important interview and was incredibly generous with her recollections of her mother's final hours. Patsy Mose Fletcher, Art's daughter-in-law, is a Washington, DC–based scholar and civil rights leader in her own right; our informal conversations at a Seattle conference and at the bar at DC's now-defunct Channel Inn were informative and insightful. Joan Fletcher, Art's adoptive daughter, and her daughter, Onna Harrison, arranged my initial access to Art's personal papers in his former house on G Street Southwest in DC.

Paul Fletcher, Art's only surviving son, has been the single most important advisor to the project. He sat for several interviews, attended the launch of my first book, and has given me much food for thought about his dad in countless conversations over the years. After he took possession of his father's papers, he and I worked closely with a team of assistants (Mercedes Chuquisengo Vazquez, Gabriel and Benjamin Sarmiento, and filmmakers H. "Lee" and Leslie Sullivan and Allen Elfman) for two weeks in the summer of 2014 to digitize the collection. I described this project in my essay "Digitizing the Fletcher Papers: A Unique Historical Experience" (*Perspectives on History*, April 2015). The 20,000-odd documents represent more than four fifths of the total sources consulted for this project.

I would also like to thank the fantastic staff at the University Press of Kansas, especially David Congdon, Michael Kehoe, and Larisa Martin, as well as peer reviewer Joshua Farrington and the anonymous peer reviewer. Of course, the mistakes are mine alone.

Not one word, not one letter, could have been written without the unfailing support of the love of my life, Lana Rogachevskaya. While simultaneously constructing her own successful career in arts administration, she has seen me through every challenge, from my first halting efforts in Charlottesville, to completion of my dissertation at the CUNY Grad Center, to publication of my first book, and most recently through the intense writing year that resulted in the current volume. Outside of myself and the extended Fletcher family, she now knows more about Art Fletcher than anyone—far more than she signed up for. Art Fletcher has likewise been a constant presence in the lives of our children, Zelda and Jerry, who are unique among their classmates in knowing more about him than they do his more famous contemporary, Dr. King.

Last, I must thank Arthur Fletcher. Thank you, Art, for doing everything I recount in this book, and so much more. The story of your life is humbling. I wish I had met you. I have done my best to give your achievements the attention they were too often denied. I hope this book will add to your legacy and help this nation live up to the promise of our founding creed: that we are all created equal.

CHAPTER ONE

ORIGINS, 1924–1945

They were having a heck of a time knocking me down.
—Arthur Fletcher, 2003

On June 26, 2005, an eighty-year-old man ascended the steps of Mother Bethel African Methodist Episcopal Church in Philadelphia, one of the oldest Black churches in the United States. Tall and broad-shouldered, his build alone did not betray his former vigor, but the close observer might have discerned a hint of the football player and soldier in his step: more spry than it should have been, as if the youth was trying to escape the prison of the old man. Within the church, only the handful of parishioners who had invited him up from his home in Washington, DC, recognized him. Perhaps they knew him as the former head of the United Negro College Fund (UNCF) who had launched the slogan "A mind is a terrible thing to waste," or perhaps as the former chairman of the United States Commission on Civil Rights who had bravely denounced his good friend, the president of the United States, for vetoing a civil rights bill. But most of the congregants had little idea who this old man was, and little knowledge of the many and myriad ways his life had profoundly shaped theirs. His name was Arthur Allen Fletcher, and he had come to Philadelphia to deliver a speech on his signature achievement, affirmative action.[1]

The next morning he walked over to the Independence Visitor Center, a few yards from the Liberty Bell, in the shadow of Benjamin Franklin's statue and Independence Hall, to deliver what would be the last speech of his life. The timing and location were poignant and historical, and he knew it. It was the anniversary of another speech he had given in the City of Brotherly Love, thirty-six years earlier, when he had come to town as assistant secretary of the Department of Labor to sign the Philadelphia Plan, the nation's first affirmative action enforcement policy. The Philadelphia Plan required government contractors to make a good-faith effort to hire skilled Black construction workers, who until then had been almost completely excluded by the unions that controlled hiring. As the old presidential adviser strolled up Independence Mall, his thoughts surely turned to that 1969 speech. His topic today, as it had been so often during these last few years, was the successes and failures of affirmative action in the three decades since its implementation. In the wake of a Supreme Court decision that had barely left affirmative action intact, Fletcher worried that time was running out to deliver on the promise of equal employment opportunity.

The location was as apt for Fletcher's principles as it was for his accomplishments. The promise of equal opportunity seemed physically embedded in Philadelphia's historical attractions. Independence Hall and the Liberty Bell represented for the old man the essence of the American dream, with all its great potential and promise. He cherished the words written there: "We hold these truths to be self-evident, that all men are created equal, that they are endowed by their Creator with certain inalienable Rights, that among these are Life, Liberty and the pursuit of Happiness.—That to secure these rights, Governments are instituted among Men, deriving their just powers from the consent of the governed." These fifty-six words encapsulated everything that Fletcher stood for: the idea that men and women could come together and form a government to safeguard an inalienable right to equality. He had always seen himself as the equal of any white man, no matter what pernicious Jim Crow laws and traditions might stand in his way. And he believed that involvement in a democratic government was the best way to tackle the problem of race in America.

The location was also poignant in a more personal way. The church he attended that Sunday, Mother Bethel, was founded by another proud independent Black man, one from an earlier era. Fletcher claimed descent (through his birth father, whom he never knew) from Bishop Richard Allen, who founded Mother Bethel in 1794 and later, in 1816, helped start the AME denomination.

As Arthur Fletcher prepared for his final speech, sitting in the pews that Sunday and strolling up Independence Mall the next morning, his thoughts surely also turned to his youth, his long-dead mother and older brother, and the adoptive father who had given him his name. He likely thought of his childhood at the opposite end of the country, far from the colonial facades of historical Philadelphia. Fletcher's life began out on the frontier of the arid Southwest, the land of the Comanche and the Apache and the Navajo, of the Santa Fe Railroad and the buffalo soldier. Fletcher's story began not in the era of affirmative action and legal equality but at a time when, as he put it, the cup of civil rights was empty—when a little Black boy was given little, and expected even less.

Edward Arthur Allen

Edna Miller gave birth to her second son, Edward Arthur Allen, on December 22, 1924, in Phoenix, Arizona. Little is known about the child's father, Samuel Brit Allen, other than that he disappeared from Edna's life shortly thereafter, never to return. His name, however, and Edna's church activism, subsequently gave his son to claim that he was descended from or somehow related to Bishop Richard Allen. More is known about Edna's first son, Earl Harris, born in 1922, although not his last name or his paternity; he was only the new baby's half-brother.[2]

Early sources for the boy who became Arthur Allen Fletcher are sparse, as they are for nearly everyone born outside of the families of the rich or famous at that time. We have a handful of faded photographs, but for the most part we must rely on information gleaned from speeches and interviews Fletcher gave and forms he completed later in his life. These are more valuable, however, for the insights they give on the formation of his identity than for their veracity. The truthfulness of the stories he told about his childhood rests more in what they say about the man he became than what they tell us about the child he had been. The formation of his identity, captured in the stories that he repeated to himself and to diverse audiences throughout the long period in his life when he had audiences, gives us insight into his decisions and activities of that later period.[3]

One such story, often told to journalists and interviewers, juxtaposed his mother's education with her actual employment. Despite her training as a schoolteacher and as a nurse, she cleaned other people's homes. This was why she left her children with a series of other families during the formative years of their development.[4] In a 1969 speech, Fletcher said,

> I would ask you to picture in your mind's eye a young mother who has arrived at a cotton field, back in 1929 . . . because she and her husband have separated, she has left her son with a family to take care of him while she goes and works as a domestic in the services of a family. She . . . has a bachelor's degree in education, and is a registered nurse, but there are no nursing jobs for people with her capability, back in 1929, so she was using her skill, if you will, as a domestic servant.[5]

One problem with this statement is that Fletcher acknowledged in a 2004 interview that his "mother had [him] out of wedlock," which contradicts the statement that "she and her husband have separated." Was Edna Miller ever married to Samuel Allen? No wedding certificate survives, or any document referring to her as Edna Allen, so we cannot be sure. There is copious documentation referring to her as Edna Fletcher (from her later marriage to Fletcher's adoptive father) and Edna Banner (from her final marriage). What we do know is that social mores regarding out-of-wedlock births—and Fletcher's desire to identify with youth from single-parent homes—changed between 1969 and 2004. In 1969 Fletcher was seeking respectability as a member of the Nixon administration; he probably thought his colleagues would look down their noses at him if they found out he was what was then called a bastard. In 2004 Fletcher was eager to maintain his status as a role model for African American youth, many of whom came from single-parent homes themselves.[6]

The reference to the "cotton field" is also curious: in only one other document—an article published in 1969 in which he told a reporter that he was "a five-year-old boy working in the cotton fields of Oklahoma"—does Fletcher link himself to the sharecropping background so common among African Americans in the growing cities of the North and West. As he delivered this speech at a meeting of the Associated General Contractors, he may have been subtly reminding his audience of their Black employees' (and potential Black employees') hardworking background and pedigree. In any event, this aspect of the story is plausible; East Texas, where Edna was born, contains an immense cotton-growing region north of Houston, and Oklahoma, one of the states in which she is said to have left her boys, includes a section of cotton country.[7]

In a 1999 open letter to the graduates of Evergreen State College in Washington, Fletcher told a similar story: "My mother had two degrees, one qualified her to be a registered nurse, and the other a [sic] elementary school teacher. But, because of racism and discrimination, based on color, she was never able to use either of her degrees, to economically speaking, up grade her standard of living and establish herself as a solide [sic] middle class citizen."[8] In an exhaustive 2003 interview, he provided still more detail:

My mother was the offspring of a Comanche Indian woman and my grandfather was a Methodist minister in Houston, Texas. . . . And . . . when her mother passed, my grandfather . . . remarried, and since my mother was half Indian, the woman he married didn't want to raise her, so he put her in Prairie View State Teachers College in Prairie View, Texas. Prairie View had an academy and Mama finished high school and then went on to college and got a nursing degree and got a . . . degree in education to teach. But . . . she was what they called a half breed, and so the black school systems didn't want to hire her to teach and so she never got a chance to use her teaching degree. She did go to Oklahoma City and do some nursing for a while.[9]

Prairie View State Normal & Industrial College—today's Prairie View A&M University—first admitted students into a four-year baccalaureate program in 1919, but it had been training Black schoolteachers from the Houston area as far back as 1879. Documentary evidence confirms that Edna was born in Houston on January 1, 1898, so while we cannot say for sure that she attended Prairie View, it is plausible.[10]

The 2003 story also does not jibe with a letter he wrote in 1990. After making an "insensitive statement" at a Black History Month celebration that year, which was misconstrued as derogatory of Native Americans, he wrote an apology letter, noting, "My late mother, whom I loved dearly, was a full-blooded Comanche Indian . . . from whom I am proud to say I take most of my courage, integrity, and my aggressive traits." It is unlikely that a "full-blooded Comanche" could have been "the offspring of . . . a Methodist minister"; it is even less likely that one could have attended Prairie View. More likely was that Fletcher, in his zeal to demonstrate that he meant no harm in his earlier remarks, confused his mixed-race mother with his Comanche grandmother.[11]

Fletcher also blamed his mother's failure to find teaching work on her personality. "I'm assuming that when Mama was young she was kind of a renegade," he told his 2003 interviewers. Black schoolteachers in the early twentieth-century South—almost all of whom were women—were held to strict moral standards, and having two children out of wedlock by two different men would be considered a gross violation of the code, regardless of formal training. So the particulars of the story, while unprovable, are also certainly plausible.[12]

What we can say for sure is that Fletcher looked to his earliest observations of his mother's employment situation to explain his understanding of racial discrimination and demonstrate his bona fides as a civil rights leader. This was especially important as he made a name for himself as a Republican politician in an era when that party was increasingly turning against the achievements of the civil rights movement.

The formation of one's identity is a complex psychological undertaking, one that is both conscious and unconscious. For Arthur Fletcher, who rose from Edna Miller's broken home to advise four American presidents, his identity as a civil rights leader and Republican politician was as dependent on the stories he chose to remember as on the circumstances, experiences, and external factors beyond his control. In that same 1969 speech, he used anecdotes from his childhood to explain the man he had become. Speaking of his mother, Fletcher continued,

> She arrives this morning to pick the boy up, and to take him with her . . . and because she was in the domestic service business, she had to leave her son with whoever would keep him. And as she moved from one family to another, she left the boy with an Indian family for awhile, with a Mexican-American family for awhile, and with various and sundry Negro families for awhile . . . consequently her son goes to seventeen different schools before he hits the eighth grade. And naturally, he was a slow learner when they finally arrived at Fort Riley, Kansas, and he went to school at Junction City.[13]

Was it a true story? Again, its factuality matters less than what it tells us of his identity. The timing of the speech was important. In November 1969, when he delivered it, Fletcher was embroiled in a battle with congressional antagonists of both parties eager to tear down his proposed affirmative action program for the building trades. In addressing a meeting of the Associated General Contractors, he sought to generate support for his policy among the powerful white businessmen in attendance. Hoping to garner sympathy born from the white guilt of privileged men who had just witnessed the racial upheaval of the 1960s, he identified himself as a worthy recipient of that sympathy. He also played on their own underprivileged backgrounds: many of them had been raised by white immigrant parents in urban ethnic ghettoes, where they had built the support networks that had resulted in prosperity. Fletcher gave them a story that they could admire—he too had pulled himself up by his bootstraps—while pointing out just how much harder it was for those born Black.

Finally, by claiming to have lived with families of diverse ethnicity in his early childhood, he embodied a diverse American inheritance. He was not just a Black man; he also sympathized with the peculiar plight of Indians and Mexican Americans—and therefore all downtrodden minority groups. He played on themes from stories with which these men were certainly familiar: Edgar Rice Burroughs's *Tarzan of the Apes* and Rudyard Kipling's Mowgli from *The Jungle Book*. Whereas Tarzan and Mowgli had been raised by different species (apes and wolves, respectively), taking on the behaviors

Class photo, Washington School, 1931. The future Art Fletcher, in his Sunday best, is in the top row, left. Arthur Fletcher Personal Papers, courtesy Paul Fletcher.

attributed to them while maintaining an innate, even noble, humanity, Fletcher had been raised by people of all races and had learned their customs, mores, and most importantly their perspectives. Fletcher gave his audience an element of voyeurism but shrewdly played to their sense of white superiority—Burroughs and Kipling were, after all, white imperialists who used jungle species as stand-ins for nonwhite races—for the benefit of a program designed to undermine that superiority.

While we have no documentary corroboration that Arthur Fletcher—or, to be more precise, Edward Arthur Allen, as he was still named at the time—actually lived with any families other than Edna's, we do have his kindergarten class photo. He attended the integrated Washington School, but no city is listed. (Tulsa had a Washington Elementary at least as early as 1954, and Phoenix still does; naming elementary schools after the first president was not uncommon.) A white teacher stands over twenty children, of whom Edward Arthur and a little girl are apparently the only African Americans. Integrated the class may have been, but the photographer (or the teacher) placed the two Black children in a back corner. Edward Arthur himself stands a bit apart, somewhat forlornly. He is the best-dressed person in the photo (including the teacher, who wears a blouse and a string of pearls). While the boys are almost universally clad in thin sweaters or open-collar shirts with shorts, and the girls mostly in casual dresses, Edward Arthur wears what may be his Sunday best—a single-breasted jacket and tie, with both buttons done. It may in fact be a suit; the pants are not visible. He was a tall six-year-old in 1931.[14]

Although we cannot draw many solid conclusions from the photo, we can make useful assumptions. For one thing, Edward Arthur is clearly over-dressed; the parents of most of the other children felt comfortable sending them to picture day in far more casual clothing. It is possible that he was raised in better circumstances than he later claimed, but more likely his mother worked extra hard to make him look presentable. Obviously having some familiarity with the "racial uplift" theories of Booker T. Washington, she did not want him to be the object of pity or derision because of either his race or her circumstances. Having an education herself, she strove to give the impression that her son had class. It is a dark, thick suit; in the South-west, it would have been uncomfortable for most of the year (although the sweaters worn by the white children indicate a more temperate climate, like that of Tulsa). It might have been borrowed or handed down from his older brother, Earl.[15]

Most importantly, the fact that he kept the photo—indeed, it is his only preteen photo—is telling. As a man, Fletcher practiced and preached the pol-itics of respectability, the philosophy that African Americans could achieve equality by assimilating into polite white culture; if only they could get jobs on an equal basis to whites, commensurate to their gifts and education, he believed, racism would fade. Here he was as a boy dressed better than the whites in his class, just as good if not better than the whites who surrounded him. He was respectable (if somewhat awkward).

At some point between the ages of six and thirteen, Edward Arthur found himself in Los Angeles. Here he got a different sort of education than that found at Washington School. "I used to roam up and down Central Avenue, which was the Black side of Los Angeles, and . . . the people you emulated then were the street hustlers. So what you saw were pimps, prostitutes, gam-blers, hustlers, you name it, and those were the only places you could go." Again, regardless of the truthfulness of the story, the recollection mattered to Fletcher's sense of identity. By placing himself in the Watts ghetto during his childhood, he reaffirmed his link to the poverty and sense of hopeless-ness that persisted there (barely four years had passed between the 1965

Watts rebellion and Fletcher's 1969 speech). Later, he used his experiences there to explain why he preferred jobs programs for minority youth over recreation programs: "I was a bad boy in the slums of Los Angeles. I broke windows on the way to the park, and I got in all kinds of mischief on the way back home again." When he said this in 1989, he was justifying his decision to remain in the Republican Party despite the evisceration of civil rights programs during the Reagan years. "The right way to handle youth is to get them to work," he told a journalist.[16]

But like Malcolm X, whose autobiography Fletcher surely read, he used his own story to light a path out of that darkness. "I used to be a shoeshine boy," he added, pointing out that despite the environment of lawlessness so prevalent in a neighborhood where the police were seen as apathetic outsiders at best, he found more legitimate pursuits than other children there. And it was his work at the shoeshine stand that connected him with role models who, he claimed, helped shape his future:[17]

> I shined shoes on the corner of 12th and Central Avenue in Los Angeles, California. And I would often get to see such people as Henry Armstrong, the great welterweight fighter; Jack Johnson, who was at one time the heavyweight champion of the world, and on that site I got to see Kenny Washington who was a great football player at . . . UCLA, and Jackie Robinson and all those guys. I was just a kid when they were getting ready to go through school. So they influenced me, although I was in a horrible immediate environment, we had the ambition to go to the coliseum and watch . . . those guys and one day visualize ourselves being there.[18]

Fletcher was indeed likely to have met or at least seen Armstrong, Johnson, Washington, and Robinson while shining shoes in Los Angeles in the mid-1930s. Armstrong won forty-five fights in Southern California between 1932 and 1938; Jack Johnson's long career and national fame surely brought him to Los Angeles during the 1930s; Washington grew up in Los Angeles and was at the University of California there in 1937; and Robinson, who also attended UCLA, grew up in nearby Pasadena.[19]

Edna recognized that for all of the positive influences young Edward Arthur might occasionally gain through serendipity, Depression-era Watts was no place for a teenage boy. "I was on my way to being a hoodlum," he later recalled. "I was headed straight to San Quentin, brother. My Auntie came and got me to take me to Oklahoma City" in 1937.[20]

It was there in 1938 that he had yet another serendipitous encounter, one he treasured for the rest of his life as critical to his spiritual development. Civil rights leader Mary McLeod Bethune, a Black New Deal official and Eleanor Roosevelt confidante, was in the midst of a national tour. According to the *Oakland Tribune,* her "itinerary includes a visit in every state of the union." She appeared at Douglas Junior–Senior High School in Oklahoma City, which Edward Arthur was attending. The school held an assembly on April 14, 1938, at which she gave an inspiring speech. "Bethune walked into the room," he later told a reporter, "and the whole audience was silent and he said he could 'feel the electricity.'" Bethune was director of the National Youth Administration's Negro Affairs Division, and she was telling children all over the country to "better themselves and live better lives." At that time the boy who later, as Arthur Fletcher, advised four presidents, was still a street-smart tough doing poorly in school. She could hardly be talking to him, could she? "But she planted the seed."

> She said, "I am as Black as the ace of spades and anything but beautiful, yet I have been summoned to the White House to advise presidents . . . I know that I am talking to someone in this auditorium who is going to grow up and advise a president of the United States, too. . . . And I came here to tell them what to tell the president when they get there." And what she told us was "Always carry a brief for Black folks. Tell him when you get there that we Negroes, individually and collectively, can be of great value to this nation."[21]

As with so many of his later recollections of events in his childhood, the specific words Fletcher attributed to Bethune indicate more about him than they do her. In Bethune's time, to be Black and to have political influence meant being a presidential advisor, but she surely hoped that by the time those children were her age, the presidency itself would be open to them. She also likely envisioned a day when the president might not necessarily be a man. Indeed, by 1991, when Fletcher told that story to an *Ebony* reporter, the Democrats had nominated a woman, Geraldine Ferraro, for the vice presidency, and a Black man, Colin Powell, was considered a front-runner to be the GOP's 1996 presidential nominee. But Fletcher, whose own run for the 1996 nomination was a protest candidacy, did not. To him, the presidency was a white, male institution. The quotation itself was likely a product of Fletcher's imagination.

But the feelings Bethune's visit stirred in him were most certainly real. When he had become a political insider and civil rights leader himself, he looked to Bethune's public *Last Will and Testament* as a model for his own legacy. Her 1955 death coincided with the start of a new national push for civil rights, after the *Brown v. Board of Education* Supreme Court decision, and the document symbolically bequeathed to the next generation—Fletcher's generation—responsibility for pursuing equal opportunity.[22]

New Name, New Life

Clearly one of the most important elements in the formation of Arthur Fletcher's identity was his name, which changed in 1938 thanks to his adoption by his stepfather, Andrew "Cotton" Fletcher. According to Arthur, his mother had met and married Cotton a few years earlier, when their lives converged near Fort Huachuca, Arizona, Cotton's duty station at the time. Cotton was a master farrier—he fitted horseshoes—and was variously assigned to the 9th or 10th Cavalry, the buffalo soldiers.[23]

Organized after the Civil War, the buffalo soldiers—units of the 24th and 25th Colored Infantry and the 9th and 10th Colored Cavalry—policed the Great Plains from 1866 to 1890 and subdued some of the most famous Indian freedom fighters, including the Apaches Victorio and Geronimo, on behalf of the white settler nation. The 9th and 10th Cavalry were mainly stationed in Kansas and West Texas, respectively, but by 1890 had been assigned to Indian Territory (Oklahoma), New Mexico, Colorado, and the Dakotas. While they often had talented commanders (almost exclusively white) and their valor was recognized by their generals, they were typically assigned inferior equipment and horses, and they endured the ire of local white civilians, who considered them little different from the hostile Indians. The occasional misbehavior of individual soldiers was blown out of proportion by the press in comparison to that of white troops.[24]

At the turn of the century, a second generation of buffalo soldiers distinguished themselves overseas. They were deployed to Cuba and saw combat in the Spanish–American War in 1899, famously helping Teddy Roosevelt take San Juan Hill, and were sent to the Philippines to assist in putting down the postwar rebellion there during the following decade. In 1916 they served under John J. Pershing in the attack on Pancho Villa's forces at Columbus, New Mexico. Nevertheless, their mistreatment worsened in the first decades of the century. White civilians wanted the Black soldiers anywhere but their own towns for fear they would socialize with white women, and their presence in southern towns resulted in several race riots.[25]

By the time he came into Edward Arthur's life, Cotton Fletcher was well into his army career. Born in 1888 in Brownsville, Texas, he ultimately became one of the best farriers in the United States Army. According to his adopted son, "he joined the army and became . . . quite good at horse shoeing. He was . . . good enough that when they wanted to put shoes on the United States polo horses, they called in my dad. . . . When they were going to put American horses in the [1932 Los Angeles Summer] Olympics, they had horse events, my dad was responsible for shoeing those horses."

Cotton Fletcher spent most of the 1930s stationed at Fort Huachuca, near Tucson, Arizona, but was increasingly called upon to travel to Fort Riley, Kansas, to train Black farriers there. Eventually he was transferred to Fort Riley, at which point he adopted Edna's boys and the family moved to nearby Junction City.[26] A military town, Junction City existed primarily to support the local army base, Fort Riley. Neighborhoods and public accommodations were segregated by custom rather than law, as was the case throughout Kansas. Schools were integrated, as in all of the state's small towns. The influence of the military was pervasive, especially in the African American community, owing to the presence of the 9th and 10th Cavalry buffalo soldiers. Federal funds, in the form of military contracts and soldier paychecks, helped the people of the town get through the Great Depression.

The marriage of Cotton Fletcher and Edna Miller was clearly life-changing for young Edward Arthur. Not only did having a mature father figure give the boy a sense of stability, but Cotton Fletcher also introduced him to military life:

> They had inter-troop and inter-regimental competition, so we got to see competitors from the time we got up in the morning to the time we went to bed at night, and it was just kind of drilled competitiveness into you and constantly challenging you not to beat the other guy, but to see how good you could be . . . and they would constantly . . . make you raise the bar for yourself, and they would coach you . . . and pretty soon that moved over into the academic arena . . . so that military environment . . . all paid off.[27]

This sense of personal competition—to "constantly raise the bar"—played an outsize role in the formation of the boy's personality and in the accomplishments of the man. Most obviously, it gave him a working ethic in his pursuits on the football field, and he took his gridiron skills all the way to a brief professional career. But it affected his personal philosophy in two other important ways: his ambition, which led him to professional success, and his moral philosophy, which shaped his political positions. He never stopped challenging himself, despite incredible setbacks in his family life and professional life, and the fact that he advised four American presidents is ample testimony to that ambition. But the sense of self-competitiveness that he learned growing up near army bases made him partial to the philosophy of self-help, which he developed into a national civil rights program, and which dovetailed with the Republican Party's antipathy to direct government aid to individuals.

One should not underestimate the importance of the name change to the development of the boy and the early priorities of the man. In 1938 Edward Arthur Allen officially became Arthur Allen Fletcher with his adoption by Cotton. He kept the surname Allen as a middle name, seeing the importance of a link to the founder of the AME Church; but he took the name Fletcher out of respect, admiration, and affection for this man who was already making so important a contribution to his upbringing. For the remaining sixty-seven years of his life, he kept the name Fletcher and did honor to the memory of the master farrier with a third-grade education, bestowing it on two wives, five children, and many grandchildren. He also passed it on to a stepdaughter, playing the role for her that Cotton had for him.[28]

Name changes among prominent individuals are not as unusual as they might seem. In the political arena, we have the example of Gerald R. Ford, one of the presidents whom Fletcher later advised. A decade Fletcher's senior, Ford was born Leslie Lynch King Jr. in 1913. Like Fletcher, he took the name of his adoptive father and became known as Gerald Rudolph Ford Jr., legally changing his name at age twenty-three. The two best-known figures of the civil rights era—Martin Luther King Jr. and Malcolm X—likewise were born with different names. Fletcher's contemporary Dr. King was born Michael King Jr., but his father changed both of their names, in honor of the Reformation churchman Martin Luther, when the future civil rights martyr was only five years old. Dr. King was referred to as "Little Mike" well into his childhood. Perhaps most famously, Malcolm Little shed his "slave name" after his jailhouse conversion to the Nation of Islam, becoming Malcolm X and eventually Malik Shabazz, adopting a family name that his children and grandchildren still proudly bear.[29]

Arthur Fletcher's two decades as a Kansan provided the crucible in which the personality of the civil rights politician gelled. His years in Junction City were formative in a number of important areas, one of the most important being football. "Thank God for football or I wouldn't have stayed in high school," Fletcher later said. Upon arrival in the town, fourteen-year-old Fletcher enrolled in Junction City High School and was promptly recruited by Coach Henry Shenk for the football squad. For two years under Coach Shenk, Fletcher learned the rules and techniques of the game, staying in shape during the spring playing basketball and running track, and growing into the six-foot-four youth known to fellow students as Big Art.[30]

In his junior year, a new coach, Robert Briggs, took over the squad and began experimenting with the players' positions. At first this meant that Fletcher warmed the bench, but in the final games of the 1941 season, as he approached his seventeenth birthday, Coach Briggs put Fletcher at halfback and found the formula that allowed Big Art to really shine. On November 15, Fletcher "went fifty-five yards for a touchdown in a 13–0 victory over Herrington," a hamlet some thirty miles south of Junction City. In the final game of the season, at homecoming against the neighboring town of Chapman on November 27, "Art Fletcher was the star, making runs of 78, 42, and 29 yards" to deliver three of the four victorious Junction City Blue Jays' touchdowns.[31]

Coach Briggs was also a stickler for academics, which pushed Fletcher and his teammates to devote time to their studies, not just sport. He "made us get an eligibility card every Monday morning, and we'd have to take that eligibility card to the teachers. And each teacher would sign a square, and if you were below a C you lost your game uniform. It was just that simple. You had to turn your eligibility card in on Thursday, we played Friday." Because he loved playing—a desire only strengthened by his successes on the grid-iron—Fletcher resolved to keep up his grades. As a result, he largely avoided the backstreet temptations of the army base town that sometimes resembled the streets of Watts, and became a good student as well as a good athlete.[32]

Playing high school football in Kansas in the early 1940s gave young Fletcher yet another lesson in the realities of race in America. Few hotels in rural Kansas served Black patrons, and none were integrated. So while white players often were allowed to stay overnight at away games, the coach's wife drove the Black players home to Junction City. That a white high school coach might stand up for his Black players in these instances was unlikely; Shenk and Briggs were focused on building their coaching careers, perhaps hoping to coach college football, and so were unlikely to rock the boat. Nor was young Fletcher in a position to make a difference; he and his fellow Black players, a minority on the team despite their fathers' collective importance to Fort Riley as buffalo soldiers, kept their heads down on the race issue lest the coach bench them as troublemakers. In any event, the high school football market was small for hotels; no individual team had the economic leverage to change the system.[33]

Another early exposure to racism came within the walls of his own school. "I did a grade by grade head count of the Black students . . . and concluded that if we voted in a block, we could elect . . . a pretty dark brown skin girl Home Coming Queen." But his budding political talent ran headlong into the entrenched institutional racism. "A white man on the . . . janitorial crew got wind of what we were up to. He immediately told Mr. Karnes the school principal about our plans. The principal . . . informed the school board members and they changed the rules for electing the queen," eliminating the chance for a Black girl to win.[34]

Ten days after Fletcher's star turn at the homecoming game against Chapman, on December 7, 1941, the Imperial Japanese Navy sent scores of kamikaze pilots to their deaths in a surprise attack on the American naval base at Pearl Harbor, Hawaii. The attack sank four battleships and damaged four others; destroyed 188 US airplanes; and killed more than 2,000 American sailors and nearly 400 soldiers, airmen, and civilians. Meant to cripple United States maritime operations in the Far East and warn off American involvement in World War II, the attack instead provoked an American resolve to fight. Calling it "a day that will live in infamy," President Roosevelt asked for, and Congress granted, a declaration of war against Japan. The empire's European allies, Germany and Italy, having already conquered most of that continent, immediately declared war on the United States, which responded in kind.

Fort Riley and adjacent Junction City now became a churning cauldron of activity as the army mustered for a global war in which the United States would play a defining role. The fort trained more than 100,000 soldiers, including boxer Joe Louis and actor Mickey Rooney; the increased activity drew major national entertainers to town like Earl "Father" Hines; and the county registrar saw a major increase in requests for marriage licenses, as young couples sought stability in the face of an uncertain future.[35]

Arthur Fletcher was no less affected by these developments. On December 7, he and a teammate, Jim Warren, "were walking up Jackson Street headed to the Hardens' house." Mr. and Mrs. William Harden, together with their granddaughters Mary and Florence, were the most prominent family on the Black side of town. Light-skinned and privileged, the Hardens had come to the area after the Civil War, probably as Exodusters—freed slaves seeking a new life in the West—and acquired land. Around the turn of the century, William Harden had secured a federal contract to deliver railroad ties for the Santa Fe Railroad, and he eventually sold significant land holdings to the government as Fort Riley expanded in the first half of

During Arthur's senior year in high school he began dating the popular Mary Harden. The couple married shortly after this photo was taken, in the summer of 1943. Arthur Fletcher Personal Papers, courtesy Paul Fletcher.

the twentieth century. Mrs. Harden operated the Black officers' club and ran an informal Black USO out of their spacious home in town.[36] Mary Harden was a year younger than Arthur Fletcher, and one of the most desirable Black girls in Junction City. Normally a kid from the backstreets of Los Angeles and Oklahoma City wouldn't have stood a chance with well-to-do Mary, but now Fletcher was a football star, and the two began dating.[37]

Fletcher was a fighter as well as a lover, going on a "suicide mission" that his teammate Warren jokingly compared to the Pearl Harbor attack. Responding to a racist provocation, Fletcher "walked into a small restaurant—filled with white soldiers—snatched one soldier from the back of the restaurant and proceeded to kick his ass!" He barely escaped the wrath of the other soldiers, melting into the backstreets of Junction City.[38]

A growing self-confidence, even bravado, was matched by Fletcher's exploits on the field. In his senior year, he led the Junction City Blue Jays to an 8–1–1 victorious season, and he was named by the *Topeka Daily Capital* newspaper as the first Black student on its all-state high school football team. A position adjustment by Coach Briggs after their first game, the only loss of the season, made all the difference. "Fletcher started as a back but after the Lawrence reverse he was shifted to end where he became the standout player of the Central Kansas League." According to scholar Mark Peterson, young Fletcher racked up "nine touchdowns over the course of the season . . . and accumulated impressive yardage even in those few games where he did not score." After the final game of the season, Coach Briggs told the *Capital* that Fletcher was "the greatest football player I've ever coached."[39]

Success on the gridiron, and the knowledge that his final season at Junction City High was over, led to Fletcher's first civil rights protest. "They had this crazy policy in Junction City High School that I don't understand today, but all seniors, black seniors, their pictures went in the back of the year-book," Fletcher later recalled. "You went to school with [the whites] all the way through, but when it was time to graduate, your picture was in the back of the yearbook." In fact, Fletcher had already appeared in integrated yearbook photos in his junior year: the 1942 *Pow Wow* shows him in a class photo for Home Room 319, as well as in team portraits for the football, basketball, and track teams, and in action shots from football and basketball games. But the senior portraits were strangely segregated; the 1943 *Pow Wow*, for Fletcher's senior year, included a portrait of the "First Chinese girl to graduate from this high school," Betty Mar, after all of the white students' portraits.[40]

Although Fletcher implied that segregated yearbook portraiture was a high school or local school board policy, more likely it was a policy of the yearbook staff, the white students who wrote and published the annual document and organized the photographs. While ostensibly under teacher supervision—and the adults should not be left off the hook—it was probably the students who decided to emulate the Jim Crow traditions of the adult world. They imposed segregation on one aspect of the teenage world over which they had a modicum of control. Further, given the fact that the school and its athletic and other activities were integrated, the very inconsequence of the policy to the overall Jim Crow social structure in Junction City lends credence to the notion that it was not an adult-imposed policy. Adults invested in the segregation of teenagers were far more concerned about separating Blacks and whites at social events like dances, which could lead to interracial dating, than in the placement of photographs in the yearbook.

Just as the students' policy was seen by adults as inconsequential, so too was the resultant boycott by Black students. When the yearbook portrait section ultimately was integrated—in the 1944 edition—the principal could enthusiastically point to it as a demonstration of racial progress with little effect on, or risk of censure from, the outside community:

When I came back [from World War II] the principal honked his horn and jumped out of the car and ran over and threw both arms around me, and . . . said "Just get in." I got in the car. He wheeled around, went down to the high school, jumped out of the car, he was almost running, and I'm limping along behind him.

When he got to his office, he snatched the '44 yearbook off of the shelf, opened it up and said "Look at this." Everybody was in there in alphabetical order.[41]

Fletcher claimed to have led the successful boycott. "I started my civil rights struggle by convincing the 13 blacks who were going to graduate from Junction in 1943, we won't put our picture in the yearbook, period." His organizing work was successful in that there are, after all, no Black students' portraits in the 1943 Pow Wow, while the 1944 edition has integrated portraits. He does not appear, however, to have been the first student to come up with the idea: the 1942 Pow Wow, from his junior year, also contains no portraits of Black seniors; the boycott started before Fletcher's involvement. But leadership by the young football star seems to have made the difference for the victory, and Fletcher learned an important lesson for future civil rights activity. "I began to realize that if you put the pressure on, decent people will do the right thing." White people were therefore not enemies but potential allies. The real enemy was racism, which could be fought with arguments and peaceful actions, not just youthful ass-kicking (which, while temporarily satisfying, in the long run led only to places like San Quentin). Fletcher promised to never again resort to violence—outside of the football field and the battlefield, of course. Aside from one uncorroborated incident, we have no evidence that he ever did.[42]

Fletcher himself had the opportunity to do the right thing soon after graduation: Mary was pregnant. The couple had been dating for the better part of a year, and despite Mary's Catholic faith, she had given herself to her lover as a wife to a husband. Birth control was unavailable and abortion was illegal, and Mary and Art had engaged in the one component of baby making that teenagers in love can least control. Arthur married Mary Harden, and his new bride moved in with the Fletchers at 384-B Riley Place, in noncommissioned officers' housing on base.[43]

Arthur later told his son, Paul, as he pushed him out of the nest when Paul turned eighteen in 1967, that he had learned from his father, Cotton, that a young man needed to make his own way in the world. Based on addresses listed on official forms, Cotton's philosophy does not seem to have been as strict as Fletcher later maintained. Arthur and Mary remained with Cotton and Edna for the remainder of the school year and into the summer of 1943.[44]

Fletcher was inducted into the army at Fort Leavenworth, Kansas, on August 7, 1943, and was transferred to Fort Knox, Kentucky, for infantry basic training with a quartermaster trucking regiment. "I turned 18 on the 22nd of December '42, so I got my draft card. And actually, I scored well enough on the . . . entrance examination that I was qualified to go to OCS [Officer Candidate School], but they also wanted me to go in the Navy. I can swim, but I ain't about to get in nobody's Navy, brother."[45]

His pregnant wife stayed with her in-laws. On October 6, at 6:47 in the morning, Mary made Arthur a father, giving birth after five hours' labor to a healthy baby girl, Phyllis Edna Fletcher. Art listed his "usual occupation" on the birth certificate as "PVT, 521 QM Trk Regt (a)"—a soldier in a trucking regiment.[46]

Fighting Man

Arthur Fletcher joined the army during one of the most trying tests of its history: the war against Nazi Germany, fascist Italy, and imperial Japan. The Germans had conquered nearly the entire continent of Europe, as well as France's vast North African empire, and the Japanese had conquered the Philippines and much of the Pacific and Eastern Asia. After Pearl Harbor, President Roosevelt deployed the navy and marines to the Pacific and the army to North Africa, invading Casablanca, Morocco, in November 1942. The Germans, faced with increasing difficulty in the east against the Soviet Union, did not have the resources to effectively defend against the attacks in Africa. By the time Fletcher enlisted the following August, Allied forces had pushed the Germans out of North Africa and into Sicily.

Fletcher's training in the fall of 1943 at Fort Knox, Kentucky, therefore took place in an atmosphere of confidence that the Allies would soon prevail. His memories of his time there are more of football than maneuvers: "I was over in the bed one night . . . and sure enough, they were practicing football. . . . So I watched them for two nights. The third night I walked over to the coach and I said I'd like to see if I could try out. . . . I beat my chest and I told him I was all-state Kansas, and . . . he said 'There's no high school players out here.'"[47]

In fact, however, the issue had less to do with Fletcher's qualifications than his race. The army was segregated, and Kentucky, where Fletcher was being trained, was very much a Jim Crow state; indeed, the army paid so little attention to the qualifications of its "colored" soldiers that it released Black felons from prison to serve alongside recent high school graduates like Fletcher. Ultimately the coach was less concerned with Fletcher's abilities than the reactions of the other players and the people in the stands.

But Fletcher refused to be dissuaded, believing that if he could only just get past the first barrier and convince the coach to let him prove himself, he could get an opportunity:

> So I go back over and I make him an offer . . . I will put on the blocking aprons, and they can block me, I'd be the cannon [fodder] for them. They could block me, and I could warm up the passes. He said "Okay."
>
> So the next night I put on the blocking apron and played the cannon fodder role. [After a few hits, the coach] finally said "You know . . . they're going to have a hard time knocking you down." And . . . they were having a heck of a time knocking me down.

Still, the coach would not let an African American play football with white soldiers in Kentucky. It took yet more convincing and a team crisis, but Fletcher was getting closer. His persistence was slowly paying off: they issued him a uniform and put him on the line. Now he had the opportunity to show everyone that they were wrong to segregate the races, wrong to discriminate against Black people. If you want to win a football game, if you want to run a successful company, if you want to win an election, you use the best players and workers and strategists you can find, regardless of their race.

> So I went running out on the field. You should have heard the catcalls. This is in Kentucky in '43. . . . The first play out of the bag . . . I knew they was coming at me. There was something we knew then . . . when a guard or a tackle puts his weight on his knuckles . . . the knuckles are white . . . that means he is going to go straight ahead. . . . I hit that guard. Made him . . . do a belly, and when he got back in the middle of that belly, boy, I loaded on him. The ball went one way, his helmet went the other. I made the team.[48]

Black servicemen in World War II had various experiences, but they fared somewhat better in the army than the other services. In the navy, they were relegated to menial tasks aboard ship; they were banned altogether from enlisting in the marines until 1942 (and even then kept far from enemy lines). In the army, however, Black soldiers served as tankers, artillerymen, engineers, infantry, cavalry, and even pilots. Almost all nevertheless experienced discrimination during stateside training, often including violence and in a few cases actual pitched battles with white soldiers and townspeople. They then faced overseas duty where they were given the least attractive assignments. Black officers were humiliated, and white commanders were often promoted simply to avoid their having to take orders from Black officers, making promotions for Blacks rarer. Black tank operators played a crucial role in General George Patton's push into Germany, and Black infantry units in Italy were renowned by their peers, but General Mark Clark blamed them for setbacks and refused to report their gallantry in the face of enemy fire.[49]

Other individual stories illustrate the variety of the African American experience in World War II. Historian John Hope Franklin was denied an appointment as a War Department historian despite his Harvard PhD. His equally intelligent (if less educated) brother, "drafted by a segregated army," was assigned to peel potatoes. Future major league baseball player Jackie Robinson, who completed Officer Candidate School at Fort Riley, was court-martialed for refusing to move to the back of an army transport bus. Whitney Young, on the other hand, found his vocation during the war, intervening successfully between Jim Crow–enforcing white officers and resentful Black soldiers. He went on to use these skills when he led the National Urban League (NUL).[50]

Fletcher, for his part, was qualified to enroll in Officer Candidate School based on his entrance examination at Fort Leavenworth. Upon completion of basic training at Fort Knox, he applied for that option and was transferred into the Army Specialized Training Program (ASTP). "They wanted me to stay [at Fort Knox], but I wanted to be an officer. One thing I wanted was my dad to salute me. He was still in the Army, and I wanted to come home with them bars on."[51]

The ASTP was a short-lived program designed to train potential officers and replace, on college campuses, the depleted ranks of Reserve Officers Training Corps cadets who had been inducted into active duty after Pearl Harbor. Inductees who scored high on entrance examinations, as well as noncommissioned officers willing to start again at the rank of private, were assigned to a rigorous training program at colleges throughout the United States. According to author Louis E. Keefer, "The standard work week was 59 hours of 'supervised activity,' including a minimum of 24 hours of classroom and lab work, 24 hours of required study, 5 hours of military instruction, and

6 hours of physical instruction." Many Blacks started ASTP, but most were washed out and transferred to the 92nd Colored Infantry at Fort Huachuca, Arizona, based on the false assumption that the unit had a lower average IQ than white infantry units and could use an influx of smarter Black soldiers. The program had its zenith just as Fletcher was completing his training at Fort Knox: as one ASTP veteran recalled, "ASTP enrollment peaked at about 140,000 in mid-December of '43."[52]

Setbacks in the Allied invasion of Italy that fall (where the Italian government had overthrown fascist Benito Mussolini and the Germans had occupied the north), coupled with the mobilization of Allied forces in Britain in preparation for an amphibious invasion of France, led officials at the War Department to view ASTP as a waste of manpower, both in terms of the men in training who were being kept from the front lines and in terms of the experienced soldiers administering the program. "At the peak of the programs at 227 colleges, there were 1794 officers and 3345" enlisted men charged with training the students, all kept safely stateside, mainly engaged in paperwork. The bulk of the program was shut down on February 18, 1944, and most of the students were returned to active duty as privates. Another Kansan who later achieved success in politics, Bob Dole, enrolled in ASTP after a year and a half at the University of Kansas; he was one of the few who was transferred to actual Officer Candidate School at Fort Benning, Georgia, where he earned a commission as a second lieutenant.[53]

Fletcher left his training regiment at Fort Knox in January 1944 with orders for ASTP in one of the colleges out west. "But when I got to California," he later told an interviewer, "they were ready for the invasion" of France. "They closed down the ASTP. They didn't need any more officers." He was reassigned to the 3209th (Colored) Quartermaster Service Company out of San Bernardino. On March 10, 1944, the unit left California by train, arriving five days later at Camp Myles Standish, Massachusetts, home of Boston's point of embarkation for the European theater of operations. They left Boston on March 2, joining tens of thousands of soldiers who made the dangerous crossing through a German submarine–infested Atlantic. They arrived at Crewe, Cheshire, England, on April 5, and two weeks later, on April 20, 1944, they were attached to General George Patton's Third Army.[54]

The segregation of the American army, and obvious racial tensions in the ranks, gave the British pause. As Fletcher recalled, "The English used to ask, 'How in the world, with all this animosity between American troops, how in the world are you going to beat anybody when you go to Germany?'" While later civil rights advocates lamented the lost opportunities for interracial bonding in the trenches and foxholes, the army brass didn't see it that way. "We were fighting a war and the generals didn't have time to get into some kind of social adjustment thing," Fletcher said. "They had a war to win. So rather than try to deal with the social issue," Black soldiers were kept separate from whites both on and off base. "They simply said, 'We won't have them go in to town the same night. [White troops will] go to town one night and [Blacks] on the other night.' And I often got to go to town both nights because I could play the trumpet."[55]

The nineteen-year-old soldier's prowess, as it turned out, was not limited to sports. This polymath had learned the trumpet in Junction City, from soldiers at Fort Riley:

Being an Army brat there's always somebody wants to teach you something, always, and that's how I learned to play the trumpet. When I went over to band practice [at Fort Riley], the warrant officer said, "You want to learn to play a horn, boy?" And I said, "Yes, sir." So he called my dad . . . and said, "That boy of yours is over here at band practice all the time. Send him over here . . . and we'll issue him a trumpet," so they issued me a trumpet, and I used to practice with the 9th Cavalry band. That's how I learned to play the trumpet. Then I joined the high school band.[56]

His musical talent came in handy while stationed in Britain in 1944. "I was attached to an organization called Seventeen Special Services . . . a 17-piece band and a 45-minute floor show, and I traveled all over England and into Scotland and all over to Ireland playing one-night stands."[57]

As preparations for the amphibious invasion commenced, the Third Army was sent to East Anglia and Kent, in England's southeast, not far from the strait of Dover, the narrowest point in the English Channel. The idea was to convince the Germans, who respected the brusque, no-nonsense General Patton more than any other American leader for his victories in North Africa and Sicily, that the invasion would be in the Nord-Pas-de-Calais region, directly across from Dover. In fact, Patton's Third was not part of the D-Day invasion at all, which surprised the Wehrmacht on June 6, 1944, in Normandy, some 200 miles away.[58]

As the invasion commenced and the casualties began returning, Fletcher kept on playing trumpet. "What we would do is play the hospitals in the morning, play for different British groups in the afternoon. In the evening we played at the USOs." Notwithstanding the carnage on the Normandy beaches, Fletcher's war so far was more play than work. "Before going to bed, depending on where we were, we would play an hour for a shift coming off of a defense factory or an hour for the shift going in."[59]

But the happy days of playing trumpet in England soon came to an end. With the beachfront secure, the many battalions in Patton's Third Army made the crossing throughout July in preparation for the push to liberate France. "All of a sudden some guy came by and told us, 'Art Fletcher?' I said 'Yeah.' 'You got a trumpet?' I said 'Yeah.' 'Turn it in.' I said 'What?' He said, 'The gig's over, brother, you're going back to your outfit, and you're getting ready to go over.'" Fletcher traded his trumpet for the armband of a military policeman, crossing the English Channel from Hiltingbury, Hampshire, and landing at Utah Beach on July 18, 1944.[60]

Fletcher's unit, the 3209th Quartermaster Service Company, was attached to XV Corps. On July 19, 1944, they moved inland toward Avranches, then marched southeast to the vicinity of Le Mans, which they reached by August 16. In doing so, they assisted in the encirclement of the Argentan–Falaise pocket, which held the bulk of Wehrmacht forces in France. Unfortunately, General Omar Bradley, Patton's commanding officer, refused to allow XV Corps to press north from Le Mans to Caen, which would have closed the circle. The Germans escaped and were able to regroup at Metz, in the eastern province of Lorraine. Fletcher's group, "engaged in graves registration work," moved on two weeks later to Villeneuve-Sur-Auvers, about thirty miles south of Paris; two weeks after that, on September 6, they moved east to the Nancy area, south of Metz, where they remained through October.[61]

As a trucking specialist, Fletcher was assigned to the Red Ball Express. Beginning on August 25, with the liberation of Paris, mostly African American soldiers loaded trucks with ammunition and other supplies for Patton's combat units and drove them to the battle lines, returning with corpses. "When Gen. Patton said for you to be there," recalled driver James Rookard, "you were there if you had to drive all day and all night. Those trucks just kept running. They'd break down, we'd fix them and they'd run again." The Red Ball Express lines, two-lane highways converted for one-way use to avoid accidents, extended east from Saint-Lô in Normandy through Paris and then eastward to the battle lines near Metz.[62] According to reporter Rudi Williams, on an average day, nine hundred fully loaded vehicles were on the Red Ball route around the clock, with drivers officially ordered to observe sixty-yard intervals and a top speed of twenty-five miles per hour. At the Red Ball's peak, 140 truck companies were strung out, with a round trip taking fifty-four hours, as the route stretched nearly 400 miles to First Army and 350 to Patton's Third. Some drivers had machine gunners attached, but most were armed only with a single carbine.[63] Fletcher, for his part, recalled that the Red Ball Express was a dangerous job:

> After the sun went down . . . you can't turn your lights on when you're running the gauntlet, so a truck is leaving every five minutes, sometimes a little longer there so if one got hit [from bombs dropped by the Luftwaffe] it wouldn't stack them all up. And if you tried to go off the highway and go around, you'd run into mine fields . . . you'd go out and blow your truck up . . . you had to have your mirror up, your windshield up, because it would [make] some kind of reflection.[64]

Indeed, Fletcher's company saw combat on October 9, enduring two casualties (one killed in action).[65]

But it wasn't all bombs and bullets. "Rookard . . . said the only fond memory he has is that of the French people, who treated African Americans nice. 'Some of the white soldiers told the French people that black soldiers had tails and stuff like that,' he said. 'But other than that, our company didn't have too much . . . discrimination.'" Fletcher concurred, noting the response from French children to whom he gave candy: "They were very nice, great big smile on their face."[66]

With the capture of Metz in November 1944, Fletcher's unit moved into the town's north and west suburbs, billeting at Dommary-Baroncourt on November 2; Piennes on November 14; and Uckange on November 29. There they were put to work "handling ammunition at railheads . . . until the tactical situation drew the unit into Belgium in the vicinity of Bastogne," reported Fletcher's company commander, First Lieutenant Alvin E. Weber.[67]

The tactical situation to which Lieutenant Weber referred was the Germans' last major counteroffensive on the Western Front. In what is now known as the Battle of the Bulge, the Wehrmacht moved through large swaths of southern Belgium, recapturing St. Vith and surrounding Bastogne on December 21. While Fletcher was about 200 miles away from the fighting at that time—in fact, he posed, smiling, for a birthday photograph the next day—the Battle of the Bulge put him in grave danger. Allied casualties were so high at the Bulge that General Patton decided to integrate his infantry units. Fletcher was headed for the front line. On December 30, the 3209th was reassigned to Belgium and headed north into the Ardennes Forest.[68]

Fletcher had a somewhat different take on the decision to integrate the combat units. There were bilingual Germans dressed as American soldiers at the Bulge, with "a little signature on their coat and on their sleeves."

Other copies of this photograph state that it was taken in Nancy, France, on his birthday, December 22. Arthur Fletcher Personal Papers, courtesy Paul Fletcher.

On that first break-through, they were dressed in American uniforms, and the Germans could see those and they knew they were Germans. But we didn't, so that first wave they killed more American soldiers . . . at Bastogne than you could imagine.

It was then that Eisenhower decided that one way to know if he's in an American . . . is he's Black. So they began to move the Black troops to the front in Bastogne like you've never seen.

There is no evidence that General Eisenhower or General Patton integrated combat forces because of German soldiers dressed as Americans; given the sheer numbers needed that terrible winter in the Ardennes, removing white soldiers from the front lines would have been disastrous. However, Fletcher's story is based on an actual German scheme to send English-speaking SS spies behind enemy lines, which he likely learned about years later from books in his voluminous library.[69]

Regardless of Patton's motives, the integration took place, and Fletcher's company narrowly avoided combat in the Bulge. They spent January 1945 in Longlier, Belgium, and moved up to Bastogne in February in preparation for the assault across the German border. On March 7, 1945, Patton's troops captured an intact bridge over the Rhine at Remagen and quickly established a bridgehead, moved five divisions across, and raced north to capture Cologne, about thirty-five miles downriver.[70]

It is here, on March 21, 1945, that Fletcher's war came to an end. "I got hit in the chest and blood came out of my hip . . . I took small arm fire," he told his 2003 interviewers. Earlier he said that he was shot while walking alone at night "down a street in a small village in western Germany," adding, "I could have been hit by friendly fire; I could have been hit by Germans . . . I don't know." The official report characterized his wounds as "non-battle injury" due to "artillery shell, fragments, afoot or unspecified . . . not inflicted by self or another person," giving grounds for denial of a Purple Heart medal. But the shrapnel passed through his spleen, causing serious damage. He was evacuated to a field hospital in Brussels and then to England for months of treatment. "I got four operations over there and a fifth one at" Fitzsimons Army Medical Center near Denver, Colorado, where "they patched up the muscle in my hip."[71]

From his hospital bed, Fletcher requested, and was given, an honorable discharge. "I had planned to follow [my father's] path and stay in the army and become a career military man myself," he later told the 1999 Evergreen College graduating class. "However, my parents not only said no, they both said hell no. And, they were firm about it. . . . My mother insisted [that] Black Veterans would be the country's 20th century pioneers of freedom." Despite all the lost promise of her own education, Edna Fletcher demanded that her son come home and get a college degree.[72]

In the first twenty-one years of his long life, Arthur Fletcher's experiences, lessons, and actions gave a preview of the man he would become. His birth out of wedlock and years in the backstreets of places like Los Angeles and Oklahoma City gave him an understanding of life as a Black boy in makeshift families, all too common for those he later represented as a civil rights leader and political appointee. His adoption by Cotton Fletcher and move to

Kansas brought him into his life's crucible, where experiences in Junction City on the gridiron, in the classroom, and in the civil rights arena—as with the yearbook boycott—were but the first in a series of life-changing events that made him a man who could bridge the gap between the White House and the ghetto, between the president and the gang leader. After early exposure to the sheltered world of the buffalo soldiers at Fort Riley, his own military service, while mostly fun with football and music, reminded him that the segregated army did not just separate the races but discriminated against Blacks and other minorities. Yet he learned the importance of persistence and came to define persuasion as resistance. He met his obligations while reminding those around him that the Black man could be more than a menial laborer. His discharge was honorable, his integrity intact.

Fletcher's parents—birth, adoptive, and spiritual—played an outsize role. Edna taught him resilience, that despite life's hard knocks (and she had seen more than a few), he must keep getting up. He used this on the college gridiron and as a professional football player. It kept him going later, when he followed her lead and became a college graduate but couldn't find a job while his white classmates took lucrative management positions. Cotton Fletcher, meanwhile, gave him more than a name; he gave him an ethic. With his third-grade education, natural talents, and hard-won skills, Cotton taught Arthur that hard work always won out, and that one shouldn't look outside for help, but within. And his spiritual mother, Mary McLeod Bethune, whom he only saw once when she spoke to his junior high school class, impressed on Fletcher the importance of government as a vehicle for achieving civil rights, and pushed him to join a generation of leaders who opened up untold possibilities for African Americans.

It is also evident that in those first twenty-one years of his life, Fletcher experienced and learned to overcome psychological trauma in three areas. First, early in his life, his mother provided somewhat lackluster parenting—when she left him with relatives, friends, and even, it seems, casual acquaintances—notwithstanding the excuses he later made for her. Second, he experienced mistreatment by individual and systemic racism, including his time in the Watts ghetto, the incident with the high school yearbook, and the institutional racism of the segregated army. Finally, thanks to the first two traumas, he experienced shame. What is remarkable is that he overcame these traumas. He avoided hoodlum life, developed resilience, and tamed a natural and understandable desire for revenge against those who wronged him. Thanks largely to his ability to channel his emotions into the controlled violence of the football field and battlefield, he developed a capacity to sustain humiliation without being destroyed, and an ability to not take insults personally.

During the war, Fletcher became a husband and a father; upon his return from the army, he learned that he now had a second daughter, Sylvia Jean, born in 1945. He had immediate responsibilities to Mary and their daughters that often took priority over, and sometimes conflicted with, his ideals. But one of the things that made Fletcher a good husband and father was his drive to make America a better land for Black people, a land of truly equal opportunity, where his daughters could aspire to far greater achievements than his mother.

Arthur Fletcher often likened the progress of the civil rights movement to filling a glass of water. In 1924, the year of his birth, the civil rights glass was empty. By the time he left the army, thanks to Bethune and dozens of other civil rights leaders beyond the scope of this story, the civil rights glass was a quarter full. He resolved to use his life to help fill up that glass. The obvious obstacles were external: the arrayed forces of Jim Crow—legal, social, financial, and traditional—stood in the way. But first, as he returned to Kansas after the war to assume the role of husband and father, limping from his wound, he needed to tackle internal obstacles. These proved far more difficult to overcome.

CHAPTER TWO

A TERRIBLE THING TO WASTE, 1946–1960

Once Fred [Hall] convinced me that politics was not about social
justice, I started trying to figure out a way to make some money.
—Arthur Fletcher, 2003

Arthur Fletcher left the army with one thought on his mind: to play football. He knew that he had the talent, discipline, and drive to be a great player, but he also knew, having faced discrimination in high school and in the army, that the odds were stacked against him. Colleges throughout the nation—not just in the Deep South—often refused to play against integrated squads. Where Blacks were allowed to play, they faced difficulty getting housing and meals on the road. Unable to room and dine with their teammates weakened team cohesiveness and limited Black players' accomplishments on the gridiron.

College and Civil Rights

After being transferred back to the United States for treatment at Fitzsimons Army Medical Center near Denver, Colorado, Arthur Fletcher was discharged from the army in October 1945. He took a job as a painter's helper at the hospital while completing his convalescence. In April 1946, thirteen months after his wounding, he boarded the Union Pacific train line home to Junction City to reunite with his wife, Mary. The couple now had two children: Phyllis, born in 1944, and Sylvia, born in 1945. Mary soon became pregnant with their third child, Arthur Jr., born in 1946. In an era before the popular availability of home refrigeration, Fletcher took a job running deliveries for Junction City Ice and Cold Storage Company, owned by an old acquaintance: high school football scout Ray McMillin. His full recovery was evident on the job; his war wound bothered him not at all as he carried 300-pound blocks of ice up flights of stairs to residential customers.[1]

Fletcher wanted to do more than deliver ice. He wanted to play football, and the key to that was to play college ball. As GIs returned from active duty, four years' worth of high school graduates, delayed by the war, were now competing across the nation for starting slots. The competition was fierce. And unlike most other potential recruits, Fletcher had a wife and growing family to feed.

His race did not help matters. Black collegiate athletes had been barely tolerated at Big Ten schools before World War II. After 1930, when Blacks began to be recruited in significant numbers, they faced severe restrictions. They rarely served as team captain, despite popularity with their teammates and proven athletic prowess. On the road, they faced difficulty rooming at the same hotels and dining at the same eateries as the rest of the team, and at school they faced difficulty securing financial aid and finding adequate housing. Collegiate social life also posed a challenge: there were virtually no Black women on campus, and they faced the consternation of coaches and alumni—and potentially worse from the locals—when they dated white women. The prospects for employment after college served to further discourage potential Black players. Between 1934 and 1945, no Blacks played on any professional team, and coaching at all levels was virtually closed as a career path. Unlike in baseball, where Black players could at least look to employment in the Negro Leagues, no parallel opportunity existed in football. But soon after Fletcher was discharged, the Los Angeles Rams signed African American UCLA grad Kenneth Washington to start in the 1946 season. A second professional league, the eight-team All-American Football Conference, founded in 1944, was energetically recruiting Black players. The optimistic Fletcher looked hopefully to participate in fully integrated professional football, with teams in every major city of the nation, after his expected graduation four years hence.[2]

Fletcher first considered playing for the University of Denver. While he was convalescing at nearby Fitzsimons, the Denver Pioneers won the 1945 Mountain States Conference championship. The conference itself had been integrated since 1939, when the Colorado A&M Aggies fielded John Mosley, but the Pioneers remained defiantly all white, warning off a Fletcher application. Indeed, Denver was one of the last in the conference to integrate, not doing so until 1949, when they fielded James Jordan. Instead, Fletcher returned home to Junction City.[3]

Indiana University coach Bo McMillin had coached the Kansas State University football team in nearby Manhattan, Kansas, to the brink of a Big Six championship in 1933 (they won it the year after he left). McMillin still had family in the area; in fact, his brother, Ray, owned Junction City Ice and was Fletcher's boss. "I worked the summer as an ice man, and when it was time for football practice to start, he gave me a $300 check and said 'get going,'"

Fletcher later recalled of the helpful Ray McMillin. He brought toddler Phyllis, baby Sylvia, and pregnant Mary to Bloomington, where he tried out and made the team. But he quickly ran into trouble. "Bloomington, Indiana, at the time was as bad as Biloxi, Mississippi, where blacks are concerned. Couldn't find a house anywhere." Indeed, the second Ku Klux Klan had found fertile ground in Indiana, even electing a governor there in 1924. Fletcher was faced with the choice of keeping his family in "hostile territory" or giving up his dream of playing football.[4]

Although his focus was on football, these setbacks were formative for the future civil rights leader. "The very enemy I fought against [in Germany] could buy a house and I couldn't, could go to state institutions of higher learning and I couldn't," he later told a reporter. "That had more than an indelible marker on my conscience. . . . I decided I am not going to be denied my citizenship after I laid my life on the line."[5]

As it happened, Washburn University in Topeka, an hour east of Junction City, had just hired a promising new football coach. Although Washburn's Ichabods hadn't won a championship since 1931, Coach Dick Godlove was looking to build the Washburn squad into a "small college powerhouse" in the Central Independent Conference (CIC), which included schools throughout Kansas, Nebraska, and Missouri. Here Fletcher had another connection, through his old high school coach. "I get this call from Bob Briggs who knew Dick Godlove. He and Dick were in the Navy together." It wasn't a Big Ten school and therefore didn't appear to hold out the promise of a lucrative professional career, but at least he could get a good education and keep his football dream alive. Knowing Fletcher was virtually destitute, Briggs advanced Fletcher the money to bring his family back to Kansas.[6]

Fletcher found postwar Topeka a hotbed of civil rights intellectual and political activity. African American Topeka lawyer Elisha Scott was determined to use the victory in World War II to help achieve civil rights victories at home. Well connected to the political powers in the Republican-dominated state capitol, Scott was impressed by the rhetoric of national civil rights leaders like A. Philip Randolph, Walter White, and Lester Granger, who had popularized the notion of the Double-V campaign during the war. Scott resolved to meet every train carrying returning GIs to Topeka. Whenever he saw a Black veteran disembark, he pulled the young man aside to impress upon him the benefits of education, self-pride, and perseverance. Often he helped Black vets sign up for benefits under the GI Bill, and he remained available to help these young men readjust to civilian life.[7]

He had his work cut out for him. Notwithstanding its abolitionist history, race discrimination in Kansas was not limited to segregated sections of high school yearbooks. A midwestern variant of Jim Crow, Kansas segregation was somewhere between de jure and de facto, but it was certainly real.[8] As one former state attorney recalled of Topeka,

> The restaurant where I took many of my meals displayed a sign that read, "Colored and Mexicans served in sacks only." Movie houses were segregated—one for blacks and five or six for whites—although in the Grand, one of the city's top theaters, I remember a section in the balcony, sometimes called "nigger heaven," reserved for black moviegoers.
>
> At . . . the church we attended I encountered a black man of my own age whom I had known at the university, where he was recognized as a good student, ambitious for a professional career. In 1950 he was a church janitor.[9]

Black graduates of Kansas' public colleges typically left the state; in essence, the state was subsidizing the education of Black professionals employed elsewhere. Most famously, the unfair effects of elementary school segregation in Topeka soon gave rise to the *Brown vs. Board of Education* case, which Scott's own sons litigated.

The GI Bill of Rights, ostensibly color-blind, nevertheless was designed to limit the ability of Black veterans to take full advantage of its offerings. A key provision allowed local authorities to dole out the funds, and the Deep South states notoriously prevented African Americans from using them to any significant degree. Elisha Scott used his connections to the office of Republican governor Andrew Schoeppel to ensure that Black Kansas veterans were able to attend college on the GI Bill in their state.

Since he had disembarked in Junction City, an hour west of Topeka, Arthur Fletcher did not meet Elisha Scott at the train station when he left the army. Indeed, it is unclear exactly when the two met, but the respected community elder did meet Fletcher soon after his return from Indiana, and he took a keen interest in Fletcher's education and professional development throughout his college career. In particular, he introduced Fletcher to another powerful connection, state supreme court justice William A. Smith, who helped the young student get part-time jobs at and near the state capitol. Justice Smith, according to scholar Mark Peterson, "was known for his generosity" in the African American community as a white ally in the cause of equality in and around Topeka, both for providing cash to struggling Black students "and in arranging patronage employment with the state."

The Fletchers in 1949, at veterans' housing in Topeka: Art, Mary, Phyllis, Sylvia, Art Jr., and Paul. The next year would see the birth of Phillip. Arthur Fletcher Personal Papers, courtesy Paul Fletcher.

Through Smith, Fletcher secured jobs as a doorman when the legislature was in session and as a student worker for the state highway department when it was not. Indefatigable and energetic, he also waited tables at the nearby Jayhawk Hotel, a popular hangout for local politicos; worked nights during the off-season at Morell Packing Company cleaning out dog food machines; and in the spring of his senior year was an aide at the Topeka state hospital.[10]

At the statehouse, Fletcher received an education to rival his coursework at Washburn. He learned the ins and outs of Kansas state government—how bills were argued, coalitions formed, and budgets apportioned. He learned that the soft currency of government work was personal connections, and that these could always come in handy down the road. "Listening to the lobbyists and watching them write their kind of papers that end up in legislation just kind of helped to drive home the point that Scott [was] trying to make," Fletcher later recalled. "You've got to get public policy on the books in the State before you can [make a difference]. If there isn't a statute on the books somewhere that authorizes you . . . the chances of . . . getting it done is not going to happen."[11]

Jobs in hand, Fletcher installed his family in public housing at 1309 East Lake Street, in an integrated (but predominantly Black) neighborhood in

Topeka, a short drive from campus and from his jobs. Mary delivered Arthur Jr., the Fletchers' first son, in 1946; a fourth child, Paul, was born in 1948.[12] His family saw little of him. Despite the demands of his several jobs, he devoted as much time to his classwork as he did to his efforts on the gridiron, majoring in sociology (although he also enjoyed political science and history) and earning mostly As and Bs. He joined the Young Republicans, becoming vice chairman of the Washburn chapter and then vice chairman of the state chapter. "My inclination to get involved came from [Elisha] Scott ... insisting ... 'I want you to run for ... that vice chairman seat' that was kind of earmarked for blacks at all city and county committees." In addition to football, he spent three seasons on the Washburn track team, and he pledged Omega Psi Phi, one of the Divine Nine traditionally African American fraternities and sororities.[13]

He also managed to find time for civil rights activity. When he and James Warren, a friend from Junction City now also playing for Washburn, discovered that they were unwelcome at the after-game varsity dances, they shouldered their way in:

> And then they moved the varsity from the campus to a private hall, and the owner ... said that the black students could not come ... so ... James Warren and I gathered up the black students—it wasn't over 150 of us—and we all went out to the door and threatened not to let anybody else in ... unless we can get in. And we ... got the class president and demanded that [he] find out whether there was anybody in that student body that didn't want the members of the football team and the rest of the black students to attend the dance. It was put to a kind of a vote right out there, and of course, it was just impossible for them to say no. We had beat Emporia State Teachers College that night, 21 to nothing; and Warren and I had made all the points. The net result ... was that we integrated the varsities.[14]

Certainly the most important civil rights action to take place in Topeka during Fletcher's years at Washburn was the buildup to the original *Brown v. Board of Education* case. Kansas school segregation laws were peculiar. Unlike in the Deep South, where separate schooling was required, Kansas law permitted local school boards to maintain separate facilities, but only at the elementary level, and only in "cities of the first class"—that is, with populations greater than 15,000. There were twelve such cities in the years immediately after World War II, and school boards in ten of them maintained segregated elementary schools. Only Kansas City, by exception, was permitted segregated high schools. Further, most observers agreed that education within the segregated schools in Kansas was fundamentally equal. Of course, these "cities of the first class" were those where the Kansas Black population was concentrated, and the issue in *Brown* was not inequality within the school but in the innate hardship caused by requiring young Linda Brown and children like her to travel across town while their white neighbors went to school nearby. In Topeka, white, Hispanic, and Asian American students attended neighborhood schools while Black youngsters and their parents could choose from among four Black schools. Linda Brown had to leave home exceedingly early to walk down the street and across railroad tracks to catch the school bus the city provided—and if she missed it, she'd miss instruction. Her white neighbors attended Sumner School, just around the corner, and often returned home for lunch. In 1950 Oliver Brown attempted to register Linda at Sumner School and was rebuffed.[15]

Fletcher's connection to the *Brown* case has been the subject of some dispute. He certainly was a Black parent in Topeka at the time that Oliver Brown and other members of the local National Association for the Advancement of Colored People (NAACP) decided to bring the lawsuit; he was certainly involved in local civil rights initiatives; and no one has disputed his claimed connection to two of the three lawyers for the plaintiffs—Charles and John Scott—through their father, Elisha. Given his gregarious personality, growing fame as a Washburn football star, and interest in civil rights, it is likely that Fletcher met and discussed school segregation with Charles and John Scott while they were completing their studies at Washburn Law School. John graduated in 1947, when Fletcher completed his freshman year, and Charles a year later. Like Fletcher, both had served in World War II. "So if anybody asks you what—where the seed corn for Brown versus the School Board of Topeka, where did it start? It started right over here on Washburn's campus with guys in the Law School," Fletcher said, and then it moved "down to the Jordan Patterson Post, which was the black American Legion here on Fourth Street." Four decades later, Linda's sister, Cheryl Brown Henderson, who ran the Brown Foundation in Topeka, acknowledged his "inextricable link to the individuals who worked to make the Brown decision a reality," and Fletcher claimed to have helped raise money for the case in "1954 while teaching in a rural elementary school in Kansas."[16]

It is there, however, that Fletcher's verifiable and likely connections with the case ended, despite his claim very late in life that he had been "one of nine original litigants." (He confused the number of parents with the

Little Rock Nine; in fact, there were thirteen litigants in the Topeka case, and none named Fletcher.) Although he was a Black Topeka parent, he and Mary did not send their children to public elementary schools. Mary was Catholic, and Art had agreed to raise the children in that tradition. So when their firstborn, Phyllis, two years younger than Linda Brown, entered kindergarten in the fall of 1949, they enrolled her at the local Catholic school. Unlike the white public elementary schools, which excluded Black children but admitted Hispanics, the "white" Catholic elementary schools excluded Hispanics but admitted Blacks. Also, while the seed may have been planted in 1947 and 1948, when Fletcher's undergraduate years overlapped with Charles and John Scott's years at Washburn Law, the case itself began with a fund-raiser on November 9, 1950, after the unsuccessful attempt of Brown and twelve other parents to enroll their children at white public elementary schools that fall. Indeed, in a 1990 speech in Kansas City, Fletcher alluded to a close connection to the case, but he went only so far as to say that he had friends at the meeting: "I only wish that my good friends who sat in a room in 1950 and fought about whether we should file Brown versus Topeka could be here to see this."[17] As we shall see, Fletcher was nowhere near Topeka in fall 1950, and it is highly unlikely that he returned for the fund-raiser or was consulted at the time by those involved.

Star of the Gridiron

Fletcher's jobs and civil rights activities were, of course, secondary to his football career at Washburn. He spent his freshman year, the 1946 season, on and off the field. Coach Godlove, himself new to the team, sought to find the best place for Fletcher, who was listed as an end. Fletcher started out strong, providing two of the three touchdown receptions for Washburn's opening-day victory over Emporia State. Washburn went on to win the first six games, but not the final three, ending the season with a 6–2–1 record. Still, Fletcher was one of three Washburn Ichabods to make the *Topeka Daily Capitol*'s all-conference team.[18]

It was in his sophomore year, the 1947 season, that a star was born. After the second game of the season, a *Washburn Review* sports editor named Fletcher the lineman of the week, and the *Emporia Gazette* noted that the Washburn "line is built around Art Fletcher, [a] 215-pound colored giant at end." For the fifth game of the season, against St. Benedict's Men's College in Atchison, Kansas, Godlove "moved husky Art Fletcher out of the line [and] inserted him in the backfield in an effort to gain more scoring punch,"

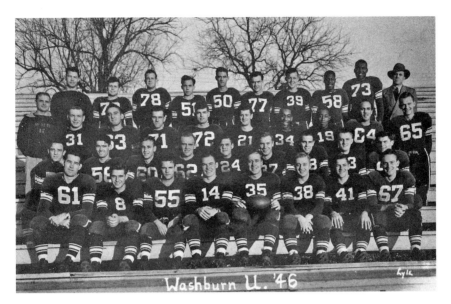

Washburn University football team portrait, Art's freshman season, 1946. He is number 73, *top right*, next to the coach, Dick Godlove. Arthur Fletcher Personal Papers, courtesy Paul Fletcher.

reported the *Kaw* yearbook. "The strategy paid off, as Fletcher was harder to stop than a Santa Fe Streamliner. He scored two of our touchdowns on straight power plays," contributing to a 26–6 victory. At least one local Black teenager, normally a St. Benedict's fan, recalled being "silently overjoyed for the achievements [he] made that evening in beating the Ravens who . . . had not integrated their team." Fletcher and white back Leroy Harmon were clearly the stars of that 7–1 season. He only made the second string of the all-conference team that year, owing to a plethora of excellent ends, according to the *Iola Register*. One columnist worried that racism would block Fletcher's admission to the top college football honors but noted that he technically hadn't been snubbed yet because he was only a sophomore. The *Kaw* included a picture of four opponents trying to tackle "Big Art" Fletcher, rushing yards against Nebraska's Peru State College in a 12–6 Washburn victory, with the provocative caption "It takes 4 to stop Fletcher."[19]

At an away game at Fort Hays State College, Fletcher had particular difficulty off the field. In his freshman year, he wasn't allowed to stay in the same hotel as the rest of the team. Coach Godlove insisted that this ban end, later telling a reporter that "the hotel wanted our business bad enough they gave in. I think Art was the first Negro ever in that hotel." But when they admitted him in 1947, they wouldn't let him eat breakfast in the restaurant where other guests could see him, so "I went to Art and asked him how he would like breakfast in bed. [He] thought that was great because he was a pretty well balanced individual and understood the situation." When the Fort Hays college cafeteria refused to serve Fletcher, Godlove demanded that it shut down, then serve the Washburn team its meal alone, reopening only after all the Ichabods had left. After the game, racist students burned Fletcher in effigy, and when they faced Washburn in Topeka, it was even worse: "Reports hitting the desk indicate that the [Fort Hays] Tigers do not do all of their fist-fighting on the practice field, according to Mr. Art Fletcher, colored end for the Ichabods. Fletcher came out of the fracas at Topeka with a broken nose, supposedly inflicted when it came in violent contact with a balled-up fist on the end of a Tiger arm."[20]

That Fletcher "was a pretty well balanced individual and understood the situation" speaks volumes about not only the developing relationship between Coach Godlove and his rising star but also the deep-seated nature of racist attitudes among even the most well-meaning whites, and Fletcher's growing expertise in achieving and excelling despite it. For Godlove, Fletcher's quiet acquiescence and forced smile at the prospect of breakfast in bed marked him as a "good Negro," one who would accept society's racial proscriptions without a fight. In this formulation, discrimination was a white problem, which whites alone were responsible for solving. Godlove's expedient compromise allowed him to feel good about his own racial attitude despite the fact that as a coach in a conference that included all-white teams, he was abetting continued discrimination. Continued exclusion from the hotel's restaurant and Godlove's willingness to compromise on the matter were surely painful and frustrating for Fletcher, but he knew that his continued ability to play football was dependent on the coach seeing him as a "well balanced individual."

Fletcher's junior-year season, during the fall of 1948, appears from available sources to have been more lackluster for the team. Fletcher, however, continued to excel. At a loss against the Washington University Bears in St. Louis, "Washburn made her best drive of the game in the final quarter, from her own 15 to the Bears' 20 for 65 yards. . . . Art Fletcher, fleet Ichabod back, was outstanding in this drive." At a 20–19 "upset" against the Omaha University Cardinals, Fletcher scored the second of three touchdowns for the team, with Leroy Harmon scoring the other two. One impressive victory, however, came at homecoming on October 22. Fletcher scored an astounding five touchdowns, leading the team to beat St. Benedict's, 53–0. But the Ichabods lost their final game, despite two Fletcher touchdowns and more

Washburn possessions than their Southwestern Moundbuilder opponents. They ended the season in fourth place, with Fletcher returning to the first string of the all-conference team and ranking fourth nationally among small-college rushers.[21]

The Washburn Ichabods had a truly outstanding season in Fletcher's senior year, earning a 7–2 record and sharing the championship with the Pittsburg (Kansas) State University Gorillas. Fletcher, now cocaptain with Leroy Harmon, was no less outstanding. After rushing more than 700 yards for the season, Fletcher was named one of three Washburn players to the all-conference team, the only all-conference player to earn a unanimous vote from the judges.[22]

After making the first two touchdowns in a preseason 31–13 victory over Doane College in Crete, Nebraska, Fletcher really "caught fire" in the third game, his "scintillating thrusts into the line" nonetheless failing to bring victory. But that 14–19 loss against Emporia State Teachers College, in which "Washburn . . . got two touchdowns in the third period [and] Art Fletcher plunged for the first one after Washburn returned a punt to Emporia's 35," was Washburn's last of the season. The next week they beat the Omaha University Indians 13–6, with Fletcher scoring one touchdown. Then they beat Pittsburg 27–19. According to the *Topeka Daily Capitol*, the "big gun in the Ichabods' ground offense was big Art Fletcher. The long-legged Junction City tailback cracked Pittsburg's line for top yardage throughout the night, twice going over for Washburn touchdowns." The sports editor gushed, "Fletcher definitely had a busy evening. The lanky tailback carried the ball 23 times to go 113 yards for an average of almost five per try. To boot he had one run of 34 yards called back by a Washburn penalty and also took one pass for 17 yards." Fletcher, Harmon, and rising star Gene Brooks led Washburn to three more victories: against St. Benedict's, 21–6; Kansas City's Rockhurst College by an incredible 60–0; and Fort Hays, 35–13. Rockhurst was the homecoming game at Washburn's Moore Bowl, in which Fletcher scored two touchdowns and was "the reliable ground gaining ace."[23]

The final game of the season, in Winfield, Kansas, against the Southwestern College Moundbuilders, was a true nail-biter. At halftime, Washburn was down 13–0, but the Ichabods roared back to win 21–20. "Fletcher showed his running ways quickly in the fourth quarter," reported the *Topeka State Journal*. "Harmon plowed for 10 yards to the Builder 41. A long pitchout to Fletch caught Southwestern napping and the high-stepping Negro outran the field for 40 yards but was nailed on the one. On the next play Fletcher tallied over right tackle. Harmon split the posts again and Washburn took a safe lead,

21–13." While Fletcher was a star, he was also a team player. His was the winning touchdown, but Harmon's extra point won the game: Southwestern made a touchdown with extra point in the game's last minute, and if not for Harmon's kick would have tied the score. Wrote Sam Jackson, student sports editor, "Coach Dick Godlove was so happy that he couldn't stop the tears from flowing. He laughed, cried, and hugged each of his players."[24] A week later, Pittsburg State won their final game, tying Washburn for the CIC championship, but Fletcher was in a position to share: "Don't be surprised," wrote Jackson, "if you read about Leroy Harmon and Art Fletcher playing Pro football next year. Big Fletch has already got a tryout contract from the Los Angeles Rams."[25]

Fletcher had spent his years at Washburn looking at developments in professional football with eager anticipation. In 1946, during his freshman season, the Los Angeles Rams broke the color barrier, signing Kenneth Washington seven months before Jackie Robinson became the first Black major league baseball player. The fledgling All-America Football Conference (AAFC), founded in 1944 to challenge the dominant National Football League (NFL), started play in 1946 with eight teams and was more welcoming of Black players, hiring thirteen by 1949. Two leagues were also growing in even more egalitarian Canada, further adding to the "seller's market."[26] Indeed, the growth and integration of the professional sport were very encouraging, as Fletcher recounted with what is likely an apocryphal tale:

> I'm having scouts come look at me from the Los Angles Dons [AAFC], from the Brooklyn Dodgers [AAFC], from the Chicago Rockets [AAFC] and at the same time I'm getting a call from Canada. Every year I got a call from Canada wanting me to come up there and play . . . I get an offer for five thousand dollars in my freshman year, I get an offer for ten thousand dollars . . . my sophomore year, got an offer for fifteen [as a junior,] so I know twenty is coming.[27]

Then the bottom fell out. The AAFC folded after the 1949 season, and only three of its teams—the Cleveland Browns, San Francisco 49ers, and Baltimore Colts—merged into the NFL. Making matters worse, the anticipated full integration had yet to arrive. The Colts still excluded Black players, blaming intense racial animus in their city, and no prior NFL team other than the Rams and the Detroit Lions had more than one Black player. Going into the 1950 season, therefore, Black professional football players were still a tiny minority in the sport. Further, the competition for pro slots in

1950 turned out to be even tougher than for college slots in 1946. Whereas in '46 Fletcher was competing against four classes of high school graduates delayed by the war, now he was competing not only against the best of those—now college graduates themselves—but also laid-off professionals from defunct teams. "So the market is crowded with 33 players who already had at least one year of pro experience," Fletcher later told an interviewer. "I finished in 1950 and that's the big year of GI Bill graduates, and there [were] some goodies who finished school in 1950." There had been a flip to a "buyer's market," and every pro slot was precious.[28]

The claim by *Washburn Review* sports columnist Sam Jackson in November 1949 that "Big Fletch has already got a tryout contract from the Los Angeles Rams" is probably based on Fletcher's own statements to Jackson. Pro scouts did visit college games, even on occasion small college games like those of Washburn's CIC, but pro tryouts in that era were as often the result of personal connections and pluck, and the plucky Fletcher had a connection to the Rams. His mother, Edna, had relocated to Santa Ana, California, not far from the Rams' training camp at Redlands University. Given the skills he was learning at the Kansas statehouse and the personality traits that would later serve him well, it is likely that Fletcher had gone to meet the coaching staff during a summertime visit before his senior year.[29]

In any event, while any tryout contract was surely conditional on need, and likely evaporated in spring 1950 after the AAFC collapse flooded the market, Fletcher was determined to become the third Black player for the Rams. After graduation he, Mary, and their four children moved in with Edna in Santa Ana:

I go over there and watch them practice for two days and then walked on. I told the coach who I was, and he says, "We're interested in you and a guy named Bill Litchfield that played down at Emporia State [another CIC school]. What's he doing?" I said, "I don't know, I'll tell you what I'm doing. I'm trying to get on this football team." So he said, "Check your health and come and talk to our doctors." And the next day I took the health examination and they issued me a football uniform for the Los Angeles Rams.

Fletcher was signed onto the roster. After a July scrimmage against the Washington Redskins, who were training at nearby Occidental College, Rams "End Coach Red Hickey said he was 'pleasantly surprised' by the showing of a new candidate, Art Fletcher of Washburn College of Kansas. Fletcher, a rangy Negro weighing 203, walked into camp the other day unannounced and asked for a trial. He lives in nearby Perris where L. B. Mayer's horse factory used to thrive."[30]

Fletcher continued to play exhibition games with the Rams through the summer, and he distinguished himself whenever given the opportunity. "We've got two promising rookies in Johnny Smith and Art Fletcher," Hickey told the *Los Angeles Times*. "Fletcher . . . has done everything asked of him, both on offense and defense." Fletcher did well despite the team's lackluster performance on the field that summer. In a lopsided 14–49 loss to the Philadelphia Eagles, he scored one of the Rams' two touchdowns. "The only display of sustained zeal by our bedraggled local heroes came in the fourth quarter . . . when Norman Van Brocklin completed [a pass to] Art Fletcher. Art scored the touchdown, making a nifty catch right in the westside coffin corner . . . on a 28-yard throw." Against their neighbor Redskins again they lost 14–17, but "got another chance with six minutes to play when Art Fletcher, promising rookie end, flopped on Bartos' fumble on the 'Skin 32.'" New head coach Joe "Stydahar was tickled by the excellent showing of three rookie linemen, Guards Stan West and Bill Lange and End Art Fletcher." Tickled enough, apparently, to give Fletcher a shot at the end of August in a San Antonio exhibition game against the Baltimore Colts. Jerry "Williams . . . hot footed it 85 yards for the touchdown with Fletcher applying the key block on the Colt nine-yard line." In fact, at one point Fletcher made three blocks in a single play, including one on future hall of famer Art Donovan. The Rams won 70–21.[31]

But he was cut from the roster—waivered, in the parlance of the game— just before the start of the regular season. In his place, the Rams kept Bob Boyd, an African American sprinter from Loyola University of Los Angeles (now Loyola Marymount). Fletcher later claimed that Boyd's selection was based on his having graduated from a local Catholic college: "They knew that if they kept him, he would draw the Catholic crowd to come see Los Angeles whenever they were there." There may have been some truth to this. Despite management's great expectations of the sprint champion alternately dubbed "the dash king," "the Loyola flash," and even "Seabiscuit"—a reference to the champion race horse—Boyd's performance that summer was less than stellar. In fact, during the 14–17 loss to the Redskins in which Fletcher recovered a fumble, the team might have won if not for another fumble—by Bob Boyd. Nevertheless, Boyd went on to play eight seasons with the Rams, distinguishing himself in particular in 1954, when he made the NFL's All-Pro team and played in the Pro Bowl.[32]

Back in Kansas, at least one sportswriter sympathized:

West coast football writers . . . are burning over the dismissal of Art Fletcher . . . from the roster of the Los Angeles professional club. Fletcher . . . joined the pro ranks when he graduated from Washburn last spring, and the west coast writers thought that he was the best looking end on the Ram squad. Which didn't stop the management from giving Fletcher the boot. . . . Evidently the big boy had looked terrific in early season games, and the writers thought that he was being given a raw deal.

In fact, the waiver had nothing to do with Fletcher's performance or Boyd's popularity. Head coach Joe Stydahar wanted to convert star defensive left halfback Elroy Hirsch, alternately known as "the Wausau Wiggler" and "Crazy Legs," into an offensive right end—Fletcher's position. That, plus a surfeit of ends, made Fletcher superfluous. The best that the "West coast football writers" themselves could say of Fletcher was that he made a "noble effort."[33]

As happened so often in his life, Fletcher got a second chance. In that September 2 game in San Antonio against the Colts, he had impressed the Baltimore coaches. The Colts had been a 1947 replacement team in the AAFC, filling a gap left by the defunct Miami Seahawks franchise. Unlike teams in more cosmopolitan Miami, however, the Colts excluded Black players owing to the more overt racism in Baltimore—a city segregated by law. "There was no hotel I could go to, no restaurant I could go to," said Fletcher of the town. (In fact, he did register at an all-Black hotel, the York, but was forced to leave when the league commissioner discovered gambling taking place there.) The Colts had no Black players; neither did any other professional sports team in the city. Black Baltimoreans hungered to see players of their own race on the field, however, arguing that the money they paid for football tickets was just as good as that of whites. When the Colts president told the editor of a Black-owned newspaper that he had "genuine interest in bringing on colored talent," sales of 1950 season tickets to Black patrons saw a significant increase. But the idea seemed stillborn in the 1950 summertime exhibition season, as the most attractive available Black players—George Taliaferro of the now-defunct Los Angeles Dons and Buddy Young of the now-defunct New York Yankees—were both quickly snapped up by the New York Bulldogs. (Taliaferro and Young eventually landed with a resurrected Colts team in 1953.)[34]

Finally, in October, after Arthur Fletcher had been off the field for three weeks and was, by his own admission, out of shape, the Colts signed a contract making him the first Black athlete on any professional sports team in the history of Baltimore. On October 15, 1950, Fletcher took the field as Number 53 in the green-and-silver uniform of the original Colts in a home game against the Philadelphia Eagles (which they lost, 14–24). During the final seven minutes, with the Colts down, "Art Fletcher, Negro end from Los Angeles, broke into the Colt lineup. The big fellow played well on defense," reported the *Baltimore Sun*. The following week, the Colts took on Fletcher's former teammates in Los Angeles, and Fletcher gave a decent—if not outstanding—performance, despite a lopsided 27–70 loss. "A pass, [Y. A.] Tittle to Art Fletcher, was good to the Ram 16 and three plays later Burk connected with Mutryn in the end zone." Head coach Clem Crowe told a reporter that Fletcher "already handles himself better than any defensive end we have on the roster."[35]

In fact, the Baltimore job represented quite an opportunity for Fletcher. Whereas the Rams had too many ends, the Colts had too few; Fletcher went from being a small fish in a big pond to a big fish in a small pond. The local press, eager to tell his story, played up the arrival of the city's first Black pro player. "This week the Colts signed a 6-foot-four-inch wingman who has displayed in practice his billing as a sprinter as well as an end. The new man is Art Fletcher, 210-pound Negro end from Washburn College," wrote Cameron Snyder of the *Sun,* adding that Fletcher's "mere presence has added more pep and vim to the Colt workouts." Coach "Crowe accounts for this uplift in spirits with the advent of Fletcher to the fact that the team now feels it has an end who can go all the way. Heretofore, the Colt ends were limited to catching short passes." So eager was the coach to play Fletcher— and Fletcher to take the field—that he flew him across the country the day he bought Fletcher's contract, rather than wait to have him join the team during the Colts' West Coast trip the following week. As a member of the starting lineup, Fletcher found himself giving his first professional interview. "We can beat the Rams," he told the *Sun's* James Ellis. "They've got good men but not as much spirit as we have." Gushing reporter Snyder added, "The 210-pound 6-foot-four-inch Negro has given the Colts a shot where they needed it most."[36]

Breaking the color barrier was a mixed experience for Fletcher. His hiring was denounced by angry white racist fans, decrying what they saw as an attack on "the Maryland way of life." But Fletcher had good relationships with his teammates. "Art Donovan, who was one of the tackles, Art and I got along pretty good. [Y. A.] Tittle was a quarterback, and [Y. A.] and I got along because I was his receiver." Still, "it was more tolerance than acceptance."[37]

Coach Crowe had hired Fletcher to please the local African American community, but he was loath to use him too much, fearing a box office backlash by the majority-white population. Fletcher later also claimed that his war wound scar—visible in the locker room every day of practice—made the coaches worry that he might keel over on the field. Despite two completions against the Rams on October 22, "Art Fletcher, incidentally, may not get another chance on the attack," wrote the disappointed James Ellis of the *Sun*. "The big Negro end is not proving consistent as a receiver. He was awarded a starting assignment against the Rams and was so tense when the ball came at him he dropped two passes in the clear that might have gone for touchdowns." Coach Crowe agreed. He fired him in the lobby of a Beverly Hills hotel.[38]

After less than three weeks playing for Baltimore, including only a single home game and the honor of having finally broken the city's color barrier, Fletcher's professional football career was over for good. "Pro football . . . at that time was still full of color prejudice," summarized his well-meaning college coach, Dick Godlove, some years later in a letter of recommendation. "While he was good enough to play, he shortly had the intelligence to get out of it and started making an effort toward a more stable career. . . . He returned to Topeka and went about the serious business of trying to raise his family on a good standard."[39]

The 1950 season, lackluster for Fletcher, was disastrous for the Colts. Quarterback Tittle, who went on to stardom with the San Francisco 49ers and New York Giants, called the 1950 Colts "the worst professional football team in history." The team ended the season with an abysmal 1–11 record, their only win coming in a home game against the Green Bay Packers on November 5. "What really was disastrous is at the end of that season the Colts went out of business," said Fletcher. Declining box office receipts forced the team to fold after only a single season in the NFL. Colts football would return to Baltimore after a two-year hiatus, but with a completely different team. The blue-and-white-clad New York Bulldogs, renamed the Yanks in 1951, spent the 1952 season as the Dallas Texans; ejected from the Cotton Bowl midseason for poor sales, they then played without a home field, folding at season's end. In 1953 most members of that team brought those colors to a new home in Baltimore as the Colts, which remained in the city until a 1984 relocation to Indianapolis.[40]

Fletcher's five years on the college and professional gridiron, despite his setbacks in the job market and the frustrations of the 1950 season, nevertheless constituted a successful chapter in his life. College football taught him that hard work, when applied to existing talent, could bring success. He diligently worked at his off-campus jobs to make ends meet for his growing family. Wisely, he never neglected his studies, ensuring a better chance at a secure future regardless of how his football career worked out, later noting that "going to Washburn was the greatest decision I ever made."[41] But when he was on the field, either in practice or in a game, he focused on developing his skills with the pigskin. The result was college stardom, as reflected by the multiple articles about his exploits in student newspapers and in local Topeka periodicals, pages and pages about him in the Washburn *Kaw* yearbook, and the opportunity to make a career at the sport. They taught him the benefits of persistence: discouraged at Indiana University, he returned to Kansas and excelled at Washburn. Then, discouraged by the collapsed job market, he refused to quit. "After you give up, then what? So what use is giving up? You might as well keep on trying."[42] Defying the 1950 pro football buyer's market, not to mention the long odds against Black players at the time, he walked on at the Rams training camp, resulting in exhibition season employment—and recruitment by the Colts. They taught him to be a team player: working with Coach Godlove and the Washburn squad, he achieved success; but with Baltimore, brought on as the token Black and barely used, he saw the Colts collapse in an abysmal season that cost them their franchise.

That experience with the Colts also gave him firsthand knowledge of the limitations that racism placed on him. No matter how talented and determined he was, there were always racist whites who worked against him. Sometimes this racism was overt, as in hotels refusing to house him, restaurants refusing to serve him, and fans refusing to fill seats for him; sometimes it was covert, as with Coach Clem Crowe telling him that it was his war wound scar that prevented his making the Colts' starting lineup (the wound never bothered him when he was delivering ice or, more importantly, excelling as an Ichabod and as a Ram). Still other times it was unconscious, as with the well-meaning Dick Godlove's offering breakfast in bed to avoid a confrontation with a recalcitrant hotel.

But perhaps most importantly, his college years taught him the importance of mentorship. His affectionate, almost filial relationship with Coach Godlove had brought him great success at Washburn, but in Los Angeles and Baltimore, he was on his own; he learned to equate his chances at success to connections with powerful white patrons. And thanks to his connections at the Kansas statehouse, they had prepared him for his next adventure.

Apprentice

After his October 1950 release from the Colts, according to a job application he completed two decades later, Fletcher was unemployed and living at "Rural Rt # 4, Perris, Calif.," presumably with his mother Edna, wife Mary, and four children. A fifth child, Phillip, was born to the Fletchers in 1951. Perhaps Fletcher worked part time in his mother's barbecue restaurant in Riverside; perhaps he traveled to Canada that summer to make one more try at a pro football career (he later claimed to have either played or tried out for the Hamilton, Ontario, Tiger-Cats, but he did not appear on their roster). Mary surely was unhappy with the situation, living with her mother-in-law in an unfamiliar area for two years while raising five small children. Her support system was in Kansas, where, as a light-skinned daughter of a fairly well-to-do African American family, she certainly felt more at home. In November 1951, they returned to Junction City, and Fletcher went back to delivering ice for Ray McMillan.[43]

This time it stung. Fletcher was grateful to McMillan for the job, and indeed he kept it for more than two years. But he could not escape the fact that he was a college graduate delivering ice while whites from his graduating class at Washburn were already moving into management positions. In March 1953, he took a second job, as a tire builder at Goodyear in Topeka. Goodyear surely had jobs in Junction City, but he endured the hour-long commute along US Route 40 because his own connections were in the state capital. Fletcher gave up his job at Junction City Ice in the summer of 1953 and moved his family back to Topeka, installing them at 1220 Locust Street, a short walk from his old stomping grounds at the statehouse. He had high hopes for promotion to foreman at Goodyear, but when a position came open, he was rebuffed: such jobs didn't go to Blacks, he was told.[44]

If someone like Fletcher—a wounded veteran, college graduate, and local celebrity—couldn't get promoted to foreman at Goodyear Tire in a college town in a nonsouthern state like Kansas, clearly something was wrong. This was worse than unfair. But unlike his mother, who had no allies in the 1920s to help her get more appropriate employment, Fletcher was in the right place at the right time. The Scott brothers had recently filed Oliver Brown's case against the school board, and the NAACP Legal Defense and Education Fund, led by the formidable Thurgood Marshall, had combined it with other cases in the South that they were bringing to the Supreme Court. Indeed, Black Topeka had already achieved success, electing new school board members who forced through a vote integrating the Topeka elementary schools ahead of the 1954 decision. In this heady atmosphere, Fletcher became active in the Kansas state Republican Central Committee on the advice and recommendation of Elisha Scott. Thanks to a combination of his football celebrity and white Republicans' well-intentioned (if infantilizing) eagerness to demonstrate egalitarianism, he rose quickly through the ranks.[45]

Fletcher's employment prospects improved thanks to his involvement with the GOP Central Committee. Unlike in the Deep South after *Brown*, where integration often meant the displacement of Black teachers, Topeka schools were hiring, and Fletcher was politically positioned to take advantage of the opportunity. He enrolled in Kansas State University's postgraduate correspondence program in education in the fall of 1953, earned a teaching certificate, and became principal of the new Pierce Addition Elementary School for the 1954–1955 school year. Fletcher was finally moving up, in a solid career, and it was thanks to his political connections. That summer, when he learned that Lieutenant Governor Hall, a liberal Republican from Dodge City who favored equal employment opportunity for Blacks, was running for governor, Fletcher threw all of his copious energy into getting Fred Hall elected.[46]

Fred Hall was a 1934 recipient of a National High School Achievement Scholarship, which he used to take a bachelor's degree at the University of Southern California. At USC he became president of the Young Republicans Club, and after graduation in 1938 he stayed on to earn a law degree, which he completed in 1941. Like many of his generation, he signed up for military service after Pearl Harbor. Rejected as physically unfit for active duty, he spent the war in Washington as assistant director of the Production and Resource Board for the Combined Chiefs of Staff (later known as the Joint Chiefs). In 1944 he returned to Dodge City, where he worked for a law firm, chaired the Ford County Young Republicans, and from 1946 to 1949 served as county attorney. In 1950 he ran for lieutenant governor, the only resident of western Kansas among a field of eight seeking the GOP nomination. Described as "pugnacious, strong, aggressive, ambitious and fiercely independent," he won the nomination and the general election, and on January 8, 1951, he was sworn in as Kansas' thirty-first lieutenant governor.[47]

Hall served two terms as lieutenant governor, earning "a reputation as a trouble maker, even within his own party, and was constantly at odds with Gov. Ed Arn." The offices of governor and lieutenant governor were independently elected in Kansas, and the centrist Arn often found himself opposed by the liberal Hall. While campaigning for his own reelection in 1952, Arn actively worked to oust Hall. He won his own campaign but was unsuccessful in his attempt to replace Hall; their struggles continued.[48]

With Arn leaving office after a customary two terms (there were no legal term limits in Kansas until 1974), Hall resolved to take his place. His 1954 gubernatorial campaign exposed divisions within the party: Arn's moderate/conservative faction included most of the state senators. But the savvy Hall waged a progressive campaign in a state whose Republican electorate was not yet ready to endorse conservatism. His platform included support of a state Fair Employment Practices Commission (especially important to the party's Black voters) and opposition to the antilabor right-to-work movement, which sought to prevent unions from collecting fair-share dues from nonmember workers. He earned key endorsements from the state party chairman, who agreed to manage his campaign; state supreme court justice William A. Smith; and even "the grand old man of GOP politics in Kansas," former governor and 1936 Republican presidential nominee Alfred "Alf" Landon.[49]

Arthur Fletcher's return to Topeka in the spring of 1953 coincided with the rise of Fred Hall, and his relationship with Hall allowed him to develop the talent he had first discovered during his years at Washburn: politics. Fletcher's experience as a doorman at the state capitol when the legislature was in session, and at the state motor vehicle and highway department when it was not, had given him a unique internship in the workings of state government; his time as a waiter at the Jayhawk Hotel had schooled him on the personal side of politics—how alliances were forged and deals were struck. His political apprenticeship with Hall now gave him further insights into the realities of political work and fortified him with advanced skills and background in the craft—skills he used for the rest of his life.[50]

Fletcher first met Hall while at Washburn, through the good graces of Justice William Smith. The progressive jurist, who had helped Fletcher get his first jobs in state government during his college years, was also an early patron of Hall's. Now Fletcher was a rising star in the Republican Central Committee, and Hall was running for governor against the Arn-supporting regulars. For a liberal like Hall to win the statehouse, he not only needed to win the Black vote but he also needed to register Black voters who had previously been politically apathetic. It was here that Fletcher helped. Outside of the state's three largest cities—Kansas City, Wichita, and Topeka—the largest concentration of Blacks was in the rural southeastern corner of the state. Fletcher knew the area well, having played college ball against teams down there in Pittsburg and Fort Scott. According to political scientist Mark Peterson,

> In the 1950s blacks in this area were largely without political voice. Most of the families had come to the area following the Civil War to work in the coal mines owned by the Missouri, Kansas, and Texas Railroad Company and the Atchison, Topeka, and Santa Fe Railway. During the late summer and fall of 1954, Fletcher . . . used his . . . notoriety derived from his athletic career at Washburn to meet with and mobilize members of that isolated black population. In the course of a few months, Fletcher said, with $5,000 in campaign money and a salary of $75 a week from Hall's campaign war chest, he motivated ten thousand heretofore non-participating black adults to register and then vote for Fred Hall for governor.[51]

Hall beat Arn's favorite in the GOP primary, former state senator George Templar, and went on to win the general election "by a margin of 40,000 votes" over Democrat George Docking.[52]

Fletcher's work was a critical aspect of Hall's gubernatorial victory, and Hall was impressed by the young man's passion, drive, and charisma. Hall also needed to keep the campaign promises Fletcher had been making on his behalf to the Black voters in Kansas' southeast. One such constituent, Earl Thomas Reynolds of Coffeyville, wrote soon after the election to request that the new governor appoint Blacks to state positions on an equal basis to whites. Blacks "have received an unusual amount of consideration during the brief time I have been" governor, Hall replied to Reynolds. "I have employed a Negro woman as an office secretary, there have been numerous Negro people working in jobs created by the legislature being in session, Art Fletcher recently received an appointment—all in all considering the few openings there have been so far, I believe recognition has been shown as called for." That spring the new governor asked Fletcher to leave his position at Pierce Addition Elementary and work full time in his administration.[53]

Fletcher's official job in the Hall administration was assistant public relations director for the state highway department. This made sense given his experience there as a student worker. Unofficially, however, Fletcher was Hall's right-hand man on all matters concerning African Americans. He liaised with the hostile legislature on fair employment legislation, chaired a state commission on equal opportunity, and became vice chair of the GOP Central Committee.[54]

2-28-55

Earl Thomas Reynolds
Attorney At Law
Coffeyville, Kansas

Dear Mr. Reynolds:

In reply to your recent letter concerning consideration of Negroes, I thank you for your comments.

I am a little surprised, however, that you seem unsure as to my attitude on the matter. I think you will find through a minimum of investigation that they have received an unusual amount of consideration during the brief time I have been in my present position.

I have employed a Negro woman as an office secretary, there have been numerous Negro people working in jobs created by the legislature being in session, Art Fletcher recently received an appointment---all in all, considering the few openings there have been so far, I believe recognition has been shown as called for.

such would be

maybe As for the Third District, I realize perhaps what you say is true; but is a matter which must be worked out pretty much on the local level there.

My best personal regards,

Fred Hall
Governor of Kansas

FH:JK

Not long after Fred Hall's election as governor of Kansas, he appointed Fletcher to the State Highway Department. Kansas State Historical Society; special thanks to Mark Peterson.

Fletcher helped make clear that on equal employment opportunity, the Hall administration was a departure from the prior regime. A case in point was that of Mrs. Edwyna Dones of Topeka, an African American who had been denied a job as a social worker by the Shawnee County Board of Commissioners. Her complaint to the State Board Against Discrimination met with approval and was referred to the governor's office. Governor Arn had ignored it; Hall picked it up and tasked Fletcher with investigating the case. Fletcher concluded that Mrs. Dones "is qualified as her score on the examination indicates [and] is well thought of by her co-workers and that she and her husband are highly regarded by their neighbors," adding "the majority of her co-workers and neighbors are white." Knowing that his audience went beyond the sympathetic governor to the hiring board that had earlier denied her a job, and that his memo could eventually be used as evidence in legal proceedings, Fletcher added that "in my opinion there is nothing in this file nor in her personality make-up to indicate that she is a trouble maker or race conscious." Hall asked that the board reconsider the case.[55]

We know little else about Edwyna Dones, including the ultimate disposition of her case. However, Fletcher's words on the recommendation are telling. What was his definition of "trouble maker"? What did he see as "race conscious"? Few Kansas Blacks in the 1950s, given the pervasive racial discrimination, could avoid race consciousness; Fletcher himself was race conscious, as surely was Mrs. Dones. And the very act of protesting discrimination—as Fletcher had several times in his life already, and as Mrs. Dones had in filing her complaint with the State Board Against Discrimination—made trouble for the white supremacist system and the whites who benefited from it. Most whites pretended that the system was as egalitarian as the Declaration of Independence promised, and resented those troublemakers who reminded them that it was not. The recommendation indicates that Fletcher had learned by 1955 that he could be equally effective at undermining the system by using the language of the oppressors as through direct confrontation.

The most important lessons Fletcher drew from his apprenticeship with Hall, however, had nothing to do with the actual nuts and bolts of governing, equal opportunity, or even the political wheeling and dealing he had first observed at his college jobs at the statehouse and the Jayhawk Hotel. His political connections had elevated him from tire builder to school principal to statewide appointee in less than a year, and it was now clear to the young father of five that politics was lucrative. "Once Fred [Hall] convinced me that politics was not about social justice," he later said, "I started trying to figure out a way to make some money."[56]

The position of assistant public relations director for the Kansas state highway department during construction of the Eisenhower interstate highway system proved a plum assignment, to say the least. Anyone who wanted a highway construction contract, or just desired a connection to the liberal governor, sought to get in good with Fletcher. His first foray into the business world using his connections was to open the Esquire Motor Company, a used-car business for soldiers and airmen. Recognizing that servicemen needed affordable cars in an increasingly suburban society, he approached the credit unions at Fort Riley back in Junction City and Forbes Air Force Base just outside Topeka. He convinced the loan officers there to preapprove member soldiers and airmen, and arranged similar preapprovals for workers at his former places of employment, notably Goodyear Tire (management there had an interest in getting employees into cars) and the meatpacking plant he'd worked at in college. Checks in hand from prospective buyers, Fletcher purchased cheap cars by the dozen at auction in Kansas City, then turned around and sold these to the preapproved servicemen at a profit, processing title, registration, and even insurance, all for a fee. Thanks to his political job at the department, he knew supervisors at every local DMV office in the state. And with his considerable influence over highway contractors, he always had places to park his overstock.[57]

A second venture stretched Fletcher's political muscles even further. His father, Cotton, had been a member of a segregated post of the American Legion in Junction City, which had brought in top-name Black entertainers such as Cab Calloway, Count Basie, and Duke Ellington. With the integration of the military and the aging of the previous generation of vets, this had slowed to a stop. Fletcher reached out to the leader of the chapter and looked into the files, where he found the contact information for a booking agent in New York City.

So I got on the phone and called him and asked him who he could provide me with. He said. . . . "Who do you want?" I said, "Who you got?" He said, "I've got Ray Charles." . . . I said, "What do I have to do?" He said, "Send me an advance and I'll send you the contract. . . . He was coaching me from . . . New York. He said, "Paper the place, the telephone post, the barber shops, wherever folks go . . . sell enough tickets to take care of your . . . advance and make your profit at the door, and if you sell enough advance tickets, those who pay at the door, they're going to pay an increased price. You'll clean up."[58]

Fletcher then contacted the commandants of army, air force, and national guard bases and armories in Kansas and the four adjoining states to contract their auditoriums. All of these commandants had an interest in pleasing Fletcher, not only for his general connection to the state government but for his job at the highway department in particular: they wanted to ensure that new highways linked to their bases, and they wanted backroom influence over who won those contracts. Fletcher booked major Black entertainers and sold a limited number of cut-rate advance tickets to pay the booking agent and the performers, drumming up interest in the show. The commandants kept the parking concessions, and Fletcher's profits, as predicted, came from selling scores of higher-priced tickets at the door. Before long Fletcher was presenting entertainers to mostly Black audiences throughout the region. "Long story short, boy, when Ray Charles came to that . . . auditorium, there were people around the corner. When it was ready to close, they was still trying to get in."[59]

While these ventures were of questionable ethics, at the time there was nothing illegal about any of this. Still, the picture we get of Arthur Fletcher during his political career in Kansas is of a politically savvy man who had learned to use his connections to power for his own monetary gain. While we should not judge this behavior so harshly as to claim that he was more self-serving than the venal white politicians of the day (much as earlier versions of history condemned Black Reconstruction-era politicians while ignoring Confederate treason and white Southern politicians' corruption, and World War II commanders treated Black soldiers' infractions more harshly than those of whites), neither should Fletcher be allowed a free pass for the same reason. But it is important to contrast the opportunism of the young Fletcher with the selfless civil rights advocate he later became.

Indeed, much consternation regarding Fletcher's schemes should be reserved for those who abetted them. The credit union officers at Forbes Field and Fort Riley were no doubt responsible for at least a few loan defaults among the servicemen who bought Fletcher's cars. And no penalties seem to have befallen any of the commandants who provided free auditoriums for Fletcher's productions. They pocketed cash from parking lot concessions on land owned by the federal government, and they improved their professional reputations to boot by smoothing out any potential bumps in nearby highway construction. Fletcher had joined a system that, as scholars Martin and Susan Tolchin have shown, can be corrupt from top to bottom.[60]

It should be noted that the only independent corroboration of Fletcher's political opportunism during this era had nothing to do with money. In the summer of 1956, when his patron, Fred Hall, was facing a challenge for the statehouse from within his own party, Fletcher was mentioned as one of two Kansas highway department employees accused of conducting political activities during working hours. The evidence, innocuous enough, was that "the letterhead of the Shawnee County Hall for Governor organization . . . included the names of [personnel director] Frank D. McGrew, Jr. and Arthur Fletcher [who] is employed in the department's public relations department." Both "submitted their resignations from the Hall for Governor Committee today," but state highway director Frank Harwi called it "another odious and deliberate political maneuver by the 'slander squad' to discredit the administration of Gov. Fred Hall and mislead the people of Kansas."[61]

In fact, Fletcher was learning from one of the best. Fred Hall's single term as governor was "one of [the state's] most controversial." His administrative style earned him enemies, and he quarreled with members of the state legislature from both parties. In 1956 Hall lost his reelection bid to a conservative primary challenger, and the internecine feud scuttled the Republicans' chances in the general election. What followed was an unethical, if legal, maneuver known as the triple play. On January 3, 1957, lame duck Fred Hall accepted the resignation of his ally, state supreme court chief justice William Smith (whom he had elevated from associate justice less than a year before). He named as Smith's replacement associate justice Walter G. Thiele. He then resigned as governor so that his lieutenant governor and ally could name him to replace Thiele on the court. Still, Hall's real passion was for the more lucrative statehouse, and in 1958 he resigned his lifetime appointment to run for governor again. In a replay of the events of 1956, he lost the GOP primary, but again he so divided his party that the Democratic incumbent was reelected. This was the first time in the history of the state that the Republicans lost two gubernatorial races in a row, and Hall was roundly blamed.[62]

It wasn't Hall's corruption so much as his staunch liberalism that earned him the increasing ire of his copartisans. In fact, the divisiveness was the result of larger forces than Hall's admittedly outsize personality. The Republican Party of Kansas, as in other states, was undergoing an internal battle for control between moderates and liberals on the one hand and conservatives on the other. The moderates were represented at the national level by Governors Thomas Dewey of New York and Earl Warren of California, and by President Dwight Eisenhower after his 1952 election. The conservative faction, meanwhile, was led by Senator Robert A. Taft of Ohio until his death in 1953. At that point conservatives coalesced around a number of figures, including senators Joe McCarthy of Wisconsin, William F. Knowland of California, and Barry Goldwater of Arizona.

At issue was the Republican Party's very viability. The political influence of President Franklin Roosevelt remained paramount for a generation after his death in 1945; the consensus among a majority of Americans was that Roosevelt and the Democrats, champions of left-of-center policies, including the union-legalizing Wagner Act and Truman's integration of the armed forces, had rescued the nation from Republican neglect (the Great Depression) and right-wing totalitarianism (World War II). The result had been five consecutive Democratic presidential terms (1933–1953), only broken by the election of war hero Eisenhower, and Democratic dominance of Congress, briefly halted for a single term in 1953 thanks to Eisenhower's coattails.

Moderate Republicans like Dewey claimed that in such a political environment, the Republican Party could remain viable only by acquiescing to the accomplishments of the New Deal while offering somewhat more moderate versions of Democratic policies. Conservatives like Taft, on the other hand, promoted repudiation of the New Deal, arguing that voters should have a real alternative to the Democratic program, even if it meant losing elections. The conservatives, while still in the political wilderness both in the party and the nation, were nevertheless heartened in these years by the rise of a vigorous intellectual movement. Writers such as Friedrich Hayek, Russell Kirk, Ralph de Toledano, and William F. Buckley Jr., the young editor of the *National Review,* promoted overlapping conservative theories including libertarianism (a distrust of the state), traditionalism (a desire for a premodern order), and laissez-faire capitalism (antipathy to market regulations).[63]

In the Kansas Republican Party, a significant liberal faction to the left of the moderate supporters of Dewey and the state's long history of progressive Republican leadership made this conflict more acute. The Democrats of Kansas, meanwhile, were similar to the Dixiecrats of the Deep South, and therefore hostile to liberalism. Progressives looked to the state's territorial origins as a violent battleground between Republican abolitionists (like the followers of John Brown) and fire-eating representatives of the slaveocracy. In such an atmosphere, liberals like Fred Hall found great electoral successes tempered by fierce rivalries with the growing conservative faction.

These battles paved the way for unprecedented Democratic victories like that of George Docking (and his son, the only Kansas governor to serve four terms in office) until the Kansas Democrats came more to resemble the left-of-center, pro–civil rights national party of the post–Lyndon Johnson era, and the conservatives cemented their ascendancy over the Republican Party.[64]

Much more so than the liberal Fred Hall, it was a conservative from the small western town of Russell who came to represent the trajectory of postwar Kansas Republicanism. Whereas Hall's political career was a flash at the end of the state's progressive Republican history, the career of Bob Dole was a long, slow burn that achieved much greater, and longer-lasting, success as his faction achieved dominance in the party, both in Kansas and nationwide. A member of the Kansas House of Representatives from 1950 to 1952 while he completed his law degree at Washburn, Dole spent the Hall years away from Topeka as Russell County attorney—not unlike Hall's own internship as Ford County attorney after the war. His gradual rise resumed in 1960 when he was elected to represent Kansas's Sixth District in the US House of Representatives; in 1968, riding Richard Nixon's coattails, Dole was elected to represent Kansas in the United States Senate, where he remained for three decades.

With Hall and the rest of the party out of office, Fletcher's political influence evaporated. One by one the commandants who hosted his entertainment programs abandoned him, seeing no further profit in his connections. "Next thing I know, Fred gets beat, and when Fred gets beat . . . the word went out, and . . . I couldn't get an auditorium anywhere." After several cancellations of shows for which he had already paid a substantial, nonrefundable advance to the booking agent in New York, Fletcher found himself practically penniless. "When I look around again, they came and got my cars and flat put me out of business. And I couldn't find a job in Topeka anywhere, not only Topeka, anywhere in Kansas."[65] Like Hall, Fletcher had seen a rapid, bright rise to fortune and influence. And like Hall, it appeared that his time for fortune and influence had ended.

Nadir

In the spring of 1957, Arthur Fletcher found himself $15,000 in debt (more than $125,000 in today's dollars) without any income or job prospects. Still, he resolved not to declare bankruptcy. Topeka race car driver John R. Peach, whose son had attended Washburn with Fletcher, "cosigned a note to take some of the more demanding creditors off Fletcher's back." As Peach later recalled, "I knew I'd get my money back." He had at least as much confidence as Fletcher himself, who noted, "I refused to take bankruptcy because I knew that once I did I'd be dead. I knew I could come back if I was given a little time." To keep food on the table and make his mortgage payments, he went back to the dead-end job at Goodyear Tire.[66]

Having failed, as he saw it, first as a professional football player and now as a politician, Fletcher still thought that his college degree, teaching certificate, and sports knowledge should matter. "I studied the theories and techniques of coaching football, basketball and track," the three sports he had played in high school. However, the seemingly impenetrable barrier of racism stood in his way, even among otherwise well-meaning individuals. "I presented myself to school board after school board after school board in the state of Kansas and the answer was 'you are ready, but we're not.'" Desperate, he asked his old coach, Dick Godlove, for a job at Washburn. Godlove gave him a job as assistant coach, making him one of the first African Americans to coach football at a predominantly white college. Put in charge of the ends and given some scouting responsibilities, Fletcher found that even this was not the panacea he anticipated. In the 1958 season—his second as a coach for the team—he got into a fistfight with a player who called him a nigger, according to his son, Paul. But he still had further to fall.[67]

In early 1959, ex-governor Hall threw Fletcher a lifeline, buying him a ticket to Sacramento and arranging a job interview at Aerojet General, a rocket and missile manufacturer there. He came out for the pro forma interview and received a job offer for the position of "Engr. Proj. Ass't 'A' (1311) D," which Fletcher later described as "controller of records and reports for the Solid Rocket Plant, Management Control Division." In other words, the job was in public relations, the very sort of post given to ex-politicians by government contractors seeking to show current politicians that they would be taken care of once out of office—if they ensured that relevant laws and regulations remained conducive to increased profits. He settled his affairs in Kansas, selling the house, paying off the mortgage, and paying an overdue state tax bill, and moved Mary and the kids to Sacramento. Fletcher thought his problems were solved, but they had only just begun.[68]

Many millions of people have moved west to California since the first gold rush of 1849, but few have found the big nuggets, and fewer still have been able to capitalize on them. The Fletchers were not among the lucky few. The first indication of the problems that lay in store came while on the road. Like the Joads in Steinbeck's *Grapes of Wrath*, they traveled west along Route 66 to visit with grandmother Edna along the way. But unlike the fictional Joads, who were white, the Fletchers had difficulty getting service at restaurants. Mary, who could pass for white, went in and ordered the food and brought it back to the car where Fletcher and the children were scrunched down, out of sight. This was not entirely unexpected; once during their prior sojourn in Riverside, a policeman had pulled them over: he wanted to know what a Black man was doing driving with a "white" woman in the front seat. A natural politician, Fletcher had calmly explained that his wife was a light-skinned African American while the children cowered in the back, dumbfounded and afraid by the most overt instance of racial hate they had yet encountered—notably in California, and not in Kansas.[69]

During the 1950s, the California Republican Party was experiencing tensions similar to those in Kansas, but with much higher stakes nationally. With thirty-two electoral votes—then the second most in the nation—California politicians who won statewide elections often saw themselves as presidential timber. Just as often, internal feuds stymied their fantasies. In 1958 US Senate Republican leader William F. Knowland, a newspaper scion from Oakland, chose to run for governor to better position himself for a 1960 presidential bid. (At that time, no sitting senator had won the presidency in decades.) The less popular Republican governor, Goodwin Knight, who as lieutenant governor had inherited the statehouse when President Eisenhower nominated Earl Warren to be chief justice of the Supreme Court, resolved to run for Knowland's Senate seat rather than face his deep-pocketed challenger. These two decisions are together known as the Knight–Knowland switch. Both failed: the voters, led by the labor movement opposing a Knowland-backed antiunion right-to-work proposition also on the ballot, rejected the candidates' contempt of the electorate. Democrats Clair Engle and Edmund "Pat" Brown were elected senator and governor. With Knight and Knowland out of the way, Vice President Nixon, another Californian, easily won the state's delegates to the 1960 Republican National Convention, and its thirty-two electoral votes in the general election, losing the presidency to John F. Kennedy in a squeaker.[70]

It was into this milieu of acrimony and defeat that Fred Hall and Arthur Fletcher stepped when they moved to Sacramento in 1959 to rebuild their shattered careers. The absence of entrenched leadership in the state party after the defeat of Knight and Knowland gave Fred Hall an opening, and he quickly rose to head the California Republican Assembly. But his progressive politics did not endear him to the growing conservative majority, especially strong in Southern California, which later culminated in the 1966 election of Ronald Reagan. Hall ran a quixotic campaign for United States Senate in 1962, obstinately (and bravely) championing Democratic-backed state fair housing legislation. He lost the primary and returned to Kansas to practice law, dying virtually destitute in 1970.[71]

For Fletcher, on the other hand, a return to politics seemed inconceivable in 1959. His family's problems worsened as they settled into their new home at 1200 Los Robles Boulevard in one of Sacramento's new developments northeast of downtown. A beautiful neighborhood with palm-lined streets, they were its only Black family, and many of their white neighbors resented their presence. Fletcher drove their only car to his job at Aerojet in neighboring Rancho Cordova, and when the kids were in school, Mary found herself alone and stranded. She received death threats from the neighbors, in person and over the phone. If her experience was similar to that of other Black families in such "defended" neighborhoods around the country, according to historian Thomas Sugrue, she likely also had to deal with such nuisances as broken windows and dogs being allowed to defecate on her lawn. By the summer of 1959, the family had had enough. They moved to Demaret Drive, on Sacramento's south side. The problems persisted, and they moved again in October to McLaren Avenue, on the other side of the airport, where there were already a few Black families. But this presented a new problem: with each move, Fletcher's commute to Aerojet was getting longer. At the same time Mary's mental health was deteriorating.[72]

The decline in Fletcher's fortunes had taken a toll on Mary's stability. The fancy lifestyle afforded the family of a successful state politician, entertainment promoter, and used-car salesman had been just fine for Mary, who was accustomed to being well-to-do. Light-skinned, well born, and popular, as we have seen, Mary had been attracted to the young athlete for his ambition as much as for his charm and charisma. Mary's family had long been prominent in the Black social circles of Junction City. Her maternal ancestors, the Bells, had owned much of the land that the army bought in the early twentieth century as Fort Riley expanded. Her grandfather, William Harden, had been a contractor on the Santa Fe Railroad and later had an ice supply contract with the army; he was clearly one of W. E. B. Du Bois's "talented tenth." So it had been a particular shock to Mary when Fletcher's political empire came crashing down around him. The constant traveling; being uprooted from family, friends, and lifestyle; and the racist threats and attacks in Sacramento had also taken their toll on the thirty-four-year-old mother of five. She had worked at the Menninger Clinic in Topeka, so she had a passing familiarity with psychiatric theory and practice, and she knew that she needed help. She asked her husband to check her into Napa State Hospital to be treated for clinical depression.[73]

In fact, however, Mary's collapse was a long time coming. She had a history of emotional and mental health difficulties, which she seemed to have inherited from both sides of her family. Although the record is unclear, there appear to have been suicides on both her mother's side—the Bells—and her father's—the Hardens; in addition, her father's side had apparently wrestled with alcoholism for three generations. She and her sister, Florence, had been raised by her grandparents because her mother had tried to drown them in a bathtub as infants.[74]

Mary also had to deal with concerns about the paternity of her second daughter, Sylvia, born in 1945. Given that Fletcher had left for Europe in March 1944, it seemed unlikely to family members and close friends that he had fathered Sylvia, although he signed her birth certificate upon his return to Junction City. Despite the doubts he surely had—late in life he told his son, Paul, that he believed his brother, Earl, to have been Sylvia's father—there is no indication that Fletcher treated Sylvia any differently than he did his other children. The others noticed that Sylvia had a darker skin tone than they, and they teased her about it, but because Mary had a light skin tone this would not seem to indicate anything about Sylvia's paternity. Mary did develop a closer relationship with Sylvia than with her other children, although this may have had more to do with complementary personalities than any sense that she was biologically different than the others.[75]

The question of Sylvia's paternity speaks volumes about Arthur Fletcher. When he returned from Europe to discover the apparent infidelity of his wife and what he took to be betrayal by his brother, few would have blamed him for abandoning the marriage then and there. He could have walked away and started fresh, but he didn't. He was influenced by a combination of personal and social factors. First, his own adoptive father had demonstrated, by treating Arthur and Earl as his own sons, that genetic ties were not required for family ties. As an African American, he inherited the tradition of fictive kin, unofficial adoption by various "aunts" and "uncles" to lessen the trauma of separation during slavery. Second, being a husband and father in 1946 was already integral to Fletcher's sense of identity and manhood. His early childhood, juxtaposed with his teen years as the adoptive son of the responsible Cotton Fletcher, had taught him to cherish family unity. Third, his love of Mary, which he maintained during their long separation by the war, pushed him to forgive this single, albeit major, indiscretion.

Suspecting that Sylvia was not Fletcher's biological child, however, was not necessarily to attach blame to Mary; because of constricted communications during military operations in France and Belgium, the couple temporarily lost communication. Mary may have feared her young husband dead. Nevertheless, Arthur's safe return would likely have triggered intense feelings of guilt.[76]

Increasingly concerned about Mary's declining emotional state, Fletcher gave up his job at Aerojet in April 1960 and moved the family to Berkeley to be closer to her treatment center at Napa. He had no permanent job prospects, but there is anecdotal evidence that Richard Nixon's presidential campaign organization sent him to talk up the Nixon–Lodge ticket in the Midwest that summer (although he left the period from April to December 1960 blank on a subsequent job application, and there is no mention of him in the campaign records at the Nixon Library). His children later recalled that he secured a job with Goodyear Tire in Berkeley. In any event, he put no stock in such dead-end jobs for the long term. He obtained a provisional California teaching certificate and applied for a job at Berkeley High School.[77]

The early 1960s was a dangerous time for psychiatric hospitalization. The spartan accommodations at Napa, evocative of the 1975 film *One Flew Over the Cuckoo's Nest*, were depressing in themselves, housing upwards of twenty patients per room in rows of beds without privacy. To make matters worse, psychiatrists were experimenting with a wide variety of psychotropic medications, including some, like LSD, that have since been banned for their dangerous hallucinogenic properties. They were also more likely to use female patients as their subjects because women tended to be more compliant and trusting of authority figures. Finally, researchers did not have the ethical restrictions then that are now in place: consent was not required, and review boards were nonexistent. Much of the research was informal, even ad hoc, with psychiatrists often doing what they pleased. Mary, who soon apparently found herself on several psychotropic drugs, was released on her own recognizance on weekends.[78]

On Friday, September 30, 1960, while at home alone, Mary received a phone call from the principal of Berkeley High School. Fletcher had been tentatively offered a teaching job there but had not yet signed the contract. In the interim, the principal had done some checking into Fletcher's background. Learning of his civil rights activities in Kansas, he had decided that Fletcher was a troublemaker. He rescinded the job offer.[79]

When Fletcher got home, Mary didn't tell him about the call. But he could tell that something was bothering her, that she seemed more depressed than usual. The next day, Saturday, October 1, Fletcher decided to take Mary to the movies to cheer her up. They drove over the Bay Bridge into San Francisco, a short ride from their home at 1339 Francisco Street. Alarmingly, Mary wondered aloud what it might be like to jump off the bridge. The trip seemed to have done her some good; she seemed content. Unfortunately she had entered a dangerous mental state. Often when a suicidal person comes to the final decision and devises a method for carrying it out, she becomes calm, even happy, seeing in the impending suicide a means of retaking control.[80]

The following day, Sunday, October 2, around 1:30 PM, Mary went out—to buy some vegetables, she said. Sylvia asked if she could go with her, as usual, but Mary refused, insisting she go alone. She drove onto the bridge, according to the *Oakland Tribune,* slowed down "on the Oakland side of the Yerba Buena Island tunnel and waved other automobiles past. Then she stopped the vehicle, jumped out and vaulted over the railing."[81] Fletcher recalled the scene at home:

> I'm sitting at the typewriter doing some writing, and the next thing I know the radio said . . . that the 214th person had jumped off the Bay Bridge. And I looked at it, there was something strange. . . . All of my kids came in about 15 minutes before that announcement. They'd never done that before.
>
> They all came in and sat on the sofa and didn't say a word . . . and we looked at each other, and I just went on back, and they just sat there quietly.
>
> And in about ten minutes the police knocked on our door and said, "Are you Mr. Fletcher?" I said "Yeah." "Would you come out for a minute?" I said "yeah." They said "Your wife has just killed herself, jumped off the Bay Bridge." So I had to go back in and tell the kids and then go over to the morgue and look at the body, and sure enough it was her.[82]

The end of Mary's life proved the nadir of Fletcher's, but its impact was more immediately obvious on her children, who never fully recovered from the tragedy. The oldest child, Phyllis, in eleventh grade in school, started shoplifting. Like her mother, Phyllis had been popular in Kansas, with a large circle of friends. She had regularly attended social events at Topeka's segregated YMCA, and she had been dating a popular high school football player before the move to California. She too had become accustomed to a certain lifestyle, with expensive clothes and the like, and the family was now unable to maintain that—so she started shoplifting. Also, as the oldest,

Phyllis was expected to be a role model for her younger siblings, and after her mother's death she found that pressure overwhelming. "I'm not trying to be the example," she once said. "I'm trying to be me." In 1962, three weeks before she was scheduled to graduate from high school, Phyllis hitchhiked her way to Chicago and then to New York City, maintaining little contact with the family thereafter. Her younger siblings called her "the nomad."[83]

Sylvia, the Fletchers' second child, outwardly handled Mary's death best, but the internal scars remained. The only one who had visited her mother regularly at Napa, and the last to see her mother alive, she took over the housekeeping and found her refuge in books. School became, as she later put it, her escape.[84]

Arthur Jr., in ninth grade when his mother died, had a talent for drawing and for music, and he developed a passion for jazz. He ultimately became accomplished on the drums, piano, flute, saxophone, and bass, but he just wanted to get away from home. He spent as much time as he could around the University of California campus and the thriving jazz scene along Telegraph Avenue. This was the era of the beatniks, and Art Jr. was particularly drawn to the W. E. B. Du Bois Club. He started smoking, and lost a full scholarship to the Art Institute of San Francisco after being caught with a cigarette. He nevertheless pursued his talent for music and began touring the country as soon as he could get away.[85]

The Fletchers' second son (and fourth child overall), Paul, started getting into fights with other children in school. In seventh grade when his mother died, he spent a year in juvenile hall for participating in a civil rights march with Art Jr., the day after the police in Birmingham, Alabama, attacked protesters with dogs and fire hoses. He graduated from high school functionally illiterate—sadly all too common in the East Bay's predominantly Black schools, but not what one would expect from the son of a former Kansas state official and college graduate.[86]

The child on whom Mary's suicide had the greatest impact was Phillip, the "baby." Only nine years old at the time of his mother's death, he was "the apple of her eye," according to his father. Phillip had already been getting into fights in school, along with his brother, Paul. He was left back a grade, got into more fights, and was sent, like Paul before him, to juvenile hall. Fletcher then sent him to a military school in Virginia, where Phillip responded to hazing with more violence: according to Paul, one day in the school's cafeteria he put a fork through another boy's hand after the boy tried to steal his dessert. Phillip ran away from school, started taking drugs, and became involved in petty crime.[87]

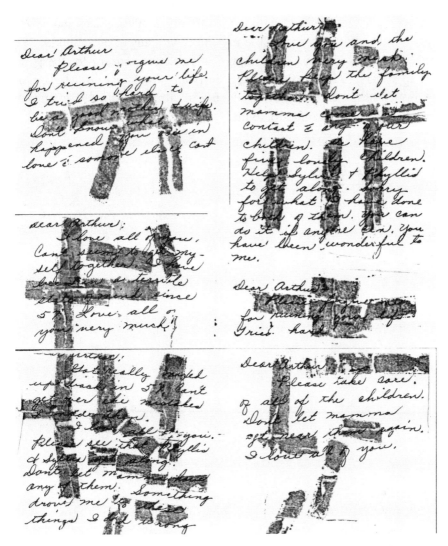

Mary Fletcher tried several times to compose a suicide note to her "Dear Arthur," urging him to "forgive me" and "keep the family together." Arthur Fletcher Personal Papers, courtesy Paul Fletcher.

Mary had attempted several times to complete a suicide note to her "Dear Arthur"; the drafts she left, torn to pieces and then painstakingly reconstructed with Scotch tape, presumably by her widower, were an attempt to absolve Arthur of guilt for "ruining your life. I tried so hard to be a good mother & wife. Love you and the children very much." She may have killed herself in an attempt to save her children from the mental illness she believed she had inherited from her own mother. "Please keep the family together. Don't let Momma come in contact with any of our children. We have five lovely children." She expressed particular concern for the girls: "Help Sylvia and Phyllis to get along. Sorry for what I have done to both of them." But she also expressed confidence in him: "You can do it if anyone can. You have been wonderful to me."[88]

CHAPTER THREE

MOON SHOT, 1961–1969

The name of the game is to put some economic flesh and bones on Dr. King's Dream.
—Arthur Fletcher, 1969

Mary's death resulted in the disintegration of Art Fletcher's family and proved the nadir of his life. But recovery is a critical human characteristic. Fletcher had never shared Mary's depression and was able to find the bright side of any situation. This trait helped him recover from the tragedy; it also helped him see the best of American society despite his many encounters with discrimination. Art Fletcher always believed things would get better. If Mary's suicide was a far worse experience than most people face, Fletcher determined to make an equally extraordinary recovery.

His recovery—one might even call it a rebirth—took place in the decade of the 1960s. The nation also experienced something of a rebirth during that decade. The baby boomer generation, entering adulthood, seemed to collectively resolve that society needed to change. The new, young president told them to "ask not what your country can do for you, ask what you can do for your country"—a call to service that many interpreted as an admonition to make a more inclusive society. Particularly galvanized by Kennedy's assassination in 1963, the nation's youth, across the political spectrum, doubled down on their commitment to effect change. Civil rights protests moved from courtrooms and buses to the streets of cities in the South and the North, and then to the steps of the Lincoln Memorial, where a young preacher, who also suffered a martyr's fate by decade's end, asked the nation to "be true to what you said on paper," to honor the Constitution's commitment to equality. When the federal government responded with more paper—the Civil Rights Act of 1964—the peaceful protests pushed for an even stronger Voting Rights Act of 1965. Violent protests, the product of frustration, pushed bureaucrats to enforce existing laws. Young women encouraged their mothers to join them in protesting gender inequality, and a sexual revolution swept the nation's college campuses and elsewhere. Conservatism, too, saw a youthful infusion, with young Republicans devouring

William F. Buckley Jr.'s *National Review* and others joining more militant groups like the John Birch Society. Hanging over it all was the threat of being drafted and sent to fight and die in Vietnam.[1]

The 1960s was also the decade when men first walked on the moon. In September 1962, President Kennedy announced that "we choose to go to the moon in this decade and do the other things, not because they are easy, but because they are hard."[2] He did not live to see it, but as he promised, within the decade, Neil Armstrong set foot on the moon, capping a successful moon shot.

Arthur Fletcher's trajectory during the 1960s was no less fantastic. Out of the ashes of tragedy, the underemployed thirty-five-year-old single parent found better employment, remarried and constructed a new family, and left California for a small town in the desert of southeastern Washington State. There he threw off the last vestiges of venality and used his skills for the betterment of his people, becoming a unique hybrid of civil rights leader, politician, and white-collar professional. Like the space program, he had setbacks along the way. But Kennedy had said that the "goal will serve to organize and measure the best of our energies and skills," and so it was for Fletcher. When Kennedy made that speech, Fletcher had barely recovered from the shocking loss of his wife. When men landed on the moon, he was assistant secretary of labor for employment standards and advisor to the president of the United States.

Back to School

Each of the Fletcher children dealt with the death of their mother in his or her own way, some better than others, but all remained haunted by her absence. For Mary's widowed husband, however, it was his strong commitment to civil rights and his natural facility as a politician that helped him deal with the loss of his wife and the slow, steady breakup of his family. In late 1960 Fletcher found himself an underemployed single parent. With help from his mother, who had owned a restaurant in Riverside, California, he opened up a restaurant of his own, Fletcher's House of Barbecue. But it never attracted a regular clientele, fell into arrears for failure to file sales taxes, and closed after less than six months. Without the school job he had been promised, he fell back on the hustling skills he had developed on the backstreets of Los Angeles and Oklahoma City. He got a job managing a small building, but there were months when he was unable to make his own rent, spending his time in the ghetto west of San Pablo Avenue, avoiding agents of the landlord, Nakamura Realty. He correctly assumed that Nakamura would not evict a single parent who usually paid the rent on time (and paid it all eventually).[3]

But as he began to interact with his neighbors, mostly unmarried mothers, he realized that being a single parent was something he shared with many of them. And as they came to know him, they realized he was different: his education, background, and connections were his ticket out of the poverty in which most of them were trapped. They sought his advice, and he became a community leader in a way that he had never been as a political appointee back in Kansas. "At that time," he said,

> I understood the difference between what an education had done for me and . . . what a lack of education had done to and for the people living next to me who were on public payrolls. In other words I knew I had no business [being] there. . . . But being there . . . and having two girls and three boys, I was in a position to understand the depth of pain and suffering and the confusion and the struggle that a single head of a household was experiencing as he or she tried to raise kids by themselves.[4]

Fletcher found his calling in a bootstrap self-help civil rights philosophy that he encapsulated with the phrase, "I'm as willing to help you as you are willing to help yourself." Joining a tradition going back to Booker T. Washington's National Negro Business League (which Fletcher later helped resurrect as the National Black Chamber of Commerce), and combining it with the self-help philosophy of Dale Carnegie, Fletcher's movement was informed both by the advances of the civil rights era and his own political experience.[5]

In the early 1960s, after decades of planning and building, it seemed as if the moment had arrived for a mature civil rights movement to finally put an end to the scourge of de jure Jim Crow in the South and combat de facto segregation elsewhere. After the victories in the Supreme Court and the public outcry after Chicago youth Emmett Till was lynched in Mississippi, local leaders and Atlanta preacher Martin Luther King Jr. had led a successful boycott in Montgomery, Alabama, integrating the city's buses, and President Eisenhower had forcibly integrated a high school in Little Rock, Arkansas.[6]

The mainstream movement coalesced into four major organizations, two new, two old. The Congress of Racial Equality (CORE), founded in 1941 by James Farmer and Chicago college students, organized lunch-counter sit-ins and Freedom Rides to integrate the interstate bus system; the Southern

Christian Leadership Conference, led by Dr. King, organized nonviolent direct action to dramatize the violence that sustained the system. The two older organizations, meanwhile, were revitalized and transformed by new leadership: the youthful Whitney Young rose within the ranks of the National Urban League (NUL), and in the 1960s, as its leader, transformed it from a staid corporate jobs bank into a dynamic vehicle for equal employment opportunity; Roy Wilkins, civil rights bureaucrat and negotiator extraordinaire, ascended to the helm of the NAACP and pulled the competing organizations under a single umbrella, the Leadership Conference for Civil Rights, ensuring that he, Young, King, and Farmer were invited to meet with President Johnson in 1964 to strategize passage of the late president Kennedy's civil rights bill.[7]

How did Arthur Fletcher go from being an underemployed single parent to a civil rights leader? Unlike King and Farmer, he didn't have the support of a church or college group, and unlike Young and Wilkins, he hadn't climbed the ranks of an existing civil rights bureaucracy. He did it by using his own skills and talents, building a new kind of civil rights organization in his own unique way. His new self-help civil rights mantra became not only what encouraged others to pull themselves out of poverty but also what would build his organization and his status as a leader. He grew his support from the grass roots, using sweat equity, and he utilized his skills at making connections with corporate and political institutions to build external support. He drew up contracts and bylaws, and he solicited advisory board membership from captains of industry. He also sought political office to bring his ideas to higher levels of influence.

Fletcher's first political foray after Mary's death came the following year, when fellow Washburn alumnus Burnell Johnson asked him to join Berkeley's Citizens Steering Committee for the local school bond initiative. The initiative had failed fourteen times in a row, and when the committee realized that Fletcher was the only member with any political experience, they elected him chairman. This time the initiative failed by less than 1 percent— the closest it had ever come to passage.[8] Fletcher's service on the Citizens Steering Committee paid off nevertheless. Burnell Johnson also happened to be the personnel director for the Berkeley Unified School District, and no derogatory reports from Kansas could replace what he had just seen and heard with his own eyes and ears. In September 1961, Johnson arranged a job for Fletcher as the special needs teacher at Burbank Junior High, Berkeley's all-Black middle school.[9]

Teaching inner-city, underprivileged youths, Fletcher developed a self-help curriculum centered around the book *Think and Grow Rich* by Napoleon Hill, which advocated mental discipline as a means to success. Unlike his stint at Pierce Addition Elementary in Topeka, which he had abandoned as soon as he was offered a more lucrative political position, this time he threw himself into the work. He volunteered as a temporary gym teacher and developed a joint after-school program with the local YMCA for "a hard core group of young men who were potential school drop outs and constantly presented discipline problems," winning the youths over with his can-do attitude and tales of his own personal experiences. He took a group of kids to the local water utility to show them the opportunities for employment, emphasizing the work ethic of the employees there. One student, who went on to earn a doctorate from the University of Iowa, later told him that "you provided the tools . . . to have confidence in yourself that you can make it in the modern world. It would be hard, the odds were against us, but we must not give up." Clearly Fletcher's recent tragedy was influencing his approach to teaching.[10]

With his finances stabilized, Fletcher became active in the Alameda County Republican Central Committee and the California Republican Assembly, where he was made chairman of the Civil Rights Committee. Following in the footsteps of Black activists such as Betty Hill, who founded the (Black) Women's Republican Study Club in Los Angeles in 1929, and Crispus Attucks Wright, a prominent Beverly Hills Black Republican who fought restrictive covenants and supported boycotts of businesses that discriminated in hiring, Fletcher set to work building a Republican organization in liberal Democratic Berkeley, and in 1962 he declared his candidacy for the Republican nomination for state assembly.[11]

Democrat William Byron Rumford had held Berkeley's seventeenth assembly seat since 1949. In this liberal, college-centered district, therefore, Fletcher's skin color was not a factor in the race, but his political affiliation was. Before he faced Rumford in the general election, Fletcher needed to win a primary in a state with a peculiar primary tradition.[12]

Dating back to the Progressive-era reforms of Governor (and later Senator) Hiram Johnson, California primaries were designed to generate maximum interest and involvement among both the electorate and the candidates. Candidates were not required to be members of a party and could run in as many primaries as they wished; primary ballots did not list party affiliations. The result was widespread cross-listing, whereby a candidate sought the primary nomination of both major parties. It was by just such a strategy that Earl Warren, who presided over the *Brown v. Board* decision as chief justice of the Supreme Court, won reelection as governor. A moderate Republican in a majority-Democratic state, Warren won both major-party primaries, winning his 1946 reelection bid with an astounding 91.8 percent of the vote.[13]

William Rumford, Fletcher's Democratic opponent, was no stranger to cross-listing himself. After his initial 1948 election, he sought and won the nominations of both parties in each biennial election from 1952 through 1960, and won 100 percent of the vote in every general election from 1950 to 1960. The entrance of Fletcher into the 1962 race may have warned Rumford off a cross-listing attempt. Rumford now faced a political veteran (albeit one of Kansas politics). With neither party organization allowed to make an endorsement, the energetic newcomer had the advantage—at least in the primary. Fletcher handily won the Republican nomination (despite 444 write-in votes for Rumford), and with the end of the school year that June, he began an earnest campaign for the general election. With the help of his children, Paul and Sylvia, Fletcher campaigned hard. Sylvia worked the campaign office while Paul and his father drove around the district with a bullhorn and a large sign. They wore thin the skin on their knuckles, rapping on doors. They distributed leaflets. And they attracted the attention of an old political hand, now back on the California campaign trail.[14]

Richard Nixon was running for governor against Pat Brown, who was seeking reelection to a second term. Considering that the former vice president and presidential nominee had won several statewide races there, and considering that Brown was polling poorly, Nixon expected an easy walk into the governor's mansion. Of course, he didn't really want to be governor of California; he hoped to use the job as a springboard for a second try for the White House in 1964. But California was changing. A growing conservative insurgency, which centered in Nixon's own Orange County and which echoed the growing nationwide conservative insurgency especially strong in the West, saw Nixon as part of the old-guard establishment. They mounted a primary challenge in the person of state assemblyman (and John Birch Society activist) Joe Schell, who took more than one third of the Republican votes, and when Nixon refused to kowtow to his demands for his proposed platform, Schell refused an endorsement, imperiling Nixon's general election chances.[15]

Nixon therefore had to fight hard, and he had to seek funds from party leaders back East. His advisor, H. R. "Bob" Haldeman, decided that Fletcher could be put to good use. Most African Americans in California were expected to vote for Pat Brown, but Nixon had civil rights bona fides from his years as vice president (leading the President's Committee on Government Contracts, which focused on the same area of civil rights as Fletcher's

Revised Philadelphia Plan years later). Art Fletcher could be used to bolster Nixon's reputation in the state's Black community. Haldeman sent Fletcher "on a fact-finding trip East" (read: fund-raising with civil rights–supporting Wall Street Republicans) and arranged a meeting between the two candidates. "I am not sure we want to make a press conference out of this . . . it should be a meeting between the two, with Fletcher to announce afterwards whatever they agree should be said . . . let Fletcher know that RN hopes to get with him Friday, and find out what times would be possible."[16]

There is no evidence that Fletcher's work for Nixon made a difference: the former vice president lost the gubernatorial race 52 percent to 47 percent. He threw a temper tantrum at a subsequent press conference ("You won't have Dick Nixon to kick around anymore"), undermining his chances for a serious 1964 presidential run. But Nixon's support seems to have helped Fletcher. Considering that Republicans constituted only a small minority of the Berkeley electorate (or perhaps because many voters stayed home, certain that Rumford would win reelection), Fletcher did fairly well, winning an impressive 25.2 percent of the vote.[17]

As he was getting his political life back on track, Fletcher put his personal life back on track as well. He moved the family—Sylvia, Art Jr., Paul, and Phillip—to a more affordable bungalow in North Oakland and started classes at San Francisco State College for a full teaching certificate. To save money and eat more healthily (he was diagnosed with diabetes at age forty), Fletcher joined the Consumers' Cooperative of Berkeley, a member-owned grocery store selling healthy and organic products that by the early 1960s was "the second largest urban cooperative in the United States." While shopping at the Berkeley co-op in 1964, he met Bernyce Hassan, a divorced mother working there as an accounting clerk. The two started dating and were married in April 1965. A week later, they moved to Pasco, Washington, where Fletcher had been offered a job as director of a new community organization.[18]

While the marriage brought new children into Fletcher's family—Bernyce's teenage daughter, Joan, and Joan's baby daughter, Onna—it came with a cost. Arthur's daughter, Sylvia, did not approve of the match. This was partially out of a sense of loyalty to her own late mother; Sylvia had been the closest to Mary of all the children. By the same token, Bernyce apparently did not care much for Sylvia, who had replaced Mary as the family housekeeper and was the strongest female competition for her new husband's affections. Sylvia moved in with her grandmother, Edna, rather than follow the rest of the family north. Art Jr., having secured a toehold in the Berkeley jazz scene, stayed behind as well.[19]

Higher Horizons

On August 12, 1965, the streets of the Watts section of Los Angeles, California, erupted in five days of violence. Angry about a racist police force and frustrated by the failure of recent federal equal employment legislation to translate into actual jobs, young Black men in Watts attacked police officers and looted local businesses. Sadly, the result was a worsening of conditions, as devastated local Black businesses laid off workers and the authorities imposed martial law. In the following two long, hot summers, equally violent rebellions swept through Black neighborhoods in Cleveland, Newark, Detroit, Rochester, and Chicago—but not in Pasco, Washington.[20]

Part of the tricity area in the desert east of the Cascades—Richland, Kennewick, and Pasco, Washington—East Pasco in the late 1960s looked like any other Black neighborhood in the nation, but with tumbleweeds. It had a concentrated, impoverished, largely unemployed young Black male population living almost exclusively east of the railroad tracks that split the city along Oregon Avenue. The city had an all-white police force that often seemed bent on participating in the local drug trade rather than in its interdiction. Young Black men were exploited for some of their talents, but only to the extent that this didn't violate the racial status quo. The local Columbia Basin Community College, noted for the best junior college football and basketball teams in the state of Washington, recruited its mostly Black squads nationally and put them up in a local hotel owned by the coach. But no attention was given to these players' schoolwork. A far cry from Washburn's Dick Godlove, the coach kicked them out of the hotel at the end of each season and sent them home, reportedly to prevent their dating local white women.[21]

The region as a whole was segregated and defiantly racist. The Hanford Nuclear Reservation, just northwest of the tricity area, was the largest local employer and had attracted most of the Blacks who moved there, but the Black workers—mainly given menial jobs at the plant—were forced to live in East Pasco. Kennewick, just across the Columbia River, was totally white. Although possibly apocryphal, some African American residents remember a prominent sign on the westbound side of the bridge that warned Black people against entering Kennewick after dark. In Yakima, about an hour's drive west, the John Birch Society controlled a newspaper that reportedly included employment advertisements that blatantly and brazenly said "we don't hire niggers."[22] Pasco had all the ingredients for a violent, deadly conflagration—but now it also had Art Fletcher.

Fletcher was looking for an opportunity to build a civil rights organization to serve as a launching pad for his self-help civil rights philosophy. He also was looking to relocate to an area with a stronger Republican Party, as California, at least from his Berkeley vantage point in early 1965, seemed in the midst of a Democratic resurgence. Eastern Washington, notwithstanding its overt racism and the fact that it was what Fletcher and others defined as "a southern community in attitude," was Republican country.[23]

Economically, the tricity area was a typically western combination of company town and federal largesse: the Hanford plant, the region's largest employer, was a federal installation run by myriad government contractors—big companies like Battelle-Northwest and Douglas United Nuclear. This presented an opportunity for Fletcher to build a jobs program with funds from the federal government's war on poverty while developing relationships with prominent local members of corporate boards. Fletcher ignored the irony of accepting federal funds from a Democratic presidential administration while building a Republican network to further the cause of self-help civil rights. He just wanted the program to work, regardless of the politics.[24]

On June 1, 1965, Fletcher assumed the post of director of Higher Horizons, telling reporters from the local *Tri-City Herald* that his job was to "assist pre-school age and in-school youngsters who are having a difficult time adjusting, assist dropouts and adults with an on-the-job training program" and to "improve neighborhood appearances with a beautification program." Higher Horizons, "the first project of its nature to become fully operational in . . . the Pacific Northwest Region," was the brainchild of Hanford scientists—white, liberal residents of Richland—and the Black community of East Pasco, in particular the leaders of the local YMCA. Relying on federal funds, the ostensible purpose of the program was to work in concert with the state employment security administration, vocational educational department, and Columbia Basin Community College to secure work for entry-level job seekers and train borderline employees—those who could reasonably aspire to a higher skill level—so that they could enter local industry and earn better wages.[25]

Fletcher developed a skills bank—a list of qualified East Pasco residents for use in referrals to local jobs. He launched a tutoring program and a weekly public information film series. He created a temporary day care center to help parents receiving job training and sent volunteer teaching aides into local schools to handle noninstructional tasks, freeing up teachers for more instructional time. "The effort was an immediate success, which led the school district to consider sponsoring the effort itself." Higher Horizons started with an $86,000 federal grant under the Manpower Development Act, and the expectation among YMCA and Hanford organizers that the money was to be extended over three years. Fletcher's salary was $12,000 per year.[26]

The most enduring program Fletcher created that first summer was the neighborhood watch committee. Fletcher divided East Pasco into twelve zones of two square blocks each, and he designated two volunteer block captains for each zone. More than crime prevention, their job was to identify unemployed working-age youths on their blocks and encourage them to sign up for Higher Horizons services. He solicited help from twelve "well-educated individuals (negroes) who live in Richland" to serve as "block coordinators"; they connected youths with employers and training programs. The block coordinators immediately identified thirty-five people whom they thought they could help, and they convinced nine to submit applications for training and/or employment.[27]

The project ran into difficulty almost from the get-go. Higher Horizons rented space in Whittier Elementary, a school recently shuttered after a CORE lawsuit alleging segregation. They leased the principal's office, two classrooms, and the cafeteria. Fletcher arrived to find temporary staff working without office furniture. But deeper problems followed. Fletcher found his efforts stymied by interagency conflict. Local officers of state agencies refused to treat with respect anyone involved in the program, stated that job trainees should not report to Higher Horizons staff, and instructed local newspapers not to write as if their agencies had any connection to the program. Fletcher attributed this to "race prejudice," noting that "the supervisors in question, both the retired Army officer and the instructional staff supervisor, were Caucasians who had never before been called upon to either take orders from or cooperate with a Negro in a supervisory capacity . . . this is a southern community in attitude . . . southern folkways, mores, and stereotypes . . . reinforce the resistance of the supervisors in question." Print attacks by local John Birchers forced Fletcher to defend the program on several occasions. His son, Paul, drove him over the mountains to Olympia, the state capital, while he slept so as to be fresh for his meetings there.[28]

Fletcher evinced a brash, combative style when under attack. When the moderate *Tri-City Herald* editorialized against waste and unsanitary conditions at the day care center, complaining that all the children there were Black when another day care center in one of Pasco's predominantly white sections had recently been shuttered for illegal segregation, Fletcher responded that he "could care less about integrating a community. . . . We need services, whether integrated or segregated. We need active participants, not passive recipients. These people need a center here, and they need to learn how to run something like this."[29]

Fletcher's use of block captains and zones, and his refusal to prioritize integration for its own sake, was designed to evoke white homeowner rhetoric and activities of the era. In cities throughout the country, postwar whites without the option of suburban flight "defended" their neighborhoods against integration by forming "protective" organizations. Among other activities, these used block captains to organize white resistance. White newspaper boys would sound the alarm, and the captains would mobilize their neighbors for violent attacks on new Black homeowners. But Fletcher's scheme consciously turned the white racist version on its head. Instead of fighting to maintain an ethnic homogeneity, Higher Horizons used these tactics to pursue employment opportunities.[30]

The coup de grâce for Higher Horizons ultimately came in the ineptitude of the men who had created it before Fletcher had arrived. The YMCA officials who hired Fletcher had told him that it was a three-year project. Fletcher was therefore surprised to receive a phone call in December 1965 from an official at the Department of Labor in Washington, DC, wondering why termination documents had not been filed, as the project was slated to end on January 6, 1966. Fletcher quickly cobbled together an extension request and was granted temporary funds over the opposition of state agencies. But in September 1966, barely a year after he had come to Pasco, Higher Horizons ceased to exist, and Fletcher was out of a job—again.[31]

The collapse of Higher Horizons in 1966 corresponded with events in California that surely made Fletcher consider returning to Berkeley, where his mother, two children, and many friends still lived. It was a banner year for Golden State Republicans, with actor and conservative spokesman Ronald Reagan defeating Pat Brown's bid for a third term as governor. Even in liberal Berkeley, GOP fortunes seemed to be changing for the better. The Democrats in Sacramento had gerrymandered a state senate district for Assemblyman Byron Rumford, who handily won the Democratic primary but then lost the general election to perennial local Republican candidate Lewis Sherman by only 800 votes. The voters of the East Bay rebelled against being taken for granted by their Democratic elected officials in 1966 in much the same way the voters of the state had rebelled against the Republicans of the contemptuous Knight–Knowland switch in 1958. Tom Berkeley, publisher of the *Oakland Post,* an influential African American newspaper, had refused to endorse Rumford, later stating "that it was too bad [Fletcher wasn't] here to run against Byron as he felt sure that [he] could have beaten him this time." Lew Sherman, the new Republican state senator, added that if Fletcher had "remained in California, it is my conviction that he would now be high up on the staff of the Governor-Elect."[32]

It is uncertain how eagerly Fletcher would have accepted a high-ranking position with Reagan at that time. The new governor's campaign had capitalized on suburban white fear after the Watts rebellion, and Reagan, who had been a Goldwater supporter, was in the vanguard of the New Right, battling moderates for control of the party. Fletcher clearly stood with the moderates as the conservatives increasingly welcomed the support of unreconstructed white southerners at the national level. Still, after the collapse of Higher Horizons, Fletcher could hardly but be wistful at news of the Republican ascendance in the Bay Area.[33]

Cooperative Self-Help

To bring food to the table and keep up with their mortgage payments, Fletcher's wife, Bernyce, took a clerical job for Battelle-Northwest at the Hanford plant, and Fletcher became an employee relations specialist (read: minority recruiter) for Douglas United Nuclear and eight smaller Hanford contractors. After taking correspondence courses in divinity, he obtained a license to preach in Baptist churches and wrote sermons on human rights, which he often delivered to large white congregations for honoraria. Said one observer, "He had the audiences rolling in the aisles with laughter and two minutes later they'd have tears in their eyes."[34]

City manager Horace Menasco also hired Fletcher as a temporary consultant to submit an application to make Pasco a "demonstration city" in the federal Model Cities program. Fletcher hoped that the grant could be used to develop light industry in East Pasco to build employment opportunities, noting that local unemployment stemmed partially from the absence of fathers, many of whom were leaving Pasco from April to October for abundant summertime jobs in Alaska. These were the very months when youngsters needed the most supervision, especially during this era of urban rebellion. Fletcher proposed an industrial park in close proximity to the residential sections of East Pasco, supporting light industry like window manufacturing and cereal processing. He had seen similar programs work in the East Bay cities south of Oakland in Alameda County, where the workplaces were outwardly attractive so that workers were encouraged to live within walking distance. But the bottom line was that they bring jobs to the neighborhood. "If Model Cities doesn't get some of these East Pasco people off [the government] dime, nothing will," Fletcher told a reporter. He wanted government programs to improve opportunity rather than dole out individual aid.[35]

However, the place where Fletcher increasingly put his energies was his new civil rights organization, the East Pasco Self-Help Cooperative. The co-op, a for-profit institution to establish business opportunities, employment, and training for local residents, built on a premise dear to Fletcher's heart: that Black people, working together, could rise out of the depths of inner-city poverty. This had been a guiding feature of his own story, and with the co-op, Fletcher sought to imprint that ethos on the Black community of Pasco.[36]

The co-op was born out of the Higher Horizons neighborhood watch committee. This unique group, formed to find jobs for the chronically unemployed, had quickly expanded into a proactive program to identify neighborhood problems and encourage residents to work together to devise solutions. Higher Horizons had always had difficulty coordinating with other agencies, and when the funding dried up, Fletcher and the zone coordinators and block captains realized that they did not need federal funding to continue what was essentially a volunteer program. So the neighborhood watch program continued, but he knew it could do more. The zone coordinators—middle-class Black professionals from Hanford—formed the co-op's initial steering committee and investing group on February 26, 1966, raising an initial $5,000 in stock shares by the end of the following month. Fletcher also used his connections with the corporate leaders of the tricity area—connections that he had developed while directing Higher Horizons and that he had used to secure employment for himself and Bernyce when Higher Horizons ended—to create a parent organization: Promoters and Underwriters of Self-Help Enterprises and Related Services, or PUSHERS, Inc.—a conscious play on words designed to take ownership of language resonant of the growing scourge of inner-city drug use.[37]

The use of a not-for-profit corporation to provide a high-powered advisory board for the for-profit co-op was another example of the pragmatism that served Fletcher well. Although a committed Republican, Fletcher was not a conservative, and he saw nothing wrong with either the nonprofit idea or the cooperative premise. Further, PUSHERS was an opportunity to bring important players into the room: local business executives with the financial wherewithal to bring the co-op's programs to fruition if the organization failed to secure government funding.

Still, the co-op represented a risky proposition for Fletcher. Although he had cobbled together sufficient consulting and contracting jobs to keep up his mortgage payments (he had bought three homes in East Pasco as white neighbors took flight from the rapidly integrating neighborhood), to stay in Pasco now meant turning down more lucrative employment opportunities. "He was virtually assured of an appointment to fill a vacancy on the State Prison and Parole Board," according to one reporter; the job came with a salary of $17,500, more by half than his former Higher Horizons salary. "However, it meant moving to Olympia," the state capital. "He feared this would cause the co-op to fold. So he rejected it," over Bernyce's objections. Then he was offered "a $14,500-a-year job fighting poverty in Utah." Instead, he accepted the position of co-op business director for a nominal one-dollar salary, throwing his few eggs in the co-op's basket. He did keep his job at Douglas United Nuclear.[38]

As ever, Fletcher turned the positives of the existing situation to his—and in this case the co-op's—advantage. The first Blacks to move into the area, during World War II, had come mostly from the South to do unskilled work at the Hanford plant. As an incentive, the federal government had given these early settlers plots of land just east of Pasco. At the time the land was virtually worthless, but now highway construction was planned for the area. Building on his experience as deputy state highway commissioner back in Kansas, Fletcher argued that this land could be leased to shipping and warehousing businesses looking for lucrative locations adjacent to the right-of-way. He convinced the local landowners to let the co-op broker leases for the land. In turn, the landowners used their profits to buy stock in the co-op, which funded Black-owned start-ups.[39]

One critical concern to co-op members was the status of the Higher Horizons day care center. This program had been launched to provide supervision for the children of the beneficiaries of Higher Horizons programs, who otherwise could not take advantage of its job training and employment opportunities. Now Higher Horizons was gone, but its beneficiaries still needed this assistance or the gains of the program would be lost. The Pasco YMCA agreed to temporarily house the day care center on the condition that the co-op assume responsibility for its operations. Fletcher applied for federal funding for the center from the Office of Economic Opportunity. The application was cosponsored by the Morning Star Baptist Church, whose pastor, Reverend F. A. Allen, had agreed to serve as chairman of the co-op's board (and eventually house the center). Fletcher also wrote a grant for funds from the Washington State Department of Health.[40]

Fletcher with an unidentified man (possibly Reverend F. A. Allen of the Morning Star Baptist Church) working at the East Pasco Self-Help Cooperative service station. Arthur Fletcher Personal Papers, courtesy Paul Fletcher.

The co-op's first profit-generating business was a service station, with a contract with Texaco Oil. Fletcher established a service station committee, including one professional accountant who donated his services, and leased an existing underutilized gas station in East Pasco. Supplies were obtained at cost from Texaco and from a Richland service station going out of business; they hired a manager for $100 a week, an assistant manager for $95 a week, and an attendant for $90 a week, and they sublet one of the station's three service bays to an independent mechanic who doubled as a part-time attendant. The service station opened on September 17, 1966, and quickly became the automotive stop of choice for local motorists, many of whom, being co-op members, deservedly considered themselves co-owners; still others, curious, joined the co-op as a result. After thirteen months, total sales at the service station were more than $64,000, of which more than $4,000 was profit for the co-op. While relatively small, any profit was a boon in that the establishment was providing jobs for three neighborhood residents. Further, dividends were not planned: members saw their investments as benefiting their community rather than their personal finances, and profits were continually reinvested in additional projects, leading to more employment and training opportunities for their children and their neighbors' children, building community equity.[41]

These profits led to the co-op's most remarkable achievement. The $4,000 was used as down payment for an eight-acre commercial site, on which the co-op planned to construct "a number of businesses, such as a laundromat, barber shop, branch bank, hardware store and drugstore . . . and education center and [co-op] offices." The first building was a permanent home for the service station, which would no longer need to pay rent, thereby increasing profits considerably to allow for rapid repayment of the loan. Construction, with materials purchased at cost from sympathetic local suppliers and labor supplied almost exclusively free of charge by co-op members (which Fletcher called sweat equity), commenced in September 1967, and the new service station was completed the following May, just as the co-op was awarded a $95,000 grant from the US Department of Commerce.[42]

The service station was followed by a butcher, a sewing shop with a contract to repair uniforms for the Hanford plant, a welding shop that converted flatbed trucks for use in local farming, and a housing development for the landowners who had leased their land. The activity of the co-op was not limited to private enterprise: the block clubs helped keep the streets safe and encouraged residents to take pride in the appearance of the neighborhood. They successfully pushed the city to fix streetlights and oil the roads, and they helped local residents install indoor plumbing to eliminate outhouses. When local professionals offered financial assistance, Fletcher asked them to contribute their skills instead, which provided free legal, accounting, and even plumbing services for the organization and its projects. Thus, the co-op's skills bank differed from that of Higher Horizons in that the earlier one was about matching the unemployed with jobs in the community while the new one matched professionals with co-op needs.[43]

While the long-term goal of Fletcher's activities was a better life for the residents of East Pasco and his short-term goal was their increased employment, Fletcher's activities on a day-to-day basis were not unlike his business ventures while in the Hall administration a decade earlier and his teenage experiences in the Watts ghetto. He successfully channeled the street smarts of the Depression-era shoeshine boy, the drive he had developed on the gridiron, and the wheeling-and-dealing instincts he had honed as a used-car salesman and entertainment promoter. The difference was one of motivation. Fletcher was no longer concerned with enriching himself, or even simple survival. Instead, his selfless goal was to use his skills and talents to enrich the community.

Fletcher's successor at the co-op, Nat Jackson, likened it to the work of Reverend Leon Sullivan in Philadelphia.[44] Sullivan, like Fletcher, rose from poverty to become a prominent moderate Republican civil rights leader who espoused self-help as the key to economic uplift. While Fletcher pursued football and politics and only came to the ministry as a sideline in his forties, Sullivan pursued a career as a Baptist preacher. He made his way from his childhood in Charleston, West Virginia, to New York City, where he attended Union Theological Seminary and took a graduate degree in religion at Columbia University before becoming assistant minister at Adam Clayton Powell's Abyssinian Baptist Church in Harlem. In 1950 he took the pulpit of Zion Baptist in Philadelphia, a congregation growing with the Second Great Migration. As elsewhere in the North, the best-paid local jobs were reserved for whites, despite their employers' dependence on African American consumers. In 1958 Sullivan organized Philadelphia's Black pastors to call on their parishioners to boycott these establishments—a program he called "selective patronage"—which led to the integration of large local employers like Tasty Baking Company.[45]

Building on the success of selective patronage, Sullivan founded Opportunities Industrialization Center (OIC), a skills training and educational institute in Black North Philadelphia that spread to several cities throughout the United States with funding from the war on poverty. Whereas Fletcher built on his experiences to create economic opportunity in the co-op, Sullivan built on community activism to create an educational institution in the OIC. Sullivan and Zion Baptist also established Black-owned businesses, including the Progress Plaza shopping center, not unlike the co-op's profit-generating ventures in East Pasco. At the same time, Martin Luther King

Jr. established Operation Breadbasket in Chicago, under the leadership of Jesse Jackson, to build a "don't buy where you can't work" program similar to Sullivan's selective patronage campaign.[46]

Unlike Pasco, most OIC cities experienced violent uprisings in the late 1960s. These may not have been preventable by even the best work of Reverend Sullivan—and indeed the rebellions were compelling evidence for the need for OIC's work. Further, the tricity area had a population of only about 50,000—significantly smaller than OIC cities like Newark, which had about 375,000, and a fraction of the size of others like Detroit, Philadelphia, and Los Angeles, each of which totaled over one million inhabitants. Nonetheless, the contrast is telling because—unlike even similar-size towns like Rochester, New York—Pasco avoided major racial violence. After the 1968 assassination of Martin Luther King Jr., when several cities experienced disturbances, Pasco "Negroes and whites prayed together for peace and brotherhood," and an article in the *Tri-City Herald* treated Fletcher as the most important leader of Pasco's Black community in that regard. Later there was boycotting of targeted establishments practicing racial discrimination; whereas in Philadelphia, Sullivan's movement began with boycotts and moved on to self-help, Fletcher's Pasco began with self-help and moved on to boycotts.[47]

Fletcher's work in Pasco also had much in common with that of Floyd McKissick, who succeeded James Farmer as leader of CORE in 1966. The first African American graduate of the University of North Carolina–Chapel Hill Law School, McKissick took CORE in a more militant direction, publicly espousing Black power and expelling white activists from the organization. Under his leadership, CORE rejected the notion that civil rights could be achieved through integration, only different by degree from Fletcher's statement, responding to an attack on the all-Black Higher Horizons day care center, that he "could care less about integrating a community." Like Fletcher, McKissick saw economic empowerment as the key to Black power. He advocated the creation of Black-owned industrial and business concerns, even declaring that "Black capitalism . . . takes precedence over job training programs and general education." He left CORE in 1968 to found Soul City, a North Carolina town peopled with African Americans, with businesses owned by African Americans and streets named for African Americans and civil rights themes. McKissick and his handpicked successor at CORE, Roy Innis, like Fletcher, worked well with white moderate Republicans owing to their devotion to self-help and capitalism. Also like Fletcher, McKissick and Innis formed alliances with former vice president Richard Nixon and

New York governor Nelson Rockefeller, who would rise to the presidency and vice presidency, respectively. Finally, like Fletcher, their eventual break with the Republican leadership resulted from the rise of the conservatives, in McKissick's case North Carolina's Jesse Helms, who vociferously opposed Soul City.[48]

Like OIC and Soul City, Fletcher's co-op faced entrenched obstacles. Whereas Higher Horizons was stymied by bureaucratic feuds, the co-op faced an enemy of a more immediate sort. Fletcher was increasingly finding his community-building efforts hamstrung by the local police force. More than simply racist, some of the officers stationed in predominantly Black East Pasco were actively profiting from kickbacks from drug dealers. At the time East Pasco and Yakima were local centers of the state's illegal drug trade, and the drugs themselves were a powerful temptation to the very youngsters the co-op was created to assist. For all of the success of the co-op, Fletcher faced a looming problem: How does one build a thriving community when the police, the most visible agents of local government, are actively working to undermine your activities?[49]

Fletcher faced other opponents in his quest to strengthen the Black community of East Pasco in 1967. He had become a locus of the growing split between what NUL director Whitney Young called the "responsible" civil rights leadership and the "irresponsible leadership." Between the older generation of leaders, like Reverend Martin Luther King Jr., who focused on integration and nonviolence, and the younger generation, like Stokely Carmichael of the Student Nonviolent Coordinating Committee and Huey Newton and Bobby Seale, who founded the Black Panther Party in Oakland that year. They saw such leaders as King and Young as gradualist Uncle Toms. During the summer of 1967, as the news reported increased racial violence elsewhere in the nation, Fletcher was as concerned about the impact of "irresponsible" Blacks as he was about white racists.[50]

Fletcher had his own definition of the dichotomy between "responsible" and "irresponsible" leaders. For him it was not a question of militancy but of degree. Proudly claiming the "militant" label, he explained, "The difference between a militant and extremist is the militant wants a share in developing a neighborhood while extremists are trying to burn them up." But those "who use violence and crime in the battle for equality" were gaining ground. "The longer nothing is done, the more extremists are able to convince persons to their points of view," he said. "This force must be converted to technical militancy—the training of minorities with the know-how to fill these jobs."[51]

To address his increasing concerns about the difficulties faced by East Pasco, Fletcher decided to run for Pasco's city council in 1967. A resident for barely two years, his newcomer status paled beside the fact that if elected, he would be the first Black to serve on that body—and the first to serve on any city council in the entire state of Washington in the twentieth century. Ignoring his own skin color—something most local white voters obviously could not do—Fletcher campaigned in the nonpartisan, at-large election (the race was citywide rather than to represent a particular neighborhood) on a typical moderate Republican platform for the era. In his printed candidate statement, Fletcher noted that "Pasco is now experiencing a . . . tremendous economic growth cycle," advocating "the full development and utilization of our human and natural resources." To the African American community, this was code for equal employment opportunity, but his decision to not specifically mention civil rights was an attempt to woo white voters ambivalent about voting for a Black man.[52]

Fletcher quickly came under fire from both left and right. According to his son, Paul, local Black Panthers called him an Uncle Tom, likening him to King and Young for his willingness to seek change from within the system. On the other hand, he received actual death threats from racist John Birchers. No stranger to politics, he took it all in stride. When the midnight phone calls came in, he calmly told his trembling son to "ask who's calling."[53]

It is worth pausing at this point to examine Fletcher's motives. While his city council run was ostensibly the next step in a program for uplifting the minority residents of East Pasco and for better securing their civil rights, his background as a campaign worker, political appointee, and candidate in his own right suggests that he had moved to Pasco primarily with political advancement in mind. He left Kansas in 1959 when the dominant conservatives in his party blacklisted him and his patron, Fred Hall; arguably he moved to California to seek an electorate more interested in Black leadership. Then in 1962 he found his party affiliation made political success unlikely, especially in the Bay Area. Had he moved to eastern Washington—staunchly Republican—to eliminate this partisan obstacle?[54]

Although it is likely Fletcher would have eventually run for office again, in Pasco or elsewhere, the evidence from 1967 does not support a carpetbagger charge; nor does his continued support from Pasco residents in the years—and in his political activities—that followed. Most of his relocations were more circumstantial than deliberate. The move from Kansas to California was for economic rather than political opportunity: Fred Hall had found him a good job with Aerojet. Fletcher gave up that good job for a worse one in Berkeley—not to run for office but to keep the family close to his wife, Mary. Then in 1965, when he got the Higher Horizons opportunity, leaving the junior high school in Berkeley to oversee job training programs in Pasco seemed to him a logical step in developing his self-help civil rights program. While his party affiliation commended him to corporate leaders, the racism of the tricity area, which created the need for Higher Horizons and the work of a man like Fletcher, minimized any African American's chances for political advancement; after all, no Black had been elected to any city or statewide office there since the nineteenth century. Finally, Fletcher didn't actually see himself as a political winner. His campaign in 1967, as in 1962, was an uphill battle; he measured success not by victory but the percentage of votes he received above his natural constituency (be that Republicans, as in Berkeley, or Blacks, as in Pasco), and in the concurrent strengthening of his organizational endeavors. He wanted to win but expected to lose.

In short, Fletcher ran for Pasco City Council primarily to raise visibility and support for the co-op. Were he to win, he planned to use his political influence to pursue equal rights in Pasco; otherwise, he hoped the attempt would bring the co-op to statewide attention and lead to the growth of the program. He and his supporters therefore saw his candidacy as a win-win proposition.

Just who were his supporters? Certainly everyone who had worked closely with him at Higher Horizons, or had been helped by its programs, and everyone connected to the co-op, including its funders. As for the Blacks of the local community, he acknowledged that their support, when he could get it, was fickle. Claiming to have the trust of only "15–20 per cent of the Negroes in the ghetto area of East Pasco," he candidly told a reporter from the *Seattle Post-Intelligencer* that "I'm a great guy if they have problems I can solve . . . I'm great until the next problem I can't solve."[55]

As in Kansas and California, Fletcher was also not without friends in high places. His work at the co-op had caught the attention of the staff of Governor Daniel Evans, a young, moderate Republican who had been elected to his first term in 1964. In the fall of 1966, at the urging of a member of the Pasco school board, Evans reached out to Reverend Allen, chairman of the co-op's board, and arranged a visit. Allen deferred to Fletcher to make the plans, and Fletcher created a day to remember, with a reception, songs from the church choir, a lengthy explanation of the co-op's work, and an Evans keynote. As Evans recalls,

In those days, a lot of pressure was for the government to do this and that, and here was a program run by a guy who said "we've got ourselves to blame if we can't get things done." The next time I visited the area, I went out to see the program and met Art Fletcher. He was a big, handsome guy with a deep voice, and more importantly he could really communicate . . . his philosophy was not to turn away government help, but to use it and multiply it by what [local Blacks could] do.[56]

Clearly Fletcher had made an impression, and soon the two were corresponding, with Evans striking out his secretary's typed "Mr. Fletcher" and replacing it with his own handwritten "Art," a sign of growing familiarity.[57]

That trust paid off in the city council race. Only days before the November 7 election, Evans named Fletcher to his newly formed State Advisory Council on Urban Affairs. Under the coordination of Washington's secretary of state, A. Ludlow Kramer, the purpose of the council was "to find solutions to the problems brought about by our rapid urban growth." Fletcher used the appointment to promote his campaign, contacting the *Tri-City Herald* and issuing an updated candidate's statement: "As an advisor . . . I will have access to studies, facts, and essential resources needed to control and direct growth and will be able to make them available to Pasco. . . . My appointment . . . implies that I have the . . . leadership ability and record of achievement needed to be of real service."[58]

Fletcher handily won the election by a vote of 888 to 617, taking 59 percent of the electorate. The Black ex–football player beat a white ex–baseball player, Pete Migun, to become the first Black member of the Pasco City Council and one of the first two Blacks on any Washington State city council in the twentieth century (Sam Smith simultaneously won a seat in Seattle). "It's another first for Pasco," his wife, Bernyce, told a reporter. "Art and his fellow councilmen will make Pasco a most desirable place for each of us to live in and be proud of."[59]

Fletcher was out of town on Election Day, touring the campuses of Black colleges in the South to recruit potential new Hanford employees. On his return he participated in a panel discussion on race relations at a Unitarian church in Kennewick. The reporter in attendance for the *Tri-City Herald*, Web Ruble, got two articles out of the event for the next day's edition. His calm report on the panelists' discussion of racial progress in employment, "Race Relations Not 'Rosy' Here," was published in the interior pages, but his salacious recounting of the discussion of police relations with the Black residents of Pasco, "Fletcher Blasts Pasco's Police," made the front page.

Quotations attributed to Fletcher included "Pasco police need a course in human relations, and I'm going to do something about it"; policemen are "always over in the Negro community, or chasing Negroes out of city parks in other parts of town"; "courses in human relations are necessary because police are unable to distinguish the trouble-makers from others"; and "police just don't know how to handle the situation . . . that's why they need training, baby."[60]

While it was true that police corruption had been one of the more important reasons for Fletcher's city council bid, in fact most of the quotations had been taken out of context or wrongly attributed. Fletcher immediately reached out to the new police chief, A. L. McKibben. The story was poorly reported, he told him, noting that some of his comments had been in reference to police forces around the country, in particular Houston, the site of recent clashes with Black students at Texas Southern University; other comments had actually been made not by him but by one or another of his fellow panelists. "I did not 'BLAST' Pasco's police," he said. Ever politic, Fletcher claimed to not blame the reporter: "I must admit that he was working under very trying circumstances. There were four people on the panel, and each had a great deal to say during the two-hour session." In his personal, detailed letter, he commended the new chief for not commenting to the reporter and assured him that "should I have a charge to level at you and/or your staff . . . I will discuss the matter with you before making it a public issue." Fletcher ultimately found Chief McKibben amenable to his concerns about cleaning up the drug corruption in East Pasco, and from all available evidence, the two had a positive working relationship during Fletcher's time on the council.[61]

Fletcher continued to offer advice and support for the co-op from his new position in political leadership, even as he added citywide concerns to his portfolio, such as leadership of a school bond initiative and the Tri-Cities Merit Employment Council, an affiliate of the federal Plans for Progress affirmative action program.[62]

Action for Washington

Arthur Fletcher now came into the orbit of Sam Reed, executive director of the State Advisory Council on Urban Affairs. A recent graduate of the master's program in political science at Washington State University, Reed cochaired an organization called Action for Washington, a group of politically active youngsters looking to strengthen the tenuous hold of moderate

Republicans on the statewide party. Most importantly, they wanted to help reelect two moderate leaders, Governor Evans and Secretary of State A. Ludlow Kramer. Evans and Kramer had each been elected for the first time in 1964, and both were young: in 1967, Evans was forty-two, and Kramer—the youngest secretary of state in Washington history—was only thirty-five. Reed believed the party had an opportunity to secure a moderate Republican majority in Washington for a generation by developing the interest of young people turned off by what they saw as the extremism of both left and right during the 1960s.[63]

To build momentum, Reed hoped that Action for Washington could endorse a full slate of statewide candidates early in the race—before the primaries—that would work well as a team to inspire younger voters. To complement Evans and Kramer, he needed Republican candidates for attorney general and lieutenant governor. When Seattle attorney (and descendant of the Gorton's Fish founder) Slade Gorton agreed to run for attorney general, Reed was especially interested in recruiting a candidate for lieutenant governor with a youthful vigor, charisma, and charm. He decided that Arthur Fletcher was his man.[64]

By the spring of 1968 Reed had been working with Fletcher for several months on the Council on Urban Affairs. Like Governor Evans, Reed was particularly impressed with Fletcher, and after visiting Pasco and asking around, his suspicions were confirmed: here was a man who could captivate a crowd, and he had statewide campaign experience to boot (albeit from Kansas). What's more, Fletcher's race did not strike Reed as a political handicap. Given the times, it seemed especially appropriate to woo younger white voters. If elected, Fletcher would be Washington's first Black statewide office holder—and the first Black lieutenant governor in any state since Reconstruction. The Democratic state legislature was about to pass new civil rights legislation, and Fletcher's nomination would remind voters that the Republican Party—the party of Lincoln—had historically been at the forefront of the battle for equal rights. Finally, he saw Fletcher's flamboyance, energy, and Baptist-preacher speaking style as the ideal match for the country-club Gorton. Reed convinced Action for Washington to endorse him as part of the slate.[65]

When Reed first asked him to run, Fletcher laughed out loud, as Reed describes it, "in that deep, booming laughter of his." The concept of a three-year state resident, first-term city councilman from a veritable backwater running to be a heartbeat away from the statehouse did indeed seem ridiculous, not to mention that a primary win seemed statistically impossible:

John Birchers, for instance, far outnumbered Blacks in the state Republican Party; indeed, Blacks totaled only 2 percent of the state population. Even if he were to win the nomination, Fletcher faced an uphill battle against the popular three-term Democratic incumbent, John Cherberg. Still, Reed promised the support of Action for Washington, and he reminded Fletcher that his background was hardly typical of a first-term councilman. And after all, Fletcher reasoned, so what if I lose? As with the city council race, the proposition was win-win for his main goal, promoting self-help civil rights to wider audiences.[66]

In March 1968 Fletcher announced that he was "considering running for the post" and that after an upcoming trip to Seattle to explore potential financing and organizational help, "if it seems promising, between now and June, I will announce." He sent a courtesy letter to Governor Evans, explaining his qualifications and arranging a meeting with him and the state party chairman. Evans, for his part, refused to make an endorsement in the primary, not wanting to play favorites—smart politics because Fletcher's victory was by no means assured, and Evans needed the dedicated support of the eventual nominee in the general election campaign. He did allow that Fletcher was "a good man with good ideas" and that he "would be a credit to any office for which he chose to run." A subsequent report on Action for Washington claimed that "the Pasco Councilman was known to be the Governor's personal favorite."[67]

Martin Luther King Jr.'s assassination on April 4 pushed Fletcher to action. Telling the *Centralia Daily Chronicle* that "the shooting had prompted him to enter the race," he asked Seattle physician Ray Smith to set up a Citizens for Art Fletcher committee and accepted an invitation from the Spokane County Republican Convention to address their April 27 meeting.[68]

Responding to an Associated Press questionnaire sent to the state's two new Black city councilmen, Fletcher deliberately zoomed out to address the national urban crisis, saying that the biggest challenge for President Johnson was keeping the peace at home rather than winning the Vietnam War abroad; that the solution to domestic strife lay with the promotion of grassroots programs rather than asking industry to form committees (which had been Johnson's response to the Watts rebellion); and agreeing with the president that 1968 would be "a bad summer."

The underlying motivation for the questionnaire, of course, was an attempt to tease out the position of the "respectable" Black leadership in an era when the civil rights movement seemed to be devolving into violent rebellion. Fletcher responded tellingly, emphasizing the importance of a

Black "silent majority" more than a year before Nixon popularized the term in reference to white conservatives.

> During my recruiting trips throughout the nation, I always make it a point to change from my middle class businessman's apparel into less formal attire. I then proceed to walk the streets of the ghetto, visiting pool halls, [barber] shops, eating establishments, bars and taverns and visiting the homes of friends and relatives who reside in these neighborhoods. My purpose is to observe, listen and discuss local conditions as regards to the civil rights–poverty struggle and to evaluate the impact of the national effort on the community in question. . . . There is a loud outcry within the Negro ghetto which claims that the professional, highly skilled, highly qualified, so-called middle classed Negro is a traitor to the cause and has deserted the brothers in the ghetto. I have also found that there is a great deal of discussion and disagreement among all classes as to whether the claim is valid or that the break is clean. I have observed that those who [espouse] the desertion point of view are definitely in the minority.[69]

This response speaks volumes about Fletcher's place in the Black community. As a college-educated, white-collar professional, Fletcher oscillated between two worlds: that of the boardroom—an overwhelmingly white domain—and that of "authentic" Blackness. His "less formal attire"—presumably including dungarees—would have made him feel more at home in "the streets of the ghetto." He clearly struggled at times to reconcile these dual identities and took personally the charge that men like him were "traitor[s] to the cause." As a Republican in an increasingly Democratic demographic, he carried additional baggage and felt even more defensive. In response, he focused on the opinions he saw as that of the silent majority of African Americans.[70]

Notwithstanding his job as a minority recruiter and his position as a city councilman, however, it was his identity as a civil right leader that mattered most to Fletcher. In fact, he eschewed the moderate label, using it only in comparison with Goldwaterite conservatives. Otherwise, he considered himself a "practical militant." Racism and discrimination were a cancer on the body politic, and moderation in their presence, to paraphrase Goldwater, was no virtue. "First, baby, understand, there are no moderate Negroes. There are extremists and practical militants," he said. "For the past few years the practical militants have been paralyzed by extremists like Stokely [Carmichael] and Rap [Brown]. They've been afraid to get with the white power structure for fear of being labeled 'Uncle Tom.'" Fletcher saw practical militancy as seeking radical change in the racist order from within the existing system, rather than attacking it from the outside. But he was not a marcher, however effective that technique; his organizing efforts were aimed at strengthening Blacks' economic and political power.[71]

Fletcher knew that his successes in Pasco and his developing statewide presence was giving him a moment in the spotlight, and he resolved to exploit it for all it was worth. This was what he had been waiting for at least since his nadir in the Berkeley ghetto, and that he had been training for since his days waiting tables at the Jayhawk Hotel and working the doors of the Kansas state capitol. Over the first four decades of his life, he had developed an answer to "the race question"—what W. E. B. Du Bois had said would be "the problem of the twentieth century"—and the nation seemed to finally be listening. In May Governor Evans invited him to Seattle to address a traveling panel of the Republican Governors Association, where he out-lined the history and achievements of the co-op, and suggested that similar programs could be implemented to positive effect throughout the nation.[72]

Fletcher formally announced his candidacy on May 3, issuing a state-ment stressing his seriousness (important under the circumstances). He explained how he would extend his self-help labor and civil rights theories, noting that he was seeking executive office (rather than a seat in the state legislature, a more appropriate next step for a city councilman) because he wanted to pursue his theories year round (state legislators only served part time). "The people in my district know about the program and after a legis-lative session I would have little if any opportunity to explain it elsewhere." He stayed true to his self-help theme, advocating that citizens "go back to the grass roots where the problems are and lend themselves personally to help people organize and develop the implements to be self-sustaining."[73]

Despite a few endorsements, the campaign fizzled early on for want of funds and media attention, not to mention poor coordination. On more than one occasion Fletcher missed his appearances at important fund-raisers. In one telling example, he reported,

At 12:00 noon yesterday (June 18) I left my office, took care of some last minute details, stepped into my car at 1:55 pm, and drove at brake-neck speeds [sic] from Pasco to Seattle [about 225 miles]. Once in Seattle, I took the ferry to Bremerton. I was going there under the assumption that a dinner and cocktail hour was being held in my behalf. I was also told that the persons sponsoring the affair would meet me at the ferry-dock in Bremerton and take me to its location. . . . However, we failed to make connections . . . I arrived in Bremerton alone, without an escort, and at loose ends. I tried desperately to make contact with several of the Republican party officials from that area, but all to no avail. I later learned that the affair was being held in Winthrop and not Bremerton, that it was well attended and that the sponsoring parties were quite disappointed at my failure to appear.

Because of problems like this, Fletcher gave serious consideration to suspending his campaign; he even drafted a letter to Governor Evans to that effect. But because he was still running unopposed, he decided to stick it out.[74]

Governor Evans, meanwhile, doubled down on his quiet efforts to support him, realizing that a Fletcher nomination could help his own reelection campaign demonstrate its relevance and moderation in the face of a challenge from the Democratic state attorney general, John O'Connell. Scheduled to be the keynote speaker at the Republican National Convention in Miami that August, Evans boldly arranged for Fletcher to address the party's platform committee, hoping that the national exposure would help Fletcher's campaign back home. When New York governor Nelson Rockefeller visited Seattle in July, campaigning for the Republican presidential nomination, Evans—a declared Rockefeller delegate—set up a meeting between Fletcher and Rocky to pitch his "so-called Fletcher plank" for self-help civil rights.[75]

Theodore H. White, that great dry chronicler of presidential elections, has pointed out that "in actual fact, all platforms are meaningless," while nevertheless conceding that the "writing of a platform does indeed flatter many people, gives many pressure groups a chance to blow off steam in public, [and] permits the leaders of such pressure groups to report back to their memberships of their valiant efforts to persuade." So it was for civil rights organizations. The records of the NAACP, for instance, contain copious folders on advocacy surrounding the quadrennial national platforms of both parties. And so it was for Fletcher. This was an opportunity for a politician heretofore bound by state and local politics to make an impact on the national level, to show some of the great movers and shakers of the national party who he was and what he was capable of doing. If he could garner their support, it might yet revive his moribund primary bid back home in Washington—and more. In his speech, Fletcher discussed in detail the co-op and its relevance to Republican—and indeed American—values, charming the approximately 100 delegates of the platform committee. The result was a self-help civil rights plank in the 1968 Republican platform that closely tracked Fletcher's testimony:

> An essential element of economic betterment is the opportunity for self-determination—to develop or acquire and manage one's own business enterprise. This opportunity is bleak for most residents of impoverished areas. We endorse the concept of . . . capital, technical assistance and insurance for the establishment and renewal of businesses in depressed urban and rural areas. We favor efforts to enable residents of such areas to become owners and managers of businesses and, through such agencies as a Domestic Development Bank, to exercise economic leadership in their communities.[76]

Of course, Fletcher's was not the only interesting Republican primary race in 1968. That summer, former vice president Nixon was again engaged in a tough race for the presidential nomination. The moderate wing of the party was represented by Rockefeller, and the conservatives by a fellow Californian, Governor Ronald Reagan. With a strong record on civil rights stemming from his chairmanship of President Eisenhower's Committee on Government Contracts, his public opposition to the disastrous war in Vietnam, and memories of his 1960 near win still fresh in the minds of voters, Nixon hoped to stake out a strong middle position. His support of Goldwater in 1964, he hoped, would pacify the party's right wing; he desperately wanted to avoid a repeat of 1962, when John Bircher dissent assured his loss to Pat Brown. To deflect a challenge from the moderates, meanwhile, meant supporting a civil rights program that could prevent and fight urban violence while at the same time demonstrating sympathy with the achievements of the civil rights movement. Nixon endorsed self-help civil rights legislation proposed by CORE and began casting about for potential Black advisors.[77]

In Miami Beach the nomination went to Nixon on the first ballot, and Governor Evans, a good soldier, endorsed the nominee and arranged for him to meet with Fletcher. Although Fletcher had met Nixon during the 1962 campaign, he had never worked one-on-one with the new presidential nominee. The two hit it off, and Nixon invited Fletcher to confer with him in San Diego the following week.[78]

It was expected that Blacks would largely vote for the Democratic nominee out of loyalty to President Johnson, who had successfully pushed three major civil rights bills through Congress. Black voters had been trending Democratic since 1932, but their Republican numbers had been especially negligible in 1964, when the GOP nominated ultraconservative Arizona senator Barry Goldwater. On August 17 in San Diego, Fletcher met with Nixon; his running mate, Spiro Agnew; his campaign staff coordinator, Glenn Olse; "and others." Also in attendance for a photo opportunity was basketball superstar Wilt Chamberlain. The candidates and campaign officials talked all day with Fletcher about Black capitalism and strategized winning more of the Black vote. Nixon announced an upcoming speech on the subject of civil rights, "Bridges to Human Dignity," and the group agreed to form a national campaign task force on the subject, with Olse inviting Fletcher to serve as a member and advisor.[79]

We should not underestimate the importance of this moment. After three decades, Fletcher was fulfilling the prophecy he claimed Mary MacLeod Bethune had made to his junior high school class in Oklahoma City: someone in this room will advise presidents. Bethune had also charged her young audience, according to Fletcher, to always hold a brief for Black people. The Olse task force was exactly what Fletcher believed Bethune had envisioned: the opportunity to discuss and recommend civil rights policy to the next president of the United States.

But Fletcher knew he had not yet reached his personal zenith, and he resolved to get back to work. For now, that meant winning his own nomination for lieutenant governor. The San Diego conference was reported in several newspapers around Washington. "I'm urging Mr. Nixon," Fletcher told the *Spokane Spokesman-Review*, "to deliver plans for implementing programs . . . not promising pie-in-the-sky programs, but rather implementing action plans." And he followed up by detailing his speech before the Republican National Committee (RNC) platform committee at regular campaign events around the state.[80]

Action for Washington, for their part, now went into high gear on behalf of Fletcher. The clean-cut, moderate college students who constituted the rank and file of the organization saw Fletcher's candidacy as "a genuine crusade," the opportunity to strengthen their preferred wing of the party, fight for a candidate who combined civil rights with the idea of self-help, and give the lie to the growing sentiment, among John Birchers and leftists alike, that African Americans had no place among Republicans. The summertime was perfect for employing college students, and dozens went to work for Fletcher. The candidate responded in kind, taking the time to nurture and mentor his eager helpers, whom he saw as the future of his party. So while

Fletcher gave the Action for Washington campaign workers experience in a real political campaign, they gave him a sense of purpose within the party that he carried beyond the 1968 race and through the rest of his career: the idea that African Americans still had a role to play in the party, and that he could find support in great numbers among eager white allies.[81]

Fletcher now finally had an opponent in the Republican primary, Bill Muncey, who likewise had no problem getting good press, in his case from built-in name recognition as a champion hydroplane driver. Other than declaring his candidacy, however, Muncey announced no plans for how he would use the office and proposed no program: his campaign strategy appeared to be simply to trade on his celebrity and coast to the nomination. In this, he was not unlike prior successful candidates for the office: a popular columnist noted, "Muncey's name is better known among the independent voters, and name familiarity has been a major item in the race for the office each time it has changed hands in the last 36 years." He refused to debate Fletcher, shrewdly arguing that "to those Republican candidates who feel that intra-party debate is necessary, I suggest that the real debate and challenge should be to the 12-year Democrat incumbent." Still, close observers perceived that this primary race was different; the *Renton Record Chronicle,* for instance, called the Fletcher–Muncey race "the one to watch." As primary day approached, Muncey's absenteeism in the face of Fletcher's earnest activity began to rankle. The Associated Republican Women evaluated both candidates and endorsed Fletcher after Muncey missed a joint appearance to instead race a hydroplane, making his priorities clear. On the eve of the primary, one columnist, endorsing Fletcher, wrote, "Why Muncey filed isn't really clear to political observers, since he hasn't waged any campaign at all." The *Bellingham Herald* called the contest a "close battle," and a University of Washington poll showed Fletcher with a slight lead.[82]

On September 17, Fletcher defeated Bill Muncey 2–1 for the Republican nomination, winning the primary in every single county of the state. Like California, Washington had an open primary; voters of any (or no) party affiliation could vote for any candidate, and the results did not indicate the party affiliation of the voters. It is possible that Fletcher's victory in some areas—notably Seattle, Tacoma, and Spokane—was the result of Democratic and other liberal voters' crossing over, but demographic voting data from Seattle, which contained more than half of the state's African American voters, has been difficult to parse. Predominantly Black East Pasco—likewise an overwhelmingly Democratic area—chose Fletcher in the primary by 142 votes, more than all other candidates in both parties combined. More remarkable

Governor Dan Evans with Fletcher, probably at a primary-night party, September 17, 1968. Arthur Fletcher Personal Papers, courtesy Paul Fletcher.

was Fletcher's showing in the rural counties, especially those where he even outpolled the Democratic incumbent, John Cherberg, such as Yakima County, in the south-central part of the state, and tiny Wahkiakum County in the southwest. The expected white backlash did not materialize significantly to change the results of the nomination. Fletcher was now the first statewide major-party nominee of color in the history of the state of Washington.[83]

The Fall Campaign

With the full Action for Washington slate having secured nomination, Sam Reed and his young colleagues organized several events on college campuses throughout the state. In early October, Fletcher and attorney general nominee Slade Gorton embarked on a fly-in tour, occasionally joined by the incumbent Republican secretary of state, Lud Kramer. Their speeches were specifically designed to appeal to the sensibilities of baby boomer students, with Gorton sounding almost like a liberal: "We have demonstrations and violence not because we are moving backward but because we are moving forward." Added Fletcher: "Law and order will flow when justice prevails." The students, for their part, listened intently to Washington's first Black major-party nominee for statewide office. One editorial lauded the students at Yakima Valley College, who gave "not even a boo or a catcall" during the Gorton and Fletcher speeches: "That's the kind of demonstration that is a joy to watch."[84]

Although the team got on well, Fletcher's charisma actually made the other candidates on the slate seem dull by comparison. None wanted to follow him in the speaking order, and it made sense for Fletcher to speak last because the post he sought was senior to those of Gorton and Kramer. But all were pleased by his draw: at each campus, students came out by the hundreds to hear him. "It was great because Art Fletcher could draw 400 people where I could draw 40," Gorton recalled. "It was also awful because it didn't matter whether I spoke first or second because I was a complete after-thought to the wonderful orations Art would come through with." This played directly into Sam Reed's plans. Despite the fact that most college students still could not vote (the Twenty-Sixth Amendment, which lowered the voting age to eighteen, was not ratified until 1971), Reed hoped that the youthful energy and vigor demonstrated by the candidates would generate enthusiasm among the students, who would do campaign work in the short term and become moderate Republicans in the long term.[85]

Fletcher also found a complimentary and supportive running mate in Dan Evans. A civil rights liberal and fiscal moderate, Evans was a good fit for Fletcher's ideology. When the governor, at an open meeting at Seattle's predominantly Black East Madison YMCA, was confronted by seven teenage Black power advocates—one of whom almost went so far as to threaten his life—Evans asked for a concrete list of requests for how the state government could help the community. As a result the state opened a multipurpose community center that combined social and health services. When Evans spoke that fall at a public meeting at Seattle's predominantly Black Garfield High School, he again proved his civil rights bona fides, facing down the Black Panthers with whom he shared the podium and winning over a hostile crowd with his frankness and candor about race. On police brutality, he said, "We ought not condemn the entire police force for the actions of some just as an entire community ought not be condemned for the actions of some." Having kept his promise to vote for Rockefeller at the national convention but fallen into line to endorse Nixon afterward, he was asked the awkward question about endorsing his race-baiting California colleague, Ronald Reagan, if the latter had been picked by Nixon for the vice presidency. "Let's put it this way," Evans said. "I'm glad I didn't have to make that choice."[86]

Evans was able to publicly support Fletcher now that the primary was behind them. Not only did the governor agree to campaign as part of a Fletcher–Gorton–Kramer slate with the support of Sam Reed's Action for Washington, but he also made resources available to ensure that Fletcher did not suffer a repeat of the previous June's doldrums. This was easier after Evans's opponent, Democratic state attorney general John O'Connell, became embroiled in a gambling scandal involving multiple trips to Las Vegas, thus making Evans practically a shoo-in for reelection. Another member of the slate, Lud Kramer, was also far ahead in the polls. So Kramer agreed to work full time on Fletcher's campaign, and he volunteered his own organization to support it. Evans and Kramer brought a who's who of powerful Republican donors and operatives to the table, including *Marine Digest* publisher and Seattle port commission president John Haydon and state senator Joel Pritchard, also of Seattle. Massachusetts senator Edward Brooke, the first African American to win a statewide election since Reconstruction, headlined a Fletcher fund-raiser in Seattle on October 28. In a particularly telling moment, as Richard Nixon visited Seattle on his only trip to the state that fall, available sources note that the only topic of conversation between the governor and the presidential nominee was how they could support Fletcher's campaign.[87]

Fletcher's support was not, however, limited to the rich and powerful. Most donors provided small amounts of money but critical moral support for Fletcher and his campaign staff. Fletcher proved a cipher on which his white supporters, seeking catharsis from the racial turmoil of the 1960s, could project their varied hopes and dreams for American race relations. And project they did, Democrats and Republicans alike. "I think the Negroes should have the right to work in stores," wrote Richard H. Smith of Mt. Vernon, enclosing fourteen cents. Mr. and Mrs. B. Flynn of Seattle, sending $5, wrote that they "were greatly impressed with his views and feel he has the right answers to our problems. We were also impressed with his appearance and dignity"—such compliments being equivalent to the old "credit to his race" trope. "It's not because you're white, nor is it because you're black—it's because you're YOU and for what you stand for," wrote Roy Butler of Bellingham, a $1 donor, who added that in the presidential race, "I will vote for the lesser of two evils: H.H.H." (Hubert H. Humphrey, the Democratic nominee). For these supporters, Fletcher represented an

Washington secretary of state A. Ludlow "Lud" Kramer managed Fletcher's 1968 campaign for lieutenant governor. Arthur Fletcher Personal Papers, courtesy Paul Fletcher.

opportunity to remain liberal on civil rights while decrying what they saw as the extremism of the left. White northern liberals constructed an identity that decried southern Jim Crow but ignored their own subconscious racism and the institutionalized racism of their communities.[88]

While Fletcher's "up by the bootstraps" story was certainly compelling to voters—one newspaper called him a "former shoeshine boy"—his opponent also had an interesting Cinderella background. Like Fletcher, John Cherberg had been a college football star, in his case at the University of Washington. And like Fletcher, he had then turned to coaching. After bringing teams from two different Seattle high schools to championship victories, he returned to the University of Washington to coach the freshman team there. Unlike Fletcher, who faced the handicap of racism, Cherberg continued to advance in college coaching. After an undefeated season, he was made UW head coach. Then his luck ran out, and after losing a few games, "certain alumni" organized to fire him. The losing fight to save his job gave Cherberg a taste for politics, and when the lieutenant governor position fell vacant in 1956, he filed for it, defeated well-known opponents in the Democratic primary, and won the general election. He supplemented his $10,000 state salary by managing a small radio station in Seattle. By 1964, after two terms, he had built a reputation as a fair, if somewhat undynamic, presiding officer of the state senate, but as his governors never died in office or resigned from it, he did little else.[89]

For Fletcher, defeating Cherberg would be no easy task—but then, winning the primary had also seemed difficult at the outset. The primary voting results boded well for Fletcher to give Cherberg a run for his money. He had hoped to get within 100,000 votes of Cherberg on primary day, and actually came within 40,000. While Republicans were said to have turned out more strongly for the primary than Democrats, and while it remained to be seen whether Muncey's voters would go to Fletcher out of party loyalty, switch to Cherberg for racist or other reasons, or simply stay home, the nearly two-month-long general election campaign presented both candidates with opportunities. Impartial observers predicted a tight race. At least one prominent Democrat, Seattle's state assemblyman, David Sprague, publicly agreed that Cherberg was vulnerable. As their poll numbers converged in late October and the race grew tighter, Fletcher naturally grew more confident; he was riding the coattails of both Dan Evans and Richard Nixon. Shelby Scates, a popular columnist with the *Seattle Post-Intelligencer,* added to the incumbent's woes by contrasting him poorly with the dynamic Fletcher. After watching Cherberg address a group of college students, the report was telling. "There was still a handful of students to listen as he ticked off the seven committees on which the lieutenant governor sits. Feet shuffled when he got to the Data Processing Advisory Committee. . . . There was little interaction. Fletcher leaves a group like this talking to themselves, Cherberg leaves them indifferent."[90]

Fletcher continued, but amplified, his primary campaign strategy now that he was facing the incumbent Democrat. This came down to flogging three issues: Cherberg's chairmanship of the state senate rules committee; Fletcher's intention to make the position a full-time job; and Cherberg's continued refusal to debate. At issue with the senate committee was the rule that senators could vote on legislation in secret, which Fletcher decried as undemocratic, pointing out that voters had a right to know how their representatives were voting. As lieutenant governor, Cherberg served as chairman of the rules committee, and Fletcher harped on his failure to abolish the rule. Next, the position of lieutenant governor was part time, with Cherberg serving only during the legislative session and remaining on call should there be a vacancy in the office of the governor. Fletcher

Fletcher supporters Ann Hanson and her son, Max. Arthur Fletcher Personal Papers, courtesy Paul Fletcher.

called this wasteful and promised to travel the state as a full-time officer of the state government, proposing and implementing solutions to the state's problems. Last, Cherberg refused to debate, despite Fletcher's repeated calls for him to do so.[91]

Cherberg's responses to these points were perfectly logical. On the matter of the senate rules committee, he said, "I serve as rules committee chairman because the senators want it that way and not by virtue of any law. . . . The lieutenant governor also has no voice in determining whether or not voting . . . is done openly or in secret." On his status as part time, "Every candidate I've run against has in his platform to make it a fulltime job," he protested. "Actually, the duties have been greatly expanded since I became lieutenant governor." And on his refusal to debate, Cherberg said, "I'm the incumbent. I'm not going to pay for advertising and then split it with someone." But despite the logic and clarity of these points, polls showed the race tightening. Clarity alone cannot win an election; to capture the voters one must play their song, and Cherberg proved tone-deaf. When the Fletcher campaign dispatched a photographer to get a shot of Cherberg's empty statehouse desk and found his office door locked, Cherberg labeled it a campaign stunt and offered to make his office available in the future to any Republican photographer. But Fletcher won the point.[92]

Despite Fletcher's growing momentum, Cherberg did have one major advantage besides incumbency and name recognition: he was white. In a year when the ultraconservative George Wallace was mounting a racist third-party presidential campaign with substantial (if not statistically significant) support in Washington State, Cherberg subtly played the race card to pick up votes from rural and suburban whites who feared that the civil rights movement, and its increasing militancy, challenged their perceived supremacy. "For what it's worth I do mention from time to time my Yugoslav ancestry. . . . My father left there when he was 12 years old as cabin boy on a four-masted sailing ship and never returned. It's funny, some people think I'm Scandinavian or Jewish because of my last name. And people 'vote ethnic' even more than they vote party." This was a naked plea for the very same white ethnic vote that Nixon was courting with his own not-so-subtle race talk. The implication was, let's debate my (gentile) ethnicity, but remember that Fletcher is Black, and he's not one of us. The "cabin boy" story, meanwhile, both appealed to the aquaculture enthusiasts of the western half of the state and reminded voters that Fletcher's ancestors had crossed the Atlantic on a very different sort of ship.[93]

Cherberg also found a way to link Fletcher to government handouts despite Fletcher's antipathy to them. "As a former teacher," the *Vancouver Columbian* put it, Cherberg "feels society should extend 'the full educational experience to anyone and everyone who can profit from the experience,' and indicated he feels there should be no additional welfare programs." The implication was that African Americans were uneducated, perhaps uneducable, and dependent on taxpayer support—more than a decade before Reagan won the presidency partly by characterizing Black inner-city mothers as welfare queens. This was an old canard, of course; racist whites had justified slavery during the late antebellum period by claiming that uncivilized Blacks needed the "stability" of a plantation system (that was in fact notable for enforced instability); now, according to this theory, welfare programs were evidence that Blacks were not ready for independence and freedom, and by extension should not be elected to public office.[94]

Cherberg—or at least his supporters—also used media influence to weaken Fletcher's appeal. In addition to his management position on a local radio station, Cherberg held a public relations job at KIRO-TV, which he temporarily left for the campaign. Clearly, however, his colleagues there numbered among his most fervent supporters. When the Fletcher campaign

Fletcher for lieutenant governor rally. Courtesy Kathy Keolker.

produced a thirty-minute paid television program, "The Fletcher Story," KIRO-TV was the only station in the Puget Sound area that refused to air it, claiming there was no time (although they found time for a program on Democratic gubernatorial candidate John O'Connell).[95]

The 1968 campaign in Washington State included two moments of historical serendipity: Fletcher's encounters with former child actress Shirley Temple and future serial killer Ted Bundy. Temple, the Depression-era child star now going by her married name, Shirley Temple Black, had become active in Republican politics in 1967 with a failed bid to represent California's Eleventh Assembly District. In October 1968, she visited Seattle to endorse Fletcher and the rest of the "Action Team." Ms. Black's endorsement actually seems to have lost Fletcher at least one vote: "Though a Democrat I fully intended to vote for Art Fletcher," wrote someone with an apparent grudge against the aging, curly-haired celebrity, "but after hearing over the air of his appearance on the platform with Shirley Temple Black, I had second thoughts. It is not only how good a man is, but the company he keeps!" The screed reached the Fletcher committee scribbled in the margins of a campaign fund-raising flyer. Black, for her part, remained active in Republican politics; she later served as ambassador to Ghana under President Ford and to Czechoslovakia under the first President Bush.[96]

Fletcher's interactions with Ted Bundy, who subsequently murdered at least thirty young women "in seven states between 1974 and 1978," and who went to the electric chair for his crimes, was a by-product of his endorsement by Action for Washington. The group actively recruited clean-cut, politically moderate college students to serve in the Republican campaigns, as most could not yet vote. Bundy had attended college in Seattle, and despite dropping out in early 1968, he managed to become a Washington delegate to the Republican National Convention in Miami, pledged to Rockefeller. Paul Fletcher called him a "typical Young Republican . . . a little Yuppie in blue blazers and penny loafers." Nattily attired, polite, and affable—the very traits he later used to gain the confidence of his victims—Bundy became Fletcher's driver, shuttling the candidate around the state to various campaign events, even acting as a sometime bodyguard when the death threats against the candidate were deemed serious, "sleeping," he later told true crime author Ann Rule, "in a room close by. He wanted to carry a gun, but Fletcher vetoed that," although longtime Fletcher family friend Kathy Keolker reported that Bundy was indeed armed with a pistol on nights when there had been a spike in death threats.[97]

Voters in 1968, it must be remembered, had recently seen the assassination of two major national figures: Martin Luther King Jr. in April and Robert F. Kennedy in June. The sense that public lives were at risk was palpable. After the election, a number of Cherberg voters said they hadn't voted for Fletcher for two reasons, both of which came down to a fear of violence. Voters have told Dan Evans over the years that they voted for Cherberg out of a fear that an assassin might kill Evans to make Fletcher governor. Other voters have told Sam Reed that they were afraid for the safety of Fletcher. These fears were not unfounded: shortly after the 1968 election, Seattle Urban League director Ed Pratt was gunned down on his doorstep in a manner reminiscent of the assassination of NAACP leader Medgar Evers in Jackson, Mississippi, five years before. Fletcher understood the risks, having been told that "the best way to avoid [being assassinated] is to stay out of public life," but he saw his work as too important to give in to such fears.[98]

With Fletcher again taking death threats over the phone, rumors from anonymous sources swirled that the East Pasco Self-Help Cooperative was a failure; that Fletcher was lying about his football career; and most notably, in a ploy certain to resonate with white conservatives, that Fletcher had "been arrested on several felony charges." An FBI check failed to support any of the spurious charges, labeling Fletcher, in a strange play on words, "brighter than white." But donations to the campaign slowed, and Fletcher found himself taking too much time talking about the past and not enough about the future. The final blow came late in the campaign, when racist, George Wallace–endorsing *Yakima Eagle* editor Don Tait circulated a pamphlet guaranteed to bring racists to the polls. It pictured Fletcher mowing his lawn in a sweaty T-shirt with the caption, "Meet your new governor," claiming a GOP conspiracy to make him governor after Evans won a federal appointment in an expected Nixon administration.[99]

Still, by Election Day Fletcher had nearly closed the gap. Early returns on Wednesday, November 6, showed Fletcher behind Cherberg by only 38,477 out of nearly a million votes counted. By November 7, Cherberg's lead had increased to 55,181 votes. While a tight margin, indeed the closest any Republican had yet come to beating the incumbent, it was nevertheless too wide to generate a state-funded recount. Fletcher could have paid for a recount himself, and some of his supporters, believing he had indeed won, urged him to do so. But the funds of what had always been a largely shoestring campaign had run out; a subsequent bank statement showed a balance of $77.04. Fletcher conceded to Cherberg and announced that he was moving to Olympia anyway to work as an urban affairs adviser to Governor Evans, who like Kramer and Gorton had won his own election. Ironically, the (full-time) staff position paid $16,500 per year, significantly more than the post of lieutenant governor, which paid only $10,000.[100]

In contrast to Fletcher's popularity among moderate Republicans, it is difficult to gauge Fletcher's support among African American voters in the state. Longtime activist Eddie Rye Jr. noted, "I absolutely think that if Blacks had voted for him or voted at all he would have won." Family friend Kathy Keolker reports of campaign events that "I wasn't always the only white face, but sometimes I was." If East Pasco—admittedly where he was best known—was any indication, significant numbers of Black voters split their ballots to vote for him. In Franklin County's First and Seventeenth Districts—the only area of the county he won—voters chose Democratic presidential nominee Hubert H. Humphrey over Nixon, and Democratic US senator Warren Magnuson over his Republican challenger, each by more than a 7–1 margin; the limping Democratic nominee, John O'Connell, bested Dan Evans among these voters nearly 2–1. But these Democrats switched for Fletcher, choosing him over Cherberg by practically the same margin.

Fletcher's showing elsewhere in Franklin County might also be telling as to his overall popularity among Republicans in the Evergreen State. The county split between the parties, choosing the Republican nominees for president, house of representatives, and secretary of state, and giving the win to the Democrat in the senate, governor, and lieutenant governor contests. While Fletcher's victory in the primary over Muncey in Franklin County appears to have been partly the result of Black Democrats crossing over and voting in the Republican primary, his defeat there in the general election appears to have been at least partly the result of racist Republicans crossing over and voting for Cherberg. He lost "because he was Black," argues Keolker, "and the state was not ready for a Black man."[101]

In an era when the Republican Party, at least at the national level, was turning to the right—most notably with Nixon's Southern Strategy and Reagan's rising popularity—Action for Washington did not succeed in creating a generation of moderate Republicans. Yet despite his failure to win a majority of votes cast, it was ironically the losing member of Sam Reed's slate who seems to have had the greatest impact. According to Reed—who eventually became a three-term secretary of state himself—the dwindling moderate Republicans in Washington State still called themselves "Fletcher Republicans" as late as 2010.[102]

As for John Cherberg, Fletcher's dignified, dependable opponent who defined a somewhat boring office, he went on to win reelection four more times. At his retirement in 1988 he had served for thirty-two years under five governors, making him the longest-serving lieutenant governor in the history of the United States.[103]

Winning While Losing

Fletcher's defeat happened at an auspicious moment for his party. After eight years in the political wilderness, Republicans again held the White House, with Richard Nixon elected over Vice President Hubert H. Humphrey on the left and George Wallace on the right. Among African Americans, Nixon had polled only 5 percent, however, continuing the party's downward slide among voters of color. The new president developed the so-called Southern Strategy, White House advisor Harry Dent's plan to woo the traditionally Democratic white South to the Republican Party. In retrospect, this plan ultimately replaced Black votes with those of white racists, a move cemented with Governor Reagan's 1980 decision to begin his presidential campaign in Philadelphia, Mississippi, the site of three of the most infamous killings of the civil rights era. Still, the president-elect had a record of commitment to the cause of civil rights and integration—and in any event, with all the advances made in that cause in the preceding few years, it would have appeared downright unseemly for Nixon to not at least have a subcabinet official who was Black (of course, by the end of his presidency, appearances were the least of his problems). CORE founder James Farmer became an assistant secretary in the Department of Health, Education, and Welfare (HEW), and Samuel C. Jackson, the Washburn alumnus who had reported Fletcher's gridiron exploits, took the same title at the Department of Housing and Urban Development (HUD). But Fletcher now had a celebrity that Jackson lacked, and his self-help program—part of the very platform on which Nixon had been elected—held an immediacy and relevance to professed Republican values not shared by Farmer's CORE; indeed, by 1969 the organization had moved to the left of Farmer's leadership under Floyd McKissick and Roy Innis. Special consideration was thus given to Fletcher, who now was seriously considered for a White House post or even a cabinet-level position. Fletcher's moon shot moment had arrived.[104]

On November 25, Fletcher accepted a temporary position with the transition team. John Ehrlichman, a top Nixon advisor, asked him to develop a nationwide proposal for implementing local Black capitalism programs: "Your own knowledge of the subject matter must be as good, right now, as we can hope to derive over a period of a month or so from 'field surveyors' going in and talking to the Reverend Leon Sullivan and others." The administration was "anxious to demonstrate small accomplishments in relatively short time spans," Ehrlichman added, "rather than undertake a survey to make broad promises for long-range achievement." Eager to please, Fletcher drafted an interagency plan, including a protocol for the Small Business Administration (SBA) to deliver targeted funds to existing local programs. Three months later, with some revisions, President Nixon used the idea to create the Office of Minority Business Enterprise in the Department of Commerce.[105]

For all his accomplishments, Fletcher's ascent was almost scuttled by Ehrlichman's first impression. After their initial meeting in Washington, DC, Ehrlichman told a colleague that Fletcher "is extremely articulate, cannot spell and has dirty fingernails." In fact Fletcher was dyslexic, and the comment on his hygiene may tell us more about Ehrlichman than Fletcher; further, the "articulate" assessment belies a racist condescension. "He is not cabinet caliber. He should be favorably considered for a role which will put him in the field making contacts with black communities and white business leaders. I would imagine that he is a relatively poor administrative executive." John McClaughry agreed: "We have some negative readings from several sources. . . . I frankly was shocked, after collecting all of the favorable references [from Governor Evans and others in Washington State] to find him opinionated, excitable, and not too bright," noted Nixon's special assistant for community affairs. "Our decision in this shop, at least for now, is *not* to submit his credentials to cabinet officers looking over black appointees."[106]

Discussions back in Washington State of a more positive nature nevertheless also served to decrease the chances that Fletcher would be moving to the nation's capital. Another member of the Action for Washington slate, Lud Kramer, was also being considered by the Nixon team for a possible federal appointment. In February 1969 the *Bellingham Herald* lauded Evans's decision to appoint Fletcher to a paid position on his urban affairs advisory committee, and urged the governor to go even further: "There's talk in Olympia that Secretary of State Lud Kramer is angling for a major job with the Nixon administration, and that Fletcher may be in line for Kramer's present position," which under the state constitution fell to Evans to fill. "Either way," the editorial continued, the "bulky ex–football star could still be effective . . . in cooling sticky situations as well as promoting racial progress." A month later, as rumors began to swirl that Fletcher was meeting with cabinet members in the Nixon administration, the Walla Walla county attorney, who had managed Fletcher's local campaign and had close ties to Governor Evans, wrote the president in the hope that Nixon would consider this as he made his final appointments. There is no record of a reply, but if Kramer was offered a position with the new administration, he did not accept it. He continued to serve as secretary of state and chair the state Commission on the Causes and Prevention of Civil Disorder, which later that year released an influential report to which Fletcher had made a major contribution.[107]

Fletcher himself turned down at least two federal job offers. He rejected a staff appointment with a United States congressman, worrying that "it would take him out of circulation," and he also refused an appointment to the Bureau of Indian Affairs, in the Department of the Interior (presumably proffered on the basis of Fletcher's background as a westerner and son of a buffalo soldier). He made it known that his chief interests were labor and education, and that he wanted a position with executive authority. He had a meeting with Michigan governor George Romney, who was the secretary designee of HUD, for a possible job in that department, but that post, as we have seen, went to his college friend, Sam Jackson.[108]

Ultimately the "old man," as one of his advisors called him, ensured that Fletcher was a part of his new administration. While it is questionable whether Nixon remembered Fletcher from their brief interaction during the 1962 campaign, the two had developed a rapport at the Miami convention and the subsequent San Diego retreat. In consultation with George P. Shultz, dean of the University of Chicago's graduate school of business and secretary designee of the Department of Labor, the president offered Fletcher the position of assistant secretary of labor, with responsibility for administering the wage and hour regulations of a national workforce of over 80 million people, and a salary of $38,750 per year (nearly four times Cherberg's $10,000). Fletcher met with Shultz and told him he'd take the job if the secretary agreed to add the Office of Federal Contract Compliance (OFCC) to his portfolio. Tasked with enforcing the nondiscrimination clause in federal contracts and Title VI of the Civil Rights Act of 1964, the OFCC had the frankly awesome power to revoke federal contracts and debar contractors from bidding on future work. Under the Johnson administration, the OFCC had reported directly to the secretary of labor, but Shultz agreed to place the OFCC under Fletcher's supervision, and on March 21, 1969, Fletcher accepted the job.[109]

Arthur Fletcher achieved his moon shot through tenacity, hard work, and a positive attitude. As with his earlier successes in Kansas, he had plenty of help along the way—Burnell Johnson, Sam Reed, Dan Evans—but a major part of his success was his ability to recognize and cultivate these relationships.

Mary's suicide had left Fletcher with a commitment to do something better with his life, and by the end of the decade it was clear that he had accomplished that. But it had also left him with, as he later put it, "a controlled rage." One of the last things Mary told him was that she felt he had "been blackballed from the employment arena altogether," and indeed it had seemed so in the fall of 1960, when the former Kansas state deputy highway commissioner was again working as a tire builder.[110]

Although most people, regardless of race, never endure such a tragedy as the suicide of a spouse, Fletcher was not alone in his rage over the effects of discrimination. As James Baldwin put it in 1961, "To be a Negro in this country and to be relatively conscious, is to be in a rage almost all the time. So that the first problem is how to control that rage so that it won't destroy you." Fletcher, at least, had controlled his rage.[111] He had taken this controlled rage to Burbank Junior High, where he had used it to inspire at-risk youth; he had brought it to Pasco, where it fueled the fire of the East Pasco Self-Help Cooperative. He had continued to use it for his own motivation as he sought public office at increasingly high levels. Now he was entering an entirely different arena, with incredibly high stakes. As assistant secretary of labor, he was responsible for executing provisions of the Civil Rights Act of 1964, using the formidable power of the federal government to ensure equal employment opportunity for the entire nation.

Nixon had hired Arthur Fletcher at the Department of Labor for political reasons: Black self-help was an attractive, Republican-sounding idea that allowed him to demonstrate a passing interest in civil rights without actually committing to major change.

But Fletcher had other ideas.

CHAPTER FOUR

THE MAN WITH THE PLAN, 1969–1971

As anyone who has dealt with Art Fletcher knows, he is very
difficult to control.
—Charles "Chuck" Colson, 1971

In March 1969, when Arthur Fletcher accepted an appointment as a subcabinet officer in the Nixon administration, he became one of the top Blacks in the United States government. He had come a long way from Junction City, Kansas, and as we have seen, his path to this pinnacle of power had been strewn with obstacles. But these obstacles—especially his experiences in the Topeka and Berkeley ghettoes—had prepared him for the task that lay ahead. Although Nixon's advisors saw Fletcher's appointment as deflecting the accusation that the Nixon administration would be lax on civil rights, in fact Fletcher saw his role as one of consolidation and expansion of the achievements of the preceding decade. He would build on the legislative accomplishments of the 1960s—the Civil Rights Act of 1964 in particular—to write and enforce a new definition of affirmative action: mandatory integration. He knew how to spot a hole in the defense and push through for a touchdown.

What Arthur Fletcher found in the workforce whose wage and labor standards he was charged with overseeing was all too familiar: the exclusion of Blacks from the most skilled, lucrative jobs. With the Revised Philadelphia Plan, Fletcher forced the building construction trades, at least, to reckon with their history of discrimination. At first, owing to Nixon's desire to seem in favor of civil rights, Fletcher found support from the president and was able to fend off attacks on his programs. But the skilled construction unions proved a tough nut to crack. Despite a history as a Democratic constituency, the support of the president's Vietnam War policy by the rank and file made them a tempting target for White House political operatives focused on Nixon's reelection bid. In a Northern version of the developing Southern Strategy, whereby the Republican Party was reorienting itself to court suburban white voters, the White House ultimately jettisoned Fletcher's affirmative action program in the hope that the hard hats and other work-ing-class northern whites would vote Republican.

Discrimination in the Building Trades

In 1957 a navy veteran named Henry Clayton Lee, who had served as an "electrician's mate" on board the USS *Saratoga*, returned home to Phila-delphia to find the local Electrician's Union closed to him. In 1958 skilled mason Thomas Bailey was denied a job on a hospital building site in New-burgh, New York, because he wasn't a member of the union. When he tried to gain admittance to the union, he was told that he first needed a job. In 1962 air force veteran James Ballard, applying for an apprenticeship with the New York City Sheet Metal Workers Union, was shown a tall stack of applications and told to wait his turn. After passing a state aptitude test with high marks, he still was not admitted. Henry Lee could not join the electricians' union, Tom Bailey could not work on union mason jobs, and James Ballard could not become an apprentice sheet metal worker for the same reason Arthur Fletcher could not be a football coach—because they were Black. In the 1950s and 1960s the building trades were notoriously segregated throughout the United States, with precious apprentice and jour-neyman slots going most often to the sons and nephews of existing white members and the vast majority of Blacks in the industry confined to the less skilled trowel trades or to less lucrative nonunion work.[1]

The building trades operated with tremendous visibility and extreme unfairness. Although the sector was not the most discriminatory of employ-ment pursuits, it operated literally in the public eye: much of their work was done outdoors, on city streets and highly visible projects like the St. Louis Memorial Arch, San Francisco's new BART system, academic buildings at Cleveland's Case Western Reserve University, and a new US Mint building in Philadelphia. The postwar building boom, coupled with white flight to the suburbs, meant that urban construction projects were increasingly taking place in Black neighborhoods. Meanwhile, much of the lucrative work was partially or wholly funded by the federal government—in other words, by tax dollars collected from Americans of all races.[2]

The first major push by civil rights leaders to force the government to spend fairly came just before the United States joined World War II. Hop-ing to avoid a planned march on Washington in 1941, President Roosevelt issued Executive Order 8802, creating a Fair Employment Practices Com-mission for wartime spending. Thousands of Blacks streamed into war production facilities in the South and migrated north and west for even better opportunities. The end of the war brought a return to the prewar status quo, and Congress ended the experiment. Several northern states established their own fair employment commissions. President Truman required that all government contracts include a clause requiring equal employment opportunity, and he established a President's Committee on Government Contract Compliance to enforce the clause. Presidents Eisenhower and Kennedy assigned Vice Presidents Nixon and Johnson, respectively, to head up the same group under slightly different names, but these committees did little more than investigate and use moral persuasion on captains of industry. The most touted of their programs was Kennedy's Plans for Progress, which required that members—federal contractors—draw up detailed plans for integrating their companies. The prize for having a staff lawyer draw up a plan for progress was an invitation to a White House cocktail party, but the penalty for not actually implementing it was virtually nil.[3]

The problem was twofold. First, in government, which funded federal contracts, the contract officers at the various agencies prioritized project completion over workforce integration. The idea that a committee ("President's" or otherwise) could herd all those cats was overly ambitious, to put it mildly. Second, in employment, local unions ran hiring halls that referred members to jobsites; the contractors did not control their own employment practices.[4]

A series of events in 1963 created an inflection point. As protesters campaigned against de jure segregation in Birmingham, Alabama, Blacks protested at a school construction site in Philadelphia, forcing the mayor there to integrate city-funded construction. President Kennedy sent Congress a civil rights bill that integrated public accommodations (the focus of the Birmingham protests). Congress added language on employment (the focus in Philadelphia). That summer, in Philadelphia and cities throughout the nation, Blacks picketed jobsites, sometimes resulting in violent clashes. The leaders of the mainstream civil rights movement, meanwhile, joined by sympathetic union leaders who also wanted to integrate employment, engaged in an alternative form of political pressure: the (completely peaceful) March on Washington for Jobs and Freedom, first planned in 1941. From the steps of the Lincoln Memorial, speakers white and Black pleaded with the government to act against all forms of discrimination.[5]

After John Kennedy was killed, the new president, Lyndon Johnson, combined his predecessor's desire to pass civil rights legislation with his own political savvy. The following spring, thanks to protests from below and pressure from the new president above, Congress passed the Civil Rights Act of 1964. The new law's Title VI prevented government expenditure on any racially discriminatory program or contract, and its Title VII guaranteed equal employment opportunity in private sector employment. To implement the act, Congress established the Equal Employment Opportunity Commission (EEOC) and the president issued Executive Order 11246, creating the Office of Federal Contract Compliance (OFCC), which reported to the secretary of labor. The OFCC was given the sweeping authority to revoke contracts and debar contractors from future bidding for failure to ensure equal opportunity in their hiring and promotion practices.[6]

The OFCC spent the remainder of the Johnson administration developing experimental programs to force construction contractors, if not unions, to integrate the skilled trades. It employed twenty area coordinators around the country who analyzed employment patterns and worked with local civil rights groups to determine the number of skilled Black workers denied union employment on government contracts. At one point in 1967 OFCC shut down all federal construction funds for the entire Cleveland area, forcing contractors to develop a method of reporting minority man-hours for each project—an additional column on the "manning table," which had previously broken down man-hours only by skill, not race. In Philadelphia in 1968, the area coordinator instituted the "Operational Plan for Philadelphia," which required prospective contractors to include projected minority man-hours in their actual bids, before the contracts were even awarded.[7]

Prior efforts to integrate the building construction trades in Philadelphia had produced mixed results. In 1967 the local electricians admitted eleven minority youths to their apprentice class in an attempt to boost their 1 percent minority journeyman population (consisting of fourteen people), and the plumbers' union formed an apprenticeship class that was 10 percent nonwhite. The Sheet Metal Workers Union, with an all-white membership of 1,200, accepted two Black journeymen and three Black apprentices under a court order. But Black Philadelphians, including skilled construction workers employed in less lucrative, nonunion construction, constituted just under one third of the city's population. At that rate of integration, it would be centuries before minorities achieved union membership approximating their citywide share of the population. Meanwhile, there was no shortage of federal contract construction work in the Philadelphia area, which had a total 1967 allocation of more than $300 million. Clearly the OFCC had good cause to pursue an affirmative action program to integrate the Philadelphia building trades.[8]

Contractor and union complaints about the OFCC's activities in Cleveland and Philadelphia reached the ears of their congressional representatives, who ordered the General Accounting Office to conduct an investigation. In November 1968, Comptroller General Elmer Staats ruled the Philadelphia Plan illegal under federal procurement law, calling it "arbitrary and capricious" to deny a contract to a low bidder who was unwilling to estimate minority man-hours. The backsliding was immediate: federal contracting agencies and contractors in Philadelphia abandoned the manning table requirements. One union, the steamfitters, jettisoned the program's apprenticeship requirements, causing the city's board of education to ban the union from using its classrooms to train apprentices. The city of Philadelphia and several local universities began work on their own affirmative action programs, and the OFCC area coordinator attempted to manage these activities while working on a revision of the program to meet the comptroller general's objections. Civil rights groups demanded that contractors—at least those working on projects in Black neighborhoods—continue operating under the program. When these entreaties fell on deaf ears, they resumed protests and planned visits to congressional offices, promising civil disorder. The local skilled unions, meanwhile, welcomed the respite from the federal demand to integrate; fewer workers meant higher wages. By early April 1969 the plumbers had won a significant wage increase, and the carpenters, bricklayers, steamfitters, and roofers threatened strikes to obtain the same. Integration, however, was back to square one.[9]

The Revised Philadelphia Plan

Like Henry Lee, Tom Bailey, and James Ballard, Arthur Fletcher knew well the pain and shame of job discrimination. He had learned it in childhood, when his mother, Edna, cleaned houses instead of teaching children. He had seen it himself—again and again—when he was denied work befitting a college graduate and instead had to build tires or clean dog-food machines. And he knew its cost: he blamed it for the death of his first wife.[10]

But he also knew how to fight it. In Washington State he had learned to leverage local political connections and influence to secure jobs for Higher Horizons trainees and co-op members' children at the local atomic power plant. He had watched with increasing interest, and acted with increasing agility, as government officials began implementing aspects of civil rights and war on poverty legislation. Now he was coming to the other Washington, the nation's capital, to use the memory of that pain and shame and the experience he had gained to bring the fight to the aid of the entire nation's minority workforce. Legislation had brought civil rights to the fifty yard line. Enforcement, Fletcher thought, would score the touchdown of full economic equality.

Fletcher deliberated carefully before accepting the job at Labor. He researched the recent work of the department, learning about the activities of the OFCC and the efforts in Cleveland and Philadelphia. He researched his bosses and colleagues, Secretary Shultz, Undersecretary James Hodgson, and Solicitor Laurence Silberman, finding them open to using their authority to help minority workers. What's more, Fletcher had a personal connection to the travails of Philadelphia Black construction workers; his second wife, Bernyce, was a native of the city and had brothers in the industry.[11]

Fletcher moved quickly to bring in people he knew and trusted. He asked Pasco city manager Horace Menasco to serve as his deputy and tapped an old friend, San Francisco lawyer and political operative John Wilks, as director of OFCC. Rounding out the team were Alfred W. Blumrosen, a law professor on leave from Rutgers University whom Fletcher poached from his latest position as an equal employment consultant at HUD, and Nelson I. Crowther, a negotiator with a strong understanding of both Department of Labor policies and the conditions on the ground in multiple areas under the department's purview. Fletcher came to depend on Crowther's skills as a speechwriter as his own skills as an orator took him around the country stumping for OFCC policies, the administration's civil rights activities, and the role of Blacks in the Republican Party.[12]

There was no shortage of work for the new assistant secretary. Even before his confirmation by the Senate, Shultz and Hodgson tasked him with analyzing the equal employment compliance activities of major federal contractors. In May 1969 the navy awarded a $118 million contract, and promised nine more of similar dollar amounts, to Ingalls Shipbuilding of Pascagoula, Mississippi, a company that had fallen short in its integration attempts and had already seen an affirmative action plan rejected by the Maritime Administration. In a similar situation at Newport News Shipbuilding and Drydock Company in Virginia, Blumrosen reported to Fletcher a "probable blatant violation of the EEOC conciliation agreement." Part of the problem was that while the navy awarded these contracts, the Maritime Administration—a separate agency—was responsible for enforcing equal employment opportunity. Fletcher ruled that the navy officials were trying to circumvent the authority of OFCC. It took more than a year of arguing with contract officers

Department of Labor senior staff, 1969. Seated at center is the secretary of labor, George P. Shultz. Arthur Fletcher Personal Papers, courtesy Paul Fletcher.

at the navy, while the contractors dragged their feet, before Ingalls and Newport News finally submitted acceptable affirmative action plans.[13]

Even as he was haggling with contracting agencies, Fletcher got a couple of early boosts in the estimation of Secretary Shultz and Undersecretary Hodgson. In May 1969 Black workers at Bethlehem Steel's Sparrows Point Facility came to Washington to protest discrimination in hiring and promotions by their employer, a major federal contractor on the Baltimore waterfront. They demonstrated in front of the Department of Labor, and their leader demanded a meeting with Secretary Shultz, who was not in town that day. Fletcher, on the other hand, was available; he had recently returned from a visit to Sacramento for his daughter Sylvia's wedding. He brought several members of the group into his office. Quickly establishing a rapport and an atmosphere of trust, he promised to visit the facility and conduct an investigation. In early June, after visiting the plant, Fletcher declared the company out of compliance with Executive Order 11246, and he pushed management and the contracting agency to develop an agreement to ensure enforcement of equal employment opportunity.[14]

Of course, Fletcher had been hired in part for his charm and political skills, so it came as no surprise that he could defuse fraught situations like the one presented by the Sparrows Point workers. What most impressed Shultz and Hodgson was his policy legerdemain, and the opportunity to further prove himself in this area came from the same case. The OFCC had appointed Reverend Dexter L. Hanley of the Georgetown University Law Center to develop a conciliation agreement between the Black workers and Bethlehem Steel. Impressed by Hanley's equal opportunity hiring provisions, Fletcher wrote, "I wish, however, to advise the panel that I have reservations concerning . . . the Company-Union proposal of relief on seniority." Black workers were being prevented from transferring to more lucrative, skilled departments within the plant by unnecessary aptitude tests and educational requirements, which Fletcher judged irrelevant to the jobs. When they did transfer, they lost all seniority, subjecting them to increased risk of layoff or demotion (and thereby removing the incentive and discouraging them from applying). The final agreement did not resolve the question, and the exasperated Hanley stated unequivocally that it was Fletcher's concerns on behalf of the Black workers that had prevented conciliation. Clearly Fletcher was holding his own with experienced government lawyers; he was no lightweight, and his background as an employment consultant for Douglas United Nuclear was coming in useful. Ultimately his opinion on seniority was upheld by the Supreme Court: two years later, in *Griggs v. Duke Power Co.*, the Court held that irrelevant educational requirements and aptitude tests were a violation of Title VII; as a result, Bethlehem Steel conciliated the seniority question to Fletcher's satisfaction.[15]

The most visible and controversial policy Fletcher worked on, of course, was the Revised Philadelphia Plan. With the original "Operational Plan for Philadelphia" now all but abandoned after Comptroller General Staats's declaration that it was illegal, in May 1969 Fletcher discussed the program with his advisors. All agreed that the plan should be revised to address the General Accounting Office's objections, implemented, and enforced.[16]

Staats had said that the program was too vague: it was unfair, he claimed, to expect bidders to estimate the number of minority man-hours for a project without giving them specific guidelines in the request for bids. Fletcher reasoned that creating specific requests for minority employment on each project met that objection, but he also worried that too much specificity might be seen as an unfair racial quota, which was illegal under Title VII. The team came up with a "goals and ranges" formula: contracts let under the Philadelphia Plan promised to employ minority journeymen and apprentices in each of the skilled trades according to a specific percentage goal, to be gradually increased over three years as apprentices graduated and increased the ranks of available minority journeymen. To defray the quota concern, Fletcher inserted a good-faith clause, which allowed contractors to remain in good standing under the program as long as they made a good-faith effort to meet the minority hiring goals. He clarified that simply asking the unions to provide skilled Black workers was not an adequate demonstration of good faith, as racial exclusion among the skilled unions was common knowledge among contractors. Solicitor of Labor Silberman assured Fletcher that Title VII prohibited exclusionary quotas—used to limit the hiring of people from protected minority groups—rather than inclusionary goals, which brought workers from protected groups in. But as an added precaution, Silberman sent the proposal to the assistant attorney general for civil rights, Jerris Leonard, who replied on behalf of the Department of Justice that "we find [the plan] to be consistent with the . . . Civil Rights Act of 1964."[17]

On June 27, 1969, Fletcher traveled to Philadelphia and announced implementation of the Revised Philadelphia Plan. "Every government contractor," he said, "must realize that he has the responsibility to provide equal access to money spent by the federal government. This is true in Philadelphia and is equally true in every city and town throughout the United States." He stated that the program would take effect on July 18; that OFCC would hold hearings in late August to determine the specific goals and ranges; and that it would be the first in a nationwide series of similar programs. That same day he signed a memo to the "heads of all agencies" of the federal government ordering contract officers to implement the program.[18]

A number of factors contributed to Fletcher's forceful implementation of the Philadelphia Plan and later versions around the country. First, after a lifetime of observing and experiencing job discrimination, Fletcher saw implementation of the program in Manichean terms: integrating the building trades was absolutely right, and those who opposed the plan were absolutely wrong. He believed that it was honorable, proper, and his duty to those who had been wronged by the racist system to doggedly pursue what was right. Fletcher also had a sense that the time for affirmative action had arrived. A decade of protests and favorable legislation had created the opportune moment to translate words into action. Legislation would become regulation, and Blacks would get jobs from which they had been excluded.

Events around the country during the summer and fall of 1969 served to keep the issue of building trades' segregation in the news and Fletcher's travel itinerary full. In particular, the situations in Pittsburgh, Seattle, and Chicago placed the mistreatment of skilled Black workers—and the recalcitrance of the building trades unions—in sharp relief.

In Pittsburgh, where African Americans represented 16 percent of the population but only 1 percent of the skilled building trades, contractors, unions, and civil rights groups reached an uneasy truce with a combination of union-sponsored and community-sponsored programs to integrate the trades. The union program, apprenticeship outreach, was a national plan touted by the AFL-CIO as an alternative to government programs, though largely dismissed by civil rights groups in Pittsburgh and elsewhere. They put more stock in the community program known as Operation Dig, a conscious play on words combining military and construction terminology with street jive. Operation Dig had been developed with the support of contractors and local government officials following a rebellion there after the assassination of Martin Luther King Jr. in April 1968. This program sought to train hard-core unemployed inner-city residents, almost all of whom were Black, for skilled construction work. But in August 1969, facing challenges from the unions, the contractors withdrew their support, citing uncertainty in the quality of the training. Civil rights activists responded with a campaign they called Black Mondays, mobilizing supporters to picket key construction sites around the city and shut down all construction work for one day of the week. On Monday, August 25, the protest turned violent as policemen and white workers clashed with protestors, resulting in "forty-five persons, including 12 policemen . . . injured," according to the *Wall Street Journal*. Later that week, all sides agreed to talks, and discussions and protests continued sporadically throughout the fall. In November OFCC officially intervened, threatening a mandatory "Philadelphia-style" plan if the parties could not agree to an acceptable affirmative action plan. By mid-December, with labor columnist Victor Riesel calling Fletcher "frank in his fury over what he considers discrimination against black workers by the nation's—indeed, the world's—highest paying industry, building and construction," OFCC reported that the groups were close to a deal that promised 1,250 more Black construction workers over the next five years.[19]

Fletcher monitored the developing situation in Seattle even more closely, owing to his familiarity with the city and its political leaders; he also knew that John Ehrlichman was watching, as it was the presidential advisor's hometown. The most active protestors in Seattle were Black subcontractors, who organized their own training programs but found themselves shut out of contracts by discriminatory unions and white general contractors. In late

August, just as Pittsburgh protestors were holding the first Black Monday, Black workers, contractors, and community members successfully shut down three government-funded construction projects in the city. The Seattle Model Cities program administrators, working with local government officials, the OFCC, and the Black subcontractors, developed an affirmative action training program, which the general contractors on the affected sites agreed to implement. But white workers walked off the job. One Black subcontractor suffered a beating by three white men outside a local YMCA. By September, with construction still halted, several local unions demanded that the government end the training program and authorize back pay for union workers who had missed work. The county executive, contractors, civil rights and union leaders met in "marathon" sessions to resolve the issue of training, and Model Cities agreed to fully fund the program—to no avail.[20]

Sporadic protests, violence, and talks continued in Seattle throughout the fall, with construction resuming in fits and starts; Black contractors prepared charges of unfair labor practices against the unions, and the county executive and OFCC recommended that the Department of Justice file a pattern or practice lawsuit against the unions under Title VII. In October the unions developed a weak affirmative action program, which the local Model Cities director told Fletcher was "completely unacceptable to the Black and minority community." The director of the local Urban League asked Fletcher to order that all federal funds be withheld from Seattle construction projects, as had been done in Cleveland in 1967. After the protests were again met with violence, this time at a project at the Seattle–Tacoma airport, Fletcher resolved to take action. He put together a meeting of all interested parties at the Seattle chamber of commerce several days after Thanksgiving, and arranged his own speaking schedule so he could attend. When the unions refused to participate, Fletcher encouraged the parties to work with Model Cities to develop a program without union involvement, and they agreed to the Seattle Multi-Employer Affirmative Action Program. But with the unions continuing to withhold approval, integration in the Seattle building trades remained uncertain.[21]

If Pittsburgh set the tone and Seattle attracted the most attention, Chicago proved the most violent. Black protestors there, asking for more Black apprentices and foremen on projects in Black neighborhoods, shut down a whopping twenty construction sites in the city, affecting $80 million, mostly from HUD. According to the local Urban League chapter, minorities represented only 3 percent of all construction workers in the city; eleven of the nineteen construction unions had less than 1 percent minority membership, and two (the lathers and sprinkler fitters) had no minority members at all. Familiar names from the civil rights movement led this fight: Ralph Abernathy, C. T. Vivian, and Jesse Jackson, colleagues of the late Dr. Martin Luther King Jr. Jackson, arrested at one jobsite, consciously evoked King's "Letter from Birmingham Jail" with a jailhouse letter of his own: "We do not seek to take white jobs. But neither do we intend to allow whites to keep Black jobs while we are passively quiet and docile. . . . There will be no more rest and tranquility until our just pleas are heeded."[22]

As with King's earlier attempt to integrate the Chicago suburbs, however, the violence there during the fall of 1969 was the work of white racists. HUD threatened to pull all funding until work resumed, and Fletcher announced hearings in the city for September 24–25. Because of the concurrent trial of the Chicago Seven protestors who had disrupted the 1968 Democratic National Convention there, the federal courthouse was unavailable, so Fletcher reserved the Lincoln–Douglas Room at the La Salle Hotel. But despite the room's name, which evoked the history of great debates on race, the location was not conducive to a controversial hearing. "I walked into the room to find it packed with white construction workers. Downstairs, a thousand hard hats picketed," Fletcher later recalled. The hard hats "would not let the witnesses into the hearing room, or even into the hotel. The Chicago police were behaving very gently toward the pickets, and would not help us in any way. There was no federal police present [sic]." When Fletcher tried to deliver his opening statement, which explained that the purpose of the hearing was to take testimony from all parties to the construction dispute, he was shouted down by union men, mostly hostile, with at least one threat ("let's work it at night"); the transcript repeatedly refers to "a chorus of boos." With 300 people in a room limited by fire code to 150, and another 200 reportedly filling the hallway outside, the hotel manager asked that the hearings be postponed for reasons of fire safety. Fletcher, Wilks, and the other Labor personnel were packed away to spend the night in another hotel under armed guard.[23]

Consulting with federal officials at the United States customhouse, Fletcher hastily arranged for the hearings to take place there the next day. Unable to disrupt the hearings inside that fortified building, the "cursing, flag-waving, beer-drinking white construction workers," as one reporter called them, perpetrated mayhem in the streets outside. They blocked all entrances, chanting "Blacks yes, gangs no," an apparent reference to the Conservative Vice Lords street gang, which doubled as a civil rights organization and included among its members youngsters involved in the construction site protests. Searching for Fletcher, white construction workers falsely identified another tall Black man as him, whom they beat savagely. Other workers set on a Black motorist and pummeled his car, and still more surrounded another group of Black passersby, who fired warning shots in the air and were themselves arrested. The police mostly looked on. The few other arrests came after white protesters attacked a group of white women counterprotesting in favor of civil rights. (This represented progress of a sort: historically, white women who have challenged the racial status quo have been deemed unworthy of protection by white authorities.) Fletcher and his aides only barely managed to get in through a back entrance, "followed into the building by catcalls and obscenities," he later reported."[24]

The hearings did successfully take place at the customhouse on September 25 and 26, and with OFCC assistance, the contractors, civil rights groups, and union leaders came to a tentative agreement the following month to admit 1,000 new minority workers into the building trades in 1969–1970 and another 4,000 in 1970–1971. But the violence in Chicago was an augur of things to come, as rank-and-file white construction workers, fearing for their jobs in a contracting economy and emboldened by their brothers' willingness to take to the streets, made themselves heard in opposition to affirmative action.[25]

The Battle in Congress

The violence in Chicago did have a positive effect on Fletcher's policy: it resulted in President Nixon's decision to defend the Philadelphia Plan. A Quaker by upbringing, the president believed in civil rights policies insofar as they didn't interfere with his main priority: getting reelected. As long as Fletcher's activities were focused on northern and western cities, Nixon could continue to pursue the Southern Strategy: the goal of winning the southern white vote by stalling on issues related to de jure Jim Crow, such as school integration.[26]

At the start of his administration, Nixon still hoped to woo a larger share of the Black electorate by 1972. Blacks were a traditionally Republican constituency, remembering Emancipation and seeing Republicans as the party of Lincoln. White northern construction workers, on the other hand, were a traditionally Democratic constituency, remembering the New Deal and seeing the Democrats as the party of Franklin Roosevelt. While it's true that the Southern Strategy was part of a realignment whereby the GOP came to represent the social interests of white working-class conservatives and drive away the vast majority of Black voters, North as well as South, this sea change was not fully apparent in 1969. Meanwhile, Nixon worried that wage increases in the construction industry were driving uncontrolled inflation, and he saw a strong economy as paramount to his reelection bid. What also surely effected Nixon's thinking was the fact that, as Fletcher later recounted, skilled white workers making time-and-a-half overtime pay a significant portion of their annual earnings meant that the hiring of more skilled Black workers at the regular hourly wage would allow contractors to realize significant payroll savings and profits; the largest contractors were also some of the most important GOP donors. Sociologist John David Skrentny has written that the administration's position on civil rights was characterized, to quote an Ehrlichman phrase, with "liberal zags and conservative zigs." For the time being, hoping to win Black votes and divide the civil rights and labor rights leadership, Nixon tacitly supported Fletcher's programs, especially when they had the concurrence of Secretary Hodgson and Attorney General John Mitchell, as with the Philadelphia Plan.[27]

Nixon's support was important as the forces of the construction industry status quo mobilized against the Philadelphia Plan. The first major attack on the program came from a familiar antagonist: Elmer Staats. The Department of Labor had consulted with the General Accounting Office in June before issuing the Revised Philadelphia Plan to ensure that the new version comported with procurement law. The comptroller general nevertheless ruled the revised plan illegal on August 5, 1969. This time, although he found that it was consistent with procurement law—his actual legal domain—Staats determined that the "goals" of the program were in fact quotas, which violated Title VII of the Civil Rights Act of 1964, the legal foundation on which the Philadelphia Plan was built. Although the General Accounting Office had never before pronounced on matters unrelated to procurement law, Staats argued that because he had found the plan illegal under Title VII, he could not in good conscience authorize payment for any contracts let under the program.[28]

With Staats having fired the first shot, several United States senators from both parties now made public their opposition to the Philadelphia Plan. They did so from a variety of perspectives. Republican Paul Fannin, the Arizona conservative who had replaced 1964 presidential nominee Barry Goldwater, saw the program as too harsh on contractors, and he wanted any affirmative action program to instead take aim at unions. Republican Everett Dirksen, architect of a compromise with President Johnson that had allowed the Civil Rights Act of 1964 to go forward, saw in the Philadelphia

Plan exactly the sort of quota system he had sought to prevent with language he had inserted into Title VII. As a senator from Illinois, Dirksen was also no doubt intensely watching the Chicago jobsite protests that August, worried about his next reelection bid (although he died just as the congressional battle was beginning, on September 7, 1969). His Democratic House colleague, Roman Pucinsky, agreed, complaining, "The heavy hand of the federal government setting up quotas is not the answer." Democrats Samuel Ervin of North Carolina, John McLellan of Arkansas, and Robert Byrd of West Virginia, for their part, opposed the Philadelphia Plan both out of partisan antipathy for the policies of a Republican president and out of sectional opposition to integrating anything anywhere, reasoning that if it could happen in Philadelphia, it could happen in Raleigh, Little Rock, or Charleston. Nevertheless, in keeping with changing expectations for public statements, they couched their positions in color-blind language. McLellan, for instance, decried the argument that the Philadelphia Plan pointed to "goals" rather than quotas as "a subterfuge," while Ervin complained that the program would "discriminate against workers who are not members of any minority group," beginning the long, spurious tradition of calling affirmative action "reverse racism." Even moderate Republican Pennsylvania senator Richard S. Schweiker opposed the plan, out of a concern that it might undermine ongoing efforts to conciliate voluntary agreements between the building trades and civil rights groups. Fletcher and Shultz consistently maintained that any contractor with an approved affirmative action plan was excused from the Philadelphia Plan; more likely Schweiker was triangulating, like Nixon, out of concern for his next reelection campaign, and being on the ground in Pennsylvania, he drew the opposite conclusion to that of the president (and after all, Nixon eventually changed his mind).[29]

Of course, Fletcher's program did not lack for supporters either. These included all six senators from New York, Massachusetts, and Michigan: Republicans Jacob Javits, Charles Goodell, Edward Brooke, and Robert Griffin, and Democrats Ted Kennedy and Philip Hart, as well as Indiana Democrat Birch Bayh, New Jersey Republican Clifford Case, and Hawaii Republican Hiram Fong. While the list of the program's supporters, like that of its opponents, was bipartisan, notably absent was any support from the South, reflecting the antipathy of most southern whites to any civil rights measures and belying the sincerity of the plan's southern opponents. Supporters noted that while the comptroller general could make pronouncements on procurement matters unrelated to procurement law, the Civil Rights Act of 1964 designated the Department of Justice as having interpretive authority. Attorney General John Mitchell agreed with Solicitor of Labor Silberman and his own deputy for civil rights, Jerris Leonard, that the Philadelphia Plan was a reasonable regulation for the enforcement of the act. They also expressed concern that allowing Staats's ruling to stand would set up the General Accounting Office as a virtual fourth branch of government.[30]

Outside of Congress, the Philadelphia Plan faced strong opposition from the AFL-CIO's Building Construction Trades Department and from AFL-CIO president George Meany, himself a former skilled construction worker. At their annual meeting in Atlantic City, the Building Construction Trades Department executive council called the Philadelphia Plan a "quota system, no matter how it may be dressed up in legal verbiage." Meany stated that there weren't enough skilled Blacks to fill the positions the program created, disingenuously ignoring the fact that the unions were also discriminating in their training programs and were therefore directly responsible for the shortage of skilled Blacks. Despite strong endorsements from both mainstream and Black-oriented newspapers like the *New York Times* (whose editors called it a "sounder course" than protests), the *Boston Globe* (anything less was "token compliance"), the *Philadelphia Inquirer* ("a significant step toward equality"), the *New York Amsterdam News* ("positive move"), and the *Washington Post* ("reaching towards decency and fairness"), Fletcher received only tepid support from civil rights organizations, with the NAACP seeing Nixon's support as political gamesmanship that would result in few actual new jobs for Blacks.[31]

Despite Staats's ruling and the pending congressional showdown over the program's legality, Secretary Shultz held firm in his support. So Fletcher pushed forward, holding hearings with the director of the OFCC, Wilks, in Philadelphia to determine the specific goals and ranges and announcing full implementation of the plan on September 29, less than a week after the Chicago hearings. He found more than 1,200 qualified Blacks ready to be hired in the skilled trades and at least another 5,000 eligible for training. He assigned Wilks and the Philadelphia area coordinator to develop a training program using local schools, and he worked out a deal with Temple University to train Black contractors. After jetting off to a manpower conference in Dakar, Senegal, picking up gifts for his wife, Bernyce, on his return layover in Paris, on October 23 Fletcher announced the awarding of the first contract under the Philadelphia Plan. An "addition to the Children's Hospital and Child Guidance Center" would be constructed by Bristol Steel and Iron Works of Richmond, Virginia, for HEW. Leon Panetta, responsible for that department's civil rights initiatives, had been champing at the bit to award contracts under the program since August.[32]

Bristol had been the low bidder in any event; but in early November, after HEW passed over the low bidder on a project at Villanova University Law School for a failure to project compliance with the Philadelphia Plan, Staats announced that he was suspending all payments to Bristol and any other company awarded a contract under the program, mailing letters to that effect to all current federal contractors in the Philadelphia area.[33]

Senators Ervin and McLellan, two southern Democrats opposed to the Philadelphia Plan, convened hearings on the program in the Senate Judiciary Committee's Subcommittee on the Separation of Powers, which Ervin chaired. Ervin invited Staats to testify, along with Secretary Shultz and Assistant Attorney General Leonard; EEOC chairman William H. Brown and Fletcher were asked to submit written opinions on the plan. Ervin's racism was thereby put on full display: he invited the white officials to testify in person but requested only written comments from the Black officials (including Fletcher, the man directly responsible for the program). The intention was not to gather information surrounding potential legislation—the ostensible purpose of committee hearings—but to provide Shultz and Leonard with a tongue-lashing for giving their Black subordinates too much leeway.[34]

Staats, who was greeted approvingly by the senators, testified that regardless of the distinction between goals and quotas, prospective contractors felt pressure to hire Black workers at the expense of better-prepared whites. This may have been true, but "McLellan and Ervin hammered away at Leonard and Shultz in an attempt to get them to concede that that plan impose[d] racial hiring quotas . . . and therefore violate[d] Title VII," wrote *Washington Post* staff writer Spencer Rich; John Herbers of the *New York Times* reported that Ervin "held the tip of his fountain pen in his line of sight, drew a bead on Mr. Leonard and quoted the language of Title VII," noting that it was "as clear as a noonday sun on a cloudless day" that "the Philadelphia Plan requires quotas that are based on race." But Shultz and Leonard held their ground, as did Brown and Fletcher in their written statements, Brown stating that it was "only fitting that the government lead the way in this most important area."[35]

Notwithstanding the subcommittee hearings, the full Judiciary Committee did not report a bill outlawing the Philadelphia Plan out of concern that such legislation would give too much authority to the comptroller general. It fell to another southern Democrat to try to kill the program. In December, at Staats's urging, Senator Robert Byrd of West Virginia quietly introduced a

Enjoying victory after the congressional battle over the Philadelphia Plan with the solicitor of labor, Laurence H. Silberman. Arthur Fletcher Personal Papers, courtesy Paul Fletcher.

short rider into a supplemental appropriations bill designed to give financial aid to victims of a recent hurricane. The rider gave the comptroller general the final authority to rule on all matters related to public expenditures. This was parliamentary trickery at its finest. The House of Representatives had already approved the hurricane relief bill, and Byrd's rider joined several minor amendments made in the Senate; given the proximity to the Christmas break and legislators' desire to go home, Byrd expected that the bill would be approved by the Senate—and the amendments, including his rider, approved by the House—in short order. The president would be forced to sign the bill or face the political fallout of failing to support the victims of a natural disaster.[36]

But Byrd and the Philadelphia Plan's other Senate antagonists failed to predict how skillfully Nixon would defend Fletcher's program. During his first year in office, the president had already developed a reputation as hostile to civil rights, what with his nomination of unreconstructed southerner Clement Haynsworth to the Supreme Court, his dismissal of Clifford

Alexander as head of the EEOC, and his waffling on the question of enforcement powers for that commission. The Philadelphia Plan was his administration's only tangible civil rights initiative, with the political bonus for Nixon of potentially splitting two Democratic-leaning constituencies (labor and civil rights). Although the president faced Democratic majorities in both houses of Congress, Dick Nixon had a few tricks up his sleeve. After senators Javits and Fong failed to remove the Byrd rider from the appropriations bill by having it declared "non-germane," Nixon mobilized the House minority leader, Gerald Ford, to defeat the amendments in the lower chamber. He convened a meeting of Republican legislative leaders and their wives in a White House dining room on December 22, 1969, knowing Fletcher would turn on the charm—which he did. The president then gave a press conference alongside Shultz and Fletcher announcing his support, and explaining the importance, of the Philadelphia Plan. Further, once the House had rejected the Byrd rider, he threatened to call Congress into session during the holiday if they failed to pass the House version of the appropriations bill. He had turned the tables: not only had he prevented the hostile senators from quietly passing a law supporting Staats, but he had also placed them in the position of being labeled opponents of hurricane relief if they insisted on the Byrd rider. The gambit worked: the Senate voted to approve the House version and go home for Christmas. Arthur Fletcher's Revised Philadelphia Plan had survived its first major challenge. "Art," Fletcher recalled Nixon saying, "you won."[37]

Power and Possibility

At the start of 1970, Arthur Fletcher found himself an in-demand player on the national stage. Having implemented the Philadelphia Plan, and seen the defeat of congressional attempts to stymie it, his travels—already a major feature of his job—took on the tone of a victory tour. Despite the tension of the preholiday showdown over the Byrd rider, he began the year rested and refreshed. After a post-Thanksgiving whirlwind junket, during which he gave speeches and interviews in Atlanta, New York, Phoenix, Chicago, and Baltimore in addition to the meetings in Seattle, Fletcher had taken a ten-day vacation—at home with Bernyce in Columbia, Maryland. But he was not long at rest. In January he spoke at a teachers' symposium in Chicago the day after all parties signed the affirmative action plan for construction there, and in Boston he met with members of the Massachusetts advisory committee to the United States Commission on Civil Rights, along with other

Fletcher's longest political friendship was with George H. W. Bush, seen here with Fletcher at the Republican National Committee, September 10, 1973. Arthur Fletcher Personal Papers, courtesy Paul Fletcher.

local elected officials, who had been demanding a Philadelphia Plan of their own. (One of these was Father Robert Drinan, who won a seat in Congress later that year; Drinan became known as the Mad Monk when he introduced the first impeachment charge against President Nixon in 1973 and argued strenuously for impeachment in the House Judiciary Committee in 1974.) Then it was off to Las Vegas to receive an award from the National Black Newspaper Publishers Association. After that he went to Buck Hill Falls, Pennsylvania, to receive the George Washington Medal of Honor from the conservative Freedoms Foundation at Valley Forge. Ostensibly the prize was for his prior work in Pasco, but given the events of 1969, it was more likely in recognition for his support of President Nixon and his insistence that the GOP was still welcoming of African Americans. Drawn to the false mantle of color-blindness, conservatives were increasingly sensitive to charges of racism, especially after the 1964 Goldwater debacle and the rise of the John Birch Society. Fletcher, hardly conservative, was a safe Black they were comfortable honoring. Secretary Shultz and Bernyce joined him at the event, and Nixon sent a personal letter of congratulations.[38]

It was during this time that Fletcher's most important political friendship began. He had exchanged letters briefly the previous spring with a Houston congressman named George Bush on the topic of discrimination in the off-shore oil rig industry; now Bush told Fletcher to feel free to use his local office while in Houston. "I just wanted you to know that . . . if, for some reason, you'd like to do any work there, call your office, or use our facilities in any way, please be assured the door's wide open." Congressman Bush had bravely gone against the will of his own district's voters by supporting President Johnson's fair housing bill in 1968, despite his earlier support of Goldwater's position on civil rights legislation—that it was a violation of free enterprise rights. What Fletcher found particularly attractive in Bush was that he was a rising Republican star, and a southerner to boot (albeit one transplanted from New England), willing to buck the party's conservative, anti–civil rights trend. Bush's civil rights stance, honestly come by from his observations of Black servicemen returning from the war to face discrimination, made him appear almost a resurrected Fred Hall, but with key differences. Bush was independently wealthy from both his Greenwich pedigree and his personal success as a Texas oil wildcatter, and he was therefore not in politics for his own financial benefit. Bush also coupled a natural political instinct inherited from his senator father with genuine friendliness, self-lessness, and loyalty.[39]

The awards and requests for appearances did not abate, and Fletcher considered how to parlay his increasing national stature into increased authority, either within the administration or in elected office. This was a midterm election year, and the president was looking to decrease Democratic majorities in both houses of Congress, if not actually flip one or both to Republican control. Additionally, a bipartisan (albeit small) antiwar coalition in Washington State was looking to mount a challenge to hawkish Senator Henry M. "Scoop" Jackson. Given Jackson's strong civil rights bona fides, it was thought that only a Black candidate could unseat the popular Democrat. The idea was not far-fetched: at the time, the only African American in the Senate, Edward Brooke of Massachusetts, was also a Republican.[40]

But Brooke's background and experience were quite different from Fletcher's. Whereas Fletcher was raised in the ghettoes of the Southwest by a single mother and occasionally by friends and relatives, Brooke grew up in what he described as a "cocoon" of middle-class Black life in the LeDroit Park neighborhood of Washington, DC. Whereas Fletcher attended the integrated Washburn University after the war, Brooke, five years Fletcher's senior, attended historically Black Howard University before the war. This made their wartime experience also very different: Fletcher was an enlisted man who played football and trumpet and patrolled the Red Ball Express in France; Brooke was an officer who proposed battle plans in Italy and defended soldiers in court. These activities allowed Brooke to find his calling in the law, and after the war he attended Boston University's law school. Fletcher turned to politics when football panned out and racial discrimination proscribed his opportunities in the private sector; for Brooke, politics was a natural outgrowth of his successful career at the bar. While Brooke observed racial discrimination throughout his life and sympathized with its victims (including his own father), he didn't claim to have been personally harmed by it. Brooke entered politics of his own volition, running unsuccessfully for local office. This brought him to the attention of Republican Massachusetts governor John Volpe, who, like Kansas's Fred Hall, was a rising star. But whereas Hall gave Fletcher a management job at the state highway commission, Volpe made Brooke chairman of the Boston Finance Commission, where he publicly fought corruption and gained a reformer's reputation in the press. Volpe also backed Brooke in his successful 1962 race for state attorney general and provided a very different political base than Fletcher's Black supporters in East Pasco: the Italian Americans of Boston. Brooke's appeal in Boston's Italian community was surely helped by his light skin tone and his Italian wife, whom he had met during the war (although he also maintained support in Massachusetts's Black community). Hall's fall preceded Fletcher's nadir, and Fletcher eventually moved on to more successful patrons like Dan Evans and Richard Nixon. Brooke was a rising star in his own right, and he eclipsed Volpe when in 1966 he became the first African American to win a United States Senate election.[41] In sum, the factors in Ed Brooke's Senate win were mostly irrelevant to Fletcher's electoral viability.

Although a Fletcher victory against the three-term senator Scoop Jackson was unlikely, apparently the thinking at the RNC was that Fletcher could at least force the Democrats to devote additional resources to the Washington race, increasing the likelihood of unseating more vulnerable Democratic incumbents elsewhere. One such incumbent was Texas senator Ralph Yarborough; Nixon convinced Fletcher's new friend, George Bush, to give up his seat in Congress and take on Yarborough a second time. (Bush had tried to beat Yarborough in 1964 and lost.) For Fletcher, a Senate run in Washington would further cement his good relationship with Nixon, and it would help Bush. Although he publicly announced that he was giving it serious consideration, along with an offer to run for Congress from Berkeley, California, he was careful not to be perceived as ruffling any feathers in the White House; he stated unequivocally that he was happy with his current job. Ultimately he did not run for office in 1970, but he gave speeches around the country in the service of various campaigns, including Bush's and that of Paul Eggers, who was running for governor of Texas.[42]

These and other developments contributed to Fletcher's campaign that year for a higher-ranking post within the administration. Indeed, despite his increasing concern that Blacks were not giving the president enough credit for civil rights initiatives, Fletcher saw the resignations of others as opportunities to further demonstrate his own loyalty and continue to rise in Nixon's circle. In March the HEW director of civil rights, Leon Panetta, resigned over the administration's stalling on school desegregation; at the same time someone leaked memoranda in which token White House Democrat Daniel Patrick Moynihan called for a moratorium on new civil rights initiatives, recommending a period of "benign neglect." Moynihan was already distrusted by many in the civil rights community for a 1965 report he had issued as assistant secretary of labor in the Johnson administration, in which he was perceived to blame persistent inner-city problems on a matriarchal African American social order dating back to slavery. Subsequent statements by Ehrlichman that the problem was the leaks rather than the content served only to inflame the situation. Ehrlichman already saw the administration's civil rights activities as a political liability, and he viewed the developing war on drugs as a way to stigmatize the African American community as part of the southern (and northern white suburban) strategy.[43]

Fletcher seized the moment, writing a thoughtful letter asking Nixon to publicly reiterate his commitment to civil rights, and the president did so by inviting thirty-five Black administration employees to the White House for a ninety-minute meeting in the cabinet room. Although the White House had to scour the roster to find enough Black staffers, the requisite photo, later trumpeted by the RNC as evidence of the administration's commitment to its Black constituents, showed Fletcher seated at the president's right hand—exactly where he wanted to be.[44]

On June 10, as a reward for his work on the Philadelphia Plan fight, Nixon named Shultz head of the new Office of Management and Budget, and he designated Undersecretary Hodgson his replacement as secretary of labor. Given Hodgson's close involvement with the development, implementation, and defense of the Philadelphia Plan, the president's choice was a vote of confidence in Fletcher's work, and it indicated a desire for continuity at Labor. Nixon could have appointed another assistant secretary—he was in fact developing a relationship with Bill Usery, assistant secretary of labor for labor–management relations, an important component in wooing the white working-class vote—but this would have telegraphed a desire that Labor should emphasize other programs. He also could have brought in an outsider to shake things up. He did not. By the same token, the president did not appoint Fletcher to the job; a cabinet-level position for a Black man at that time would have undermined the Southern Strategy. Promoting Hodgson was shrewd politics: the president maintained support of his administration's only civil rights program without damaging his efforts to court white southerners.[45]

Hodgson's promotion did leave a vacancy directly above Fletcher: the position of undersecretary of labor. A number of prominent people around the country (probably at Fletcher's urging, although there is scant evidence for this) wrote Nixon to suggest that Fletcher either be tapped as undersecretary or, after African American White House advisor Robert Brown announced his resignation in July, take over that job. The San Francisco regional director for the NAACP, an Alameda County, California, Republican group, a slew of GOP congressional candidates from all over the country, and even the mayor of Wichita, Kansas, wrote Nixon on Fletcher's behalf, but ultimately the president named the solicitor of labor, Laurence Silberman, as undersecretary, and Stanley Scott as his token Black White House advisor. Because Silberman had also been an important supporter of the Philadelphia Plan in 1969, this was a further move by the president to preserve the existing regime at Labor without ruffling Jim Crow's feathers.[46]

This political balancing act became more complicated by the hard hat riot of the spring of 1970. After several students were killed at Kent State University in Ohio protesting the Vietnam War, the New York city council lowered the flag at City Hall to half-staff, and about 1,000 sympathetic antiwar activists marched in downtown Manhattan. They were set upon by about 200 counterprotesting construction workers. As in Chicago the previous September, the police mostly observed from a safe distance as the hard hats mercilessly beat the college students, invaded city hall to force the flag back up to full mast, and stormed neighboring Pace University in pursuit of fleeing protestors. Nixon, who had earlier scolded antiwar protestors, responded to the violence by inviting leaders of the construction unions to a meeting at the White House. They brought a hard hat as a gift for the president and told him they supported his Vietnam War policy; thus began Nixon's efforts to win the white northern working-class vote permanently for the GOP.[47]

Nixon's embrace of these fascists did not go unnoticed by the civil rights community. At the annual NAACP convention in Cincinnati that summer, the chairman, Stephen Spottswood, decried the administration as the most "anti-Negro" since that of Woodrow Wilson, linking his embrace of the hard hats to the Moynihan memos and Panetta resignation. NAACP labor secretary Herbert Hill drilled down in his own speech, accusing the president of abandoning the Philadelphia Plan in favor of the hard hat vote.[48]

Fletcher was livid, but more at the NAACP attack than Nixon's apparent embrace of the hard hats. He took Clarence Townes of the RNC and Sam Jackson of HUD and jetted out to Cincinnati. Ostensibly the three Black Republicans went to campaign on behalf of the US Senate bid of Robert Taft Jr. and in support of Charles Collins, a fellow Black Republican running for the Ohio state senate, but Fletcher was really there to rebut Spottswood and Hill. At a press conference outside the convention hall, Fletcher lost his cool. Although he made a good argument, he went off script, accidentally referring to the goals of the Philadelphia Plan as quotas. According to reporter James L. Adams,

> Fletcher grabbed a fistful of microphones to assert: "I took it upon myself to come here to respond to Herb Hill's statements and to refute them." . . . Fletcher said the Philadelphia Plan was still working and that following the meeting of President Nixon with the "hard hats" in May, the Washington Plan was propounded, June 1. "The Washington Plan goes even further than the Philadelphia Plan in that it effects 11 unions instead of five, it requires a *quota* of 35 per cent blacks instead of 20 and the contracts of all federal contractors—even those on non-federal jobs—must be in compliance with the plan." [emphasis added]

Other administration officials gave a more measured response but delivered essentially the same message. White House civil rights specialist Len Garment sent Spottswood—and several reporters—a long telegram citing the Philadelphia Plan and the overall number of Black government appointees as evidence of the administration's commitment to racial progress, and John Wilks gave an interview denying that the administration had abandoned the Philadelphia Plan in favor of white construction workers.[49]

While Fletcher was wrong on the merits—the administration did have a poor overall civil rights record—his anger at Spottswood and Hill was in keeping with his personality and strategy. He was a team player, after all, an organization man, and even though the NAACP leaders at the core of their arguments wanted to make Fletcher's position and the Philadelphia Plan stronger, he viewed an attack on Nixon as an attack on him. His strategy had always been that of the insider; he believed that he could best effect change by working with those in power, not by publicly criticizing them. But he failed to see that the external criticism was as important as his own work, and that it could even serve to strengthen his position within the administration and his ability to champion affirmative action and other civil rights policies. Further, by amplifying the NAACP complaints, he fed into the developing notion among GOP strategists that African Americans were a lost constituency and that Fletcher represented a dwindling, insignificant remnant whose ideas were easily dismissed. In this case, and especially because he mistakenly referred to the goals as quotas, silence in Cincinnati would have been more prudent.[50]

In the wake of the NAACP flap, Fletcher told Garment that the administration needed to propound a clear civil rights strategy to avoid the appearance that it was, as Bishop Spottswood had put it, "anti-Negro." He sent him a program, developed in tandem with Al Blumrosen, to use federal regulations to achieve full nationwide equality of employment opportunity by the end of the 1970s, and he began delivering a speech to that effect, coauthored by Nelson Crowther, to audiences all over the country. He hoped that the sympathetic Garment would push the president to implement the program. Of course, given the political reality of the Southern Strategy, Nixon and his closest political advisors had no intention of nationally publicizing a coherent civil rights program, certainly as long as George Wallace was threatening a primary challenge or third-party run in 1972, as it would serve only to alienate southern and working-class whites without winning enough Black votes to deliver any individual state.[51]

Fletcher's relationship with President Nixon and the White House led him to move beyond self-confidence into overconfidence. He failed to see that Nixon's primary motivations were political: far more than the president liked Fletcher personally, Richard Nixon craved power for its own sake. The president's genial treatment of Fletcher led the latter to think he had the total confidence of the administration at all levels. On the multiple occasions when Nixon invited Fletcher and his wife, Bernyce, to the White House, where they were sometimes even seen on the second floor—an honor usually reserved for close friends of the first family—it was easy for Fletcher to interpret this as unqualified support from the chief executive. More likely they were there to demonstrate Nixon's purported racial egalitarianism. As we have already seen, his appointment was made despite the concerns of John Ehrlichman and others far closer to Nixon than he. Such men were poised to move against him as soon as his programs lost their political expedience.[52]

For now, however, the administration's strategy was for the president to avoid public statements on civil rights in favor of speeches focused on the economy and the war in Vietnam, where he could play the reassuring national father while simultaneously appealing to voters' patriotism. Junior members of his administration quietly defended discrete civil rights programs like the Philadelphia Plan in court and in the Black community (as with Fletcher's speeches), and Garment and Fletcher pushed back against periodic attacks from the left, as with their response to Spottswood and Hill. Given the continuity-based staffing decisions at Labor in June, it seems unlikely that the president actually wanted to abandon his only real civil rights initiative in pursuit of the hard hat vote, which was as yet a new, uncertain constituency. Union leaders were staunch Democrats, and the best he could hope for from men like George Meany in the 1972 race was official neutrality. Finally, thanks to other developments in Fletcher's OFCC, Nixon had another ace to play in winning the votes of the rank-and-file white unionists: the Hometown Plans.[53]

The Chicago hearings the previous September, and the hard hat melee in the streets outside, had produced an official alternative to the mandatory, federally imposed programs like the Philadelphia and Washington plans. This Chicago Plan, developed in consultation with the building trades, contractors' organizations, local civil rights groups, and local government officials, and with the approval of the Department of Labor, fulfilled a promise Fletcher made whenever he spoke on construction integration: that local parties who developed their own acceptable affirmative action programs were exempt from the mandatory, federally imposed plans. The Chicago Plan proposed to train and hire several thousand skilled Black workers over the next few years, and as Fletcher announced the planned expansion of the Philadelphia Plan to as many as twenty cities by the end of 1970, the Chicago Plan became a model for a local alternative that came to be dubbed the Hometown Plans. In many cities this option proved attractive to all parties, but for the unions in particular it suggested an escape from the actual integration of the Philadelphia Plan with a process they hoped to dominate through their influence over local elected officials. Ultimately most Hometown Plans proved a sham, and OFCC would eventually replace many with mandatory versions. But for the time being, it was a business-as-usual alternative that Nixon pointed to when building trades leaders accused him of singling out their industry for "forced" affirmative action.[54]

For the most part, the Hometown Plans met the legislative and regulatory requirements of the OFCC, at least on paper. While there was a degree of

With Jesse Jackson, July 11, 1970. Arthur Fletcher Personal Papers, courtesy Paul Fletcher.

negotiation involved with each, OFCC approved most of them, only imposing a mandatory plan in cases where the local parties failed to agree to a program. And while subsequent investigations and academic studies showed that the Hometown Plans were indeed failures in comparison to the mandatory versions, paper compliance usually took the immediate heat off the unions and contractors.[55]

For Fletcher, the first indicator that the building trades were using the Hometown Plans as an out to avoid compliance with real affirmative action came in July 1970. Invited to address Operation Breadbasket/Chicago, an offshoot of the late Martin Luther King Jr.'s Southern Christian Leadership Conference led by Jesse Jackson, Fletcher attended the event accompanied by Bernyce and delivered his speech on ending economic discrimination during the 1970s.[56]

Jesse Jackson had a similar background to that of Fletcher. Both were born out of wedlock (although Jackson knew and maintained a good relationship with his birth father); both had attended college and experienced discrimination there; both had been star athletes (Jackson was offered a minor league baseball contract and was quarterback at North Carolina A&T); both were natural politicians (Jackson was student body president); both were deeply guided by the church (Jackson pursuing a ministerial degree and following that career path); both were captivating in the pulpit and at the lectern; and both were politically open-minded: the most important thing for both men was the success of the movement, and while Fletcher worked within his party to achieve that, Jackson's partisan affiliation remained fluid well into the 1970s. Initially their differences were superficial: Jackson was from the Deep South rather than the Midwest, and his apprenticeship was with Martin Luther King Jr. rather than a white politician. While Fletcher was building Higher Horizons and the co-op, and nurturing his connections with white corporate directors, Jackson was marching with Dr. King and John Lewis from Selma to Montgomery. These differences widened with time: Fletcher's credibility among everyday African Americans was increasingly suspect thanks to his continued public identity as a Republican, while Jackson's presence at Dr. King's assassination, and his literal covering in the slain leader's blood (he even wore the bloody shirt to speeches), earned him King's mantle as unofficial leader of the national civil rights movement. While the two were friendly, there was also a generation gap. Jackson, a baby boomer, represented the public protests of the 1960s, while Fletcher, middle-aged by 1965, symbolized the tactic of private negotiation and compromise. In interviews with Fletcher's son, one detects a strong hint of resentment at Jackson's fame in comparison with Fletcher's.[57]

Fletcher and Jackson were by now well acquainted, having shared the 1970 National Black Newspaper Publishers Association's John B. Russwurm award. Jackson, who had gone to jail in 1969 in Chicago protesting discrimination in the building trades, complained at the Operation Breadbasket event that "no jobs have been made available to blacks and no recruitment centers set up" in the six months since the signing of the Chicago Plan, and he asked Fletcher to conduct an investigation. As a result Fletcher and Wilks began moving forward with a proposal to convert the Chicago Plan to a mandatory, Philadelphia Plan–style program.[58]

That the unions were using the Hometown Plans to evade affirmative action became even more apparent with the New York Plan, the epitome of the sham alternative. Developed by local building trades head Peter J. Brennan, who had organized the city hall rally that became the hard hat riot, the New York Plan was everything the other Hometown Plans—let alone the Philadelphia Plan—was not. First, it was unilateral: none of New York's copious civil rights organizations was involved, nor were any local government officials (although the mayor and governor, both Republicans, eventually gave it grudging approval). Second, it was very limited. It projected a training program for fewer than 1,000 minority trainees (compared to the Chicago Plan, which promised more than 4,000 trainee slots), and contained no requirement that contractors set any goals for minority hiring. Most egregiously, the plan provided for a separate training facility for minority trainees—in other words, it proposed a segregated educational program even as school districts throughout the South were being expected to integrate.[59]

Naturally Fletcher and Wilks disliked Brennan's New York Plan, and they thought they could prevent its implementation and replace it with a multilateral Hometown Plan for New York, or an imposed plan like that of Philadelphia. In this sentiment recent experience was their guide. After the defeat of the Byrd rider in Congress, they had negotiated strong affirmative action agreements in Kansas City and Seattle—the latter being an especially difficult case, as the building trades there had held out for many months against the entreaties of Governor Evans and in the face of multiple visits by Fletcher—and imposed a plan in Washington, DC, when the parties there failed to agree.

Fletcher and Wilks were mistaken, as Meany and Brennan looked to use their growing influence with President Nixon to make their stand with the New York Plan.[60]

"The Old Order Is Collapsing"

The final, successful attempt of the building trades to neuter the Philadelphia Plan began just as the program was achieving its first modest successes. Although initially contractors were evading the program's requirements with so-called motorcycle compliance (the shuttling of token Black workers between jobsites to fool government inspectors), following the defeat of a contractor lawsuit and the first contract revocations for noncompliance, by January 1971 the OFCC was able to report to Fletcher "that most contractors can and do meet the goals."[61]

Arguably it was the very success of the program and Fletcher's growing self-assurance that caused his downfall and the end of aggressive affirmative action enforcement by the Nixon administration. Fletcher was giving speeches all over the country, often more than a dozen a month, to great acclaim. He was sitting for interviews on nationally syndicated television shows, and the new chairman of the RNC, Bob Dole, was actively seeking his transfer to a permanent job with him to replace the recently departed Clarence Townes as director of minority outreach. Dole invited Fletcher to address a meeting of the RNC, and he was not disappointed. Fletcher wowed the almost entirely white crowd with lines like, "Yes, we have a Southern strategy, a Northern strategy, a Cornbelt strategy, a Rocky Mountain strategy, a Pacific Coast strategy. The Democrats do, too. I am not concerned as to whether the President has a Southern strategy or not. I am concerned about the character of that strategy." He got a standing ovation. Dole ended the meeting with, "Let me say one thing for Art Fletcher. You don't have to say much for Art Fletcher, but let me predict you are going to hear a lot more about Art Fletcher in the weeks and months ahead."[62]

It was in this context that Fletcher began to deliver his new stump speech for 1971, cowritten by Crowther, "The Old Order Is Collapsing." In it he said that unions were losing control of construction hiring because of their failure to integrate; that mandatory affirmative action programs were being extended to every city with a Hometown Plan that had failed to see progress, and that the program retained the support of the Department of Labor, attorney general, Congress, courts, and the president. He connected a Nixon suspension of the Davis–Bacon Prevailing Wage Act, which required all contractors in each region to pay their workers the local prevailing wage, with his own campaign to integrate construction. (Actually Nixon did this as a temporary anti-inflation measure; he rescinded the order by early May.) Aware of the history of employers using Blacks as strikebreakers, however, Fletcher was careful to urge contractors to not use affirmative action as an excuse to break unions.[63]

When he gave the speech before local chapters of the Associated General Contractors—union employers—it was not particularly controversial. After all, he was mostly crowing about the Philadelphia Plan's accomplishments, and there was nothing in it that was explicitly antiunion. As always, Fletcher was decrying the racist practices of some unions, not unionism in general. He personally championed the role of industrial unions, especially, in espousing social change. The problem was that he didn't tailor the speech for specific audiences. When he gave the speech to the nonunion Associated Builders and Contractors—where lines like "the era of union domination of the employment pattern in the construction industry is over" surely garnered loud applause—the speech was spun by the leaders of the skilled construction trades as antilabor. This, coupled with the fact that he had accidentally or absentmindedly crossed at least two picket lines during his tenure as assistant secretary of labor, gave significant ammunition to the enemies of affirmative action.[64]

It didn't take long for attacks to materialize. On March 16, 1971, influential labor columnist John Herling excoriated Fletcher in print, comparing the speech, as delivered to the nonunion contractors, to letting a fox into a chicken coop. And on March 23 the Sheet Metal Workers national president denounced Fletcher in a letter to Nixon, arguing that his mischaracterization of the president's Davis–Bacon decision made the administration look antiunion.[65]

Secretary Hodgson, on the other hand, came to Fletcher's defense in a reply on behalf of Nixon, citing the very speech that had caused the ruckus: "On page eleven . . . Assistant Secretary Fletcher specifically warns against the civil rights movement becoming 'perverted into an anti-labor, anti-worker movement.'" Hodgson reiterated that his and Nixon's support of Fletcher "has not waned but has become more confirmed with the passage of time." Liberal labor columnist Victor Riesel also defended Fletcher, noting that leaders of the Sheet Metal Workers Union and other organizations calling loudest for his ouster headed unions with tiny Black memberships— that is, they were the ones with the most to lose from affirmative action— and that Fletcher was not calling for an end to union control of hiring where the trades were actually integrating. Riesel went so far as to give Fletcher a guest column. "Is the Philadelphia Plan a union busting device? No," Fletcher wrote.

> The present problem has been created by the failure of a number of construction unions to represent minority workers or to allow them to join locals. The answer for the unions is to organize this labor supply, let minorities in and allow them to participate. More Philadelphia-type plans are an alternative. Other alternatives are to have all black unions or to encourage black contractors to do more and more Federal construction work. These black contractors are largely non-unions simply because the locals will not accept their employees as members.[66]

But White House political operative Charles "Chuck" Colson was becoming concerned. The future Watergate conspirator told senior presidential advisor H. R. "Bob" Haldeman that Fletcher's speech had the potential to weaken Nixon's tenuous support among the hard hats and "Middle America," and he recommended that they transfer him to a more advisory, honorary position where he could do less damage to the president's 1972 reelection fight. "Assuming we do survive this one, we certainly cannot afford another major confrontation with the Building Trades over a gut issue," he said.[67]

Fletcher still had friends in high places. His old boss, George Shultz, now head of the Office of Management and Budget in the White House, was concerned that Colson might be judging the situation too quickly. He knew the kind of hardball that the building trades could and would play to keep control of hiring and training—and he knew Fletcher. But he also understood the politics, and he agreed to talk to Hodgson about the situation and line up support at Labor for a Fletcher transfer to a position without enforcement authority.[68]

Unaware of the growing concern in the White House, and confident of Hodgson's support, Fletcher boldly continued his offensive against the segregated trades: "We shall impose plan after plan in cities where the hometown solution doesn't work," he said, even as George Meany continued to defend the Chicago and other Hometown Plans, calling them "vastly superior to any government-imposed quota system."[69]

Reading this exchange in the *Wall Street Journal* on May 6, 1971, and noting that the cities to be targeted for mandatory plans were all in key battleground states for the 1972 election, Colson told Haldeman that it "may very well represent the last straw." Of course it should have been obvious that the areas with the densest population—key electoral regions—were also those with the largest proportions of Black people and most instances of discrimination. But Colson was not looking to achieve racial equality; he was looking to keep the "old man" in office. Fearing to "antagonize millions of union members and George Meany," he argued that unionist antipathy toward Fletcher had reached the point where he could no longer be an effective conciliator. He recommended that the New York Plan be immediately approved, and that they brainstorm other jobs for Fletcher. He stated the political situation plainly: no civil rights program helped the president increase his share of the Black vote (10 percent in 1968), and they should try harder to win over white union voters.[70]

The next day Colson called Nixon on the telephone to discuss the building trades and the concerns of George Meany and their other leaders. "Fletcher just sends Meany up the walls," Colson told the president, explaining that the labor leader was concerned that the administration, "not you, Mr. President, but the administration," was trying to completely restructure the building trades, and he strongly recommended that Nixon meet with Meany to cool tempers. Nixon, for his part, thought that Fletcher was right on the merits but not on the politics. "The building trades needs [change] but hell, why fight that battle? That's somebody else's battle. There's no votes in it for us! . . . We don't get anything from it, pick up any Negro votes . . . not one damn vote." "No," Colson replied, "but we turn off the Italian carpenters in Pittsburgh and the Irish in New York."[71]

Meany was in town, so the president invited him to the Oval Office. After exchanging the usual pleasantries, Meany told Nixon that Fletcher "made a great speech to the nonunion contractors, and he looked awfully stupid." He defended the skilled building trades, of which he himself was a member, noting that discrimination was "not a pattern" but isolated cases. Nixon clarified that the views of Arthur Fletcher did not represent the views of his administration, and he reiterated his "great respect for the people that are in those trades." Overall the tone of the meeting was pleasant, that of a respectful politician wooing the leader of a major, heretofore antagonistic constituency. That Fletcher was "right on the merits," on which Nixon and Colson agreed, did not come up. President Nixon had sold out the Philadelphia Plan to the hard hats—as Herbert Hill had predicted a year earlier at the NAACP convention.[72]

Colson continued pressuring his bosses. On May 27 he told fellow operative Fred Malek that "we only have about 30 days to work on this before the building trades are irretrievably lost to us politically," suggesting that Fletcher be appointed to the US Court of Appeals for the Armed Forces. On June 4, he told advisor Ken Cole, "I can't tell you how much this particular situation worries me politically." On June 7 he reported to Ehrlichman that the situation was "deteriorating" and that he thought that Fletcher was deliberately undermining the Hometown Plans and refusing to ratify the New York Plan. "In my opinion we are being sabotaged. . . . We are simply allowing the bureaucrats to drag us into a situation that can politically be devastating," noting that unemployment in the building trades was "now close to double the national average; this is notwithstanding a building boom. The obvious inference is that we are training many more minority apprentices than there are jobs to be filled." Furthermore, with the administration perceived as backing down on other civil rights measures, such as school integration, the building trades were feeling singled out, he argued. Colson advocated a centralized, White House–dictated policy. Two days later he sent Ehrlichman an article from the *St. Louis Post-Dispatch* wherein Fletcher decried the hard hat riots as racist, noting, "This is just the kind of thing that gives us incredible political problems and I think would be terribly upsetting to the" president.[73]

At some level Colson's arguments were both understandable and constitutional, in that the president was elected to be the chief executive officer of the federal government; his advisors could argue that their policies reflected the democratic will of the people. But on the other hand, the modern republic has a nonpartisan bureaucracy so that its policies do not blow back and forth with the fickle electoral wind. Also, instead of looking to satisfy those racists who felt singled out, why not strengthen other civil rights programs? In other words, by pushing to remove Fletcher, Colson was using the administration's overall bad civil rights posture as an excuse to make it even worse.

Whereas Nixon saw the political utility in having an outspoken civil rights advocate on the team, all Colson saw was an uncontrollable firebrand. After Democratic senator (and presidential front-runner) Edmund Muskie publicly ruled out naming a Black running mate in 1972 and New York governor Rockefeller botched the handling of the prison rebellion at Attica, Fletcher gave another clear-eyed but impolitic speech. On Muskie, Fletcher said, "The Democrat party has its own Southern strategy which is based on a whites only policy," calling for the Democratic National Committee to issue a formal apology to "the nation, and especially its Black members." Noting "an absence of Black prison guards" at Attica "while 50 per cent of the inmates are Black," and that "Night Sticks are called 'Nigger Sticks' and the word 'Nigger' is used to mean 'prisoner' in the prison and community," Fletcher chided Rockefeller for not meeting with the inmates during their takeover of the prison, as had the governor of Maryland during a recent rebellion at a prison in his state. Colson exploded, focusing not on the truth of Fletcher's remarks but on the possibility that they could cost Nixon white law-and-order votes. Again, Fletcher was right on the merits, but "as anyone who has dealt with Art Fletcher knows, he is very difficult to control," Colson told a confidant. "He blew it."[74]

Colson now arranged for Nixon to meet with Peter Brennan, the head of the New York building trades, on July 2, 1971. The Nixon tapes here are instructive as to the position of building trades leaders on Fletcher as well as Nixon's own concerns. "Some of the Blacks are satisfied progress is being made and other Blacks are starting up," Brennan told the president. "Now what is this fellow Fletcher, this appointee of yours, I'm sure you're not responsible for what he's doing right now. . . . People are trying to do the right thing and being harassed." Nixon turned to Colson. Fletcher "apparently has taken a position that goes beyond what the law requires, correct?" Colson: "He means very well but he gets carried away with his rhetoric." Brennan continued, "It's not a question of fighting discrimination, we all want to fight discrimination. But [Fletcher's] speech to the contractors' association, 'we have broken the back of the building trades unions' . . . our people feel that the president wants to break the unions. . . . Fletcher sees himself as a new Martin Luther King, and this is something you cannot control, we cannot control." Nixon, for his part, wanted to pacify Brennan, knowing that he was fighting for critical votes from a constituency that favored his Vietnam policy and saw the late Dr. King not as a hero but as a troublemaker:

> I think for example the problem in the Fletcher case, [where] the Blacks are concerned, we've done more than anybody else, and they don't . . . appreciate it. We'll still do what's right, but on the other hand, let's not have any illusions about all this, and we're going to . . . stop this rhetoric, and I don't want anything said by anybody in this administration that takes off on the people that are supporting us in the foreign policy area.

In other words, if the white construction workers continued to support his Vietnam policy and voted for his reelection in 1972, he would unofficially withdraw support for the Philadelphia Plan. "With regard to the specifics," he told Colson, "get the New York thing worked out.[75]

Brennan felt great after the meeting: "You tell the president there's 250,000 of my boys out there and by god, we're with him," he told Colson. "He was just delighted with what you said," Colson reported to the president. Elated about the votes but concerned about Fletcher, Nixon replied, "Fletcher shouldn't say those things, we've gotta get him out of that line of fire and put him in the National Committee or something." On that topic, Colson had good news. "He agreed this morning—while we were meeting, he was meeting with Ehrlichman." Nixon's ducks were lining up:

> It's a great idea and it gives him more opportunity, they can pay him a little more money, and . . . put him on the road, to not just talk about [the Philadelphia Plan]. He is a good political property but that thing about the hardhats was . . . he thinks the Philadelphia Plan helps us. The Philadelphia Plan is right, but it hurts us. . . . Shultz and Garment and the other guys are often, "isn't it great that we have the Philadelphia Plan?" And I says fellas, it's fine that we're getting these Blacks into the jobs, but boy it's killing us with our constituency!

"They're now beginning to realize that it hasn't worked either," Colson replied, either disingenuously or out of ignorance of the program's successes. But he took it further, still seeing civil rights only through the lens of the president's political prospects: "You can't force these things . . . you've done it so beautifully with the schools, we should be using the same technique in this area." Remarkably, but unsurprisingly given the Southern Strategy, Colson saw the administration's lackluster handling of school integration as a success, despite the resignations of Leon Panetta and James Farmer and a State of the Union walkout by the Congressional Black Caucus (CBC). But Nixon refocused on the action item, seeking concrete support from Brennan and Meany: "Get that New York Plan approved—get something approved before his meeting if you can." "I will, Mr. President, [but] the Fletcher news is probably the biggest thing we can do for them when that happens. They'll understand it." Nixon concurred, but cautioned, "We don't want a big story out that we canned Fletcher or anything; Fletcher wants to do this."[76]

The White House arranged a temporary appointment for Fletcher as an alternate delegate to the 26th regular session of the United Nations under the permanent representative, George Bush, whom Nixon had appointed to the UN after his failed Senate bid the previous fall. After that, everyone expected Fletcher to go to work for Bob Dole at the RNC. For the time being, Fletcher and Bernyce moved into tony digs in New York's Plaza 50, a stylish new building at 155 East 50th Street, walking distance from the UN, Broadway theaters, and fashionable shopping.[77]

"Fletcher wants to do this," Nixon said. To what degree? It was clear by the summer of 1971 that it was impossible for Fletcher to stay in the Department of Labor. He was roundly despised by white labor leaders and the skilled white rank and file alike. And as a staunch Republican and Nixon supporter, few in the civil rights movement rose to defend him. He had been attacked by Herbert Hill on the left for the perceived weakness of the Philadelphia Plan, and by Peter Brennan on the right for its strengths. Despite the support, he found little practical assistance from his boss; James Hodgson was not the inside player his predecessor George Shultz was and could not effectively defend him. What's more, the frantic schedule of speaking events, exhilarating though each appearance may have been, was taking its toll on Fletcher's health, and it may have contributed to the oversight of delivering the fatal speech word for word to the nonunion contractor audience. But Fletcher took his removal in stride, looking forward to bringing his civil rights message to the international stage. As always, he took comfort in his successes and chose not to dwell on his defeats; tomorrow was another day. After all, as he later told an interviewer, his thirty months as assistant secretary of labor was a longer than average stint in a political appointment at that level.[78]

Another interesting quotation from that day at the White House also bears analyzing. "Fletcher sees himself as a new Martin Luther King," said Brennan, who disliked the ideas and activities of both men. Fletcher was an avid admirer of Dr. King and his work, and he acknowledged King as the unofficial leader of the movement from the mid-1950s until his 1968 assassination. But whereas the mainstream movement—and Dr. King himself—had focused on southern integration from the *Brown* decision through at least 1963 and had then turned to voting rights and eventually economic rights, Fletcher had been focused on economic rights for most of his adult life. Although his earliest civil rights action—the integration of the yearbook—had carried no economic impact, his argument in college, in professional football, and in his earliest job seeking in Kansas had been that integration was secondary to economic access. By the time he entered the Nixon administration in 1969, with the three major civil rights acts of the 1960s already signed, these arguments had become mainstream, as demonstrated by the work of Leon Sullivan, Floyd McKissick, Roy Innis, and others. Unlike those leaders, however, Fletcher had access to the highest corridors of power. He was now in a position to take on the mantle of national civil rights leadership. To that extent he saw his work as an extension of Dr. King's earlier efforts, but he never publicly compared himself to the martyr.

Of course, Nixon's calculus had little to do with Fletcher's resemblance to Dr. King. He decided that Fletcher had served his purpose and had become a liability in his present position. The expected split between labor and civil rights leaders over the Philadelphia Plan had failed to materialize; the AFL-CIO had opposed Nixon's nomination of anti–civil rights judge G. Harrold Carswell to the Supreme Court in 1970—the first time the organization had opposed such a nomination on anything other than labor grounds—but the president was nevertheless winning supporters among rank-and-file white workers by the day. Even the leadership was coming around, and George Meany ultimately handed Nixon a gift, refusing an AFL-CIO endorsement for 1972 Democratic presidential nominee George McGovern and paving the way for Nixon to win a large share of the working-class vote in his successful reelection bid. The labor rights coalition didn't need to be split for Nixon to win; he just needed to use the war in Vietnam and racist code to appeal to white workers.[79]

Days after Fletcher's transfer was announced, OFCC director John Wilks, acting no doubt on orders from the White House, approved the New York Plan, and Department of Labor official Joseph Loftus told the press that the Chicago Plan would not be replaced with a mandatory version after all. Months later, Fletcher's vacated position at Labor still hadn't been filled.

Knowing that the highly qualified John Wilks was unlikely to get White House approval, closely tied as he was to Fletcher, Secretary Hodgson recommended Chrysler personnel manager Lowell Perry, who had been the first Black assistant coach in the National Football League, and who had the support of the leaders of AFL-CIO. But White House staffers, including Colson, blocked Perry from consideration. John Ehrlichman noted that "it's very bad political judgement to put another black in this job because it would stamp that job as a Black job, and . . . a Black should not be administering the Philadelphia Plan, at least for a while, until we get well with the unions." Nixon agreed: "I am inclined to frankly not put a Black in that job," he told Ehrlichman. "The Building Trades are still a tension for us. . . . It doesn't help us at all. . . . Believe me, there isn't a goddamn thing I can do" to generate greater support in the Black community. "I could, you know, take a second wife, marry a Black, it would not help . . . let's not kid ourselves." Ultimately he appointed a white manager from the Olin Corporation, Richard J. Grunewald, who took office in January 1972 and served unremarkably through the rest of Nixon's administration. Nixon asked for Hodgson's resignation in early 1973 in favor of the leader of the hard hat revolt, so instrumental in Fletcher's removal. In exchange for delivering his members' votes in 1972, Peter Brennan became secretary of labor. Strong enforcement of affirmative action in the building trades was effectively dead.[80]

After nearly three years with the Nixon administration, Fletcher could point with some justified pride to his accomplishments. Most importantly, he had redefined and enforced affirmative action and become a national figure, giving well-received speeches in cities all over the country. Politically, however, his utility to Nixon and the Republican Party was to support a very important lie the party was telling the nation: that it still stood for racial equality. By allowing Fletcher to enforce the Philadelphia Plan—within limits—the Nixon administration could say that it was continuing and expanding the civil rights initiatives of the previous administration even as it was actually curtailing civil rights policies in other areas.

The abandonment of the cause of civil rights by the party of Lincoln was a century in the making. In many states, Fletcher's Kansas included, the GOP had served as the only alternative to a local Democratic Party dominated by white supremacists. The Reconstruction-era Black politicians had all been Republicans, as was the first new African American member of Congress in the twentieth century, Oscar De Priest, elected in 1928 to represent Chicago's South Side.

This is not to say that most Republicans were liberal—far from it. In the nineteenth century they were the party of northern industry and finance, and their platforms by the mid-twentieth century were clearly right of center on most issues. But as we have seen, the postwar era saw a fierce battle for control of the Republican Party between its conservative wing, led by midwesterners and southwesterners like Ohio senator Robert Taft and Arizona's Barry Goldwater, and its moderates, led by eastern establishment Republicans who called themselves liberals: New York governors Thomas Dewey and Nelson Rockefeller. Most conservative Republicans were no more overtly racist than their moderate counterparts; outside of Dixie, after all, it was not considered polite to espouse white supremacy, however such men may have taken their socially ordained positions for granted. In such an environment, men like Fletcher made easy friendships with men like Bob Dole of Kansas and George Bush of Texas. The hint of noblesse oblige on Bush's part, inherited from his staid Connecticut upbringing, certainly didn't hurt.

The Democrats also had a long-simmering internecine feud between conservatives and liberals, but in their case the conservatives were overt racists. They had threatened to bolt the party in 1948 under the Dixiecrat banner after the nomination of Harry Truman, who had announced integration of the armed forces and favored equal employment opportunity in government contracts. When President Johnson signed the Civil Rights Act of 1964, the trickle of these southern conservatives into the Republican Party became a waterfall. As they grew more important to the Republican electoral calculus, their natural allies within the Republican Party—the midwestern and southwestern conservatives—saw their opportunity to take permanent control. Republican liberals left to join the Democrats, and the Dixiecrat tail eventually came to wag the Republican dog. Every potential Republican presidential nominee from 1968 onward saw the need to woo the South, especially when threatened by third-party candidates from the region, and that meant a wink and a nod at efforts to slow down or even stop the progress of civil rights. It was here that Nixon's Southern Strategy originated. Even as the Republican Party captured Dixie, it became a slave to it.[81]

Events in the nation's cities after 1964 also made for fertile ground for the GOP among working-class whites outside of the South. For decades, the rank-and-file white members of the American Federation of Labor had largely voted their class interests, pulling the lever for Democrats. But during the 1960s many working-class whites, their unions bringing middle-class stability, began to see the Democratic Party as the coddlers of the inner-city rebel and the campus revolutionary, and economic concerns gave way to social fear. Republican candidates who could learn to speak in the coded vernacular of the color-blind racist could pick off votes here too.[82]

As Fletcher prepared to leave the Nixon administration in 1971, he was not unaware of this political calculus. Nevertheless, he remained a loyal Republican. He exemplified what William Whyte would call in his 1972 book *The Organization Man*: his principles played second fiddle to his loyalties, in this case to the Republican Party in general and to his patrons in particular—men like Fred Hall, Dan Evans, and Richard Nixon. These loyalties had gotten him into trouble before; indeed, when it came to his relationships with Hall and Nixon, Fletcher defined the phrase "loyal to a fault," refusing to see the corruption so apparent to others.[83]

Arthur Fletcher perceived a clear path to bring the Republican Party back to its founding principle of racial egalitarianism: encourage more Blacks to vote Republican and more Black leaders to work with Republican administrations. As he left the Department of Labor, it was on this prospect that he focused his endeavors.

CHAPTER FIVE

ROLLER COASTER, 1971–1979

There's nothing between the lines. My message is on the line every inch of the way.
—Arthur Fletcher, 2003

If Arthur Fletcher's rise during the 1960s recalled the space program, with incredible forward progress tempered but not dissuaded by setbacks along the way, his political career in the decade after he left the Department of Labor was more like a roller coaster. Whereas during the 1960s his relationship with the Republican Party was marked by patient loyalty, during the 1970s Fletcher focused on slowing the exodus of African Americans from the GOP. The party was growing, but as he discovered, its gains were from segments of the population hostile to the causes he championed.

Still, even as the Republican Party ran away from Fletcher's positions much faster than he could keep up, it didn't shake his faith. This wasn't so much naivete on his part but rather a dedication to principles he believed could still work to pull the party in a more productive and racially egalitarian direction.

New York Interlude

Fletcher's stint as alternate delegate to the United Nations began with UN Week in late September 1971 and extended through the regular session, which ended in December. During this time the permanent representative, George Bush, and the deputy permanent representative were joined by three other delegates and five alternates. These included Congressmen Charles Diggs of Michigan and Edward Derwinski of Illinois, presidential adviser Pat Moynihan, astronaut Alan Shepard, the president of the National Federation of Republican Women, and three permanent employees of the US Mission to the UN.[1]

Fletcher and African American congressman Diggs were sent to New York to demonstrate to the world that the United States was racially egalitarian, and once there, Fletcher became an outspoken advocate for international human and civil rights, unafraid to take on America's most vociferous enemies. In a story he later recalled with relish, he stared down the Russian ambassador at a meeting of the High Commission on Human Rights. Fletcher pushed the ambassador on the question of refuseniks, the Soviet Jews who had been denied the right to emigrate to Israel. The Soviet ambassador saw the Americans as hypocrites; indeed, he claimed that Jews were treated better in the Soviet Union than Blacks in the United States. In a speech in the committee room on October 26, 1971, Fletcher boldly retorted, "My country is simply not interested in having the representatives of totalitarian governments lecture us on the liberties of American citizens." He told the Russian ambassador that since 1945, the founding of the United Nations, "the record shows that 40,000 [African Americans went to Africa] to visit, and when the visit [was] over, 40,000 [came] home. How many Jews will leave Russia and come home?"[2]

Having been tipped off by Bush, Nixon watched the speech on television at the White House. Always impressed by Fletcher's oratorical skills, and still eager to use him for political benefit, the president sent Fletcher overnight to Hawaii to deliver an important speech to the International Junior Chamber of Commerce (known colloquially as the Jaycees) on the US stance on Red Chinese recognition at the UN. (Despite Nixon's announced forthcoming trip to China, the administration still officially opposed mainland Chinese membership in the UN, continuing to recognize that of the rump Taiwanese holdout.) Normally such an assignment would have been given to Nobel Peace Prize–recipient and Howard University political scientist Ralph Bunche, but Bunche was now on his deathbed, and Fletcher was on deck. What he didn't know was that he was expected to prepare his own remarks. As Fletcher later described it, "We get on the plane and I have a good time, drink me some Bloody Marys and Lord knows what else, so I'm feeling pretty good. When the plane lands [there were] three dozen people from the press waiting for me to get off . . . the [Jaycees] president said, What are your remarks? We have to translate them into four languages. So I called the White House, and [they] said, Art, you write it." Scrambling, with hours to go before the speech, Fletcher went to the local press office for the *Honolulu Times*, requested several articles to review, and banged out a speech. "The audience was flabbergasted. One, A black guy? Is there a message in this? Nixon sent a black guy to welcome us to the United States, and did you read that speech? It was straight ahead. There's nothing between the lines. In the diplomatic arena, the message is between the lines, not on the line, and my message is on the line every inch of the way."

The very next morning, the White House called and told Fletcher that he was to give a noon press conference to explain the previous night's Jaycees speech:

> They said, Well, Art, that speech you gave last night, you got to explain it. I said, I'm not writing another speech. They said, However you want to do it.
>
> . . . So that's exactly what I did. I got up before an audience of 3,600 people from around the world. I . . . explained how we in the civil rights movement got legislation on the books, got ourselves appointed to political positions inside [the] administration, and we hadn't developed the sophistication yet to know how to talk between the lines . . . I stood there and answered questions for . . . over an hour. And when I got through . . . to my shock . . . I got a . . . standing ovation. I must have had to stand up at least five times. And it was the direct talk that they appreciated.

According to Fletcher, upon his return, he was offered a permanent position with the UN delegation. But Fletcher turned Nixon down, citing the same health problems that ultimately felled Ralph Bunche:

> When you're there you have to go to at least five receptions a night. . . . If you don't eat, it's an insult. . . . The next morning you all come back and debrief, [w]hat was the Indian delegate talking about over this event . . . what was the Pakistani delegate talking about with that. . . . And you don't have an option, you don't want to get surprised . . . anyway, you're going to eat [and] drink yourself into bad health. I'm already a diabetic then, and I didn't want to do anything that would cause that problem to become more complicated.

Because Fletcher continued to accept jobs involving cocktail parties, dinners, and travel, however, one cannot help but wonder about the veracity of this statement. But he went on to say, "I just didn't feel comfortable . . . interpreting policy that I didn't have a chance to help give input into. You wait for the message to come from Washington and then try to get on the floor and try to sell it, and I just said no, thank you." This excuse appears more salient, as he found being a spokesman for other people's policies unappealing. Fletcher had tasted authority at the Department of Labor. He had been given the opportunity to make an impact, and he wanted similar responsibilities in his next job.[3] The job offer—there is no record of it in the Nixon archives, but a White House spokesman did confirm to a *New York*

Times reporter that Fletcher "was offered other positions" and was "highly regarded within the administration"—was in keeping with Nixon's regard for Fletcher as a "good political property."[4]

Fletcher didn't have to wait long for his next job opportunity, and as with the permanent job offer at the United Nations, tragedy paved the way. Whereas the job offer at the UN resulted from the death of the stately Ralph Bunche, Fletcher's next job offer stemmed from the untimely death of the longtime executive director of the National Urban League (NUL), civil rights icon Whitney Young, who had drowned the previous March in Nigeria. Young had been one of the four civil rights leaders to meet with President Johnson to strategize a pathway for the 1964 Civil Rights Act.[5]

After a brief interlude under the leadership of Harold R. Sims, the NUL appointed United Negro College Fund (UNCF) executive director (and later Clinton intimate) Vernon E. Jordan Jr. to the post. Jordan announced that he would leave the UNCF effective January 1, 1972, giving their board of directors, which consisted of presidents of historically Black colleges and universities, time to find a successor. And Jordan already had someone in mind: Arthur Fletcher.[6]

Fletcher, however, was not interested in leaving politics. He wanted to return to Washington, DC, as a congressman from Washington State. Action for Washington, the group comprising his young allies back home, were urging him to run against Democrat Brock Adams for the Seventh District seat in Seattle. Fletcher had a grudge in this case; Adams had supported local construction unions in 1970 when he was trying to implement an affirmative action plan there. But the Seventh District was majority Democrat; although Fletcher had relocated his official residence to the city in 1970, few seriously thought he stood a chance against the popular four-term congressman. He also considered contesting the Fourth District seat, back in the tricity area, held by freshman Democrat Mike McCormack of Richland. This particular seat had previously been held by Republicans since 1943, and he could use his connections in the White House for assistance; the president was eager to help allies win seats in a hostile Congress.[7]

Fletcher also considered a Senate run. In an interview in December 1971 he claimed that he had been sent to the United Nations by Ehrlichman and Haldeman, with Nixon's blessing, to add international experience to his domestic accomplishments and position him for a 1974 challenge to Democratic senator Warren Magnuson of Washington. (They may have hinted as much to him to soften the blow of his being fired from the Department of Labor.) He had even "given some serious thought to going into the California

A 1969 photo with Richard M. Nixon in the Oval Office; note from Stanley Scott in top-right corner dated December 1971. Arthur Fletcher Personal Papers, courtesy Paul Fletcher.

or Wisconsin [1972 presidential] primaries, but not on the basis that I'm challenging President Nixon . . . simply using this as an opportunity to present my views" and "to help pave the way for white Americans to accept the idea of a Negro president or vice president." He noted that Black New York Democratic congresswoman Shirley Chisholm was similarly planning a demonstration presidential bid. As Fletcher explained to a reporter, "She's going to have a lot of votes on that first ballot, brother," adding that a bid of his own would remind Blacks that they had a voice in the GOP too.[8]

As in 1970, however, Fletcher's various campaign ideas were not to be. The smooth-talking Vernon Jordan gave Fletcher the hard sell and arranged for him to meet UNCF founder Frederick D. Patterson and board chairman Morris Abram, a civil rights attorney and former president of Brandeis University. They explained that this was a job that would take Fletcher all over the country; running the New York–based national office held second status to attending fund-raising events and cultivating political connections.

Comfortably ensconced with Bernyce at Plaza 50, the stroll to the "Building for Equal Opportunity" that the UNCF shared with the Urban League at 55 East 52nd Street was, if anything, an even shorter commute than that to the UN. Fletcher accepted the job, telling Nixon that it was "one of the most influential national leadership positions in the Black community."[9]

Nixon sent Fletcher off well, becoming the first US president to write a personal check to the UNCF. Presidential advisor Stanley Scott, now the highest-ranking Black in the government, gave him a picture of Nixon shaking hands with Fletcher in the Oval Office, with a note scrawled across the top: "To Art, A great guy to have on any team—To your credit, we'll miss you more than you'll miss us—Best Personal regards, Stan Scott, The White House, Dec. 1971."[10]

Fletcher hit the ground running at UNCF, delivering fund-raising speeches in Atlanta, Omaha, and Philadelphia in his first two months alone. The ex–football player liked to be physically active, and the UNCF schedule, unlike the UN schedule, didn't usually require attendance at more than one cocktail party or dinner per night.

He announced an unprecedented fund-raising goal of $50 million by 1975, with a 1972 goal of $12.5 million, an increase of nearly $3 million over 1971. This was not chump change. The UNCF raised funds to help mostly first-generation African American college students pay their tuition and associated costs, and in doing so assisted the historically Black colleges and universities in their quest to remain relevant and fiscally viable in the post–Jim Crow era, when the most academically talented Black youngsters were expected to attend the newly integrated formerly all-white schools throughout the South. The amount Fletcher proposed was indeed unprecedented: if realized, it represented nearly a third of all donations since the UNCF's 1944 founding (which then totaled $120 million).[11]

On March 13, 1972, the UNCF announced its new advertising slogan, "A mind is a terrible thing to waste," which brought the UNCF into newspapers and televisions for the first time and made the organization a household name. The slogan had been in the works for several months. At the end of Vernon Jordan's tenure, the organization had become a client of the non-profit Advertising Council, which developed public service announcements and had helped UNCF secure the pro bono assistance of the prestigious advertising firm Young & Rubicam, who tasked account executive Forest Long with developing a slogan. When Fletcher assumed his post at UNCF, development of the slogan was in its final stages. As Fletcher recounted,

Within less than 30 days [of starting work at UNCF], I was called over to the offices of Young and Rubicam. . . . Once there, I was shown a copy of the ad they wanted me to sign off on. It said, "A mind is a hell of a thing to waste." My immediate reaction was "That won't fly." Why? Because at the time [the UNCF schools were] sponsored by various African-American Christian religious denominations. . . . Therefore, I knew the word "hell" in an advertisement that was supposed to promote black education would be totally unacceptable. . . . We tossed around a host of words . . . *awful, sad, horrible, stupid, pity,* etc., [and] finally settled on the word *terrible,* and went with it.

Young & Rubicam was ready to launch the slogan, the Ad Council needed Fletcher to start a public campaign explaining it, and Fletcher, as he remembered it, didn't have the time to soothe potential tensions among board members. "I said, you know, 'You all appointed me to be the Executive Director. The clock is running,' so I didn't do all that internal campaigning." He filmed the first television commercial ads that summer, and the slogan took off.[12]

With the launch of the new slogan, Fletcher became comfortable and confident in his position at UNCF and decided to permanently relocate to the New York area. He and Bernyce began looking at houses in suburban New Jersey, but they found racial segregation as oppressive there as anywhere else. Realtor Ted Brunson found them a spacious three-bedroom Dutch Colonial in the leafy suburb of Rutherford, but noted, "I don't know if I have done you any justice by inquiring into this house. I am well known in the town as a human rights activist and as a black man the price may have gone up." That summer the Fletchers signed a three-year lease on a new apartment in Lincoln Plaza, on the Upper West Side between Central Park and Lincoln Center—no less fashionable than their prior digs at Plaza 50, and still a comfortable twenty-minute walk from the UNCF office. And Fletcher sought and won election to the steering committee of the National Urban Coalition, a civil rights organization based in New York.[13]

Fletcher continued traveling and raising money for the UNCF that spring, calling its member colleges "a vital and indispensable national resource." He spoke in Raleigh and Cincinnati; keynoted the "A mind is a terrible thing to waste" campaign kickoff in Princeton; and was the main speaker at a fund-raising event in San Antonio. He gave the commencement speech at Kent State University, two years after the deadly shooting of student protestors there by members of the National Guard. "Minorities and women will not be excluded nor limited," he said. "Your generation should see to it that no stone is left unturned in sharing these job opportunities for those who were left out in the decades of the 50s and 60s." He also wrote a successful $95,000 grant from the Luce Foundation for management training for the UNCF staff.[14]

In the summer Fletcher secured a $2 million gift from a Richmond businessman for UNCF member institution Virginia Union University, "described as the largest single contribution ever presented" to the school. At a New Orleans convention of the Links, a charitable organization led by Black women, Fletcher accepted their check for $68,000 for the UNCF. He announced the "1–10–75" program, whereby one million Blacks would each pledge $10 a year through 1975, adding that the nation needed to get beyond "first nigger syndrome"—in other words, to get beyond the first Black person to hold a particular job. At the Republican Party's quadrennial convention, where Richard Nixon was nominated for a second term as president, Fletcher convinced the RNC platform committee to adopt a plank supporting historically Black educational institutions. In the fall Fletcher gave speeches for UNCF in Kansas City, San Francisco, and St. Louis, and in the winter he spoke in Oklahoma City and Miami. The total amount raised in 1972, one reporter noted, was $11.2 million, which didn't quite meet the $12.5 million goal, but still represented "an increase of nearly $2 million over the previous year."[15]

And then they fired him. Board chairman Morris Abram requested his resignation effective no later than March 1, 1973, offering a severance package of three months' salary.[16]

Available sources point to several possible reasons for Fletcher's being asked to leave UNCF. While he was raising unprecedented funds, Fletcher had remained active in Republican politics. Nixon had appointed him to chair a committee of the White House Domestic Policy Council in 1971, and he agreed to stay on after his resignation from the government so that he could lead an economic discrimination study. This alone should not have presented a problem, as Fletcher's job at UNCF was only helped by continued access to powerful people in the government. He stated bluntly that he wished to leverage his experience in contract compliance at the Department of Labor to push defense contractors, all of whom now needed to meet the affirmative action standards he had enforced, to make UNCF a priority recipient of their donations. Further, the nature of the work helped Fletcher maintain connections with people working on the root problems of continued discrimination in the United States—problems for which UNCF and its member colleges were part of the solution. Fletcher had made this clear to the board when they offered him the job.[17]

But there was more. At the Republican National Convention, Fletcher circulated a flyer petitioning for his election to chair the party's national committee. This full-time job, which ultimately went to his friend, George Bush, would have resulted in his resignation from the UNCF; a former director of UNCF predicted that Fletcher would "leave soon to return to his first love, Republican politics." However, the notion that Fletcher could win the chairmanship in 1972 was preposterous, and he surely knew it. Serious contenders for that position typically lobby behind closed doors rather than circulate flyers; when the party holds the White House, as it did in 1972, the president tends to make the pick. The purpose was publicity for Fletcher, which led to his greater success as chief fund-raiser for the UNCF. Fletcher's disregard for immediate advancement in the party was made even more clear the next month, when he and Vernon Jordan wrote simultaneous open letters to both major party presidential nominees challenging their campaigns to more directly address civil and economic equity for minorities. This was not the behavior of someone looking for another job in the Nixon administration but rather of someone doing his job for the UNCF. The import of writing simultaneously with Jordan was to unite their respective organizations (which shared office space in midtown Manhattan) in pushing Nixon and his opponent, Democrat George McGovern, to promise more on civil rights.[18]

Fletcher also headed the 1972 Washington state delegation to the nonpartisan National Black Political Convention in Gary, Indiana. The convention took the overall tone of African American sentiment of the day, typified by Jesse Jackson, Stokely Carmichael, and Andrew Young, all of whom were, to varying degrees, on Fletcher's political left. Fletcher's influence, however, was seen in resolutions championing self-help and entrepreneurship. Joined in Gary by former protégé John Wilks, Fletcher had supporters among Republican attendees like Curtis T. Perkins of the National Council of Afro-American Republicans, who urged the RNC to include more Blacks on committees at the Republican National Convention.[19] But this hardly distracted from his duties as UNCF executive director.

Fletcher's relationship with the forty college presidents whose institutions comprised the membership of the UNCF was always shaky. This would have been true with any new executive director, as the UNCF restricted individual colleges' fund-raising activities according to rules that the presidents themselves had created. Presidents, especially newer presidents, saw the executive director in New York as a meddler in what had become a college president's primary mission. Further, Fletcher's launch of the ad campaign without fully vetting the slogan with the presidents, along with these mostly southern Blacks seeing the westerner Fletcher as a cultural outsider, resulted in a distrust of him from the outset.[20]

Finally, there was his invitation to Vice President Spiro Agnew to deliver the keynote address at a UNCF dinner for business executives. Despite an early reputation as a moderate Republican and a supporter of Nelson Rockefeller for the presidential nomination in 1968, Agnew had quickly moved to the right to serve as President Nixon's political attack dog. By the spring of 1973, when Fletcher was fired from UNCF, Agnew was one of the most divisive men in American politics: 35 percent of Republicans supported the former Maryland governor for the 1976 presidential nomination, making him the front-runner; yet for Democrats he was increasingly a bête noire. For Fletcher, Agnew was the key to high-level fund-raising. His borderline racist public comments ("Negroes have historically been charged with running down neighborhoods"; "If you've seen one slum, you've seen them all") were less important to Fletcher than his connections to power and money. For the UNCF board of directors, however, the Agnew invitation was "the straw that apparently broke the camel's back." Several members threatened to resign unless the event was canceled and Fletcher sacked.[21]

It is possible that Fletcher's termination had nothing to do with the Agnew invitation or any of Fletcher's other political activities during his tenure at the UNCF. In her 2007 book *Envisioning Black Colleges: A History of the United Negro College Fund,* scholar Marybeth Gasman makes no mention of Fletcher in the text, referring only to an interim director who served between Vernon Jordan's departure and the hiring of Fletcher's successor, Christopher Edley:

> Upon arrival at the Fund in 1973, Edley "found chaos and inefficiency but moderate success in fund raising despite that." Edley had expected to find some of this based on the fact that the Fund had been led by an *interim director* for about a year [emphasis added]. Also, during an interview with [board chairman] Morris [Abram], Edley had asked about the status of the fund . . . and [Abram] had responded by saying, "Last year we raised ten million dollars. If you don't come, we probably will raise nine million dollars."

On the basis of these fund-raising figures, Edley's interview with Abram appears to have occurred in late 1971 or early 1972, at least a year before

Fletcher was fired, and before Fletcher had defied these expectations and raised more than $11 million.[22]

Additional evidence points to Abram and Jordan having actively courted Edley before Fletcher's initial hiring. Gasman notes that they took Edley, "the candidate of choice to succeed Jordan . . . to an intimate dinner" at which they discussed his "thoughts about Black colleges, and about the United Negro College Fund"; when Edley stated that he wouldn't leave his current post at the Ford Foundation, Abram called "McGeorge Bundy, the President of the Ford Foundation (and former Kennedy administration insider)" to arrange a two-year leave of absence. The machinations between UNCF and the Ford Foundation to obtain Edley's services may account for Fletcher's fourteen-month tenure at UNCF; it is entirely possible that Jordan, Abram, and Patterson, waiting for Edley, hired Fletcher with the express purpose of firing him as soon as Edley was ready to take the job.[23]

However possible these scenarios, the reality is that after the launch of the new ad campaign, Fletcher was no longer the right man to lead UNCF. As a result of the UNCF becoming a household name, the average dona-tion size was decreasing even as the total amount collected increased; in other words, the ad campaign was bringing in a significant amount of small donors, whereas previous gifts had mainly been from major givers like the Rockefeller Fund. Appealing to large donors remained important, but UNCF needed an operations overhaul, and Fletcher was not prepared to do this. He was a dynamic speaker and a politician with high-level political and corporate connections, but he was not a detail-oriented manager capable of overhauling a nationwide organizational system for soliciting and pro-cessing small gifts. In his previous managerial jobs, at Labor and the East Pasco Self-Help Cooperative, he had been the ideas man, leaving the details to others. He had received dozens of small donations during his campaign for lieutenant governor of Washington State, but it was John Haydon and the rest of Ludlow Kramer's organization who had collected the checks and sent the acknowledgments. Chris Edley was less flamboyant and less polit-ically connected, but he was more capable, thanks to his decade at the Ford Foundation, of instituting the top-down reform necessary for converting the UNCF into a modern fund-raising organization.[24]

Fletcher acknowledged the authority of Abram and the board to fire him but registered his dissatisfaction with their proposed termination settle-ment. It was simply insufficient under the circumstances. He had, as he saw it, been fired for strictly political reasons, which the board all but acknowl-edged, and given Fletcher's public statements and well-known political loyalties before taking the job, he viewed the action as patently unfair. The board had known Fletcher's status as a loyal Republican and had hired him anyway—to demonstrably good effect, Fletcher pointed out: he had presided over the single largest fund-raising year in the history of the organization, and with Nixon's reelection, Fletcher's high-level political contacts promised continued growth. Further, Fletcher had taken a risk with the job. Expecting to lead the UNCF for the foreseeable future, he had secured a three-year lease on his new Lincoln Square apartment—not an inexpensive location— that he was now obligated to pay despite his lack of New York employment. And while his talented predecessor Vernon Jordan had left UNCF for the better visibility, higher profile, and solid civil rights leadership post as head of the NUL, Fletcher had expressed every intention of staying. One columnist even expressed sorrow for Fletcher's successor, noting that the job was not an easy one to keep: "I am sorry Chris Edley agreed to accept this hot potato of a job. I'm afraid it will burn his fingers good."[25]

In public, however, Fletcher was gracious. His resignation letter, addressed to the board, college presidents, and national staff, promised to "continue to support the Fund, its mission, both spiritually and financially, and . . . your cause with all of the energy I can muster." He called Edley "a trusted, personal friend, one I hold with high regard and esteem. Both his character and his professional credentials are outstanding, to say the least. . . . It is my opinion that he could be the best director the Fund has ever elected." The letter earned him praise from numerous member college presidents (more than he had received during his tenure), as well as a number of private individuals, including Kenneth Clark, the influential African American child psychologist who had contributed crucial testimony to the *Brown v. Board* case. Perhaps as a result of this outpouring of support, Abram offered a more substantial severance package: six months' salary and benefits.[26]

Fletcher, as he later put it, "quietly slipped out the side door and opened my business [Arthur Fletcher & Associates] and became a . . . labor standards consultant to 20 of the top Fortune 500 companies." He gave an initial workshop on affirmative action requirements for General Electric at their Crotonville Institute in New York, and apparently he was a hit: "GE then decided . . . that I should fly to five different cities, and they would bring in people that sold them products . . . and run workshops for them. So I went to Minneapolis and went to Chicago, Cincinnati, Denver, and a couple of others." More work quickly followed. He delivered presentations to Mutual of Omaha; Sears, Roebuck and Company; and US Steel. After that, "I got on the college circuit . . . 42 different campuses across the country." His bottom-line message: "Affirmative Action is here to stay."[27]

Fletcher also returned to paid political work. He and Bernyce moved back to Washington, DC, where his friend, George Bush, now chairman of the RNC, gave him a job focusing on—what else?—minority outreach. Fletcher, whom Bush called "the most articulate Black spokesman in America," replaced another Kansas Black, Edwin T. Sexton Jr., who moved over to the Office of Minority Business Enterprise (which had been based on a program Fletcher had developed for John Ehrlichman back in December 1968). Fletcher drafted a speech for President Nixon to deliver at a meeting of the National Academy of Engineers, and shortly thereafter he assumed duties not dissimilar to those he had undertaken for UNCF: delivering speeches. Ultimately the goal was less about drumming up Black votes for Republican candidates and more about inspiring people to donate money to what Fletcher portrayed, either falsely or naively, as a Republican Party committed to racial egalitarianism.[28]

Interestingly, after his years with the Nixon administration, Fletcher had earned the grudging support of one of his early critics there, while more natural allies now expressed concerns. White House operative Ehrlichman, who had rejected Fletcher in 1968 only to be overruled by the president-elect, now expressed confidence that Fletcher would be a good fit with Bush at the RNC. On the other hand, Nixon's Black advisors, Robert Brown and his replacement, Stanley Scott, disagreed. Presidential advisor Larry Higby relayed their concerns: "Fletcher is somewhat of a maverick . . . undoubt-edly an effective spokesman, and is a team player most of the time . . . an excellent choice, if he can be controlled by Bush. I question whether George can do this." Fletcher was indeed "a team player most of the time," and this phrase would encapsulate his relationship with the Republican Party for the next two decades. Higby's concern that Bush could not control Fletcher proved prescient decades later. But for now, the White House approved the appointment, and Fletcher held the job until Bush left the RNC to become ambassador to China in September 1974.[29]

Side Projects

It was while Fletcher was working for Bush at the RNC that he published *The Silent Sell-Out: Government Betrayal of Blacks to the Craft Unions.* The book was a brief history of the government's battle to secure equal employment opportunity from Fletcher's perspective. He started writing it during the spring of 1971, when he was still at the Department of Labor, and completed the draft manuscript in the spring of 1972 while at the UNCF. Hastily written and poorly edited, it was, like so many of Fletcher's activities after leaving the Nixon administration, an attempt to keep himself in the national spotlight. In it he displayed what he had learned about how the federal government worked. He faulted the civil rights leadership for not putting pressure on government to ensure proper enforcement of Title VII of the Civil Rights Act of 1964, in essence accusing them of resting on their laurels after the signing ceremony. At some level this was fair, in that the leaders of the NAACP, NUL, Congress of Racial Equality (CORE), and Southern Christian Leadership Conference were initially charmed by President Johnson into thinking that the law itself was the accomplishment (which for Johnson it was).

His arguments broke down in their naked partisanship. Rather than attempt to remain objective, Fletcher began with the conclusion that the Johnson administration had failed to enforce Title VII but that under Nixon, and in particular under his own supervision of the Office of Federal Contract Compliance (OFCC), the real, honest hard work began. This resulted in a contortion of facts.

First, in chapter 6, "The Silent Sell-Out: The Failures of 1967–1968," Fletcher described what he called "the dreary story of inept inaction which characterized most of the period of 1967–1968." The Department of Justice, which had "the power to sue in federal court to eliminate patterns and practices of employment discrimination . . . filed [its first case under Title VII] in February 1966, eight months after the law became effective, but 20 months after it had been passed." The members of the EEOC were not appointed until ten months after the act was passed, giving them "less than two months to prepare to enforce the statute. . . . The result was a rush job, and the agency was not able to cope effectively with the masses of complaints which poured in. . . . Rather than giving the complainant the key to the court house door, the Commission directed the complainant on a long tour before he went to court." Fletcher reserved his harshest assessment for the Johnson-era OFCC, the agency that he later controlled: it "did not effectively supervise the various purchasing agencies, and . . . was unable to . . . control the actions of the major employers," he wrote. "The OFCC floundered inconclusively, developing different programs in several cities, but implementing none of them in a systematic, orderly way. There was simply a series of improvised approaches to community pressures, each of which was labeled a 'plan' with the name of the city attached."[30]

That these statements were purely partisan was evident from Fletcher's own words. While he decried the EEOC as having been unable "to cope effectively with the masses of complaints which poured in," he nevertheless noted,

> The EEOC did adopt some very advanced approaches . . . the concept that the complainant had to agree before a settlement could be reached . . . the concept of a written agreement which specifically altered discriminatory systems . . . written decisions as to whether there was reasonable cause to believe an employer or union was discriminating. This . . . helped to lay the foundation for a broad definition of discrimination . . . which has now been adopted by the Supreme Court . . . EEOC developed and implemented the reporting requirements which [made] programs such as the Philadelphia Plan possible. This is an impressive list of conceptual accomplishments.[31]

Fletcher was describing an EEOC that worked hard to combat employment discrimination, making his attack on their complaint backlog a non sequitur.

It would be surprising if after his tenure at Labor he was truly unaware of the limitations of his arguments as regards the Department of Justice. When he stated that Justice filed its first pattern or practice lawsuit "eight months after the law became effective," he was referring to a St. Louis case which OFCC officials spent months developing before handing over to the attorney general only after union intransigence became clear. Comprehensive lawsuits such as these often took many months to develop—as Fletcher well knew from his experience trying to integrate the building trades in Seattle. The result in St. Louis, Fletcher surely recalled, was a decisive victory.[32]

His statement that "the OFCC from 1965 through 1968 had all the powers to be an effective regulatory agency, but did not use them" was likewise not borne out by evidence of which he was certainly aware. On May 18, 1967, OFCC stopped the flow of 48 million federal dollars, shutting down every federally funded or federally assisted construction project in Cleveland, and ultimately forcing all construction contractors there to show how they were resolving discrimination at their work sites. Calling this but one of "a series of improvised approaches . . . each of which was labeled a 'plan' . . . so vague and indefinite, that they did not succeed in influencing the course of discrimination in the trades" left out the obvious point that these "improvised approaches" taught the bureaucrats in the Department of Labor how to handle the various stalling tactics of the contractors and the unions, and also how to deal with the intransigence of federal contracting agencies. These "vague and indefinite" plans had culminated in the original Philadelphia Plan, issued before Nixon's election and Fletcher's appointment.[33]

In chapter 7, "The Construction Industry, 1969–1971," Fletcher painted a picture of successes under his own leadership in juxtaposition to the failures of the previous administration. Here he told the story of the Revised Philadelphia Plan, its opposition by the comptroller general, the fight in Congress, and the contractors' failed lawsuit. He portrayed clear heroes and villains, and indeed his nonacademic writing style made the story perhaps more thrilling than the current author's own treatments of the subject.[34]

Two of Fletcher's heroes were unlikely in retrospect: Nixon, whose actual motivation was not equal employment opportunity but political Machiavellianism; and Attorney General John Mitchell, who was simultaneously engaged in the sort of nefarious deeds that culminated in the Watergate burglary. Fletcher depicted Nixon as everything his predecessor in the Oval Office was not: he "publicly and privately placed his political weight against the [Byrd] rider, and began to round up votes in the Senate to kill it. This was . . . unprecedented for President Johnson had never intervened to help an agency trying to enforce these laws." Aside from the fact that Johnson used his legislative skills to push through the civil rights legislation in the first place, Fletcher took it on face value that Nixon was genuinely in favor of the Philadelphia Plan for nonpolitical reasons. But this was belied by his own words on the next page: "The civil rights movement in the Legislature has long been spearheaded by the 'leadership conference,' a loose coalition of liberal, labor and civil rights groups, which . . . was shattered by the debate on the rider to kill the Philadelphia Plan." Fletcher was inadvertently explaining Nixon's political motivations behind his support of the plan. As for John Mitchell, according to Fletcher, he "rose to the challenge and came to the Labor Department for a widely publicized press conference . . . determined to support the equal employment program . . . because he believed in it." Thanks to Mitchell's intervention, "the roadblock raised by the Comptroller to the Philadelphia Plan was effectively pushed aside." In fact Mitchell vigorously supported the plan only because it served the political interests of the president.[35]

Other heroes in Fletcher's version of the story made more sense. These included the solicitor of labor, Laurence Silberman, who argued "that the Philadelphia Plan was legal and did not violate the 'no quota' provisions" of Title VII; the OFCC Philadelphia area coordinator, "who was largely responsible for [the Philadelphia Plan's] creation"; and Alfred Blumrosen, who "produced the concept which made it possible to develop the national plan."[36]

But no greater hero emerged in these pages than Fletcher himself. His most heroic moment, however, was not in connection with his order that the Revised Philadelphia Plan be implemented in June 1969, nor his efforts to defend it the following winter, nor in its implementation in 1970. Rather, it was the September 1969 hearings in Chicago. "Waves of violence swept construction sites in the city," he wrote accurately. "Workers carried pistols in their lunch boxes. . . . We faced the elementary forces of life, racism and fear of loss of jobs. . . . The FBI had picked up a rumor of the threat of physical violence."[37]

The real sellout, as we have seen, was Nixon's disavowal of the Philadelphia Plan in favor of the hard hats, Fletcher's transfer from executive authority, and the appointment of Peter Brennan as secretary of labor. But Fletcher didn't see it that way. "In the summer of 1971, I felt that I had brought the OFCC to the brink of effectiveness. At that point, the President suggested that I should move to a larger stage—the United Nations. From there, I believed I might get into another position from which I could see more of my ideas through to fruition."[38]

Why did Fletcher write such a slanted and blatantly partisan account of the battle for equal employment opportunity? The easy answer—to encourage more African Americans to support candidates of his party, his role at the RNC at the time of the book's publication—was only part of it. He also sought to play up his own role in the origins of affirmative action. By downplaying, even dismissing, the activities of the OFCC and other government entities before his own involvement, Fletcher was making the case that real progress on civil rights came only—if surprisingly—from a Republican administration for whom a minuscule number of African Americans had voted. The result was an account that was easily dismissed for its partisanship and thereby failed to serve its purpose, which was to play up Fletcher's role.

This was unfortunate, because Fletcher actually was a hero in the struggle for equal employment opportunity. If he had not embellished his own role, and if he had acknowledged the positive developments of the years that preceded his appointment and the politics that resulted in his removal, the book would have made the recollections of his heroism far more believable. This paradoxically would have better served the purpose of recruiting more Black Republicans, as he might have received his just accolades from both sides of the political aisle, better setting himself up as a positive Republican role model. The book might have also attracted the attention of a more mainstream publisher than the Third Press, with better editing and promotional resources, compounding its importance and better positioning Fletcher for future opportunities with national civil rights organizations. Furthermore, had it not been so overtly partisan, he might not have been taken for granted by his fellow Republicans in the following decades, perhaps eventually resulting in a cabinet-level appointment.

But we should not be too hard on Fletcher. When he published *The Silent Sell-Out* he was holding on to his position of influence by his fingernails. If not for his friendship with Bush he would not have had any political position at all. It was also still too early for Nixon to be safely criticized from within the party, as the administration was not yet consumed by the Watergate scandal. Had Fletcher published a critical book, a spiteful—and still powerful—Nixon might have ordered Bush to fire him from the RNC. Had he waited just a few months, he not only would have been safe denouncing the president but would even have had Bush's support in doing so: the chairman wrote the president on August 4, 1974, recommending that he resign in the face of impeachment over the Watergate cover-up. "I believe this view is held by most Republican leaders across the country," Bush told Nixon. The president resigned the next day. Bush and Fletcher learned the news while meeting with Thomas Kleppe, the head of the Small Business Administration (SBA).[39]

Fletcher also found time during his stint at the RNC for a more personal pursuit. In 1974 he established the Society for Victorious Living (SVL), incorporated as a nonprofit in the District of Columbia. The "chief objective of the society," Fletcher later wrote, "is that of raising monies to establish a . . . scholarship and financial aid fund." Having obtained a license to preach in Pasco from the Southern Baptist Church, Fletcher had been further impressed by the work of the UNCF; indeed, he later wrote that his year with UNCF "was the most enjoyable year of my life." The SVL combined his spirituality with his newly discovered love of fund-raising. "Irrespective of sex, race, color, national origin, or religion," Fletcher wrote, students would "achieve a higher level of God-consciousness and . . . develop their inborn potentials into . . . professional abilities so they can care for themselves and help God manage the universe." In short, the SVL was an institution for the promotion of religion, education, and civil rights, which Fletcher hoped would keep him in the forefront of the civil rights movement.[40]

Fletcher's renewed focus on spiritual matters was prompted by a new tragedy in his personal life. His oldest son, Arthur Jr., died in early 1974 from complications resulting from Hodgkin's disease. The young Arthur's reputation as a jazz musician had blossomed in Berkeley during the late 1960s, and he had a brief, exciting career in the European jazz scene cut short by his diagnosis in January 1970 while on tour in Denmark. He was fortunate to have a father so highly placed in public service; the labor attaché to the US embassy in Copenhagen arranged for him to be flown back to the United States for treatment. He was in and out of hospitals for the remainder of his life, continually benefiting from his father's influence. In 1972 a UNCF donor advanced the funds for surgery. After Art Jr.'s death at the heartbreaking age of twenty-seven, Chairman Bush—who himself knew the pain of the loss of a child—called for a moment of silence at the April 1974 RNC meeting.[41]

As part of his work at the SVL, Fletcher developed the Victorious Living Creed, a series of eight spiritually uplifting tenets, each building on the logic and faith of the last. Each tenet of the creed begins with the statement, "I believe my living will not be in vain." This speaks to Fletcher's deep, driving fear that his life would be without consequence or meaning, that he would not be remembered. It was this fear (among other factors) that drove him to his successes and caused him to pursue public service. This fear was rooted in his early childhood and his ancestry.

Arthur Fletcher was not born Arthur Fletcher, as we know; he never knew his birth father, Samuel Brit Allen. That man may have lived a long or a short life; he may have been rich or poor, educated or not. Fletcher never knew more about his birth father than he did his African ancestors. But even the relatives whom he did know seemed to die in obscurity, mainly because of the pervasive racism that sought to diminish and erase the achievements of African Americans. His mother wanted to teach; instead she cleaned houses, and as far as Fletcher was concerned, her various employers never really knew her and didn't remember her; she was expendable. This had instilled in Fletcher a desperate desire to leave a record of his existence. To some extent all of his exploits on the gridiron and in government stemmed from this drive.[42]

The first two tenets of the creed, "I believe my living will not be in vain because I am convinced I am made in God's image and that his power dwells within me," and "I am convinced that there is a God and I trust in his love, justice and mercy," make clear Fletcher's belief that he was made in the image of a loving, just, powerful, and merciful god. At the same time as he was acknowledging his fear, Fletcher envisioned a method for overcoming it. With a god's omnipotence, a man can do anything, but when tempered with a sense of "love, justice and mercy," such a man will use his power for good. Rather than finding motivation in resentment and revenge for the evils perpetrated on his people by the racist society, Fletcher sought to love and treat with mercy his enemies—unreconstructed southerners and other racists—but he never forgot the importance of justice. When he found himself in a position of power, he became a tough advocate for equal opportunity.[43]

The third tenet, "God put me here to be his servant and I am to be an instrument of his will during my sojourn on earth," is the most problematic of the creed. Major organized religions like the Catholic Church imposed their official interpretations of god's will on their adherents, keeping personal visions in check. With the advent of Protestantism, the relationship with the deity no longer required the interpolation of an officiant, stunting the hierarchy's dominance. But this tenet is redeemed in the context of Fletcher's vision of God as loving, just, and merciful. Not seeing his god as vengeful, Fletcher sought reconciliation—in other words, he would "be an instrument of his will" for love and justice rather than revenge. Antagonists decried affirmative action as vengeful, but he didn't see it that way. The Philadelphia Plan required 'that Blacks be considered for union membership and employment on an equal basis, rather than give them an unfair advantage.

The fourth, fifth, sixth, and seventh tenets of the creed offer a prescription, based again on Fletcher's own experiences, for developing and building on one's natural talents to the betterment of self, family, and society. The fourth tenet reads, "God provided me with one or more gifts and talents, and that with my own efforts and his help, plus the aid of education and training, I can develop my gifts and talents into skills, technical or professional abilities and be rendered able to do some of the world's work," referring to Fletcher's athletic and political abilities. The fifth tenet, "If I try, God will help me find ways to use my skills, technical or professional ability in service to his cause," posits that talent and training are insufficient without great effort. In California, after Mary's suicide, Fletcher had already seen how far he could go on the basis of talent and training alone. Faced with the disintegration of his family, his life and faith were shaken to the core. It was his effort campaigning for the school bond initiative and his subsequent assembly race that made possible the job offer to lead the Higher Horizons program in Washington State. Likewise, it was his hard work in Pasco that led to his successful city council bid, and his strenuous efforts on the campaign trail in 1968 led to his appointment to the Department of Labor. The sixth and seventh tenets, "In serving God's cause, I will be able to sustain my own life and be of benefit to mankind and humanity in the process" and "In serving God's cause and sustaining my own life and being of benefit to mankind and humanity, my deeds, private and public, will become building blocks out of which a victorious life is built," build on the developing momentum of the creed. "God's cause," for Fletcher, was to use his talents and skills, nurtured by training and made potent by effort, to serve the betterment of mankind. Here we see the transformation wrought by the tragedy of Mary's death in stark relief. Fletcher's first foray into politics, back in Kansas, had been devoted to his own financial enrichment; any benefit to his community was merely a happy by-product. But in 1961, with his career in ruins and his family falling apart, he flipped the script, making community his cause and financial gain the by-product. He resolved to use his political skills for the betterment of his fellow man and became a civil rights community organizer. For the remainder of his long life, Fletcher never forgot what it was like to be a single parent in that Berkeley ghetto. He maintained an impressive income for most years after that, but his goals were never again rooted in the desire for personal wealth but instead in his community. Indeed, as we have seen, he gave up more lucrative opportunities to run the East Pasco Self-Help Cooperative for a $1 salary.[44]

Finally, the eighth tenet of the creed, "By following this creed my life's work will be dedicated to God, and my lifestyle will become a light, a guide and example that my family, friends, acquaintances and others might use in fulfilling their destiny during their sojourn on earth," returns to his confrontation with his deepest fear that his life will have been in vain. Tying it all together as a raison d'être for the SVL, the creed represented Fletcher's highest aspirations for his own personal fulfillment and a self-help mantra for African Americans to take advantage of the new opportunities delivered by civil rights legislation.[45]

But the SVL sputtered as a serious fund-raising program. For one thing, the language Fletcher used in SVL literature was poorly chosen for fund-raising. "God-consciousness" and "help God manage the universe" were not phrases that typically appealed to nonsectarian educational donors; Fletcher's professional life, meanwhile, was secular, which did not appeal to evangelical Christian groups. As in his politics, Fletcher was basically stuck in the middle: he believed deeply in the role of faith in education, but he believed just as much in equal opportunity and so could never allow himself to favor one religious sect over another. The goal was equal education of the nation's youth: Protestant, Catholic, Jewish, or Muslim, the practice mattered less than the faith in a supreme being as provider of human potential. This meant that he could not successfully appeal for funding to any specific religious group. Further, the SVL competed with Fletcher's work as an affirmative action consultant, his eventual forays into federal contracting, and his continued political appointments and electoral attempts. Ultimately the SVL remained on Fletcher's back burner, often handled by his wife, Bernyce, when she wasn't otherwise occupied with her own professional endeavors.[46]

Fletcher and Ford

Vice President Spiro Agnew's October 10, 1973, resignation on charges of tax evasion had required that President Nixon invoke the recently ratified Twenty-Fifth Amendment to the Constitution and nominate a new vice president. With such a nomination requiring a majority vote in both houses of Congress, each of which were controlled by the loyal opposition and with whom the president had an antagonistic relationship (indeed, members of Congress were already laying the groundwork for his impeachment), Nixon needed a nominee who had the trust and respect of significant numbers of congressional Democrats. He settled on the House minority leader, Gerald R. Ford, whose years in Congress had earned him respect from his colleagues across the aisle.

On November 20, 1973, the House Judiciary Committee, considering the Ford nomination, called Arthur Fletcher to defend Ford's civil rights record in sworn testimony. Currently the RNC's director of minority outreach, Fletcher had just returned from a labor conference in England. He made two arguments. First, during the battle over the Philadelphia Plan in Congress, Ford's support had helped when it mattered: he had mustered Republican support in the House to recommit the Byrd rider to the Senate, resulting in its defeat. Second, in response to concerns about Ford's lackluster civil rights voting record (28 in favor, 26 opposed), Fletcher pointed out that Presidents Truman and Johnson had been forgiven earlier racist legislative activity on the understanding that they had to win elections in the South among a more racist constituency. He stated that settlement trends for rural southern migrant whites in Michigan had forced Ford to behave similarly in his northern state, and should warrant the same forgiveness. If this excuse worked for Democrats, he noted provocatively, it was good enough for Republicans too. Fletcher was careful to add that he didn't agree with the excuse in general, only that Republicans should get the same treatment as Democrats. Congress approved Ford's appointment as vice president the following month.[47]

Of course, Nixon and his advisors were by now consumed with covering up the notorious Watergate Hotel burglary of January 1972, wherein operatives of the Committee to Re-Elect the President had broken into the headquarters of the Democratic National Committee in order to plant listening devices and steal damaging information on potential Democratic nominees. While the president did not personally order the burglary, he had nurtured the atmosphere of win-at-all-costs lawbreaking from which it stemmed and had explicitly authorized an illegal cover-up. In the summer of 1974, facing impeachment, Nixon resigned. Gerald Ford, the nation's first unelected vice president, became the nation's first unelected president on August 9.

Within a day of Nixon's resignation, Fletcher's supporters began lobbying the new president to appoint him to a prominent post in the administration. In particular, Black Republicans were looking for Fletcher to be the first Republican cabinet-level African American. (Democrat Lyndon Johnson had appointed the first Black cabinet official, Robert C. Weaver, to head the new HUD in 1966.) "Now that Vice President Ford has become President, he has the opportunity to substantially clarify his administration's concern for all Americans by naming blacks to the top advisory level for the first time during our Republican regime," wrote Henry Lucas, a prominent Black dentist from San Francisco. "Needless to say Art Fletcher would be my first choice." From a Black accountant in Kansas City: "Just a note to urge you to support Art Fletcher's appointment as Counselor to the President . . . and in elevating that position to cabinet level. It will be difficult to find a man more qualified and knowledgeable." And an Oklahoma City pastor wrote, "Creating a cabinet-rank post of Black Counselor to the President would serve to franchise a minority and provide the faith in government needed to help carry this nation forward. We urge the consideration of Mr. Arthur Fletcher. . . . He is . . . qualified in international diplomacy, economics, labor and domestic affairs to provide the leadership . . . needed in that position."[48]

Fletcher received an endorsement from a prominent civil rights leader as well. Reverend Leon Sullivan of Philadelphia, the founder of the OIC, wrote Ford to say, "There are a number of Black Americans who might serve you well. . . . However . . . I want to especially note the unique roll [sic] that Mr. Arthur Fletcher has played as a Black Republican who relates effectively with the Black community on behalf of the philosophy . . . that is consistent with yours. I trust that you will give serious consideration to including him on your staff." The OIC national director, Chicago activist Maurice Dawkins, who had been one of the organizers of the 1963 March on Washington, added that "my deep and sincere concern for . . . your Administration . . . leads me to make a strong categorical recommendation. Mr. Arthur Fletcher

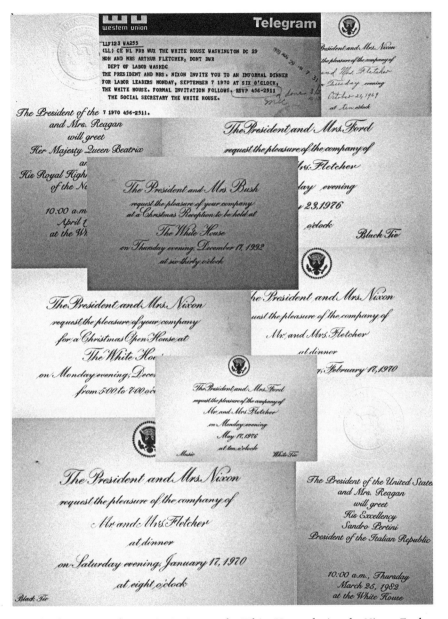

The Fletchers received many invitations to the White House during the Nixon, Ford, Reagan, and Bush administrations. Arthur Fletcher Personal Papers, courtesy Paul Fletcher.

undoubtedly would be outstanding as a 'Mr. Outside' working with Stanley Scott as a 'Mr. Inside.' The role of political leader visibly campaigning yet tied in close as part of your top strategy team fits Art like a glove."[49]

Fletcher's most prominent endorsements for a position in the Ford administration came from important inside sources. Referencing the recommendation of San Francisco dentist Henry Lucas, George Bush reached out to William Scranton, the former governor of Pennsylvania and now a member of the Ford transition team. "His suggestion regarding Black involvement and his suggestion regarding Art Fletcher have my full concurrence," Bush wrote. And an unknown White House political operative, possibly Dick Cheney (the memo was found in the Cheney Collection at the Ford Archive), the assistant chief of staff, called Fletcher an "Excellent and Loyal Black" while discussing various possible political appointees.[50]

Fletcher himself, who had likely orchestrated the recommendation letters to Ford and his team (although I could find no direct evidence of this), was quick to demonstrate to the new president how he could be of assistance. Sending Ford a newspaper article detailing wastefulness in the office of the postmaster general, Fletcher wrote, "Dear President Ford, This appears one day after your speech where you spoke of cutting down on 'Govt Spending.'"[51]

Fletcher also got a leg up from presidential advisor Stanley Scott, who brought him and other leaders representing "a cross-section of the Black community" into the White House to make a presentation to the president. He asked Fletcher to "bring with you a brief position paper on what you perceive to be the ten most pressing problems facing Blacks and the poor in this nation." At the meeting, Ford asked Fletcher to follow up with him later on an issue pertaining to minority education, and Fletcher gladly complied. Then, at Ford's invitation, Fletcher participated in a White House think tank on extending economic opportunities to members of minority groups. Ford also appointed Fletcher to the President's Commission on Personnel Interchange, which facilitated transfers of executives between government and private-sector work, and in that capacity Fletcher was able to make some hiring recommendations of his own.[52]

Ultimately, however, the politics of appointing top-level African Americans in a Republican administration were the politics of tokenism, and after naming William T. Coleman as secretary of the Department of Transportation (the second Black cabinet member in history), Ford was disinclined to name another Black to a senior appointment. "Your name has come highly recommended to me from several sources," wrote the special assistant to the president, David J. Wimer. "However, the government job situation is very tight at present, and I am not currently aware of an appropriate opening for you." When Bush headed off to China, Fletcher left the RNC and focused full time on his consulting business, Arthur Fletcher & Associates, and registered with the SBA, where he sought protected status as a minority-owned company.

To stay close to the action, he purchased a townhouse on G Street Southwest in the District of Columbia. He and Bernyce kept their suburban home in Columbia, Maryland, which they had bought in 1969, but the G Street location was less than a ten-minute walk from several federal offices. It was also not far from the Channel Inn, a popular watering hole for Black politicians and government workers. Fletcher often entertained clients there and spent evenings at the bar keeping tabs on government happenings.[53]

Fletcher's allies kept up the pressure, working to ensure that when Stanley Scott left the White House in late 1975, Fletcher got that job. Leon Sullivan told Ford that with "the crisis that our nation faces . . . as regards race relations in America [the] judgement and experience of a man like Mr. Arthur Fletcher could prove most valuable" and sent a more detailed note to the White House chief of staff, Donald Rumsfeld, expressing his "deep concern that a strong man like Fletcher be chosen [for] maximum effectiveness in communicating . . . the genuine and sincere efforts of President Ford to solve the problems of all Americans. . . . Mr. Fletcher has demonstrated his ability to do just that." Forecasting that Republicans could be competitive for the Black vote in the next presidential election, Sullivan added, "His role would be regarded . . . as one of the most important ones in the critical days leading to November 1976."[54]

Arthur Fletcher was similar to Gerald Ford in a number of ways. Both were midwesterners from medium-size cities: Ford hailed from Grand Rapids, Michigan, a town not unlike Junction City, Kansas. Both were college athletes: Ford was a star football player for the University of Michigan. Both were coaches: Ford at Yale while in graduate school. Like most men of their generation, both served in World War II, Ford in the navy in the Pacific. And unlike most men of their generation, both pursued political careers: Ford, a lawyer, mounted a successful insurgency against Frank D. McKay, the Republican powerhouse of Grand Rapids, entering the United States Congress. Both men were charismatic and ambitious, but not of the presidency: Ford's aspiration was to be Speaker of the House, while Fletcher knew that for most of his lifetime, Black men "need not apply" for the highest office in the land. Yet both men ran for president.[55]

Fletcher and Ford also had similar political views. Ford considered himself a "midwestern conservative," which presidential historian Douglas Brinkley has defined as open to government spending on domestic programs that make clear "How much will it cost? What does it do? How does it help?" This was a temperate fiscal conservatism in opposition to the antigovernment ethos represented by former California governor Ronald Reagan. For Ford and Fletcher, an abundance of caution moderated—but did not eliminate—an instinct to use government for positive social change. One example of this in practice was Ford's response to New York City's fiscal crisis. The president initially balked at bailing out the city, but he ultimately approved loan guarantees when city leaders demonstrated that they had a solid plan for recovery.[56]

There is also evidence for the portrayal of Ford as a champion of civil rights from within the system, not unlike Fletcher. As House Republican leader during the 1960s, Ford actively opposed recruiting segregationist southern Democrats into the Republican Party. "We must firmly resist," he declared, "the takeover of our party by any elements that are not interested in building a party, but only in advancing their own narrow views."[57]

But the similarities between Ford and Fletcher ended when it came to how the government could promote civil rights. For Fletcher, ending racial discrimination represented a priority on par with national defense, and he saw the robust enforcement of federal civil rights regulations as an absolute necessity. His views on the matter were tied to his patriotism: as far as Fletcher was concerned, the failure of the United States to fully utilize the potential of its population by discriminating in housing, education, and employment opportunities for African Americans left America weaker and more vulnerable to its Cold War antagonists. Fletcher certainly favored self-help programs over what he saw as government handouts, but only a massive government response could end the problems caused by racism. Ford, on the other hand, was a gradualist on civil rights, seeing it as one of many domestic problems, its programs requiring a more thorough review before implementation and enforcement. He preferred public relations approaches with negligible government costs, like the observance of Black History Month, which he made an official national tradition in February 1976.[58]

Having resolved to win election to the presidency in his own right, Ford faced a series of difficult choices. He had enjoyed a brief honeymoon after taking the oath of office, one largely based on his unassuming personality and clear differences from the man he had replaced. He gained additional popularity with his choice of former New York governor Nelson Rockefeller to succeed him as the nation's second unelected vice president, but the

Vice President Nelson Rockefeller speaking at Fletcher's swearing-in ceremony, February 1976. Bernyce Fletcher accompanies her husband; longtime ally John Wilks is seated on right. Arthur Fletcher Personal Papers, courtesy Paul Fletcher.

honeymoon ended with his granting of a "full, free, and absolute pardon unto Richard Nixon for all offenses against the United States." Many in the press and public suspected collusion (although historians have largely borne out Ford's explanation that a Nixon trial would distract the nation from the major problems still to be tackled, among them fighting inflation and ending the war in Vietnam). Ford's electability continued to suffer as he developed a reputation as President Klutz—falling on the ski slopes, injuring himself swimming, bumping his head repeatedly on his helicopter door, and tripping while exiting Air Force One.[59]

Normally a sitting president is a shoo-in for his party's nomination, but Ford's position was shaky. His fluctuating popularity, coupled with his unelected status—after a career in the House of Representatives he had never won a statewide vote—made him ripe for a credible primary challenge from the party's right wing. As Reagan mulled such a challenge, Ford made ineffective stabs at winning over that constituency, vetoing a school lunch bill and a prounion picketing bill, and forcing Rockefeller to withdraw from consideration for the vice presidential nomination.[60]

The hiring of Fletcher was not a strategic move in response to the conservative challenge. When it came to personnel, Ford's strategy meant dumping Rockefeller, not hiring an African American moderate. There is also no indication that the decision to hire Fletcher was in any way based on forward thinking as regards the general election: the Democratic front-runners in December 1975 did not include the eventual winner, former Georgia governor Jimmy Carter; the civil rights credentials of the main contenders at the time—Scoop Jackson, Walter Mondale, Lloyd Bentsen, Mo Udall, and of course Ted Kennedy—were sufficiently strong enough to render the possibility of a Republican challenge to the African American vote virtually moot. Rather, the appointment appears to have been simply an expedient replacement for the departing Stanley Scott.[61]

On January 29, 1976, Ford commissioned Fletcher as his deputy assistant for urban affairs. (Press Secretary Ron Nessen, making the announcement, stressed disingenuously that "urban" was not a synonym for "Black.") Fletcher's immediate supervisor was presidential advisor James Cannon, and he became a member of the Domestic Policy Council. Vice President Rockefeller administered the oath of office, and the Council of 100 Black Republicans, a Washington lobbying group, held a reception for Fletcher at the Capitol. Fletcher met with the president, Cannon, and White House chief of staff Dick Cheney to discuss his role in the administration, and he got to work advising the president on urban affairs.[62]

Fletcher drafted a mission statement for his job, stating that his five objectives were

1. To advise President Ford with reference to urban policies and programs all for the purpose of helping him succeed as the Nation's Chief Executive.
2. To help the President turn his State of the Union Message into an action program.
3. To help the President implement the policies and program called for in his State of the Union and Budget Message as well as his promise to live within the budget.
4. To do those things necessary and essential to winning public approval and support for the President's policies and programs.
5. To help draft a Presidential policies paper concerned with urban affairs.

The mission statement also included an ambitious plan for Fletcher to meet with Ford every two weeks "for the purpose of reporting to and advising him on my activities and to offer observations, suggestions, and recommendations for his consideration," and "to make a minimum of twenty public appearances throughout the nation between March 1 and April 30, 1976, all for the purpose of winning support for [Ford's] proposals and initiatives."[63]

Fletcher didn't get his desired biweekly meetings with the president. He was given an office in the Old Executive Office Building and put to work, and his "observations, recommendations, and suggestions" were typically channeled through Cannon and Cheney. He was given a copy of the "Presidential Issues Book," a confidential biweekly tome, and encouraged to submit items.[64]

But he did get to travel—a lot. Between February 19 and December 16, Fletcher made sixty-seven appearances in thirty-eight cities. Fletcher traveled so frequently in his first two months alone that he made a formal request to the White House travel office that, because of his football-player build, he be allowed to fly first class, as he had while assistant secretary of labor. (The request was denied by the fiscally prudent Ford White House.)[65]

Some of these appearances were in response to invitations to President Ford; presidents receive far more speaking invitations than they can possibly accept, and relevant members of the staff are sent to represent the president at such functions. Fletcher, as the senior Black administration official, was the go-to guy when invitations came from predominantly African American groups. In other cases, it was Fletcher who was invited. But at every appearance, the message was the same: whatever your concerns, President Ford shares them.[66]

One incident from Fletcher's travels on behalf of the Ford administration bears recounting, as it demonstrates the limits of his loyalty and juxtaposes his position as Ford's advisor on Black issues with his prior experience as an alternate delegate to the United Nations. On August 3, 1976, at Vernon Jordan's invitation, Fletcher participated in a panel called "The Case for Republicans" at the annual conference of the NUL.[67] Secretary of State Henry Kissinger had been invited to give a keynote address, and as Fletcher recalled, Kissinger blew it:

We were at the big Hilton Hotel in downtown Boston, and . . . there were two wall banks of elevators, and this wall they reserved for Kissinger and his folk, and that hotel was packed, so all of the delegates had to [share the other elevators]. And by the time they got up to change their clothes to come down to hear him speak they were fuming.

And then he spoke, and during the Q and A he was asked about the [lack of] Blacks in [the State Department]. He made the suggestion that you have to be real intelligent to work at the State Department. You can imagine how that went over.[68]

For the secretary of state to imply that he saw Blacks as intellectually inferior—at a convention of the NUL, no less—undercut Fletcher's efforts encouraging Blacks to vote for GOP candidates. At Fletcher's panel the next evening, which he shared with Democrats including former vice president Hubert Humphrey, irate Urban Leaguers confronted the senior elephant in the room, demanding that Fletcher account for Kissinger's insensitivity. But Fletcher, in this case, refused to support his fellow Republican:

> I said, you know, "I am not Kissinger. My name is Art Fletcher and . . . I'm 6 foot 4. I don't know how tall he is. I played football, I don't know what he played," and then I said, "There's no way I'd tie up that bank of elevators. I don't understand why he did that, and since you asked me, I'm curious to know why he made a foreign policy speech before a domestic organization."[69]

Newspapers missed the point. "Kissinger Scolded by Black Ford Aide," blared a headline in the next morning's *Philadelphia Bulletin,* potentially putting Fletcher in hot water with his supervisors.[70] While this doesn't appear to have concerned Cannon, Cheney, or Ford, it did attract the attention of Vice President Rockefeller, who called Fletcher onto the carpet as soon as he returned to Washington.

But Fletcher was having none of it. "I said, 'Do you want to know the truth, Mr. Vice-president? . . . He's got Blacks on his staff over there that he should have had with him . . . and he should have been briefed by them before he came there, and they could have told him about the audience, what to expect . . . so he created the problem for himself, and I see no need to apologize to him or to you, sir.'" Rocky got the message, and he apparently ensured that it was delivered to the secretary of state, because Kissinger soon changed his tune: "Two weeks later . . . Kissinger [and I] spoke to the [OIC conference], about 8,000 people there . . . he came over and shook my hand and said, 'You were right, you were right.' And then he turned around and he said, 'look,' and he had about five Blacks with him. And to his credit, he made a tremendous speech."[71]

Fletcher's vindication in his Kissinger affair was in keeping with the way he saw his position at the White House. He was grateful to have the job, but he refused to compromise his principles; he stood up for what he believed in. As he had when he was a member of the United Nations delegation, he said what he actually felt, without expecting people to read between the lines. Sometimes this got him into trouble, but more often it earned him grudging respect and even admiration. He was not your typical politician.

Spirit of '76

Neither, for that matter, was Ronald Reagan, who formally declared his candidacy for the Republican presidential nomination on November 20, 1975, and after narrowly losing the New Hampshire primary, took the party on its own roller-coaster ride. First Ford was up and Reagan down, then Reagan came back and Ford saw looming defeat, then Ford fought his way back on top again. The battle between the two camps exemplified the larger battle between conservatives and moderates in the GOP, a battle that often revolved around competing visions of race and civil rights.[72]

The Southern Strategy clearly played a role in Reagan's campaigning in the South in the spring of 1976. Two primaries in particular bore this out. In North Carolina, Reagan's victory was the work of ardent segregationist Senator Jesse Helms, who publicly decried federal expenditures on a health center run by Soul City founder Floyd McKissick and supported by the moderate governor, James Holshauser, a Ford loyalist. Helms also circulated an implicitly racist flyer that insinuated that the president's vice presidential pick would be African American Massachusetts senator Edward Brooke. Reagan's appeal to the racist elements in the party so concerned the Ford committee that sheaves of documentation on the North Carolina race were sent to Fletcher, Ford's senior African American advisor, for comments and advice. Texas, meanwhile, was a crossover state, allowing voters to vote in either primary regardless of affiliation, and Reagan was hoping for a large amount of conservative Democrats to support him in the Republican race. The Texas conservatives' candidate of choice, George Wallace, was still contesting the Democratic nomination, but by this point—the Texas primary was on May 1—former Georgia governor Jimmy Carter had all but secured it for himself. Reagan won the Texas Republican primary thanks to these first Reagan Democrats.[73]

Reagan's appeal to conservative Democrats represented larger forces in American politics during this era. For more than two decades both major parties had been struggling to define their identities. Party affiliation was determined for most Americans by a combination of parents' loyalties, education, social class, economics, and race, and party regulars and loyal-ists, often with complex feelings about a multitude of political issues, prior-itized those that allowed them to feel comfortable in one or the other party. The result in the early postwar era had been two big tents, each containing strong leaders from both ends of the political spectrum. The Democratic Party contained die-hard southern segregationists like Senator Strom Thur-mond and African American liberals like Congressmen William Dawson and Adam Clayton Powell; the Republican Party contained eastern establish-ment moderates like Rockefeller, midwestern commonsense conservatives like Ford, and New Right conservatives like Reagan. In 1948 Thurmond's Dixiecrat insurgency nearly denied reelection to Democratic president Tru-man, who had integrated the armed forces; in state after state during the 1950s and 1960s conservative Republicans like Arizona's Barry Goldwater battled moderates (like Dan Evans of Washington) and liberals (like Fred Hall of Kansas) for control of their party. In 1964, when Democratic presi-dent Johnson signed the Civil Rights Act, he put in motion the final stage of the African American political migration out of the party of Lincoln. At the same time, as he himself noted during the signing ceremony, white south-erners hostile to integration would now feel even more estranged from the Democratic Party. Southern whites did not tilt the South solidly Republican until 1988, but their increased numbers did tilt the scales within the party in favor of the conservative faction, eventually making it inhospitable to lib-erals even as the number of conservative Democrats dwindled. This process was incomplete in 1976, but by the 1990s it was increasingly evident in the polarization between a liberal to moderate Democratic Party and a conser-vative Republican Party.[74]

Ronald Reagan's bid for the Republican nomination in 1976—and his crossover appeal to conservative Democrats—was emblematic of these trends. This is not to say that Reagan was more racist than Ford or any other Republican moderate. While it's true that in 1980 Reagan used the Southern Strategy as an explicit part of his campaign strategy, beginning with a speech in Philadelphia, Mississippi, the site of the killing of three civil rights work-ers in 1964, and later as president attacked the federal government's civil rights enforcement mechanisms by gutting the Commission on Civil Rights and appointing the hostile William Bradford Reynolds as assistant attorney general, in 1976 Reagan was concerned that he not be labeled a southern apologist, and when he learned of the Edward Brooke flyer in North Caro-lina, he moved quickly to quash it.[75]

Notwithstanding these trends, Fletcher's appointment did prove electorally fortunate for Ford. During the primary season, having an African American on the domestic council, advising on urban affairs, and speaking before largely African American audiences around the country shored up Ford's reputation as a responsible moderate; the minimal national press for Fletcher's activities ensured that he could develop support in cities without affecting perception among rural conservative Republicans. Indeed, although the archival evidence of Fletcher's activities on behalf of the primary campaign is sparse, we do have him begging off at least one appearance owing to the rigors of supporting the president's reelection efforts, suggesting that "perhaps we could reschedule this after the primary elections are over with."[76]

This was especially important in Reagan's home state of California, where a significant showing by Ford would not only yield the incumbent a handful of delegates but also hand his challenger a highly visible black eye. In a nomination race that eventually came down to about two dozen undeclared delegates, perception was everything. Ford's team strategized that although the president would not win the state, they could use their superior funds to force Reagan to campaign heavily there while neglecting important races back East. Reagan couldn't afford anything short of a landslide in California, and Fletcher's activities helped keep the former governor busy.[77]

Fletcher made two trips to the Bay Area before the California primary: a four-night trip to the East Bay in early May (his longest visit to a single metropolitan area during his year in the Ford White House), followed by a one-night trip in early June. In May he served as keynote speaker at a public policy conference. He returned on June 3 to speak at the Marcus Foster Institute, an Oakland nonprofit focused on facilitating higher-education opportunities for inner-city youth, garnering letters of appreciation from the Oakland school superintendent and the mayor of nearby Concord.[78]

The nomination ultimately came down to Mississippi's thirty uncommitted delegates. The state party subscribed to the winner-takes-all unit rule, whereby all delegates voted on the first ballot for the candidate who won an overall majority of the delegates. Although the conservative majority of the Mississippi delegates supported Reagan, the thirty (mostly young and moderate) alternates could vote on procedural matters—like suspending the unit rule. Ford's team went to work building a majority among these sixty combined delegates and alternates to suspend the unit rule and thereby peel away a handful of delegates, while the Reaganites, who needed all thirty votes, focused on keeping the unit rule intact.[79]

Reagan then made a fatal mistake: he named a moderate running mate, Pennsylvania Republican Richard Schweiker. For the general election,

Schweiker would have been an excellent choice, offsetting Reagan's hard-line conservatism. But with the nomination still in play, the Mississippi delegates saw it as a betrayal. Cutting off their nose to spite their face, they suspended the unit rule. Then, at the convention in Kansas City, the Reaganites squabbled over strategy and squandered their last chance. When Ford won floor votes on a disputed platform plank and a procedural rule, the tide turned decisively. Ford won the nomination on the first ballot. After the vote, despite a "chorus of nays" nearly as loud as that of the ayes, the House minority leader, John Rhodes, chairman of the convention, declared Ford's nomination unanimous.[80]

At this point Rhodes called the vice president to the podium. Rockefeller then delivered his last major political speech, nominating Kansas senator Bob Dole for the vice presidency. This was followed by a seconding speech by Peggy Pinder, delegate of Iowa. Rhodes then introduced Senator Paul Laxalt of Nevada for what he said was the "final seconding speech."[81]

Either Rhodes made a mistake or what happened next was unplanned. Indeed, national political conventions during the 1970s were hardly the scripted affairs they later became. Dole, knowing Fletcher's oratorical skills, probably insisted on it. In any event, after Laxalt concluded his brief speech, Rhodes said, "The chair now recognizes a personal friend of Senator Bob Dole, the Honorable Arthur Fletcher, a special assistant to the President and former Assistant Secretary of Labor, Art Fletcher."[82]

Fletcher's speech seconding the Dole nomination, the only address at the convention by an African American other than Senator Edward Brooke, was as long as those of Pinder and Laxalt combined. But more important than its length was its meaning. This was his opportunity to speak on behalf of African Americans to an audience containing nearly every candidate for the Republican presidential nomination for the next three decades, to remind them that in this era of racist backlash and conservative resurgence, the party still had a role to play in civil rights. Fletcher seized the moment.

> Mr. Chairman, fellow delegates, when I was asked to make a seconding statement in support of Senator Bob Dole for the Vice Presidency on the Republican ticket, I . . . called friends across the country and asked them to tell me what they would like for me to say. . . . And they said to me, "Remind them . . . that we should be and are a thankful people . . . for 200 years of freedom and liberty . . . a thankful people to have a Constitution and a system of government that is self-renewing. [Applause.]
>
> "Remind them that under our system . . . wherever they have made a

mistake, they have gone back and corrected it; and in the process of cor-
recting that mistake, made it possible for you to speak to them tonight.
. . . [Applause.]

"Also remind them that we . . . are a thankful people to have a President who . . . could steady our ship safely home from one of the most
difficult periods in the Nation's history."

Let me say that again . . . Mr. Ford . . . brought courage . . . integrity
and . . . the capacity to . . . make the lonely decisions that only he could
make. . . . [Applause.] . . . Let me say to you . . . that right now the people
are singing our song. They are convinced that the solutions to our problems are not in Washington, D.C.; that if they are to be solved, they will
be solved at the city, state and local level.

They are singing our song, which means this, that we should elect the
ticket of Ford and Dole so that we can implement the kinds of programs
that are a remedy to our problems and continue to lay the foundation that
will endure . . . another 100 years of security and endurance. . . . Finally,
let me say that it is important that we have a Republican Party, a strong,
powerful Republican Party . . . I am proud then to place Robert Dole's name
in nomination for the Vice Presidency of the United States. [Applause.][83]

As in Miami Beach in 1968, Fletcher had decisively staked out a position
at the forefront of the moderate wing of his party. In seconding his friend
Bob Dole's nomination for the vice presidency, he was supporting a conservative, but the timing had more to do with Dole and Fletcher sharing a common background in the Sunflower State than it did Fletcher's own politics.
He was a Ford man more than a Dole man, but he was a team player, and
therefore a party-line man. Eager for the visibility of the national podium,
he seconded the candidate he was told to second.

Going into the general election, Ford suffered from more than a twenty-
point deficit against the Democratic nominee, Jimmy Carter. No incumbent
had ever won against such odds, but his team nonetheless developed a solid
strategy. The president campaigned by making statements from the White
House Rose Garden in an attempt to demonstrate his competence and take
full advantage of his incumbency, trading on the respect everyday Americans held for the office of the president. Running mate Bob Dole would play
the attack dog, channeling Agnew in 1968 and Nixon in 1952, attacking
Carter in the hope that the Democrat would commit gaffes. Ford would participate in three televised debates, where he hoped to demonstrate his command of foreign and domestic policy, and paint Carter as inexperienced and

untrustworthy. In the final two weeks he would leave the White House for an exhaustive campaign schedule culminating in his hometown of Grand Rapids, Michigan.[84]

The GOP actually had a good opportunity to increase its percentage of the Black vote in 1976. In addition to Fletcher's seemingly tireless footwork on the issue, the Carter nomination provided an opening. As president, like Johnson before him and Clinton after, Carter proved that white southerners could be effective advocates for civil rights. But as a candidate, his record in 1976 was unclear. To be elected governor of Georgia in 1970 he had to win a significant segment of the white racist vote, resulting in his general avoidance of civil rights issues. During this period none other than Jesse Jackson, the leader viewed by many in the movement as the ideological and organizational heir to Martin Luther King Jr., entertained the idea of supporting Ford. But as we have seen, Ford was in the same position in 1976 on race as Carter had been in 1970: lest he lose more support among conservatives, he could not openly embrace the civil rights movement, let alone someone like Jesse Jackson.[85]

Fletcher's activities on behalf of the Ford campaign became more prominent as the president pivoted back toward the political center. Eager to whittle away at the Democrats' lock on the African American vote, and seeking to blunt the conservatism of Dole, Fletcher prepared a detailed memorandum briefing the president on minority issues before the presidential debates, and he made several speeches in key states with significant African American and urban populations. He spent five nights in Texas (Beaumont, Dallas, and Houston) and four nights in New York and environs (New York City, Rochester, Hempstead, and Newark, New Jersey). Both New York and Texas ultimately went to Carter, but Fletcher was dispatched there in the hope that he could help generate the Electoral College margin for the president; indeed, had Ford taken New York alone, or Texas and one other small state, he would have kept the presidency. Fletcher spent a total of thirty-six days on the road between the end of the convention on August 19 and Election Day on November 2, just shy of half his time, culminating with a trip to Chicago on November 1 to assist in a final push in the key midwestern swing state of Illinois, which Ford won. But it was not enough. Ford won 241 electoral votes to Carter's 297, and lost the election.[86]

Contemporary observers, including Jesse Jackson, entertained the possibility that Ford might have retained the presidency by choosing as his running mate Edward Brooke, the African American senator from Massachusetts. Indeed, it is possible that this choice would have resulted in Ford's winning Brooke's home state, which brought fourteen electoral votes. It probably also would have won Ford the Black vote nationwide—a result for which Arthur Fletcher was working very hard—and which might have won Ford a number of other states. But vociferous racist attitudes at the prospect of a Black man being a heartbeat away from the White House—especially since four of the previous seven vice presidents had become president—might have cost Ford as many electoral votes as the choice won him.[87]

In his final weeks in the White House, Fletcher was sufficiently confident of his standing in the party to mount a second, more serious campaign to be chairman of the RNC. Unlike his earlier bid in 1972, when he was only trying to generate publicity for himself and the UNCF, now he had significant support. One of seven candidates for the position, his campaign earned a newspaper endorsement in Kansas and support in Washington State. After he addressed a forum of the Northeast region's state chairs, he was considered a serious contender: his nomination on the floor of the meeting came with several impassioned speeches from supporters, and he was not eliminated in the first round of voting. But he was not the lame-duck president's choice: that distinction went to James Baker, the future secretary of state who had directed the presidential campaign (and who soon withdrew). After three rounds of voting, Fletcher's initial 22 votes (out of a total of 161), which had placed him third in a field of five, gave way and the chairmanship went to Senator William Brock of Tennessee.[88]

Despite his personal popularity, Fletcher's candidacy was quixotic. With Nixon's Southern Strategy and continuing attempts to win over riot-fearing northern working-class whites, the idea that President Ford would support, let alone that the RNC would elect, an African American chairman in the 1970s was far-fetched. Republicans knew on which side their bread was buttered. But the importance of Fletcher's candidacy was in the attempt. It kept him near the forefront of discussion within the national party apparatus so as to best prepare for his next political foray.

As with most appointed members of the government, Fletcher was not returning with the new administration. Ford accepted Fletcher's pro forma resignation on January 19, 1977, thanking him for his "tremendous spirit of optimism and dedication to the great work that will continue to be ours." Despite his candidate's near miss, Arthur Fletcher emerged from his second tour of duty in the federal government in a very different position than he had been a year earlier. His position with the Ford administration was significantly more visible than the role he had played at the RNC with George Bush. Although he could not boast regular, unfettered access to the president, he had been a member of Ford's Domestic Policy Council and a top African American in the administration.[89]

Fletcher and Barry

Because of his heightened visibility, Fletcher resolved to remain in Washington (despite intimations after a trip to Coeur d'Alene that he might relocate to Idaho to open a restaurant, and the repeated urging of his wife, Bernyce, to retire to Pleasantville, New Jersey, to "go back to teaching or lecturing"). He returned to his post as head of Arthur Fletcher & Associates and devoted some time to the SVL. In 1978 he decided to run for mayor of Washington, DC.[90]

The office was a relatively new one. The District of Columbia had always been subservient to the will of the United States Congress, which had established it during the early republic so that the security of the federal government would not depend on any individual state. Until 1974 the residents of the city—by then majority African American—had enjoyed no democratic control over the city's government; its chief executives were appointed by the president of the United States. The 1973 District of Columbia Home Rule Act established that the residents of Washington would elect their own city council and mayor, and the following year Walter Washington, who had been appointed mayor-commissioner in 1967 by President Johnson and retained by President Nixon, narrowly defeated former EEOC chairman Clifford Alexander in the Democratic primary, then went on to trounce Republican Jackson Champion in the general election.[91]

In 1978 a slew of Democratic opponents, as well as prominent members of the press, decried Mayor Washington for fiscal mismanagement. Portions of the city were fast becoming run down. Like most major cities, Washington, DC, was undergoing white flight to the suburbs, shrinking the municipal tax base. Whereas other cities could appeal to their state governments for assistance, Washington, DC, was beholden to Congress, whose members did not depend on votes from its residents for reelection.

City council chairman Sterling Tucker and council member and civil rights leader Marion Barry declared their intention to challenge Mayor Washington in the Democratic primary, but Fletcher expected that the incumbent would nevertheless win the nomination. In his estimation, Tucker and Barry would split the reform vote in the city's poorer wards, while the mayor would dominate the more affluent wards and take enough additional votes elsewhere to eke out a victory.[92]

May 1978: Fletcher, Bernyce at his side, throws his hat in the ring for mayor of Washington, DC. Arthur Fletcher Personal Papers, courtesy Paul Fletcher.

Fletcher focused on the general election. If Jackson Champion was the Republican nominee again, Walter Washington would easily consolidate Tucker's and Barry's reformist supporters and be reelected. But a Republican could win if the party nominated someone with Fletcher's stature who could take on the reform mantle. He announced his campaign for the Republican nomination and moved quickly to secure support in the primary race, lining up endorsements from such party luminaries as George Bush and Ronald Reagan. Paul Hays, chair of the DC Republican committee, organized a fund-raising dinner with RNC chair Bill Brock as keynote speaker.[93]

In addition to the question of the district's fiscal management, three issues animated the race for mayor. The first was a major construction project to be located in the historic Mount Vernon section in northwest Washington. Proponents in real estate envisioned upscale shopping with adjacent high-end hotels and restaurants, leading to an increase in local property values. Originally called Eisenhower Center, by 1978 the project was referred to as Civic Center despite the lack of government institutions to be located there. (It ultimately became known as City Center.) The project promised increased municipal tax revenues, but the real reason the three major Democratic candidates—Washington, Tucker, and Barry—gave it their support was that their campaigns were largely funded by real estate interests sympathetic to the project, according to the *Washington Post*. In their support, however, each worried that the eventual Republican nominee could use the project against him in the general election, as it was seen by many in the city's poorer neighborhoods as a "boon for landowners"; they hoped to avoid it as a campaign issue. Fletcher did not oppose the project, but he made it just such an issue, seeing an opportunity to score populist points. "I think the Center will be a plus for the city but [it] ought to be a private investment, and there ought to be a referendum," he told the *Post*.[94]

A second issue in the campaign was the notion that the district might legalize gambling, which Fletcher ardently opposed. During the 1970s and early 1980s, cities across the nation wrested control of the illegal numbers games popular in African American ghettoes, replacing them with regulated lotteries. Fletcher disliked both the illegal and legal versions, seeing them as preying on those who needed precious funds for their own uplift. Casino gambling he opposed for moral reasons. His opponent in the primary, Jackson Champion, favored both the establishment of a lottery and legalization of casinos; on the Democratic side, Marion Barry endorsed gambling. (Washington, DC, legalized a lottery in 1982 but did not legalize casino gambling.)[95]

A third highly charged issue of the campaign centered on congressional representation. Not being part of a state, the District of Columbia had no representation in the federal government. In 1971 Congress established a nonvoting seat for a representative of the district. In 1978 the district leaders mounted a campaign for a constitutional amendment to establish full representation for the district on par with the states, a step that some hoped might lead to eventual statehood—indeed, district residents ratified a state constitution in 1982. The problem with congressional approval ultimately boiled down to the district's population being heavily weighted in favor of the Democratic Party, and the necessity of winning sufficient Republican support for the measure. Nevertheless, there were a number of factors that worked to convince Republican members of Congress to vote in favor of full representation. One was idealism: the notion that all Americans had the right to representation. Another was that district residents paid federal taxes yet had no say in federal spending. Finally there was the political argument that Fletcher was making privately in the offices of Senate Republicans: that their support of the measure was critical to his goal of building a viable two-party system in the district. On August 22, 1978, the Senate approved a constitutional amendment—previously approved by the House—granting full representation to the district. The measure passed by a single vote, with forty-eight Democrats and nineteen Republicans voting in favor.[96]

Shortly after the vote, the nonvoting congressional representative, Walter Fauntroy, and one of the Democratic mayoral candidates, Sterling Tucker, traveled to California as part of a lobbying trip to convince state legislatures to ratify the amendment, but they didn't invite any Republicans from the District of Columbia. Fletcher decried this as having turned the question "into a partisan issue. And one of the problems we're now into is that the Republicans in the state of California . . . are slowing it up." Fletcher was right, and the *Washington Post* editorial page agreed. California—and most other states—never ratified the amendment.[97]

While Fletcher handily won the Republican nomination on primary day (garnering nearly 8,000 out of approximately 9,000 Republican votes cast), the results on the Democratic side were not what he expected. The months of ganging up on Walter Washington had paid off too well: the incumbent placed third in a tight race. Despite some irregularities resulting in the subsequent resignation of the election commissioner, Marion Barry emerged the victor.[98]

Marion Barry was an experienced politician with a long record as a civil rights leader. Like Fletcher, he had experienced the early loss of his father, but was profoundly influenced by a stepfather. He grew up in Memphis, and like Fletcher he had an organizational awakening protesting for civil rights around a local issue: the unfair treatment of Black paperboys denied a prize after winning a contest. Like Fletcher and Dr. King, Barry was older than the students of the 1960s movement, but unlike Fletcher, he joined them in that decade, putting his body on the line. In Nashville for graduate studies at Fisk, he was arrested several times trying to integrate lunch counters. He became the first chairman of the student nonviolent coordinating committee and participated in the voter registration activities in Mississippi during Freedom Summer. He relocated to Washington, DC, where he gradually moved from civil rights protests to civil rights politics, and in 1972 was elected president of the school board. With DC home rule in 1974, he sought and won an at-large city council seat. Fletcher's ascension to the Pasco City Council in 1967 had also involved an at-large seat, but his status with local Republicans allowed him to thread the needle in a majority-white city. For Barry, civil rights bona fides were far more important in majority-Black, overwhelmingly Democratic DC. Barry also had the status of a local hero:

he survived a gunshot wound during a siege of the DC government building by a Nation of Islam sect. He would make a far tougher opponent, and one very different than the more moderate Walter Washington, whom Fletcher had expected to face in the general election.[99]

Fletcher responded with bravado. "I'm gonna play to win and I'm gonna play well, and I intend to be the next mayor." But this barely masked his frustration: he had to completely change his strategy in the wake of Mayor Washington's defeat. No longer could Fletcher play the populist for the reformers' votes; now he had to move in the opposite direction to win support among Democrats who had voted for Walter Washington. If he could galvanize the city's 26,000 Republicans and win most of the incumbent's nearly 30,000 supporters, then he could still engage Barry in a highly competitive race. Indeed, according to one reporter, prominent supporters of Mayor Washington and Chairman Tucker began "talking privately about Fletcher's candidacy in ways that have all the markings of a possible 'Anybody-but-Barry' Movement."[100]

Barry agreed that Fletcher posed a threat. He "was careful not to declare himself mayor-elect . . . and said he would now dedicate himself to getting out a victory vote in the November general election when he faces Republican challenger Arthur Fletcher." Barry self-consciously saw his victory as an upset and feared that Fletcher could pull off a similar trick. When a reporter interviewing Barry noted "that a Fletcher victory in November would be the first time a Republican has overcome a gargantuan Democratic registration to become mayor, Barry retorted: 'Well, it's the first time in history I've upset all these other candidates, too.'" His aides cautioned against "taking the November election for granted," and he moved to consolidate his support with Walter Washington and extend an olive branch to Tucker, even as the final primary votes were being counted.[101]

Fletcher garnered the support of more than a dozen local Baptist ministers thanks to his oratorical skills and his opposition to gambling. According to the *Washington Post*,

> At yesterday's press conference, more than a dozen churchmen came to the pulpit to announce their support for Fletcher, including the Rev. Andrew J. Allen, pastor of First Baptist Church of Deanwood, and the Rev. Raymond Robinson, pastor of Israel Baptist Church, who formally announced Fletcher's endorsement by the Committee of 100 Ministers. . . . The Rev. John J. Koger, pastor of New Bethany Baptist Church . . . pulled a $100 bill from his wallet and contributed it to the Fletcher campaign.

"Take this. That's good money," he said, stretching his arm toward Fletcher. "And there's some more where that came from."

He made an all-out, albeit failed, push to win the cab driver vote (they were staunch supporters of incumbent Walter Washington), whom he thought might be swayed away from Barry. He demanded public debates with the Democrat, threatening to argue with an empty chair, as he had in 1968 when he ran for lieutenant governor of Washington State, and Barry agreed to attend a few. By mid-October, Fletcher could credibly claim that "the requests for appearances are coming so fast that I really can't cover them all."[102]

Fletcher had a plan. He had an experienced campaign manager (John Wilks, his old friend from Berkeley who had followed him to Washington in 1969 to direct the OFCC and who had worked on campaigns in the Bay Area since the late 1950s). He had loyal supporters, including his son, Paul, who took a leave of absence from his job as a probation officer to work on the campaign. He even had momentum. What he needed was money, and a handful of hundred-dollar bills from local ministers fearing the loss of Bingo revenue wasn't going to cut it. As of October 15, his campaign had "raised only $28,444—one tenth as much money as Barry." He had hoped that his connections with the RNC would help, but in this he was gravely disappointed. Despite his arguments that a well-funded campaign would result in a viable two-party system in the district—arguments echoed by popular African American columnist William Raspberry—Fletcher's appeals for party funding fell on deaf ears. After all, 1978 was also a midterm election year, and the RNC, hoping to build momentum for a challenge to Democrats at all levels of government in 1980, spent its money on competitive congressional races elsewhere. The party was also uninterested in too visible a show of support for Fletcher; as with his bid for RNC chairman the previous year, Fletcher was trying to gain support from a GOP actively wooing unreconstructed white southerners and northern working-class whites. In the campaign for Republican cash, as in his campaign for mayor overall, Fletcher never really stood a chance. The lack of funding sent the campaign into a vicious cycle. Unable to generate much publicity, he was unable to garner sufficient support to develop "ward coordinators or precinct captains," refusing, when asked by a reporter, "to name those he says he has. His campaign workers, he said, are chipping in money to pay for posters." In the end Fletcher's campaign collected only $69,064, compared to more than half a million dollars in the Barry war chest. Even the main Democratic contenders who lost the primary to Barry—Sterling Tucker and Walter Washington—raised five times as much as Fletcher.[103]

To be sure, there were national Republican leaders willing to be quoted favorably on Fletcher and his campaign, and even make personal donations. "Art Fletcher has demonstrated his commitment to a two-party system and the Republican Party," Bob Dole told the *Washington Post,* which called him "a close political associate of Fletcher." Dole continued, "He can go only one way and that's up. We need forward looking responsible black leadership in the Republican Party." Reagan advisor Lyn Nofziger told the *Post* that "even if he is not elected, if he runs an effective campaign and if Black Republicans say here's a guy we can respect, I really think there's a chance we could rally Blacks around him. He has a chance through this thing to seize the Black leadership in the party, and I hope he does that."[104]

The press, too, was mixed on Fletcher, even within a single publication. Despite an editorial endorsing Barry, in which the *Washington Post* denounced Fletcher's campaign as "shabby," one of the paper's correspondents wrote a flattering article on the eve of the election, calling Fletcher "a black 'Rocky,' up against the celebrated champion. . . . Just as Apollo Creed was supposed to flatten the unranked challenger . . . so Barry was to devastate any sacrificial lamb the GOP offered. But Fletcher, 53, is far more lion than lamb. He loves a fight and, like Rocky, is battling Barry for the full 15 rounds."[105]

By the evening of the final debate, the campaign had devolved into dirty tricks and name calling. Bernyce wrote family friend Kathy Keolker, "You have never seen an environment like the one here in DC. The game-playing, pettiness, distrust, disrespect & fear would blow your mind." Fletcher complained, "There are people going to houses where they're holding functions for me, taking the license numbers off of cars, putting them on cards, calling people late at night." Barry, for his part, denied the accusation; he accused Fletcher of "Nixonian fear tactics." According to Paul, Fletcher and Barry nearly came to blows: Fletcher "always took off his glasses when he was getting ready to fight. Barry tried to intimidate [him. He] took off his glasses and said 'son, I played professional football and kicked ass for a living, and if you come across that table you're gonna' get an ass-whuppin.'" The moderator managed to calm the tension.[106]

On Election Day, Fletcher did better than expected, winning nearly one-third of the total vote in a city where Republicans constituted only 10 percent. Unsurprisingly, he did best in the seven most affluent precincts of

Ward 3 along Rock Creek Park in the northwest, including American University Park, where he won 68 percent of the vote. But the election was Barry's. The final tally gave Fletcher 28,048 votes, or 28 percent of the total, to Barry's 69,933, or 69 percent. Senator Dole wrote in consolation, "I know from experience that it is far better to win than to lose and I hope you won't be discouraged by the outcome." Bernyce, however, was privately glad of the outcome, telling Keolker, "Truthfully, I'm glad he lost. He would have 'killed himself' trying to do a decent job."[107]

In his final months with the Nixon administration, his sights set on a political career back in Washington State, Arthur Fletcher had hoped that the 1970s would be a time of consolidation: of the nation as a post–Jim Crow land of equal opportunity, the ghettoes disappearing in the wake of good jobs and fair housing; of the Republican Party as an interracial big tent led by men like Nelson Rockefeller, George Bush, and Edward Brooke; and of his own career as a rising star and role model in both. It was his drive for consolidation in these areas, as much as serendipity and luck, that called him to lead the UNCF, work at the RNC, publish *The Silent Sellout*, develop his affirmative action consulting business and the SVL, challenge Kissinger's unconscious racism, campaign tirelessly for Ford's reelection, deliver the speech of his career at the 1976 Republican National Convention, and run for RNC chairman in 1977 and mayor of Washington, DC, in 1978.

Although the party was racing away from what Fletcher stood for much faster than he could keep up, it didn't shake his faith the way one might expect. This wasn't naivete; rather, Fletcher held fast to his principles and believed that he could still pull the GOP in a more productive direction. In all three of his goals, however, the decade proved disappointing. Continued inequality and poverty as well as the decline of the cities developed in tandem with a racial backlash leading unreconstructed southerners and northern white working-class voters into the Republican Party. The conservatives seemed ascendant. The UNCF fired him, the SVL fizzled, and Ford lost to Carter. In 1979 Nelson Rockefeller was dead, Edward Brooke was out of office, Marion Barry was mayor of Washington, and Fletcher's book was out of print.

There were plenty of things that kept Arthur Fletcher up at night in 1979, but he did have one cause for hope. In George Bush he saw a panacea. Here was a man who, like Fletcher, spent the 1970s working to consolidate his goals for the nation, the party, and his own career. Here was an experienced leader and skilled politician, a civil rights moderate and fiscal conservative who combined a Northeast establishment upbringing with a Texan's charm, and who had proven experience bridging the two sides of the Republican Party. At the United Nations and at the RNC, Fletcher and Bush had become friends. Now, after enduring his own roller-coaster ride in the 1970s, George Bush was running for president.

CHAPTER SIX

BUSH FOR PRESIDENT, 1980–1989

*It is unrealistic to talk about a color-blind society when we know it
is not color-blind, has not been, and is not likely to be.*
—Arthur Fletcher, 1990

The decade of the 1980s began with incredible prom-
ise for Arthur Fletcher. Despite the severe setbacks and swings in fortune
he had experienced during the 1970s, he looked hopefully to the election
campaign of his friend, George Bush, to reinvigorate his own efforts to bring
African Americans into the Republican Party and push back against the
New Right, which he blamed for the defeat of Gerald Ford in 1976. But that
movement's popular leader, Ronald Reagan, was also running for president.
A Reagan victory would bring Fletcher's party back into the seat of power—
but threatened to set back Fletcher's cause for years.

Campaign '80

Arthur Fletcher supported George Bush for president for a variety of reasons, but certainly the two most important were Bush's political moderation and the pair's decade-long friendship. Despite Bush's adopted home in
the Deep South, he was, like his father Senator Prescott Bush, a product of
the New England Republican Party—far more Rockefeller Republican than
Goldwaterite. As a congressman he had stood for civil rights, voting in favor
of President Johnson's fair housing bill, and he explained the importance of
fairness to a hostile crowd in Texas. He and Fletcher had first met in 1970,
when Fletcher was traveling the country stumping for the Philadelphia Plan
and Bush, at Nixon's behest, was running for Senate. They had become
close in 1971 while working at the United Nations; in 1973, when Fletcher
was fired from the United Negro College Fund (UNCF), it was Bush who
provided a safe landing, hiring Fletcher to work at the RNC. Both Bush and
Fletcher had experienced the devastating death of a child—Bush in 1953,
losing his daughter to leukemia, and Fletcher in 1974, losing Art Jr. to Hodgkin's disease. Bush's call for a moment of silence at the April 1974 RNC

meeting in honor of Art Jr. was no doubt preceded by unrecorded private discussions in which the chairman expressed his understanding and sympathy, further cementing their friendship. Barbara Bush and longtime Bush confidant James Baker attended Fletcher's swearing-in ceremony at the White House as a new member of the Ford team, and it is likely that Fletcher lobbied, however unsuccessfully, for Bush to be Ford's running mate that year. What's more, Bush was objectively the best-qualified candidate for the nomination, with experience in both Congress and the executive branch, including stints as ambassador to China and director of the CIA. Fletcher's agreement in early 1979 to cochair the District of Columbia's "George Bush for President" committee was an easy call.[1]

The idea that Fletcher might instead support front-runner Ronald Reagan in the primaries was a nonstarter. Although the two had crossed paths and were cordial, Reagan's New Right represented for Fletcher everything that had been going wrong in the Republican Party; it also undercut his efforts recruiting Black voters. Reagan's appeal to unreconstructed southerners, white-flight suburbanites, and skilled white workers—the hard hats Fletcher had battled over the Philadelphia Plan—made him unpalatable. Like many Americans at the time, Fletcher saw Reagan's background as a Hollywood actor as limiting his competence for the presidency, notwithstanding his proven ability to compromise while governor of California. It was, after all, the height of irony that the star of such second-rate fare as *Bedtime for Bonzo*—a film about a chimpanzee—could have come as close to the presidency as he had in 1976 while fine Black statesmen like Edward Brooke were not seriously considered for even the vice presidency. Fletcher also blamed Reagan for Ford's defeat in 1976—having weakened him in a grueling primary contest and siphoned off conservative support in the general election—and therefore Fletcher's own absence from political office in the intervening years.[2]

Of all the other candidates for the 1980 Republican presidential nomination, only Bob Dole might have competed for Fletcher's political affections. Despite Dole's conservatism, Fletcher appreciated the Kansan's support during and after his 1978 mayoral campaign, and indeed the two had been friendly at least as far back as 1971, when the senator had tried to recruit the Department of Labor firebrand to work at the RNC. But Fletcher's personal and political ties to Bush were far stronger. He committed himself to winning the District of Columbia's delegates for his former boss.[3]

In the first weeks of 1980 it appeared that Fletcher had backed the winning horse in the race. Bush won the Iowa caucuses by a tight margin and declared that the momentum was his (he called it his "Big Mo" in what one historian has called his "garbled patrician syntax"). The press declared him the challenger and developed a narrative of Bush as underdog. The candidate and his wife, Barbara, hearing that Bernyce Fletcher was in the hospital for a minor operation, wrote from campaign headquarters in Houston that she should "get well in a hurry because 1980 is going to be a great year for all of us and we want you involved."[4]

But the tide quickly turned. Reagan was the better campaigner by far, a natural with the press and the camera. Seasoned by his 1976 near miss, the Californian waited patiently for his opportunity. It was not long in coming. He and Bush had agreed to debate one-on-one in Nashua, New Hampshire, at an event sponsored by a local newspaper. Claiming to be worried that such sponsorship violated campaign finance laws, Reagan funded the event himself and, unbeknownst to Bush, invited four other candidates. When he learned of the deception, Bush—already on the stage—refused to debate the other four, claiming a violation of the rules. Reagan walked in with the others and protested that all voices should be heard. The moderator ordered Reagan's microphone turned off, and Reagan, simultaneously feigning self-righteousness and playing the victim, retorted, "I paid for this show. I'm paying for this microphone, Mr. Green."[5]

It was a master stroke (notwithstanding that the moderator's name wasn't actually Green). At a time when Americans were suffering under astronomical inflation and recession, gripped by a sense that the decisions that most affected their lives were being made by far-off, inaccessible bureaucrats and effete eastern establishment types, Reagan's masquerade of innocence struck a chord when juxtaposed with Bush's staid insistence on following the rules—and not just with New Hampshire's voters. From that moment, the nomination was practically sewn up.[6]

Bush fought on, winning tight races in Massachusetts and Connecticut in March. He denounced Reagan's economic plan as "voodoo economics," and won two more large states by wide margins: Pennsylvania in April and Michigan in May. His only other victory, thanks in no small part to Fletcher's popularity and hard work, was a largely meaningless win in DC. But Reagan took more than twice Bush's total number of votes nationwide, and the overwhelming number of delegates to the convention. Bush stopped campaigning on May 26 and endorsed Reagan's nomination shortly thereafter.[7]

The July Republican National Convention represented an opportunity for Arthur Fletcher to find a way to support Ronald Reagan in the hope of influencing the nominee's vice presidential pick and getting himself a government appointment—ideally as secretary of labor—after the hoped-for Reagan victory in November. Given Reagan's conservatism and the antipathy toward him by the civil rights community—which dated to his 1966 guber-natorial campaign, in which he advocated harsh tactics in dealing with the Watts rebellion—such a pivot required verbal gymnastics. Calling President Carter and independent candidate John Anderson similarly "right of center," Fletcher agreed that the RNC platform was conservative, but he defended its plank on urban policy, which focused on empowering government contrac-tors rather than welfare. "I liken Reagan to Nixon going to China," the *Washington Post* quoted Fletcher as saying on the eve of the convention. "Reagan is the only conservative who could reach out to the Black community and they would accept him. It will be interesting to see if he does that."[8]

Indeed, despite Fletcher's disappointment at the defeat of his favored can-didate, he was feeling his influence at the convention. Reagan was expected to pivot to the political center for the general election, and that meant that the RNC would be putting the convention's Black delegates center stage. The nearly all-Black DC delegation, which Fletcher chaired, was the sin-gle largest group of African Americans at the Detroit event. One episode makes the point. After Reagan skipped the NAACP convention that month in Miami, Fletcher organized his fellow Black delegates to threaten to walk out of the convention hall unless the RNC invited the NAACP president to speak. In any event the organization's leader was no stranger to Republi-cans. Although no longer a member of the GOP, Benjamin Hooks shared Fletcher's feeling that Blacks should be active in both parties. The walkout would have been symbolic, for the delegates planned to immediately turn around and reenter the convention hall, but the potent threat of Blacks walk-ing out of the RNC on national television was enough to convince Reagan's advisers to allow the Hooks speech. Fletcher himself was called on to make the convention's first motion from the floor, a routine matter which passed without objection.[9]

Fletcher also claimed outsize influence in convincing the Reagan team to add George Bush to the ticket as his running mate. Reagan was determined to split the ticket, not the party; in other words, as a conservative himself, he would pick a moderate. Although a number of names were entered into nomination from the convention floor, Reagan and his advisors had whittled the list down to three several days before the convention: Senator Howard Baker of Tennessee, George Bush, and—in one of modern political history's stranger twists—the former president, Gerald Ford.

Each of the possibilities posed a problem. Baker had said he didn't want it; Bush had said he did, but he had publicly insulted Reagan on the campaign trail for his incompetence. Ford, meanwhile, now three and a half years after his presidency had ended, was very popular, having taken on the gravitas that often accompanies ex-presidents. Further, Ford was viewed as a moderate in the popular imagination, thanks in no small part to his protracted showdown with Reagan in 1976. The Reagan team saw a Ford vice presidency as a winner, but Ford had intimated that he didn't want it. Nevertheless, wily former secretary of state Henry Kissinger opened the door, suggesting that they might be able to work out a power-sharing deal that Ford could accept.[10]

Fletcher, learning that Ford was under consideration rather than his own favorite, George Bush, rallied his Black Republican troops to sway the decision. Coughing up their own money, they ordered buttons and placards bearing the phrase "Reagan–Bush," which they wore and waved during the first two days of the convention, before the running mate decision was announced. Worried that it might come down to an open convention vote, Fletcher worked the hall and later claimed to have received the pledge of every single one of the party's 121 Black delegates to vote for George Bush for running mate. After Bush's convention speech endorsing Reagan, the Black delegates led a standing ovation, waving their Reagan–Bush placards from various points throughout the hall. The impression was overwhelming support for a Bush vice presidency.[11]

Of course, the decision as to who should be the running mate, in this as in nearly all major party conventions during the twentieth century, belonged to the presidential nominee. By the same token, the role of the vice president, beyond the constitutional duty of serving as president of the Senate, was likewise the president's to determine. Walter Mondale, the incumbent, was a policy wonk, and Carter often included him in policy-related discussions. Spiro Agnew, on the other hand, had been used by Nixon primarily for public relations: he became the conservative attack dog while Nixon strove—poorly, in the final analysis—to appear above the fray.[12]

The question of a Ford vice presidency ultimately turned on the ability of the aspiring president and the former president to come to terms on Ford's role in the new administration. Would it be a copresidency? Would Ford enjoy unfettered decision-making authority on certain areas—foreign policy, say—without presidential oversight? Ford had been a president, had judged himself fairly good at the job—and had beaten Reagan before. To come out of his lucrative retirement (which oscillated between skiing in Vail, rounds of golf in Rancho Mirage, and feel-good speeches for significant honoraria) to be a traditional vice president for a former Hollywood actor did not appeal to him. Given Reagan's age, the prospect of Ford becoming a successor president a second time was a real, tempting possibility, but he only was interested if he could be a hyperpowerful veep. As a former president, only real authority in the administration interested Ford, and this was the heart of the proposal Kissinger brought back to the Reagan team.[13]

Reagan wanted to win the presidency, but not at the price of such a significant amount of presidential power. He thus rebuffed Kissinger's proposal; Ford would not be the running mate. That left George Bush, who had belittled Reaganomics and expressed disdain and contempt for Reagan on the campaign trail. But putting aside such internecine strife for party unity was a tried-and-true campaign strategy; further, naming Bush to the bottom of the ticket would quiet those pesky moderates—moderates like Arthur Fletcher and his 121 Black delegates. On the second night of the convention, Reagan called Bush and offered him the spot. Bush's assistants assembled a handful of supporters to give nominating and seconding speeches; they included Art Fletcher.[14]

Knowing that he had a tendency to elaborate, the RNC gave Fletcher only one minute, and so his speech was significantly shorter than the one he had delivered for Dole four years before:

> Mr. Chairman, ladies and gentlemen, I stand before this convention to second the nomination of a man who is uniquely qualified to help Governor Reagan and the Republican Party reach out across this great land and enlist all Americans in our crusade. Ours is a crusade for jobs, for economic growth, for opportunity, and for peace.
>
> I know this man will join Governor Reagan on this most important quest.
>
> I had a chance to work under his leadership at the United Nations and when he was the chairman of our party. I know he is a man of character, a man of determination. He is a man who is concerned for those who are less fortunate in our society. He is a man who wants to make the American dream a dream of reality for all Americans.
>
> Ladies and gentlemen, it is my distinct honor and pleasure to second the nomination of the next Vice President of the United States, Ambassador George Bush.[15]

What is noteworthy here is Fletcher's focus on Bush, the candidate whose nomination he was actually seconding. The two mentions of Reagan were as regards the role of the running mate: "help Governor Reagan" and "join Governor Reagan." This was quite different—in addition to the length—from the seconding speech he gave in 1976 for Dole, in which Fletcher had focused on his own role as a spokesman for African Americans and on the poignancy of being asked to speak at a convention during the bicentennial year. When he got down to discussing the nomination, he spent far more time on the qualifications of Ford as president than he did on Dole's fitness for the vice presidency.[16]

The reason would have been clear to even the most casual observer at the time: Fletcher's preference of Bush for the presidency. Whereas in 1976 he had been called on to second Dole's nomination because he was a Kansan, he was far more comfortable talking about Ford, whom he served directly in the White House and whose positions were more moderate than Dole's. This time around he was a Bush man rather than a Reagan man, and his speech reflected that. Although for Bush the vice presidency was a consolation prize, for Fletcher the speech was a victory lap for the hard work he had put in winning the DC primary for Bush and his self-perceived influence over Reagan's decision on the ticket.

Shortly after the convention, Reagan kicked off his fall campaign in Philadelphia, Mississippi, the site of the 1964 murders of civil rights workers James Chaney, Andrew Goodman, and Michael Schwerner. He gave what was by then his standard speech on federalism, championing the importance of the states over the authority of the federal government. To give such a speech in California was one thing; to do so at the Neshoba county fair was to implicitly side with the unreconstructed white southerners who had fought against the civil rights movement and to undercut their support of the incumbent native son, Georgian Jimmy Carter. On the one hand Reagan was shoring up his base, nodding to the former Democrats who had brought the conservatives lasting victory within the Republican Party. On the other hand he was appealing to the northern and western Democrat backlash voters: the working-class whites who resented affirmative action, and the suburban whites who had fled the cities during and after the 1960s.[17]

The Neshoba county fair speech preceded the worst weeks of the campaign for the Reagan team, what election chronicler Theodore White called "Reagan's weeks of near-disaster." The speech energized the base but brought in few new voters; further, it undercut in one fell swoop the hard work that Fletcher and others had done the previous decade to shore up Black support for Republican candidates. The next day Reagan went to New York City to address the National Urban League (NUL) convention, but he was actively jeered when he toured an inner-city neighborhood in the South Bronx. The Democrats had their convention the following week, and they took the momentum, painting Reagan as the candidate of reaction who favored theoretical states' rights over tangible civil rights.[18]

Obviously the Mississippi speech did not go over well with Fletcher, but he soldiered on, knowing that a Reagan victory would put his friend George Bush—who earnestly supported civil rights—a heartbeat away from a presidency held by a septuagenarian. Fletcher also knew that Reagan's sagging poll numbers would force him to switch gears and advocate more civil rights–friendly policies as he pivoted to the center for the final months of the campaign. In this he was not disappointed. The Reagan campaign created an urban affairs task force, chaired by conservative San Diego mayor Pete Wilson, but which included such prominent Black Republicans as Gloria Toote, Nathan Wright, and Arthur Fletcher. Reagan also deployed Fletcher on a Truth Squad, a group including former defense secretary Melvin Laird, Wyoming senator Alan Simpson, and Ford's economic advisor, Alan Greenspan, which visited such swing states as Pennsylvania and Florida in an attempt to counter negative press depictions. When journalist Tony Brown asked all three major candidates to comment on Black colleges, only Reagan replied, noting, "Under the leadership of Art Fletcher, one of my advisors and the former executive director of the UNCF, the slogan 'a mind is a terrible thing to waste,' was developed. Today, Black colleges are needed more than ever to make sure that talented minds are not wasted."[19]

Ultimately Reagan won in a landslide, thanks mainly to economic concerns and the perception that the former California governor would bring a new vigor to an Oval Office perceived to have developed a "malaise" under Carter. But African Americans continued to move toward the Democrats, with only 14 percent supporting Reagan, down from Ford's 17 percent in 1976. Majority-Black Washington, DC, gave its three electoral votes to Carter. Of the swing states Fletcher had visited, Reagan won Florida by a 2–1 margin. The race was tighter in Pennsylvania, but even there, Reagan's victory probably had little to do with Fletcher's activities. Carter kept the support of the two big cities, Philadelphia and Pittsburgh.[20]

Disappointed

The Reagan–Bush victory ushered in a heady time for Fletcher. Key members of the transition team pushed for him to get a major appointment in the new administration, like secretary of labor or UN ambassador. Columnist and former Nixon speechwriter William Safire recommended that Blacks get a variety of top positions in the Reagan administration, rather than have a single "special assistant for blacks" as had Nixon and Ford; he recommended Fletcher in particular for such a job. The top African American on the transition team, Melvin Bradley, was particularly concerned that Fletcher and others get important jobs because they "paid a price, personally, for urging Blacks to vote for Reagan." George Bush attended a party at which he "literally gushed praise" for Fletcher, noting, "I've worked with Art Fletcher in many incarnations. . . . You've got to be careful he doesn't boss you around. If there's a better speaker around, I don't know where he is. When I need advice, I turn to Art Fletcher at the top of the list."[21]

In the meantime, Fletcher waited. As a minor player on the transition team, he began to position himself as a potential go-between for Mayor Marion Barry and the new administration. Trading on his connections, he billed himself as a lobbyist on behalf of a variety of government-contractor clients, and he registered to represent the government of Guyana in its economic dealings with the Reagan administration. He advised Bush on appointments to the office of the vice president, and he served as an honorary cochairman of the vice presidential inaugural ball at the Smithsonian (Bernyce was listed as a member of the hostess committee).[22]

But the expected top-level job did not materialize. On February 4, 1981, Reagan appointed Raymond Donovan as secretary of labor (later replaced by former RNC chair Bill Brock) and Jeane Kirkpatrick as ambassador to the United Nations. One by one the various cabinet and subcabinet positions filled up, and indeed few went to Blacks. Like Ford, Reagan did not go beyond tokenism in his cabinet appointments, naming only Samuel R. Pierce as secretary of HUD. Other prominent African American Republicans received only temporary or ad hoc initial appointments. Affirmative action opponent J. Clay Smith Jr. became acting chairman of the Equal Employment Opportunity Commission (EEOC), for example; liberal Republican Jewel Lafontant was asked to head a transition team to overhaul the US Commission on Civil Rights (to disastrous results).[23]

Reagan claimed his tokenism and appeal to unreconstructed southerners and white suburbanites was not rooted in race prejudice. He often repeated stories about how his Protestant mother and Catholic father had taken in Black boarders during his childhood; how his father had refused to stay in a hotel that didn't admit Jews; how he had protested segregation in baseball while he was a radio announcer in the 1930s. For Reagan, as with his political predecessor, Barry Goldwater, and his philosophical forebear, Milton

Friedman, civil rights laws imposed state authority on matters that would be better worked out eventually through the good graces of caring white people. He bought into the myth of an innocent white majority, residing mostly in the North and West, embarrassed by culpable white southerners whom they would eventually shame into better behavior. He conveniently explained his rejection by the overwhelming majority of Black voters with a "Democratic Party/Federal Government Handout" slave plantation analogy: "The Negro has delivered himself," he said in 1976, "to those who have no other intention than to create a federal plantation and ignore him."[24]

In fact, the better plantation analogy was demonstrated by those Black Republicans who got the permanent slots in Reagan's administration: conservatives willing to toe the party line, who "espoused a philosophy," according to sociologist Philip S. Hart, "indistinguishable from the right wing of the Republican Party." These included Clarence Thomas, who took the helm of the EEOC in 1982; Thomas Sowell, appointed to the Economic Policy Advisory Committee; Clarence Pendleton, chairman of the Commission on Civil Rights; and neoconservative professor Shelby Steele and conservative activist Robert Woodson, who formed something of a Black brain trust. If these men represented Reagan's figurative plantation, "happy slaves" toiling in the fields of the political backlash, white assistant attorney general William Bradford Reynolds was the overseer. Appointed to lead the agency responsible for enforcing legal remedies for Jim Crow like voting rights, equal employment opportunity, and school integration, Reynolds "unabashedly opposed both civil rights laws and the Supreme Court decisions that affirmed them," recalled Mary Frances Berry, who added that he "flat out refused to enforce laws intended to remedy race discrimination."[25]

Clearly, if unsurprisingly, the administration reflected the values of the conservative president rather than the moderate vice president. Fletcher, for his part, could not reconcile himself with this distasteful, if predictable, turn of events. The feeling was mutual. For two years he did not receive a presidential appointment, and when he did it was not to a position of any great influence.

Fletcher should not have been surprised. As the next eight years proved, the Reagan administration was abysmal for civil rights, and there was no political reason for such a team to allow a staunch supporter of affirmative action like Fletcher—with a proven track record for speaking his mind—anywhere near public policy. They were happy to have him shill for them, as when, during the campaign, he swallowed hard and made the case that Reagan could be trusted to do the right thing for African Americans once in office. But the Reagan team, like the Nixon team, was far more interested in using coded racist language to court the votes of unreconstructed white southerners, suburbanites, and skilled laborers. Unionists had ironically suffered most from the effects of Republican policies like Ford's refusal to sign a common-situs picketing bill, but they were made to blame people of color instead.[26]

This was not a new strategy. "Here's how I would approach that issue as a statistician, as a psychologist—which I'm not," Reagan political strategist Lee Atwater told Case Western Reserve University professor Alexander Lamis in 1981. "It's how abstract you handle the race thing. In other words you start out—and now, y'all don't quote me," he said:

> You start out in 1954 by saying "nigger nigger nigger." By 1968 you can't say nigger, that hurts, it backfires, so you say stuff like, uh, forced busing, states' rights and all that stuff. And you're gettin' so abstract now you're talking about cutting taxes, and all these things you're talking about are totally economic things, and the byproduct of them is blacks get hurt worse than whites. And subconsciously maybe that is part of it. I'm not saying that, but I'm saying that if it is getting that abstract and that coded, uh, then we're doing away with the racial problem one way or the other, uh, you follow me? 'Cause obviously sitting around saying, uh, we wanna cut taxes, we wanna cut this, and we want—is much more abstract than even the busing thing, um, and a hell of a lot more abstract than "nigger nigger."[27]

Atwater knew the depth of white racism—unconscious, overt, and otherwise—and was an expert at using it to turn out the vote. Like John Cherberg in 1968, who referred to his "Yugoslav ancestry" and his father's migration on a "four-masted sailing ship," he knew exactly how to appeal to the racist majority without saying the N word.

In his euphoria over the prospect of a restored Republican White House, Fletcher had ignored these race-baiting warning signs. He had refused to admit the truth: that the campaign represented the worst political instincts of conservatives in the Republican Party. But faced with the denial of a top appointment and the rise of Reynolds and the Black conservatives, Fletcher was forced to admit that the Reagan administration stood for everything he had been fighting in the party since his days with Governor Hall in Kansas.

Fletcher's wife, Bernyce, did somewhat better in the early years of the Reagan administration. She first got a job as an administrative assistant in the office of the secretary of labor, but she was quickly transferred to the Old Executive Office Building to work at the Office of Private Sector Initiatives. From there it was a short hop across the plaza to the East Wing, where in January 1982 she became administrative assistant to James Rosebush, the aptly named chief of staff to the first lady. Nancy Reagan was suffering from an image problem, having arranged for an expensive (if privately funded) renovation of the White House during a tough recession. Including an African American woman on her staff—a move that garnered some small mention by the Washington, DC, press—was part of a makeover designed "to temper her elitist image," to make her appear more like Betty Ford and less like Marie Antoinette. Among various clerical duties, Bernyce handled logistics for a European trip in March 1982, and she arranged for well-wishers to get autographed photos of the first lady. She worked in the East Wing for one year, at which point she left the federal service to help her husband with Arthur Fletcher & Associates, his contracting company.[28]

Arthur Fletcher & Associates (AF&A) proved yet another area of frustration for Fletcher during the first years of the Reagan administration. Contrary to his expectations, his connections to the White House did not help. He had founded the company in 1974, during his stint working for Bush at the RNC, to give a corporate base to his work as an affirmative action consultant for major corporations like Sears, General Electric, Marriott, AT&T, and IBM. He listed himself, Bernyce, and Rutgers professor Alfred Blumrosen, his colleague from the Department of Labor, as the company's principals. The Small Business Administration (SBA) had a program known as 8(a), which gave companies owned by women and members of minority groups a leg up through set-asides, selected no-bid contracts, and the like, so that after graduation (usually after five years in the program) they could compete on an equal basis with more established contractors. An old friend, Black Kansas Republican Leroy Tombs, had his own company registered with 8(a) as a food services, janitorial, and security contractor on the Alaska pipeline; Tombs turned Fletcher on to the program and made AF&A a subcontractor. During 1976 Fletcher put AF&A on hiatus and resigned his position as CEO to avoid a conflict of interest while serving in the Ford White House. On returning to the private sector in 1977, he attempted to register AF&A with the 8(a) program to pursue projects similar to those completed by Tombs. But the SBA had the business listed under its "professional services" category, and his application was repeatedly denied. Fletcher later claimed that the Carter administration had ordered the SBA to blackball him during these years for his outspoken stance as a Black Republican, but there is no evidence

On the African trip: Bush and Fletcher with President Joseph Mobutu of Zaire.
Arthur Fletcher Personal Papers, courtesy Paul Fletcher.

to support this; more likely it was simply the result of a slow-moving federal bureaucracy. In 1980 he officially asked that the SBA change the company's status from "professional services" to "housekeeping," the category which covered Tombs's company, and then, after Tombs got a major contract to run food services for the army at Fort Leonard Wood, Missouri, to "base maintenance/facilities management service." After completing a lengthy form in which he described his personal experiences with racial discrimination, in May 1982 Fletcher was finally admitted into the 8(a) program.[29]

While his White House connections did little to advance his business interests, having a friend housed at the Naval Observatory did give Fletcher a unique opportunity to travel. In November 1982 the vice president and Mrs. Bush made a trip to Africa for state visits to seven nations, and they took

April 13, 1983

Dear Art:

I hope that the enclosed photographs will bring

back many pleasant memories from a very enjoyable

trip.

                    Sincerely,

sorry they are mostly of me

From George Bush: "Sorry they are mostly of me." Arthur Fletcher Personal Papers, courtesy Paul Fletcher.

Fletcher along as part of the official entourage. The group cut a swath across the continent, visiting Cape Verde, Senegal, Nigeria, Zaire, Zambia (later known as the Democratic Republic of the Congo), Zimbabwe, and Kenya. On the return trip they stopped in Bermuda before the vice president departed for yet another state visit, to the Soviet Union. Fletcher had previously visited Africa only once, for a conference in Nigeria while he was assistant secretary of labor. Bush ostensibly invited him because their time together at the UN had given Fletcher foreign affairs experience; more likely the vice president had simply wanted to surround himself with Black friends during the trip.[30]

The next month, *Jet* magazine published a photo of Fletcher and Bush posing on either side of Prime Minister Robert Mugabe of Zimbabwe, surrounded by three other African Americans from the delegation. Some months later Bush sent Fletcher more than a dozen photographs, hoping they "will bring back many pleasant memories from a very enjoyable trip," and adding by hand that he was "sorry they are mostly of me."[31]

In early 1983 Fletcher was able to secure a $7 million contract to handle food services at Fort Leonard Wood, an army base in Missouri. Sources for how he accomplished this are incomplete, but it appears to have been due to connections with the appropriations officers at the base, forged through his friendship with Leroy Tombs. With paperwork in hand showing the 8(a) status of AF&A, Fletcher was designated the recipient of a no-bid contract. His own salary as CEO and his portion of the profit would have netted him as much as half a million dollars, much of which he hoped to use to get the SVL, the inner-city nondenominational self-help project he was now calling the National Christian Technical Institute, off the ground.[32]

However, the contract was not to be. The white-owned KP Services Co. of North Carolina, which had previously held the contract, complained through their lawyers to powerful senator Jesse Helms, who asked the SBA to investigate. The SBA then canceled the AF&A contract, noting that Fletcher could not take advantage of the 8(a) program without applying for contracts directly through its office. Fletcher appealed to his own political connections, notably Senator Alan Simpson, with whom he had worked during the Reagan campaign, and of course the office of the vice president. A White House staffer, ordered to look into the matter, told Bush that he thought the SBA wasn't being fair to Fletcher. But neither Simpson nor Bush exercised influence on the matter to the degree that Helms had. Fletcher's problems with the SBA simply weren't high enough priorities for his friends to risk a public feud with Helms, however sympathetic they were. Helms was a Reagan ally, going back at least as far as the 1976 election, when he ran racist pro-Reagan campaign ads in North Carolina. The SBA did give Fletcher a consolation prize, awarding AF&A a much smaller $2 million contract running food services for several dining halls at Fort Belvoir, Virginia, with annual salary and profits for Fletcher estimated at about $150,000.[33]

On May 18, 1983, while fighting to keep the Fort Leonard Wood contract, Fletcher had a heart attack. He made a full recovery, but he apparently did not take it as the warning sign it was. Having already suffered from diabetes for more than fifteen years, and being only fifty-eight years old, this should have spurred him to improved diet and exercise. Instead, after his release from the hospital, Fletcher plunged back into his work, sending the labor secretary, Bill Brock, a proposal for a pilot project for food service training on June 11. He seems to have been eager to get the incident behind him as quickly as possible, and he did not refer to it in any correspondence at the time.[34]

Shortly after his recovery, he discovered why he had encountered so much difficulty getting a job with the Reagan administration: he had been black-balled by a powerful White House advisor. In the August 1983 edition of *Washingtonian* magazine, reporter Fred Barnes explained that Lyn "Nofziger was able to bar black Republican Arthur Fletcher . . . from any administration job, pointing to Fletcher's attack on Reagan's civil-rights stand." Fearing that this might affect his consulting business, Fletcher wrote a letter decrying Nofziger's statement and noting his long history supporting Republican candidates, including Reagan. He addressed it to the president and vice president over Bernyce's signature, and ostensibly from Bernyce's perspective ("Art, for his part, is willing to turn the other cheek . . . but I am not"). Presumably he was concerned that he would appear petty if he sent an angry reply himself. Bernyce sent copies to "Elected Members of Congress," the RNC chair, and "Other Prominent Republicans." Senator Simpson and former defense secretary Melvin Laird thanked her for their copies, noting their positive experiences campaigning for Reagan with Fletcher during the fall of 1980. Arkansas congressman Ed Bethune told White House chief of staff James Baker that the Fletchers deserved a reply, but none was forthcoming.[35]

Consolations

Notwithstanding Nofziger's statements, 1983 was the year in which Fletcher's connections to the Reagan administration finally began to pay off, albeit in a small way. In February the president appointed him to a vacancy on the Pennsylvania Avenue Development Corporation (PADC) and designated him vice chairman.[36]

The PADC had been founded by an act of Congress in 1972 in response to growing concerns that the corridor between the Capitol and the White House had fallen into severe decay. This portion of the avenue in northwest DC was the traditional parade route taken by presidents immediately after inauguration. In 1961 President Kennedy, walking to his new home, remarked that the boulevard had become an eyesore unbefitting its prominence in the capital of a global superpower. He authorized an ad hoc committee, which morphed into a "President's Council," and then under President Johnson into a "Temporary President's Commission on Pennsylvania Avenue," with each group having greater authority than the last. They succeeded in designating the avenue and its surrounding blocks a national historical site, but they failed to attract significant interest from developers. Local residents' groups expressed concern about redeveloping the area, having learned from the bitter experiences of other cities that urban renewal all too often meant "Negro removal." In 1972, at the urging of President Nixon and his advisor, Daniel Patrick Moynihan (who had been involved in the project since the Kennedy administration), Congress established the PADC as "a wholly owned Government Corporation," with a $200 million appropriation. Members included several appointed "from the private sector by the President" as well as five "heads of federal agencies," along with the DC mayor and city council chairman. The PADC developed a master plan, acquired properties, and forged corporate partnerships to facilitate investment.[37]

From the start Fletcher developed an excellent working relationship with the corporation's new chairman. A corporate lawyer and longtime DC resident, Henry Berliner had been Fletcher's predecessor as chairman of the DC delegation to the RNC in 1972 and 1976. His connections to local real estate interests made him a good choice for PADC chair, as these were necessary to put the corporation's master plan into action during its critical second decade. Fletcher's concerns with protecting the interests of Black tenants, meanwhile, and background enforcing affirmative action in building construction, made the two a well-rounded team. During their six-year tenure at the helm of the PADC, the corporation approved plans for, or saw to fruition, several important projects with which visitors to and residents of the district have since become familiar. These included a new park at Market Square with a refurbished navy memorial; a restored Willard Hotel; the Bob Hope USO Building on Indiana Avenue; and restored facades on Gallery Row. The PADC preserved the Old Post Office and designated Western Plaza for its reincarnation as Freedom Plaza in honor of Martin Luther King Jr.[38]

Fletcher became the chair of the corporation's affirmative action advisory committee. In that capacity he analyzed the affirmative action compliance reports of the existing general contractors and subcontractors as well as those bidding on new projects; recommended board action to ensure continued compliance for those who had effective compliance postures; and proposed timelines for those not yet in compliance.[39]

He was well suited to the work. He was enforcing policies that he himself had authored while with the Nixon administration, but meeting transcripts also show a collegial temperament, attention to detail, passion for getting it right, and determination to champion minority and female contractors. They also make it clear that his more recent experiences as a small business owner, coupled with his advancing age, had given him the wisdom and the steady hand to act as an effective intermediary between the PADC and the contractors. He enjoyed being in a position of government authority again, and he relished the opportunity, however small, to make an impact on public policy. His good nature came through most clearly when Mayor Barry was in attendance; their jocular ripostes showed no lingering ill will over the 1978 race.[40]

Fletcher's professional life continued to incrementally improve. The secretary of transportation, Elizabeth "Liddy" Dole, contracted AF&A to hold a "procurement fair" in Atlanta. The wife of Senator Bob Dole, Elizabeth Dole's tenure at the Department of Transportation was most notable for her approval and promotion of new regulations requiring center brake lights on cars (known then, to her embarrassment, as Liddy Lights). A new law required that the DOT set aside 10 percent of the federal gasoline tax to fund opportunities for minority- and women-owned businesses, and Dole wanted Fletcher to get the word out to eligible companies. After his mixed experience with the SBA 8(a) program, Fletcher certainly was prepared to offer advice. Assisted by his son, Paul, he booked representatives from various government agencies to reserve booths in the event space at Atlanta's Westin Peachtree Plaza on July 20, 1983, to discuss their contracting opportunities and the processes for obtaining them, then set about promoting the event to potential participants.[41]

The first fair was so successful at attracting potential business owners that Elizabeth Dole contracted AF&A to hold similar procurement fairs in twenty cities in 1984. Records do not indicate the degree to which attendees actually obtained contracts, and so we cannot be sure exactly how successful the program was in that regard. But they generated good press for Dole and her corner of the Reagan administration, received rave reviews from attendees and agency representatives, and gave Fletcher the opportunity to show Republicans in action on behalf of Black entrepreneurs. Advertising the program with the millennial fervor he so often brought to speeches, he told a reporter, "This is no time for faint hearts. This is the one opportunity, and you better get it while it's in front of you or you can forget it . . . tell the Congress, the president and others that they weren't wrong when they set aside $7.8 billion for minority and women entrepreneurs."[42]

Fletcher combined his experience organizing these procurement fairs with his position as vice chair of the PADC to develop a procurement fair for Washington, DC, in September 1985. Initially intended for women and minority contractors interested in obtaining subcontracts on existing and future PADC projects, Fletcher was able to expand it to include opportunities for contracts with other government entities in and around the district thanks to the interest of agency representatives on the PADC board. The most important of these was Jack Finberg, who represented the General Services Administration at the PADC. The General Services Administration, as I have noted elsewhere, was "responsible for overseeing, among other things, the construction and maintenance of the federal government's physical plant in the nation's capital." As a result, the PADC procurement fair was one of the most successful Fletcher organized. Ecstatic, PADC chairman Berliner commended Fletcher: "No better person is suited to reaffirm our commitment to the rights for all Americans than Art Fletcher, who has been so active in the field."[43]

Marking Time

Fletcher did not actively campaign during the 1984 presidential election. His work organizing the procurement fairs, managing AF&A's food service contract at Fort Belvoir, and his vice chairmanship of the Pennsylvania Avenue Development Commission were more than enough to keep him busy in his sixtieth year. He remained nonplussed with the Reagan administration, both because he had largely been shut out at the policy level and because his experience was typical of moderate Black Republicans.[44]

His relationship with George Bush remained strong. When his old Washburn chum and former Nixon appointee Sam Jackson died of cancer at age fifty-three, it was Fletcher who delivered remarks at the funeral on behalf of the vice president. And the Bush family never forgot to include the Fletchers on their Christmas card list. (The Reagans sent them Christmas cards only during Fletcher's years on the PADC.)[45]

But the vice president didn't need his help this time around. Bush's position on the ticket was never in doubt; he had greatly impressed Reagan early in the presidency by refusing to land his helicopter on the White House lawn during the crisis when Reagan was shot. The Reagan–Bush ticket won reelection in 1984 in a landslide despite garnering only 9 percent of the Black vote (down from 14 percent in 1980). The only places where the Republicans lost were Minnesota (the home state of the challenger, former vice president Walter Mondale) and Fletcher's DC.[46]

Jesse Jackson's campaign for the 1984 Democratic presidential nomination also played a role in Fletcher's decision to sit this one out. The disciple and adviser to Martin Luther King Jr., who early on laid claim to the slain civil rights leader's mantle, had adopted his mentor's avoidance of partisanship for the first decade after the assassination. He focused instead on building his own civil rights organization, the Rainbow/PUSH Coalition, based in Chicago. In 1976 Jackson openly postulated that the GOP might win the Black vote by naming Massachusetts senator Ed Brooke as Ford's running mate. But in 1984, galvanized by the downright hostility of the Reagan administration, and seeing in the race an opportunity to boost his own popularity and strengthen the reach of his organization, Jackson entered the Democratic primary race. He was the first Black candidate for the presidency to contest primaries in every state (skipping only Puerto Rico), and he won a few: South Carolina, Louisiana, Mississippi, and Washington, DC. He took second place in Maryland and third place—after Mondale and Senator Gary Hart—in nearly every other. He took nearly one-fifth of the popular vote, and he stayed in the race until the convention.[47]

Fletcher was fascinated by Jackson's candidacy. As a longtime political insider, he had always viewed the chances of an African American winning the presidency as worse than negligible; he believed that the best way for Blacks to achieve political influence was to befriend and influence white elites like George Bush, who actually stood a chance. Even a white Hollywood actor had a better chance at the presidency than a Black man, no matter how politically savvy. Fletcher's views reflected the same popular wisdom that had kept Ed Brooke off the 1976 ticket.

Jackson's 1984 candidacy did not prove to Fletcher that a Black man could win the presidency (and sadly Fletcher did not live to see the historic 2008 election of Barack Obama). But it did demonstrate two things to him. First, it proved that Blacks had decisively moved into the Democratic Party. The quadrennial November elections reflected the preferences of voters for particular candidates, but Jackson's showing in the primaries reflected the growth of the Black vote within that party. Second, Jackson's candidacy confirmed something Fletcher had been saying all along: Blacks could influence a political party from within.

The 1984 Democratic convention made for a stark contrast with the 1964 Democratic convention. In 1964, when the nomination of the incumbent Lyndon Johnson was hardly in question, a segregated Mississippi primary prevented the seating of an integrated delegation from that state. The Freedom Summer protests moved north to the convention in Atlantic City, but party leaders forged a compromise based on tokenism. By 1984, however, thanks to the Voting Rights Act, the concerted efforts of Black Democrats, the popularity of Jesse Jackson, and the Republicans' embrace of unreconstructed white southern and suburban Democrats, the Democratic convention and platform clearly reflected the influence of African American concerns.[48]

As Fletcher saw it, Jackson's campaign demonstrated that Blacks could successfully integrate a previously hostile political party, and he became increasingly interested in using this as a model for the GOP. In the immediate aftermath of Reagan's reelection, he penned two essays and gave interviews on the subject to syndicated columnist William Raspberry and former congressman turned TV host Julian Bond. Submission of his articles to the

Washington Times gave him no traction (they were far too long for publication in the opinion pages). But conservative pundit and former Nixon speechwriter Pat Buchanan, despite disagreeing with Fletcher's motives, nevertheless respected the effort and recommended that he submit them for publication in venues that allowed more long-form writing. Ultimately he did not publish them, but seeing an uptick in speaking requests, he reworked their themes into his speeches.[49]

His argument was that African Americans whose political and social views dovetailed with much of the Republican platform should not write off the Republican Party as hopelessly intolerant and opposed to civil rights any more than they should write off the United States for the same reason. Rather, they should see the challenge much as they saw the challenge of Jim Crow: something to overcome. Join the Republican Party despite the strength of the conservatives, he argued; then fight, as he was doing, from within.

That increased numbers of Black Republicans might decrease African Americans' tenuous influence in the Democratic Party—in other words, that a racial minority might only be large enough to influence a single party—did not concern him; he was a GOP partisan and saw it as Black Democrats' job to focus on integrating the Democratic Party, not his. But such a concern should have informed his thinking; the distribution of unreconstructed southerners and white suburbanites was also a zero-sum game, and as long as the majority of them were voting for Republican candidates, their influence would be felt by GOP decision makers. Furthermore, he hoped that by continued exposure to civil rights ideas, hostile whites would eventually come around.

A third option—political independence—presented no concrete examples of success. The most prominent Black political independent in the 1980s, whom historian Quintard Taylor called a "significant twentieth-century profile in political courage," was Nebraska state senator Ernie Chambers. Elected during the height of the Black power movement, Chambers had much in common with Fletcher: an impatience with the racist status quo, an openness to a wide variety of programs to achieve civil rights, a willingness to call it as he saw it, and a refusal to join the Democratic Party despite the demographic trends. Chambers won supporters in his north Omaha district and among members of the state's unicameral legislature much as Fletcher often did: one at a time, with persistence. While he eventually would become the longest-serving state senator in Nebraska history, his inability to win a statewide race in some ways mirrored Fletcher's own disappointments. Fletcher at least continued to have friends in high places.[50]

After the 1984 presidential election Fletcher was given the opportunity to bury the hatchet with the UNCF. He had continued to contribute to the fund through the years, and he served on its DC committees whenever asked; he was proud of his year as executive director, especially with the incontrovertible success of the "a mind is a terrible thing to waste" ad campaign. In December 1984 he was named interim cochair of the *Lou Rawls Parade of Stars* telethon to benefit UNCF, which aired on DC's channel 20 on December 29. This sixth edition of the annual event was the first to run a full twelve hours. Cohosted by singer Marilyn McCoo and *Tonight Show* personality Ed McMahon, the shindig included fifty entertainers and was headlined by "Kool & The Gang, Billy Dee Williams, Mr. T, Donna Summer, Bill Cosby and Dianne Carol [*sic*]." Fletcher convened a fund-raising team at the PADC conference room and successfully appealed to President Reagan, who made a personal donation and recorded a greeting from his holiday vacation.[51]

Fletcher's success cochairing the event, no doubt coupled with his experience with the procurement fairs, led to his being asked to chair the 1985 UNCF annual campaign in Washington. He lined up Labor Secretary Bill Brock to chair a job fair on June 11, secured support from the White House, engaged African Methodist Episcopal bishop John Hurst Adams to conduct a "prayer breakfast," and recruited representatives from corporations like IBM to staff the job fair booths. Fletcher's continued devotion to UNCF, despite his having been fired in 1973, impressed his replacement, executive director Chris Edley, still in the post after fourteen years. When Edley was interviewed for a Columbia University oral history project that July, he had only good things to say about Fletcher, noting that "he has remained kind and helpful." In the following year, 1986, they "named the second annual UNCF Job Fair in [his] honor."[52]

Sadly for Fletcher, his newfound success with UNCF was not reflected in his professional life. The Department of Transportation (DOT) procurement fairs dried up in 1985, and the PADC fair was something of a last hurrah in that regard. More importantly, things were not going well with AF&A's food services contract at Fort Belvoir. Despite receiving numerous letters of commendation from unit commanding officers and an additional small contract to provide cafeteria services at Carlisle Barracks in Pennsylvania, the company's activities came under fire from the on-site contracting officer.

Fletcher's first two years supplying cafeteria services to the Army Corps of Engineers training facility at Fort Belvoir had gone well for him and the company. From October 1983 to September 1985, AF&A took in $2.26 million, employed 157 workers, paid more than $400,000 per year in officer salaries (including Fletcher's own), and saw profits totaling $329,000. The successes of the first two years led to a second two-year contract for $2.4 million.[53]

The problems began in the summer of 1986, when a routine inspection resulted in several demerits for menu substitutions, recipes not being followed, and food not being properly thawed. The company was fined tens of thousands of dollars. Fletcher's on-site manager, Raleigh Harden, protested the demerits, arguing point by point that in all cases the company was following the proper procedures. The contracting officer, Lydia Bryant, ignored Harden's letter; by October, the parties were talking past one another. Bryant complained that "performance has continued to deteriorate"; Harden, for his part, claimed that Bryant was editing inspection reports to paint the company in an even worse light. Meanwhile, ironically, the accolades continued to flow. AF&A was selected to represent Fort Belvoir in an armywide food service competition after a surprise inspection by the training and documents division, which was independent of the contracting officer; a colonel told the director of logistics that the inspected dining facility was being run "in a dedicated and professional manner." Nonetheless, Bryant declared on December 1, 1986, that "the deficiencies are valid." When Fletcher requested that the military police investigate security at the site, noting Harden's complaints of pilferage, Bryant reprimanded him for not first going through her office.[54]

Because the company continued to earn high marks from disinterested observers, and because the contract (and AF&A's membership in the SBA 8[a] program) was due to expire in the fall of 1987, it appears that Bryant was building a paper trail to deny AF&A a further extension. There is insufficient evidence to definitively explain her motivations. Perhaps she had a connection to another company that sought to replace AF&A; perhaps she simply didn't get along with Harden. Another AF&A manager, Teresa Greene, wrote Fletcher, "It is my interpretation that the plan is to throw the contract back to the streets for the remaining option years. [Bryant's] visits appear to have been designed to find fault, and not look at the operation objectively." Fletcher believed that Bryant singled him out for being a Black Republican, although there is no evidence for this. An appeal to SBA earned Fletcher a one-year extension in 8(a), a threatened lawsuit earned him the money docked for previous demerits, and in June 1987 Bryant finally changed her "inspection rating . . . to satisfactory." But on October 1 Bryant summarily terminated the contract. Fletcher's desperate appeal to President Reagan was simply referred to the Department of Defense, where it fell on deaf ears.[55]

Overall, the Fort Belvoir contract earned Fletcher a handsome salary and secured a tidy profit for AF&A. The Fletchers now owned three homes—in Columbia, Maryland, G Street in southwest DC, and a getaway in Pleasantville, near Atlantic City, New Jersey—and it had allowed them to significantly pay down their mortgages. Although he had unfairly lost the contract, which he attributed to political discrimination, he emerged from the situation believing ever more strongly in the importance of programs like SBA's 8(a) minority set-asides.

Despite the setback, Fletcher had another reason for cheer. In the midst of these difficulties he received a letter from a longtime friend and sometime patron: "I would be honored to have your support for my presidential candidacy, the greatest challenge of my public life," wrote George Bush. Fletcher's own greatest challenge lay ahead: to help his friend become president, and to work within a new Republican administration to further the cause of civil rights.[56]

Campaign '88

Going into the 1988 presidential election, George Bush had a problem. He needed to appear conservative enough to win nomination from what was now the party of Ronald Reagan without significantly damaging his reputation as a moderate for the general election. Warning signs appeared early: New York congressman Jack Kemp, more conservative than Bush, saw his campaign falter when he was perceived by white conservative voters as too sympathetic to the concerns of Black people. Given Bush's track record on civil rights, he needed a strong lift. He won Reagan's endorsement and promised a skittish Republican electorate that he would continue the Gipper's policies. This proved crucial; despite his own moderation, he was able to paint his only serious opponent, conservative Bob Dole, as a liberal on taxation. After coming in third in Iowa (behind Dole and televangelist Pat Robertson), Bush campaigned hard in New Hampshire. The result was the reverse of his experience against Reagan. New Hampshire proved as much Dole's frustration in 1988 as it had been for Bush in 1980. Afterward Dole took only four other states (including his native Kansas), Robertson won a total of four, but Bush swept the rest of the nation, at long last winning the Republican presidential nomination that he had desired since at least as early as 1973 and that he had been actively seeking since 1979.[57]

Fletcher's support of Bush during the primary season was focused, as in 1980, on winning him the delegates from the District of Columbia. After a Bush fund-raising dinner with Black Republicans at the Sheraton Washington on March 21, Fletcher told a reporter that Bush and Black Republicans "have in common . . . a clear recognition that the unfinished business of the civil rights movement of the '60s and '70s is economic empowerment." Fortunately, given Fletcher's advancing age (he was now sixty-three), winning the DC primary was a cakewalk. It took place on May 3, by which point Dole and all the other serious contenders had withdrawn from the race and pledged their delegates to Bush.[58]

While Fletcher was closely attuned to the need for Bush to win the support of conservatives to snag the nomination, he also wanted to position Bush to win the Black vote in November. He told Bush that he "can set the Black Political Campaign Agenda . . . if we move now while the window is still open," forwarding a newspaper clipping on the growing appeal of self-help remedies for inner-city poverty. "'Self-help' is conservative talk;—it is GOP talk," he wrote. "If we 'strike while the iron is hot' . . . it will not cost you any conservative votes."[59]

Other pundits saw an opportunity for Bush in the Democrats' rejection of Jesse Jackson in 1984 and in the subsequent snubbing of Jackson and members of the Congressional Black Caucus (CBC) by the party's inner circle. Black conservative Robert Woodson noted that African Americans "have done themselves a major disservice with their dog-on-the-grave loyalty to one party—a party that has come to take them for granted." He urged the GOP to "reach out and provide an alternative to what might kindly be called Democratic indifference," arguing in the *Atlanta Journal-Constitution* that "Republicans should advance policies and initiatives that stimulate investment and business development in low-income neighborhoods" and "vigorously support the privatization of government services in ways that generate increased business and job opportunities for black Americans." (Underestimating Fletcher's loyalty to Bush, an acquaintance forwarded this article to him during the primaries with a note asking him to "pass this to Bro[ther Bob] Dole: If he complies I'll support him!!")[60]

Syndicated columnist William Raspberry, who had been following Fletcher's career with admiration since the Nixon administration, concurred that the Black vote represented an opportunity for the GOP, if they played it right. "The Democrats are losing their vise-grip on black voters, but the Republicans haven't figured out how to take advantage of the opportunity," he wrote. "One black Republican, Arthur Fletcher . . . has argued that blacks ought to integrate the party the way they integrated southern restaurants in the '6os. The perception of hostility 'didn't stop us from integrating the schools or hotels or lunch counters,' he has said." And Murray Friedman, the Democratic vice chairman of the United States Commission on Civil Rights, wrote, "It is never wise to put all one's eggs in the same basket, so it's a mistake for any ethnic or religious group to throw all its support to one political party." Of Fletcher's strategy to integrate the GOP, Friedman said, "That's not a bad idea either."[61]

The GOP wasn't the only party looking to recapture a lost constituency. The popular perception of George Bush as an effete, elite, out-of-touch Ivy Leaguer gave the party of Jefferson and Jackson an opportunity to run to the right and recapture the Reagan Democrats. New York governor Mario Cuomo, seen as a national security hawk, appealed to those who espoused this line of thinking, but he declined to run. Former Colorado senator Gary Hart, who had placed second in 1984, was an early front-runner, as he was seen as an experienced pragmatist, but his campaign faltered after a sex scandal. Tennessee senator Al Gore, a moderate, took seven primaries, but the real contest ended up in the liberal camp, between Massachusetts governor Michael Dukakis and civil rights activist Jesse Jackson. Making his second national try, Jackson had learned well the lessons of 1984. A Jackson victory was still a long shot, but he avoided his earlier mistakes (like his anti-Semitic "Hymietown" remark) and ended the race a strong second, hoping to force himself onto the ticket as running mate. Given that the Democrats had nominated the first woman for vice president in 1984, Geraldine Ferraro, a Dukakis–Jackson ticket certainly seemed plausible.

Unfortunately for Jackson and his supporters, the running mate calculus in the Democratic Party was similar to that of the Republicans. In 1988 each party nominated for president a member of its own left wing; each nominee saw the need to pick a running mate who could run to his right. The moderate Bush picked conservative J. Danforth Quayle; the liberal Dukakis picked moderate Lloyd Bentsen (who had coincidentally ascended to the Senate by beating a young congressman Bush in 1970).

With Bush having won the nomination, Fletcher's role in the 1988 Republican National Convention was far less exciting than it had been eight years earlier. Fletcher gave Bush his full support. He understood why the running mate needed to be a conservative, so there was no organizing Black delegates, no threatened walkout, no protest. His one speech at the convention was a simple paragraph in which he introduced one of the scheduled speakers:

In the late '70s, a sure laugh was simply to say the word "Cleveland." That once proud city on Lake Erie had become a rust belt, ran on potholes, and for recreation the citizens [would] go down to the river to watch it burn. Not to mention the fact that the city was completely bankrupt and without credit. That was the situation when a new Republican mayor took office in 1979. Using innovative public and private partnerships, persuading eight Democrats for every Republican in the election, the entire City Council which was 100 percent Democrat, that mayor created a renaissance in the city of Cleveland. And today Cleveland is a marvel of urban renewal and growth. And that mayor has established a national reputation for really knowing how to manage. Once again Cleveland is an all-American city, thanks to the remarkable efforts of this determined Republican. I give you George Voinovich, the Mayor of Cleveland.[62]

The seasoned observer might have detected a hint of wistfulness in Fletcher's tone; after all, the accomplishments of Voinovich tracked the path Fletcher had planned for his own stillborn mayoralty in Washington, DC.

Despite his friendship with the nominee, Fletcher no longer had any significant political influence in his party; eight years of Reaganite conservatism had taken their toll. But he was still there, a relic of his party's past. He looked to a Bush victory to reinvigorate the moderate civil rights Republicanism he championed and to give him another opportunity to fight for his beliefs at the highest levels of power.

Dukakis and Bentsen came out of the Democratic National Convention with a seventeen-point lead in the polls. Bush was in a deep trough, and at first he sought to shore up his traditional support from the Black community. Fletcher, he knew, could be useful here. Bush convened a meeting of top DC African Americans, including the president of Howard University, Dr. James Cheek, and he brought Fletcher along. According to a reporter from the *New York Times,* Bush told the group, "We are not writing off anybody this year. . . . I am familiar with historic voting trends, but we are going to try to turn that around. We have a good shot, we have a chance if I get my message of commitment and fair play out across the country." He added, "I have to show who I really am to overcome certain perceptions out there."[63]

But campaign manager Lee Atwater had a very different strategy for reversing Bush's flagging poll numbers. Acquainted with Fletcher as a fellow member of the PADC board of directors, Atwater's vision was opposed to nearly everything Fletcher stood for. He set out to capture the same voters he had won for Reagan in 1980: unreconstructed southerners chafing at the end of Jim Crow (and the recent establishment of a national holiday to honor their favorite villain, Dr. Martin Luther King Jr.); skilled white workers resentful over a perceived loss of privilege; and white suburbanites who had fled what they saw as crime-infested cities now rife with the crack cocaine associated with ghetto residents.[64]

Atwater took his cue from D. W. Griffith's 1915 film *Birth of a Nation*, which portrayed a monstrous Black man, Gus, attempting to rape an innocent white woman (when historically the rape of Black women by white men was far more prevalent), and which led to a resurgence of the Ku Klux Klan. Atwater found his own Gus in William Horton, a convicted murderer and rapist originally from South Carolina. While serving a life sentence without the possibility of parole for a Lawrence, Massachusetts, murder, Horton was released multiple times on weekend furlough as part of a program that Dukakis supported. On his tenth such furlough he did not return; he went to Maryland, where he raped a white woman and assaulted her fiancé.[65]

Al Gore had first raised the issue of Dukakis's support of the furlough program during the primaries, but Atwater took it to a new level, supporting television advertisements that showed a mug shot of the unshaved Horton, renaming him "Willie" to evoke male genitalia, and warning in no uncertain terms that a vote for Dukakis was a vote against white female sexual innocence. Bush, to his credit, objected to ads which implicitly likened him to a white knight of the Ku Klux Klan who promised to save America from the scourge of Black male monsters, and he demanded they be pulled; but he did not object to the resulting poll numbers. By mid-September he had taken the lead, and Dukakis never recovered. Bush was elected to the presidency, and in January 1989 he became the fortieth person to hold that title.[66]

Fletcher's elation at his friend's election was tempered by his grave disappointment at the methods. His work promoting the Republican Party to African Americans had again been betrayed—this time by the campaign of the very man he had so long supported as a moderate voice of reason. No stranger to the rough-and-tumble of electoral politics, Fletcher understood that the Horton ads were distasteful to Bush personally, but they certainly, he felt, put the "evil" in necessary evil.

Still, Fletcher knew the heart of this man who would now be president. Bush had good intentions on civil rights, and Fletcher did his best to convey that to anyone who would listen—and to fight those within the campaign and the administration who tried to turn Bush against civil rights for political opportunism. In a pattern that replayed throughout the Bush presidency, Fletcher saw the triumph of the racist ads as one lost battle; he picked up his sword and prepared for the next. The effort to secure civil rights was a long war.

Certainly the most effective way for Fletcher to fight that war was to secure a top spot in the administration. Columnist William Raspberry agreed, arguing that Bush had an opportunity to win Black support for his administration through the appointment of Black advisors and cabinet members. Fletcher lost no time in pressing the advantage of his friendship to the president-elect and others in his transition team. When he learned that Bush family friend (and former Reagan chief of staff) James Baker had been named secretary of state, he told him that he and Bernyce "indeed feel comfortable knowing you are at the helm assisting our good friend President-Elect George Bush achieve the status of a great president." Baker's reply was personal; he took a standard "Thank you very much for your congratulatory note" form letter, crossed out "Mr. & Mrs. Fletcher" in favor of a handwritten "Art & Bernice [*sic*]," and added at the bottom, again by hand, "Happy Holidays to you both from Susan & me."[67]

Although one supporter wrote Bush recommending that Fletcher be tapped to chair a panel on minority business initiatives, Fletcher had higher aspirations. He wanted to be secretary of labor and pick up where he left off when he left the Nixon administration. And unlike in 1980, when the incoming president was a conservative and his friend's influence was minimal, this time Bush was president. The *Washington Post* listed Fletcher among five prominent Blacks being considered for top posts, and he secured powerful endorsements for the Labor job from the private sector as well as from a prominent—conservative—member of Congress. None other than Strom Thurmond, former Dixiecrat nominee for president and one of the architects of Nixon's Southern Strategy, told transition personnel head Chase Untermeyer that "those who have contacted me on Mr. Fletcher's behalf feel he would ably serve the Administration and fulfill any trust reposed in him. Therefore I request his qualifications to serve as Secretary of Labor receive your careful consideration."[68]

Without access to the private correspondence between Thurmond and "those who have contacted me," we can only conjecture as to his motives. Perhaps the old segregationist firebrand made this recommendation for reasons peculiar to his own political situation back home in South Carolina, aiming to shore up support with the Black business community there, where Fletcher was well known. Perhaps he was hoping to curry favor with an administration headed by someone he knew all too well to be to his left on civil rights. Perhaps he was simply ignorant, or forgetful, of how contrary were Fletcher's positions on civil rights issues to his own—especially affirmative action.

Whatever Thurmond's motives, Bush took his and the other recommendations, as well as his own political instincts, seriously enough to consider Fletcher for the position. Thanks largely to the Horton ads, he had garnered a mere 11 percent of the Black vote nationwide, only a slight uptick from Reagan's 9 percent in 1984 but significantly less than the 14 percent Reagan had taken in 1980. He knew that he needed to reach out to African Americans to be the president of all the people, and he wanted very much to win reelection in 1992 with a larger percentage of the Black vote. On Friday, December 16, Bush invited Fletcher into the Oval Office for a meeting to discuss the appointment.[69]

Bush's decision was likely swayed by another meeting he had just after the weekend. Union leaders had traditionally been consulted on these appointments, as organized labor was considered the most important constituency of the Department of Labor. What's more, by now white skilled unionists were considered a critical component of the Reagan Democrats who had helped elect Bush to the presidency. On Monday, December 19, Bush met with AFL-CIO president Lane Kirkland (the late George Meany's successor) as well as the organization's secretary-treasurer, Thomas Donohue. Because presidents no longer recorded their Oval Office conversations since the tapes had been so damaging to Nixon, and because Lane Kirkland's files at the AFL-CIO archives are not yet open to the public, we cannot be certain what was said. But Kirkland and Donohue had long been powerful leaders in organized labor, and they surely remembered Fletcher's work on the Philadelphia Plan. It is highly likely they gave the president what amounted to a veto of a Fletcher appointment. Five days later, on Christmas Eve, Bush announced that he was instead nominating Elizabeth Dole to the post.[70]

Bush kept Fletcher close through the winter of 1989, knowing his old friend's disappointment in having been passed over for the Labor job. Naturally Fletcher and Bernyce were invited guests at the "Bicentennial Inaugural," as the Bush team billed the presidential inauguration (1989 marked 200 years since George Washington's first inauguration, but the actual anniversary was in March). And he took them for a ride on Air Force One soon after. But Fletcher didn't want a comfortable retirement as one of Bush's "secret ten" Black friends; he wanted a job.[71]

He didn't have to wait long. On January 30 a White House official contacted the security office to request a routine FBI background check on Fletcher, stating that he was "our tentative selection for Chairman of the

Commission on Civil Rights." Bush hoped the Fletcher appointment would reinvigorate an agency that had sadly languished during the Reagan years. On March 20, 1989, twenty years after his first federal appointment, the White House publicized that decision to the general approval of the press and civil rights community.[72]

The problem now was actually getting Fletcher onto the commission. Because Reagan had attempted to eviscerate the agency in 1983, Congress had passed a law to ensure that it remain strictly independent of any branch of the government so that it could submit nonpartisan reports on the government's civil rights activities. As such, the president could appoint four of the eight members—and Congress the other four—but only upon a vacancy. The president could designate any member of the commission as chair, but the incumbent, William Allen, a Republican appointed by Reagan, refused to resign despite his recent involvement in a bizarre scandal (and the unanimous vote by the other commissioners to censure him). None of the terms of the Republican presidential appointees expired until November, and in the meantime powerful members of Congress were announcing that they might not vote for the commission's reauthorization. For the time being Fletcher's appointment was in limbo.[73]

Eager to get started, and ever the optimist, Fletcher made use of the surge in press coverage to take on the mantle of the government's civil rights watchdog without a formal appointment. Political and civil rights organizations, government groups, and universities were clamoring to hear the presumptive chairman-designee's take on the future of civil rights in a new Republican administration. The invitations came from all across the country, and he accepted with relish. Not since his year in the Ford administration had he traveled so much. He took advantage of the fact that without an actual government job he was free to accept private funds for his speeches, and charged between $1,500 and $10,000, depending on what each group could afford. He gave interviews to any reporter who asked. "Rather than wait to get named, I have suited up and started playing," he told one audience, referencing his vigorous youth on the gridiron. He accepted invitations from the American Contract Compliance Association; the Minority Enterprise Development Committee of Rochester, New York; the Black McDonald's Operators; Mankato State University in Idaho; the Illinois Department of Transportation; and others. In total he gave fifteen speeches in 1989, earning $28,475 in honoraria. At every appearance he made use of his years of experience in government and the private sector to give attendees the confidence that they could use civil rights legislation and affirmative action regulations to better themselves and their communities. He always mentioned his friendship with President Bush, but he avoided political hucksterism; he let the fact of his designation to chair the Commission on Civil Rights speak for the administration's commitment to do right by African Americans. He received numerous letters of appreciation from attendees, all wishing him well in his forthcoming work reinvigorating the commission.[74]

On October 12, 1989, the idiosyncratic incumbent commission chairman, William Allen, after giving an inflammatory speech opposing civil rights for homosexuals, finally resigned the chairmanship. President Bush accepted in a terse letter. But Allen didn't resign his membership on the commission, which he held through 1992. Fletcher's appointment, and Bush's formal designation of him as chair, would have to wait yet another month for a vacancy. Still, things were moving in the right direction: shortly after Allen's resignation, the House of Representatives authorized a $5.7 million appropriation for the commission. Although this was significantly less than the $9 million they needed to be fully functional, and a far cry in real dollars from their most active years in the 1960s, the Commission on Civil Rights had a shot at doing the good work it had been created to do. With Fletcher expected to soon be at the helm, all signals pointed to its revitalized role as the government's civil rights watchdog.[75]

Fletcher headed out to Yakima, Washington, to speak at a local church on November 3 and then deliver a more formal address at a conference sponsored by the SBA the next day. One of the organizers hoped that his "visit to Yakima will spark the multiracial alliance necessary to help rebuild and integrate [predominantly Black] South East Yakima with the rest of the community." During the address at the church, he started to feel chest pain. He soldiered on and finished the speech but then asked to be taken to the hospital.[76]

Arthur Allen Fletcher was admitted to St. Elizabeth Medical Center in Yakima, Washington, where he was evaluated, diagnosed with cardiac arrest, and underwent triple bypass surgery.[77] The chance to chair the Commission on Civil Rights seemed to be slipping from his grasp. But in his war against injustice and intolerance, he had one more battle yet to fight. With his health declining, he needed to make every moment count.

CHAPTER SEVEN

MAN OF RAGE, 1990–1995

If you want peace, you have to work for justice and fair play.
—Arthur Fletcher, 1992

On March 3, 1991, five officers of the Los Angeles Police Department brutally beat motorist Rodney King, a parolee fleeing a charge of driving while intoxicated. The incident was recorded by a local resident, George Holliday, and when the tape went public, even police chief Daryl Gates was astonished: "I stared at the screen in disbelief. I played the . . . tape . . . twenty-five times. And still I could not believe what I was looking at. To see my officers . . . beat a man with their batons fifty-six times, to see a sergeant on the scene who did nothing to seize control was something I never dreamed I would witness." Chief Gates's "disbelief" may seem naive in the era of Eric Garner, Alton Sterling, and Philando Castile, as new technologies expose existing realities. In 1991 the Sony Camcorder was the latest technology and was far from ubiquitous, but Holliday's tape nevertheless exposed the reality of police brutality. Four of the five officers were charged with assault and use of excessive force. What was perhaps more astonishing came a year later, when the officers were acquitted despite the video evidence. The incident revealed not only the depravity of police treatment of Black people but also the injustice inherent in the justice system. Two nights of rebellion ensued—the worst in Los Angeles since the 1965 Watts uprising.[1]

The Rodney King verdict shattered Arthur Fletcher's view of race relations in America. Until that moment his civil rights struggle had focused on economic equality rather than other areas of civil rights such as public accommodations, voting, housing, and schooling. Partly this was because of his early experiences as a college graduate in Kansas, before he became active in the state GOP, when he was unable to find professional work because of his race. Partly this was because his signature issue was affirmative action in employment—the Philadelphia Plan. Still another factor was that his own experiences with those other types of discrimination were (mostly) brief and tangential. He was raised during the Great Depression in communities that, while largely segregated, were close enough to white neighborhoods that he could observe white poverty. He attended integrated schools. He was never denied the right to vote and hold office, and in Berkeley he lost the state assembly race not to a white but to another Black man. His few experiences with segregated public accommodations came while traveling, as when he was refused service while moving his family to California. Congress had passed civil rights legislation against those types of discrimination, so he concluded that if only Blacks could increase their earnings, they could fully take part in all that American society had to offer—as he had. Although he was gravely concerned that far too many African Americans had been left behind in the ghettoes, he was convinced that good jobs—and the ability to compete for them on an equal footing—would help them out of that life.

Rodney King's beating, the verdict, and the subsequent rebellion were a reawakening for Arthur Fletcher. His rhetoric almost immediately began to change. He still focused his policy speeches on what he knew best—equal employment opportunity—but now he began talking about America as a racist nation, and he called himself a man of rage. No amount of money in Rodney King's pocket would have saved him from that thunderclap of night-sticks or convicted those cops. Now, as chairman of the United States Commission on Civil Rights, Fletcher was in a position to do something about it.

The United States Commission on Civil Rights

The United States Commission on Civil Rights (USCCR) was established in 1957 as part of the first civil rights act in nearly a century. Congress gave the temporary commission two years to investigate the state of civil rights in the nation, particularly in the South, but it waited nearly a year before appropriating funds or confirming Eisenhower's appointees.

The initial commission was chaired by John A. Hannah, president of Michigan State University, and included five other distinguished commissioners. They held hearings in the South to investigate voting rights violations, analyzed complaints of obstacles to school desegregation, submitted a final report, and prepared to close down their staff operations. But the nation's concerns with civil rights, and the movement led by Dr. King and others, was growing stronger. In 1959 Congress extended the commission's term, and continued to do so in increments ranging from two to five years.[2]

Because the commission initially had only a two-year mandate, no term limits were set for the chairman or the other commissioners. The law simply said that they were appointed by the president with the advice and consent of the Senate. Nevertheless, after John F. Kennedy was inaugurated in 1961,

Hannah and the other commissioners sent the new president their resignations, knowing that they would be ineffective without explicit support. Kennedy, for his part, refused to accept the resignations, fearing bad press; and after all, he knew the nonpartisan group wanted to stay on. Thus began a decades-long dance wherein the USCCR claimed independence but each new president attempted to shape the activities of the commission to support his own civil rights agenda.[3]

President Kennedy was incrementally more committed than Eisenhower to civil rights, and his staff worked with the USCCR to draft the Civil Rights Act of 1964. After Kennedy's death, President Johnson aggressively pursued civil rights legislation, and the resulting Voting Rights Act of 1965 was partly the result of USCCR hearings. Johnson's very enthusiasm for civil rights ironically endangered the independence of the commission, with the president at one point designating Vice President Hubert Humphrey as a civil rights czar with authority over all of the administration's civil rights agencies, including the USCCR. The civil rights laws of the 1960s also called into question the need for the USCCR at all, now that specific areas of civil rights came under the purview of new subcabinet offices. In response, the USCCR refocused its own mission as a watchdog observing them all.[4]

During his first term, President Nixon formally respected the commission's independence. He accepted Hannah's resignation in 1969 only because the founding chairman earnestly wanted to step down. He elevated to the chair longtime commission member (and president of Notre Dame University) Reverend Theodore Hesburgh, and he pressed Congress for an increased budget allocation for the agency. By his second term, however, the USCCR was becoming a thorn in his side. In late 1972 he unexpectedly accepted Hesburgh's pro forma resignation, which historian Mary Frances Berry called "killing the messenger." For fourteen months the commission was rudderless, but in 1974 the Senate approved Nixon's appointee, Arthur Flemming, as chair. Over the next six years the moderate Flemming restored the commission's independence and prominence as an investigative, deliberative, reporting watchdog, serving under three presidents.[5]

It was precisely this activity that worried officials in the incoming Reagan administration, especially senior White House advisor Edwin Meese and special assistant to the attorney general (and eventual chief justice of the US Supreme Court) John Roberts. Two 1981 commission reports in particular raised hackles: one, dear to Arthur Fletcher's heart, recommended the continuation and strengthening of affirmative action remedies; the other addressed police brutality around the country.[6]

Reagan himself was at best apathetic on civil rights for African Americans, but advisors like Meese, Roberts, and Assistant Attorney General William Bradford Reynolds shaped his policy. These conservatives looked to the market for remedies; they saw racism as an accident of history that would work itself out over time. Meanwhile, they believed, African Americans and women were to get no special treatment and no contract set-asides, and police practices were best left to states and localities.[7]

It didn't take long for Reagan to move against the liberals on the commission. After Nixon had unexpectedly accepted Hesburgh's resignation in 1972, commissioners and chairs no longer submitted pro forma resignations after presidential elections. So Reagan fired Chairman Flemming and replaced him with Clarence Pendleton, the first African American chairman of the commission. Flemming and another commissioner, both loyal Republicans, agreed to leave quietly. The Pendleton choice was Machiavellianism at its finest. The White House got credit for naming a Black man to lead the commission, but because Pendleton was an anti–affirmative action conservative who was willing to serve as the administration's lapdog rather than lead a robust watchdog, the agency was effectively neutered.[8]

Reagan's next move against the commission came in October 1983, when he summarily fired Carter appointees Mary Frances Berry and Blandina "Bambi" Ramirez. Unlike Flemming, the two fought their terminations. The 1957 Civil Rights Act, which had established the commission, held that the president could not fire commissioners other than for misbehavior in office, and these terminations were clearly based on politics. Berry and Ramirez sought an injunction. Congress intervened, expanding the commission to eight members serving fixed six-year terms. Four were appointed by the president without requiring Senate approval, and four were appointed by Congress. No more than two of the presidential appointees could be of the same party as the president, and the four congressional appointees would be chosen by the Democratic and Republican leaders of the House and Senate—one each. The president would name the chair and vice chair from among and with majority consent of the commissioners, as well as the staff director, also with the commission's consent. Reagan signed the law, and Congress reappointed Berry and Ramirez.[9]

The liberals had won their fight to remain on the commission, and they had ostensibly secured its independence, but the hostility of a Reaganite staff director and the relative incompetence of the chairman spelled continued acrimony. The new appointment process and term limits also meant that control of the USCCR oscillated between conservatives and liberals thenceforward. Commissioners spent more time fighting each other and not enough fighting for civil rights.[10]

The USCCR shortly added embarrassment and a public loss of respect to the list of their problems. When Chairman Pendleton died in 1988, Reagan named Commissioner William Allen as his replacement, and a bare majority of Republican appointees confirmed him in a 5–3 vote. The next year, even as President Bush announced his intention to seat Fletcher in the chair, Allen brought the commission to a historic low point. A prominent member of an organization that helped white parents adopt Native American children, in early 1989 he was arrested in Phoenix on suspicion of kidnapping a Native American girl whom he had questioned on a nearby reservation. The other commissioners unanimously voted to censure their chairman. Allen, for his part, ridiculously compared his actions to Rosa Parks's 1955 refusal to change seats on a segregated Montgomery bus. He instead pushed the commission to consider polarizing items from his conservative agenda, and in early October he addressed an anti–gay rights' group, where he "gave an incendiary speech titled 'Blacks? Animals? Homosexuals? What Is a Minority?'"[11]

After nearly a decade of abuse and neglect by the Reagan administration, the commission descended into chaos. Liberal members thought that Allen should resign; the conservatives suggested that all of the commissioners should resign. Allen said that the Bush administration consisted of "country club Republicans . . . and their caddies," ironically likening Arthur Fletcher to an Uncle Tom. (In fact, if anyone was carrying water for "country club Republicans," it was the Reaganite Allen.)[12]

The October 27, 1989, meeting of the USCCR demonstrated how far the agency had fallen from its heights under the leadership of Hannah, Hesburgh, and Flemming. Demonstrating a very different dynamic than the Pennsylvania Avenue Development Commission meetings, where old adversaries Fletcher and Marion Barry got along just fine, the members of the USCCR couldn't agree on even the simplest questions. Members left the room, claiming illness, to break quorum and prevent votes they didn't like, then returned, "feeling better," when the offending item was no longer under discussion. Clearly the next chair faced a difficult job bringing order to the commission, let alone getting it to actually advocate for civil rights and serve as a rights-enforcement watchdog.[13]

On November 29, 1989, the expiration of the term of a Reagan appointee finally allowed Bush to formally appoint Fletcher to the commission. The only problem was Fletcher's health; he spent November in Yakima recovering from triple bypass surgery, and then he spent the holidays in Portland, Oregon, at the home of a business acquaintance, for further convalescence. But the doctors assured him that with proper diet he would make a full recovery, and he accepted the appointment. Letters of congratulations now followed the "get well soon" correspondence Fletcher had received from all over the country. A poignant and ironic handwritten note arrived from former president Nixon:

Dear Art,
I was delighted to read about your appointment as Chairman of the Civil Rights Commission.
Based on my evaluation of your outstanding service in my administration I believe the President could not have appointed a better man.
You must be prepared to take a lot of heat from critics on both the left & right. But you have demonstrated that you can dish it out as well as you can take it!
With warm regards,
RN.

Jesse Jackson wrote less ironically via telegram, using more flowery language, but with essentially the same message:

Your appointment to the head of the Civil Rights Commission is a welcome sign. It is a bright light in darkness. As you remain true to your historical sense of justice, remember the destiny of our nation in a greater measure weighs in the balance of the work of the Civil Rights Commission. Your strength is needed. If you remain true to yourself and what you know to be right, if you put the Republic above Republicans and democracy above Democrats, you will serve us well. You will serve the nation well at a time when a sense of justice is needed. I look forward to working with you in the days ahead. Keep hope alive.

On February 26, 1990, by a telephone poll conducted by the acting staff director, every member of the commission voted to confirm Fletcher as chairman—except William Allen, who explained that his was a protest vote against "gratuitous insults and deliberate misrepresentations" by the White House on his own resignation the previous year. Nixon and Jackson were right: Fletcher had his work cut out for him.[14]

No sooner had Fletcher convened his first USCCR meeting than chest pains put him back in the hospital. An examination at George Washington University Medical Center showed that the operation in Yakima had been faulty, and surgeons needed to go in again. Intermittent health problems continued through the better part of 1990, but Fletcher did manage to attend a welcoming ceremony for new USCCR members on the White House lawn on May 17, the anniversary of the *Brown v. Board of Education* decision.[15]

Knowing that the commissioners needed to get along with one another to make an impact on civil rights, Fletcher worked quickly to turn their formal respect for him into a personal respect and even camaraderie. They were a varied group. In addition to William Allen, returning commissioners included Mary Frances Berry, a historian at the University of Pennsylvania steeped in radical and feminist thought. Berry had been initially appointed by President Carter, survived her firing by Reagan, and then been reappointed by the Democratic Speaker of the House, Tip O'Neill, in 1986. She greeted Fletcher at his first commission meeting with a kiss. Esther Buckley, a high school science teacher from Texas, had been appointed by Reagan in 1983 and then reappointed by Reagan in 1986. Blandina Ramirez, director of the Office of Minority Concerns at the American Council on Education, was, like Berry, a Carter appointee who survived the 1983 firing; she had been reappointed in 1987 by the Senate president pro tempore, John Stennis, a Democrat.

Fletcher was one of four new faces at the commission. His fellow initiates included Knights of Columbus vice president Carl Anderson, a Republican appointed by Democratic House Speaker Tom Foley. Russell Redenbaugh, a corporate executive from Philadelphia who had been blinded in an accident at age seventeen, became the first disabled member of the commission after he was appointed by the Senate majority leader, Bob Dole, who was himself disabled. Finally, Charles Pei Wang, a New York–based Asian American civil rights leader and president of the China Institute in America, was a Democrat appointed by President Bush and designated commission vice chairman.[16]

The presence of two holdovers from the Carter era, two from the Reagan era, and four new members, with a rough partisan balance, had the potential to push the agency back into the chaos that had prevailed during William Allen's scandals. However, over the next three years, the group got along fairly well and were in sufficient agreement on enough commission activities to earn the grudging respect of the members of Congress who held the commission's purse strings and controlled its periodic reauthorization. This was mainly the result of Fletcher's positive attitude; he had enough experience in politics to know not to sweat the small stuff, and because he hadn't been party to the previous internecine battles, he saw almost everything as small stuff. Another important factor was his politics. As a civil rights liberal he sympathized with the positions taken by Mary Berry, Bambi Ramirez, and Charles Wang; but as a Republican he could relate to Esther Buckley, William Allen, Russell Redenbaugh, and Carl Anderson. Beginning with an all-day retreat in early May 1990, Fletcher worked hard to develop personal relationships with his new colleagues.[17]

Fletcher also occupied the sweet spot between the Republican administration and the Democratic Congress, and he used that position to effectively champion continued reauthorization and funding of the USCCR. At the start of his chairmanship Congress had passed a bill extending the life of the commission for only six months and had allocated a mere $5 million for its operations—barely enough to keep it going. Influential congressmen like Representative Don Edwards of California, chair of the House Judiciary Committee's subcommittee on civil and constitutional rights, and Senator Paul Simon of Illinois, who chaired the Senate Judiciary Committee's subcommittee on the Constitution, had grown exasperated by the commission's inactivity during the Pendleton and Allen years. Fletcher labored to change that dynamic and was moderately successful. He testified before the committees about the importance of the USCCR as a well-funded national watchdog. He emphasized that only increased funding could allow them to maintain the national office, hold hearings, and deliver reports. Also of critical importance were the regional offices, which oversaw the state advisory committees—the frontline on the battlefield of civil rights. Slowly over his years as chairman he wrested additional funding from Congress, earning an annual budget increase of more than 50 percent as well as extensions of the commission's authorization through 1994. When he reopened the Midwest regional office in Chicago, Fletcher was pleased that Senator Simon accepted his invitation to keynote the event. As Charles Wang later recalled, "We were able to accomplish quite a bit under his able leadership."[18]

The commission needed all the funding, consensus, and external support it could muster. In 1989 the Supreme Court had made several decisions that called into question Fletcher's signature achievement for the Nixon administration: affirmative action. In response, liberal members of Congress drafted a new civil rights bill. The USCCR needed to campaign to convince the president to sign it—a tall order.[19]

Civil Rights Vetoed

Four Reagan appointees on the Supreme Court—William Rehnquist (appointed by Nixon and promoted to chief justice by Reagan), Anthony Kennedy, Sandra Day O'Connor, and Antonin Scalia—joined alternately by Ford appointee John P. Stevens and Kennedy-appointed swing voter Byron White, significantly damaged affirmative action in 1989. In *City of Richmond v. J. A. Croson Company,* a January 1989 decision written by O'Connor, the Court outlawed a minority set-aside program for municipal contracts. In *Wards Cove Packing Company v. Atonio,* a June decision written by White, the Court allowed a company to require unnecessary skills or credentials, undercutting the 1971 *Griggs v. Duke Power Co.* decision. Also in June, in *Martin v. Wilks,* written by Rehnquist, the Court found that an affirmative action consent decree had resulted in "reverse discrimination."[20]

President Bush greeted these decisions with resolve to continue pursuing affirmative action remedies—a hopeful sign. The *Croson* decision "didn't kill all set-asides, and it didn't kill off affirmative action." In what could only have been music to Arthur Fletcher's ears, he said, "I want to see our SBA program go forward vigorously. . . . I will not read into [*Croson*] a mandate to me to stop trying on equal employment and on affirmative action generally." It surely helped that unlike his predecessor, Bush had a personal friend who had benefited from that very SBA program, the 8(a) minority contract set-aside program. By the time Fletcher took over as chairman of USCCR, Bush took pride in a 70 percent approval rating among African Americans.[21]

Conservative elements within the administration, however, argued differently. The deputy attorney general for civil rights, Donald Ayer, testified in early 1990 before a House subcommittee in opposition to laws that would correct the Court's decisions on affirmative action. Clearly, as Fletcher put it, "the battle for the president's mind" was underway, and those on the right wing were wasting no time in making their case.[22]

Supporters of affirmative action had powerful allies of their own. These included Massachusetts senator Ted Kennedy and California congressman Gus Hawkins, who jointly sponsored legislation to reverse the 1989 decisions. The Kennedy–Hawkins bill, otherwise known as the Civil Rights Act of 1990, explicitly clarified the definition of "disparate impact" as defined in *Griggs,* putting the burden of proof in employment discrimination cases explicitly on the employer. Addressing the "reverse discrimination" complaints in *Martin v. Wilks,* the bill prohibited challenges to consent decrees by affected employees and job applicants. Addressing *Wards Cove,* the bill expanded the prohibition against discriminatory seniority systems "whether or not that discriminatory purpose is apparent." Among other aspects of the measure, the bill increased the potential punitive damages victims of employment discrimination could claim, and it outlawed discrimination on the basis of prior drug use (fast becoming a substitute for explicit racial discrimination thanks to the inner-city crack cocaine epidemic).[23]

Conservative attorney general Dick Thornburgh advised President Bush to veto the bill, stating that it would permit "surreptitious quotas." A columnist at the *Washington Times* agreed, decrying the bill as Fletcher's handiwork because he was the author of the Revised Philadelphia Plan (there is no evidence that he was consulted in its drafting).[24] In fact, the bill contained no language allowing employment quotas; its drafters even went so far as to reiterate the antiquota passage from the 1964 Civil Rights Act: "Nothing in . . . this Act shall be construed so as to require, permit, or result in the adoption or implementation of . . . quotas by an employer . . . on the basis of race, color, religion, sex, or national origin."[25]

Bush, for his part, "desperately wanted to sign a civil rights bill," eager to further distance himself and the Republican Party from the civil rights backsliding of the Reagan administration. He also hoped to take advantage of his high approval rating among Blacks, which he enjoyed to a great extent because of appointments like Fletcher's. He convened a meeting at the White House with prominent African Americans, including Ralph Neas of the Leadership Conference on Civil Rights; Benjamin Hooks of the NAACP; Julius Chambers of the NAACP Legal Defense and Education Fund; National Urban League (NUL) director John Jacob; John Wilks, Fletcher's Office of Federal Contract Compliance (OFCC) director during the Nixon administration; and Fletcher himself. But the president's chief of staff, John Sununu, seeking a veto, also invited members of Reagan's Black brain trust, Robert Woodson and Professors Walter Williams and Glen Loury, whom Fletcher called "superconservatives." In a press conference afterward, Woodson lambasted the bill, strangely claiming that "poor blacks are being sacrificed on the altar of affirmative action" (as if the correlation of rising poverty rates since the civil rights era equaled causation by the advent of affirmative action policies).[26]

From his influential perch as chairman of the Commission on Civil Rights, Fletcher made an all-out effort to convince the president to sign the bill. He gave interviews to every reporter who would listen, and many did. He told *New York Times* reporter Maureen Dowd that the bill "had goals, not quotas," repeating a line he had first given in 1969, but adding new material from his more recent experience as a small business owner: "A quota is a flat number that has to be satisfied irrespective if a person can do the job. . . . A goal is what all business pursue." Addressing Ann Devroy of the *Washington Post,* he called "the issue of quotas . . . a non-argument," adding that it was a "red herring." He went on *Meet the Press* with Jesse Jackson, and he delivered the same message to *USA Today.* He published a thoughtful op-ed in the *New York Times,* urging the president to sign the bill and arguing that the twenty years since implementation of the Philadelphia Plan had shown the quota argument to be moot.[27]

He lined up support at the USCCR. They ordered a staff report, and in June they voted 5–3 for a statement that said the commission "strongly supports the efforts of Congress in drafting the Civil Rights Act of 1990" and urged "Congress to pass and the President to sign the proposed legislation," but they unanimously insisted "that Congress clarify the legislation" to ensure that it not be misinterpreted on quotas. Specifically, they asked Kennedy and Hawkins, the original sponsors, to include a preamble disallowing quotas in the hope of highlighting the fact that the bill already disallowed quotas in its actual text.[28]

Fletcher drafted an uncharacteristically short letter to Bush. He compared the president's choice on the Kennedy–Hawkins bill to President Lincoln's decision to issue the Emancipation Proclamation, when "a disenfranchised nation became whole. Today, Mr. President, as a result of over 125 years of civil rights struggles, accomplishments, and setbacks, our country is disenfranchised once again. You . . . can make it whole again by signing the Civil Rights Act of 1990 . . . in the Abraham Lincoln bedroom."[29]

As the final vote on the bill approached in October 1990, the president faced mounting pressure from both sides, including Fletcher, whose rhetoric toughened. After Ku Klux Klan leader David Duke took 60 percent of white votes in his failed bid for a United States Senate seat from Louisiana, Fletcher worried that the White House saw this as further evidence of the need to woo unreconstructed white southerners. He told a *USA Today* reporter that he feared Bush would cave in to the same forces within his administration that had supported the Horton ads two years earlier. He called a compromise bill sent to Congress by Sununu, which Kennedy rejected, "an absolute outrage. It would take us back to the 1940s. I cannot believe anyone sincere about civil rights could have proposed such language."[30]

Ultimately, however, Bush swallowed the quota canard hook, line, and sinker. In vetoing the bill on October 22, he followed the spurious advice of former USCCR commissioner Morris Abram (who as chairman of the United Negro College Fund [UNCF] in 1973 had fired Art Fletcher). "If I were still practicing law," Abram wrote snarkily, "I would love the 'Civil Rights Act of 1990.'" Arguing that "it holds the employer guilty until proven innocent [and] denies individuals their day in court," he claimed that "while it may enrich some lawyers, it will impoverish the principle of equality for all Americans." (Abram found himself opposed in this by the Jewish Anti-Defamation League, which had historically opposed quotas; like Fletcher, the league could not find a legal basis for quotas anywhere in the bill.)[31]

The picture we get from this episode is one of a president who was being directed too easily by his advisors, rather than the other way around. Had Bush actually read the bill—it was only seventeen pages long—he would have seen that it did not authorize quotas. Yet years later he still maintained, even after having signed a nearly identical bill in 1991, that "despite my pleas, Congress passed a quotalike bill, and I promptly vetoed it." A president is constantly busy and must depend on his advisors to do a significant amount of his reading. Perhaps he was distracted by foreign policy that week, as (among other things) he had ordered a troop buildup in Saudi Arabia in response to Saddam Hussein's invasion of Kuwait that August. But considering that he "desperately wanted to sign a civil rights bill," cherished his historically high approval ratings among African Americans, and was being urged to sign the bill by his "old friend Art Fletcher" and other Blacks in the administration, the least he could have done was read it before vetoing it.[32]

Despite his moderation, the president had refused to purge the Reaganite conservatives from the government. Reagan's support—and the support of his followers—had been a critical component in Bush's winning coalition. Appointments like Fletcher's represented only marginal changes, while the right wing continued to be very influential in his administration.

That Fletcher did not exercise the degree of influence he had sought was disheartening. Team player that he was, however, he soldiered on, knowing he had yet more influence in his current position than at any time since the Nixon administration.

The impression of an administration rudderless on civil rights was further enforced that December, when Michael L. Williams, assistant secretary for civil rights in the Department of Education, announced that colleges and universities could no longer earmark scholarships for minority students. Such scholarships had been a critical component in affirmative action efforts by higher education institutions seeking to provide more opportunities to disadvantaged students and to diversify their campuses. "The Title VI regulation," however, Williams wrote, "includes several provisions that prohibit recipients of [Department of Education] funding from denying, restricting, or providing different or segregated financial aid . . . on the basis of race, color, or national origin." The Office of Civil Rights "interprets these provisions as generally prohibiting race-exclusive scholarships." Williams was a Black Texan opponent of affirmative action who had recently replaced Reaganite Clarence Thomas at the Department of Education (after the president had elevated Thomas to the United States court of appeals). One reporter called Williams "a movement conservative with [a] zealous commitment to abstract logic."[33]

The response was quick and uniform. The *New York Times* editors called the move a "devastating signal." Suzanne Ramos of the Mexican American Legal Defense and Education Fund called it "very dismaying." Jesse Jackson called the decision "morally wrong." Virginia governor Douglas Wilder, the first African American state governor in history, asked Bush to reverse the policy, noting that "these programs remain an integral part of our educational system." NAACP head Benjamin Hooks said that "to say we are appalled . . . is to understate our position." Even Lyn Nofziger, the conservative former Reagan aide who had worked assiduously to keep Fletcher out of that administration, called it "a dumb move" (presumably from a political rather than moral calculus).[34]

Fletcher wrote to Bush on behalf of the USCCR urging him "to take a strong stand in support of affirmative action in the recruitment of minority students, including the use of minority-targeted scholarships." To the press, Fletcher again defended affirmative action programs like race-based scholarships: "It is unrealistic to talk about a color-blind society when we know it is not color-blind, has not been, is not now, and is not likely to be."[35]

At the USCCR, the official commission response to the Williams ruling was hard fought. The general counsel drafted a letter to the president stating that "the law does permit educational institutions to make reasonable use of minority-targeted scholarships when necessary to overcome the effects of discrimination, or to achieve the legitimate and important goal of a culturally diverse student body." But Commissioner William Allen stood in opposition, arguing, in essence, that Williams was right, and that a culturally diverse student body could be achieved without resorting to race-based scholarships. Fletcher and Mary Frances Berry took him to task, and with the concurrence of Vice Chairman Wang and Commissioners Esther Buckley and Russell Redenbaugh, approved the general counsel's draft letter with only a few changes as to tone.[36]

In the run-up to the Gulf War, President Bush certainly did not need another domestic black eye. Further, as a longtime donor to the UNCF, Bush cherished his connection to Black higher education. He fired the secretary of education, Lauro Cavazos, a Reagan holdover. But Assistant Secretary Williams, who kept his job, held fast to his interpretation of policy. A meeting with White House officials resulted in only a partial reversal: Williams announced that the previous policy remained in effect while the administration conducted a review. In reply to Fletcher's letter, White House aide Roger Porter told him that "the president's commitment to minority education remains unshakable. He believes in the importance of these scholarships and that they should be preserved as best they can." After Bush named former Tennessee governor Lamar Alexander as secretary of education, Porter followed up with Fletcher again, eager to keep the independent commission's independent-minded chair on the Bush team. He noted that Alexander "believes in the importance of these scholarships" and "intends to review this matter carefully immediately upon his confirmation."[37]

While Fletcher hoped to maintain his long-standing friendship with Bush, he did not hesitate to criticize the administration. The Gulf War presented another opportunity. Speaking in Kansas at a Martin Luther King Day event, Fletcher said the slain leader, had he lived, would have opposed the Gulf War. "He'd take the same line on the Persian Gulf as he did on Vietnam," said Fletcher of King. "But he'd make a stronger point about who was doing the fighting, in terms of the high numbers of blacks and Hispanics that make up the military."[38]

Fletcher's outspoken opinions, at odds with those of the president and his chief advisors, earned him the sobriquet "conscience of the administration" among reporters; they also earned him the ire of those selfsame advisors. Assuming the boss shared their antipathy to Fletcher's heresy, Chief of Staff Sununu and White House counsel C. Boyden Gray began to maneuver against Fletcher, much as Chuck Colson had twenty years before. The difference was that this time, not only was Fletcher a personal friend of the president but also this president tolerated disagreement. As demonstrated by his apparent failure to read the Kennedy–Hawkins bill, Bush relied on his advisors to brief him before he made major decisions, but the Williams minority scholarships debacle had apparently proven to the president the need for a dissenting opinion, the value of devil's advocacy. On civil rights, Fletcher played that role. So when Bush learned that Sununu had removed Fletcher's name from a White House invitation list for a Black History Month event, the president ordered it restored.[39]

Bush's personal support of Fletcher paid off in the chairman's tortured decision to endorse the nomination of Clarence Thomas to the Supreme

With Bush in the Oval Office, ca. 1990. Their friendship remained strong despite Fletcher's criticism of administration decisions. George Bush Presidential Library.

Court. When Bush first nominated Thomas to replace the retiring and ail-ing Justice Thurgood Marshall, Fletcher withheld judgment, expressing concerns about the nominee's stance on affirmative action in particular. He earned hearty laughs at the NAACP convention the following week when he announced that White House operatives had specifically asked him to shill for the nominee at the oldest civil rights organization's annual gathering. But he did ask the group to withhold judgment for the time being so that the Senate could have time to complete its investigation. Nonetheless, the NAACP opposed the Thomas nomination. Influential African American journalist and history professor Roger Wilkins, who had served as an assis-tant attorney general in the Johnson administration, also opposed Thomas, noting that Bush could have made a far better choice and offering specific suggestions from among Black Republicans: "Had President Bush nom-inated William T. Coleman Jr., a Black Republican who was in President Ford's cabinet . . . I would be doing cartwheels down Pennsylvania Avenue," he wrote. "Louis Sullivan, the US Secretary of health and human services, and Art Fletcher, chair of the US Commission on Civil Rights, [also] meet that test." (Although Fletcher was never considered, the nomination of a Supreme Court justice without a law degree was not unprecedented.)[40]

Nevertheless, after three weeks of wrestling with the decision, on July 26 Fletcher decided to endorse Thomas despite the nominee's continued refusal to endorse affirmative action. "In his heart of hearts he knows how he got where he is," Fletcher said, telling the Reuters news service that Thomas "has benefited from the dramatically improved opportunities environment created by the employment affirmative action enforcement movement and . . . has ridden it all the way to the top." Fletcher hoped that Thomas would claim a new freedom with the lifetime appointment and revert to a more liberal understanding of civil rights than he had so long espoused as part of Reagan's Black brain trust. The president, for his part, was ebullient at Fletcher's loyalty. In a handwritten note, Bush wrote, "Dear Art—I was so pleased you endorsed Clarence—He's a good man. Love to all—Off to Moscow—George Bush." Perhaps fearing embarrassment were he to change his mind, and perhaps simply following Bush's lead, Fletcher did not rescind his endorsement even after former Equal Employment Opportunity Commission (EEOC) staffer Anita Hill credibly accused Thomas of sexual misconduct. Thomas was confirmed to the bench on October 15, 1991, and proceeded to join the Court's Reaganite bloc in opposition to affirmative action. Proven wrong, Fletcher mostly avoided mentioning Thomas in interviews or correspondence thereafter, but he did once slip: after a 5–4 decision limiting affirmative action in 1995, Fletcher told a reporter from *Jet* magazine, "As far as I'm concerned . . . Justice Thomas, who is Black, is leaning over to try and think White."[41]

"Man of Rage"

The Clarence Thomas nomination was only one item on Fletcher's calendar during 1991, a year that proved tumultuous for him and for the commission he led. In March came the brutal beating of Rodney King in Los Angeles; in May, after a Cinco de Mayo celebration, the shooting of a Salvadoran man in the Washington, DC, neighborhood of Mount Pleasant led to two nights of violent clashes between Latino youths and the police. Fletcher told a reporter that the United States had "the worst climate for civil rights in at least 40 years." In August Fletcher went to Germany and toured the US military installations there on a joint USCCR-NAACP venture, paid for by the NAACP's European branch, to investigate discrimination in the armed forces. The organization also paid for Bernyce to go with him; the shoestring USCCR budget, which required that Fletcher use his own home as his office for eight months out of the year, could pay for none of it. Fletcher's subsequent report, which found rampant discrimination against minority service personnel and their dependents, prompted a major Department of Defense investigation and a flurry of activity in the White House where the staff had hoped to capitalize on the successful Gulf War in Bush's reelection bid. It also led to a 1992 invitation for Fletcher to conduct a similar investigation at military bases in the Far East. The USCCR, despite its threadbare budget, resolved to hold hearings in DC on the Mount Pleasant uprising, refocused its attention on the issue of racial tension in local communities, and urged all potential contenders for the 1992 presidential election to eschew the use of race-baiting campaign techniques.[42]

In 1991 the USCCR also snatched victory from the jaws of defeat when President Bush signed a civil rights bill virtually indistinguishable from the one he had vetoed the previous year. Thanks to Fletcher's improving health, this time the commissioners were able to discuss and plan their approach to the bill early, and they worked their contacts on Capitol Hill, in the press, and at 1600 Pennsylvania Avenue to promote its passage and signing. Although Bush initially decried the legislation as another "quota bill," Fletcher got to the press early to contradict that notion.[43]

Congress passed the bill just shy of the votes needed to override a potential veto, but the president did not want to go down in history as having vetoed two civil rights bills. He also may have thought that his nomination of conservative Clarence Thomas provided sufficient cover on the right. However, when it became apparent that the president was going to sign the bill into law, White House counsel C. Boyden Gray and other advisors fought a rearguard action. They prepared a signing statement for Bush that threatened the end of all federal hiring guidelines, effectively undermining the purpose of the act—and ending affirmative action. When three cabinet members protested and journalists started asking questions, the White House press secretary, Marlin Fitzwater, disavowed the statement on Bush's behalf, and it was not issued. There is no evidence that Bush saw it, and at the signing ceremony, Bush said simply, "I support affirmative action. Nothing in this bill overturns the government's affirmative action program." Gray then disingenuously wrote in a *Washington Post* op-ed that the 1991 bill was fundamentally different from the one that Bush had vetoed in 1990, claiming that in this one, Congress had removed the possibility of quotas. The incident served as further evidence of the machinations of conservatives within the Bush administration. Although Bush compromised on the bill in an attempt to win Black approval going into an election year, the activities of his staff served to undermine that possibility.[44]

The flurry of press attention over his advocacy on behalf of the 1991 Civil

Rights Act brought Fletcher more professional success. He received nearly as many lecture invitations as he had during his years with the Nixon administration. The commission's formal independence from the administration, and the fact that he received only a half-time salary as chairman, allowed him to continue to collect honoraria; as usual, he charged only what the organizations could afford, with rates ranging from "travel expenses only" all the way up to $5,000. As he continued to build connections around the country in support of his eventual goal—establishing a nondenominational inner-city religious civil rights organization—he made other connections for his own professional advancement.[45]

The most important of these was at the University of Denver. In June 1990 Fletcher delivered the commencement address at DU and received an honorary degree from the university he had once hoped to attend. Times had changed: thanks to affirmative action and diversity efforts, not only did the school's sports teams now include star Black athletes, but minority students and faculty were a major part of the campus community. Conversations with Chancellor Daniel L. Ritchie and business school dean R. Bruce Hutton led to Fletcher's appointment as distinguished professor of business administration and founding director of a new Center for Corporate Social Policy, with an annual salary just under $100,000. Fletcher wanted very much to have an academic position, noting that the most effective prior USCCR chairmen had been accomplished professors (even William Allen was on the faculty at Harvey Mudd College). Fletcher seized the opportunity and moved to Denver in the summer of 1991.[46]

It was while Fletcher was fund-raising for his new center at the University of Denver in April 1992 that he heard the shocking news of the acquittal of the police officers in the Rodney King beating and the subsequent rebellion in South Central Los Angeles. In his official capacity he reiterated a commitment to justice for Rodney King but antipathy to violence as a response; he wrote the Department of Justice requesting that the Office of Civil Rights investigate the case for possible federal charges against the officers involved. (The Department of Justice did indeed prosecute four of the officers in federal court for violating King's civil rights; a racially mixed jury later found two of them guilty.) But he was increasingly troubled by the verdict, stating that he was "under controlled rage." He called on President Bush to be "heroic" by taking dramatic action not seen since President Johnson announced the war on poverty; the HUD secretary, Jack Kemp, urged the president to do something "extraordinary," calling the uprising "a cry for help."[47]

But Fletcher and Kemp were rebuffed by the White House. Falling under the sway of his conservative advisors—who presumably saw him as needing to look tough on race issues again to win renomination—Bush blamed the social programs of the Great Society for the unrest. "If I said a year ago that these programs weren't working, perhaps I have been vindicated," he said. "It is a very appropriate time to rethink whether we've done it just exactly right in the past, whether it's the Great Society or all the way up to this administration."[48]

Fletcher was livid. Noting that the USCCR "has submitted economic development proposals to the White House and Congress 'that would have prevented much of what is going on now,'" Fletcher told TV journalist David Brinkley that "this program has drawn nothing but a yawn. We've been unable to get anyone to listen to us." He told a reporter from the *St. Petersburg Times* that "if you want peace, you have to work for justice and fair play. For some strange reason we've had a difficult time doing that."[49]

Fletcher's involvement in Bush's 1992 reelection campaign was minimal. Although the president faced a challenge from the right in the person of former Nixon speechwriter Pat Buchanan, who represented a segment of the party increasingly angry after Bush broke an earlier ill-advised pledge ("read my lips: no new taxes"), Fletcher's help was not necessary for the president to win either the District of Columbia's delegates or the nomination, and he was not sufficiently established with the Colorado Republican Party to make much difference there either. In any event, Fletcher was far too busy with his day job in Denver and his part-time (if higher profile) job as USCCR chairman to actively campaign. Although he wanted to see his friend reelected— not least because it might have extended his chairmanship, perhaps into the twenty-first century—he found the rhetoric of the Democratic challenger more in line with his own positions, especially after the Rodney King uprising. Arkansas governor Bill Clinton, like Fletcher and Kemp, did not see the Great Society as the problem but blamed instead presidential inaction: "We can do better than the Great Society, but now we're doing nothing, so we're doing worse than the Great Society," he told the *New York Times*. "We need things that will let people at the local level shape their future in everything from houses to jobs to safe streets. But we can't do better with a do-nothing approach."[50]

Clinton's youthful vigor, charm, and charisma, combined with voter fatigue after twelve years of Republican rule, made for a tough reelection fight for the older, more reserved Bush, who increasingly appeared out of touch (as when he responded to an economic downturn by going out to buy socks). Bush refused to engage in race baiting, perhaps in response to the

1991 call from the Commission on Civil Rights, but this left him vulnerable to an attack from the moderate southern Democrat, who won his own home state of Arkansas (and five other southern states) with a country boy's charm. In foreign policy, Bush's victory in the Gulf War was perceived less as the work of his own foreign policy, lining up allies for an unprecedented coalition, and more the work of skilled General H. Norman Schwarzkopf, who decried the president's decision to not occupy Iraq. Although Bush had masterfully navigated the end of the Cold War and collapse of the Soviet Union, the expected peace dividend had yet to materialize. Bush mustered only 37.4 percent of the popular vote and 168 votes in the Electoral College, and lost the presidency.[51]

For Fletcher, Bush's loss of the White House was only a small part of increasing problems, both personal and professional. Despite a year of diligently working his contacts, he failed to raise adequate funds for the University of Denver's Center for Corporate Social Policy to even cover his own salary at the university. By the spring of 1993 he was "no longer on DU's payroll." He blamed it on his focus on the Rodney King rebellion and donors' waiting to see the results of the presidential election, but the reality was that, as with his work at the UNCF in 1972, he was not a hands-on fund-raiser but rather a big-picture dreamer. He could envision a successful Center for Corporate Social Policy at DU, but he lacked the day-to-day management expertise to motivate others at the crucial work of development, and unlike in his food-service contracts, he could not hire subordinates with the requisite skills. His poor fiscal decisions also affected his personal finances; despite his contracts, public speaking fees, and substantial salaries, he failed to pay his hospital bills from his 1983 heart operation, let alone the more recent procedures in 1989 and 1990, and he went into arrears on the rent for the AF&A office space in Hyattsville, Maryland. Longtime family friend Kathy Keolker said his one weakness was "money management." Although he eventually paid everything off, in the meantime his bills were sent to collection agencies.[52]

Further, Fletcher's home life was in shambles. He and Bernyce were largely estranged; she hadn't come to Denver with him. Keolker notes that Bernyce often took time away from Art and a political world she despised, escaping to her house in Pleasantville, New Jersey, or to visit with Keolker in the Seattle suburbs. But this appears to have been a more substantial break. In early 1993 Fletcher offered to take a second mortgage on the G Street home in Washington, DC (by now it was worth far more than they had paid for it) to buy out Bernyce's share and use the house as a headquarters for his National Christian Technical Institute/Society for Victorious Living. Bernyce's reply may have been by telephone, as there is no record of any further discussion of this, but Fletcher never bought her out, nor did they ever use the house for that purpose.[53]

Struggle

In early 1993 Fletcher was exhausted. At sixty-eight years old, the pressures of his position between liberal Democrats in Congress and conservative advisors of a moderate Republican president had taken a toll. It wasn't easy on his health to be a man of rage. Knowing that his relationship with the White House would become more strained now that his friend was no longer in the Oval Office, he accepted that he was not long for his own job. "I expect President Clinton to name his chairperson to the commission," he told a group of congressional freshmen. In the meantime, however, there was work to be done: investigating inmate deaths in Mississippi prisons, publishing a report on the Mount Pleasant uprising, assisting Jesse Jackson's investigation into discrimination in professional sports, and forwarding discrimination complaints to appropriate agencies. Civil rights in the United States were far from secure.[54]

Fletcher did ask Bush, during the lame-duck months, to replace two presidential appointees on the commission whose terms were expiring: Esther Buckley and William Allen. Worried that the commission would not be able to make a quorum—the congressionally appointed terms of Mary Frances Berry and Bambi Ramirez were also up—Fletcher recommended that Bush reappoint Buckley and replace Allen with Wilfredo Gonzalez, the staff director who was resigning to take a position in the private sector. Bush's director of personnel, Reaganite Constance Horner, instead selected herself and Robert P. George, an antiabortion professor of politics at Princeton, and Bush acquiesced. As for the other expiring seats, Ramirez decided she had had enough and did not seek reappointment. She was replaced by former California supreme court justice Cruz Reynoso. House Speaker Tom Foley reappointed Mary Frances Berry. Staff director Gonzalez appointed as his acting replacement Bobby Doctor, a Democrat and the director of the USCCR southern regional office in Atlanta, pending an appointment to that post by President Clinton.[55]

The new political alignment at the USCCR weakened the consensus Fletcher had worked so hard to develop. During the Bush years the moderate Fletcher had been the glue that held together the commission's conservatives and liberals. Now that a Democrat was in office, the new conservative appointees joined with Carl Anderson to form an obstinate conservative bloc opposite liberals Mary Frances Berry, Charles Pei Wang, and Cruz Reynoso, with Russell Redenbaugh oscillating between the right and the center. Because Fletcher was increasingly seen as a lame duck chairman, a rump holdover from the Bush era despite his staunch civil rights activism, his ability to calm the tensions among the commissioners weakened with each passing month. Fletcher could have exercised more leadership with the conservatives, as he had during the first three years of his term. But now, scrambling to maintain his income, he was often absent from commission meetings, leaving Vice Chair Wang to preside. Nonetheless, despite the political differences, commission meetings for most of 1993 were far from rancorous. Three years of Fletcher's hard work meant that the group would not easily revert to the state of dysfunction that had prevailed during William Allen's tenure in the chair.[56]

Fletcher planned to remain on the commission through the end of his term in 1995, but he was looking for a dignified exit from the chair that would foster collegiality among the commissioners and allow continuity of his own efforts. The leading voice among the commission's liberals—and also the longest-serving commissioner—was Mary Frances Berry, but Fletcher worried that she would not work well with the conservatives. On the other hand, Vice Chairman Wang was a Democrat appointed by Bush thanks to commission rules limiting the number of appointments from the president's own party. Fletcher thought that Wang's political views and experience on the commission might make him an attractive candidate; the fact that he would be the commission's first Asian American chair was an added bonus. Wang, for his part, liked the idea; he saw his chairmanship as a "natural succession" and thought he could "make a difference." He and acting staff director Bobby Doctor went so far as to arrange meetings with members of Congress from both parties to gauge support. They found little, but what mattered most were the feelings of the president—who nominated the chair—and the commissioners, who confirmed the nomination. To ensure that Wang would get the required votes from among the commissioners, Fletcher convinced the conservative bloc to agree to Wang's leadership. Five of the eight commissioners—Fletcher, Wang, Anderson, George, and Horner—thus wrote Clinton asking that the president designate Wang as chairman. They also asked that he designate Democrat Bobby Doctor as permanent staff director—a request that, when publicized, resulted in numerous letters of recommendation from prominent Democratic politicians. A White House staffer replied that their suggestions would "receive every consideration."[57]

What followed was one of the more distasteful episodes of Fletcher's tenure as chairman. The members of the Congressional Black Caucus (CBC) had historically been important allies of the commission. Their existence was intimately connected to the USCCR. The commission had advocated uncompromisingly for the Voting Rights Act of 1965, which had made it possible for more African Americans to be elected to Congress; in 1971 the growing numbers in the House had formed a caucus. The CBC had likewise been staunch advocates for a robust commission. Learning of the letter to Clinton requesting that the president designate Wang and Doctor as chair and staff director, however, founding CBC member John Conyers Jr. went on the warpath, urging his "CBC Colleagues" to push Clinton to reject "any extension of the Reagan–Bush hegemony" and designate Mary Frances Berry as chair. His letter did not mention Wang, but it specifically decried the notion of Clinton naming Bobby Doctor as staff director. (Possibly Conyers was worried that in openly opposing Wang he might alienate Asian Americans.) That this came after Conyers had opposed increasing the USCCR's budget allocation made it even more galling.[58]

Fletcher was furious. The father of affirmative action hated being lumped in with the Reaganites, and he resented the implication that his tenure as chairman had followed the policies of President Bush in lockstep. As he saw it he had convinced three conservative commissioners—two of whose terms on the commission would not expire until after Clinton's own first term as president—to accept a Democrat as chair and another Democrat as staff director for the sake of maintaining a good working relationship on the independent commission during a Democratic presidency—no small feat. Now he was being accused of playing politics. "My civil rights record will match and equal any of them," Fletcher said. Later he added that Conyers made him so mad he wanted to "punch him out" despite his personal dislike of violence.[59]

Mary Berry, for her part, was hardly playing it cool. Admirably putting principle above her own self-interest in desiring the chair, she decried Clinton's decision to withdraw the nomination of the competent—if controversial—Lani Guinier as assistant attorney general for civil rights. If Clinton "clearly intends to move to the right," she said, "I'd be the last person he'd be interested in having [as USCCR chair], and I'd be the last person interested." But her designation was strongly supported by the chairmen of the congressional committees who held the commission's purse strings, Congressman

Don Edwards and Senator Paul Simon, who threatened to withdraw support for the commission altogether unless Clinton named Berry forthwith. They were joined in their support of Berry by Congressman Kweise Mfume, Raul Yzaguirre of the National Council of La Raza, and the fourteen members of the Congressional Hispanic Caucus.[60]

Clinton delayed his decision on the chairmanship through the summer. But with his poll numbers in the African American community flagging after the Guinier incident, he needed the support of the CBC. On September 27, 1993, Clinton designated Berry USCCR chairperson, Cruz Reynoso as vice chair, and a former staffer from Congressman Don Edwards's office, Stuart Ishimaru, as staff director. That Ishimaru was a Japanese American was seen as a nod to Asian Americans meant to obviate any potential resentment in that community over his rejection of a Wang chairmanship.[61]

Given the antipathy of the conservative bloc, Berry and Cruz could not muster the requisite five votes for confirmation without Fletcher's consent. They had the tentative support of Wang and Redenbaugh, who read the tea leaves and saw Berry's ascent as inevitable. But without Fletcher's vote, that made only four. Despite having received her vote in 1990, Fletcher announced that he was withholding his vote on Berry's confirmation.[62]

Fletcher claimed honest motives. On the designation of Ishimaru as staff director, he believed that it would compromise the integrity of the commission and make it beholden to Congressman Edwards (who had tried to cut USCCR funding after Fletcher endorsed the Clarence Thomas nomination). He also worried—with good reason—that under Berry the commission would devolve into partisan bickering. But another claim he made, that he was withholding his vote to get the White House to pay adequate attention to the commission, didn't hold water. There is no evidence that the commission under Fletcher received any less official attention from the Clinton White House than it had from the Bush White House. In fact, White House counsel Alexis Herman personally contacted Fletcher to inform him of the Berry designation and to ask him, on behalf of the president, to resign; Fletcher could not claim, as had William Allen four years earlier, that the administration was ignoring him. The difference in treatment was simply personal. Bush was Fletcher's personal friend and invited him to social events; Clinton was not and did not.[63]

In fact, by withholding his vote, Fletcher was sinking to Congressman Conyers's level. He stopped being the innocent nonpartisan, interested only in commission unity, and offered to support Berry only if the White House offered Charles Wang and Bobby Doctor jobs in the administration. After all the work he had put into rebuilding the commission and restoring its gravitas, Fletcher was blackmailing the president of the United States and holding the commission hostage.[64]

This behavior did not go unnoticed. Jesse Jackson wrote Fletcher a scathing letter comparing him to George Wallace by accusing him of "stand[ing] in the civil rights door and block[ing Berry's] nomination." After listing Fletcher's many civil rights accomplishments, Jackson added, "It seems incongruous that you would cap your career in such an unfair manner." The rhetoric may have been overblown, but the sentiment was right. Having already announced his willingness to step aside, Fletcher needed to approve Clinton's choice.[65]

Berry herself was less harsh, noting in a 2018 interview that she saw Fletcher's behavior as expected political gamesmanship, which had become par for the course after the Reagan administration's attempted gutting of the commission. It didn't change "my longstanding fondness for Arthur," adding that he "got a lot of good things done. The Mount Pleasant hearings, his work with the Rodney King hearings." But after she had arranged liberal support for his chairmanship in 1990, she was disappointed.[66]

When he carefully analyzed the situation, Fletcher recognized that his position was untenable. Clinton had no intention of rescinding his designation of Berry as chair, so Fletcher could not get Wang elevated. The best his intransigence might have accomplished would have been a default extension of his own chairmanship until the end of his commission term in 1995, but this would have made the agency completely ineffective. Despite its statutory independence, history had shown that the USCCR could not get much done without a working relationship with the White House. What's more, according to Berry, Congressman "Edwards threatened to defund the commission if they refused to support the White House slate." Besides, Fletcher was exhausted and no longer wished to be chair. It had taken a toll on his health and his marriage. He wrote a positive reply to Jesse Jackson, ignoring the Wallace reference, thanking him for being "the only Democrat, public figure or civil rights leader of national stature to acknowledge my contribution to the civil rights movement." He added "I . . . will treasure your letter for those kind words of recognition for the rest of my days." On November 19, 1993, Fletcher joined Commissioners Berry, Reynoso, Wang, and Redenbaugh in a 5–3 vote approving Berry's and Reynoso's designations as chair and vice chair, respectively. The commissioners did not, however, approve Stuart Ishimaru as staff director.[67]

Mary Frances Berry's personality and career were simultaneously alien and admirable to Fletcher. Like Fletcher, she had known separation from her parents, having briefly been left in an orphanage. Also like Fletcher, she was a college graduate. Other than a mutual dedication to civil rights, however, they had little else in common. Whereas Fletcher had grown up in the West, Berry was from the South, growing up in Nashville. Whereas Fletcher attended a predominantly white midwestern college, Berry attended Fisk, a historically Black college in the South. Whereas Fletcher, with five children to support, had pursued sports and politics after graduation, Berry went directly into graduate school at Howard University, another prominent historically Black college. After completing her doctorate in history at the top-tier University of Michigan, she joined the professoriate, rising quickly; by the age of thirty-eight she was chancellor of the University of Colorado. As we have seen with Fletcher's appointment at the University of Denver, this was a career path Fletcher found admirable but also alien. Furthermore, the world of academia had taught Berry the power of directness; she was often impolitic, with little interest in bridging political divides with conservatives whose behavior she saw as antithetical to civil rights. This personality trait was anathema to the more deliberative but no less earnest Fletcher. As Wang put it, "Berry is a professor, so she treated everybody like her students. She would lecture us . . . rather than see us as her colleagues."[68]

Berry's assumption of the chair preceded a remarkable series of events. First, she removed the acting staff director, Bobby Doctor, sending him back to the southern regional office in Atlanta. General counsel Lawrence Glick advised the commission that Berry did not have the legal authority to do this without a vote—at which point Berry gave him a pink slip as well. When Fletcher and other commissioners protested, Berry explained that because Doctor had never been confirmed by a vote, she could remove him without a vote. As for Glick, she had fired him for incompetence; a lawyer herself, her interpretation of the statute contradicted his.[69]

The commission resumed the partisan acrimony last seen during William Allen's chairmanship. Berry requested and received from the president the designation of Stuart Ishimaru as acting staff director. When Fletcher and four other commissioners forced a vote on Ishimaru, Berry turned condescending: "If . . . we wish to vote that . . . dogs are cats or apples are oranges . . . I [won't] stand in the way of the Commission voting [but] any vote that is taken is ineffective legally." When pressed to hire outside counsel for impartial interpretation, Berry said the commission could not afford it. Fletcher asked if they could request pro bono advice, and Berry said that would be illegal. Only an internal staff lawyer, she claimed, could render an alternate interpretation. Of course, she had fired Glick for doing just that.[70]

Commissioner George took Berry to court, arguing that the president did not have the authority to unilaterally name an acting staff director, and the US district court agreed; Ishimaru was removed. Berry then announced that the commission could not meet without a staff director to prepare an agenda. This was a bridge too far for Commissioner Redenbaugh, who now joined Fletcher and the conservative bloc in a motion to vest executive authority in the commissioners themselves and bring Bobby Doctor back, but as deputy staff director. In frustration, Berry pointed out that all five commissioners voting to take executive authority had been appointed by Republicans. Commissioner Anderson noted that it was the first time a USCCR chair had accused commissioners of voting out of partisanship. Berry and Reynoso threatened to walk out. Matters had clearly spiraled out of control. Berry couldn't accept the return of Doctor; the conservative bloc wouldn't accept Ishimaru. Redenbaugh and Fletcher brokered a compromise. Berry apologized, the conservatives withdrew the motion to bring back Doctor, and all agreed to give President Clinton a month to name a compromise staff director (which he did).[71]

While Berry bore ultimate responsibility for the decline in collegiality among the commissioners, and certainly added to it with her intransigence over the Ishimaru appointment, it would be unfair to assign all the blame to her. President Bush had irresponsibly saddled the commission with staunch Reaganites in his final days in office. Berry might have appealed to Fletcher, as an elder statesman, to conciliate the conservative bloc, but his behavior in the final weeks of his chairmanship made that difficult. For her part, Berry refused to hold a grudge. The conservative appointees, she later said, "knew how to leverage power . . . they could keep us from doing a lot of things that we wanted to do. . . . I don't blame them for that. The way they went about it was reprehensible, but I understood it."[72]

Except that it didn't have to be that way. Established in an era when support for—and opposition to—civil rights was bipartisan, the commission wasn't supposed to be beholden to the fickle political winds, to change leadership each time the White House changed hands. Nixon had broken that precedent by firing Hesburgh, and Reagan undermined it with multiple terminations. Bush, faced with William Allen's incompetence and censure, had little choice but to push him out of the chair.

In 1993 Clinton had the opportunity to restore the commission's independence—by leaving it alone. There were no scheduled vacancies among the presidential appointees until 1995; Fletcher was a dynamic, competent moderate with civil rights bona fides; and the vice chair and acting staff director were Democrats. Notwithstanding Fletcher's exhaustion, the staff director ran the day-to-day activities at the agency, and Fletcher, spelled occasionally by Wang, could easily have been effective for the two years remaining in his term.

Berry might not have asked for the job in 1993, either. She had been reappointed by congressional Democrats to a term scheduled to expire in 1999; Fletcher's was scheduled to expire in 1995. Clinton could have smoothly appointed her chair in 1995 and acquiesced to her recommendation for a new staff director. Had they waited, the collegiality fostered by Fletcher's continued leadership might have allowed her to develop a working relationship with commissioners George and Horner, and perhaps they would have blocked her less frequently once she became chair. As it was, the commission under her leadership accomplished little before 1999, when the last Reaganite terms expired.[73]

Here again, however, we should not be too quick to judge either Berry or Clinton. The devolution of commission comity was attributable to the increasing partisanship throughout the country since the 1960s. By 1993, Republicans were more and more likely to view Democrats as their enemies rather than the patriotic opposition, and vice versa. This atmosphere prompted a *USA Today* writer to label Democrat Wang as "part of the cabal of GOP appointees" and report that Doctor had "gotten into bed with the enemy." It also led to congressional threats to defund the Fletcher-era commission and pressure on Clinton to elevate Berry. Fletcher's leadership kept the commission productive and amicable during the Bush years, but this was an aberration, not the rule.[74]

Fletcher for President

The November 1994 midterm elections resulted in a Republican majority in both houses of Congress for the first time since the 1950s. Congressman Newt Gingrich of Georgia, the principal architect of the election campaign, became Speaker of the House on January 4, 1995. Gingrich immediately set out to implement his conservative Contract with America, a series of bills that, among other things, threatened to end affirmative action.[75]

A recent case demonstrated that affirmative action was vulnerable. In Piscataway, New Jersey, in 1989, a tight high school budget had required that one teacher be laid off. According to conservative columnist Charles

Krauthammer, "the two with the least seniority . . . had identical records: hired on precisely the same day in 1980, with equal academic credentials and with similarly favorable progress reports since." The school board terminated the white teacher and retained the African American, arguing that she was the only Black teacher in the department despite an overall Black student population of approximately 50 percent. The white teacher sued, and won, mainly because the school board "conceded from the start that this was not a remedial act," and that "there was no history of discrimination in the Piscataway school district"—a point with which Black parents and jobseekers certainly disagreed. On appeal, the Bush administration had sided with the white teacher, but in 1995 Deval Patrick, Clinton's assistant attorney general for civil rights, filed a brief on behalf of the district, arguing that faculty diversity was an appropriate goal for a school with so diverse a student body. To conservatives, the case seemed prima facie evidence that affirmative action was unfair to white people.[76]

Sensing the popular mood, Republican senators (and presidential front-runners) Bob Dole and Phil Gramm jumped on the Gingrich bandwagon and promised to repeal affirmative action. Bill Clinton, worried about his reelection prospects, announced a review of all government affirmative action programs, including contract set-asides for minority- and women-owned firms. State legislatures in California, Washington, and Pennsylvania took up similar bills, and in Oregon the governor ended most affirmative action programs by executive order.[77]

At some level, there may have been a sense that avoiding race-baiting in 1992 had cost the Republicans the White House. Candidates like Dole and Gramm saw affirmative action as a safer form of Willie Horton–style campaigning and attempted to use it as a wedge issue; like Nixon, they hoped to split the white working class from African Americans. Of course, they didn't publicly admit that; instead, one conservative columnist accused Bill Clinton of using "quotas" as a wedge issue against *them,* looking to mobilize the Black vote. Dole, who had supported the Philadelphia Plan in 1969 and favored minority set-asides for much of his career, claimed that he still supported equal employment opportunity but now favored, as he put it, "a color-blind America."[78]

Fletcher grew worried. Now seventy years old, his signature issue was under attack from both sides of the political aisle. He wrote a personal letter to Dole, his friend of decades. "I am disturbed, as well as deeply disappointed, over the position my party of fifty years is taking on this vital issue," he told Dole, adding in an open letter to congressional Republicans that "affirmative action is too critical to the nation's immediate and foresee-able future for me to sit on the sidelines as a casual observer. . . . I intend to . . . make my position known and help you and other GOP members of the Congress arrive at a decision that is fair and equitable to all concerned: women and minorities, and white males too." He urged Dole to call him; as he was leaving for a visit to Kansas City, he listed telephone numbers where he could be reached on the road.[79]

Reflecting the political skill that ultimately brought Dole the GOP nomination, the Senate majority leader was sensitive to maintaining his alliances with men like Fletcher. "As you know, Art," he replied cordially, "I have supported every major piece of civil rights legislation since I was first elected to Congress." But he went on to distinguish between what he saw as legitimate and illegitimate affirmative action policies:

> If affirmative action means remedying proven past discrimination against specific individuals, then I'm all for it. If affirmative action means recruitment of qualified minorities and women to give them an opportunity to compete, without guaranteeing the results of the competition, then I'm for that too. But if affirmative action means quotas, set-asides and other preferences that favor individuals simply because they happen to belong to certain groups, then that's where I draw the line.

Despite his kind tone, Dole was repeating the very canard that affirmative action opponents had invented in the 1960s: that it was about unfair quotas and hiring unqualified minorities and women at the expense of better-qualified whites. After centuries of whites receiving favorable treatment simply because of their race, the idea that equality of opportunity could actually be accomplished by asking individuals to prove specific cases of past discrimination was a red herring. More galling still was that Dole saw his letter as the last word on the subject. Fletcher had asked for a phone call so that he could explain his views; Dole's reply was written, and despite including a line thanking Fletcher for "your willingness to share your concerns and views with me," it was calculated to keep his old friend—and his opinion on affirmative action—at arm's length.[80]

For Fletcher, affirmative action was not an abstract political issue. It meant real jobs and contracts, the livelihood and success—or failure—of real people. He had spent decades trying to convince the Republican Party of the importance of those real people, that they were at least as important as the white skilled workers, suburbanites, and unreconstructed southerners whose votes party leaders fetishized. With every Republican candidate opposed to affirmative action, and with President Clinton waffling on the subject, Fletcher resolved to take the only step that might save the programs he so prized. He decided to run for president.

Fletcher was not naive. He knew he stood little chance of winning the Republican nomination, let alone the White House. But he also knew that by adding his name to the list of candidates he commanded significant press coverage, which he could use to highlight the importance of affirmative action programs. What's more, as a candidate he would not be asked to endorse Bob Dole, and he could thereby avoid the ticklish question of snubbing his friend on the one hand or abandoning his principles on the other. Last, since his replacement as chairman of the Commission on Civil Rights, he had been drifting from the limelight; if he were ever to raise funds sufficient to form a national institution to combat inner-city poverty, which he still hoped to do against all odds, he needed to be a major national figure—and command the honorarium levels to which he had grown accustomed.[81]

In April 1995 Fletcher informed the press of his expected candidacy, set about putting together a campaign staff, and opened a bank account for Fletcher for President. By the end of June, as he prepared for a formal announcement speech at Independence Hall in Philadelphia, he had established a midwestern campaign office in Kansas City (while running the national headquarters out of his G Street home in Washington, DC) and secured the services of his fellow USCCR commissioner, Carl Anderson, as the campaign's legal advisor. He coined the slogan "give me five and keep it alive" to solicit small donations, and he announced a national Freedom Ride bus tour, consciously evoking the civil rights struggles of the 1960s. Acknowledging his age (at seventy he was already older than Reagan had been in 1980) and the rigors of a presidential campaign, he planned a part-time schedule, alternating weeks on the hustings with weeks at rest.[82]

As one of only two African Americans in the race (the other was Reaganite former assistant secretary of state Alan Keyes), and the only one who favored affirmative action, Fletcher got a lot of positive press for his shoestring campaign. Major news outlets like the *New York Times, Wall Street Journal, Washington Post, Los Angeles Times, USA Today,* and even the *Times of London* devoted articles to his candidacy, as did local newspapers throughout the country. He sat for interviews with National Public Radio, the *MacNeil-Lehrer NewsHour,* and Tom Snyder's *Late Late Show* on CBS.[83]

Nevertheless, Fletcher's campaign did not have sufficient supporters to get his name on any primary ballot, so he took it day by day, viewing the race primarily as a publicity exercise rather than a serious presidential campaign. By midsummer 1995 he had pinned his hopes on the CityVote Urban Straw Poll, a nonbinding referendum taking place in twenty-three cities around the country. Retired journalist Walter Cronkite lent gravitas to the event by agreeing to serve as its honorary chairman. The major candidates ignored it; for them the risk of losing momentum far outweighed any potential benefit, especially when it came to the Republican front-runners, who feared they were too unpopular in the cities. But the ghetto was Fletcher's natural base, and he hoped that a strong showing in the poll, scheduled for November 7, 1995, would give him the needed momentum to keep campaigning, at least into the early primaries.[84]

The Fletcher campaign garnered neither major financial backing nor any significant traction in the polls, but by October Fletcher could claim victory of another sort. Anti–affirmative action bills had failed in the states where they were being considered, and they failed to move forward in the US Congress. New polls showed that the majority of Americans favored various versions of the policy, and President Clinton concluded his internal study and decided to leave affirmative action alone. Even front-runner Bob Dole stopped talking about it, signaling that affirmative action would not be used as a wedge issue in the campaign after all.[85]

Fletcher came in dead last in the November 7 CityVote Urban Straw Poll, garnering only 241 votes nationwide, compared to 24,890 for Bob Dole and 2,786 for Alan Keyes. Colin Powell—who wasn't running—did best among Republicans, claiming 38,205. This was mainly because the poll, like an open primary, was available to all voters regardless of party affiliation; the inner-city overwhelmingly went for Clinton (who took 91,763 votes), and the more affluent neighborhoods split among Clinton, Dole, and Powell. As for Fletcher, the press attention and campaign donations dried up; if he couldn't even garner support in a straw poll that the major candidates ignored, then there seemed little point in continuing. He told journalist Simeon Booker that he was exhausted. His final official act of the campaign came months later, when he made the painful choice to boycott the 1996 Republican National Convention over the RNC's decision to include an anti–affirmative action plank in the Dole–Kemp campaign platform.[86]

The year 1995 was one of mixed blessings in Fletcher's personal life. First, to their mutual satisfaction, he and Bernyce reconciled. She joined him on the campaign trail in August, and the couple resumed sharing hotel rooms.[87]

But in November, a week after losing the CityVote Urban Straw Poll, having already lost his first wife and oldest son, Fletcher experienced a third personal tragedy: the untimely death of his youngest child. Phillip Fletcher had never recovered from his mother Mary's suicide. His behavior problems in school escalated to more serious—and violent—criminal activity, and he spent much of his adult life in prison. What is perhaps most striking about Phillip's story is that he ultimately had, according to his daughter Phyllis, "fourteen children by thirteen different women around the country." Trying desperately to replace the mother from whose arms he had so tragically been ripped at such an early age, and at the same time unable to process his anger at a mother who had abandoned him, for most of his life Phillip failed to develop lasting relationships, leaving a string of abandoned mothers and babies in his wake. (His aforementioned daughter, Phyllis, it should be noted, attended Columbia University and became an on-air host for Seattle Public Radio.) Although he finally settled down and married in 1986, Phillip was never able to kick his drug habit, and he continued to run into trouble with the law. On November 11, 1995, his wife, Juan-El, found Phillip dead of a heroin overdose.[88]

Phillip Fletcher was exactly the sort of person his father wanted to help with Victory Hall, his planned nonprofit inner-city institute. Phillip's tragic death brought home for Fletcher what he saw as his own failure: his inability to translate the victories of the civil rights era into equality of opportunity for all Americans. That the rise in homelessness, joblessness, drug abuse, and despair in the ghettoes was not his fault, and that it had developed thanks to the policies of Nixon, Reagan, and even Bush—and despite the herculean efforts of Jesse Jackson, Vernon Jordan, and Benjamin Hooks—were immaterial to the sense of personal responsibility Fletcher felt. Well into his eighth decade, however, he no longer boasted the stamina he had brought from the gridiron to the Oval Office.

Less than two years after Phillip died, Fletcher lost his eldest child. His daughter, Phyllis, had been the first to leave the household in 1961 and for many years was without contact with her father and siblings. In 1969 Phyllis married Leroy Palmer in Georgia, and by the early 1970s the couple was living in Greensboro, North Carolina, selling "handcrafted earrings." When she applied for a loan from the SBA in 1971, an officer there told her father, then at the Department of Labor, that "she has a good product, can't keep up with orders . . . will help her with her application." She appeared after that in the records only obliquely, after her son, Doc, was involved in a car accident in 1995. She died of AIDS in 1997 at age fifty-four.[89]

To Arthur

[signature: Geo. W. Bush]

Despite George W. Bush's conservatism, Fletcher admired the new president's faith-based initiatives program and remained loyal to the family. Arthur Fletcher Personal Papers, courtesy Paul Fletcher.

In the final years of his life, as the dream of Victory Hall receded further and further from reality, Arthur Fletcher focused less on his own abilities and more on transferring his knowledge to the next generation of civil rights leaders. He remained active in various projects and schemes, including two terms as chairman of the National Black Chamber of Commerce and the formation of Fletcher's Financial Services, an undercapitalized venture meant to stimulate bidding by Black contractors. In 1998 he took a booth at an NAACP convention to sell copies of his self-produced VHS tape *Affirmative Action: The Real Truth,* and after the election of George W. Bush he sought funding for his Friends of America's Future organization from the White House Office of Faith-Based and Community Initiatives. But increasingly he saw himself as part of a continuum of civil rights fighters, as a "keeper of the flame" for the next generation. Like his hero, Mary McLeod Bethune, he saw his mission as informing the young of the good works of the old, and of those, like Martin Luther King Jr. and Whitney Young, who had not shared his good fortune to become old. He continued to give speeches in cities all over the country until the week he died, when he spoke at Mother Bethel Church in Philadelphia. Even then he was preparing to travel for a week of speeches in England.[90]

As we have seen, the tragedies that befell some of the civil rights movement's greatest leaders were reflected in Fletcher's own family. In addition to his first wife, three of his children died before he did. But as with the transfer of the flame to the next generation of civil rights leaders, Fletcher transferred some of his best qualities to his two surviving children. His second child, Sylvia, became an educator and by 2003 was running a spousal abuse support center in Sacramento. Paul, his fourth child, attended the University of Washington, ran for King County Council in Seattle and the state legislature in Alaska, worked for HUD secretary Jack Kemp during the George H. W. Bush administration, and went on to head the Evansville, Indiana, housing authority. He married Patsy Mose, a Washington, DC–based author and historian, and the couple had two children, Tino and Om. In his father's final years, Paul joined him in an educational venture, Fletcher's Learning Systems Inc.[91]

Arthur Allen Fletcher died of heart failure on July 12, 2005. In an obituary, the *Washington Post* called him "a maverick Republican," a line echoed by several other newspapers. The *Topeka Capital-Journal* called him "a beacon of change." He was lauded in Congress, ironically by Democrats. Senator John Kerry, then the most recent Democratic presidential nominee, said Fletcher "never missed an opportunity to advance the interests of underserved people throughout the nation," adding, "His legacy lives on in all of us who believe in the struggle for racial and gender equality and who continue to fight for equal opportunity for all." In a posthumous reconciliation of Fletcher's relationship with the CBC, so wounded during the 1993 fight over Mary Berry's chairmanship of the Civil Right Commission, California representative Barbara Lee called him "a true pioneer in the movement for racial and socioeconomic equality."[92]

At his funeral, more Democrats chimed in with gushing praise. Clinton appointee Alexis Herman, the first (and as of this writing, only) African American secretary of labor, called Fletcher "truly, in spirit, the first African-American secretary of labor . . . a powerful reminder . . . that all of our children—whether they are on the honor rolls or the welfare rolls—that they belong to us, and that we have to pass on the legacy of education and skill-building to make sure that they, too, can sing America." Eleanor Holmes Norton, the District of Columbia's nonvoting delegate to the House of Representatives, said that Fletcher "didn't believe in being on the inside just to be on the inside. . . . Once he got on the inside, [he] believed that his challenge, his duty, was not to go where his party was, but to bring his party where he was." And Jesse Jackson, in a letter read at the ceremony, wrote, "Just as Moses had an impact inside of Pharaoh's house . . . with his sheer brilliance and against heavy odds, Arthur Fletcher became the father of affirmative action as we know it today. He was a minority, but with a true majority vision for all America."[93]

Longtime president of the National Council of Negro Women, Dorothy Height, said Fletcher "made clear to all who would listen that affirmative action was not about quotas but was about opening access and opportunity to all Americans." Height represented an organization founded by Mary McLeod Bethune, one of Fletcher's earliest civil rights inspirations; her words at his funeral brought his life full circle. Among Republicans, Maryland's African American lieutenant governor, Michael Steele, noted, "Art Fletcher . . . taught us that it wasn't enough to have a seat at the lunch counter; it was more important to own that lunch counter." In a letter, President George W. Bush called "Arthur's record of civic leadership . . . an inspiration to all, and a lasting legacy. Our nation is grateful for his many years of dedicated public service." Perhaps the best of the many pithy summations of Fletcher's long life came from Reverend Jeremiah Wright, the fiery pastor presidential candidate Barack Obama later disowned. In his eulogy Wright likened Fletcher to the biblical Nathan, advisor to King David and King Solomon on the plight of the common man. Clearly, despite Fletcher's decades of loyalty to the Republican Party, his influence had been felt across the political spectrum.[94]

Fletcher himself, despite his many defeats, gave a positive depiction of his life's achievements while sitting for an interview at Washburn University in 2003:

So when they ask me, "What is it that would make you feel that the journey was worthwhile?" It was figuring out how to get the federal government and contractors to agree to use everybody in their work force who has the guts, the will, the tenaciousness to develop their skills and make a contribution. So on my tombstone, just put "Fulfilled. The cat did his number."[95]

CONCLUSION

The Conundrum of the Black Republican

When you are sitting in the dressing room, taking off your
uniform after the ball game is over, only you know whether you
played a good game or not. The score doesn't really tell it.
—Arthur Fletcher, 1993

The story of Arthur Fletcher mirrors the decline of
the Republican Party's concern for the civil rights of people of color and
women during an era of renewed promise when it came to those very same
civil rights. His singular achievement—affirmative action in skilled union
employment—happened at a singular moment, the early Nixon administration, when civil rights were still an important concern for Republican leaders. His rise to that achievement, that moment—and the subsequent decline
of civil rights advocacy within the party—are an important component of the
story of racial progress in the United States.

Arthur Fletcher often likened the struggle for civil rights to the filling of
a cup with water. At the time of his birth, that cup contained only a sip, and
the metaphorical drinker—the African American—was dying of thirst. The
ongoing work of the civil rights leaders of his childhood years, like W. E. B.
Du Bois, Marcus Garvey, and his all-important Mary McLeod Bethune, filled
a quarter of the cup. Fletcher and his generation, which included Rosa Parks,
Martin Luther King Jr., Leon Sullivan, James Farmer, and Roy Wilkins, filled
the cup by half, thanks to their steadfast devotion to egalitarian principles
and insistence that government leaders respond to the desperate cries of the
people for civil rights legislation and enforcement. Fletcher remained active
during the rise of the next generation, which included Jesse Jackson, Floyd
McKissick, Ralph Neas, and Mary Frances Berry, but his optimism turned to
rage as the cup stubbornly refused to fill. Too many whites, joined by a new
generation of collaborators like Clarence Pendleton, Thomas Sowell, and
Clarence Thomas, believed that the filling of the cup meant the depleting

of white rights. In fact it did not; the founding documents of the American republic promised that every group could enjoy a full cup of civil rights. If Fletcher's metaphorical cup was depleting anything, it was white privilege, the noxious system by which elites had kept the working classes fighting among themselves since the time of slavery, and which most whites refused to admit even existed.

Arthur Fletcher, Civil Rights Republican

Arthur Fletcher shared many components of his upbringing with the better-known leaders of the civil rights movement. He worked cotton fields in his youth like Fannie Lou Hamer, knew the ghetto like Malcolm X, was raised by an educator like James Farmer, saw service in the segregated army like Whitney Young, and played football like Paul Robeson. He even claimed a minister among his forebears like Martin Luther King Jr. But as with the differences caused by his regional origins, he stubbornly marched to the beat of his own drum, like the pioneers and buffalo soldiers of his fond imagination.

Whereas scripture gave Dr. King guidance to pursue success for himself and become a leader of the movement, for Fletcher it was football. The sport of rugged individualism tempered by teamwork appealed to Fletcher's frontier sense of self, helped him find his place in the world of his youth, and gave him purpose. A football player is a fighter, a warrior. Fletcher developed a philosophy of controlled, channeled violence. His broad frame and imposing height lent a physical strength, but the gridiron taught him to channel his anger into short, controlled outbursts against the opposing team. This helped him deal with the racist slights he experienced—such as hotels and restaurants refusing to serve him—with equanimity. He would show them who the better man was not by lashing out in anger in the moment but by using that anger to push through to the end zone, whether literal or metaphorical.

Given his background in the Southwest and the influence of his adoptive father, Cotton Fletcher, his father-in-law, William Harden, and his political patron, Elisha Scott, it is not surprising that Fletcher became a Republican. While the Democrats were making inroads among African Americans at the national level thanks to President Roosevelt's New Deal, in Kansas as in the Deep South, that party was still closely associated with Jim Crow. However, he didn't become a Republican simply because of the negatives associated with Kansas Democrats; nor did he become a Republican by default. As we have seen, the factors that shaped his personality and his take on civil rights also shaped his politics.

A switch to the Democratic Party might have been appropriate during his years in Berkeley. This was his personal and professional low point, with his political connections dry and the national civil rights mantle being taken up energetically (at least from 1963) by a Democratic president who in the space of five years signed equal employment, voting rights, and fair housing legislation. The Republican Party, meanwhile, was moving to the right, and their appeal to racist southerners, so prominent in the 1964 Goldwater campaign, only grew.

But Fletcher's loyalty to the Republican Party remained logical throughout. In 1962, with William Byron Rumford's path to the Democratic nomination for California's Seventeenth Assembly District seemingly unstoppable, being a Black Republican made sense for Fletcher in his first turn as a candidate in his own right, and his interests lay in building the Berkeley GOP both as a counter to Democratic dominance in the Bay Area and as a force in the California Republican Assembly, where he was slowly building respect, influence, and friendships.[1]

It was not simply self-interest that kept Arthur Fletcher in the Republican fold as more and more African Americans abandoned the party. Despite the growing rift between Republican electoral strategies and the interests of civil rights advocates like Fletcher—a rift later epitomized by Nixon's Southern Strategy—Fletcher's political ideology was better suited to the Republican Party than the Democratic. While he approved of the civil rights legislation that Democratic president Lyndon Johnson pushed through Congress and signed—and indeed would later find himself responsible for enforcing the equal employment sections of the 1964 Civil Rights Act—Fletcher's was an individualist orientation. He believed that personal success came through personal effort. His civil rights philosophy was a self-help philosophy. He did not oppose government assistance for the needy—he certainly met more than a few truly needy single parents in the Berkeley ghetto—but he wanted such assistance to be used only as a stopgap measure; he worried that too much of it bred dependence and sapped the will to work.[2]

Joshua D. Farrington, in his 2016 book *Black Republicans and the Transformation of the GOP,* described the Black Republicans of Fletcher's era (and Fletcher himself) as middle and upper class, in favor of a two-party system, and in favor of political solutions to racial inequality. While Fletcher was not raised in the middle class, he did have much in common with the partisans Farrington described, and it was they who helped him become middle class through connections forged during and after college. Fletcher's individualism and patriotism, furthermore, made him a good fit with other Black Republicans, among whom he remained popular until his death.[3]

Arthur Fletcher most certainly did not become a Republican—or remain so—because he was a conservative. Fletcher subscribed to none of the tenets of postwar Republican conservatism as understood by Ohio senator Robert Taft, leader of the conservative wing of the Republican Party until his death in 1953: opposition to large federal government, federalism, and isolationism.[4] As demonstrated by his development and implementation of the Philadelphia Plan, Fletcher saw a robust federal government as the guarantor and enforcer of civil rights legislation, distrusted states' abilities to protect the rights of Black people, and was unafraid of federal power on this issue. At the United Nations he supported a dynamic, engaged foreign policy to promote the ideal of an egalitarian United States for the advancement of human rights everywhere, especially in Africa and the Soviet Union. He was also proud of his military service during a war that gave the lie to isolationism and effectively ended it as a viable American foreign policy.

Fletcher's peculiar brand of politics perfectly suited him for the job at the Department of Labor. His rejection of the direct-aid model gave him the perspective to view the private sector as ground zero in the civil rights struggle. For Fletcher the role of government was not to employ people directly (except when it came to the military and a lean bureaucracy) but rather to facilitate private employment—set the stage, create the environment, and get out of the way to let the market work. Where he differed with conservatives was that he believed the federal government should spend significant funds in doing so. After his experiences with Higher Horizons and the Pasco co-op, the Philadelphia Plan was right up his alley. Here was a program needing minimal funding, one that used existing federal contracts to cajole major employers into developing integration plans.

Had Fletcher been successful in permanently integrating the skilled building trades, it would have benefited more than a handful of skilled underemployed Black workers. The middle class—Black and white—was built on skilled union labor. In the automobile industry, in places like Detroit and Dayton, African Americans successfully integrated the skilled trades and built middle-class lives in the postwar era. But in the building trades whites stubbornly held onto their privileges, and the potential for a Black middle class was lost. While the Philadelphia Plan only affected a handful of workers in each city where mandatory versions were implemented, it had the potential to set a completely different tone. If Fletcher had been successful, the other areas of industrial life might have fallen like dominos. This would have meant more Black middle-class families and fewer who suffered from inner-city poverty. But it wasn't a zero-sum game: more dollars in the pockets of African Americans would have meant more consumer spending, more construction, and more jobs overall. Continued employment discrimination instead contributed to an economic downturn. The whites who so desperately clung to their privileges would have been better off had they accepted integration. Idle Black hands were truly terrible things to waste.

The opportunism with which Fletcher greeted Nixon's ascendance, and the loyalty he displayed toward the disgraced former president was the same opportunism and loyalty that kept him in the Republican Party. He never left the party even as the party left him. Fletcher's loyalty ran against the increasingly obvious reality that being a Black Republican was his greatest electoral handicap. Each time he ran for office, what kept him from victory was the fact that every major sector of any given electorate had reason to mistrust him. Whites worried that affirmative action would take away their jobs, and Blacks saw him as a stand-in for increasingly hostile white conservatives. He could win primaries for a variety of reasons, as in his 1962 California State Assembly bid (the dearth of Republican politicians in the Bay Area), his 1968 Washington lieutenant governor race (his sports-celebrity opponent's lack of interest), and his 1978 try for mayor of Washington, DC (the perceived incompetence of his opponent), but nearly always failed in the general election. In 1962 and 1978 Fletcher lost because of his party, in 1968 because of his race. Only in 1967 did he successfully navigate a general-election victory, in an at-large city council race in a Republican area where sufficient white voters overcame their fears and acknowledged his appeal.[5]

Beyond his loyalty and political moderation, Fletcher became trapped in the Republican Party by his own prominence. The examples of politicians who actually switched parties in this era did not give Fletcher any cause for emulation. No sitting Republican senator left the party during Fletcher's years in national politics, and the Democrats who became Republicans—Strom Thurmond and Richard Shelby—were unreconstructed white southerners. John Connally, the former Texas governor who successfully navigated a party switch, was probably denied a spot as Ford's running mate in 1976 because the act demonstrated a lack of the very loyalty prized by party leaders, and presumably party voters. Outside of partisan politics it was easier, of course: NAACP leader Benjamin Hooks, for instance, successfully left the Republican fold, following most of that organization's membership. Another notable Black Republican who switched parties—Ralph Neas, an advisor to Edward Brooke and Minnesota senator Dave Durenberger—did not achieve political success afterward, although his long career as chairman of the Leadership Conference on Civil Rights was suggestive of the path Fletcher's might have followed had he somehow continued to lead the United Negro College Fund (UNCF).

Whereas Fletcher remained in the Republican Party despite its increasing conservatism, Clarence Thomas embraced it. A generation younger, Thomas's childhood had much in common with Fletcher's. His earliest years were spent in deep poverty, especially after abandonment by his father. What changed him, as for Fletcher, was the presence of a strong surrogate father: his maternal grandfather, Myers Anderson, who owned a thriving fuel oil and ice company in Savannah. Like Fletcher, Thomas went from early childhood in an all-Black community (Pin Point, Georgia, part of the Sea Island Gullah region) to teen life in a mixed one; he was the only Black student in his high school. Like Fletcher, he was connected to the Catholic church: Fletcher married into it and raised his children in it while Mary was alive; Thomas was raised in the church and even considered the priesthood, attending seminary. Like Fletcher, he was involved with civil rights protest activity at an early age; for Thomas it was a walkout over racially discriminatory punishments for behavioral infractions at his college in Worcester, Massachusetts. Thomas learned early on the value of hard work and adopted a version of Fletcher's self-help civil rights mantra.[6]

Important differences in career choice and civil rights philosophy, however, resulted in a divergence in political success. First, Thomas went directly from college into law school, graduating from Yale Law in 1974; while Fletcher took some correspondence courses in the law during the late 1960s to help him work on the contracts at the Pasco co-op, he never seriously entertained the idea of becoming a lawyer.[7]

Second, and most importantly, Thomas developed an antipathy to affirmative action, Fletcher's signature program. He was admitted to Yale Law because of an increased Black quota, and after facing derision in his legal career from white employers, he came to doubt his diploma's value. Fletcher would have argued that Yale needed to admit more Black students to overcome an entrenched history of racism in admissions, and that lowering LSAT and college GPA requirements was a necessary countermeasure to overcome the inherent inequality of those standards. Because the graduates of Yale and other top-tier law schools controlled the top tier of jurisprudence—from corporate law firm partnerships to the Supreme Court—they needed to admit more Black students so that African Americans could have increased access to those corridors of power. Thomas, on the other hand, saw it as shameful that he was admitted with a lackluster academic record and gave a lackluster academic performance once there. He blamed himself, while Fletcher blamed the system. But that Yale law degree, despite his rejection of its value, was nevertheless the key to Thomas's success. In one of the great ironies of history, Clarence Thomas fulfilled Arthur Fletcher's vision of affirmative action with his 1991 ascension to the highest court in the land, then joined the conservative majority in the Court's continuing assault on affirmative action.[8]

On the topic of party fealty, it is also worth comparing Fletcher to his opposite number in the 1976 presidential campaign. While Fletcher was fighting for Black votes for a Republican, an increasingly difficult prospect despite Ford's moderate record on civil rights, Andrew Young was campaigning for a Georgia planter from a party whose appeal to African Americans was steadily growing. Unlike Fletcher, Young was originally from the Deep South—New Orleans—and was raised by two professional parents. Young moved away from the South after college, where he settled into a comfortable life as a minister with the National Council of Churches in New York City. Whereas Fletcher followed a political path into civil rights work, Young followed a civil rights path into politics. In 1960, after watching the Nashville student sit-ins on TV, Young relocated to Atlanta to join Martin Luther King Jr.'s organization. Benefiting from the Voting Rights Act, which he had helped pass by participating in the march from Selma to Montgomery in 1965, he ran for Congress in 1970, and after a tight loss, he tried again and won in 1972. In 1976, as a member of the CBC, he defended Carter, campaigned for him in the general election, and was rewarded with an appointment as the first Black ambassador to the United Nations. There he took positions similar to those Fletcher had espoused during his own UN stint in 1971. Like Fletcher, after his president's eventual loss, he ran for mayor of his adopted city. His accomplishments as Atlanta's mayor during the 1980s read like Fletcher's hopes for Washington, DC: he capitalized on and strengthened the existing infrastructure and workforce to build major public–private partnerships to expand the tax base and improve social services. His successes in office, however, were the result of initial successes at the ballot box, and unlike Fletcher, he became and remained a Democrat. As we have seen, this was something that Fletcher could not do; nevertheless, Young's story represented for Fletcher another path not taken because of his loyalty to the Republican Party.[9]

The Conundrum of the Black Republican

In his 2013 book *Republicans and Race,* historian Timothy N. Thurber chronicled the decline of African American membership in the Republican Party during the first three postwar decades. Although never quite as welcoming of Blacks as the popular imagination would have it, the GOP's story is one wherein the southern tail—a small minority in the party during most of that period—came to wag the Republican dog. In this telling, the moderates and conservatives after the war were fighting for control of the party, but the moderates retained the upper hand through the Eisenhower era. However, any political party will take votes where it can get them, and the civil rights legislation of the 1960s gave the conservatives an opening. The old Dixiecrats, increasingly disenchanted with the Democratic Party, began to move toward the GOP. Once in the party, these unreconstructed southerners joined and expanded the conservative wing, bringing it to dominance.[10]

Mary C. Brennan saw an adherence to laissez-faire economics as more important than race. In her 1995 book *Turning Right in the Sixties,* Brennan noted that the conservative Goldwaterites saw Nixon's 1960 loss as an opportunity to build a viable alternative to New Deal liberalism and not rely on "personality candidates" like Eisenhower, elected thanks to his popularity as a World War II general. Despite the loss in 1964, the Goldwaterite victory in the primaries rekindled conservatives' belief that the party could turn to the right, and they resumed their internecine battle to accomplish this. For Rick Perlstein, on the other hand, it was a gradual switch during the tumultuous 1960s that pushed voters to prioritize moral values over economic concerns. Racism was a trap that the GOP walked into as Democrats were increasingly associated with housing integration and softness on inner-city crime. Middle American white homeowners and skilled unionists, linking these issues, began to see the GOP as a viable alternative.[11]

Although the tail did indeed come to wag the dog—the conservative ascendancy resulted in the rise of Ronald Reagan—it did not become the dog. Unreconstructed southerners like North Carolina senator Jesse Helms did not gain control of the party so much as they allowed southwestern and midwestern conservative Republicans to do so—like Ronald Reagan, Bob Dole, John McCain, and Paul Ryan. To date the party has yet to nominate a real southerner to the presidency (Eisenhower was born in Texas but raised in Kansas; George W. Bush was raised in Texas but born and educated in Connecticut). Unreconstructed white southerners took on the kingmaker role in Republican politics, but they did not become kings themselves.

After 1980, with the rise not only of the white conservative Reaganites but also the new Black conservatives, it was increasingly clear that Fletcher's faction had lost. But as any talented politician knows, there are no permanent losers in politics. Fletcher knew that the Republican Party could flip back to moderation as quickly as it had been lost to the conservative wing. He postulated that Blacks should join the party to integrate it, much as they had integrated hostile high schools and lunch counters during the civil rights era, and indeed as they had integrated the Democratic Party after 1964. The fact that it didn't happen—indeed, as the rise of Donald Trump has demonstrated, racist elements within the party were even stronger in 2016 than they were in 1980—does not mean Fletcher was wrong.

Radical change such that Fletcher was proposing within the Republican Party, however, is prone to failure, and Fletcher's position within the party was increasingly quixotic. He was less and less an obvious fit with party leaders, who, as he told an interviewer in 1995 in frustration, advocated "hard-nosed economic development . . . in the suburbs [but] become sociologists when it comes to the depressed neighborhoods."[12] Success in his bid for chairman of the RNC in 1977 seems impossible in retrospect—despite his coming in third on the first ballot—as RNC members by then knew which way their party's wind blew. President Ford would never have endorsed such a candidacy. Nor could the RNC actively support Fletcher's mayoral run the following year, as that would have required a diversion of resources to the increasingly disdained urbanity, which conservatives saw as throwing good money after bad. It was different three decades later when Maryland lieutenant governor Michael Steele was elected RNC chairman; demographic changes and the election of Barack Obama briefly forced the party to acknowledge that alienating minorities might be a losing strategy in the long run. The brevity of Steele's tenure—and the advent of the Tea Party and Trumpism—is evidence that the party has yet to come to terms with this issue.

The Republican Party's embrace of southern votes also need not have resulted in an embrace of nationalist and racist policies. While it's true that unreconstructed white southerners moved almost en masse from the Democratic to the Republican party after President Johnson signed the 1964 Civil Rights Act, ultimately replacing Black voters and moving the party decisively to the right on race, it didn't have to be that way. There could have been room for both moderate Blacks (who might have even been conservative on non–civil rights issues) and the descendants of the Dixiecrats, if party leaders had affirmatively led unreconstructed white southerners into ideological reconstruction—or at least to compromise on some of their racist beliefs. Instead, moderate and conservative alike, they pandered to them, alienating and isolating moderate Black Republicans in the process.

What should they have done? They should have followed the lead of Harry Truman, who overcame his own bigotry to integrate the armed forces; Dwight Eisenhower, who integrated Little Rock High School even as he saw civil rights issues as a nuisance; and Lyndon Johnson, the good ol' boy who pushed Congress to pass the Civil Rights Acts of 1964, 1965, and 1968. Nixon should not have abandoned the Philadelphia Plan for the hard hats; Colson was wrong, and they would have supported his reelection anyway because of his Vietnam policy and their Cold War machismo. Instead, as Arthur Fletcher advocated in 1971, the Southern Strategy should have focused on developing the southern economy for people of all races. Working together, whites might have come to accept Blacks in their workplaces and neighborhoods, just as they had in the armed forces. Ultimately, starting with Nixon, Republican leaders didn't lead on race; they followed.

With the rise of the New Right, one of the remaining cards moderate Republicans could play was that of "faithful party service," and it was this that returned Fletcher to government work in the Bush administration. Formerly a phrase used to explain why moderates accepted right-wingers, the conservatives who dominated the party after 1976 understood that moderate Republicans who had demonstrated faithful party service could be trusted, in office, to employ and promote conservative people and ideas. Their ability to win made them tolerable. This helped Ford secure the 1976 nomination; it likewise propelled Bush to the top of the ticket in 1988, and his election victory allowed for the return to public office of other faithful moderate Republicans like Fletcher. Although Bush kept numerous conservative Reaganites in his administration, his failure to demonstrate sufficient fealty to conservative values (i.e., rescinding his "no new taxes" pledge) resulted in the 1992 Buchanan revolt and contributed to his subsequent loss to Clinton.

As time went on, however, conservatives were less interested in tolerating loyal moderates. The 1988 Bush nomination was something of a last gasp for the idea. His namesake son had to run to the right to win nomination. Indeed, George W. Bush consciously looked to Reagan, rather than his own father, as a presidential role model, which helped him win reelection in 2004.

Similar to Eisenhower, Ford, and Bush, moderate Black Republicans like Art Fletcher, observing and concerned by the rise of the New Right, remained loyal in the hope that faithful party service would win them support. Fletcher exemplified this, as did Colin Powell. But moderate Black Republicans, like their white counterparts, lost the race for the support of white conservative Republicans to a new breed of conservative Black Republicans. Clarence Thomas eclipsed Arthur Fletcher, and Ben Carson eclipsed Colin Powell.[13]

Arthur Fletcher represented a political direction that the Republican Party rejected. He saw in African Americans, who shared the family values lauded by his friend George Bush, a vast untapped market for the party. The church-going, civil rights liberal, fiscally moderate, and socially conservative Blacks of the rising middle class—and even the strivers of the ghetto who eschewed personal aid in favor of institutional assistance like affirmative action and contract set-asides—represented to him the potential rebirth of the party.

But the conundrum remains. Bush's waffling on civil rights issues, from the veto of the 1990 civil rights bill to the Clarence Thomas nomination, wasn't encouraging. Eager to win the white conservative vote, Dole decried affirmative action in 1995. More recently, conservative Republicans have engaged in various voter suppression techniques, from the intimidation of Black Florida voters in 2000 to spurious accusations of voter fraud and the push to require state identification at polling places. Republican presidents continued to nominate conservative jurists to the Supreme Court; five of them ruled in the 2013 *Shelby County v. Holder* case that African American voters no longer needed protection from Jim Crow state laws designed to keep them from the polls, eviscerating a core provision of the 1965 Voting Rights Act. The historic election of Barack Obama in 2008, meanwhile, further cemented Democrats' hold on the Black vote.

Most modern prominent Black Republicans are decidedly of the conservative minority within a minority. These ideological heirs to Reagan's Black brain trust include Senator Tim Scott of South Carolina, who embodies the antiunion attitudes with which George Meany and Peter Brennan once tarred Arthur Fletcher. Clarence Thomas consistently joins the anti–civil rights conservatives on the Supreme Court. Other less intellectual African American conservatives, sensing a void, have moved directly from business into presidential politics, but they falter in attempting to apply their particular expertise to the world of political leadership. These include former Godfather's Pizza CEO Herman Cain, briefly a front-runner for the 2012 presidential nomination, and accomplished pediatric neurosurgeon Ben Carson, President Trump's secretary of HUD. While conservatives should have a home in even a big tent, the prominence of these men in the party, rather than the far larger group of Black moderates, signals Arthur Fletcher's failure to integrate it.

Whatever their flaws, one could hardly accuse conservatives of having developed a losing strategy. In a nation rapidly becoming less white, less male dominated, and less heteronormative, the adoption of policies and ideologies deemed harmful to immigrants, women, and people of color has served instead to galvanize a lurking reactionary base that modernity has failed to soften. The Republican Party, despite its explicitly retrogressive agenda, won six of the eleven presidential elections after Watergate. From 1995 to 2018, a Republican was Speaker of the House in all but four years. With the 2016 election of Donald Trump, Republicans and their appointees took control of every branch of the United States government. Jim Crow, sometimes dressed up in an alt-right version as Professor James Crowe, continues to be an effective campaign operative and political power player.

Arthur Fletcher realized too late that his party had left him behind and had thoroughly betrayed his values. Only after the Rodney King verdicts did he shift from loyalty to confrontation, from quiet lobbying to public rage. But by that point, at the end of his career, he had become a relic of an all-but-forgotten Republican past. Far more than in solid accomplishments, his legacy is in the road not taken. That said, although the score showed a clear loss for his team, he most certainly played a good game.

INTRODUCTION

1. David Hamilton Golland, *Constructing Affirmative Action: The Struggle for Equal Employment Opportunity* (Lexington: University Press of Kentucky, 2011).

CHAPTER 1. ORIGINS, 1924–1945

1. Stephanie and Eric Stradford to Michael Williams, June 24, 2005 (Arthur Fletcher personal papers, digitized by and in possession of the author [hereafter G Street], box 112, folder 3, 425–426); Mother Bethel African Methodist Episcopal Church order of worship, June 26, 2005 (G Street, box 8, folder 4, 82–83); and Independence Visitors Center, "36th Anniversary of the Affirmative Action Enforcement Movement" program, June 27, 2005 (G Street, box 112, folder 4, 5–6).

2. Arthur Fletcher speech, November 19, 1969 (G Street, box 80, folder 3, 587–615); Geoffrey Gould, "Black Nixon Aide Prods Labor Plan," *Staten Island Advance,* March 3, 1971; Fletcher application for government employment, December 1975 (G Street, box 15A, folder 2, 1023–1048); and Paul Fletcher interview by and in possession of the author, April 2, 2011.

3. "Anderson," photograph, 1931 (G Street, box 77, folder 1, 178); unknown photographer, photograph, n.d. [1935] (G Street, box 68, folder 1, 13).

4. Virginia Olds, "Fletcher Spells Plan," unknown publication (G Street, box 39, folder 1, 59); Gould, "Black Nixon Aide Prods Labor Plan."

5. Fletcher speech, November 19, 1969.

6. Fletcher interview by Linda Furiate, December 6, 2004 (G Street, box 15A, folder 2, 1797–1808).

7. Olds, "Fletcher Spells Plan"; "The United States—Cotton Region, 1897," from Jacques W. Redway and Russell Hinman, *Natural Introductory Geography* (New York: American Book Company, 1897), 38, reproduced at Maps Etc., http://etc.usf.edu/maps/pages/2600/2626/2626.htm. References to "Edna Fletcher" and "Edna Banner" can be found in G Street, passim.

8. Fletcher open letter, n.d. [1999] (G Street, box 68, folder 5, 90–115).

9. Fletcher interview by Washburn University Department of Political Science, April 9, 2003 (Mabee Library, Washburn University, Topeka, KS), tape 2a, transcript, 194–195.

10. Adam Fairclough, *A Class of Their Own: Black Teachers in the Segregated South* (Cambridge, Mass.: Belknap Press, 2007), 278; "History of Prairie View A&M University," PVAMU, https://www.pvamu.edu/.

11. Fletcher to Theresa M. Kerrigan, March 26, 1991 (G Street, box 16, folder 1, 1082); Fletcher interview by Washburn University, tape 2a, transcript, 194. This assumes his mother had any Native American background at all; DNA evidence, used most famously by the scholar Henry Louis Gates Jr., has shown that many

African American claims to Native American heritage are unfounded. Gates, *Finding Your Roots: The Official Companion to the PBS Series* (Chapel Hill: University of North Carolina Press, 2014).

12. Fletcher passport application, October 5, 1969 (G Street, box 124, folder 1, 67–68); Fletcher employment application, December 1975 (G Street, box 15A, folder 2, 1023–1048); and Fletcher interview by Washburn University, tape 2a, transcript, 195.

13. Fletcher speech, November 19, 1969.

14. "Anderson," photograph; "George Washington Elementary School, Tulsa, OK," Classmates.com, http://www.classmates.com/.

15. Louis R. Harlan, *Booker T. Washington: The Wizard of Tuskegee, 1901–1915* (New York: Oxford, 1983); Booker T. Washington, *Up from Slavery* (New York: Penguin, 1986); Jacqueline M. Moore, *Booker T. Washington, W. E. B. Du Bois, and the Struggle for Racial Uplift* (Wilmington, Del.: Scholarly Resources, 2003); Henry Lewis Suggs, "The Washingtonian Legacy: A History of Black Political Conservatism in America, 1915–1944"; and Walter A. Friedman, "The African-American Gospel of Business Success," in *Black Conservatism: Essays in Intellectual and Political History,* ed. Peter Eisenstadt (New York: Garland, 1999).

16. Gould, "Black Nixon Aide Prods Labor Plan"; Adele Ferguson, "Art Fletcher Still Ideal Nominee," *Yakima Herald-Republic,* n.d. [November 1989] (G Street, box 15A, folder 2, 340).

17. John deYonge, "Former Shoeshine Boy Advises GOP on Ghetto Tactics," *Seattle Post-Intelligencer,* September 19, 1968; Fletcher interview by Washburn University, tape 1, transcript, 2.

18. Fletcher interview by Washburn University, tape 1, transcript, 2–3.

19. "Henry Armstrong," BoxRec, http://boxrec.com/; *Unforgivable Blackness: The Rise and Fall of Jack Johnson,* dir. Ken Burns (Florentine Films, 2005); "Kenny Washington, American Football Player," *Encyclopædia Brittanica,* https://www.britannica.com/; and Arnold Rampersad, *Jackie Robinson: A Biography* (New York: Knopf, 1997), 36, 40–41.

20. Fletcher interview by Washburn University, tape 2a, transcript, 201; Mark Peterson, "The Kansas Roots of Arthur Allen Fletcher: Football All-Star to the 'Father of Affirmative Action,'" *Kansas History* 34, no. 3 (2011): 226. He later gave his address for 1937–1938 as 328 East 6th Street, but Oklahoma City is on a compass grid; it has a Northeast 6th Street and a Southeast 6th Street, but no East 6th Street. No trace of any Depression-era housing exists in either location today; an interstate highway now dissects these fully gentrified neighborhoods, one of which is the swank Boathouse District. Fletcher employment application, December 1975.

21. "Mrs. Mary McLeod Bethune Addresses Social Workers," *Pittsburgh Courier,* August 1, 1936; Lena M. Wysinger, "Activities among Negroes," *Oakland Tribune,* March 27, 1938; Laura Randolph, "A Message to Americans: Civil Rights Commission Chief Leads Crusade for Racial Harmony," *Ebony,* July 1991; Fletcher to Margot James Copeland, October 21, 1994 (G Street, box 119, folder 1, 6–11); Fletcher

notes, n.d. [1996] (G Street, box 53, folder 1, 837); and Suggs, "Washingtonian Legacy," 96. The quotation is from Randolph.

22. Mary McLeod Bethune, "My Last Will and Testament," May 18, 1955 (Papers of President Gerald R. Ford, Collection of Arthur Fletcher, box 2, "National Council of Negro Women, Inc." folder); Louis Gray, "Civil Rights Chief Keynotes Seminar; Admonishes Blacks to Invest Money," *Oklahoma Eagle,* June 7, 1990; Bob Honeyman, "JCHS Grad No. 18 on List of Influential African-Americans," *Junction City Daily Union,* November 26, 2000; Fletcher interview by Washburn University, tape 2a, transcript, 166, 204; Fletcher interview by Linda Furiate; and Peterson, "Kansas Roots of Arthur Allen Fletcher," 226.

23. Fletcher passport application, October 5, 1969; Fletcher employment application, December 1975; Fletcher interview by Washburn University, tape 1, transcript, 1.

24. William H. Leckie, *The Buffalo Soldiers: A Narrative of the Negro Cavalry in the West* (Norman: University of Oklahoma Press, 1967), 98–100, 228–229, 258–260; Garna L. Christian, *Black Soldiers in Jim Crow Texas, 1899–1917* (College Station: Texas A&M University Press, 1995), xiii.

25. Christian, *Black Soldiers in Jim Crow Texas,* 19–20, 85–86, 157, 173–178.

26. Fletcher passport application, October 5, 1969; Honeyman, "JCHS Grad No. 18"; Fletcher interview by Washburn University, tape 1, transcript, 1, and tape 2a, transcript, 196.

27. Fletcher interview by Washburn University, tape 1, transcript, 5–6.

28. Fletcher speech, November 19, 1969; Fletcher passport application, October 5, 1969; and Fletcher employment application, December 1975.

29. *The Autobiography of Malcolm X, as Told to Alex Haley* (New York: Random House, 1964); Douglas Brinkley, *Gerald R. Ford* (New York: Times Books, 2007), 1–4; and Tanya Mohn, "Martin Luther King Jr.: The German Connection and How He Got His Name," *Forbes,* January 12, 2012, https://www.forbes.com/.

30. Peterson, "Kansas Roots of Arthur Allen Fletcher," 228.

31. *1942 PowWow* (Junction City Junior–Senior High School Yearbook), June 1942, digital copy in possession of the author; Olds, "Fletcher Spells Plan"; Fletcher employment application, December 1975; and Peterson, "Kansas Roots of Arthur Allen Fletcher," 228–229. The Fletcher quotation is from Olds; the report of the Herrington and Chapman games is from the *1942 PowWow.*

32. Fletcher speech, November 19, 1969; Fletcher interview by Washburn University, tape 1, transcript, 6.

33. Peterson, "Kansas Roots of Arthur Allen Fletcher," 228.

34. Fletcher speech before the Chicago Black Chamber of Commerce, July 23, 2004 (G Street, box 111, folder 3, 341–345).

35. Peterson, "Kansas Roots of Arthur Allen Fletcher," 229.

36. "Fletcher Named to Labor Post," *Junction City Union,* March 15, 1969; Gould, "Black Nixon Aide Prods Labor Plan"; Jim Warren to Fletcher, December 7, 2001 (G Street, box 23, folder 8, 123); Paul Fletcher interview by and in possession of the author, July 30, 2010; Paul and Sylvia Fletcher interview by and in

possession of the author, December 28, 2010; Peterson, "Kansas Roots of Arthur Allen Fletcher," 226–227; "Fort Riley History," Legends of America, https://www.legendsofamerica.com/; "Fort Riley History," My Base Guide, http://www.mybaseguide.com/; and "History of Fort Riley," ArmyBases.org, http://armybases.org/.

37. Kansas State Board of Health, birth certificate for Phyllis Edna Fletcher, October 6, 1943 (G Street, box 6, folder 1, 91); Fletcher draft letter to California Board of Parole, n.d. [early 1990s] (G Street, box 103, folder 3, 293–312), and "Fletcher Named to Labor Post"; Warren to Fletcher, December 7, 2001.

38. Warren to Fletcher, December 7, 2001. Warren's identification of Fletcher with the hated Japanese was indicative of the mixed feelings many African Americans had about fighting in support of a racist nation.

39. Gene Kemper, "Topping Captains All-Star Prep Team," *Topeka Daily Capital*, December 13, 1942; "Arthur Fletcher on All-Kansas Team: Junction City High School Boy One of Two Best Football Ends in State," *Junction City Union*, December 14, 1942; Fletcher interview by Washburn University, tape 1, transcript, 12; and Peterson, "Kansas Roots of Arthur Allen Fletcher," 229–230.

40. *1942 PowWow*; Fletcher to Jack Norman, January 4, 1993 (G Street, box 102, folder 4, 71–73); Bob Honeyman, "Man's Civil Rights Efforts Began at JCHS," *Junction City Daily Union*, September 19, 1999; Fletcher interview by Washburn University, tape 1, transcript, 11–12; and Peterson, "Kansas Roots of Arthur Allen Fletcher," 230. The 1943 portraits can be found in "Junction City High School Class of 1943 50th Reunion" program, May 28–30, 1993 (G Street, box 109, folder 2, 10–95).

41. Honeyman, "Man's Civil Rights Efforts Began at JCHS"; Fletcher interview by Washburn University, tape 1, transcript, 13; and Peterson, "Kansas Roots of Arthur Allen Fletcher," 230. The quotation is from the Fletcher interview.

42. *1942 PowWow*; Fletcher interview by Robert Wright, January 21, 1971 (Moorland-Spingarn Library Special Collections, Howard University, Washington, DC, NIDS #3.178.222); Fletcher to Norman, January 4, 1993; Honeyman, "Man's Civil Rights Efforts Began at JCHS"; Fletcher interview by Washburn University, tape 1, transcript, 12–13; and Peterson, "Kansas Roots of Arthur Allen Fletcher," 230.

43. Kansas State Board of Health, birth certificate for Phyllis Edna Fletcher; Fletcher employment application, December 1975.

44. Kansas State Board of Health, birth certificate for Phyllis Edna Fletcher; Paul Fletcher interview by and in possession of the author, September 25, 2010.

45. Kansas State Board of Health, birth certificate for Phyllis Edna Fletcher; United States Army Fifth Service Command Station List, January 15, 1944 (Records of the Adjutant General's Office Station Lists, RG407, box 74, "Fifth Service Command September, 1943" folder, National Archives and Records Administration [NARA], College Park, MD); US War Department Final Payment Work Sheet for Arthur A. Fletcher, October 19, 1945 (National Personnel Records Center [NPRC] Request No. 2-20671104597, NARA, St. Louis, MO); War Department Enlisted Record and Report of Separation Honorable Discharge, October 19, 1945 (NPRC Request No. 2-20671104597, NARA St. Louis); Fletcher veteran preference claim, June 25, 1969 (G Street, box 15A, folder 2, 1049–1050); Fletcher employment application, December 1975; Fletcher questionnaire, January 3, 1995 (G

Street, box 111, folder 1, 32); Fletcher interview by Washburn University, tape 1, transcript, 15; Richard C. Hong to Fletcher, July 15, 2005 (G Street, box 118, folder 4, 221); Peterson, "Kansas Roots of Arthur Allen Fletcher," 231.

46. Kansas State Board of Health, birth certificate for Phyllis Edna Fletcher.

47. Fletcher interview by Washburn University, tape 1, transcript, 15–18.

48. Olds, "Fletcher Spells Plan"; Fletcher interview by Robert Wright; and Fletcher interview by Washburn University, tape 1, transcript, 15–18. A "sweep," according to author Jerry Butler, "was a handoff right or left . . . parallel to the line" of scrimmage. *Pass Receiving in Early Pro Football: A History to the 1960s* (Jefferson, N.C.: McFarland, 2016), 252–253. John T. Reed, in "Dictionary of American Football Terms" (http://www.johntreed.net/fbdictionary.html), defines "belly play" as "to run a path that goes slightly backward and away from the line of scrimmage before coming back toward the line of scrimmage as in a swing pass route."

49. Mary Penick Motley, *The Invisible Soldier: The Experience of the Black Soldier, World War II* (Detroit: Wayne State University Press, 1975), passim; Neil Wynn, *The Afro-American and the Second World War* (New York: Holmes & Meier, 1975), passim; Hondon B. Hargrove, *Buffalo Soldiers in Italy: Black Americans in World War II* (Jefferson, N.C.: McFarland, 1985), passim; Charles W. Sasser, *Patton's Panthers: The African-American 761st Tank Battalion in World War II* (New York: Pocket Books, 2004), passim; and Thomas A. Guglielmo, "A Martial Freedom Movement: Black GIs' Political Struggles during World War II," *Journal of American History* 104, no. 4 (2018).

50. Jackie Robinson, *I Never Had It Made* (New York: Putnam, 1972); Dennis C. Dickerson, *Militant Mediator: Whitney M. Young Jr.* (Lexington: University Press of Kentucky, 1998), 32–33; John Hope Franklin, *Mirror to America* (New York: Farrar, Straus and Giroux, 2005), 107, 130; and John Vernon, "Jim Crow, Meet Lieutenant Robinson: A 1944 Court-Martial," *Prologue* 40, no. 1 (2008).

51. Fletcher interview by Washburn University, tape 1, transcript, 18–19.

52. Motley, *Invisible Soldier*; Louis E. Keefer, "The Army Specialized Training Program in World War II," Pierce-Evans.org, http://www.pierce-evans.org /ASTP%20in%20WWII.htm; and Phillip Leveque, "ASTP: The Army's Waste of Manpower," 89th Infantry Division of World War II, http://www.89infdivww2 .org/.

53. Keefer, "Army Specialized Training"; Leveque, "ASTP"; "A Few Notable ASTP Alumnus [*sic*]," archived at the Internet Archive Wayback Machine, https:// web.archive.org/web/20040123222552/http://humber.northnet.org/488thengi neers/ASTP.html; and "Robert J. Dole Facts," YourDictionary.com, http://biogra phy.yourdictionary.com/.

54. Alvin E. Weber, organizational history of the 3209th Quartermaster Service Company, n.d. [January 1945] (Records of the Adjutant General's Office RG407, WWII Operations Reports, 1940–48, box 18020, "QMCO-3209-0.1 1944" folder, NARA, College Park, MD); Fletcher interview by Washburn University, tape 1, transcript, 19. Fletcher's honorable discharge certificate gives the departure date at March 21 (NPRC Request No. 2-20671104597, NARA St. Louis).

55. Fletcher interview by Washburn University, tape 1, transcript, 25, 27.

56. Fletcher interview by Washburn University, tape 2a, transcript, 200.

57. Fletcher interview by Washburn University, tape 1, transcript, 26.

58. Carlo D'Este, *Patton* (New York: HarperCollins, 1995), passim.

59. Fletcher interview by Washburn University, tape 1, transcript, 26.

60. Weber, organizational history; Fletcher interview by Washburn University, tape 1, transcript, 26–27.

61. Weber, organizational history; Martin Blumenson, *Breakout and Pursuit* (Washington, DC: US Army Center of Military History, 1961), 506–522.

62. Grigsby to Fletcher, December 12, 1969; Fletcher interview by Washburn University, tape 1, transcript, 19–20; Rudi Williams, "African Americans Gain Fame as World War II Red Ball Express Drivers," DoD News, February 15, 2002, http://archive.defense.gov/. The Rookard quotation is from Williams.

63. Williams, "African Americans Gain Fame."

64. Fletcher interview by Washburn University, tape 1, transcript, 22.

65. Weber, organizational history.

66. Williams, "African Americans Gain Fame"; Fletcher interview by Washburn University, tape 1, transcript, 22.

67. Weber, organizational history.

68. Picture of Fletcher by unknown photographer, December 22, 1944 (G Street, box 95, folder 4, 572); Weber, organizational history; D'Este, *Patton*, 726; and Wynn, *Afro-American and the Second World War*, 35–37.

69. John Toland, *Battle: The Story of the Bulge* (New York: Random House, 1959), 15–16; Charles B. MacDonald, *A Time for Trumpets: The Untold Story of the Battle of the Bulge* (New York: HarperCollins, 1985), 32; and Fletcher interview by Washburn University, tape 1, transcript, 21.

70. Weber, organizational history.

71. Weber, Morning Report, March 23, and 32nd Evac Hospital Admission and Disposition Reports, March 23 and April 24, 1945 (NPRC Request No. 2-20671104597, NARA St. Louis); Fletcher veteran preference claim; Fletcher employment application, December 1975; Fletcher questionnaire, January 3, 1995; Donna St. George, "Arthur Fletcher," *Philadelphia Inquirer*, November 12, 1995; Honeyman, "Man's Civil Rights Efforts Began at JCHS"; Fletcher interview by Washburn University, tape 1, transcript, 21–23; NPRC Report, July 18, 2005 (NPRC Request No. 2-20671104597, NARA St. Louis); and Peterson, "Kansas Roots of Arthur Allen Fletcher," 231. Unfortunately, most individual personnel records were destroyed in a 1973 fire at the NPRC in St. Louis, and Fletcher's unit history is incomplete. Marta G. O'Neill and William Seibert, "Burnt in Memory: Looking Back, Looking Forward at the 1973 St. Louis Fire," *Prologue*, Spring 2013, https://www.archives.gov/files/publications/prologue/2013/spring/stl-fire.pdf.

72. War Department Enlisted Record and Report of Separation Honorable Discharge (NPRC Request No. 2-20671104597, NARA St. Louis); Fletcher veteran preference claim; Fletcher employment application, December 1975; Fletcher questionnaire, January 3, 1995; Fletcher open letter, n.d. [1999]; Richard C. Hong to Fletcher, July 15, 2005; and Peterson, "Kansas Roots of Arthur Allen Fletcher," 231. The quotation is from Fletcher's open letter.

1. Arthur Fletcher application for government employment, December 1975 (G Street, box 15A, folder 2, 1023–1048); Fletcher interview by Washburn University, tape 1, transcript, 23, 41; and Paul Fletcher interview by and in possession of the author, April 2, 2011.

2. John Behee, *Hail to the Victors!* (Adrian, MI: Swenk-Tuttle Press, 1974), 34–39, 76, 87; Alan H. Levy, *Tackling Jim Crow: Racial Segregation in Professional Football* (Jefferson, N.C.: McFarland, 2003); and Fletcher interview by Washburn University, tape 1, transcript, 44–45.

3. Fletcher to Daniel L. Ritchie, July 5, 1990 (G Street, box 103, folder 3, 193–194); University of Denver *Kynewsibok* yearbook, 1940–1949, analyzed by Stephen Fisher, archivist, University of Denver, August 23, 2016.

4. Richard M. Godlove to R. S. Himmelright, December 30, 1966 (G Street, box 134, folder 4, 165–168); Fletcher interview by Washburn University, tape 1, transcript, 41–42; and Peterson, "Kansas Roots of Arthur Allen Fletcher," 231. Bo McMillin went on from Bloomington to the pros, becoming head coach of the Detroit Lions in 1948. Frank Finch, "Scouting the Pros," *Los Angeles Times*, August 6, 1950.

5. St. George, "Arthur Fletcher."

6. Sam Jackson, "Ichabod Sports Hylites," *Washburn Review*, November 18, 1949; Fletcher interview by Washburn University, tape 1, transcript, 42; and Peterson, "Kansas Roots of Arthur Allen Fletcher," 231–232.

7. Fletcher interview by Washburn University, tape 1, transcript, 35–36.

8. St. George, "Arthur Fletcher."

9. Paul E. Wilson, *A Time to Lose: Representing Kansas in* Brown v. Board of Education (Lawrence: University Press of Kansas, 1995), 60, 67.

10. Saralena Sherman, "Fletch Has Own Team," *Topeka Daily Capital*, November 4, 1949; Gould, "Black Nixon Aide Prods Labor Plan"; Fletcher application, December 1975 (G Street, box 15A, folder 2, 1023–1048); Fletcher interview by Washburn University, tape 1, transcript, 36, 38, and tape 2a, transcript, 202; and Peterson, "Kansas Roots of Arthur Allen Fletcher," 233.

11. Fletcher interview by Washburn University, tape 1, transcript, 131.

12. Fletcher application, December 1975; Paul Fletcher interview by the author, April 2, 2011.

13. Washburn University *Kaw*, June 1950 (G Street, box 154, folder 3, 88–90, 120); Ron Colliver, "Fletcher Predicts Cliff-Hanger Win," *Topeka Daily Capitol*, September 19, 1968; Fletcher interview by Washburn University, tape 1, transcript, 129; Peterson, "Kansas Roots of Arthur Allen Fletcher," 233.

14. Fletcher interview by Robert Wright, January 21, 1971 (Moorland-Spingarn Library Special Collections, Howard University, Washington, DC, NIDS #3.178.222). Other sources verify that this happened but not Fletcher's specific role in it: "Council Homecoming Plans Disrupted: Celebration is Shifted to Later Game; Change in Plans Caused by Acres Segregation Rule," *Washburn Review*, October 7, 1949, and "Congratulations, Ichs," *Washburn Review*, October 21, 1949, note that the campuswide policy, at least, was changed before Fletcher arrived at Washburn.

15. Wilson, *Time to Lose*, 4, 5, 14, 15, 18, 39, 40; Fletcher interview by Washburn University, tape 1, transcript, 117.

16. Nicholas K. Geranios, "His Loss Was Turned into a Win: Racist Smears Cost Fletcher Election, but Formed a Career," *Yakima Herald-Republic*, December 26, 1989; United States Commission on Civil Rights, "Arthur A. Fletcher," n.d. [June 1990] (G Street, box 51, folder 2, 2–10); Cheryl Brown Henderson to Fletcher, February 26, 1991 (G Street, box 101, folder 6, 271); Fletcher interview by Washburn University, tape 1, transcript, 30; "*Brown v. Topeka Board of Education:* The Washburn Connection," *Washburn Lawyer*, Spring/Summer 2004, http://washburnlaw .edu/publications/washburnlawyer/issues/42-2/04-07.pdf. While there has been little corroboration of Fletcher's story that Scott helped him obtain employment in Topeka, there is significant evidence that he did obtain these positions, and it is unlikely that he could have done so without help. I find no reason to doubt Fletcher's claim that this help came from Elisha Scott.

17. Mary Sanchez, "Civil Rights Official Recalls Struggles with Racism," *Kansas City Star*, n.d. [July 1990] (G Street, box 22C, folder 3, 735); Wilson, *Time to Lose*, 100; Ric Anderson, "Many People Part of Local Case: Thirteen Parents Representing 20 Children Signed Up as Topeka Plaintiffs," *Topeka Capital-Journal*, May 9, 2004; and Gail Parsons, "Arthur Fletcher's Triumph: JCHS Grad is Father of Affirmative Action," *Junction City Daily Union*, May 16, 2004.

18. "E-Staters Drop Grid Opener to Ichabods, 20–12," *Emporia Gazette*, October 5, 1946; Hugh Fullerton Jr., "Sports Roundup," *Atchison Daily Globe*, October 25, 1946; "Hornets Place Two on All-Conference Eleven: Goldsmith and Litchfield are Honored—Scales on Second All-Star Team," *Emporia Gazette*, December 3, 1946; and "Ichabods Drop Final Game to Southwestern: Outplay but Fail to Outscore Builders," *Washburn Review*, December 6, 1946.

19. "Hornets to Face Washburn Team Here Saturday: Game Is Expected to Have Important Bearing on Central Conference Crown," *Emporia Gazette*, October 3, 1947; "Blue Meets Hornets in Conference Tilt: Ichabods at Top Strength for Important Game; Both Squads Impressive in Early Contests," *Washburn Review*, October 3, 1947; "Ottawa, Baker Tie for Conference Lead," *Emporia Gazette*, November 1, 1947; "Central Conference All Stars," *Iola Register*, December 1, 1947; "Four Hornets on All-Central Team Selected by AP: Sadowshi, Short, Litchfield, Corey Are Nominated—Two on Second Team," *Emporia Gazette*, December 1, 1947; Ed Shupe, "Sport Shafts," *Emporia Gazette*, December 9, 1947; Washburn University *Kaw*, June 1948 (G Street, box 154, folder 2B, 160–164); and Stu Dunbar, "Just as it Seems to Me," *Topeka State Journal*, n.d. [August 1948] (George H. W. Bush Presidential Records, Counsel's Office, White House, box 1, "Chairman Arthur Allen Fletcher Commission on Civil Rights" folder). The quotation is from George B. Kerford to Fletcher, June 16, 1992 (G Street, box 111, folder 3, 119–121).

20. "Sport Shafts," *Emporia Gazette*, November 13, 1947; Ron Colliver, "Fletcher Hopes Voters Ignore 'Paint Job,'" *Topeka Daily Capitol*, September 17, 1968; Fletcher interview by Washburn University, tape 1, transcript, 52–54.

21. "Ichabods Drop 0–20 Game to Washington," *Topeka Daily Capitol*, October 10, 1948; Claude Hays, "Washburn Overwhelms St. Benedict's, 53–0: Ich Blasts

Win Homecoming, Fletcher Racks Up Five Touchdowns as Topekans Roll Up Air, Ground Yardage," *Topeka Daily Capitol,* October 23, 1948; "Ravens Lose to Washburn," *Atchison Daily Globe,* October 23, 1948; "Omaha University Upsets Washburn, 20–19: Last-Minute Field Goal Effort Fails to Bring Washburn Win," *Topeka Daily Capitol,* October 30, 1948; "Ich Backs Rank High in Offense Totals," *Washburn Review,* November 12, 1948; "Builders Slap Blues into CIC 4th Place; Convert Point to Win 14–13," and Art Schaaf, "Hornets Take Second Straight Crown; Ich's Season Marred by Losses," *Washburn Review,* November 19, 1948; "Name CIC Grid All-Stars: Top Honors Won by 7 Hornets," *Atchison Daily Globe,* November 24, 1948; "Central Conference All Star Teams," *Iola Register,* November 26, 1948; and Washburn University *Kaw,* June 1949 (Mabee Library, Washburn University, Topeka, KS).

22. "Washburn Moves to First CIC Win, Upsetting P-State 27–19," *Topeka Daily Capitol,* October 16, 1949; Washburn University *Kaw,* June 1950 (G Street, box 154, folder 3, 53, 212, 216–217); and Colliver, "Fletcher Hopes Voters Ignore 'Paint Job.'"

23. "Easy Wins for Pitt and Washburn," *Iola Register,* September 17, 1949; "Emporia State Beats Out Washburn 19–14," *Hutchinson News,* October 3, 1949; "Hornets Down Ichs in Strong First Half," and Jackson, "Ichabod Sports Hylites," *Washburn Review,* October 7, 1949; Jackson, "Ichabod Sports Hylites," *Washburn Review,* October 14, 1949; "Washburn Edges Omaha Indians in 13–6 Thriller," *Washburn Review,* October 14, 1949; "Washburn Moves to First CIC Win"; and Washburn University *Kaw,* June 1950 (G Street, box 154, folder 3, 211–220).

24. "Washburn Nips Builders, 21–20; Second Half Rally Gets First CIC Crown Since '31," *Topeka Daily Capitol,* November 12, 1949; Jackson, "Ichabod Sports Hylites," *Washburn Review,* November 18, 1949; and Washburn University *Kaw,* June 1950.

25. Jackson, "Ichabod Sports Hylites," *Washburn Review,* November 18, 1949.

26. Levy, *Tackling Jim Crow,* 97–98; Fletcher interview by Washburn University, tape 1, transcript, 44–45.

27. Fletcher interview by Washburn University, tape 1, transcript, 81–90.

28. John F. Steadman, *Football's Miracle Men: The Baltimore Colts' Story* (Cleveland, OH: Pennington Press, 1959), 39; Levy, *Tackling Jim Crow,* 97–100; Fletcher interview by Washburn University, tape 1, transcript, 45–46.

29. Frank Finch, "Washington Redskins Hit Town Today," *Los Angeles Times,* July 16, 1950; Fletcher interview by Washburn University, tape 1, transcript, 45.

30. "Stydahar Riled over Ram Scrum," *Los Angeles Times,* July 30, 1950; Fletcher interview by Washburn University, tape 1, transcript, 45–46.

31. Finch, "Washington Redskins Hit Town Today"; Finch, "Tom Fears Called Last Word in Ends," *Los Angeles Times,* August 9, and "'Skins Take Third Upset Win in Stride," *Los Angeles Times,* August 17, 1950; Paul Zimmerman, "Redskins Triumph before 90,135 Fans: Rams Upset, 17–14, as Times Game Lures Largest Pro Crowd," *Los Angeles Times,* August 17, 1950; Finch, "Rams Wake with 17–14 Hangover," *Los Angeles Times,* August 18, 1950; Finch, "Eager Eagles Hand Rams Worst Setback: Crowd of 24,119 Sees Locals Swamped, 49–14," *Los Angeles Times,* August 31, "Rams Murder Colts, 70–21," *Los Angeles Times,* September 3, 1950;

"Rams Humble Colts, 70–21: Local Eleven Scores First but Then Is Outclassed," *Baltimore Sun*, September 3, 1950; and John Steadman, "For Fletcher, Colts' Cut Unkind, but It Started the Ball Rolling," *Baltimore Sun*, February 1, 1998.

32. "Bob Boyd Joins Up with Ram Gridmen," *Los Angeles Times*, July 12, 1950; "Loyola Alumni Plan Dinner for Bob Boyd," *Los Angeles Times*, July 15, 1950; Finch, "Gridders Buckle Down: Rams, Redskins Start Polishing Rough Edges for Times Classic," *Los Angeles Times*, July 20, 1950; "Rams, Redskins Boast 24 Coast Grid Stars" and Al Wolf, "Sportraits," *Los Angeles Times*, July 23, 1950; Finch, "Ram Scrimmage Slated Tomorrow," *Los Angeles Times*, July 24, 1950; Zimmerman, "Sportscripts," *Los Angeles Times*, August 1, 1950; Finch, "Scouting the Pros," *Los Angeles Times*, August 6, and "Rams Wake with 17–14 Hangover," *Los Angeles Times*, August 18, 1950; and "LMU Hall of Famer Bob Boyd Passes Away," LMU [Loyola Marymount University], July 6, 2009, http://www.lmulions.com/.

33. Finch, "Fred Gehrke, Two Rookies Cut by Rams," *Los Angeles Times*, September 12, and "Now It Can Be Told—The Hirsch Story," *Los Angeles Times*, September 20, 1950; Ed Shupe, "Now Hear This," *Emporia Gazette*, September 21, 1950.

34. Steadman, *Football's Miracle Men*, 39–58; "Buddy Young Dies in Auto Mishap," *The Day* [New London, CT], September 6, 1983; Charles K. Ross, *Outside the Lines: African-Americans and the Integration of the National Football League* (New York: New York University Press, 2000), 125–126; Ted Patterson, *Football in Baltimore: History and Memorabilia* (Baltimore, MD: Johns Hopkins University Press, 2000), 105; and "George Taliaferro," Pro Football Reference, https://www.pro-football-reference.com/.

35. Jesse A. Linthicum, "Colts Display Alert Game: Tight Pass Defense and Hard Tackling Cheer Crowd," *Baltimore Sun*, October 16, 1950; James Ellis, "Los Angeles Rams Triumph over Colts by 70–27: High Scoring Contest Sets Two Records; Winners' Point Total Greatest in 31 Years of NFL," *Baltimore Sun*, October 23, 1950; James Ellis, "Billy Stone May Be Used: Colt Back Is Ready for Spot Duty Against Forty-Niners," October 28, 1950; Madison Harvey, "Profile of a Bay Area Leader: Leader with Muscle in His Thinking," *Oakland Post*, n.d. (G Street, box 124, folder 1, 289–290); Colliver, "Fletcher Hopes Voters Ignore 'Paint Job;'" Rex Adkins, "Big 'Breakthrough' Man," *San Francisco Chronicle*, March 23, 1969; Steadman, "For Fletcher, Colts' Cut Unkind"; Fletcher interview by Washburn University, tape 1, transcript, 47, 81–93, and tape 2b, transcript, 8; and "Arthur Fletcher," Pro Football Reference, https://www.pro-football-reference.com/. Colts owner quoted in Ross.

36. Cameron C. Snyder, "Depleted End Corps Forces Colts' Assistant into Action," *Baltimore Sun*, October 11, 1950; "Fletcher Sold to Baltimore," *Los Angeles Times*, October 12, 1950; Linthicum, "Sunlight on Sports," *Baltimore Sun*, October 12, 1950; Snyder, "Negro Player to Join Colts for Test Here: Crowe Expects to Use Art Fletcher against Eagles Sunday," *Baltimore Sun*, October 12, 1950; Snyder, "Colts Polish Aerial Game: Tittle and Burke Toss Passes in Offensive Drill," *Baltimore Sun*, October 14, 1950; and Ellis, "Watner Challenges Blaik to Pit Army Against Colts," *Baltimore Sun*, October 22, 1950.

37. Ross, *Outside the Lines*, 125–126; Fletcher interview by Washburn University, tape 1, transcript, 48.

38. Ellis, "Colts Speed Up Practice: Coach Clem Crowe Calls Drill 'Best in Long Time,'" *Baltimore Sun*, October 26, 1950, and "Billy Stone May Be Used"; Snyder, "Colts Suffer End Shortage: Injuries to Nowaskey, Owens Typical of Misfortunes," *Baltimore Sun*, November 30, 1950; and Steadman, "For Fletcher, Colts' Cut Unkind."

39. Godlove to Himmelright, December 30, 1966.

40. Steadman, *Football's Miracle Men*, 62–63, 70–81; Y. A. Tittle with Kristine Setting Clark, *Nothing Comes Easy: My Life in Football* (Chicago: Triumph Books, 2009), 74; Patterson, *Football in Baltimore*, 105; and Fletcher interview by Washburn University, tape 1, 01:49:00–01:50:00.

41. Fletcher interview by Washburn University, tape 1, transcript, 23–24.

42. Fletcher interview by Washburn University, tape 1, transcript, 57.

43. Harvey, "Profile of a Bay Area Leader"; Colliver, "Fletcher Hopes Voters Ignore 'Paint Job;'" Adkins, "Big 'Breakthrough' Man"; Fletcher interview by Washburn University, tape 1, transcript, 91; and Hamilton Tiger-Cats Player Rosters for 1951 and 1952," CFLdb Statistics, https://stats.cfldb.ca/.

44. Fletcher application, December 1975; Isabel Wilkerson, "Remedy for Racism of Past Has New Kind of Shackles," *New York Times*, September 15, 1991; and Paul Fletcher interview by the author, July 30, 2010.

45. "Ruppenthal to GOP Helm," *Atchison Daily Globe*, and "Takes Over GOP Task," *Iola Register*, August 31, 1954; Colliver, "Fletcher Hopes Voters Ignore 'Paint Job'"; "Councilman May Run for Lt. Governor," unknown publication, n.d. [1968] (G Street, box 13, folder 3, 156); Adkins, "Big 'Breakthrough' Man"; Wilson, *Time to Lose*, 18–19; and Fletcher interview by Washburn University, tape 1, transcript, 129.

46. Kansas State College transcript for Arthur Fletcher, November 17, 1954 (G Street, box 124, folder 1, 291); "WU Grid Star Has Self-Help Idea," *Topeka Daily Capitol*, August 3, 1968; Fletcher résumé, n.d. [1996] (G Street, box 23, folder 8, 160–163).

47. Fletcher interview by Washburn University, tape 1, transcript, 135; Peterson, "Kansas Roots of Arthur Allen Fletcher," 235; "Governor Records—Hall, 1955–1957," Kansas Historical Society, https://www.kshs.org/; "Frederick Lee Hall," National Governors Association, https://www.nga.org/.

48. Peterson, "Kansas Roots of Arthur Allen Fletcher," 235–236; "Governor Records—Hall"; "Frederick Lee Hall"; and "Edward Ferdinand Arn," National Governors Association, https://www.nga.org/.

49. Peterson, "Kansas Roots of Arthur Allen Fletcher," 236; "Governor Records—Hall."

50. Sherman, "Fletch Has Own Team"; Gould, "Black Nixon Aide Prods Labor Plan"; Fletcher application, December 1975 (G Street, box 15A, folder 2, 1023–1048); Fletcher interview by Washburn University, tape 1, transcript, 36, 38, 131, 202; and Peterson, "Kansas Roots of Arthur Allen Fletcher," 233.

51. Peterson, "Kansas Roots of Arthur Allen Fletcher," 236–237.

52. Peterson, "Kansas Roots of Arthur Allen Fletcher," 236.

53. Earl Thomas Reynolds to Fred Hall, February 11, 1955, and Hall to Reynolds, February 28, 1955 (Records of the Office of the Governor, Fred Hall Collection,

Kansas Historical Society, Topeka); and Peterson, "Kansas Roots of Arthur Allen Fletcher," 236.

54. Harvey, "Profile of a Bay Area Leader"; Burnell E. Johnson to R. S. Himmelright, December 27, 1966 (G Street, box 134, folder 4, 169–170); Colliver, "Fletcher Hopes Voters Ignore 'Paint Job'"; "They Liked the 'Paint Job,'" editorial, *Topeka State Journal*, September 19, 1968; Adkins, "Big 'Breakthrough' Man"; Fletcher interview by Robert Wright; Fletcher application, December 1975; Fletcher résumé, 1996; and Peterson, "Kansas Roots of Arthur Allen Fletcher," 237.

55. Edwyna G. Dones to Kansas State Board Against Discrimination, n.d. [1954], Malcolm B. Higgins to Hall, April 8, 1955, Fletcher to Hall, n.d. [May, 1955], and Hall to Shawnee County Board of Commissioners, May 13, 1955 (Records of the Office of the Governor, Fred Hall Collection).

56. Fletcher interview by Washburn University, tape 1, transcript, 152.

57. Clarence J. Malone to Fletcher, June 29, 1959 (G Street, box 151, folder 1, 131); Fletcher interview by Washburn University, tape 1, transcript, 152–153; Peterson, "Kansas Roots of Arthur Allen Fletcher," 237–238.

58. Fletcher interview by Washburn University, tape 1, transcript, 154–155.

59. Fletcher interview by Washburn University, tape 1, transcript, 153–156; Peterson, "Kansas Roots of Arthur Allen Fletcher," 238–239.

60. Martin Tolchin and Susan Tolchin, *To the Victor: Political Patronage from the Clubhouse to the White House* (New York: Random House, 1971), and *Pinstripe Patronage: Political Favoritism from the Clubhouse to the White House and Beyond* (London: Routledge, 2015), passim.

61. "Harwi Sees No Danger to Road Aid," *Iola Register*, July 25, 1956.

62. "Political Notes: Hall's Fall," *Time*, August 20, 1956; William A. Smith to Paul R. Shanahan, December 31, 1956 (Records of the Office of the Secretary of State, Oaths of Office, 1923–1957, box 2, Kansas State Archives, Topeka); Fred Hall to Shanahan, John McCuish oath of office, and Fred Hall oath of office, January 3, 1957 (Secretary of State Oaths of Office, 1923–1957, box 2); "New Assistant Secretary for Labor Named," *Potters Herald*, May 1, 1969; Fletcher interview by Robert Wright; Homer E. Socolofsky, *Kansas Governors* (Lawrence: University Press of Kansas, 1990), 200–203; Peterson, "Kansas Roots of Arthur Allen Fletcher," 237–239; Frank Morris, "The New Justice in Kansas: Judicial Selection and the Governor's Race," KCUR 89.3, September 12, 2014, http://kcur.org/; "Governor Records—Hall"; "History of the Kansas Supreme Court Justices," Kansas Judicial Branch, Justice Listing, http://www.kscourts.org/; and "George Docking," National Governors Association, https://www.nga.org/.

63. George H. Nash, *The Conservative Intellectual Movement in America since 1945* (New York: Basic Books, 1976), passim; Rick Perlstein, *Before the Storm: Barry Goldwater and the Unmaking of the American Consensus* (New York: Hill & Wang, 2001), passim; James Worthen, *The Young Nixon and His Rivals: Four California Republicans Eye the White House, 1946–1958* (Jefferson, N.C.: McFarland, 2010), passim; Michael Bowen, *The Roots of Modern Conservatism: Dewey, Taft, and the Battle for the Soul of the Republican Party* (Chapel Hill: University of North Carolina Press, 2011), 6; Michael J. Lee, *Creating Conservatism: Postwar Words that Made an*

American Movement (East Lansing: Michigan State University Press, 2014), passim; and D. J. Mulloy, *The World of the John Birch Society: Conspiracy, Conservatism, and the Cold War* (Nashville: Vanderbilt University Press, 2014), 91–93.

64. "Robert Blackwell Docking," National Governors Association, https://www.nga.org/.

65. Fletcher interview by Washburn University, tape 1, transcript, 156; Peterson, "Kansas Roots of Arthur Allen Fletcher," 239.

66. Merchants National Bank to Fletcher, January 11, 1960 (G Street, box 151, folder 1, 126); Jack Briggs, "Tri-City Scene: Fletcher Pressed for $1,800," *Tri-City Herald,* n.d. [1968] (G Street, box 81, folder 1, 75); Jim Crossley, "What Do Years Matter When Racing is Hobby?," *Dover Daily Reporter,* September 25, 1968; Fletcher application, December 1975; and "Inflation Cost Calculator," US Bureau of Labor Statistics, https://www.bls.gov/.

67. "Negro to Be Washburn Coach," *Ottawa Herald,* September 6, 1957; Speck Reynolds, "Speck Speculates," *Great Bend Tribune,* September 8, 1957; Dick Homan, "Sidelines," *Atchison Daily Globe,* November 5, 1957; Harvey, "Profile of a Bay Area Leader"; Godlove to Himmelright, December 27, 1966; deYonge, "Former Shoeshine Boy Advises GOP"; Colliver, "Fletcher Hopes Voters Ignore 'Paint Job'"; Adkins, "Big 'Breakthrough' Man"; Fletcher and Vicente Ximenes press conference transcript, n.d. [1970] (G Street, box 68, folder 5, 70–71); Fletcher, "The $19 Billion Negro Market: How to Get Your Share," draft article, n.d. [1959] (G Street, box 77, folder 2, 997–1020); Fletcher interview by Washburn University, tape 1, transcript, 93–94; Paul Fletcher interview by the author, July 30, 2010; and Peterson, "Kansas Roots of Arthur Allen Fletcher," 239.

68. Fletcher and Mary Fletcher, agreement and promissory note, April 3, 1959, State of Kansas Department of Revenue to Fletcher, May 4 and June 12, 1959, Malone to Fletcher, June 29, 1959, R. E. Marriott to David-Wellcome Mortgage Company, October 13, 1959, and Aerojet General to Fletcher, April 1, 1960 (G Street, box 151, folder 1, 123–124, 131, 136, 164, 169, 317); "They Liked the 'Paint Job'"; Fletcher application, December 1975; Fletcher, "$19 Billion Negro Market"; Fletcher interview by Washburn University, tape 1, transcript, 157; Paul and Sylvia Fletcher interview by the author, December 28, 2010; and Peterson, "Kansas Roots of Arthur Allen Fletcher," 239. In 2001, Fletcher told memoirist Stephanie Stokes Oliver that he had been run out of Kansas in a backlash against the *Brown* decision, but the chronology and other evidence do not support that. Oliver, *Song for My Father* (New York: Atria Books, 2004), 20.

69. Paul and Sylvia Fletcher interview by the author, December 28, 2010; Sylvia Fletcher to the author, March 12, 2011 (e-mail correspondence in possession of the author).

70. Robert O. Self, *American Babylon: Race and the Struggle for Postwar Oakland* (Princeton, N.J.: Princeton University Press, 2003), 87–89, 95; Worthen, *Young Nixon and His Rivals,* passim.

71. "New CRA President Cyril Stevenson Jr.," *Petaluma Argus-Courier,* and "New CRA Leader Quit Military to Lead Conservative Cause for Republicans," *Santa Cruz Sentinel,* March 31, 1965; "Fred Hall for Senate" handbill, n.d. [1962] (G Street, box

13, folder 3, 399); Don C. Smith to Fletcher, March 18, and Fletcher to Smith, April 1, 1969 (G Street, box 15B, folder 2, 758, 782); and "Frederick Lee Hall."

72. Fletcher application, December 1975; Thomas F. Sugrue, *The Origins of the Urban Crisis: Race and Inequality in Postwar Detroit* (Princeton, N.J.: Princeton University Press, 1996), 232–234; Paul and Sylvia Fletcher interview by the author, December 28, 2010.

73. W. E. B. Du Bois, "The Talented Tenth," in *The Negro Problem,* ed. Booker T. Washington (New York: James Pott, 1903), 31–75; Leckie, *Buffalo Soldiers;* "Mental Patient Leaps to Death," *Oakland Tribune,* October 3, 1960; Fletcher interview by Washburn University, tape 1, transcript, 158–159, 204; Paul Fletcher interview by the author, July 30, 2010; and Paul and Sylvia Fletcher interview by the author, December 28, 2010.

74. Fletcher draft letter to California Board of Parole, n.d. [early 1990s] (G Street, box 103, folder 3, 293–312).

75. Fletcher, questionnaire about military service, January 3, 1995 (G Street, box 111, folder 1, 32); Richard C. Hong, certification of Fletcher military service, July 15, 2005 (G Street, box 118, folder 4, 221); Fletcher interview by Washburn University, tape 2a, transcript, 206; Paul, Patsy, and Phyllis Fletcher, unrecorded conversations with the author, various dates.

76. Paul, Patsy, and Phyllis Fletcher, unrecorded conversations with the author.

77. Adkins, "Big 'Breakthrough' Man"; Jack Fischer, "In Poverty War: Negro Candidate Tells His Goals," *Spokane Spokesman-Review,* June 25, 1968; Fletcher application, December 1975; Fletcher draft letter to California Board of Parole; and Paul and Sylvia Fletcher interview by the author, December 28, 2010.

78. "Mental Patient Leaps to Death"; Stewart E. Perry, *The Human Nature of Science: Researchers at Work in Psychiatry* (New York: Free Press, 1966); and Paul and Sylvia Fletcher interview by the author, December 28, 2010.

79. Arthur Fletcher interview by Washburn University, tape 2a, transcript, 204.

80. Arthur Fletcher interview by Washburn University, tape 2a, transcript, 204; John T. Maltsberger, "The Descent into Suicide," *International Journal of Psychoanalysis* 85, no. 3 (2004): 653–668.

81. "Mental Patient Leaps to Death"; Paul Fletcher interview by the author, July 30, 2010; Paul and Sylvia Fletcher interview by the author, December 28, 2010; and Sylvia Fletcher to the author, March 18, 2011 (e-mail correspondence in possession of the author).

82. Fletcher interview by Washburn University, tape 2a, transcript, 204–206.

83. Paul Fletcher interviews by the author, July 30, 2010, and April 2, 2011; Paul and Sylvia Fletcher interview by the author, December 28, 2010; and Sylvia Fletcher to the author, April 6, 2011 (e-mail correspondence in possession of the author).

84. Paul and Sylvia Fletcher interview by the author, December 28, 2010.

85. Paul Fletcher interviews by the author, July 30, 2010, and April 2, 2011; Paul and Sylvia Fletcher interview by the author, December 28, 2010; and Sylvia Fletcher to the author, April 6, 2011.

86. University of Washington transcript for Paul Fletcher, n.d. [1970] (G Street, box 13, folder 1, 40); Paul Fletcher to Marian Wright-Edelman, March 10, 1993

(G Street, box 102, folder 4, 301); "Paul Fletcher Is Making an Impact on Society: Housing Director Says Community Key to Progress," *Evansville Courier and Press*, July 7, 2001; Paul Fletcher interviews by the author, July 30, 2010, and April 2, 2011; and Paul and Sylvia Fletcher interview by the author, December 28, 2010.

87. Egbert J. Figaro to Fletcher, July 6 and 13, 1966 (G Street, box 123, folder 34, 120–122); Peoples National Bank of Washington cashier's check for St. Emma's Military Academy, August 19, 1966 (G Street, box 123, folder 1, 182); Phillip Fletcher to Arthur and Bernyce Fletcher, n.d. [September 1966] (G Street, box 123, folder 29, 63); "Father Timassy" to Arthur Fletcher, October 7, 1966 (G Street, box 123, folder 1, 185); Clyde L. Henderson and Phillip Fletcher interview by Arthur Fletcher, n.d. [February 1967] (G Street, box 123, folder 6, 19–30); Robert D. Quant to Arthur and Bernyce Fletcher, February 9, and Carl D. Gelder to Arthur and Bernyce Fletcher, February 10, 1968 (G Street, box 123, folder 29, 61–62); Green Hill School to Arthur Fletcher, April 2, 1968 (G Street, box 123, folder 29, 57–58); Janet Pappas to Arthur Fletcher, October 20, 1969 (G Street, box 77, folder 1, 155–156); Fletcher draft letter to California Board of Parole; Phyllis Fletcher, "Sweet Phil from Sugar Hill," Transom, NPR Radio program, January 1, 2004, https://transom.org/; Paul Fletcher interviews by the author, September 25, 2010, and April 2, 2011; and Sylvia Fletcher to the author, April 6, 2011.

88. Mary Fletcher draft to Fletcher, n.d. [1960] (G Street, box 96, folder 2, 554–556).

CHAPTER 3. MOON SHOT, 1961–1969

1. "Inaugural Address of John F. Kennedy," Yale Law School Lillian Goldman Law Library, January 20, 1961, http://avalon.law.yale.edu/. On the 1960s and civil rights, see, e.g., Allen J. Matusow, *The Unraveling of America: A History of Liberalism in the 1960s* (New York: Harper & Row, 1984); Todd Gitlin, *The Sixties: Years of Hope, Days of Rage* (New York: Bantam, 1989); Hugh Davis Graham, *The Civil Rights Era: Origins and Development of National Policy, 1960–1972* (New York: Oxford University Press, 1990); and Mulloy, *World of the John Birch Society.*

2. John F. Kennedy, "We Choose to Go to the Moon," Wikisource, September 12, 1962 https://en.wikisource.org/.

3. State of California Department of Alcoholic Beverage Control On-Sale Beer License, November 2, 1961; State Board of Equalization Notice of Hearing, December 13, 1961; and Fletcher to State of California Department of Alcoholic Beverage Control, November 15, 1962 (G Street, box 151, folder 1, images 127–129); Adkins, "Big 'Breakthrough' Man."

4. Arthur Fletcher interview by Washburn University, tape 1, transcript, 158; Paul Fletcher interviews by the author, September 25, 2010, and April 2, 2011. The quotations are from the Arthur Fletcher interview.

5. Dale Carnegie, *How to Win Friends and Influence People* (New York: Simon & Schuster, 1936); Napoleon Hill, *Think and Grow Rich* (Cleveland, OH: Ralston, 1937); John H. Burrows, *The Necessity of Myth: A History of the National Negro Business League, 1900–1945* (Auburn, AL: Hickory Hill Press, 1988); Harry C. Alford to Board of Directors, National Black Chamber of Commerce, August 19 and Sep-

tember 29, 1997 (G Street, box 41, folder 2, 637–638); and Kevern J. Verney, *The Art of the Possible: Booker T. Washington and Black Leadership in the United States, 1881–1925* (New York: Routledge, 2001).

6. Recent scholarship has reemphasized the role of grassroots organizers over the traditional notion of top-down leadership by Dr. King. See, e.g., Charles Payne, "Debating the Civil Rights Movement: The View from the Trenches," in *Debating the Civil Rights Movement, 1945–1968,* ed. Charles Payne and Steven F. Lawson (Lanham, MD: Rowman & Littlefield, 2006). Additionally, Matthew D. Lassiter has argued that we need to rethink the de jure/de facto segregation dichotomy, noting correctly that segregation outside of the South was maintained by the force of law, especially as pertains to school segregation, and that northern whites have used the paradigm to declare a personal innocence of racist effects. Lassiter, "De Jure/De Facto Segregation: The Long Shadow of a National Myth," in *The Myth of Southern Exceptionalism,* ed. Matthew D. Lassiter and Joseph Crespino (New York: Oxford, 2010), 25–48. I agree that northern whites used southern Jim Crow as a mask for their own racial culpability, and that they used color-blind laws to maintain a white-dominant society. However, I still find the dichotomy useful. Southern laws were explicitly racist, and southern whites were more prone to overt demonstrations of racism, while their northern counterparts hid their racism in color-blind legislative language. Freedom Summer was directed at voting rights in Mississippi while Blacks from New York and Chicago served in Congress; Blacks in the Great Migration moved to the front of the bus upon crossing the Mason-Dixon Line. That de facto segregation has replaced its de jure cousin should not obscure the successes—however incomplete—of the movement in the South.

7. Dickerson, *Militant Mediator,* passim; Golland, *Constructing Affirmative Action,* 52–53; and Yvonne Ryan, *Roy Wilkins: The Quiet Revolutionary and the NAACP* (Lexington: University Press of Kentucky, 2014), passim.

8. Burnell E. Johnson to R. S. Himmelright, December 27, 1966 (G Street, box 134, folder 4, 169–170); Arthur Fletcher interview by Washburn University, tape 2a, transcript, 1.

9. Harvey, "Profile of a Bay Area Leader"; Richard Bergholz, "GOP Urged to Show Negroes Need for Party," *Los Angeles Times,* February 6, 1965; Burnell E. Johnson to Himmelright, December 27, 1966, and F. Carl Dwight to Himmelright, January 4, 1967 (G Street, box 134, folder 4, images 161 and 169–170).

10. Stanley L. Jamerson Jr. to Fletcher, December 13, 1994 (G Street, box 11, folder 3, 976–978).

11. Harvey, "Profile of a Bay Area Leader"; "GOP Assembly Approves Negro-Backed Job Plan," *San Bernardino County Sun,* June 10, 1963; Adkins, "Big 'Breakthrough' Man"; Arthur Fletcher, 1974 curriculum vitae (Records of President Gerald R. Ford, White House Central Files [WHCF], Name File Box 1045, "Fletcher, Arthur [1]" folder, Ford Presidential Library, Ann Arbor, MI); Myrna Oliver, "Crispus A. Wright, 87; Son of Ex-Slave Became Lawyer and USC Benefactor," *Los Angeles Times,* December 11, 2001; Arthur Fletcher interview by Washburn University, tape 1, transcript, 164; Paul and Sylvia Fletcher interview by the author,

December 28, 2010; and Joshua D. Farrington, *Black Republicans and the Transformation of the GOP* (Philadelphia: University of Pennsylvania Press, 2016), 21, 53, 143.

12. John Robert Owens, *California Politics and Parties* (New York: Macmillan, 1970); Self, *American Babylon*, 79; and "1962 Election History" and "William Byron Rumford Election History," Join California, http://www.joincalifornia.com/.

13. Owens, *California Politics;* Socolofsky, *Kansas Governors,* 200–203; Jackson K. Putnam, "A Half-Century of Conflict: The Rise and Fall of Liberalism in California Politics, 1943–1993," in *Politics in the Postwar American West,* ed. Richard Lowitt (Norman: University of Oklahoma Press, 1995), 42–63; Worthen, *Young Nixon and His Rivals,* 15–22; and "1942 Election History" and "1946 Election History," Join California, http://www.joincalifornia.com/.

14. Frank M. Jordan, *State of California Statement of Vote: Consolidated Primary Election, June 1, 1948* (Sacramento: Office of the Secretary of State, 1948), as well as June 3, 1952, June 8, 1954, June 5, 1956, June 3, 1958, June 7, 1960, and June 5, 1962; "New CRA President Cyril Stevenson Jr.," *Petaluma Argus-Courier,* and "New CRA Leader Quit Military to Lead Conservative Cause for Republicans," *Santa Cruz Sentinel,* March 31, 1965; Owens, *California Politics;* Paul Fletcher interview by the author, July 30, 2010; and "1962 Election History" and "William Byron Rumford Election History," Join California, http://www.joincalifornia.com/. The Statement of Vote for the 1950 primary election is not available.

15. Perlstein, *Before the Storm,* 165–167.

16. H. R. Haldeman to Don Mulford, July 16, 1962 (Nixon Returned Files, box 38, folder 23, NARA Richard Nixon Presidential Library, Yorba Linda, CA); Haldeman to Bill Spencer, July 21, 1962 (Nixon Returned Files, box 38, folder 27); and Golland, *Constructing Affirmative Action,* 14–22, 28–33, 41–42, 45, 49, 59, 118–119).

17. "1962 Election History"; Perlstein, *Before the Storm,* 171–172.

18. Harvey, "Profile of a Bay Area Leader"; "Fletcher Gets $15,000 Year Poverty Post in Washington," *Berkeley Post,* April 3, 1965; "Y Picks Director for Pasco Project," *Tri-City Herald,* April 9, 1965; Fletcher, "Security Investigation Data for Sensitive Position," December 1, 1975 (G Street, box 15A, folder 2, 1023–1030); Katherine Bishop, "Berkeley Journal; Who'll Sell Tofu Puffs after Coops are Gone?," *New York Times,* June 6, 1988; Karen Zimbelman, "Berkeley: Lessons for Coop Leaders," *Cooperative Grocer* 38 (January–February 1992); Arthur Fletcher interview by Washburn University, tape 2a, transcript, 206–207; John Curl, *For All the People: Uncovering the Hidden History of Cooperation* (Oakland, CA: PM Press, 2009), 194–197; and *Settlements on the Columbia River: Portland, Oregon, Astoria, Oregon, Richland, Washington, Kennewick, Washington, Pasco, Washington* (Memphis, TN: LLC Books, 2010), 57–64, 77–84, 129–140. Joan Hassan legally changed her name to Joan Fletcher; it is unclear whether there was a formal adoption.

19. Sylvia Fletcher to Bernyce Fletcher and Sylvia Fletcher to Fletcher, October 14, 1964 (G Street, box 123, folder 30, 13–17); Fletcher interview by Washburn University, tape 2a, transcript, 203; Paul Fletcher interviews by the author, July 30, 2010, and April 2, 2011; Paul and Sylvia Fletcher interview by the author, Decem-

ber 28, 2010; and Sylvia Fletcher to the author, April 6, 2011. In his novel *The Last Days of Louisiana Red* (Champaign, IL: Dalkey Archive Press, 1974), Ishmael Reed mentions Art Jr.: "We thought we'd go to eat at the Rainbow Sign and then down to Solomon Grundy's to hear Art Fletcher. He plays a soft piano, and you can sit about the fireplace. People can hear what each other say. Across the way you can see the skyline of San Francisco" (59).

20. Leonard H. Carter to Roy Wilkins, September 10, 1965 (NAACP Records, Series III, box A333, "Watts Riot" folder, Library of Congress Manuscripts Division, Washington, DC); "The Riot's Real Causes" (editorial), *Cleveland Press*, August 10, 1966; *Report of the United States Civil Rights Commission*, March 1, 1967 (Records of the Department of Labor Office of Federal Contract Compliance, Papers of the Assistant Director for Construction, box 8, "Cleveland Correspondence" folder, NARA College Park, MD); Marc E. Lackritz, *The Hough Riots of 1966* (Cleveland, OH: Regional Church Planning Office, 1968); Transcript, Ramsey Clark Oral History Interview IV, April 16, 1969, by Harri Baker (electronic copy available at Lyndon Baines Johnson Library and Museum, Austin, TX, 1–2, 8); Guichard Parris and Lester Brooks, *Blacks in the City: A History of the National Urban League* (Boston: Little, Brown, 1971), 435; Frances Piven and Richard Cloward, *The Politics of Turmoil: Essays on Poverty, Race, and the Urban Crisis* (New York: Vintage, 1975), passim; Matusow, *Unraveling of America*, 196, 215–216, 360–361; Kevin Mumford, *Newark: A History of Race, Rights, and Riots in America* (New York: New York University Press, 2007), 125, 149–150, 173; "Hough Riots," Case Western Reserve University Encyclopedia of Cleveland History, https://case.edu/ech/; and "Hough Heritage," Neighborhood Link, http://www.nhlink.net/.

21. Web Ruble, "Fletcher Blasts Pasco's Police," *Tri-City Herald*, November 10, 1967; Paul Fletcher interviews by the author, July 30 and September 25, 2010.

22. Frances Taylor Pugnetti, *Tiger by the Tail: Twenty-Five Years with the Stormy Tri-City Herald* (Pasco, WA: Tri-City Herald, 1975), 1–11; *Settlements on the Columbia River*, 57–64, 77–84, 129–140; Paul Fletcher interviews by the author, July 30 and September 25, 2010; and John Hughes to the author, e-mail, February 28, 2018. The quotation is from Paul Fletcher.

23. Fletcher, "Higher Horizons Final Report," April 1, 1967 (G Street, box 13, folder 3, 15–135); Rick Anderson, "Tri-Cities Said Far from Race-Problems Solution," *Tri-City Herald*, March 8, 1968. The quotation is from Fletcher.

24. Jack Briggs, "Daycare Center Served 13," *Tri-City Herald*, September 16, 1966; Fred W. Albaugh to Fletcher, October 19, 1966 (G Street, box 151, folder 2, 235–236); S. Koepcke to Fletcher, and Albaugh to Fletcher, November 23, 1966 (G Street, box 151, folder 1, images 3053, 3056).

25. "Athlete Assumes Y Post," *Tri-City Herald*, April 12, 1965; "$86,000 Request Approved," *Tri-City Herald*, June 12, 1965; and Paul Fletcher interview by the author, September 25, 2010.

26. "'Skill Bank' Is Planned in Higher Horizon Program," *Tri-City Herald*, April 13, 1965; and Paul Fletcher interview by the author, September 25, 2010. The quotation is from the *Herald*.

27. East Pasco Self-Help Cooperative Association Report, n.d. [1967] (G Street,

box 123, folder 1, images 199–211); Fletcher, undated paper and "Higher Horizons Final Report."

28. Fletcher, "Higher Horizons Final Report"; Paul Fletcher interview by the author, September 25, 2010.

29. Jack Briggs, column, *Tri-City Herald*, September 16, 1966; Paul Fletcher interview by the author, September 25, 2010.

30. Sugrue, *Origins of the Urban Crisis*, 234–241.

31. Fletcher, "Higher Horizons Final Report"; Jack Briggs, "'Hounds' Sniff at Fletcher," *Tri-City Herald*, September 27, 1968.

32. Sylvia Fletcher to Bernyce Fletcher, and Sylvia Fletcher to Fletcher, October 14, 1964 (G Street, box 123, folder 30, 13–17); Lewis F. Sherman to R. S. Himmelright, December 22, 1966 (G Street, box 134, folder 4, 170); Arthur L. Hillman to Fletcher, December 23, 1966 (G Street, box 151, folder 1, images 3054–3055); Bernyce Fletcher, "Application for Security Clearance/United States Atomic Energy Commission," August 9, 1967 (G Street, box 123, folder 30, 10–11); Bertram Edises to Fletcher, December 19, 1968 (G Street, box 123, folder 8, 311).

33. For the Reagan campaign's use of Watts, see, e.g., Rick Perlstein, *Nixonland: The Rise of a President and the Fracturing of America* (New York: Scribner, 2008), xii, 71, 90–91; for conservative Republicans' appeals to white southerners, see, e.g., Timothy N. Thurber, *Republicans and Race: The GOP's Frayed Relationship with African Americans, 1945–1974* (Lawrence: University Press of Kansas, 2013), 171–218.

34. Unknown author, "Story Notes," December, 1966 (G Street, box 123, folder 8, 248); Douglas United Nuclear meeting minutes, July 10, 1967 (G Street, box 76, folder 7, 587–588); Hanford Occupational Health Foundation, "Medical Examination Report for Bernyce Fletcher," July 11, 1967 (G Street, box 123, folder 1, image 167); June R. Key to Fletcher, August 30, 1967 (G Street, box 151, folder 2, 162); "Fletcher Plans Meeting for Employment Council," *Tri-City Herald*, September 24, 1967; Web Ruble, "Race Relations Not Rosy Here, Asserts Panelist," *Tri-City Herald*, November 10, 1967; Bernyce Fletcher, "Request for Transfer/Battelle Northwest," March 5, 1968 (G Street, box 123, folder 1, images 188–189); Arthur Fletcher interview by Washburn University, tape 2a, transcript, 86–87; Paul Fletcher interview by the author, September 25, 2010; Dan Evans interview by and in possession of the author, October 28, 2010.

35. "Cooperative Asks Federal Money," unknown publication, n.d. [1967] (G Street, box 81, folder 1, 74); Web Ruble, "Pasco Expects Choice by US," *Tri-City Herald*, March 29, 1967; Ruble, "Attractive Industry Included in Pasco's Model-Cities Proposal," *Tri-City Herald*, March 30, 1967; Hanford Employee Relations Committee meeting minutes, January 11, 1968 (G Street, box 76, folder 7, 580–581); and Self, *American Babylon*, 8. Several industrial concerns did eventually locate in East Pasco, but nothing quite as attractive as Fletcher envisioned. Pasco did get $1.9 million in urban renewal funds in 1968: "US Approves Contract for Pasco Urban Renewal," unknown publication, n.d. [1968], courtesy Kathy Keolker, in possession of the author.

36. Arthur Fletcher interview by Washburn University, tape 1, transcript, 170–171.

37. PUSHERS Inc. proposal, n.d. [1966] (G Street, box 21, folder 6, 1–51); East Pasco Self-Help Cooperative Association (EPSHCA) report, February 26, 1966 (G Street, box 123, folder 34, 115); Articles of Incorporation for Promoters and Underwriters of Self-Help and Related Services (PUSHERS), May 6, 1966 (G Street, box 134, folder 1, 3–6); Robert E. Jackson to Robert F. Phillips, May 18, 1966 (G Street, box 151, folder 1, image 151); Mildred C. Montgomery, "Notarized Statement," May 19, 1966, and EPSHCA meeting minutes, August 29, 1966 (G Street, box 151, folder 3, 8–12 and 14–16); Fletcher to F. A. Allen, September 2, 1966 (G Street, box 79, folder 1, 292); Robert Olmos, "East Pasco, Weary of Federal Programs, Starts Own Private Battle against Poverty," *Oregonian*, October 10, 1966; PUSHERS application for tax-exempt status, November 5, 1966 (G Street, box 134, folder 4, 157–160); Robert F. Phillips to Fletcher, November 5, 1966, and J. N. Judy to Fletcher, S. Koepcke to Fletcher, and Fred Albaugh to Fletcher, November 23, 1966 (G Street, box 151, folder 1, images 3052, 3053, 3056, 3060); EPSHCA meeting minutes, December 20, 1966 (G Street, box 78B, folder 12, 36–41); and Robert F. Phillips to Ben Phillips, August 10, 1967 (G Street, box 123, folder 1, 111–112).

38. EPSHCA meeting minutes, August 29, 1966, and June 5, 1967 (G Street, box 123, folder 30, 27); Fletcher to employee relations officers of Hanford contractors, July 27, August 8, August 14, and September 29, 1967 (G Street, box 76, folder 7, 578, 583, 585–586); Fletcher to Tri-Cities Plans for Progress Council, September 19, 1967 (G Street, box 76, folder 7, 591); Briggs, "'Hounds' Sniff at Fletcher"; and Paul Fletcher interview by the author, September 25, 2010.

39. Arthur Fletcher interview by Washburn University, tape 1, transcript, 172; Paul Fletcher interview by the author, September 25, 2010.

40. Fletcher to advertiser, May 26, 1966 (G Street, box 79, folder 1, 289); Dorothy N. Hayes to F. A. Allen, August 8, 1966 (G Street, box 79, folder 1, 290); EPSHCA meeting minutes, August 29, 1966; EPSHCA meeting minutes, December 20, 1966; Briggs, "Daycare Center Served 13"; Fletcher, "Higher Horizons Final Report"; "Homegoing of a Saint—F. A. Allen," Robert E. Houston Sr. Ministries Yahoo! Group, June 18, 2006, https://groups.yahoo.com/neo/groups/Robert HoustonMinistries/conversations/topics/647.

41. EPSHCA meeting minutes, August 29, 1966; Fletcher to Alonzo Reed, September 2, 1966 (G Street, box 79, folder 1, 293); "East Pasco Coop Launches Service Station Business," *Tri-City Herald,* n.d., and EPSHCA Report, December 10, 1967 (G Street, box 151, folder 2, 197–199).

42. EPSHCA meeting minutes, April 6, April 17, and May 16, 1967 (G Street, box 78B, folder 12, 15–16, 19–20, 23–24); EPSHCA Report, December 10, 1967; "Pasco Self-Help Gets $95,000," unknown periodical, n.d. [1968], courtesy Kathy Keolker, in possession of the author; unknown photographer, pictures of EPSHCA service station under construction, March 1968 (G Street, box 6, images 552–567); Shelby Scates, "Negro Self Help Means Exactly That in Pasco," *Seattle Post-Intelligencer,* April 14, 1968; unknown photographer, pictures of EPSHCA service station nearing completion, n.d. (G Street, box 151, folder 1, images 273–276); Jim Philip, "East Pasco's Self-Help Project Nears Reality," *Tri-City Herald,* n.d. [May 1969],

courtesy Kathy Keolker, in possession of the author; Franklin, Wakeham & Co., "East Pasco Self Help Co-operative Association, Inc., Report on Examination, December 31, 1968 (G Street, box 13, folder 1, images 1–7).

43. "Pasco Cooperative Seeks Church Grant," *Tri-City Herald*, September 20, 1967; Jack Briggs, "'Sin City' Reforms," *Tri-City Herald*, September 28, 1966; Arthur Fletcher interview by Washburn University, tape 1, transcript, 171–172; and Paul Fletcher interview by the author, September 25, 2010.

44. Nat Jackson interview by and in possession of the author, October 23, 2010.

45. Hannah Lees, "The Not-Buying Power of Philadelphia's Negroes," *Reporter*, May 11, 1961; Leon Sullivan, *Build, Brother, Build* (Philadelphia: Macrae Smith, 1969); and Farrington, *Black Republicans*, 171–172.

46. Charles Doneghy to Vincent Macaluso, n.d. [April 1967] (Records of the Department of Labor, NARA College Park, MD, Collection of the Office of Federal Contract Compliance, Papers of the Assistant Director for Construction, box 24, "Monthly Reports, 1967, January–June" folder); William F. Miller, "Negroes in Trades Is His Goal," *Cleveland Plain Dealer*, August 24, 1967; Sullivan, *Build, Brother, Build;* Stacy Kinlock Sewell, "Contracting Racial Equality: Affirmative Action Policy and Practice in the United States, 1945–1970" (PhD diss., Rutgers University, 1999); Terry H. Anderson, *The Pursuit of Fairness: A History of Affirmative Action* (New York: Oxford University Press, 2004), 58; Farrington, *Black Republicans*, 184; and Martin L. Deppe, *Operation Breadbasket: An Untold Story of Civil Rights in Chicago, 1966–1971* (Athens: University of Georgia Press, 2017).

47. "The Nation: Now Philadelphia," *New York Times*, August 30, 1964; Jini Dalen, "Pasco Negroes, Whites Join to Honor King," *Tri-City Herald*, April 6, 1968; Charles Brinkerhoff, "Pasco Racist, Says Fletcher Son," *Tri-City Herald*, n.d. (G Street, box 124, folder 1, image 319); John deYonge, "Pasco: A Dark Curtain of Racial Distrust Falls across Town," *Seattle Post-Intelligencer*, May 3, 1970; deYonge, "Pasco Blacks Want Power to Shape Their Own Community," *Seattle Post-Intelligencer*, May 1970 (G Street, box 124, folder 1, image 316); Matthew J. Countryman, *Up South: Civil Rights and Black Power in Philadelphia* (Philadelphia: University of Pennsylvania Press, 2006), 156–159, 162, 164, 166; *Settlements on the Columbia River*, 60, 79, 135; Paul Fletcher interview by the author, September 25, 2010; and Nat Jackson interview by the author. Recent scholarship has also demonstrated another cause for rebellion: in the Watts case, the riot was partially caused by a failure of Los Angeles mayor Sam Yorty and local Black community leaders to come to an agreement on the use of war on poverty funds; Robert Bauman, *Race and the War on Poverty: From Watts to East LA* (Norman: University of Oklahoma Press, 2008). In Pasco, such funds, when they were available, were quickly put to use in the community—as in the case of Fletcher's Higher Horizons program—and there is no evidence of similar conflict between community leaders and local politicians, perhaps because of Fletcher's political savvy.

48. Farrington, *Black Republicans*, 174–175, 202–203, 212, 217, 220–222. The cooperative movement also had its adherents in the South: see Greta de Jong, *You Can't Eat Freedom: Southerners and Social Justice after the Civil Rights Movement* (Chapel Hill: University of North Carolina Press, 2016).

49. Web Ruble, "Fletcher Blasts Pasco's Police," *Tri-City Herald*, November 10, 1967; Paul Fletcher interview by the author, September 25, 2010.

50. Whitney Young, TV interview, August 18, 1963 (Records of the National Urban League, Series II, box E49, "TV Interviews, 1963–4" folder, Library of Congress Manuscripts Reading Room, Washington, DC); A. Phillip Randolph, Roy Wilkins, Young, and Martin Luther King Jr., joint statement, *AFL-CIO News*, July 29, 1967; "Negro Racial Diplomats Lose to Militants, Fletcher Warns," *Tri-City Herald*, October 19, 1967; Self, *American Babylon*, 6, 10; and Paul Fletcher interview by the author, September 25, 2010. For more on Whitney Young, see Dickerson, *Militant Mediator*.

51. "Negro Racial Diplomats Lose to Militants, Fletcher Warns," *Tri-City Herald*, October 19, 1967; "Fletcher: Riot Report 'Obsolete,'" *Tri-City Herald*, March 13, 1968; "Fletcher Expects Cherberg Debate," unknown publication, October 10, 1968 (G Street, box 8, folder 5, 73); "Good That Nixon Got Few Negro Votes—'Not Tied to Old Black Leaders'—Fletcher," *Seattle Argus*, December 20, 1968; and Clyde Herring, "Employers Tour Skills Center Here," *Oakland Tribune*, August 28, 1971.

52. Arthur A. Fletcher candidate statement, *Tri-City Herald*, September 17, 1967; "Campbell–Stinson Race Undecided; Fletcher, Seattleite First Negroes to Win Council Elections in State," *Tri-City Herald*, November 8, 1967.

53. Paul Fletcher interview by the author, September 25, 2010.

54. Sam Reed, "An Analysis of the Factional Power Struggle in the Republican Party of Washington State from 1962 to 1967" (MA thesis, Washington State University, 1968), 55–125; Owens, *California Politics and Parties;* 2–16, 49–59, 75–76, 92–100, 113–132, 201–219, 292–298; and Socolofsky, *Kansas Governors,* 200–203.

55. "Negroes Feel Insecure on New Job, Says Fletcher," *Seattle Post-Intelligencer,* July 2, 1968.

56. Evans interview by the author.

57. Daniel J. Evans to F. A. Allen, October 20, 1966 (G Street, box 123, folder 34, 4); Allen to Evans, October 26, 1966, and Evans to Fletcher, November 22, 1966, and August 22, 1967 (G Street, box 151, folder 1, images 138, 147–148, 3057–3058).

58. Evans to Fletcher, October 23, 1967, and Fletcher, "Draft Candidate's Statement," n.d. (G Street, box 151, folder 1, images 157–158); "Fletcher Appointed to Urban Council," *Tri-City Herald*, November 1, 1967.

59. "Campbell–Stinson Race Undecided," *Tri-City Herald*, and "Negroes Picked in Seattle, Pasco," *Centralia Daily Chronicle*, November 8, 1967.

60. Fletcher to James H. Stewart, October 4, 1967 (G Street, box 76, folder 1, 188); Ruble, "Fletcher Blasts Pasco's Police" and "Race Relations Not 'Rosy' Here," *Tri-City Herald*, November 10, 1967; Fletcher to employee relations officers of Hanford contractors, December 1, and Patricia Cochrane to Fletcher, December 7, 1967 (G Street, box 76, folder 7, 582, 608).

61. Fletcher to A. L. McKibben, November 13, 1967 (G Street, box 151, folder 1, images 3061–3067); William T. Jones to Fletcher, August 16, 1968 (G Street, box 78B, folder 14, 8–9); Paul Fletcher interview by the author, September 25, 2010; and Dan Evans interview by the author.

62. Fletcher to Tri-Cities Plans for Progress Council, September 19, 1967, Fletcher to local leaders, January 2, 1968, Fletcher to Robert Goode, January 15, T. C. Allen to Fletcher, January 29, Goode to Fletcher, February 5, George P. Wood to Fletcher, February 14, and Fletcher to Tri-City Area Merit Employment Council Steering Committee, February 16, 1968 (G Street, box 76, folder 1, 184–185, and folder 7, 576, 589–591, 596–600, 604); "'Jobs Now' Program Proposed Here," *Tri-City Herald*, February 29, 1968; and Fletcher to Wood and Fletcher to Maxine Daly, March 6, 1968 (G Street, box 76, folder 1, 180–181).

63. Sam Reed to members of Urban Affairs Council (UAC), January 4, 1968 (G Street, box 79, folder 2, 692–710); Samuel Thatcher Hubbard Jr., "Action for Washington: A New Approach to Youth Participation in Politics," December 1969 (G Street, box 61, folder 2, 1156–1226); Sam Reed interview by and in possession of the author, November 5, 2010; "Daniel Jackson Evans," Biographical Directory of the United States Congress, http://bioguide.congress.gov/; and "A. Ludlow Kramer," History Link, http://www.historylink.org/.

64. Paul Fletcher interview by the author, July 30, 2010; Sam Reed interview by the author; and "Thomas Slade Gorton III," Biographical Directory of the United States Congress, http://bioguide.congress.gov/.

65. Washington State UAC meeting minutes, January 9, 1968; UAC Job Training and Opportunities Committee meeting minutes, January 9 and February 2, 1968, Reed to UAC members, February 13, and UAC press release, April 5, 1968 (G Street, box 79, folder 2, 658–659, 684–685, 687–691); Hubbard, "Action for Washington"; Paul Fletcher interview by the author, July 30, 2010; and Sam Reed interview by the author.

66. "Olympia to Be Home: What Are His Chances?," unknown publication, n.d. (G Street, box 8, folder 5, 81); Reed, "Analysis of the Factional Power Struggle," 60–62; Jack E. Fischer, "Negro Candidate Tells His Goals," *Spokane Spokesman-Review*, June 25, 1968; "We'll Field a Great Team: Fletcher Swamps Hydroplane Driver," *Tri-City Herald*, September 18, 1968; St. George, "Arthur Fletcher"; Dan Evans interview by the author; Sam Reed interview by the author; and John Caldbick, "1970 Census: Women Outnumber Men in Washington State for First Time; Seattle and Spokane Lose Population as Tacoma and Everett Gain; Early Baby Boomers Approach Adulthood," History Link, http://www.historylink.org/.

67. "Councilman May Run for Lt. Governor," unknown publication, n.d. (G Street, box 13, folder 3, 156); Fletcher to Evans, n.d. (G Street, box 151, folder 1, images 156–157); Evans to Robert F. Phillips, April 4, 1968 (G Street, box 123, folder 34, 6); "Evans Is Neutral in GOP Contest," unknown publication, n.d. [1968] (G Street, box 13, folder 1, image 194); and Hubbard, "Action for Washington."

68. "Schools Close: State Mourns Slain Negro," *Centralia Daily Chronicle*, November 5, 1968; Ruth Rietmann to Fletcher and Lyle Einhaus to Fletcher, April 16, 1968 (G Street, box 151, folder 2, 189–190); Ray Smith to "Fellow Republicans," May 4, 1968 (G Street, box 151, folder 2, 192–193).

69. Vincent Hoyman to Fletcher, February 28, 1968, and Fletcher to Hoyman, n.d. (G Street, box 13, folder 3, 155, 157–169).

70. On the "dual identity" of Black Republicans, see Corey D. Fields, *Black Ele-*

phants in the Room: The Unexpected Politics of African American Republicans (Oakland: University of California Press, 2016), 56–84.

71. Shelby Scates, "Self Help Means That in Pasco, *Seattle Post-Intelligencer*, n.d. [April 1968] (G Street, box 13, folder 1, 28–29).

72. Fletcher press release, May 6, 1968, and "Address to the Republican Governors Association," May 7, 1968 (G Street, box 13, folder 3, 151–154, 178–183); Malcolm B. Higgins to Fletcher, May 9, 1968 (G Street, box 77, folder 2, 767); W. E. B. Du Bois, *The Souls of Black Folk* (Mineola, NY: Dover Thrift Editions, 1994), v.

73. Fletcher, "Press Statement," May 3, 1968 (G Street, box 151, folder 2, 191); "Negro Candidate Tells His Goals"; "Candidates' Statements," *Tri-City Herald*, September 9, 1968; "We'll Field a Great Team"; "Co-op Is Key to Win, Says Fletcher," *Tri-City Herald*, September 20, 1968; Val Varney, "GOP Candidates Team Up for Campaign Fly-in Series," *Seattle Times*, October 5, 1968; "Fletcher Loses; To Leave Pasco," *Tri-City Herald*, November 7, 1968.

74. "Other Editors Say—Pasco Candidate," *Pullman Herald* (reprinted from *Kitsap County Herald*), May 22, 1968; and Hubbard, "Action for Washington." The quotation is from Fletcher to Evans (draft), June 19, 1968 (G Street, box 151, folder 1, images 3068–3069).

75. RNC press release, June 20, 1968 (G Street, box 23, folder 8, 253–259); "Fletcher's Ideas May Be GOP Platform," *Republican Call*, July 1968; "Fletcher to Meet Rocky Tomorrow," *Tri-City Herald*, July 1, 1968; Arthur L. Peterson to Fletcher, July 17, 1968 (G Street, box 123, folder 8, 249–252); "Fletcher Plan Gaining," editorial, *Yakima Herald-Republic*, July 25, 1968; Dale Nelson, "Pre-Convention Survey: Nixon Loses Ground in State; Evans May Be 'Favorite Son,'" *Aberdeen Daily World*, July 26, 1968; "Pasco 'Plan' to Get GOP Consideration," *Yakima Herald-Republic*, July 30, 1968; "WU Grid Star Has Self-Help Idea," *Topeka Daily Capital*, August 3, 1968; "Self-Help," *Seattle Shopping News*, August 22, 1968; "O'Connell, Evans Nominated for Gubernatorial Election," *Everett Herald*, September 18, 1968.

76. Theodore H. White, *The Making of the President, 1960* (New York: Signet Books, 1967), 222; "Negro Candidate Tells His Goals"; "Fletcher Presents Co-op Plan," *Tri-City Herald*, July 30, 1968; "Negro Self-Help Program Lauded," *Aberdeen Daily World*, "Pasco Self-Help Plan Told to GOP," *Columbia Basin Daily Herald*, "GOP Hears about Pasco's Negro Self-Help Program," *Seattle Times*, "Pasco Councilman before GOP Platform Committee," *Bellingham Herald*, "In the Northwest . . .," *Longview News*, and "Self-Help Concept Outlined," *Yakima Herald-Republic*, July 31, 1968; "Self-Help Concept Included," unknown periodical, n.d. [August 1968], courtesy Kathy Keolker, in possession of the author; and "Fletcher Gives GOP Outline of Pasco Plan," *Walla Walla Union Bulletin*, August 1, 1968. The quotation is from "Republican Party Platform of 1968," American Presidency Project, August 5, 1968, http://www.presidency.ucsb.edu/.

77. RNC and CORE, "Joint Press Release," July 11, 1968 (G Street, box 123, folder 3, 1–5); Nixon, "Statement," July 11, 1968 (G Street, box 123, folder 34, 68); H.R. 18715, *Congressional Record*, July 18, 1968, H7011–H7022); "Reagan Win Seen if More than 2 Ballots—Fletcher," *Tri-City Herald*, August 6, 1968; "Fletcher Says Nixon Problem Is a Black One," *Tri-City Herald*, August 18, 1968; Perlstein,

Nixonland, 64–65; Dan Evans interview by the author; and Golland, *Constructing Affirmative Action,* 14–34, 126.

78. "Negro Candidate Tells His Goals"; Arthur Fletcher interview by Washburn University, tape 1, transcript, 172–173; Nat Jackson interview by the author; and Dan Evans interview by the author.

79. Black Capitalism Conference, "Questions for Discussion," August 17, 1968 (G Street, box 124, folder 21, 21–22); "Camp Visitors," *San Jose Mercury-News,* August 18, 1968; "Fletcher Says Nixon Problem Is a Black One"; "Agnew Favorably Impresses Notables at Dinner," *Seattle Daily Times,* August 20, 1968; "Fletcher Meets with GOP Leaders," *Seattle Shopping News,* August 22, 1968; Nixon, "Bridges to Human Dignity," August 25, 1968 (G Street, box 124, folder 21, 23–36); "Fletcher Named to Nixon Group," unknown publication, September 1968 (G Street, box 8, folder 5, 100); Fletcher to Glenn Olse, and Fletcher, "Notes," September 1968 (G Street, box 124, folder 20, 21–24).

80. "Fletcher Outlines Self-Help Program," *Longview News,* August 5, 1968; "Fletcher Says Nixon Problem Is a Black One"; James Ragsdale, "Pasco Negro Rising Political Star," *Spokane Spokesman-Review,* September 19, 1968; "Fletcher Meets with GOP Leaders."

81. Hubbard, "Action for Washington."

82. "Muncey Enters Republican Race for Lieut. Gov.," *Bellingham Herald,* August 1, 1968; "In the Spotlight," *Mt, Vernon Argus,* August 15, 1968; Robert Cummings, "Evans' Convention Vote No Threat," *Kirkland East Side Journal,* August 21, 1968; "Muncey Would Debate Demos," *Olympian,* "Muncey Dodges Fletcher Debate," *Aberdeen Daily World,*" and "Political Campaign Just Barely Warm," *Renton Record Chronicle,* August 23, 1968; "Fletcher Poll Shows 3 Trends," *Tri-City Herald,* n.d. (G Street, box 8, folder 5, 90); "GOP Women Appraise Candidates," *Seattle Post-Intelligencer,* September 1, 1968; "Muncey Evaded Debate: Fletcher," unknown publication, September 9, 1968 (G Street, box 8, folder 5, 92); Peggy Reynolds, "Bill Muncey Turns Roostertail and Runs from Republican Women," *Mercer Island Reporter,* and Bruce Helberg, "Side Lines," *Belleview American,* September 12, 1968; and "90 Hopefuls in State Race," *Bellingham Herald,* September 17, 1968.

83. Dorothy Towne, "Election Results for Franklin County," September 17, 1968 (digital record, Franklin County Auditor's Office, Pasco, WA); "We'll Field a Great Team"; James Ragsdale, "Bias Falls: Fletcher Wins Nod of GOP," *Vancouver Columbian,* September 18, 1968; "Co-op Is Key to Win"; Bill Sieverling, "Primary Vote Results Hold Two Surprises," unknown publication, n.d. (G Street, box 8, folder 5, 87); John Ludtka, "Light Voter Turnout Favors Incumbents," *Ellensburg Record;* "Election Results from Throughout the Yakima Valley" and "O'Connell to Face Evans," *Yakima Herald Republic;* Judi Modie, "County Vote Follows State Form," *Vancouver Columbian;* "Statewide Election Results," *Everett Herald;* Richard Spiro, "Demos Generally Leading in Most Lewis County Races" and "Wahkiakum County Vote Tabulation," *Longview News;* "O'Connell Leads, Evans Selected: Fletcher, Cherberg Far Ahead," *Spokane Spokesman-Review;* and "Fletcher Makes Political History," *Wenatchee Daily World,* September 18, 1968; Ragsdale, "Pasco Negro Rising Political Star," *Spokane Spokesman-Review;* "How King County Voted,"

Seattle Post-Intelligencer; and "How We Voted," *Prosser-Record-Bulletin,* September 19, 1968; "Senate Race Close," *Colville Statesman-Examiner,* September 20, 1968; "Seattle Negro Wins a State Primary," *New York Times,* September 22, 1968; "Absentee Ballots Counted—No Effect," *Pasco Columbia Basin News,* September 25, 1968; "Fletcher Challenges Cherberg to Debates," unknown publication, n.d. (G Street, box 8, folder 5, 95); "Absentee Ballot Count Reveals No Change in Early Vote Trends," *Port Angeles News,* September 27, 1968; and John C. Hughes, e-mail correspondence with the author, March 21, 2018.

84. "Fletcher Sets Campaign Tour," *Tri-City Herald,* September 30, 1968; "Fletcher Links Justice with Law-and-Order Cry," unknown publication, n.d. (G Street, box 8, folder 5, 74); "Fletcher Will Visit WWSC," *Bellingham Herald,* n.d. (G Street, box 13, folder 1, image 170); "Republican Candidates to Speak on 'Violence,'" *Daily Evergreen,* October 1, 1968; "A Demonstration," *Yakima Herald Republic;* and Jack Pyle, "Fletcher, Gorton Blast Wallace Race," *Tacoma News-Tribune,* October 4, 1968; Val Varney, "GOP Candidates Team Up for Campaign Fly-in Series," *Seattle Times;* "Candidates Urge Law and Order with Justice," *Tacoma News-Tribune,* October 5, 1968; Emmett Watson, "Weekend Pilot," *Seattle Post-Intelligencer;* Huntly Gordon, "College Crowd Cheers Fletcher, Gorton," *Bellingham Herald;* "Justice and Tolerance Need Cited," *Olympia Olympian;* and "Tri-City Politics: Improved Liaison Urged for State," *Tri-City Herald,* October 6, 1968; and Hubbard, "Action for Washington."

85. Unknown authors to Fletcher, n.d. (G Street, box 124, folder 1, image 398, and folder 39, 1, and box 123, folder 1, images 104–108); Brian Miller to Fletcher, October 18, 1968, Charlie Leland to Fletcher, October 20, 1968, and Mrs. Eugene A. Sterm to Fletcher, October 26, 1968 (G Street, box 134, folder 4, 451, 457, 466); Craig A. Lindell to Fletcher, October 30, 1968 (G Street, box 124, folder 21, 16); Mike Farris, "High School Mock Election Finds Nixon, Fletcher, Evans Winning," *Tri-City Herald,* October 31, 1968; Mary Boys to Fletcher, November 3, 1968 (G Street, box 123, folder 16, 9); Lon F. Backman to Fletcher, November 5, 1968 (G Street, box 124, folder 20, 16); Sam Reed to Fletcher, n.d. (G Street, box 124, folder 41, 7); Perlstein, *Nixonland,* 582; John C. Hughes, *Slade Gorton: A Half Century in Politics* (Olympia: Washington State Heritage Center, 2011), 85; and "26th Amendment," Cornell Law School Legal Information Institute, https://www.law.cornell .edu/.

86. Don Hannula, "Negroes, Whites, Officials Face Off at Garfield Forum," unknown publication, August 23, 1968 (G Street, box 123, folder 1, image 123); Dan Evans interview by the author.

87. "Fletcher Seeking Lt. Governor Post," *Enumblaw Courier-Herald,* July 25, 1968; Huntly Gordon, "Nation's Sea Power Grows Old—Nixon," *Bellingham Herald,* September 25, 1968; Lyle Burt, "'Very Encouraged' Nixon Takes His Campaign South," *Seattle Times,* September 26, 1968; "How About that 'Teamwork'" (editorial), unknown publication, n.d. (G Street, box 124, folder 1, 361); "Briefly Noted," *Auburn Globe-News,* October 9, 1968; Scates, "Fletcher Asks Churches to Work on Ghetto Problems," *Seattle Post-Intelligencer,* October 10, 1968; "Lud Kramer Endorses Fletcher," *Edmonds Tribune Review,* October 16, 1968; "Cherberg Hit,"

Longview News, October 17, 1968; "'Spellbinding,' Fletcher Turns On All Types," *Seattle Post-Intelligencer,* October 22, 1968; Lyle Burt, "TV Programs, US Senator Boost Fletcher for Lieutenant Governor," *Seattle Daily Times,* Ocober 23, 1968; "Meet Mass. Senator Brooke," paid advertisement, *Seattle Daily Times,* October 24, 1968; and "Editorial: Evaluate the Candidates," *Vashon-Maury Island Beachcomber,* October 24, 1968.

88. Alison M. Conner to Fletcher, October 2, 1968 (G Street, box 124, folder 17, 25); Fred S. Sherbon to Fletcher, and L. S. Rocke to Fletcher, October 23, 1968 (G Street, box 134, folder 3, 106, and folder 4, 431); John A. Godfrey to Fletcher, Mr. and Mrs. C. V. Bosem to Fletcher, Roy Butler to Fletcher, Mary Hart to Fletcher, Opal M. Smith to Fletcher, and Richard H. Smith to Fletcher, October 24, 1968 (G Street, box 134, folder 4, 174, 447–448, 461–462, 464); D. Waldo Reynolds to Fletcher, Mr. and Mrs. Winfield S. King to Fletcher, Rose E. Gates to Fletcher, Mr. and Mrs. B. Flynn to Fletcher for Lieutenant Governor Committee, Kent Peters to Fletcher, Mr. and Mrs. Paul Shellenberger to Fletcher for Lieutenant Governor Committee, and Mrs. Eugene A. Sterm to Fletcher, October 26, 1968 (G Street, box 134, folder 4, 175–176, 427, 430, 434, 443, 457); Mr. and Mrs. W. E. Mitchell to Fletcher and Jack Cameron to Fletcher, October 27, 1968 (G Street, box 134, folder 4, 428, 446); Mrs. Mark Aspinwall to Fletcher, Arthur Linn to Fletcher, Virginia Miller to Fletcher, Barbara R. Stevens to Fletcher for Lieutenant Governor Committee, M. T. Allen to Fletcher, Mr. and Mrs. Orville L. Cook to Fletcher, and Mr. and Mrs. Leif Arestad to Fletcher, October 28, 1968 (G Street, box 124, folder 41, 3, and box 134, folder 4, 173, 429, 455–456, 459, 463); Jack and Jane Berfoot to Fletcher, A. M. Constans to Fletcher, Mr. and Mrs. J. A. Camenzird to Fletcher, Gladys M. Mohn to Fletcher for Lieutenant Governor Committee, Mona L. Bowman to Fletcher, Laura Jean Stevenson to Fletcher, and Edith Balch to Fletcher for Lieutenant Governor Committee, October 29, 1968 (G Street, box 134, folder 4, 435–440, 442); Mildred S. Fortner to Fletcher for Lieutenant Governor Committee, Adelina P. Lahan to Fletcher for Lieutenant Governor Committee, and D. W. Rennewanz to Fletcher, October 30, 1968 (G Street, box 134, folder 4, 177, 433, 444); John H. Eisenhauer to Fletcher, October 31, 1968 (G Street, box 124, folder 40, 8); Elizabeth E. Rawlings to Fletcher, November 1, 1968 (G Street, box 124, folder 1, images 392–395); and Helen E. Stoebel to Fletcher, November 13, 1968 (G Street, box 151, folder 1, images 228–231). On white northerners looking to support "safe" African Americans to construct a nonracist identity, see, e.g., Shannon Sullivan, *Good White People: The Problem with Middle-Class White Anti-racism* (Albany: State University of New York Press, 2014), passim.

89. DeYonge, "Former Shoeshine Boy Advises GOP"; Jack Pyle, "Cherberg–Fletcher Most Interesting Race," *Tacoma News-Tribune,* September 25, 1968; Bill Lee, "Cherberg: Proud to Run on Record," *Yakima Herald-Republic,* October 19, 1968.

90. "Statewide Election Results," *Everett Herald,* September 18, 1968; Colliver, "Fletcher Predicts Cliff-Hanger Win"; Adele Ferguson, "Half of Last Week's Winners Will Be Losers in November," *Longview News,* September 24, 1968; Pyle, "Cherberg–Fletcher Most Interesting Race"; "Olympia to Be Home"; Daryl E.

Lembke, "Fletcher Giving Cherberg Battle," *Spokane Spokesman-Review;* Ferguson, "State GOP Chairman Sees Nixon Win Were Election Held Today," *Bremerton Sun,* October 10, 1968; "Fletcher Expects Cherberg Debate"; and Shelby Scates, "State Office's 'Avis' Now Is Hottest Race," *Seattle Post-Intelligencer,* October 24, 1968.

91. Bill Munson to Fletcher, September 19, 1968 (G Street, box 78B, folder 14, 6); "Cherberg Favors Unfettered Office," *Spokane Chronicle,* September 24, 1968; "Cherberg Enters Fletcher Lair," unknown publication, n.d. (G Street, box 8, folder 5, 74, 85, 89); "Cherberg Won't Debate Fletcher," *Seattle Times,* n.d. (G Street, box 13, folder 1, image 73); "Cherberg Invites Lensman," *Tri-City Herald,* October 4, 1968; "Empty Chair Attack . . ." *Seattle Post-Intelligencer,* October 5, 1968; "Cherberg Offers 'Empty Chair' to GOP Photographers," unknown publication (G Street, box 13, folder 1, image 178); Herb Robinson, "Debate over Lieutenant Governor's Role Less Simple than It Appears," *Seattle Times,* October 17, 1968; "Cherberg Says 'No' to Debate," *Longview News,* and Mary Totten, "Defends Closed Sessions of Rules Panel: Cherberg Says Debate Format Not Good for Issues," *Everett Herald,* October 18, 1968.

92. Fletcher for Lieutenant Governor Committee, advertisement, n.d. (G Street, box 8, folder 4, 199); Shelby Scates, "47 State Candidates in Primary," *Seattle Post-Intelligencer,* September 12, 1968; "O'Connell, Evans Nominated for Gubernatorial Election," *Everett Herald,* and "Road to Win Started with Ellensburg Talk," *Tri-City Herald,* September 18, 1968; "Fletcher Sets Campaign Tour," *Tri-City Herald,* "Fletcher Accepts Bid to Debate," *Seattle Times,* and "Fletcher Challenges Cherberg to Debates," *Seattle Shopping News,* September 30, 1968; "Fletcher Links Justice with Law-and-Order Cry," "Fletcher Blasts 'Secrecy,'" unknown publication, n.d. (G Street, box 8, folder 5, 85, 89); John Haydon to voters, n.d. (G Street, box 134, folder 3, 7); Bill Sieverling, "Maggie Expenses Questioned," *Seattle Post-Intelligencer,* and "Fletcher Asks for Debate," *Federal Way News,* October 2, 1968; Varney, "GOP Candidates Team Up," October 5, 1968; "Fletcher Expects Cherberg Debate"; "Debate Due on Channel," *Vancouver Columbian,* October 10, 1968; "Cherberg Hit," *Longview News,* and Neil Modie, "Lt. Governor Role Debated," *Vancouver Columbian,* October 17, 1968; John Christenson, "Nominee Art Fletcher Appears in Bremerton," *Bremerton Sun,* and "Art Fletcher," *Vancouver Columbian,* October 18, 1968; Kay Green, "Art Fletcher: Will People Vote Because of the Man or His Race?," *Longview News,* October 21, 1968; "Candidates to Be Heard on Saturday" and "Editorial: Evaluate the Candidates"; "Ex-Player Fletcher Vies with Ex-Coach Cherberg," *Tri-City Herald,* November 3, 1968; Paul Fletcher interview by the author, July 30, 2010; and Sam Reed interview by the author.

93. Scates, "State Office's 'Avis.'"

94. Modie, "Lt. Governor Role Debated."

95. Burt, "TV Programs."

96. "Shirley Temple Black Due Here," *Seattle Times,* October 18, 1968; unknown writer to John Haydon, October 25, 1968 (G Street, box 134, folder 4, 172); "Shirley Temple," Biography, https://www.biography.com/.

97. Stephen G. Michaud and Hugh Aynesworth, *Ted Bundy: Conversations with a Killer—The Death Row Interviews* (Irving, TX: Authorlink Press, 2000), 25; Ann

Rule, *The Stranger Beside Me* (New York: Pocket Books, 2009), 19; Paul Fletcher interview by the author, September 25, 2010; and William Grimes, "Ann Rule, 83, Dies: Wrote about Ted Bundy (a Friend) and Other Killers," *New York Times*, July 29, 2015; "Ted Bundy," Biography, https://www.biography.com/; and Kathy Keolker interview, May 25, 2018, by and in possession of the author.

98. "Labor–Negro Ties Stressed as 40,000 March for King," *AFL-CIO News*, April 13, 1968; John G. Morris, "Kennedy Claims Victory, and Then Shots Ring Out," *New York Times*, June 5, 1968; Rick Anderson, "On That Tragic Day for Kennedy Life Had to Go On," *Tri-City Herald*, n.d. [probably June 8, 1968], courtesy Kathy Keolker, in possession of the author; Jeff Stevens, "January 26, 1969: The Assassination of Edwin T. Pratt," Radical Seattle Remembers, January 26, 2010, https://radsearem.wordpress.com/; Dan Evans interview by the author; and Sam Reed interview by the author. Fletcher quoted in Anderson.

99. Briggs, "'Hounds' Sniff at Fletcher"; Pat Bushey, "Fletcher Laughs at Charge: Wallaceite Says Reds Use Fletcher," *Tri-City Herald*, n.d. (G Street, box 136, folder 1, image 9); Geranios, "His Loss Was Turned into a Win"; and Hughes, *Slade Gorton*, 86.

100. "Fletcher Close Behind Cherberg," *Tri-City Herald*, November 6, 1968; "Fletcher Loses, to Leave Pasco," *Tri-City Herald*, November 7, 1968; and "Evans Dominated State Politics," *Tri-City Herald*, January 1, 1969. Garth Marston to Fletcher, January 31, Alexander Singh to Fletcher, February 4, Harold R. Blackwell to Fletcher, February 5, and Esther Schlagel to Fletcher, February 5, 1969 (G Street, box 81, folder 2, 232–234, 238); Seattle First National Bank, "Statement, Art Fletcher Campaign Fund," February 28, 1969 (G Street, box 123, folder 1, image 60); Bill Sieverling, "Fletcher Named Assistant Labor Secretary," *Seattle Post-Intelligencer*, March 15, 1969; Hubbard, "Action for Washington"; Arthur Fletcher interview by Washburn University, tape 1, transcript, 172–173; Paul Fletcher interview by the author, September 25, 2010; and Nat Jackson interview by the author. In early December, a fellow at the Brookings Institution sent Fletcher $25, "to apply to [a campaign deficit]. If you don't have a deficit," he added, "put it in an escrow for your next campaign or use it to get around the state—at 10 cents a mile it'll get you 250 miles in any direction you want to go." Stephen Horn to Fletcher, December 2, 1968 (G Street, box 151, folder 2, 194).

101. Dorothy Towne, "Election Results for Franklin County," November 5, 1968 (digital record, Franklin County Auditor's Office, Pasco, WA); Kathy Keolker interview by the author; and Eddie Rye interview by and in possession of the author, May 25, 2018.

102. Sam Reed interview by the author; "Sam Reed, Olympia, Washington," BlackPast.org, http://www.blackpast.org/.

103. "'Guv': End of a Life of Service—Former Lt. Gov. John Cherberg, 81, Remembered for Dignity, Fairness," *Seattle Times*, April 9, 1992; "John Andrew Cherberg," Washington Secretary of State Legacy Project, https://www.sos.wa.gov/.

104. The title for this section is borrowed, with gratitude, from Kenneth Osgood and Derrick E. White, eds., *Winning while Losing: Civil Rights, the Conservative Movement, and the Presidency from Nixon to Obama* (Gainesville: University Press

of Florida, 2014). "Fletcher Loses," November 7, 1968; "Fletcher Turns Down Federal Position," *Topeka Journal*, November 8, 1968; "Ex-Ichabod on Nixon's Team" (editorial), *Topeka State Journal*, March 18, 1969; Robert A. George, "Back in Black: Bush among the NAACP," *National Review*, July 12, 2000; "1968 Presidential Election," 270 to Win, https://www.270towin.com/; and Thurber, *Republicans and Race*, passim. On the "downward slide": Barry Goldwater had polled 6 percent in 1964, and Nixon had polled 32 percent in 1960.

105. Fletcher to John Ehrlichman, November 29 and December 2, 1968; Ehrlichman to Fletcher, December 5, 1968 (Papers of President Richard Milhous Nixon Returned Files, box 18, folder 12, 49–63, Richard M. Nixon Presidential Archive, Yorba Linda, CA); Fletcher to Ehrlichman, December 17, 1968 (G Street, box 13, folder 3, 377–383); Melvin B. Voorhees, "Loser Fletcher Turns Out to Be Big Winner," *Seattle Argus*; Hu Blonk, "Oroville Speaker: Mr. Fletcher Is Found," *Wenatchee Daily World*, January 17, 1969; and Nixon, Executive Order 11458, American Presidency Project, March 5, 1969, http://www.presidency.ucsb.edu/.

106. Ehrlichman to "D.C.," November 20, 1968, and John McLaughry to Ehrlichman, December 17, 1968 (Nixon Returned Files, box 18, folder 10, 58, and folder 12, 40).

107. A. Ludlow Kramer to Fletcher, April 30, 1968 (G Street, box 79, folder 2, 655); "Fletcher Will Do a Job" (editorial), *Bellingham Herald*, February 5, 1969; Arthur R. Eggers to Nixon, March 7, 1969 (G Street, box 124, folder 1, images 126–127); Kramer, *Race and Violence in Washington State: Report of the Commission on the Causes and Prevention of Civil Disorder* (Olympia: Washington State Commission on the Causes and Prevention of Civil Disorder, 1969); and "A. Ludlow 'Lud' Kramer," History Link, http://www.historylink.org/.

108. "Fletcher Loses, to Leave Pasco"; "Fletcher Turns Down Federal Position"; Edward L. Morgan to Ehrlichman, January 12, 1969 (Nixon Returned Files, box 18, folder 12, 39); and "Ex-Ichabod on Nixon's Team."

109. Voorhees, "Loser Fletcher Turns Out to Be Big Winner"; Nixon to United States Senate, March 14, 1969 (Nixon, Collection of the Department of Labor, box 5, "Executive, 1" folder); "Fletcher Named to $38,750 Post," *Tri-City Herald*, March 14, 1969; "Nixon Names WU Grid Great to Labor Post," *Topeka Capital*, "Negro Named to Key Position in Labor Department," *Philadelphia Bulletin*, and "Negro Gets Key Post in Labor Department," *New York Times*, March 15, 1969; Fletcher to George P. Shultz, March 21, 1969 (Records of the Department of Labor, Collection of Secretary George P. Shultz, box 114, "PE-4-2 Fletcher, Arthur A. [Asst Secy for Wage & Labor Standards] 1969" folder); Adkins, "Big 'Breakthrough' Man"; Arthur Fletcher interview by Washburn University, tape 1, transcript, 173; and Golland, *Constructing Affirmative Action*, 125–126. Speechwriter Patrick Buchanan affectionately called Nixon the "old man:" Perlstein, *Nixonland*, 130.

110. Elliot Carlson, "Man of 'Rage': Arthur Fletcher Sees LA Riot as Symptom of Nation's Racial Ills,"*AARP Bulletin*, June 1992.

111. James Baldwin, "The Negro in American Culture," *Cross Currents* 11 (1961): 205.

1. J. Carlton Yeldell to Julius Thomas, August 8, 1958 (Papers of the National Urban League, Series I, box A52, "Trade Union Advisory Council, 1958" folder, Manuscripts Division, Library of Congress, Washington, DC); John Dingle to Alex Wollod, May 29, 1963 (Records of the Jewish Labor Committee of Philadelphia, Urban Archives, Temple University, Philadelphia, PA, box 3, folder 14); "US Warns 200 Unions against Bias in Training," *Philadelphia Bulletin*, March 29, 1967; George D. Zuckerman, "Sheet Metal Workers' Case: A Case History of Bias in the Building Trades," *New York Law Journal*, September 8, 1969; and Golland, *Constructing Affirmative Action*, 7, 65, 107.

2. For more on discrimination in the building trades and government contracts, see Golland, *Constructing Affirmative Action*.

3. "Executive Order 8802: Prohibition of Discrimination in the Defense Industry," OurDocuments.gov, June 1941, https://www.ourdocuments.gov/; Executive Order No. 10308 and White House press release, December 3, 1951 (NUL series I, box D15, "President's Committee on Government Contract Compliance" folder); Herbert Garfinkel, *When Negroes March: The March on Washington Movement in the Organizational Politics for FEPC* (New York: Atheneum, 1959), passim; President's Committee Equal Employment Opportunity press releases, August 8 and October 31, 1961 (Papers of the AFL-CIO [hereafter Meany], RG1-038, box 78, folders 9 and 12, George Meany Archives, Silver Spring, MD); John G. Field to Lyndon Johnson, October 6, 1961 (Lyndon Baines Johnson Vice Presidential Papers, SF box 85, "PCEEO, July–December, 2" folder, Lyndon Baines Johnson Presidential Library and Museum, Austin, TX); Anderson, *Pursuit of Fairness*, 56, 64; James D. Wolfinger, "'An Equal Opportunity to Make a Living—and a Life': The FEPC and Postwar Black Politics," *Labor* 4, no. 2 (2007): 65–94; "The FEPC and the Legacy of the Labor-Based Civil Rights Movement of the 1940s," *Labor History* 49, no. 1 (2008): 71–92; Judson MacLaury, *To Advance Their Opportunities: Federal Policies Toward African American Workers from World War I to the Civil Rights Act of 1964* (Knoxville, TN: Newfound Press, 2008), 137–145, 189–196; Jennifer Delton, *Racial Integration in Corporate America, 1940–1990* (New York: Cambridge University Press, 2009), 177–191; and Golland, *Constructing Affirmative Action*, 9, 13–14, 44–45.

4. Theodore Kheel, "Report to Vice President Johnson on the Structure and Operations of the President's Committee on Equal Employment Opportunity," n.d. [probably June 1962] (NUL series II, box A48, "PCEEO, 1962, 2" folder, concluded in box A42, "PCEEO, 1964, 1" folder).

5. Malcolm Poindexter, "NAACP Leads 300 Pickets at 2 Schools," *Philadelphia Bulletin*, May 24, 1963; John F. Kennedy, civil rights address, American Rhetoric, June 11, 1963, http://www.americanrhetoric.com/; Velma Hill, "Harlem Pickets Force City Hall to Halt Project," *New America*, June 10, 1963; Milton Honig, "Discrimination Protests Rising in Newark," *New York Times*, June 16, 1963; Gertrude Samuels, "Even More Crucial than in the South," *New York Times Magazine*, June 30, 1963; Paul Lermack, "Cecil Moore and the Philadelphia Branch of the National Association for the Advancement of Colored People," in *Black Politics in Philadelphia*, ed. Miriam Ershkowitz and Joseph Zikmund II (New York: Basic Books,

1973); Countryman, *Up South;* and Golland, *Constructing Affirmative Action,* 35–37, 56–59. For the March on Washington, see Robin S. Doak, *The March on Washington: Uniting against Racism* (Minneapolis: Compass Point Books, 2008).

6. US Congress, Civil Rights Act of 1964, H.R. 7152, July 2, 1964, and Lyndon Baines Johnson, Executive Order No. 11246, September 24, 1965 (Meany RG 1-038, box 73, folder 14); Whitney Young, TV interview, December 8, 1963 (NUL series II, box E49, "TV Interviews, 1963–4" folder); and Dickerson, *Militant Mediator,* 245–246.

7. Antony Mazzolini, "US Stops Funds on Projects Here," *Cleveland Press,* May 18, 1967; OFCC proposed agenda, August 1, 1967, and summary, August 1967 (Records of the Department of Labor, OFCC Assistant Director for Construction [ADC] box 14, "FEB Meeting" folder, NARA College Park, MD); Graham, *Civil Rights Era,* 286–287; Anderson, *Pursuit of Fairness,* 104–105; Grace Palladino, *Skilled Hands, Strong Spirits: A Century of Building Trades History* (Ithaca, N.Y.: Cornell University Press, 2005), 163; and Golland, *Constructing Affirmative Action,* 92–98, 105–111.

8. Harry G. Toland, "Negroes in Trades," *Philadelphia Bulletin,* September 24, 1963; Frank Loretti to Vincent J. Macaluso, April 29, 1966, and Bennett Stalvey to Macaluso, August 26, 1966 (OFCC ADC, box 3, "Philadelphia—C" folder); Richard Levin to Philadelphia Commission on Human Rights, August, 1966 (OFCC ADC, box 14, "C1" folder); "US Warns 200 Unions against Bias in Training"; Stalvey to Macaluso, April 14, 1967 (OFCC ADC, box 14 "Philadelphia Correspondence, 1967, January–June" folder); Stalvey, monthly reports, June and August 1967; Philadelphia Chamber of Commerce press release, November 23, 1967 (OFCC ADC, box 14 "Philadelphia Correspondence, 1967, November–December" folder); Anderson, *Pursuit of Fairness,* 115–116; and Golland, *Constructing Affirmative Action,* 105–106.

9. Elmer Staats to William C. Cramer and Staats to Willard W. Wirtz, November 18, 1968 (DOL [Department of Labor] Chronological File, 1968, NARA College Park); Stalvey, monthly reports, March 1969 and April 1969 (OFCC ADC, box 24, "Monthly Reports, 1968–9" folder); and Golland, *Constructing Affirmative Action,* 115–118.

10. Carlson, "Man of 'Rage.'"

11. Fletcher interview by Washburn University, tape 1, transcript 178–179; Paul Fletcher interview by and in possession of the author, April 2, 2011.

12. Nelson I. Crowther to Fletcher, May 27, 1969 (G Street, box 76, folder 7, 91); Matryce L. Cheek to Horace Menasco, June 3, 1969 (G Street, box 123, folder 8, 291); Alfred W. Blumrosen to Fletcher, June 6, 1969 (G Street, box 81, folder 2, 170–178); "The Heady New World of Art Fletcher: Black Man, Broke in '67, Now High in Govt.," unknown publication, June 6, 1969 (G Street, box 39, folder 1, 41); Blumrosen statement, June 25, 1969 (G Street, box 78A, folder 3, 16–34); Walker Roberts, "Menasco Resigns, Joins Art Fletcher," *Tri-City Herald,* undated [July 1969] (G Street, box 81, folder 1, 70); Richard Nixon remarks, American Presidency Project, August 13, 1969, http://www.presidency.ucsb.edu/; Crowther to

Fletcher, August 18, 1969 (G Street, box 78A, folder 8, 28–34); and Fletcher to Vera J. Lincoln, October 29, 1969 (G Street, box 76, folder 7, 561).

13. McCreedy to James L. Hodgson, May 15, Bierman to Jack Gentry, May 19, and Fletcher to George P. Shultz, May 19, 1969 (G Street, box 76, folder 1, 28, 42–44); Blumrosen to Fletcher, March 25, 1970 (G Street, box 76, folder 7, 34–36); Wilks to Fletcher, April 3, 1970 (G Street, box 76, folder 7, 30); OFCC Report, May 1970 (G Street, box 81, folder 8, 260–287); OFCC Report, June 12, 1970 (G Street, box 81, folder 8, 289–310); Fletcher to Shultz, June 24, 1970 (DOL Shultz, box 163, "AD-7-3 Weekly Reports to the Secretary, 1970 [June]" folder); and "Shipbuilding Contracts Go to Va. Firm," *Washington Post,* June 28, 1970.

14. Lee Douglas Jr. to Shultz, May 5, 1969 (G Street, box 7, folder 7, 86); Fletcher itinerary, May 8, 1969 (G Street, box 79, folder 1, 333); A. P. Toner, White House brief, May 27, 1969 (Nixon Department of Labor Collection, box 1, folder 5); Naomi S. Rovner, "Negroes Promised Bethlehem Investigation: Steel Workers Spend Day Demonstrating at US Agencies," *Baltimore Sun,* May 29, 1969; and Richard Basoco, "Bethlehem's Employment Held Unfair: US Aide Cites Survey Made at Point and Key Highway," *Baltimore Sun,* June 7, 1969.

15. McCreedy to Fletcher, May 28, 1969 (G Street, box 76, folder 7, 87); Fletcher to Dexter L. Hanley, August 7, 1969 (DOL Shultz, box 69, "EEO-3 Federal Contract Compliance, 1969, August–December" folder); DOL Conciliation Agreement, August 7, and Hanley, statement, August 8, 1969 (G Street, box 76, folder 7, 132–137); Robert M. Hobsom to Fletcher, undated [April 1971] (G Street, box 76, folder 1, 109–110); Robert Samuel Smith, *Race, Labor, and Civil Rights:* Griggs versus Duke Power *and the Struggle for Equal Employment Opportunity* (Baton Rouge: Louisiana State University Press, 2008); and Golland, *Constructing Affirmative Action,* 158.

16. Stalvey to Macaluso, undated [March 1969] (OFCC ADC, box 24, "1968–9" folder; DOL press release, June 11, 1969 (Records of the Equal Employment Opportunity Commission, Collection of Chairman William H. Brown III, folder 6906, NARA College Park, MD).

17. Staats to Cramer and to Wirtz, November 18, 1968 (DOL Chronological, 1968); Laurence H. Silberman to McCreedy, May 27, 1969 (G Street, box 81, folder 2, 206–219); Blumrosen to Fletcher, June 6, 1969 (G Street, box 81, folder 2, 170–178); DOL press release, June 11, 1969; Peter H. Binzen, "US to Revise and Reinstate 'Phila. Plan' on Minority Hiring," *Philadelphia Bulletin,* June 12, 1969; Fletcher to Jerris Leonard, June 17, 1969 (Records of the Equal Employment Opportunity Commission, Collection of Chairman William H. Brown III, folder 6906); Macaluso memo for the files, June 24, 1969 (G Street, box 78A, folder 5, 60–65); Silberman to Leonard, June 24, 1969 (G Street, box 81, folder 6, 84); Leonard to Silberman, June 26, 1969 (Nixon Records, Collection of Leonard Garment [hereafter Nixon Garment], box 14, "Philadelphia Plan 2-03" folder); Fletcher to heads of all agencies, June 27, 1969 (DOL Collection of Secretary Hodgson [hereafter DOL Hodgson Secretary], box 14, "Philadelphia Plan" folder); and Golland, *Constructing Affirmative Action,* 115–118.

18. Fletcher to heads of all agencies, June 27, 1969; Fletcher speech and DOL

press release, June 27, 1969 (DOL Shultz, box 68, "EEO-1 Summary Plans & Reports, 1969, January–August" folder); "Minority Quota Ordered in Contract Bids for US Jobs," *Philadelphia Daily News,* and Martin J. Herman, "U.S Decrees New Plan for Hiring Blacks: Bid Specifications to Include Quotas; Negotiations Barred," *Philadelphia Bulletin,* June 27, 1969.

19. Irwin Dubinsky, "Preliminary Research Findings on Operation Dig," April 8, 1969 (G Street, box 13, folder 2, 361–377); Michael Stern, "Effort to Train Blacks for Construction Jobs Falters in Pittsburgh," *Wall Street Journal,* July 24, 1969; "Five Building Projects Halted in Pittsburgh by Demands of Blacks; Demonstrators at Construction Sites Seek the Placement of Negroes in Area Trade Unions," *Wall Street Journal,* August 26, 1969; Western Pennsylvania Master Builders' Association statement, August 28, 1969 (Meany RG9-002, box 10); Fletcher to Shultz, November 12, 1969 (DOL Shultz, box 46, "Weekly Reports to the Secretary, 1969 [Nov.]" folder); and Victor Riesel to Fletcher, November 13, 1969 (G Street, box 13, folder 2, 525–526).

20. Seattle Building and Construction Trades Council Resolution, and Edward L. Mueller to Fletcher, June 24, 1969 (G Street, box 13, folder 2, 666–669 and 735–743); Roger Yockey, "Skilled Jobs Demanded: Blacks Halt Garfield Pool Construction," *Seattle Times,* August 28, 1969; "Picketing Contractor Beaten by 3 Men," *Seattle Post-Intelligencer,* September 1, 1969; William Gough, "Council Had No Business in Contractor Dispute—Mooney," Jerry Montgomery, "Training Issue Resolved in Construction Dispute," and "More Jobs for Blacks" (editorial), *Seattle Times,* September 5, 1969; Michael Parks, "Court to Hear Union's Appeal of Bias Ruling," and Paul W. Staples, "Reopen Four County Projects, Unions Ask," *Seattle Times,* September 6, 1969; "Union Demands Resumption of Construction Projects," *Seattle Post-Intelligencer,* September 6, 1969; "Building Trades Won't Hire Unskilled Blacks" and "Pact Sets Up Training for Minority Workers," *Seattle Times,* September 7, 1969; Staples, "Construction Resumes, but Unions Balk," *Seattle Times,* September 8, 1969; "15 Black Trainees Hired," *Seattle Post-Intelligencer,* September 9, 1969; "Union Dispute Again May Halt Building," *Seattle Post-Intelligencer,* September 11, 1969; and "Black Labor" (editorial), *Seattle Post-Intelligencer,* September 12, 1969.

21. US District Court, Western District of Washington, Northern Division proceedings, September 17, 1969 (G Street, box 13, folder 2, 636–648); John D. Spellman to Ehrlichman, September 18, 1969 (G Street, box 80, folder 1, 327–328); Walter R. Hundley to Fletcher and Central Contractors Association to Fletcher, October 17, 1969 (G Street, box 80, folder 1, 321, 323); "Seattle," *New York Amsterdam News,* October 18, 1969; Jerome Page to Fletcher, October 21, 1969 (G Street, box 80, folder 1, 320); "US Tries New Tack to Win Blacks Jobs in Suit against Unions in Seattle," *Wall Street Journal,* November 3, 1969; Ray J. Gautier to Fletcher, November 6, 1969 (G Street, box 124, folder 1, 90–91); Orval C. Scott speech, November 11, 1969 (G Street, box 80, folder 1, 280–282); Riesel to Fletcher, November 13, 1969; Staples, "Union Group Won't Attend Minority-Hiring Talks," *Seattle Times,* November 20, 1969; Staples, "'Action Required or Else': Fletcher Issues Job-Bias Warning," *Seattle Times,* and "Documenting Job Dispute" (editorial), *Seattle Times,*

November 25, 1969; DOL press release, and Seattle Chamber of Commerce invitation list and agenda, November 25, 1969 (G Street, box 78B, folder 9, 104–106, 122–128, 132–136); "Fletcher Is Optimistic on Job Training," *Seattle Post-Intelligencer,* November 26, 1969; Fletcher to various, n.d. [December 1969]; and Seattle Association of General Contractors affirmative action plan, December 16, 1969 (G Street, box 80, folder 1, 434–441).

22. "Abernathy Leading Fight against Job Bias in Chi," *Philadelphia Tribune,* August 30, 1969; Blumrosen to Fletcher, September 8, 1969 (G Street, box 124, folder 26, 1–2); "Jesse Jackson Writes from Chicago Jail," *Philadelphia Tribune,* September 20, 1969; "Showdown on Negro Jobs in the Building Trades," *US News and World Report,* September 29, 1969; and Golland, *Constructing Affirmative Action,* 133.

23. DOL press release, September 11, 1969 (G Street, box 53, folder 1, 902–903); "US Schedules Hearing in Building Job Battle," *Chicago Tribune,* September 12, 1969; "Federal Agencies Move In to Put Out Fire of Racial Unrest," *Construction Labor Report* 730 (September 17, 1969); Samuel J. Simmons to George Romney, September 18, 1969 (G Street, box 78A, folder 9, 56–62); DOL transcript, September 24, 1969 (G Street, box 124, folder 25, 1–11); A. P. Toner to Ehrlichman, September 24, 1969 (Nixon Garment, box 86, folder 65); Coalition for United Community Action to Shultz, September 25, 1969 (DOL Shultz, box 69, "EEO-2 Information & Inquiries, 1969, September" folder); James Strong, "Fletcher Talk Delayed as 500 Jam Room," *Chicago Defender,* September 25, 1969; Fletcher, *The Silent Sell-Out: Government Betrayal of Blacks to the Craft Unions* (New York: Third Press, 1974), 70–72; Perlstein, *Nixonland,* 414–415; and Golland, *Constructing Affirmative Action,* 134.

24. DOL list of witnesses, September 25, 1969 (G Street, box 134, folder 4, 528–530); HUD press release, September 25, 1969 (G Street, box 78A, folder 3, 35–42); Seth King, "Whites in Chicago Disrupt Hearing: 5 Hurt and 9 Arrested in Dispute on Job Bias," *New York Times,* September 26, 1969; "2000 Construction Union Members Attack Negroes Outside US Building," *Philadelphia Tribune,* September 30, 1969; Shultz to Walter J. Hickel and Shultz to David M. Kennedy, October 6, 1969 (DOL Shultz, box 114, "PE-4-2 Fletcher, Arthur A. [Asst Secy for Wage & Labor Standards] 1969" folder); Shultz to Robert L. Kunzig, October 20, 1969 (DOL Shultz, box 69, "EEO-2 Inquiries & Information, 1969, October" folder); Fletcher, *Silent Sell-Out;* and Golland, *Constructing Affirmative Action.*

25. King, "Whites in Chicago Disrupt Hearing"; King, "Whites in Chicago Continue Protest: A Plan to Take More Blacks into Building Union Scored," *New York Times,* September 27, 1969; Thomas Murray and Arthur O'Neil speech, October 15, 1969 (G Street, box 80, folder 3, 629–630); Macaluso to John Wilks, October 16, 1969 (Nixon Garment, box 1, "Oct" folder); Hodgson to Joseph Loftus, October 20, 1969 (DOL Hodgson Undersecretary, box 8, "OFCC" folder); Macaluso to Wilks, October 21, 1969 (G Street, box 78A, folder 9, 54); and Fletcher, *Silent Sell-Out.*

26. Bryce Harlow to Democratic Study Group, August 13, 1969 (Nixon EEOC "EX 1969 1" folder); Shultz to Fred A. Haynes et al., September 4, 1969 (DOL

Shultz, box 69, "EEO-2 Information & Inquiries, 1969, September" folder). On the Southern Strategy, see, e.g., Graham, *Civil Rights Era;* Joan Hoff, *Nixon Reconsidered* (New York: Basic Books, 1994); Richard Reeves, *President Nixon: Alone in the White House* (New York: Simon & Schuster, 2001); Judith Stein, *Running Steel, Running America: Race, Economic Policy, and the Decline of Liberalism* (Chapel Hill: University of North Carolina Press, 1998); and Kevin L. Yuill, *Richard Nixon and the Rise of Affirmative Action* (Lanham, MD: Rowman & Littlefield, 2006).

27. "Shultz Assigned: Nixon Orders Study of Key Labor Issues," *AFL-CIO News,* March 15, 1969; DOL press release, August 11, 1969 (G Street, box 78A, folder 5, 24–26); Thurber, *Republicans and Race,* passim; and John David Skrentny, "Zigs and Zags," in Osgood and White, *Winning While Losing,* 26–27. For more on Nixon and civil rights, see Graham, *Civil Rights Era;* John David Skrentny, *The Ironies of Affirmative Action: Politics, Culture, and Justice in America* (Chicago: University of Chicago Press, 1996); and Dean J. Kotlowski, *Nixon's Civil Rights: Politics, Principle, and Policy* (Cambridge, MA: Harvard University Press, 2001).

28. Macaluso to the files, June 24, 1969 (G Street, box 78A, folder 5, 60–65); Staats to Shultz, August 5, 1969 (Nixon Garment, box 143, "Philadelphia Plan 2-04" folder); "Plan to Hire Minorities Held Violating Rights," *Associated Press,* August 6, 1969 (G Street, box 78A, folder 5, 27–28); and Richard Homan, "Minorities Job Hiring Plan to Stay Despite US Comptroller's Protest," *Washington Post,* August 12, 1969.

29. "Administration Fight on Construction Bias Opposed by US Aide: Comptroller General Contends So-Called 'Philadelphia Plan' Violates '64 Civil Rights Act," *Wall Street Journal,* August 6, 1969; "Controller Scores Negro Hiring Plan," *New York Times,* August 7, 1969; "Dirksen to Fight Minority Hiring Plan," *Washington Post,* August 8, 1969; "Unions Invited to Offer New Hiring Plan," *Philadelphia Bulletin,* August 12, 1969; "Dirksen Leads Opposition against Minority Hiring," *Washington Afro-American,* August 12, 1969; Gifford to Shultz, August 14, 1969 (DOL Shultz, box 68, "EEO-1 Summary Plans & Reports, 1969, January–August" folder); "'Philadelphia Plan' Impasse," *Philadelphia Bulletin,* August 14, 1969; Spencer Rich, "GAO to Void Contracts with Hiring Quotas," *Washington Post,* August 15, 1969; "Fannin Renews Stand against Phila. Plan," *Daily Labor Report,* October 15, 1969; William Chapman, "Ervin Assails Plan on Minority Hiring," *Washington Post,* September 28, 1969; and Rich, "AFL-CIO Joins Foes of Plan on Minority Hiring," *Washington Post,* October 29, 1969. On color-blind conservatism, see Nancy MacLean, *Freedom Is Not Enough: The Opening of the American Workplace* (New York: Russell Sage Foundation, 2006), 225–261; Delton, *Racial Integration in Corporate America,* 17–160; and *Racing for Innocence,* 1–18.

30. Paul Delaney, "Shultz Denies His Plan to Hire Minorities Violates Rights Act," *New York Times,* August 7, 1969; Rich, "GAO to Void Contracts with Hiring Quotas," *Washington Post,* August 15, 1969; John N. Mitchell to Shultz, September 22, 1969 (Nixon Garment, box 14, "Philadelphia Plan 1" folder); Office of Senator Jacob K. Javits of New York press release, October 27, 1969 (G Street, box 78A, folder 2, 3–4); *Congressional Record—Senate,* December 18, 1969, 17131–17157; and "Quotas and Goals" (editorial), *Washington Post,* December 22, 1969.

31. Damon Stetson, "Meany Doubtful on Hiring Quota Plan," *New York Times,* August 9, 1969; NAACP press release, August 9, 1969 (NAACP series 6, box A26, folder 2); "Breaking Down the Bars" (editorial), *New York Times,* August 12, 1969; NAACP press release, August 18, 1969 (NAACP series 6, box A26, folder 2); "For a 'Boston Plan'" (editorial), *Boston Globe,* August 24, 1969; "Unionists Call Phila. Plan 'Unworkable': Minority Job Quota Proposal Attacked at Hearing Here," *Philadelphia Bulletin,* August 28, 1969; "UA Head Blasts Union Critics," *Engineering News-Record,* August 28, 1969; "Race Conflict over Jobs" (editorial), *New York Times,* August 30, 1969; "Implementing the Philadelphia Plan" (editorial), *Philadelphia Inquirer,* September 4, 1969; "Labor's 2 Faces" (editorial), *New York Amsterdam News,* September 13, 1969; Martin J. Herman, "Unions Voice 'Unalterable Opposition' to Phila. Plan," *Philadelphia Bulletin,* September 22, 1969; Damon Stetson, "Building Unions Spur Negro Jobs: Defend Record in Hiring but Pledge Greater Effort—Reject Quota Plan," *New York Times,* September 23, 1969; Stetson, "Meany Criticizes Nixon on Racism: Sees Building Trades Unions in 'Whipping Boy' Role," *New York Times,* September 25, 1969; "'Don't Lower the Standards,' Meany Tells Bldg. Trades," *Los Angeles Citizen,* October 3, 1969; "Trades Score Racial Quotas in Hiring Plan," *AFL-CIO News,* October 11, 1969; Meany to Shultz, and AFL-CIO resolution, October 21, 1969 (Meany RG1-038 box 72, folder 1); "Positive on Construction" (editorial), *New York Amsterdam News,* October 25, 1969; and Golland, *Constructing Affirmative Action,* 122–148.

32. Leon E. Panetta to Fletcher, August 12, 1969 (G Street, box 76, folder 7, 808); Richard Homan, "Minorities Job Hiring Plan to Stay Despite US Comptroller's Protest," *Washington Post,* August 12, 1969; "Legalities Won't Halt Phila. Plan, US Aide Says," *Philadelphia Bulletin,* August 29, 1969; Stalvey to Macaluso, n.d. [October 1969] (DOL OFCC ADC, box 22, folder 10); Fletcher to Bernyce Fletcher, n.d. [October 1969], and Lincoln to Fletcher, October 1, 1969 (G Street, box 21, folder 5, 646, 652–653); Richard Blumenthal to Daniel P. Moynihan, October 2, 1969 (Hugh Davis Graham, *Civil Rights during the Nixon Administration,* reel 18, New York Public Library Schomberg Center for Research in Black Culture); Macaluso to Wilks, October 16, 1969 (Nixon Garment, box 1, "Oct" folder); DOL press release, October 23, 1969 (DOL Shultz, box 69, "EEO-2 Inquiries & Information, 1969, October" folder); "Philadelphia Plan Contract," *New York Times,* October 23, 1969; "'Plan' Contract Goes to Bristol," *USDL Forum* newsletter, October 31, 1969 (G Street, box 21, folder 6, 334); and Stalvey to Macaluso, n.d. [November 1969] (DOL OFCC ADC, box 24, "1968–9" folder).

33. "Minority Hiring Plan Faces Legal Challenge," *Los Angeles Times,* November 9, 1969; Delaney, "US Aide to Block Hiring Plan Pact: Controller General Will Act against First Participant," *New York Times,* November 9, 1969; and Saul Kohler, "Philadelphia Plan Awaits Showdown," *Philadelphia Inquirer,* November 11, 1969.

34. Sam J. Ervin to Shultz, October 8, 1969 (G Street, box 78A, folder 3, 76–78); "Ervin Subcommittee to Study Philadelphia Plan," *Daily Labor Report,* October 9, 1969 (G Street, box 78A, folder 3, 80–81); Ervin to William Brown, October 15, and William L. Gifford to Shultz, October 22, 1969 (G Street, box 78A, folder 3, 68, 73–74).

35. Brown to Ervin, October 24, 1969 (DOL Shultz, box 53, "1969 Correspondence, EEOC" folder); Arnold R. Isaacs, "Bias-Program Race Quota Denied: Aides to Nixon Defend Philadelphia Plan at Senate Hearing," *Baltimore Sun*, October 27, 1969; Staats testimony, October 28, 1969 (DOL Chronological, 1969, folder 1); Shultz testimony, October 28, 1969 (G Street, box 78A, folder 3, 9–15); Rich, "AFL-CIO Joins Foes," and John Herbers, "Nixon Aides Explain the Goal of Job Plan," *New York Times*, October 29, 1969; Fletcher to Ervin, October 31, 1969 (G Street, box 78A, folder 3, 4); Laurence H. Silberman legal memorandum, n.d. [November 1969] (Nixon Garment, box 143, "Philadelphia Plan 2-03" folder); "Federal Aides Step Up Bid to Halt Job Bias at Pittsburgh, Boston: Comptroller General Reiterates Opposition to the Construction Hiring Plan Set for Philadelphia," *Wall Street Journal*, November 10, 1969; Staats interview by CBS morning news, November 10, 1969 (G Street, box 78A, folder 5, 49–52); Staats to Shultz, November 12, and Silberman to Staats, November 18, 1969 (DOL Chronological, 1969, folder 1); "Staats Advises Congress of Stand on Philadelphia Plan," *Daily Labor Report*, November 18, 1969; and Shultz to Ervin, November 28, 1969 (Nixon Garment, box 143, "Philadelphia Plan 2-03" folder).

36. *Congressional Record—Senate*, December 18, 1969, 17133; George Lardner Jr., "Senate Votes against Philadelphia Work Plan; Hands Nixon Setback in Rejecting Move to Put More Negroes in Building Jobs," *Los Angeles Times*, "Senate Upholds Ruling against Anti-Bias Plan on Construction Hiring: Setback Is Seen for Nixon in Bid to Establish Minimum Job Quotas on Federal Work," *Wall Street Journal*, December 19, 1969; Lardner, "Hill Battle Is Escalating," *Washington Post*, December 22, 1969; "Philadelphia Plan Killers" (editorial) and "Nixon Acts to Save Phila. Plan which Aids Black Workers," *Philadelphia Tribune*, December 23, 1969; Robert B. Semple Jr., "Philadelphia Plan: How White House Engineered Major Victory," *New York Times*, December 26, 1969; Graham, *Civil Rights Era*, 335–340; Anderson, *Pursuit of Fairness*, 122–124; and Golland, *Constructing Affirmative Action*, 137–138.

37. *Congressional Record—Senate*, December 18, 1969, 17131–17157; Shultz and Fletcher press conference, December 18, 1969 (Nixon Garment, box 143, "Philadelphia Plan 2-03" folder); Nixon speech, December 19, 1969 (G Street, box 107, folder 5, 868–869); Shultz press conference, White House memo, and Gerald R. Ford to House Republicans, December 20, 1969 (DOL Chronological, 1969, folder 2); David E. Rosenbaum, "Shultz Appeals to House on Jobs: Urges Defeat of a Move to Halt Philadelphia Plan," *New York Times*, December 21, 1969; Nixon speech and UPI Newswire, December 22, 1969 (DOL Chronological, 1969, folder 2); "Aid to Jim Crow" (editorial), *New York Times*, December 22, 1969; *Congressional Record—House*, December 22, 1969, 40903–40921; Semple, "Congress and Nixon: Fight Grows Sharper," *New York Times*, December 22, 1969; "Nixon Assails Rejection," unknown publication, December 22, 1969 (Nixon Garment, box 143, "Philadelphia Plan 2" folder); Lardner, "Hill Battle Is Escalating"; Bryce N. Harlow to Nixon, December 22, 1969 (Graham, *Civil Rights during the Nixon Administration*, reel 18); "Jim Crow Defeathered" (editorial), *Washington Star*, December 23, 1969; Rich, "Negro Job Ratio Plan Upheld by Congress," *Detroit News*,

December 23, 1969; Warren Weaver Jr., "Congress Avoids Tie-up on Rights, Pre-pares to Quit," and Tom Wicker, "In the Nation: Quotas, Goals, and Tricks," *New York Times*, December 23, 1969; "Congress Ends Session; Nixon Gains a Victory: Senate Drops Its Bid to Kill the Philadelphia Plan for Minority Jobs in Building," *Wall Street Journal*, December 24, 1969; Semple, "Philadelphia Plan"; "President and Congress Must Not Let Racists Kill Philadelphia Plan" (editorial), *Philadelphia Tribune*, December 27, 1969; John Herbers, "Labor and Blacks Part Company," *New York Times*, December 28, 1969; Joseph Alsop, "Nixon Minority-Hiring Plan Divides Liberal Democrats," unknown publication, January 1970 (G Street, box 77, folder 1, 37); "Congress Backs Down on Philadelphia Anti-Bias Plan," *Engineering News-Record*, January 1, 1970; "Ticker," *Jet*, January 5, 1970; William Safire, *Before the Fall: An Inside View of the Pre-Watergate White House* (Garden City, N.Y.: Doubleday, 1975), 317; and St. George, "Arthur Fletcher." The quotation is from St. George.

38. Fletcher itinerary, December 2, 1969 (G Street, box 78A, folder 4, 272–273); Fletcher to Shultz, December 8, 1969 (DOL Shultz, box 114, "PE-4-2 Fletcher, Arthur A. [Asst Secy for Wage & Labor Standards] 1969" folder); "Behind the Scenes in Washington," *Sepia*, January 1970; publisher of *Las Vegas Voice* invitation, January 1970 (G Street, box 79, folder 3, 10); Nixon to Fletcher, January 6, 1970 (G Street, box 15A, folder 2, 45–47); "Fletcher Gets Award—a Bit Late," *Washington Star*, January 8, 1970; "Assistant Labor Secretary," *Los Angeles Times*, January 8, 1970; Fletcher travel voucher, February 3, 1970 (G Street, box 79, folder 1, 160–164); Chicago and Cook County Building Trades Council and Building Construction Employers Association of Chicago agreement, January 9, 1970 (G Street, box 78B, folder 18, 354–360); Fletcher itinerary, January 10, 1970 (G Street, box 79, folder 2, 559); Republican National Committee press release, January 12, 1970 (G Street, box 39, folder 1, 81); Charles L. West to Fletcher, January 12, 1970 (G Street, box 79, folder 2, 874–875); Rogers C. B. Morton to Fletcher, January 15, 1970 (G Street, box 15A, folder 2, 43–44); National Black Newspaper Publishers Association program, January 19, 1970 (G Street, box 79, folder 4, 7–8); Fletcher itinerary, January 21, National Black Newspaper Publishers Association resolution, January 22, and Boston Urban League press release, January 22, 1970 (G Street, box 79, folder 2, 861–862, 869–871, 1256–1257); Fletcher itinerary, January 28, 1970 (G Street, box 91, folder 2, 123–124); and "Sentinel Rep Attends NNPA Black Publishers' Workshop," *Los Angeles Sentinel*, January 29, 1970. On Robert Drinan, see Mark Feeney, "Congressman-Priest Drinan Dies," *Boston Globe*, January 29, 2007; and Rick Perlstein, *The Invisible Bridge: The Fall of Nixon and the Rise of Reagan* (New York: Simon & Schuster, 2014), 264. On the falseness of the conservative "color-blindness" doctrine, see, e.g., J. Morgan Kouser, *Colorblind Injustice: Minority Voting Rights and the Undoing of the Second Reconstruction* (Chapel Hill: University of North Carolina Press, 1999), and Dennis Deslippe, *Protesting Affirmative Action: The Struggle over Equality after the Civil Rights Revolution* (Baltimore, MD: Johns Hopkins University Press, 2012).

39. George Bush to Fletcher, May 23, and Fletcher to Bush, June 26, 1969 (G Street, box 80, folder 3, 788–790); Bush to Fletcher, December 17, and Fletcher to

Bush, December 19, 1969 (G Street, box 80, folder 3, 770–771); and Fletcher itineraries, January 21, 1970 (G Street, box 79, folder 2, 861–862), and March 1970 (G Street, box 123, folder 12, 1–9). The quotation is from Bush to Fletcher, December 17, 1969.

40. UPI Newswire and Fletcher press release, December 11, 1969 (G Street, box 124, folder 1, 88 and box 134, folder 4, 532–536); "Fletcher, US Labor Aide, May Run against Jackson," *Seattle Times*, December 12, 1969; and Scates, "Director of Anti-Jackson Democratic Council Resigns," *Seattle Post-Intelligencer*, December 12, 1969.

41. Edward W. Brooke, *Bridging the Divide: My Life* (New Brunswick: Rutgers University Press, 2007), passim; Leah Wright Rigueur, *The Loneliness of the Black Republican: Pragmatic Politics and the Pursuit of Power* (Princeton, N.J.: Princeton University Press, 2015), 95–97; and Farrington, *Black Republicans*, 155.

42. Fletcher draft letter to Nixon, January 1, 1970 (G Street, box 134, folder 4, 553–555); Matryce L. Cheek and Vera J. Lincoln to Fletcher, February 20, 1970 (G Street, box 79, folder 2, 1342); Love B. Johnson to Fletcher, March 19, April 15, and October 6, 1970, Lincoln to Love B. Johnson, April 23 and May 12, 1970, and Love B. Johnson to Lincoln, May 22, 1970 (G Street, box 78A, folder 9, 212, 216–222); John Fonteno to Fletcher, April 30 and June 25, 1970, and Fletcher to Fonteno, May 15 and June 9, 1970 (G Street, box 78B, folder 18, 401–404, 406); Robert L. Garner to Fletcher, August 5, 1970 (G Street, box 78A, folder 10, 56); Lincoln to the files, August 10, 1970 (G Street, box 78B, folder 18, 405); Robert H. Maier to Fletcher, August 11 and October 8, 1970, Fletcher to William C. Spaller, August 13 and September 2, 1970, and North Texas Personnel and Industrial Relations Conference program, October 1, 1970 (G Street, box 78B, folder 20, 1–2, 4, 13–16, 24); Fletcher itinerary, August 20, 1970 (G Street, box 78A, folder 10, 53); "Job Bias Key Target, Labor Official Says," *Houston Post*, August 21, 1970; Spaller to Fletcher, October 5, 1970 (G Street, box 15A, folder 2, 192–193); and Timothy Naftali, *George H. W. Bush* (New York: Times Books, 2007), 13–14, 20–22. Scoop Jackson won reelection in 1970 with 84 percent of the vote: Perlstein, *Invisible Bridge*, 625–626.

43. Daniel P. Moynihan, *The Negro Family: The Case for National Action* (Washington, DC: Department of Labor, 1965); "The Wrong Approach" (editorial), *Chicago Sun-Times*, Daniel P. Moynihan, "'Benign Neglect' for Issue of Race?," *Wall Street Journal*, and "Looking the Other Way?," *Christian Science Monitor*, March 4, 1970; Weaver, "Nixon Aide Opposes Integration of Schools if Aim Is Only Social," *New York Times*, March 5, 1970; Fletcher to Nixon, March 5, 1970 (G Street, box 80, folder 1, 193–196); Don Oberdorfer, "Moynihan's Colorful Ways Make Him Conspicuous Target," *Washington Post*, March 5, 1970; "Washington: For the Record," *Washington Post*, "Minor Memos," *Wall Street Journal*, "Text of Statement by Rights Groups and Individuals on Moynihan's Comments," *New York Times*, and Linda Charlton, "21 Rights Leaders Rebut Moynihan: Call 'Benign Neglect' Policy 'Symptomatic of Effort to Wipe Out Gains,'" *New York Times*, March 6, 1970; "US Policy on Rights Assailed," *Washington Post*, and Delaney, "Black Aides Prod Nixon on Rights: At Meeting, They Urge Him to Take Stronger Action," *New York Times*, March 7, 1970; "Key Men in the Segregation Dispute," "Is 'Benign Neglect' the

Real Nixon Approach?," "Labor: It Wants a Little More 'Neglect,'" and "Integration: A Vocally Pessimistic White House," *New York Times,* March 8, 1970; RNC newsletter, March 9, 1970 (G Street, box 80, folder 1, 160–161; "The Moynihan Memos" (editorial), "Text of a Pre-Inauguration Memo from Moynihan on Problems Nixon Would Face," and E. W. Kentworthy, "'69 Moynihan Memo to President Urged Jobs for Negroes," *New York Times,* March 11, 1970; "Moynihan's Memos: The Political Danger of Thinking," *New York Times,* March 15, 1970; David S. Broder, "Memos of Moynihan and Dent Show Nixon Crew's Thinking," *Washington Post,* and Mary McGrory, "Despair and Hope on Integration," *Washington Star,* March 17, 1970; and Dan Baum, "Legalize It All: How to Win the War on Drugs," *Harper's,* May 9, 2016. Panetta became a Democrat and went on to a long career in government and academia, culminating in a stint as defense secretary in the Obama administration; Moynihan, always a Democrat, spent three decades as a US senator from New York.

44. Rowland Evans and Robert Novak, "GOP Turns Down a 1970 Brochure Showing Blacks Appointed by Nixon," *Washington Post,* March 20, 1970; "Equal Rights Still a Myth," *Washington Post,* April 23, 1970; and "NAACP Chief Labels Nixon Hostile to Negro," *Washington Star,* June 30, 1970. Rigueur has pointed to this photograph as evidence of a Council of Black Appointees, which she labels a Nixon "Black Cabinet," an overstatement in my view; *Loneliness of the Black Republican,* figure 10 after p. 135.

45. Riesel, "Labor Man of the Year: President Nixon's Labor Deacon Gets Free Hand in Toughest Crises Coming" column, January 16, 1970 (G Street, box 13, folder 2, 494–496); Hodgson bio, n.d. [June 1970], and Vera J. Lincoln to Fletcher, June 10, 1970 (G Street, box 79, folder 2, 208–209, 1122–1123); Bernard D. Nossiter, "Hodgson Stresses Jobs for Blacks," *Washington Post,* June 11, 1970; Fletcher to James T. Hemphill, June 26, 1970 (G Street, box 79, folder 1, 58); Graham, *Civil Rights Era,* 344–345; and Golland, *Constructing Affirmative Action,* 153.

46. Leonard H. Carter to Shultz, June 11, 1970 (DOL Shultz, box 204, "PE-4-2 Fletcher, Arthur A. [Asst Secy for Wage & Labor Standards] 1970" folder); Republican Congressional Candidates to Nixon, June 11, 1970 (G Street, box 123, folder 25, 64–95); A. Price Woodard Jr. to Ehrlichman, June 12, 1970, C. J. Patterson to Shultz, June 13, 1970, Dolores McClarity to Shultz, June 13, 1970, and Ehrlichman to Woodard, June 15, 1970 (DOL Shultz, box 204, "PE-4-2 Fletcher, Arthur A. [Asst Secy for Wage & Labor Standards] 1970" folder); "York Man Named Under Secretary [*sic*]," *Philadelphia Bulletin,* June 19, 1970; "2 Blacks Reported Quitting Administration," *Los Angeles Times,* July 28, 1970; Scates, "Possible Nixon Bid Interests Fletcher," *Seattle Post-Intelligencer,* July 29, 1970; "Washington," *American Labor,* September 1970; Robert C. Maynard, "Six Top Black Officials Defend Nixon's Record," *Washington Post,* July 26, 1971; Stanley S. Scott to Garment, August 2, 1971 (Nixon Garment, box 142, "Philadelphia Plan 1" folder); and Rigueur, *Loneliness of the Black Republican,* 213.

47. Charles W. Colson to Peter Brennan, n.d. [April 1970] (Nixon White House Subject Files SMOF Colson SF [hereafter Nixon Colson] box 95, "New York City, Workers Building Construction Council" folder); Homer Bigart, "War Foes Here

Attacked by Construction Workers; City Hall Is Stormed," *New York Times*, May 9, 1970; Tom Charles Huston to Ehrlichman, May 12, 1970, White House press conference, May 26, 1970, and Colson to Nixon, May 26, 1970 (Nixon Colson box 95, "New York City, Workers Building Construction Council" folder); "Being Patriotic" (editorial), *New York Amsterdam News*, June 6, 1970; Gertrude Wilson, "Brown Shirts—Hard Hats," *New York Amsterdam News*, June 20, 1970; Colson to Nixon, September 12, 1970 (Nixon Colson box 95, "New York City, Workers Building Construction Council" folder); "Nixon and the Bums" (editorial), *Scanlan's Magazine*, September 1970; Riesel, "Soft on Hard Hats? Nixon Rejects Advisers Urging Him to Declare War on Labor," December 7, 1970 (Nixon Colson box 73, "Riesel" folder); Joshua B. Freeman, "Hardhats: Construction Workers, Manliness, and the 1970 Pro-War Demonstrations," *Journal of Social History* 26, no. 4 (1993): 725–744; Jefferson R. Cowie, "Nixon's Class Struggle: Romancing the New Right Worker, 1969–1973," *Labor History* 43, no. 3 (2002): 257–283; and Golland, *Constructing Affirmative Action*, 148–151.

48. "Excerpts from Speech by NAACP Head Calling Administration Anti-Negro," Earl Caldwell, "NAACP's Head Brands Administration Anti-Negro," *New York Times*, and "NAACP Chief Labels Nixon Hostile to Negro," *Washington Star*, June 30, 1970; UPI Newswire, June 30, 1970 (G Street, box 79, folder 2, 166); Herbert Hill speech, June 30, 1970 (NAACP series 6, box A03, "Speeches" folder); "Black Leader Charges US Gives In to Labor," *Washington Star*, n.d. [July 1970] (G Street, box 79, folder 2, 163); and Karen Heller, "NAACP Says Nixon Junks Hiring Plan," *Washington Post*, and "Construction Shut," *Philadelphia Inquirer*, July 1, 1970.

49. Heller, "Top Nixon Aide Denies Any 'Sellout' to Unions," unknown publication, n.d. [July 1970], and Martie Kazura, "Asst. Labor Secretary Fighting Many Battles," *Cincinnati Post and Times-Star*, n.d. [July 1970] (G Street, box 79, folder 1, 62–63); "Text of White House Telegram replying to NAACP Head's Criticism of Administration as Anti-Negro" and Jack Rosenthal, "NAACP Charge Called Unfair by the White House," *New York Times*, July 1, 1970; John Russell, "NAACP Charges Rebutted: Administration Calls Charge 'Disheartening,'" *Cincinnati Post and Times-Star*, July 1, 1970; Terry Adamson, "Union Bids Deal Denied by Wilks," *Atlanta Constitution*, July 1, 1970; James L. Adams, "NAACP Answered: Pro-Nixon Blacks Tell of Job Administration's Doing," *Cincinnati Post*, July 2, 1970; and Clarence L. Townes to Fletcher, July 6, 1970 (G Street, box 79, folder 2, 158).

50. William H. Whyte Jr., *The Organization Man* (New York: Touchstone Books, 1972), passim. Fletcher didn't get in any trouble with his bosses at Labor or in the White House for letting the "quota" comment slip, but it was part and parcel of an unpolished political persona that his enemies would later use against him.

51. "Fletcher Wows Urban League Audience Here," *St. Louis Sentinel*, May 30, 1970; Fletcher, "A National Goal for the Decade of the Seventies: Establishing Economic Justice (The Means to an Open Society)," speech, n.d. [June 1970] (Nixon Garment, box 88, "Fletcher, Arthur [Asst Secy of Labor] CFOA 6320" folder); Fletcher to Garment, July 7, 1970 (G Street, box 76, folder 7, 710–711); "End of Job Bias in Decade Seen by Top Nixon Aide," *Pittsburgh Press*, August 24, 1970; Scates,

"Fletcher Awaits All-out Black Parity Drive," *Seattle Post-Intelligencer,* December 11, 1970; Nixon and Colson, telephone conversation, May 7, 1971 (Nixon White House Tapes series 1, index no. 2-121); and Perlstein, *Nixonland,* 467–468, 546, 607–634.

52. Ehrlichman to "D.C.," November 20, 1968, and John McLaughry to Ehrlichman, December 17, 1968 (Nixon Returned Files, box 18, folder 10, 58, and folder 12, 40); White House Social Secretary to Arthur and Bernyce Fletcher, October 21, 1970 (G Street, box 6, folder 1, 654); Semple, "Philadelphia Plan"; White House Social Secretary to Arthur and Bernyce Fletcher, August 29, and Richard and Pat Nixon to Arthur and Bernyce Fletcher, September 7, 1970 (G Street, box 6, folder 1, 639–642, 669–670); and Victor Riesel, "'Moment of Truth' for Unions," *Las Vegas Sun,* October 5, 1970.

53. See, e.g., White House press releases, May 14, November 3, and December 15, 1969, March 10, April 20 and 30, June 3, July 3, 7, and 31, 1970, and August 15, September 23, and October 7, 1971 (G Street, box 21, folder 2, 442–445, 458–470, 481–496, 706–759, 781–789).

54. Chicago and Cook County Building Trades Council and Building Construction Employers Association of Chicago agreement, January 9, 1970 (G Street, box 78B, folder 18, 354–360); Cornelius J. Haggerty to Thomas J. Murray, January 13, 1970 (Meany RG1-038 box 107, folder 9); Fletcher to Shultz, January 14, 1970 (DOL Shultz, box 164, "AD-7-3 Weekly Reports to the Secretary, 1970 [January]" folder); Wilks proposal, January 14, 1970 (G Street, box 78A, folder 9, 95–140); Meany to Haggerty, January 14, 1970 (Meany RG1-038 box 107, folder 9); AFL-CIO press release, January 15, 1970 (Meany RG21-001 box 6, folder 20); "Chicago Minorities Pact Hailed as Pattern-Setter," *AFL-CIO News,* January 17, 1970; Tom Wicker, "In the Nation: Philadelphia, Chicago and Meany," *New York Times,* January 18, 1970; "Now the Chicago Plan" (editorial), *Rocky Mountain News,* January 24, 1970; John Herling's Labor Letter, January 24, and DOL press release, January 26, 1970 (Meany RG 21-001 box 6, folder 20); Garment to Patrick J. Buchanan, January 28, 1970 (Nixon Garment, box 142, "Philadelphia Plan 1" folder); Spark Matsanuga to Haggerty, February 2, 1970, and Henry B. Gonzalez to Andrew J. Biemiller, February 4, 1970 (Meany RG 21-001 box 6, folder 20); Meany, "To End Job Bias," letter to the editor, *New York Times,* February 7, 1970; "Labor Leader Displeased," *New York Times,* February 10, 1970; Wilks to Heads of All Agencies, February 11, 1970 (G Street, box 13, folder 2, 303–304); "Minority Job Plans Pushed by Labor Dept." and "Key to Results: 'Real Opportunities' Credited to Labor-Backed Chicago Plan," *AFL-CIO News,* February 14, 1970; "Chicago Plan Is Fairer" (editorial), *Alhambra Post-Gazette,* February 18, 1970; "Philadelphia Scrapple," *San Pedro News-Pilot,* February 20, 1970, reprinted in *Elgin Courier-News,* February 23, 1970; "Asks Nixon for 'Philly Plan' for Jobs in Buffalo," *Jet,* March 5, 1970; Richard F. Schubert to Hodgson, March 19, 1970 (DOL Hodgson Undersecretary, box 14, "Philadelphia Plan" folder); Colson to Nixon, March 23, 1970 (Nixon Colson box 20, "BT 32370" folder); Fletcher to Shultz, April 1, 1970 (DOL Shultz, box 163, "AD-7-3 Weekly Reports to the Secretary, 1970 [April]" folder); Atlanta Building Trades Council Affirmative Action Program," April 9, 1970, and Robert McGlotten to Don Slaiman, April 13, 1970 (Meany RG21-001 box 6, folder 20); Hodgson Senate testimony, n.d.

[May 1970] (G Street, box 79, folder 2, 228–240); "Labor Dept. Approves Grant to 'Chicago Plan,'" *AFL-CIO News*, May 16, 1970; Herbert Hill speech, June 30, 1970; Byron E. Calame, "Labor Department Setting Up Unit to Spur Local Solutions to Construction Job Bias," *Wall Street Journal*, July 6, 1970; "Hodgson Issues Job Bias Warning," *Washington Post*, July 10, 1970; "Minority Hiring in Construction in 2 Cities," *New York Amsterdam News*, July 11, 1970; and "In 3 More Cities: Trades Sign Pacts on Minority Jobs," *AFL-CIO News*, July 11, 1970.

55. Herbert R. Northrup proposal, February 22, 1971 (G Street, box 78A, folder 7, 37–49); "White House Plans Offensive on Job Bias in Construction Trades Until '72 Election," *Wall Street Journal*, May 6, 1971; Diana Perry, "Art Fletcher Needs Black Support—Now!," *Pittsburgh Courier*, May 13, 1971; William B. Gould, "Blacks and the General Lockout: In Spite of the Various Plans Put Forward in the Trades, Minorities Are Still Blocked," *New York Times*, July 17, 1971; Richard L. Rowan and Lester Rubin, *Opening the Skilled Construction Trades to Blacks: A Study of the Washington and Indianapolis Plans for Minority Employment* (Philadelphia: University of Pennsylvania Press, 1972); and Northrup to Fletcher, January 5, 1972 (G Street, box 77, folder 2, 842).

56. Jesse Jackson to Fletcher, June 10, 1970 (G Street, box 78A, folder 10, 208–209); Jesse Jackson and David M. Wallace press release and Operation Breadbasket press release, July 9, Operation Breadbasket pictures and press release, July 11, and Fletcher itinerary, July 11, 1970 (G Street, box 78A, folder 10, 9–32, 210).

57. Marshall Frady, *Jesse: The Life and Pilgrimage of Jesse Jackson* (New York: Simon & Schuster, 1996); Rigueur, *Loneliness of the Black Republican*, 9–10, 134, 185, 261, 271, 273, 276, 281; and Paul Fletcher, conversations with the author.

58. "NNPA Convention Highlights," *Arizona Tribune*, July 2, 1970; Operation Breadbasket pictures and press release; and "Top US Official to Probe Chicago Plan," *Chicago Defender*, July 18, 1970.

59. "Building Firms, Unions in Minority-Training Accord in New York: Plan Billed as Alternative to the Philadelphia Plan; Pilot Project in Operation," *Wall Street Journal*, March 23, 1970; "New York Plan" (editorial) and "New York Plan Gets Knocked," *New York Amsterdam News*, March 28, 1970; "New York Plan Keyed to Minority Training," *AFL-CIO News*, March 28, 1970; Peter J. Brennan to Meany, August 10, and Meany to Brennan, August 14, 1970 (Meany RG1-038 box 130, folder 4); Thomas Ronan, "Construction Men Sign Trainee Pact," *New York Times*, December 11, 1970; "The Plan Stinks" (editorial), "NYC vs. Philly," and Simon Anekwe, "NY Plan Called 'Disgrace,'" *New York Amsterdam News*, January 2, 1971; Anekwe, "Slip NY Plan into Law: Unannounced, Unpublicized" and "NALC Hits NYC Plan," *New York Amsterdam News*, January 30, 1971; Colson to Hodgson, February 2, 1971 (Nixon Colson box 95, "NYC-WBCC" folder); and Golland, *Constructing Affirmative Action*, 150–151, 153–154.

60. Fletcher to Evans, January 7, 1970 (G Street, box 80, folder 1, 279); Fletcher to St. Laurent, January 20, 1970 (G Street, box 80, folder 1, 270); Staples, "Minority Hiring: Philadelphia Plan May Be Imposed Here" and "Seattle One of Six Priority Cities for Philadelphia Plan," *Seattle Times*, February 9, 1970; "US May Impose Hiring Plan" and "Seattle Given Ultimatum on Job Plans," *Seattle Post-*

Intelligencer, February 10, 1970; Brock Adams to Shultz, February 14, 1970 (G Street, box 80, folder 1, 416–418); US District Court, Western District of Washington, Northern Division proceedings, February 17, 1970 (G Street, box 13, folder 2, 689–702); Maynard Sundt to Ehrlichman, February 19, 1970 (G Street, box 78A, folder 4, 215); "Fleming Hits Adams Statement on Hiring," unknown publication, n.d. [March 1970] (G Street, box 78A, folder 4, 213); Hullin to Fletcher, March 4, 1970 (G Street, box 78A, folder 4, 214); Eugene R. Nielson to Fletcher, April 2, 1970 (G Street, box 79, folder 2, 1227); James F. Warren to Fletcher, April 22, Fletcher itinerary, April 23, and Vera J. Lincoln to Fletcher, April 24, 1970 (G Street, box 79, folder 2, 1222, 1461–1462, 1490); Fletcher to Shultz, April 29, 1970 (DOL Shultz, box 163, "AD-7-3 Weekly Reports to the Secretary, 1970 [April]" folder); George Jackson to Fletcher, May 5, 1970 (G Street, box 13, folder 2, 688); Fletcher itinerary, May 21, 1970 (G Street, box 79, folder 2, 518–519); "Seattle Job Edict," *Washington Post,* June 18, 1970; DOL Kansas City Regional Staff Committee meeting minutes, June 29, 1970 (G Street, box 78A, folder 10, 233–235); Fletcher travel voucher, July 1970 (G Street, box 79, folder 5, 13–15); Andrew Rollins Jr. to Fletcher, July 9, 1970 (G Street, box 78A, folder 10, 236); Blumrosen to Fletcher, July 19, 1970 (G Street, box 76, folder 7, 675–680); Malcolm R. Lovell to Warren Magnuson, July 29, 1970 (G Street, box 80, folder 1, 385); Fletcher itinerary, August 1970 (G Street, box 124, folder 29, 4–12); St. Laurent testimony, August 14, 1970 (G Street, box 13, folder 2, 651–657); General and Specialty Contractors Association and Kansas City Civil Rights Groups agreement, August 20, and Ilus W. Davis to Fletcher, August 25, 1970 (G Street, box 78B, folder 20, 248–255, 306–312); Fletcher itinerary, August 30, and DOL report, August 31, 1970 (G Street, box 78A, folder 11, 5–18, 49–52); "HEW Freezes Local Building Funds: Crafts Not Complying with Plan; Penn Valley Building One of 3 Held Up," *Kansas City Call,* November 26, 1970; Joe Lastelic, "Agencies to Confer in HEW Freeze," *Kansas City Star,* December 2, 1970; Fletcher itinerary, December 3, 1970 (G Street, box 78B, folder 21, 226); and "Minorities . . . All Building Crafts Agree on Work Plan," *Kansas City Labor Beacon,* December 11, 1970.

61. Elliott Carlson, "A Slow Start: The Philadelphia Plan to Integrate Unions Called Failure by Some; Hiring Goals Still Not Met; Blacks Shifted among Jobs to Fool US Inspectors; But Backers See Potential," *Wall Street Journal,* December 3, 1970; Robert B. Brauer to Wilks, n.d. [January 1971] (G Street, box 78A, folder 7, 121–133); US Court of Appeals, 3rd Circuit opinion, April 22, 1971 (G Street, box 78A, folder 6, 138–168); and Golland, *Constructing Affirmative Action,* 159–165.

62. Scates, "Possible Nixon Bid Interests Fletcher," *Seattle Post-Intelligencer,* July 29, 1970; *Face the Nation* transcript, August 23, 1970 (G Street, box 78A, folder 9, 191–210); "Washington," *American Labor,* September 1970; Fletcher itinerary, September 9, 1970 (G Street, box 78B, folder 18, 298); Vernon R. Schreiber to Fletcher, September 18, 1970 (G Street, box 15A, folder 2, 53); Fletcher itineraries, September 26 and 28, October 3, 5, 7, 10, 13, 16, 18, 21, and 25, November 2, 8, 19, and 21, and December 3, 6, and 14, 1970 (G Street, box 13, folder 2, 176; box 77, folder 2, 298–300; box 78A, folder 9, 225; box 78B, folder 18, 104, 120, 150, 154, 165, 408–409, 425, folder 20, 97, 110, and folder 21, 132–134, 226, 234; and box

124, folder 42, 2–4); Robert J. Dole to Fletcher, February 26, 1971 (G Street, box 77, folder 2, 726); Bob Oberdorfer, "Dole Urges Black Aide for President," *Washington Post*, March 17, 1971; and Rigueur, *Loneliness of the Black Republican*, 169. The quotations are from Republican National Committee meeting transcript, July 22, 1971 (Records of the RNC).

63. "Unity," *Ohio Contractor*, February 1971; Colson to Chapin, February 25, 1971 (Nixon Colson box 95, "NYC-WBCC" folder); Harold R. Latimer to Nixon, February 25, and Jesse E. Howard to Nixon, February 26, 1971 (Nixon WHCF SF BE box 42, "GEN BE 4-2 Construction [3 of 5]" folder); Fletcher speech, March 5, 1971 (G Street, box 77, folder 2, 501–530), and March 12, 1971 (DOL Hodgson Secretary, box 147, "PE-4-2 Fletcher, Arthur A. [Asst Secy for Wage & Labor Standards] 1971" folder); "Administration Works on a Plan to Stabilize Wages," *Engineering News-Record*, March 18, 1971; C. Edward Walters to Nixon, March 31, and Fletcher to Andrew E. Dunn, May 4, 1971 (Nixon WHCF SF BE box 42, "GEN BE 4-2 Construction [3 of 5]" folder).

64. Ed S. Miller to Fletcher, November 6, 1969 (G Street, box 78B, folder 6, 1–2); Bob Ferguson, "Federal Labor Official Crosses Union Picket Line at Hotel Here," *Arkansas Democrat*, March 11, 1970; Jimmy Jones, "WR, US Official Cross Picket Line Outside LR Hotel," *Arkansas Gazette*, March 12, 1970; Fletcher interview with Robert Wright, January 21, 1971 (NIDS #3.178.222, Moorland-Spingarn Library, Howard University, Washington, DC); and Fletcher speech, March 12, 1971.

65. Herling, "Fox and Chickens," unknown publication, March 16, 1971 (G Street, box 154, folder 1, image 56); Edward J. Carlough to Nixon, March 23, 1971 (DOL Hodgson Secretary, box 147, "PE-4-2 Fletcher, Arthur A. [Asst Secy for Wage & Labor Standards] 1971" folder); Neal Gilbride, "Union Asks Firing of US Aide," *Washington Post*; "Union Chief Asks Nixon to Fire Labor Official," *Philadelphia Bulletin*; and "Union Leader Urges Labor Aide's Ouster," *New York Times*, April 5, 1971; Donald F. Rodgers to Henry C. Cashen II, April 5, 1971 (Nixon Colson box 69, "Hardhats" folder).

66. Riesel, "New Civil War: Labor Leader with 307 Blacks among His 140,000 Members Calls Black Official 'Gutter' Speaker," April 6, 1971 (G Street, box 13, folder 2, 486–487); Hodgson to Carlough, April 26, 1971 (DOL Hodgson Secretary, box 147, "PE-4-2 Fletcher, Arthur A. [Asst Secy for Wage & Labor Standards] 1971" folder); and Fletcher to Riesel, May 18, 1971 (G Street, box 13, folder 2, 476–481).

67. Colson to H. R. Haldeman, April 7, 1971 (Nixon Colson box 62, "Arthur Fletcher" folder); Perlstein, *Invisible Bridge*, 75–76, 97.

68. Haldeman to Colson, May 11, 1971 (Nixon Colson box 62, "Arthur Fletcher" folder).

69. "White House Plans Offensive on Job Bias in Construction Trades Until '72 Election," *Wall Street Journal*, May 6, 1971.

70. Colson to Haldeman, April 30, 1971 (Nixon Colson box 62, "Arthur Fletcher" folder); Colson to Ehrlichman, May 5, 1971 (Nixon Colson box 69, "Hardhats" folder); Colson to Haldeman, May 6, 1971 (Nixon Colson box 65, "Fletcher" folder); Nixon and Colson telephone conversation, May 7, 1971; and Colson to Ehrlichman, May 14, 1971 (Nixon Colson box 40, "BCT" folder).

71. Nixon and Colson telephone conversation, May 7, 1971. Bill Safire wrote that Colson said "Every speech by Art Fletcher sends Meany up the wall." *Before the Fall*, 585.

72. Nixon and Meany Oval Office conversation, May 7, 1971 (Nixon White House Tapes series 4–5, index 495-21).

73. "Official Sees Racist Ruse in Marches Backing Nixon," *St. Louis Post-Dispatch*, May 27, 1970; Colson to Fred Malek, May 27, Colson to Ken Cole, June 4, Colson to Ehrlichman, June 7, and Colson to Ehrlichman, June 9, 1971 (Nixon Colson box 62, "Arthur Fletcher" folder).

74. Fletcher speech, and UPI Newswire, September 15, 1971; Colson to Ron Ziegler and Stanley Scott to Colson, September 16, 1971 (Nixon Colson box 62, "Arthur Fletcher" folder); and Arnold R. Isaacs, "Negro Nixon Appointee Assails Muskie," *Baltimore Sun*, September 16, 1971. For more on Muskie's campaign for the 1972 Democratic nomination, see Theodore H. White, *The Making of the President, 1972* (New York: Atheneum House, 1973); for more on the prison rebellion at Attica, see Heather Ann Thompson, *Blood in the Water: The Attica Prison Uprising and Its Legacy* (Pantheon, 2016).

75. Nixon, Colson, and Brennan, Oval Office conversation, July 2, 1971 (Nixon White House Tapes series 1, index 535-5).

76. Nixon and Colson telephone conversation, July 2, 1971 (Nixon White House Tapes series 1, index 6-93).

77. Bush to Fletcher, August 20, 1971 (G Street, box 151, folder 1, 305); Garnett D. Horner, "Nixon Naming Labor Aide to UN Staff," *Washington Evening Star*, August 27, 1971; "Pasco Man Eyes UN Post," *Spokane Spokesman-Review*, August 27, 1971; Earl J. Davenport to Fletcher, August 27, 1971 (G Street, box 79, folder 2, 390); "UN Post Expected for High Nixon Black," *Philadelphia Bulletin*, August 27, 1971; White House press release, September 9, 1971 (G Street, box 154, folder 1, image 127); "Nixon Names Delegation to UN Session," *Washington Star*, and "Labor Unit's Fletcher Named Alternate Delegate to UN," *Wall Street Journal*, September 10, 1971; Fletcher to Nixon, September 10, 1971 (DOL Hodgson Secretary, box 147, "PE-4-2 Fletcher, Arthur A. [Asst Secy for Wage & Labor Standards] 1971" folder); Fletcher to Davenport, September 11, 1971 (G Street, box 79, folder 1, 128); Stanley Scott to members of the press, September 15, 1971 (Nixon Colson box 62, "Arthur Fletcher" folder); Dole to Fletcher, September 22, W. J. Trent Jr. to Fletcher, December 1, and Margie Braden to Fletcher, December 6, 1971 (G Street, box 77, folder 1, 121, 124, 126–128).

78. Vera J. Lincoln to Fletcher, February 20, 1970 (G Street, box 79, folder 2, 1342); John E. Burnett to Herbert Hill, June 8, 1970 (NAACP series 6, box G3, "1970, 2" folder); Milton Viorst, "Judging Deeds and Not the Words," *Washington Evening Star*, July 30, 1970; Herbert Hill press statement, September 7, 1970 (NAACP series 6, box G10, "Labor, Herbert Hill, Speeches and Testimonies" folder); Roger Rosenblum, "Trades Failing Minorities, US Labor Official Says," *St. Paul Pioneer Press*, July 21, 1971; Garnett D. Horner, "Nixon Naming Labor Aide to UN Staff"; and Fletcher interview by Washburn University, tape 1, transcript, 196.

79. "Official Sees Racist Ruse"; "Nixon and the Bums"; Victor Riesel, "Soft

on Hard Hats? Nixon Rejects Advisers Urging Him to Declare War on Labor," column, December 7, 1970 (Nixon Colson box 73, "Riesel" folder); Nixon and Meany, Oval Office conversation, May 7, 1971; Anderson, *Pursuit of Fairness*, 138; and Trevor Griffey, "'The Blacks Should Not Be Administering the Philadelphia Plan': Nixon, the Hard Hats, and 'Voluntary' Affirmative Action," in *Black Power at Work: Community Control, Affirmative Action, and the Construction Industry*, ed. David Goldberg and Trevor Griffey (Ithaca, N.Y.: Cornell University Press, 2010), 142, 152–156.

80. Nixon and Colson telephone conversation, July 2, 1971; Wilks to Brennan, August 11, 1971 (G Street, box 78A, folder 4, 117–119); Willie Hamilton, "Labor Dept. OKs 'Racist' Work Plan," unknown publication, August 23, 1971 (G Street, box 78B, folder 21, 87); James Strong, "US Delaying on Racial Quota Edict for Chicago Contractors," *Chicago Tribune*, August 30, 1971; "Contractor Race Quotas Delayed Here," unknown publication, n.d. [September 1971] (G Street, box 121, folder 1, 138); "Nixonites Seek a Replacement for Art Fletcher"; Nixon and Ehrlichman, Oval Office conversation, October 13, 1971 (Nixon White House Tapes series 2, index 590-3); Chuck Colson to Fred Malek, December 7, 1971 (Nixon Colson box 62, "Arthur Fletcher" folder); "US Department of Labor Annual Report" (Washington, DC: Department of Labor Publications, 1972); Monroe Anderson, "Big Wheel at Chrysler: Lowell W. Perry Manages Huge Detroit Universal Division for Automaker," *Ebony*, April 1974; Trevor Griffey, "Blacks Should Not Be Administering the Philadelphia Plan," 156; Richard Grunewald obituary, Legacy.com, http://www.legacy.com/; and "African Americans in Pro Football: Pioneers, Milestones, and Firsts," Pro Football Hall of Fame, http://www.profootballhof.com/. Lowell Perry went on to chair the EEOC under fellow Michigan football alumnus Gerald Ford.

81. Mary C. Brennan, *Turning Right in the Sixties: The Conservative Capture of the GOP* (Chapel Hill: University of North Carolina Press, 1995), passim; Naftali, *George H. W. Bush*, 5–11; Christopher Manning, *William L. Dawson and the Limits of Black Electoral Leadership* (Dekalb: Northern Illinois University Press, 2009), 64–65; Golland, *Constructing Affirmative Action*, 13; Bowen, *Roots of Modern Conservatism*, passim; Thurber, *Republicans and Race*, passim; Geoffrey Kabaservice, *Rule and Ruin: The Downfall of Moderation and the Destruction of the Republican Party* (New York: Oxford, 2012), passim; and Robert J. Dole interview by and in possession of the author, December 5, 2014.

82. Perlstein, *Nixonland*, passim; Cowie, "Nixon's Class Struggle."

83. Whyte, *Organization Man*, passim.

CHAPTER 5. ROLLER COASTER, 1971–1979
1. White House press release, September 9, 1971 (G Street, box 154, folder 1, image 127).

2. George Bush to Arthur Fletcher, August 20, 1971 (G Street, box 151, folder 4, image 3031); United States Mission to the United Nations press release, November 3, 1971 (G Street, box 134, folder 4, 486–493); United States Mission to the United Nations press releases, October 24 and 25, 1971 (G Street, box 15A, folder 2, 1298–1333 and box 134, folder 4, 494–505); Fletcher speech, October 26, 1971 (G Street,

box 95, folder 4, 22–34); William P. Rogers to Fletcher, January 4, 1972 (G Street, box 76, folder 7, 460); Arthur Fletcher interview by Washburn University, tape 2a, transcript, 63–64; and Jim McGrath on behalf of George Bush, correspondence with and in possession of the author, February 2, 2015.

3. Bernyce Fletcher to Kathy Sheppard [Keolker], November 1, 1971 (Keolker correspondence in possession of the author); John Benjamin to Fletcher, n.d. [November 1971] (G Street, box 134, folder 3, 129); and Fletcher interview by Washburn University, tape 2a, transcript, 64–65, 70–73, 79. The quotations are from the Washburn interview.

4. Offered other positions and highly regarded within the administration: Thomas A. Johnson, "Nixon Official Will Be Head of United Negro College Fund," *New York Times,* December 2, 1971; Good political property: Nixon and Colson telephone conversation, July 2, 1971 (Nixon White House Tapes series 1, index 6-93).

5. Remarks of Whitney Young at the March on Washington, August 28, 1963 (NAACP series 3, box A227, "March on Washington Speeches and Statements" folder); "Whitney Young Jr. Dies on Visit to Lagos," *New York Times,* March 12, 1971. For more on the march, see Taylor Branch, *Parting the Waters: America in the King Years, 1954–1963* (New York: Simon & Schuster, 1988); Patrick Henry Bass, *Like a Mighty Stream: The March on Washington, August 28, 1963* (Philadelphia: Running Press, 2002); and Doak, *March on Washington.*

6. Thomas A. Johnson, "No Big Shift Expected in the Urban League," *New York Times,* March 13, 1971; "Man with a Mission," *New York Times,* June 20, 1971; Fletcher to Ehrlichman, n.d. [November 1971] (G Street, box 129, folder 1, 48–53); Johnson, "Nixon Official," *New York Times,* December 2, 1971.

7. Brock Adams to Shultz, February 14, 1970 (G Street, box 80, folder 1, 416–418); "Fleming Hits Adams Statement on Hiring," unknown publication, n.d. [March 1970] (G Street, box 78A, folder 4, 213; "Negro Official Hints Candidacy," *Washington Post,* July 25, 1971; "Fletcher Keeps His Political Future Open," unknown publication, n.d. [December 1971] (G Street, box 77, folder 1, 125); and "Fletcher Quits UN for Negro Fund," *Washington Post,* December 2, 1971.

8. Donald Finley, "Black President Possible in this Century—Fletcher; Primary Campaigns Considered," *Seattle Post-Intelligencer,* December 6, 1971.

9. Fletcher to Nixon, November 16, 1971 (G Street, box 123, folder no. 1, 218–219); Morris B. Abram to member college presidents, and Fletcher to Nixon, November 30, 1971 (G Street, box 76, folder 7, 472, 490–491); Fletcher, "Statement Before the United Negro College Fund Board of Directors Meeting," November 30, 1971, and "Statement by Arthur A. Fletcher, Executive Director, United Negro College Fund, News Conference," December 1, 1971 (Records of the United Negro College Fund, RG3 fiche 1740); UNCF press release, December 1, 1971 (G Street, box 76, folder 7, 465–467); Abram speech, December 1, 1971 (G Street, box 80, folder 3, 541–543); Thomas A. Johnson, "Nixon Official Will Be Head of United Negro College Fund," *New York Times,* December 2, 1971; Pearl Atkinson to Chase Manhattan Bank, January 26, 1972 (G Street, box 76, folder 1, 241); and UNCF-NUL exhibition program, June 21, 1972 (UNCF RG4 fiche 2546).

10. Stanley Scott to Fletcher, December 1971 (G Street, box 134, folder no. 4,

image 280); Ken Cole to Rose Woods, December 6, 1971 (Records of President Richard M. Nixon, Returned File box 17, folder no. 2); UNCF press release, January 10, 1972 (UNCF RG4 fiche 2657). The amount of Nixon's contribution was not disclosed, and there is no public record of it. Stanley Scott survived Nixon's resignation and remained in the White House until he was replaced by Fletcher in 1976.

11. Fletcher, "Speech at Morris Brown College," January 1972 (UNCF RG3 fiche 1740); UNCF press releases, January 10, 1972 (UNCF RG3 fiches 1581 and 1740, RG4 fiches 2545 and 2657).

12. Robert P. Keim to Vernon Jordan, November 18, and Jordan to Keim, November 24, 1971 (G Street, box 76, folder 7, 479–481); Edward Ney to Fletcher, December 3, 1971 (G Street, box 76, folder 1, 245–246); UNCF staff meeting minutes, January 18, 1972 (G Street, box 91, folder 2, 141–143); UNCF press releases, March 13 and 20, 1972 (UNCF RG4 fiche 2657); Fletcher, "Speech at the United Negro College Fund 50th Anniversary," March 1, 1994 (G Street, box 116, folder 2, 216–220); Marybeth Gasman, *Envisioning Black Colleges: A History of the United Negro College Fund* (Baltimore, MD: Johns Hopkins University Press, 2007), 169–170; and "Young & Rubicam Honored for 'A Mind Is a Terrible Thing to Waste'" (press release), MarketWired, March 4, 2011, http://www.marketwired.com/press-release/young-rubicam-honored-for-a-mind-is-a-terrible-thing-to-waste-by-uncf-1406451.htm. The quotation is from Fletcher interview by Washburn University, tape 2a, transcript, 74–83. Gasman has a somewhat different interpretation of the origins of the phrase. She notes correctly that the slogan resulted from meetings between UNCF officials, Young & Rubicam, and the Ad Council, and Jordan's energetic courting of these external entities. However, she incorrectly places the launch in 1971.

13. National Urban Coalition Steering Committee meeting minutes, January 26, 1972 (G Street, box 123, folder 34, 161–168); Theodore Brunson to Fletcher, May 19, Fletcher to Brunson, May 30, and Pearl Atkinson to Evelyn D'Martino, September 28, 1972 (G Street, box 76, folder 1, 217–221, 256); Fletcher draft to Abram, n.d. [April 1973] (G Street, box 151, folder 4, 24–41).

14. UNCF press releases, January 10, March 9, March 13, March 20, and June 10, 1972 (UNCF RG3 fiche 1740 and RG4 fiche 2657); Fletcher, "Speech at the United Negro College Fund 50th Anniversary."

15. UNCF press releases, July 13, July 23, September 13, September 29, October 6, and December 7, 1972, and January 31, 1973 (UNCF RG3 fiche 1581 and RG4 fiche 2658); Fletcher to RNC Platform Committee, n.d. [August 1972] (UNCF RG3 fiche 1740); "Republican Party Platform of 1972," American Presidency Project, August 21, 1972, http://www.presidency.ucsb.edu/; and Art Peters, "Black Colleges Fund-Raising Job Is a Hot Potato," *Philadelphia Inquirer,* n.d. [March 1973] (UNCF RG3 fiche 1581).

16. Morris B. Abram to Fletcher, March 22, 1973 (G Street, box 123, folder 25, 29).

17. Fletcher speech, November 30, 1971 (UNCF RG3 fiche 1740); Ray Waldmann to Fletcher, February 25, 1972 (G Street, box 78B, folder 4, 82); UNCF press release, February 28, 1973 (UNCF RG4 fiche 2658); Waldmann to Fletcher and

chairs of Domestic Policy Council Working Groups on Economic Discrimination Study, and Waldmann to Nelson Crowther, June 23, 1972 (Nixon WHCF SMOF Patterson box 25, "Economic Discrimination [Fletcher Study]" folder); and Fletcher speech, March 1, 1994 (G Street, box 47, folder 2, 76–80).

18. Fletcher, "Arthur A. Fletcher, a Candidate for Chairman of the National Republican Committee" flyer, 1972 n.d. (G Street, box 8, folder 4, 2); Ethel L. Payne, "So This Is Washington: Politics and People at the Miami Beach Confab" (UNCF RG3 fiche 1581); Fletcher to Nixon and George McGovern, September 6, 1972, and Jordan, "An Open Letter to the Candidates," "To Be Equal" column (Nixon WHCF SMOF Patterson box 43, "Vernon Jordan—Art Fletcher Letters" folder).

19. "Republican Group Issues Demands for Greater Role," *Washington Afro-American,* August 22, 1972; Farrington, *Black Republicans,* 168, 208.

20. UNCF fund-raising institute minutes, December 2, 1972 (G Street, box 77, folder 2, 933–977); Fletcher to Edwina H. Whitlock, December 15, 1973 (G Street, box 76, folder 7, 413); Herman H. Long to Fletcher, December 18, 1972 (G Street, box 123, folder 25, 31–32); "Edley Named . . . UNCF Ousts A. Fletcher," Sengstacke Newspapers, 1973 n.d. (G Street, box 123, folder 1, image 3); Chris Edley interview by Martia Goodson, July 31, 1985 (United Negro College Fund Project, Rare Book and Manuscript Library, Columbia University, New York); Fletcher interview by Washburn University, tape 2a, transcript, 74–76.

21. "Edley Named to Replace Ousted Fletcher at UNCF," *Jet,* March 1973; "Edley Named . . . UNCF Ousts A. Fletcher"; Peters, "Black Colleges Fund-Raising Job Is a Hot Potato"; Jim Lehrer, "Remembering Spiro Agnew," *PBS NewsHour,* September 18, 1996, https://www.pbs.org/newshour/; Perlstein, *Nixonland,* 217, 245, 303–304, 344, 524–530.

22. Peters, "Black Colleges Fund-Raising Job Is a Hot Potato"; Gasman, *Envisioning Black Colleges,* 181. Gasman repeatedly and incorrectly spelled Abram's surname "Abrams"; I have chosen to correct this in brackets.

23. Gasman, *Envisioning Black Colleges,* 179–181.

24. UNCF fund-raising institute minutes; Wesley J. Streater interview by Sybil E. Moses, July 19, 1973 (Rare Book and Manuscript Library, Columbia University, New York); Vernon E. Jordan Jr., interview, November 30, 1981, Frederick D. Patterson Interview, 1981 n.d., and Chris Edley interview by Martia Goodson (United Negro College Fund Project, Rare Book and Manuscript Library, Columbia University, New York).

25. Fletcher to Morris Abram, draft, 1973 n.d. (G Street, box 151, folder 4, 24–41); Peters, "Black Colleges Fund-Raising Job Is a Hot Potato."

26. Fletcher to UNCF Board, College Presidents, and Staff, March 5, 1973, James L. Hayes to Fletcher, March 6, 1973, F. D. Patterson to Fletcher, March 7, 1973, Joseph A. Mehan to Fletcher and "Mary W." to Fletcher, March 8, 1973, H. George Shipman to Fletcher, March 9, 1973, William F. Kornegay to Fletcher and John Fonteno to Fletcher, March 12, 1973, Broadus N. Butler to Fletcher, March 13, 1973, Vivian W. Henderson to Fletcher, W. A. McMillan to Fletcher, and C. B. Rock to Fletcher, March 14, 1973, Herman H. Long to Fletcher and Waldo E. McNaught to Fletcher, March 15, 1973, Allix B. James to Fletcher and Richard C.

Gerstenberg to Fletcher, March 16, 1973, Kenneth Clark to Fletcher and Abram to Fletcher, March 22, 1973, and George L.-P. Weaver to Fletcher, March 23, 1973 (G Street, box 123, folder 20, 1–4, 7; folder 21, 3–8; folder 22, 1–11; folder 23, 1–3, 5, 7–9; and folder 25, 27–29).

27. Nathaniel M. Crook to Fletcher, and General Electric Company to Fletcher, December 17, 1971 (G Street, box 8, folder 4, 477–479, and box 16, folder 2, 698); Arthur A. Fletcher & Associates Application for Incorporation in the District of Columbia, August 20, 1973, Articles of Incorporation, October 23, 1974, and Fletcher to Winford Smith, June 13, 1975 (G Street, box 44, folder 2, 1065–1071). The quotations are from Fletcher interview by Washburn University, tape 2a, transcript, 77–80.

28. "Republican Is Named Kansas State Senator," *Jet*, January 14, 1965, 8; "Ticker Tape USA," column, *Jet*, July 31, 1969; Bush to Fletcher, December 24, 1971 (G Street, box 77, folder 5, 1–2); Fletcher, "Draft Nixon Speech," May 6, 1973, and Bush to Leonard Garment, May 16, 1973 (Nixon WHCF SMOF Patterson box 43, "Vernon Jordan—Art Fletcher Letters" folder); James Sexton Jr. to Garland Guice, July 11, 1973; Aspen Executive Program, July 21, 1973; Black Republican Southeastern Regional Conference Resolution, July 28, 1973; and A. B. Herrmann to Joseph M. Margiotta, August 2, 1973 (G Street, box 151, folder 2, 44–45, 78, 111, 126); Richard Allen, "Kennedy and Wallace vs. Nigger Politics," *Los Angeles Sentinel*, August 2, 1973; Rance C. Spruill to Fletcher, August 7, 1973, and Robert Wright to Nixon, August 20, 1973 (G Street, box 151, folder 2, 112, 127); Bush, "Address at Republican National Committee," September 10, 1973 (Records of the RNC); Fletcher, "Speech Notes," December 1973 (Records of President Gerald R. Ford, Collection of Arthur A. Fletcher [Ford Fletcher], box 3, "Speeches" folder, NARA Gerald Ford Presidential Library, Ann Arbor, MI); Fletcher to William O. Walker, December 28, 1973 (Records of William O. Walker Collection 197, box 2, folder 67, Howard University Special Collections, Washington, DC); Bush, "Address at Republican National Committee," September 16, 1974 (Records of the RNC); "Edwin T. Sexton, Jr." (obituary), *New York Times*, September 20, 1983; "GOPer Edwin Sexton, 60, Felled by Heart Attack," *Jet*, October 24, 1983, 16.

29. Larry Higby to Jerry Jones, April 18, 1973 (Nixon Contested Files, box 8, folder 30).

30. Fletcher, *Silent Sell-Out*, 55–61.

31. Fletcher, *Silent Sell-Out*, 57–58.

32. Edward C. Sylvester to agency heads, January 5, 1966; "St. Louis Union Group Accused of Interfering with Race Hiring Law; Labor Agency Requests Action against the Area's Building Trades Council of AFLCIO," *Wall Street Journal*, January 1966; "Unions Charged; Justice Department Files First Job Bias Suit," *Cleveland Plain Dealer*, and "US Charges Unions Deny Negroes Jobs," *St. Louis Globe-Democrat*, February 5, 1966; "End Secondary Boycott, Union Told in St. Louis; Racial Charges Pending," *Wall Street Journal*, February 8, 1966; Maury E. Rubin, "Pipefitters Local 562 Gives Advanced Job Opportunities to 10 New Negro Members Now Working on the Job in Training Program," *St. Louis Labor Tribune*, February 17, 1966; "Steamfitters' Crash Program Enrolls 10 Negroes; Men Will Be

Paid Journeymen's Wages throughout Training Project," *St. Louis Argus,* February 18, 1966; Ted Schafers, "Negro Contractor, IBEW Sign Pact," *St. Louis Globe-Democrat,* February 21, 1966; Fletcher, *Silent Sell-Out,* 61; Macaluso interview, January 4, 2008, by and in possession of the author; and Golland, *Constructing Affirmative Action,* 83–84.

33. Antony Mazzolini, "US Stops Funds on Projects Here," *Cleveland Press,* May 18, 1967; "US Stalls $43 Million in Projects Here, Citing Unions' Bias," *Cleveland Plain Dealer,* May 19, 1967; "Union Bias Halts Projects, Cleveland," *San Francisco Chronicle,* May 19, 1967; Wilkins, news conference statement, June 27, 1967 (NAACP series 4 box A21, "Civil Rights, Wilkins" folder); Sylvester to Wirtz, June 27, 1967 (OFCC ADC, box 8, "Cleveland Correspondence" folder); Graham, *Civil Rights Era,* 286–287; Anderson, *Pursuit of Fairness,* 104–105; Palladino, *Skilled Hands, Strong Spirits,* 163; and Golland, *Constructing Affirmative Action,* 94, 96, 105–119.

34. Golland, *Constructing Affirmative Action,* 103–142, and Chapter 4 of the present volume.

35. Fletcher, *Silent Sell-Out,* 64, 66–68; Perlstein, *Nixonland,* 413, 517, 545–546, 635–637, 667, 678, 680–684, 716, 722, 724; Mark Feldstein, *Poisoning the Press: Richard Nixon, Jack Anderson, and the Rise of Washington's Scandal Culture* (New York: Farrar, Straus and Giroux, 2010), 108, 145, 150–151, 202–203, 262, 292, 337; and Golland, *Constructing Affirmative Action,* 105–119, 127–142.

36. Fletcher, *Silent Sell-Out,* 5, 66, 69, 73–74.

37. Fletcher, *Silent Sell-Out,* 70–72.

38. Fletcher, *Silent Sell-Out,* 77, 81.

39. Bush to Nixon, August 7, 1974, reprinted in George H. W. Bush, *All the Best: My Life in Letters and Other Writings,* rev. ed. (New York: Simon & Schuster, 2014), 193; Jon Weston to Fletcher, October 9, 1990 (G Street, box 103, folder 3, 150).

40. Fletcher, "Victorious Living—An Idea Who's [sic] Time Has Come," n.d. [1976] (Ford Fletcher, box 3, "Society for Victorious Living" folder); Fletcher notes, n.d. (G Street, box 134, folder 2, 1–18).

41. "Au TPN Centre de Culture du Jazz a Voir," unknown publication, n.d. [1967] (G Street, box 123, folder 34, 43); B. J. Colleran to Fletcher, January 22, Fletcher to Ernest A. Nagy, January 23, Fletcher to Colleran, January 30, Nagy to Fletcher, February 6, and Nagy to Fletcher, March 6, 1970 (G Street, box 124, folder 1, 48–51, 81–84); Fletcher to C. J. Patterson, October 18, 1972 (G Street, box 76, folder 1, 257); "Laura and Tony" to Fletcher, October 19, 1972 (G Street, box 123, folder 10, 1–4); George Bush speech at meeting of the Republican National Committee, April 26, 1974 (Records of the RNC); Naftali, *George H. W. Bush,* 10–11; Paul Fletcher interviews by the author, July 30, 2010, and April 2, 2011; Paul and Sylvia Fletcher interview by the author, December 28, 2010; and Sylvia Fletcher to the author, April 6, 2011.

42. Peterson, "Kansas Roots of Arthur Allen Fletcher."

43. "Address by Assistant Secretary of Labor Arthur Fletcher at Annual Convention of Associated General Contractors," *Construction Labor Report* 808, March 17, 1971; Nick Kotz, "US Agencies Cited in Failure to Enforce Minority Jobs Plan,"

Washington Post, March 18, 1971; and Golland, *Constructing Affirmative Action,* 159–165.

44. "Mental Patient Leaps to Death"; Paul Fletcher interviews by the author, July 30, 2010, September 25, 2010, and April 2, 2011, and Paul and Sylvia Fletcher interview by the author, December 28, 2010; Sylvia Fletcher to the author, April 6, 2011; and Peterson, "Kansas Roots of Arthur Allen Fletcher."

45. Fletcher, "The Victorious Living Creed," 1975 (G Street, box 136, folder 5, 15).

46. Bernyce Fletcher, "Introduction to 'Victorious Living: An Idea Whose Time Has Come'"; and Arthur Fletcher, "Victorious Living: An Idea Whose Time Has Come," n.d. 1976 (Ford Fletcher box 3, "Society for Victorious Living" folder).

47. Fletcher, "Statement before the House Judiciary Committee," November 20, 1973 (Ford Fletcher box 1, "Hearings on the Nomination of Gerald Ford as Vice President" folder); Fletcher, "Security Investigation Data for Sensitive Position," December 1, 1975 (G Street, box 15A, folder 2, 1023–1030).

48. Henry Lucas Jr. to George Bush, August 10, 1974 (Ford WHCF Name File box 1045, "Fletcher, Arthur [1]" folder); Benjamin F. Boyd Sr. to Robert Hartmann, August 16, 1974; and Rev. and Mrs. Alonzo Ponder to Gerald Ford, August 29, 1975 (Ford Hartmann box 91, "Fletcher, Arthur" folder).

49. Leon H. Sullivan to Gerald Ford, August 15, 1974; Maurice A. Dawkins to Ford, August 27, 1974 (Ford WHCF Name File box 1045, "Fletcher, Arthur [1]" folder); "Rev. Maurice A. Dawkins, 80, Black Activist" (obituary), *Broward Sun-Sentinel,* September 28, 2001.

50. Bush to William W. Scranton, August 14, 1974 (Ford WHCF Name File box 1045, "Fletcher, Arthur [1]" folder); unknown White House operative report, n.d. [August 1974] (Ford Cheney box 12, "Transition [1974]—White House and Cabinet Personnel Report" folder).

51. Fletcher to Ford, August 19, 1974 (Ford WHCF Name File box 1045, "Fletcher, Arthur [1]" folder).

52. US Court of Appeals, 10th Circuit, *Williams v. United States,* 444 F.2d 742, June 30, 1971, Open Jurist, https://openjurist.org/; Stanley S. Scott to Fletcher, September 6, October 9, and November 1, 1974, and February 26 and March 24, 1975, White House press release, September 13, 1974 (Ford White House press releases, box 2), William M. Walker to Fletcher, April 14, 1975, Fletcher to Ford, October 22, 1974, White House interoffice memo, August 6, 1975, Fletcher to Douglas P. Bennett, September 4, 1975, and Bennett to Fletcher, October 1, 1975 (Ford WHCF Name File box 1045, "Fletcher, Arthur [1]" folder); "President's Commission on Personnel Interchange Appointment of Seven Members," American Presidency Project, May 25, 1978, http://www.presidency.ucsb.edu/.

53. David J. Wimer to Fletcher, September 30, 1974; Fletcher to Anthony C. Goode, March 24, 1981 (G Street, box 56, folder 3, 405–472); Fletcher to Daniel J. Evans, March 31, 1987 (G Street, box 87, folder 3, 178–181); Paul and Patsy Fletcher conversation with the author, July 21, 2012; and Antoinette Crosby, "DC's Black Elite Celebrate All the Good Times, and Lament the Loss, of the Channel Inn," *Washington Post,* April 11, 2014.

54. James E. Woodson to Ford, February 24, 1975, Sullivan to Ford, July 15, 1975, Sullivan to Donald Rumsfeld, July 22, 1975, and Sylvester E. Williams III to Ford, July 26, 1975 (Ford WHCF Name File box 1045, "Fletcher, Arthur [1]" folder).

55. John Robert Greene, *The Presidency of Gerald R. Ford* (Lawrence: University Press of Kansas, 1995), 2; Brinkley, *Gerald R. Ford*, passim.

56. James Cannon, *Time and Chance: Gerald Ford's Appointment with History* (New York: Harper Collins, 1994), 404; Brinkley, *Gerald R. Ford*, 122–125, 127–128, 148.

57. Brinkley, *Gerald R. Ford*, 27.

58. Fletcher, "National Goal—Equality and Parity in the Seventies," Address Before the Pennsylvania League of Cities, Philadelphia, Pennsylvania, August 11, 1969 (Fletcher, *Silent Sell-Out*, 101–113); Fletcher "Forward Together, or On Pulling the Nation Together," address draft, January 3, 1970 (G Street, box 13, folder 3, 264–289); Fletcher, "Contemporary Racism," Address Before the United Presbyterian Church General Assembly, Rochester, New York, May 24, 1971 (Fletcher, *Silent Sell-Out*, 115–121); Fletcher, "Statement before the House Judiciary Committee," November 20, 1973 (Ford Fletcher box 1, "Hearings on the Nomination of Gerald Ford as Vice President" folder); Gerald R. Ford, "Message on the Observance of Black History Month," Gerald R. Ford Presidential Library and Museum, February 10, 1976, https://www.fordlibrarymuseum.gov/; Fletcher, address draft, n.d. [1976] (Ford Fletcher box 3, "Speeches" folder); and Brinkley, *Gerald R. Ford*, 21.

59. John Osborne, "Three to Go," *New Republic*, October 18, 1975; Jules Witcover, *Marathon: The Pursuit of the Presidency, 1972–1976* (New York: Viking Press, 1977), 86, 89; and Brinkley, *Gerald R. Ford*, 63, 66–69.

60. James M. Naughton, "President Vetoes School Lunch Bill that Widened Aid; Says $2.7-Billion Measure Would Expand Programs for 'Nonneedy' Pupils; Overriding Predicted; Vote Is Scheduled Tuesday—McGovern Calls Ford's Act 'Mindless Exercise,'" *New York Times*, October 4, 1975; "Ford to City: Drop Dead; Vows He'll Veto Any Bail-out," *New York Daily News*, October 30, 1975; Lee Dembart, "President Intends to Veto Construction Picketing Bill," *New York Times*, December 23, 1975; Witcover, *Marathon*, 13, 53–57; Cannon, *Time and Chance*, 404–407; and Brinkley, *Gerald R. Ford*, 125–127.

61. Witcover, *Marathon*, 120.

62. Ron Nessen, press briefing, January 28, 1976 (Ford Nessen Briefings box 16, "January 28, 1976" folder); White House press release, January 28, 1976; Cannon to William W. Nicholson, February 2, 1976; and Nicholson to Cannon, February 5, 1976 (Ford WHCF Subject File box 33, "FG6-11-1/F Executive" folder); "Ford Hires Black Who Quit Nixon," *Philadelphia Bulletin*, January 29, 1976; Cannon to Ford, February 11, 1976 (Ford Cannon box 56, "President and Arthur Fletcher, 2/11/76" folder); Nelson Rockefeller, "Remarks of the Vice President at the Swearing-in Ceremony of Arthur Fletcher" (Ford Fletcher box 4, "Swearing-in Ceremony [Mr. Fletcher's]"); and Samuel C. Jackson to Fletcher, February 26, 1976 (Ford Fletcher box 1, "Council of 100" folder).

63. Fletcher to Cannon, February 6, 1976 (Ford WHCF Subject File box 33, "FG6-11-1/F Executive" folder).

64. Cannon to Fletcher, February 3, 1976 (Ford Fletcher box 3, "President's Issue Book" folder).

65. For Fletcher's travel itinerary, see Fletcher, "Travel Vouchers," multiple dates, 1976 (Ford Fletcher box 4, "Travel Requests and Vouchers—Travel Vouchers [1]" and "Travel Requests and Vouchers—Travel Vouchers [2]" folders); for Fletcher's request for first-class travel and its denial, see Fletcher to Cannon and Pat McKee to "Sarah," March 19, 1976, and Cannon to Phil Buchen and Buchen to Cannon, March 25, 1976 (Ford Roth box 11, "Fletcher, Art—Travel Questions" folder).

66. For Fletcher speaking as a substitute for Ford, see, e.g., Warren Hendriks to Fletcher, February 12, 1976, and Fletcher to Hendriks, February 19, 1976 (Ford Fletcher box 7, "New York—Black Athlete's Hall of Fame, New York City, 3/13/76" folder); "DM Rights Banquet to Hear Ford Aide," *Des Moines Tribune,* February 13, 1976; and Dick Parsons to Cannon, February 17, 1976 (Ford WHCF Subject File box 33, "FG 6-11-1/F Executive" folder); for Fletcher speaking after being invited by name, see, e.g., Donald Sykes to Ford, February 24, 1976 (Ford Fletcher box 4, "Speaking Engagements—Letters of Appreciation" folder); Robert Fulton to Fletcher, February 24, 1976 (Ford Fletcher box 6, "Massachusetts—Northeast Work and Welfare Conference, Boston, 3/4/76" folder); and Geneva B. Ruffin to Fletcher, February 29, 1976 (Ford Fletcher box 5, "California—Executive Seminar Center, Berkeley, 5/5/76") folder.

67. Vernon Jordan to Fletcher, May 3, 1976 (Ford Fletcher box 6, "Massachusetts—National Urban League, Boston, 8/3/76" folder).

68. Fletcher interview by Washburn University, tape 2a, transcript, 169.

69. Fletcher interview by Washburn University, tape 2a, transcript, 170.

70. Claude Lewis, "Kissinger Scolded by Black Ford Aide," *Philadelphia Bulletin,* August 4, 1976.

71. Fletcher interview by Washburn University, tape 2a, transcript, 171–172.

72. Witcover, *Marathon,* 90, 378, 398–409, 422–431; Cannon, *Time and Chance,* 406–407; and Brinkley, *Gerald R. Ford,* 137–138.

73. North Carolina Citizens for Reagan for President Newsletter, n.d. (Ford Fletcher box 8, "North Carolina [1]" folder); Witcover, *Marathon,* 410–421; "Why Reynolds Lost," *Civil Rights Monitor* 1, no. 1 (August 1985); and Mary Frances Berry, *And Justice for All: The United States Civil Rights Commission and the Continuing Struggle for Freedom in America* (New York: Knopf, 2009), 182–244.

74. Manning, *William L. Dawson,* passim; Bowen, *Roots of Modern Conservatism,* passim; and Thurber, *Republicans and Race,* passim. Christopher H. Achen and Larry M. Bartels have recently analyzed voters' motivations; see "Do Sanders Supporters Favor His Policies?," *New York Times,* May 23, 2016.

75. Berry, *And Justice for All,* passim.

76. Fletcher to Preston L. Lambert, May 11, 1976 (Ford Fletcher box 4, "Speaking Engagements" folder).

77. Witcover, *Marathon,* 429; Craig Shirley, *Reagan's Revolution: The Untold Story of the Campaign that Started It All* (Nashville, TN: Thomas Nelson, 2005), 230.

78. US Civil Service Commission Conference, "Administration of Public Policy" program, April 25–May 7, 1976 (Ford Fletcher box 5, "California—Executive Seminar Center, Berkeley, 5/5/76" folder); Fletcher Speech, June 3, 1976, Ruth B. Love to Fletcher, June 4, 1976, and Richard B. LaPointe to Fletcher, June 15, 1976 (Ford Fletcher box 5, "California—Marcus Foster Institute, Concord, 6/3/76" folder).

79. Witcover, *Marathon*, 441–455; Shirley, *Reagan's Revolution*, 288–289.

80. Witcover, *Marathon*, 476–479; Shirley, *Reagan's Revolution*, 304, 311–312; Raleigh E. Milton, *Official Report of the Proceedings of the Thirty-First Republican National Convention, Held in Kansas City, Missouri, August 16, 17, 18, 19, 1976, Resulting in the Nomination of Gerald R. Ford, of Michigan, for President, and the Nomination of Robert Dole, of Kansas, for Vice President* (Washington, DC: Republican National Committee, 1976), 438–439.

81. Milton, *Official Report of the Proceedings of the Thirty-First Republican National Convention*, 434–437.

82. Milton, *Official Report of the Proceedings of the Thirty-First Republican National Convention*, 438.

83. Milton, *Official Report of the Proceedings of the Thirty-First Republican National Convention*, 438–439.

84. Witcover, *Marathon*, 531–539.

85. Rigueur, *Loneliness of the Black Republican*, 261.

86. Fletcher travel itinerary, August 23, 1976 (Ford Fletcher box 5, "Iowa—Blacks in Criminal Justice, Des Moines, 8/24/76" folder); Fletcher to James E. Connor, August 23, 1976 (Ford Fletcher box 4, "Travel Requests and Vouchers—Requests for Travel" folder); Fletcher to Jack Marsh, September 23, 1976 (Ford Fletcher box 3, "President Ford Committee" folder); Fletcher travel itinerary, October 8, 1976 (Ford Fletcher box F15, "Fletcher, Arthur A." folder); Fletcher travel itineraries, October 22 and 23, 1976 (Ford Fletcher box 6, "Massachusetts—WVZ-TV Boston, 10/22/76" folder); Program, Governor Robert F. Bennett's Equal Employment Opportunity Conference, October 28–29, 1976 (Ford Fletcher box 6, "Kansas—Equal Employment Opportunity Conference, Topeka, 10/28/76" folder); Fletcher Travel Schedule (Ford Fletcher box 4, "Travel Requests and Vouchers—Travel Schedules" folder); Glenwood A. Johnson to Fletcher, October 28, 1976 (Ford Fletcher box 1, "Community Services Administration" folder); Ford to Fletcher, November 1, 1976 (Ford WHCF Name File box 1045, "Fletcher, Arthur [2]" folder); Witcover, *Marathon*, 562–563; Theodore H. White, *America in Search of Itself: The Making of the President, 1956–1980* (New York: Harper & Row, 1982), end pages; Cannon, *Time and Chance*, 407–408; Brinkley, *Gerald R. Ford*, 141–144.

87. Rigueur, *Loneliness of the Black Republican*, 261.

88. Fletcher, speech to Southern Regional Republican Conference, December 5, 1976 (Records of President Ronald W. Reagan, White House Staff and Office Files, Collection of Melvyn L. Bradley: Office of Public Liaison, Series 3: Minority Appointments box 22, folder OA13334, NARA Ronald W. Reagan Presidential Library, Simi Valley, CA); Wilbur Nystrom to Editor, *Bremerton Sun*, Nystrom to Fletcher, December 6, 1976, and Fletcher to Nystrom, December 15, 1976 (G Street, box 112, folder 3, 164–166); "A Man to Reckon With" (editorial), *Topeka*

State Journal, January 4, 1977; Richard M. Rosenbaum to Fletcher, January 10, 1977 (G Street, box 22C, folder 3, 305); "Ford Choice Quits GOP Chair Race," *Washington Post,* January 11, 1977; Meeting Minutes, Republican National Committee, January 14, 1977 (Records of the RNC); Thomas B. Evans to Fletcher and Tom Stroock to Fletcher, January 17, 1977, Elaine B. Jenkins to Fletcher, January 18, 1977, Frederick Lipitt to Fletcher, January 19, 1977, Herman C. Brown to Fletcher, January 21, 1977, Noel Love Gross to Fletcher, January 25, 1977, and Rudy Boschwitz to William Brock, January 26, 1977 (G Street, box 22C, folder 3, 186, 303–304, 306–308, 310); and Chuck Slocum to Fletcher, January 27, 1977 (G Street, box 112, folder 1, image 13).

89. Ford to Fletcher, January 19, 1977 (Ford WHCF Subject Files box 33, "FG 6-11-1/F Executive" folder).

90. Fletcher to Floyd A. Decker, July 6, 1976 (Ford Fletcher box 5, "Idaho—Association of Idaho Cities, Coeur D'Alene, 6/28/76 [2]" folder); Bernyce Fletcher to Kathy Keolker, November 29, 1978 (Keolker correspondence in possession of the author).

91. Home Rule for Washington, DC, brochures, n.d. [probably 1973] (G Street, box 123, folder 7, 1–4); Karlyn Barker, "District GOP Mayoralty Candidates Sure 'City Mess' Issue Will Offset Voter Gap," *Washington Post,* August 25, 1978; "District of Columbia Home Rule Act," Public Law 93-198; 87 Stat. 777, DC Code § 1-201 passim, approved December 24, 1973, http://www.abfa.com/ogc/hract.htm.

92. "Candidates' Forum," *Washington Post,* June 8, 1978; Barker, "District GOP Mayoralty Candidates."

93. Betty James, "Ex-Ford Aide Joins Race for Mayor," *Washington Star,* and Leon Dash, "Ex-Aide to Ford, Nixon Joins DC Race for Mayor," *Washington Post,* April 30, 1978; Barker, "GOP Candidate Has a Goal: Fletcher Wants to Break Democrats' Hold," *Washington Post,* September 6, 1978; Barker, "Party Shuns GOP Hopeful: Champion Runs 'People-to-People' Campaign," *Washington Post,* September 6, 1978; Kenneth Bredemeier, "Candidate Seeking Funds Widely: GOP Mayoral Candidate Asks Friends Across Nation," *Washington Post,* June 2, 1978; and Bredemeier, "GOP Backers Snub $500 Lunch with Party's Mayoral Hopeful," *Washington Post,* August 9, 1978.

94. Barker and Martha Hamilton, "Plan to Build Civic Center in Old Downtown Called a Boon for Landowners," *Washington Post,"* July 3, 1978; Barker, "District GOP Mayoralty Candidates"; William H. Jones, "Candidates' Economic Cures for City Vary," *Washington Post,* September 10, 1978; Barker, "Leahy Scolds City for Failure to Fully Air Civic Center Plan," *Washington Post,* October 13, 1978.

95. Barker, "Party Shuns GOP Hopeful"; Milton Coleman, "Responsibility of Barry Questioned by Fletcher," *Washington Post,* October 17, 1978; Matthew Vaz, "'We Intend to Run It': Racial Politics, Illegal Gambling, and the Rise of Government Lotteries in the United States, 1960–1985," *Journal of American History* 101, no. 1 (2014): 71–96; and Rachel Cooper, "Mega Millions, Powerball, and More in Virginia," TripSavvy.com, updated December 9, 2017, https://www.tripsavvy.com/.

96. Paul W. Valentine, "A Constitution Is Approved for 'New Columbia,'" *Wash-*

ington Post, May 30, 1982; "The 1978 DC Voting Representation Constitutional Amendment," DC Vote, https://www.dcvote.org/.

97. Fletcher, "For the Record," Washington Post, September 5, 1978; "The Fauntroy–Tucker Vote Fiasco" (editorial), Washington Post, September 9, 1978.

98. "Hot Mayoral Campaign Ends at Polls Today," Washington Post, September 12, 1978; Milton Coleman and Bredemeier, "Marion Barry Takes the Lead in Early Ballot Counting," Washington Post, September 13, 1978; Valentine, "Near-Final Vote Count Assures Barry Victory," Washington Post, September 24, 1978; Jack Eisen, "Embattled Elections Chairman Submits Resignation: DC Elections Chief Says She'll Step Down Dec. 15," Washington Post, October 3, 1978; and Michael Kiernan, "Some DC Democrats Eye Fletcher," Washington Star, n.d. (G Street, box 108, folder 1, image 15).

99. Jonathan I. Z. Agronsky, Marion Barry: The Politics of Race (Latham, NY: British American Publishing, 1991), 79–183; Chris Myers Asch and George Derek Musgrove, Chocolate City: A History of Race and Democracy in the Nation's Capital (Chapel Hill: University of North Carolina Press, 2017), 341–388.

100. Coleman and Valentine, "Week Wait Seen Till City Learns Primary Victor: More than 5,000 Ballots Will Be Counted Tuesday; Slow Count, Tight Race Tie Up Mayoral Primary Results," Washington Post, September 14, 1978; Valentine, "Near-Final Vote Count Assures Barry Victory," Washington Post, September 24, 1978.

101. Dash, "That Special Feeling: Factions Pay Court to Winning Barry; Barry, Mayor 'Cordially' Talk of Transition," Washington Post, September 15, 1978; Valentine and Barker, "7,000 Ballots 'Unread' by Computer in DC Primary Race: Discovery Puts Election Result in Doubt Again," Washington Post, September 22, 1978.

102. Barker, "GOP Candidate Has a Goal"; Coleman, "Fletcher Seeks Inroads on Democrats: Fletcher Seeks Cab Driver Support," Washington Post, October 8, 1978; Coleman, "Barry Aiming at 'Avalanche' in Mayor Race: Barry Rallies Supporters to Meet GOP Challenge," Washington Post, October 15, 1978; Coleman, "Responsibility of Barry Questioned by Fletcher," Washington Post, October 17, 1978; and Coleman, "Fletcher and Taxi Board: The Unmaking of a Campaign Issue," Washington Post, November 2, 1978.

103. Coleman, "Barry Aiming at 'Avalanche;'" William Raspberry, "Why Black Voters Won't Switch," Chicago Tribune, October 31, 1978; Coleman, "Election '78: The District: Mood of Weariness Prevails in DC Mayoral Contest," Washington Post, November 5, 1978; Eisen, "DC Candidates Spend $2 Million for Campaigns: Barry's Fund a Quarter of Total," Washington Post, March 15, 1979; and Paul Fletcher interview by the author, July 30, 2010.

104. Coleman, "Fighting the Odds: Fletcher Stresses Accomplishments," Washington Post, November 3, 1978.

105. Editorial, and Nick Thimmesch, "Fletcher Is Showing Spunk and Flair," Washington Post, November 5, 1978.

106. Coleman, "Fletcher Charges Barry Intimidates His Backers," Washington Post, November 2, 1978; Bernyce Fletcher to Kathy Keolker, November 29, 1978

(Keolker correspondence in possession of the author); and Paul Fletcher interview by the author, July 30, 2010.

107. Valentine, "Poor Blacks Built Landslide for Barry, Analysis Shows," *Washington Post,* November 9, 1978; Eisen, "The Official Returns from Elections Board On City's Nov. 7 Voting," *Washington Post,* December 14, 1978; Dole to Fletcher, December 18, 1978 (G Street, box 15A, folder 2, 1849); and Bernyce Fletcher to Kathy Keolker, June 9, 1980 (Keolker correspondence in possession of the author).

CHAPTER 6. BUSH FOR PRESIDENT, 1980–1989

1. Bush to Fletcher, December 17, and Fletcher to Bush, December 19, 1969 (G Street, box 80, folder 3, 770–771); Love B. Johnson to Fletcher, March 19, 1970 (G Street, box 78A, folder 9, 220–222); Republican Party of Texas newsletter, April 1970 (G Street, box 78A, folder 1, 107–112); John Fonteno to Fletcher, June 25, and Vera Lincoln to the files, August 10, 1970 (G Street, box 78B, folder 18, 402, 405); "Pasco Man Eyes UN Post," *Spokane Spokesman-Review,* August 27, 1971; Bush to Fletcher, n.d. [December 1971] (G Street, box 6, folder 1, 701–703); Bush to Fletcher, December 24, 1971 (G Street, box 77, folder 5, 1–2); Bush to Leonard Garment, May 16, 1973 (Nixon WHCF SMOF Patterson box 43, "Vernon Jordan—Art Fletcher Letters" folder); Bush to Samuel C. Jackson, August 28, 1973 (G Street, box 151, folder 2, 118); Bush speech, September 10, 1973 (Records of the RNC part 1, series B, reel 11, frames 265–290); Bush to L. William Seidman, n.d. [January 1974] (Ford WHCF Name File Box 1045, "Fletcher, Arthur [1]" folder); Bush speech, April 26, 1974 (Records of the RNC part 1, series B, reel 11, frames 650–676); Bush to William W. Scranton, August 14, 1974 (Ford WHCF Name File Box 1045, "Fletcher, Arthur [1]" folder); Bush speech, September 16, 1974 (Records of the RNC part 1, series B, reel 12, frames 18–27); Federal Executive Protective Service List of Attendees, February 25, 1976 (Ford Fletcher box 4, "Swearing-in Ceremony [Mr. Fletcher's]" folder); Fletcher press release, n.d. [1979] (G Street, box 116, folder 2, 137); "Davis" to Bob Dole's staff, June 11, 1979 (Dole Senate Personal–Political box 48, "24-Campaign Name Lists—1980 Pres Campaign RNC 1979" folder); and Naftali, *George H. W. Bush,* 10–23.

2. Reagan to Mark E. Rivers, September 27, 1974 (G Street, box 53, folder 1, 1089); Bob Heaton, "Ford Aide Hits Campaign Hate," *Wichita Eagle,* April 16, 1976; "Lesson in a Cliff-Hanger" (editorial), and Vermont Royster, "Ominous Omens," *Wall Street Journal,* August 16, 1976; and "The Trouble with Conservatives" (editorial), *Wall Street Journal,* August 17, 1976; and Perlstein, *Invisible Bridge,* 159–169, 195–196, 408–413.

3. Dole to Fletcher, February 26, 1971 (G Street, box 77, folder 2, 726); Bob Oberdorfer, "Dole Urges Black Aide for President," *Washington Post,* March 17, 1971; Ethel L. Payne, "Black Shakeup in Cabinet?," *Pittsburgh Courier,* April 17, 1971; Nixon and Dole Oval Office conversation (with others present), July 20, 1971 (Nixon White House Tapes series 1, index 540-7); Dole speech, July 22, 1971 (Records of the RNC part 1, series B, reel 11, frame 337); Robert C. Maynard, "Fletcher Sees Position at UN as Springboard to the Senate," *Washington Post,* September 7,

1971; Jacqueline Trescott, "Tense Politics and Changing Moods," *Washington Post,* October 2, 1978; Dole to Fletcher, December 18, 1978 (G Street, box 15A, folder 2, 1849); Fletcher press release, n.d. [1979]; and Dole interview by and in possession of the author, December 5, 2014.

4. Bush and Barbara Bush to Bernyce Fletcher, January 9, 1980 (G Street, box 108, folder 4, 16); White, *America in Search of Itself,* 302–303; Naftali, *George H. W. Bush,* 36–37.

5. White, *America in Search of Itself,* 31; Naftali, *George H. W. Bush,* 37.

6. White, *America in Search of Itself,* 303–304; Naftali, *George H. W. Bush,* 37–38.

7. Fletcher press release, n.d. [1979] (G Street, box 116, folder 2, 137–163); Bush speech, May 26, 1980, excerpted in Bush, *All the Best,* 297; Keith Richburg, "DC Republicans Divided at Home, Face Isolation in Detroit," *Washington Post,* July 5, 1980; White, *America in Search of Itself;* and Naftali, *George H. W. Bush,* 37-38.

8. Richburg, "From Detroit: Black Delegates from DC Lead on GOP Issues," *Washington Post,* July 16, 1980; unidentified Reagan operative to "Darrell," September 15, 1980 (Reagan Transition Files Series 4-B, box 103, "Urban Affairs Task Force/Fletcher, Arthur" folder); and Perlstein, *Nixonland,* xii, 71, 90.

9. Richburg, "DC Republicans Divided at Home"; RNC list of speakers, July 14, 1980 (Reagan Transition Files Series 3-C, box 47, "Convention [Vice Presidential Candidate]" folder); Joyce Purnick, "Hooks Urges GOP to Pursue Equality: NAACP Leader Also Asks Party," *New York Times,* July 16, 1980; Richburg, "From Detroit: Black Delegates from DC Lead on GOP Issues"; "DC Delegates Assess Accomplishments at Convention in Detroit," *Washington Post,* July 17, 1980; Felicity Barringer and Glen Frankel, "Area Delegations in Detroit: Bitterness, Pride, Politicking," *Washington Post,* July 18, 1980; and Raleigh E. Milton, *Official Report of the Proceedings of the Thirty-Second Republican National Convention, held in Detroit, Michigan, July 14, 15, 16, 17, 1980, Resulting in the Nomination of Ronald W. Reagan, of California, for President, and the Nomination of George H. W. Bush, of Texas, for Vice President* (Washington, DC: Republican National Committee, 1980), 7; and Farrington, *Black Republicans,* 2, 25, 144.

10. "DC Delegates Assess Accomplishments at Convention in Detroit"; White, *America in Search of Itself,* 320–326; Naftali, *George H. W. Bush,* 38–39; Bush, *All the Best,* 299.

11. Richburg, "DC Republicans Divided at Home"; Purnick, "Hooks Urges GOP to Pursue Equality"; "DC Delegates Assess Accomplishments at Convention in Detroit"; Barringer and Frankel, "Area Delegations in Detroit"; and Fletcher interview by Washburn University, tape 2a, transcript, 182–186.

12. Jules Witcover, *The American Vice Presidency: From Irrelevance to Power* (Washington, DC: Smithsonian Books, 2014), 362–443; Joel Goldstein, *The White House Vice Presidency: The Path to Significance, Mondale to Biden* (Lawrence: University Press of Kansas, 2016), 52–104.

13. White, *America in Search of Itself,* 320–327; Thomas M. DeFrank, *Write It When I'm Gone: Remarkable Off-the-Record Conversations with Gerald R. Ford* (New York: Berkley Publishing, 2007), 74–98.

14. White, *America in Search of Itself,* 320–327; Naftali, *George H. W. Bush,* 38–

39; Bush, *All the Best*, 299; and Jon Meacham, *Destiny and Power: The American Odyssey of George Herbert Walker Bush* (New York: Random House, 2015), 256.

15. RNC list (Reagan Transition Series 3-C box 47, "Convention [Vice Presidential Candidate]" folder); Milton, *Official Report of the Proceedings of the Thirty-Second Republican National Convention*, 480.

16. Milton, *Official Report of the Proceedings of the Thirty-First Republican National Convention*, 438–439.

17. Douglas E. Kneeland, "Reagan Campaigns at Mississippi Fair," *New York Times*, August 4, 1980; White, *America in Search of Itself*, 384.

18. Kneeland, "Reagan Urges Blacks to Look Past Labels and to Vote for Him," *New York Times*, August 6, 1980; White, *America in Search of Itself*, 384–385. The Neshoba County speech also was against the wishes of RNC chair Bill Brock, who, like Fletcher, was becoming concerned about the decline of African Americans in the party; Brock responded with targeted, moderately successful campaigns for Black votes in state races that year. Robert Mason, *The Republican Party and American Politics from Hoover to Reagan* (New York: Cambridge University Press, 2012), 269.

19. Jacqueline Trescott, "Dinner of Discontent," *Washington Post*, September 29, 1980; Reagan to Fletcher, October 7, 1980 (Reagan Transition Series 4-B box 103, "Urban Affairs Task Force/Fletcher, Arthur" folder); Reagan Bush Committee press release, October 7, 1980 (Reagan Transition Series 4-C box 125, "Press Releases—Urban Affairs Task Force" folder); "Governor Reagan Endorses Preservation of Black Colleges and Black College Day," *Buffalo Criterion*, October 8, 1980; Paul Grey, "Dem Failures Drive Blacks to 2-Party System," *News World*, October 27, 1980; Lee L. Verstandig to Fletcher, November 5, 1980, and Berncye Fletcher to Reagan, September 17, 1983 (G Street, box 118, folder 4, 245, 252–257); Reagan to members, Urban Affairs Task Force, March 13, 1981 (Reagan White House Office of Records Management [WHORM] Subject File FG-001 box 4, Case File 012557); Alan K. Simpson to Bernyce Fletcher, September 28, and Melvin R. Laird to Bernyce Fletcher, September 30, 1983 (G Street, box 118, folder 4, 242–244); and Fletcher to Alan Greenspan (draft), December 22, 1993 (G Street, box 101, folder 6, 549–554).

20. "How Groups Voted in 1976" and "How Groups Voted in 1980," Cornell University Roper Center for Public Opinion Research, https://ropercenter.cornell.edu/; "1980 Presidential General Election Data Graphs—Pennsylvania," Dave Leip's Atlas of US Presidential Elections, https://uselectionatlas.org/; and Leah Wright Rigueur, *Loneliness of the Black Republican*, 377n101.

21. Samuel C. Jackson to Edward Meese and Melvin Bradley, November 24, 1980 (Reagan Staff Bradley box OA13334, "Fletcher, Arthur" folder); William Safire, "Feeling Out in the Cold," *New York Times*, November 27, 1980; Adam Clymer, "Black Republicans Want Reagan to Remember Them," *New York Times*, December 7, 1980; Office of the President-Elect list, December 9, 1980 (Reagan Transition Series 10-B box 167, "Guest List—R/B Black Leadership 12/10" folder); Office of the President-Elect list, December 10, 1980 (Reagan Transition Series 2-E box 26, "RI-21.01 Black Americans" folder); Trescott, "Glad Tidings: Cheery Holiday Rapping at the Arrington Dixons'," *Washington Post*, December 20, 1980;

Carla Hall, "Wall-to-Wall Republicans," *Washington Post,* January 17, 1981; Trescott, "The Pupil of Power," *Washington Post,* February 6, 1981; and Trescott, "The Power and the Pulpit: The Well-Planned Ascent of Thaddeus Garrett Jr.," *Washington Post,* March 22, 1981.

22. Richburg, "City Republicans Stake Claim as Barry Link to White House," *Washington Post,* November 12, 1980; Trescott, "Sweet Victory and the Black Republicans," *Washington Post,* November 21, 1980; Edward A. Gargan, "NAACP Leaders Express Concerns about Reagan," *New York Times,* November 23, 1980; David R. Scotton to Bernyce Fletcher, January 9, 1981 (G Street, box 138, folder 4, 104); Hall, "Wall-to-Wall Republicans"; Vice Presidential Inauguration Committee invitation, January 19, 1981 (G Street, box 41, folder 1, 34–35); Trescott, "The Inaugural Weekend," *Washington Post,* January 19, 1981; Loret M. Ruppe and Scotton to Fletcher and Bernyce Fletcher, January 28, 1981 (G Street, box 16, folder 1, 1134); Nancy Bearg Dyke to Allen Lenz, and Charles F. Tyson II to L. Paul Bremer III, April 30, 1981 (Reagan WHORM Subject File CO box 63, Case File 025360); Fletcher and Government of Guyana agreement, May 29, 1981 (G Street, box 48, folder 3, 501–507); and Bush to Laurence E. Mann, June 4, 1981 (G Street, box 72, folder 2, 491).

23. Dorothy Gilliam, "Blacks Watch Reagan for Sign of Credibility," *Washington Post,* January 19, 1981; William Raspberry, "A Short List of Black Appointees," *Washington Post,* March 25, 1981; and Rigueur, *Loneliness of the Black Republican,* 292–293.

24. "Politics: Reagan Walks Out," *Daytona Beach Morning Journal,* March 7, 1966; Witcover, *Marathon,* 95–96; and Perlstein, *Invisible Bridge,* 552–554.

25. Lee A. Daniels, "The New Black Conservatives," *New York Times,* October 4, 1981; Berry, *And Justice for All,* 189–193; Michael L. Ondaatje, *Black Conservative Intellectuals in Modern America* (Philadelphia: University of Pennsylvania Press, 2010), 4, 33, 42–44; Timothy J. Minchin and John A. Salmond, *After the Dream: Black and White Southerners since 1965* (Lexington: University Press of Kentucky, 2011), 213–217, 223, 228–230; Ralph A. Rossum, *Understanding Clarence Thomas: The Jurisprudence of Constitutional Restoration* (Lawrence: University Press of Kansas, 2014); and Philip S. Hart, "Black Republicans," letter to the editor, *New York Times,* October 21, 2016.

26. Gerald Ford, "Veto of a Common Situs Picketing Bill," American Presidency Project, January 2, 1976, http://www.presidency.ucsb.edu/.

27. "Exclusive: Lee Atwater's Infamous 1981 Interview on the Southern Strategy," *Nation,* YouTube, November 13, 2012, https://www.youtube.com/. As requested by Atwater, Lamis did not release the interview; it has come to light thanks to his widow.

28. Katherine H. Shannon to Bernyce Fletcher, December 14, 1981 (G Street, box 138, folder 4, 65–68); Donnie Radcliffe, "Washington Ways," *Washington Post,* January 19, 1982; Elizabeth A. Abramowitz to Bernyce Fletcher, January 27, 1982 (G Street, box 58, folder 2, 759); Ann Wrobleski to James S. Rosebush, March 1, 1982 (G Street, box 56, folder 2, 146–147); Rosebush to Bernyce Fletcher, n.d. [April 1982] (G Street, box 108, folder 4, 18); "Mikey" to Bernyce Fletcher, May 7, 1982 (G Street, box 108, folder 4, 19); "Jeanine" to Bernyce Fletcher, June 10, 1982 (G Street, box 138, folder 1, 2); Patricia A. Russell to Bernyce Fletcher, July 13, 1982

(G Street, box 111, folder 3, 1320–1322); Paul Corvino to Nancy Reagan, September 3, 1982 (G Street, box 56, folder 2, 139); Theresa Elmore to Bernyce Fletcher, September 20, 1982 (G Street, box 108, folder 4, 17); Bernyce Fletcher to "Mrs. Batman," November 3, Thomas A. Cook to Bernyce Fletcher, November 10, and Muffie Brandon to Bernyce Fletcher, November 29, 1982 (G Street, box 56, folder 2, 137, 142, 145); Nancy Reagan to Bernyce Fletcher, n.d. [December 1982] (G Street, box 109, folder 1, 37); Catherine Rufty to Bernyce Fletcher, December 27, 1982 (G Street, box 56, folder 2, 138); Kathy Moore to Bernyce Fletcher, n.d. [January 1983] and Sheryl Eberly to Bernyce Fletcher, n.d. [January 1983] (G Street, box 56, folder 1, 3–5); Bernyce Fletcher résumé, n.d. [1983] and Bernyce Fletcher to Reagan and Bush, September 17, 1983 (G Street, 118, folder 4, 226–234, 252–257); and Betty Boyd Caroli, *First Ladies from Martha Washington to Michelle Obama* (New York: Oxford University Press, 2010), 281–282.

29. Eleanor Williams to Arthur Fletcher & Associates (AF&A), June 1, 1974 (Ford Fletcher box 1, "General Correspondence [1]" folder); Fletcher biographical sketch, September 23, 1975 (Ford Fletcher box 3, "speeches" folder); Fletcher list, n.d. [1980] (G Street, box 44, folder 2, 564); Fletcher notes, n.d. [1980] (G Street, box 124, folder 31, 1–6); Fletcher to William A. Clement and Paul Browne, February 20, and Fletcher to J. Tunstall, March 10, 1980 (G Street, box 44, folder 2, 526–562); Fletcher to Anthony C. Goode, March 24, 1981 (G Street, box 56, folder 3, 405); Frank A. Nicholas to Fletcher, January 27, 1982 (G Street, box 30, folder 2, 213); Fletcher to Small Business Administration, March 12, Fletcher to Goode, March 30, Peter Terpeluk to Fletcher, April 16, and Fletcher to Harrold Harris, May 27, 1982 (G Street, box 44, folder 2, 509–513, 578–604, 618–621); and Fletcher to James Sanders, July 22, 1983 (G Street, box 56, folder 3, 475–479).

30. Photographs by unidentified photographers, November 10–23, 1982 (G Street, box 6, folder 1, 59–60, and box 96, folder 2, 568–572, 575–589, 617, 734–737, 739–741, 743–746, 758–764, 783–786, 798–800, 816, 849–850); White House briefing book, November 10, 1982 (G Street, box 41, folder 2, 513–530); "Around the World: Bush Is Off on Tour of 7 African Nations," *New York Times*, November 11, 1982; Thomas R. Pickering to Fletcher, November 12, 1982 (G Street, box 41, folder 1, 23); Robert V. Keeley to Fletcher, and Bush to Fletcher, November 17, 1982 (G Street, box 30, folder 1, 5, 7); and Chelston luncheon menu for visit by Vice President George Bush, November 24, 1982 (G Street, box 41, folder 1, 28.

31. "Zambia's President Kaunda to Visit Reagan Next Year," *Jet*, December 27, 1982; Bush to Fletcher, April 13, 1983 (G Street, box 116, folder 2, 1).

32. Rodney A. Lewis to Scott Deniston, March 30, 1983 (G Street, box 87, folder 3, 182); Albert R. Bell Jr. to Jesse Helms, June 1, 1983 (G Street, box 30, folder 2, 220–225); and Fletcher to Bush, April 12, 1984 (G Street, box 118, folder 4, 248–251).

33. Lewis to Denniston, March 30, 1983; Bell to Helms, June 1, 1983; Jay L. Cohen to James C. Sanders, August 1, 1983 (G Street, box 87, folder 3, 185–188); Joe Bennett to Cohen, August 11, 1983 (G Street, box 30, folder 2, 231–232); J. Steven Rhodes to Bush, August 24, 1983 (G Street, box 87, folder 3, 192); Alan K. Simpson to Fletcher, August 29, 1983 (G Street, box 56, folder 3, 473); Allen C. Estes to

Fletcher, December 6, 1983 (G Street, box 44, folder 2, 1059); and AF&A capability statement, n.d. [1988] (G Street, box 56, folder 3, 579–584).

34. Fletcher to William E. Brock, June 11, 1983 (G Street, box 44, folder 2, 923–925); "Fletcher Gives Conference Speech from Hospital Bed," *Yakima Herald-Republic,* November 4, 1989; Mark Walker, "Fletcher Sings Praise of Area's Medical Care," *Yakima Herald-Republic,* December 13, 1989; Geranios, "His Loss Was Turned into a Win"; Fletcher to Robert J. Dole (draft), n.d. [April 1990] (digital copy in possession of the author); and Fletcher to Blue Cross Insurance, December 26, 1991 (G Street, box 42, folder 4, 72–76).

35. Fred Barnes, "Who's in Charge?," *Washingtonian,* August 1983; Bernyce Fletcher to Reagan, Bush, et al., September 17, Ed Bethune to James A. Baker III, September 26, Alan K. Simpson to Bernyce Fletcher, September 28, and Melvin R. Laird to Bernyce Fletcher, September 30, 1983 (G Street, box 118, folder 4, 242–244, 246–247, 252–257). Evidence that Fletcher rather than Bernyce wrote the letter is from a comparison of their writing styles.

36. Claire O'Donnell to Flo Taussig, February 2, Helene Von Damm to Reagan, February 3, and White House press release, February 3, 1983 (Reagan WHORM SF FG box 226, case file 163230); Henry A. Berliner Jr. to Fletcher, February 8, 1983 (Records of the Pennsylvania Avenue Development Commission, Board of Directors Meetings series [PADC BODM] box 13, "March 16, 1983—Board Meeting" folder, NARA College Park, MD); "3 Named to Pa. Ave. Panel," *Washington Post,* February 4, 1983; Reagan order, February 8, 1983 (PADC Board of Directors Files series [BODF] box 1, "Appointment Affidavits" folder); and Melvin L. Bradley to Fletcher, February 8, 1983 (Reagan Staff Bradley OA box 13334, "Fletcher, Arthur" folder).

37. Jean M. White, "Kennedy-Inspired 'Grand Design' for New Pennsylvania Ave. Unveiled," *Washington Post,* May 31, 1964; William M. Blair, "Fate of Panel on Restyling of Pennsylvania Avenue Is in Nixon's Hands After Congress Deletes Funds," *New York Times,* October 26, 1969; Paul Delaney, "Capital's Redevelopment Comes Under New Fire," *New York Times,* November 29, 1970; Eric Pianin, "Berry Expects to Be Out as PADC Head," *Washington Post,* January 5, 1983; and Pennsylvania Avenue Development Corporation 1985 Annual Report (G Street, box 12, folder 2, 463–482).

38. PADC program and Barbara Austin to Oliver Gasch, March 3, Thomas J. Regan Jr. to PADC board of directors (BOD), March 7, and PADC BOD agenda and resolutions, March 16, 1983 (PADC BODM box 13, "March 16, 1983—Board Meeting" folder); Reginald H. Robinson to the files, September 13, and PADC BOD meeting transcript, September 21, 1983 (PADC BODM box 13, "September 21, 1983—Board Meeting" folder); Berliner to PADC BOD, October 3, 1983 (PADC BODF box 2, "Board of Directors Correspondence, 1973–1983" folder); Berliner to PADC BOD, December 14, 1983 (PADC BODF box 2, "Board of Directors Correspondence, 1973–1983" folder); Barbara Austin to Nira H. Long, February 24, Robinson to the files, March 20, and PADC BOD meeting transcript, March 21, 1984 (PADC BODM box 13, "March 21, 1984—Board Meeting [Unlabeled]" folder); PADC BOD meeting minutes, June 20, and Dan Sawyer to Robinson, August

20, 1984 (PADC BODM box 13, "September 19, 1984—Board Meeting [Unlabeled]" folder); PADC 1985 Annual Report; PADC resolution, December 10, 1986 (PADC BODM box 19, "December 10, 1986 Board Meeting" folder); and Sabrina Tavernise, "A Dream Fulfilled, Martin Luther King Memorial Opens," *New York Times*, August 23, 2011.

39. PADC Affirmative Action Advisory Committee (AA AC) agenda, September 8, 1983 (PADC BODM box 13, "September 21, 1983—Board Meeting" folder); PADC AA AC agenda, December 6, 1983 (PADC BODM box 13, "March 21, 1984—Board Meeting [Unlabeled]" folder); PADC AA AC agenda, March 9, 1984 (PADC BODM box 13, "March 21, 1984—Board Meeting [Unlabeled]" folder); PADC affirmative action monitoring report, July 25, and PADC AA AC agenda, September 12, 1984 (PADC BODM box 13, "September 19, 1984—Board Meeting [Unlabeled]" folder).

40. PADC BOD meeting transcripts, March 16, June 20, and September 21, 1983, March 21, June 20, September 19, and October 31, 1984, March 20, June 19, September 18, and December 11, 1985, March 19, April 16, June 18, and December 10, 1986, March 18, April 1, June 17, July 8, September 16, and December 9, 1987, March 16, September 28, and December 7, 1988, March 15, June 21, September 27, October 4, 5, and 18, and November 29, 1989, and March 21, 1990 (PADC BODM boxes 13 and 16–27, folder names corresponding with meeting dates).

41. "Procurement Fair Today," *Atlanta Daily World*, July 20, 1983 (G Street, box 102, folder 4, 389); PADC BOD meeting transcript, September 19, 1984 (PADC BODM box 13, "September 19, 1984—Board Meeting [Unlabeled]" folder).

42. "Minority Business Fair Seminar Here July 20," *Atlanta Daily World*, July 13, 1984; Ann Wead Kimbrough, "Firms Owned by Minorities Sought for Procurement Fair," *Atlanta Constitution*, July 16, 1984; "Minority Business Fair Opens Friday," *Atlanta Daily World*, July 17, 1984; Kimbrough, "The Procurement Fair: 200 Minority, Women Business Owners Meet on US Contracts," *Atlanta Constitution*, July 21, 1984; "Easing the Ride for Minorities," *Philadelphia Daily News*, July 26, 1984; Reginald Owens, "Minorities Drawn to Transit Fair," *Philadelphia Tribune*, July 27, 1984; AF&A press release, August 1984 (Reagan WHORM SF PR17 box 34, case file 281174); "Bay Area Business Seminar for Women, Disadvantaged," *The Guide*, August 10, 1984; "SF Selected for Business Fair Seminars," *Oakland Post*, and "SF Selected for Business Seminars, *Berkeley Post*, August 12, 1984; "US Sponsors Minority Business Fair," *Chicago Metro News*, August 18, 1984; PADC BOD meeting transcript, September 19, 1984; Cornelius Foote Jr., "Black Leader: Reagan Can Help Our Business," *Miami Herald*, September 22, 1984; "Republican Party Seeks Black Support," *St. Louis Sentinel*, October 4, 1984; "New York City Selected as Next Site for PSDS DBE/WBE Procurement/Contract Opportunity Fair," *Med Week*, October 19, 1984; Mark J. D'Arcangelo to Fletcher, October 22, 1984 (G Street, box 58, folder 2, 609); "Procurement Opportunity Fair for New York," *Carib News*, October 23, 1984; Fletcher to Steve Rhodes, November 26, 1984 (G Street, box 104, folder 6, 104–216); Rhodes to James A. Baker, December 5, 1984 (Reagan WHORM SF PR17 box 34, case file 281174); L. R. Fulton, "Art Fletcher, Top Republican, Visits City to Promote Fair," and C. C. Campbell, "New Orleans

Host Procurement/Contract Opportunity Fair," *Louisiana Weekly,* December 15, 1984; Fletcher to Robert G. Owens, December 20, 1984 (G Street, box 44, folder 2, 202–203); Joan Ann Lopez to Fletcher, January 28, 1985 (G Street, box 87, folder 3, 127); Richard H. Doyle to Alfred Dellibovi, January 31, 1985 (G Street, box 93, folder 2, 229); Agnes T. McCann to Fletcher, February 5, 1985 (G Street, box 87, folder 3, 125); and AF&A daily mail log, November 17–December 31, 1984 (G Street, box 44, folder 2, 216–249). The quotation is from Foote.

43. PADC AA AC report, March 20, 1985 (PADC BODM box 17 "March 20, 1985—Board Meeting" folder); PADC BOD meeting transcript, June 19, 1985; Fletcher to PADC BOD, July 25, 1985 (PADC BODF box 2, "Board of Directors Correspondence, 1984–1990" folder); PADC procurement fair staff to buyers, July 29, 1985 (PADC BODM box 17, "June 19, 1985—Board Meeting" folder); Judy Pennington to PADC procurement fair participants, September 4, and PADC procurement fair agenda, September 24, 1985 (PADC BODM box 17, "June 19, 1985—Board Meeting" folder); PADC BOD meeting transcript, September 18, 1985; Pennington to PADC AA AC, December 9, 1985 (PADC BODM box 17, "December 11, 1985—Board Meeting" folder); PADC BOD meeting transcript, December 11, 1985; and Golland, *Constructing Affirmative Action,* 30.

44. William Raspberry, "The GOP's Secret," *Washington Post,* October 1, 1984.

45. Phil McCombs, "Officials Mourn Civil Rights Worker," *Washington Post,* October 2, 1982; Bush to Fletcher, December 1983 and December 1984 (G Street, box 6, folder 1, 608, 629–630).

46. Naftali, *George H. W. Bush,* 40–41; "How Groups Voted in 1980" and "How Groups Voted in 1984," Cornell University Roper Center for Public Opinion Research, https://ropercenter.cornell.edu/.

47. Rigueur, *Loneliness of the Black Republican,* 261.

48. "The Jackson Factor," *Economist,* July 21, 1984; Gitlin, *Sixties,* 152–162; and Bruce Watson, *Freedom Summer: The Savage Season of 1964 that Made Mississippi Burn and Made America a Democracy* (New York: Penguin, 2011), 255–259.

49. Sandra R. Gregg, "NAACP Attack on Reagan: Rights 'Dismantled,' Hooks Says," *Washington Post,* July 3, 1984; Raspberry, "Integration Target: The GOP," *Washington Post,* November 9, 1984; Audrey Carroll to Fletcher, November 26, Teresa P. Greene to Carroll, December 5, and Carroll to Fletcher, December 14, 1984 (G Street, box 17, folder 4, 852–853, 855); Lavonia Perryman-Fairfax to Fletcher, December 21, 1984 (G Street, box 44, folder 2, 208); Fletcher, "Art Fletcher on Integrating the GOP," January 1985 (G Street, box 30, folder 2, 416–440); Fletcher to *Washington Times,* n.d. [January 1985] (G Street, box 30, folder 2, 443); Fletcher, "On the Case for a Strategic Alliance between President Reagan and the Black Community," January 30, 1985 (G Street, box 61, folder 2, 1345–1371); Fletcher to Patrick J. Buchanan, March 14, and Buchanan to Fletcher, April 1, 1985 (Reagan WHORM Alpha box 26, "Fletcher, Arthur A. [Arthur Fletcher and Associates] [1]" folder); and Fletcher to Carroll, November 8, 1985, and Fletcher to Samuel R. Pierce Jr., June 9, 1986 (G Street, box 17, folder 4, 844–845, 847).

50. Tekla Agbala Ali Johnson, *Free Radical: Ernest Chambers, Black Power, and the Politics of Race* (Lubbock: Texas Tech University Press, 2012), passim.

51. Fletcher to Bush, December 18, 1984 (G Street, box 16, folder 2, 1398–1399); Fletcher to Steven Danzanski and Fletcher to J. Steven Rhodes, December 18, 1984 (G Street, box 44, folder 2, 209–210); Fletcher to Reagan, January 11, 1985 (Reagan WHORM Alpha box 26, "Fletcher, Arthur A. [Arthur Fletcher and Associates] [1]" folder); Fletcher to Reagan, May 22, 1985 (Reagan WHORM SF HU012 box 8, case file 304792); "Lou Rawls Debuts Parade of Stars on Television," RareSoul.com, December 29, 2012, http://raresoul.com/; and "An Evening of Stars," UNCF, http://give.uncf.org/site/DocServer/2009AEOSTimeline.pdf?doc.

52. William E. Brock to DOL staff and DOL press release, May 16, Fletcher to Reagan, May 22, and Melvin L. Bradley to Fletcher, June 20, 1985 (Reagan WHORM SF HU012 box 8, case file 304792); Kent T. Cushenberry to Fletcher, May 24, James B. Burnham to Fletcher, May 29, M. Diane Fields to John Hurst Adams, May 31, and Adams to various recipients, May 31, 1985 (G Street, box 103, folder 3, 326–329); I. Rajesway, "Recent Grads Swarm DC Job Fair; Businesses, Federal Agencies Present Array of Career Options," *Washington Post*, June 12, 1985; Chris Edley interview by Martia Goodson, July 31, 1985 (United Negro College Fund Project, Rare Book and Manuscript Library, Columbia University, New York); Thomas L. Jones to Fletcher, March 4, and Fields to Fletcher, April 14, 1986 (G Street, box 44, folder 2, 1081–1082); and Dennis McLellan, "Christopher F. Edley, 75; Former Chief of United Negro College Fund" (obituary), *Los Angeles Times*, May 8, 2003.

53. AF&A business plan, February 6, 1987 (G Street, box 87, folder 3, 145–177).

54. Fletcher to Lydia Bryant, January 22, Alexander B. Jansen to Vaughan A. Goodall, February 21, James W. Dietz to Raleigh Harden, March 26, Jeffrey R. Ponder to Fletcher, June 11, Harden to Tom Evans, July 2, Bryant to Fletcher, n.d. [September], Bryant to Fletcher, September 22, Harden to unknown recipient, n.d. [October], Fletcher to Bryant, October 14, Teresa P. Greene to Fletcher, October 23, Bryant to Fletcher, October 31, Goodall to AF&A, November 7, Fletcher to Bryant, November 10 and 14, Bryant to Fletcher, November 14, Fletcher to Bryant, November 19, Harden to Bryant, November 21, Bryant to Fletcher, December 1, Robert R. Hardiman to Director of Logistics, Army Engineer Center, December 3, Warren A. Stubli report, December 4, Bryant to Fletcher, December 11, Harden to Bryant, December 15, and B. J. Bethea to Fletcher, December 31, 1986 (G Street, box 59, folder 2, 681–688, 697–701, 715, 729–734, 736, 753–756, 758–766, 802, 804–805, 807–809); and Paul R. Somerfield to Jody L. Reath, November 17, Maurice Lane Jr. to Fletcher, December 10, and Ralph C. Morse to Fletcher, December 12, 1986 (G Street, box 44, folder 2, 1046, 1049, 1053). According to Paul Fletcher, Raleigh Harden was not related to Fletcher's first wife, Mary Harden Fletcher.

55. Bryant to Fletcher, January 8, R. S. Kem to Sandra Brown, March 9, Craig F. Lindsay to AF&A, March 13, Fletcher to Bryant and Harden to Fletcher, March 30, Fletcher to Harold Harris, April 1, Greene to Fletcher, April 15, Fletcher to Harris and Fletcher to Bryant, April 21, Bryant to Harden, June 2, Fletcher to Harry G. Karegeannes, July 27, Fletcher bill of complaint, n.d. [August], and Bryant to Fletcher, December 1, 1987 (G Street, box 59, folder 2, 670, 704–709, 713–714, 739–740, 767–793, 812–813); Robert H. Miller to Fletcher, April 21, 1987 (G Street, box 87, folder 3, 141–143); Fletcher to Thermus Baker, March 9, 1987 (G Street, box

113, folder 2, 18); Fletcher to Howard Baker, June 24, and J. Bruce King to Fletcher, August 17, 1987 (Reagan WHORM SF PQ, case file 497122); Fletcher to Reagan, September 30, and Karegeannes to Fletcher, November 2, 1987 (Reagan WHORM Alpha box 26, "Fletcher, Arthur A. [Arthur Fletcher and Associates] [1]" folder); and AF&A capability statement, n.d. [1988] (G Street, box 56, folder 3, 579–584).

56. Bush to Fletcher, February 18, 1987 (G Street, box 116, folder 2, 3–4).

57. Mark Shields, "Jack Kemp's Problem," *Washington Post*, June 11, 1987; Naftali, *George H. W. Bush*, 50–53.

58. Phil McCombs, "Black Republicans, Standing Up for Bush," *Washington Post*, March 22, 1988.

59. Tom Sherwood, "Blacks Echo Barry's Self-Help Theme: Conferees in Miami Agree on Need for Personal Responsibility," *Washington Post*, April 27, 1987; Fletcher to Bush, May 8, and Bush to Fletcher, May 18, 1987 (George Bush Vice Presidential Files, SF PL009, 479375VP).

60. Robert L. Woodson, "Democratic Indifference to Black Voters' Loyalty Is Fertile Ground for GOP," *Atlanta Journal-Constitution*, November 22, 1987; Ed Bethea to Fletcher, November 23, 1987 (G Street, box 23, folder 1, 41–42).

61. William Raspberry, "A Problem for the GOP's Maitre d'," *Washington Post*, December 14, 1987; Murray Friedman, "The GOP Has an Opportunity to Gain Black Voters," *Philadelphia Inquirer*, April 2, 1988.

62. Derrick A. Humphries to Fletcher, July 15, 1988 (G Street, box 103, folder 2, 3); Asher & Associates Inc., *Official Report of the Proceedings of the Thirty-Fourth Republican National Convention held in New Orleans, Louisiana, August 15, 16, 17, 18, 1988, Resulting in the Nomination of George H. W. Bush, of Texas, for President, and J. Danforth Quayle, of Indiana, for Vice President* (Washington, DC: Republican National Committee, 1988), 134.

63. Gerald M. Boyd, "Bush to Campaign for Blacks' Vote," *New York Times*, August 12, 1988.

64. Lee Atwater to Henry Berliner, December 6, 1988 (PADC BODF box 2, "Board of Directors Correspondence, 1984–1990" folder).

65. Paul Duggan, "The Barneses and the Horton Debate," *Washington Post*, October 28, 1988; Roger Simon, "How a Murderer and Rapist Became the Bush Campaign's Most Valuable Player," *Baltimore Sun*, November 11, 1990.

66. "Dukakis Lead Widens, According to New Poll," *New York Times*, July 26, 1988; "Survey Gives Bush the Lead over Dukakis," *New York Times*, September 21, 1988; and "Bush Gains in a New Poll of Voters," *New York Times*, October 18, 1988. Bush was the fortieth person elected president but is traditionally referred to as the forty-first president because Grover Cleveland, who served nonconsecutive terms, is counted twice.

67. William Raspberry, "Bush and Blacks," *Washington Post*, November 11, 1988; Fletcher and Bernyce Fletcher to James Baker, November 11, 1988 (G Street, box 58, folder 2, 760); and Baker to Fletcher and Bernyce Fletcher, December 12, 1988 (G Street, box 138, folder 4, 105).

68. John J. Gomez to Bush, November 21, Cathy Clardy Patterson to Bush, December 16, and Strom Thurmond to Chase Untermeyer, December 21, 1988

(Bush Presidential Records, Staff and Office Files, Counsel's Office Appointment File box 1, "Chairman Arthur Allen Fletcher Commission on Civil Rights [OA/ID 20122]" folder, NARA George Bush Library, College Station, TX); Bernard Weinraub, "Bush Plans a Drive to Recruit Minorities," *New York Times*, December 4, 1988.

69. Maralee Schwartz and Paul Blustein, "Dennis Says 'Yes' to Labor Post but Is Still Waiting for an Offer," *Washington Post*, December 20, 1988; "How Groups Voted in 1980," "How Groups Voted in 1984," and "How Groups Voted in 1988," Cornell University Roper Center for Public Opinion Research, https://ropercenter .cornell.edu/.

70. Schwartz and Blustein, "Dennis Says 'Yes'"; Gerald M. Boyd, "Elizabeth Dole Chosen by Bush for Labor Department," *New York Times*, December 25, 1988; and "Fletcher Loses Labor Bid; Others Await Appointments," *Jet*, January 16, 1989.

71. "Fletcher Loses Labor Bid"; Committee for the American Bicentennial Inaugural invitation, January 20, 1989; and "Air Force One Guest Flight Certificates," March 9, 1989 (Bush WHORM SF TR box 9, "Unscanned 071042" folder).

72. Ross Starek to Jane Dannenhauer, January 30, 1989 (Bush Staff and Office Files, Counsel's Office Appointment File box 1, "Chairman Arthur Allen Fletcher Commission on Civil Rights [OA/ID 20122]" folder); Andy Fuller, "Fletcher Picked for Rights Post," *Seattle Times*, n.d. [March 1989] (G Street, box III, folder 3, 85); "Arthur Fletcher's Distinguished Past" (editorial), *Tri-City Herald*, March 7, 1989; "Art Fletcher Tapped to Head Civil-Rights Panel: Former Pasco Councilman Will Be in Charge of Rebuilding Commission," *Seattle Times*, March 22, 1989; Ann Devroy, "Longtime Bush Ally to Head Rights Unit: President Aims to Make Commission 'Respectable Again,' Aides Say," *Washington Post*, March 22, 1989; Julie Johnson, "White House Considers Replacing Head of Civil Rights Commission," *New York Times*; David Whitney, "Bush Lists Fletcher for Rights Panel," *Tri-City Herald*; and Richard Benedetto, "Bush Has Pick for Rights Post, but Incumbent Isn't Budging," *USA Today*, March 23, 1989;

73. "Art Fletcher Tapped to Head Civil-Rights Panel"; Devroy, "Longtime Bush Ally to Head Rights Unit"; Johnson, "White House Considers Replacing Head of Civil Rights Commission"; Whitney, "Bush Lists Fletcher for Rights Panel"; Benedetto, "Bush Has Pick for Rights Post"; and Berry, *And Justice for All*, 245–246.

74. "Arthur Fletcher to Address: ACCA National Banquet," *ACCA Compliance Monitor*, August 1989 (G Street, box 18, folder 1, 1–3); Sandra J. Simon to Fletcher, August 17, 1989 (G Street, box 22C, folder 3, 614–615); Reginald Webb to Fletcher, August 24, 1989 (G Street, box 53, folder 1, 1003–1004); Margaret R. Preska to Fletcher, September 1, 1989 (G Street, box 116, folder 2, 438–439); Susan Gilmore, "'Halfway Home . . . Still Long Way to Go': Fletcher Says Civil Rights Panel Still Necessary," *Seattle Times*, September 10, 1989; Glenn Witham to Fletcher, October 9, 1989 (G Street, box 103, folder 3, 370–371); Larry E. Tadlock to Fletcher, October 10, 1989 (G Street, box 16, folder 1, 754); Mark Bennett to Fletcher, October 11, 1989 (G Street, box 72, folder 2, 456); Richard Prince, "A Republican as Civil Rights Hero for the 90s?," *Chronicle and Times Union*, October 14, 1989; Prince, "Black Activist May Take GOP Job," *Washington Press-Intelligencer*, October

15, 1989; Paul Bayless to Fletcher, October 18, 1989 (G Street, box 22C, folder 3, 619); Martha Peterson and Winfred J. Sanders to Fletcher, October 23, 1989; Peter Moore to Fletcher, November 2, 1989 (G Street, box 103, folder 3, 335); Duane Dozier, "Fletcher: 'It's Time' for Women and Minorities," *Yakima Herald-Republic*, November 4, 1989; Donald P. Horwitz to Fletcher, November 6, 1989 (G Street, box 87, folder 2, 4); Paul King to Fletcher, November 10, 1989 (G Street, box 103, folder 3, 332); Michael T. Fagin to Fletcher, November 13, 1989 (G Street, box 41, folder 2, 138); and Fletcher financial report, n.d. [December 1989] (G Street, box 138, folder 2, 2–3).

75. Julie Johnson, "Rights Chief Offers to Quit; White House Has Yet to Act," *New York Times*, October 12, 1989; Jessica Lee, "Civil Rights Chief Quits after Troubled Tenure," *USA Today*, October 19, 1989; "A Chance to Invigorate Civil Rights" (editorial), *LA Times*, October 23, 1989; USCCR meeting transcript, October 27, 1989 (G Street, box 29, folder 2, 507–554); and Berry, *And Justice for All*, 247.

76. Fletcher to Glenn Phipps, August 24, and Daniel Mullen to Fletcher, September 18, 1989 (G Street, box 53, folder 1, 1129); Duane Dozier, "Business Conference to Offer Aid to Women and Minorities," *Yakima Herald-Republic*, October 17, 1989; Dozier, "Fletcher: 'It's Time'"; Larry E. Tadlock to Fletcher, November 10, 1989 (G Street, box 16, folder 1, 754); untitled, *Austin American-Statesman*, November 12, 1989; "Briefly," *USA Today*, November 13, 1989; and Alan K. Simpson to Fletcher, November 14, 1989 (G Street, 103, folder 3, 317).

77. "Fletcher Gives Conference Speech from Hospital Bed," *Yakima Herald-Republic*, November 4, 1989; Marla Harper, "Personalities," *Washington Post*, November 4, 1989; Julie Johnson, "Long Delay Is Seen on US Rights Post," *New York Times*, November 5, 1989.

CHAPTER 7. MAN OF RAGE, 1990–1995

1. Don Terry, "Riot in Los Angeles: At the Epicenter; Decades of Rage Created Crucible of Violence," *New York Times*, May 3, 1992; Robert Reinhold, "After Police-Beating Verdict, Another Trial for the Jurors," *New York Times*, May 9, 1992; Lou Cannon, *Official Negligence: How Rodney King and the Riots Changed Los Angeles and the LAPD* (Boulder, CO: Westview Press, 1999), 20–50; Berry, *And Justice for All*, 267–268; Charles A. Gallagher and Cameron D. Lippard, eds., *Race and Racism in the United States: An Encyclopedia of the American Mosaic* (Santa Barbara, CA: Greenwood, 2014), 709; and Daniel Funke and Tina Susman, "From Ferguson to Baton Rouge: Deaths of Black Men and Women at the Hands of Police," *Los Angeles Times*, July 12, 2016. The Gates quotation is from Gallagher and Lippard.

2. Robert A. Caro, *The Years of Lyndon Johnson: Master of the Senate* (New York: Knopf, 2002), 928–998; Berry, *And Justice for All*, 10–38; and Golland, *Constructing Affirmative Action*, 27.

3. Foster Rhea Dulles, *The Civil Rights Commission, 1957–1965* (East Lansing: Michigan State University Press, 1968), passim; Berry, *And Justice for All*, 21, 40–41.

4. Berry, *And Justice for All*, 37–101; Golland, *Constructing Affirmative Action*, 76, 84–85.

5. Berry, *And Justice for All*, 132–181. Hannah quoted in Berry, *And Justice for All*, 96.

6. United States Commission on Civil Rights, "Affirmative Action in the 1980s: Dismantling the Process of Discrimination" and "Who is Guarding the Guardians? A Report on Police Practices" (Washington, DC: USCCR, 1981); Berry, *And Justice for All*, 182–190.

7. Milton Friedman, *Capitalism and Freedom* (Chicago: University of Chicago Press, 1962), 108–111; Berry, *And Justice for All*, 190–191.

8. Berry maintains that Flemming would have resigned had he been asked; as it is, he did not protest the termination. *And Justice for All*, 189.

9. *New York Times*, October 24, 1983 (entire front page); Jean Rosenbluth, "Reagan's Assault on Civil Rights Guardians," letter to the editor, *New York Times*, November 3, 1983; Berry, *And Justice for All*, 142, 179, 184–188.

10. Ninety-Eighth Congress of the United States, "United States Commission on Civil Rights Act of 1983," HR-2230 (G Street, box 62, folder 3, 113–119); "Black Leaders Are Accused of Racism," *Associated Press*, March 6, 1985; Juan Williams, "Civil Rights Commission Chairman Says He Plans to Cool His Rhetoric," *Washington Post*, March 13, 1985; US Civil Rights Commission to Thomas J. Regan Jr., n.d. [1989] (Bush Staff and Office Files, Counsel's Office Appointment File box 1, "Chairman Arthur Allen Fletcher Commission on Civil Rights [OA/ID 20122]" folder); Linda Chavez, "Commission Unneeded; Let This Watchdog Die," *USA Today*, March 28, 1989; "Day in Court; Rights Rift; Special Delivery," *MacNeil-Lehrer NewsHour* transcript, April 11, 1989; and Berry, *And Justice for All*, 187.

11. Andy Fuller, "Fletcher Picked for Rights Post," *Seattle Times*, n.d. [March 1989] (G Street, box 111, folder 3, 85); Paul Clancy, "Civil Rights Chief Rules Over Chaos," *USA Today*, March 22, 1989; Julie Johnson, "White House Considers Replacing Head of Civil Rights Commission," *New York Times*, March 22, 1989; Whitney, "Bush Lists Fletcher for Rights Panel"; "Taking the First Step" (editorial), *Los Angeles Times*, March 29, 1989; Johanna Neuman, "Rights Agency Caught in Crisis: Infighting, Conflicts Take Toll," *USA Today*, April 27, 1989; "History of the US Civil Rights Commission," *USA Today*, April 27, 1989; Ruth Marcus, "Rights Chairman in Controversy Again; Gay Groups Hit Allen's Plans to Address 'Traditional Values' Seminar," *Washington Post*, October 4, 1989; and Berry, *And Justice for All*, 241, 245–247.

12. Ann Devroy and Saundra Torry, "Civil Rights Chief: Bush Relies on 'Country Club Republicans,'" *Washington Post*, July 15, 1989.

13. *MacNeil-Lehrer NewsHour*, April 11, 1989; Marcus, "Rights Chairman in Controversy Again"; and USCCR meeting transcript, October 27, 1989 (G Street, box 29, folder 2, 507–554).

14. "Rudy" and "Faye" to Fletcher, Florence and Jim Forest to Fletcher, Janet Snodgrass to Fletcher, various signers to Fletcher, JoAnne O'Brien and Bob Hess to Fletcher, John Cashier to Fletcher, Linda Hollman Patton to Fletcher, and Stuart Troit to Fletcher, n.d. [November 1989], and various signers to Fletcher, November 4, 1989 (G Street, box 111, folder 1, 40–49, 64–67, and folder 3, 1189–1192); Frank E. Harwi to Fletcher, November 13, 1989 (G Street, box 49, folder 4, 1); Alan K.

Simpson to Fletcher, November 14, 1989 (G Street, box 103, folder 3, 317); "Saving the Civil Rights Commission" (editorial), *Washington Post,* December 7, 1989; George W. and Doris Haley to Fletcher, December 12, 1989 (G Street, box 49, folder 4, 8); David M. Nero to Fletcher, December 18, 1989 (G Street, box 103, folder 3, 438); "Bush to Name Head of Rights Panel," *St. Petersburg Times,* February 9, 1990; Amy L. Schwartz, report, February 23, 1990 (Bush Counsel's Office Appointment File box 1, "OA/ID 20122" folder); White House press release, February 23, 1990 (G Street, box 44, folder 2, 902); Nixon to Fletcher, February 24, 1990 (G Street, box 15A, folder 2, 900); William Allen to Melvin Jenkins, February 24, and USCCR voting record, February 26, 1990 (Records of the USCCR, Freedom of Information Act request, in possession of the author); James A. Fletcher to Fletcher, February 27, and Trudi Michelle Morrison, February 28, 1990 (G Street, box 16, folder 1, 730–731); Edwin Wheeler to Fletcher, February 27, 1990 (G Street, box 140, folder 4, 93); Jesse L. Jackson Sr. to Fletcher, February 28, 1990 (Bush WHORM SF PP, folder 124458); Arch Parsons, "Rights Panel OKs Fletcher as Chairman," *Baltimore Sun,* February 28, 1990; Charles C. Blake Jr. to Fletcher, February 28, 1990 (G Street, box 22, folder 3, 672–674); Delores M. Dyer to Fletcher, George E. Hicks to Fletcher, and Bill Wassmuth to Fletcher, March 1, 1990 (G Street, box 16, folder 1, 739–742 and folder 2, 315, and box 22C, folder 3, 788); Robert A. Corrigan to Fletcher and John G. Montgomery to Fletcher, March 2, 1990 (G Street, box 16, folder 1, 751, 1349); Coretta Scott King to Fletcher, Raymond H. Boone to Fletcher, Zara Hassan and Mick Welch to Fletcher, Henrietta Canty to Fletcher, and Richard A. Worden to Fletcher, March 5, 1990 (G Street, box 16, folder 1, 728–729, and folder 2, 301; box 22B, folder 2, 301; box 22C, folder 3, 789–791; and box 112, folder 3, 161); Henry Beauchamp to Fletcher, George Parker to Fletcher, and Lydia J. Davis to Fletcher, March 6, 1990 (G Street, box 16, folder 1, 1370; box 42, folder 7, 179–180; and box 118, folder 4, 240); and Donald P. Schnacke to Fletcher and Mehrdad Karimi to Fletcher, March 7, 1990 (G Street, box 16, folder 1, 733–734 and box 41, folder 2, 275).

15. Fletcher to Bush, March 6, 1990 (Bush WHORM SF PP, folder 120345); Robert J. Dole to Fletcher, March 19, 1990 (G Street, box 101, folder 6, 196); Fletcher to Bush, April 16, 1990 (G Street, box 22C, folder 3, 174–176); "Arthur Fletcher on Job Despite Bypass Surgery," *Jet,* April 16, 1990; photographs, May 17, 1990 (G Street, box 49, folder 2, 270–271); and White House press release, May 17, 1990 (G Street, 102, folder 2, 34–36).

16. USCCR board member biographies, June 1990 (G Street, box 51, folder 2, 2–10); Neal Devins, "The Civil Rights Commission Backslides," *Wall Street Journal,* October 19, 1990; and Charles Pei Wang interview, January 3, 2017, by and in possession of the author.

17. William Allen to Melvin Jenkins, February 24, 1990; USCCR meeting transcript, March 2, 1990 (Records of the USCCR); Arch Parsons, "New Chairman of Rights Panel Seeks Consensus," *Baltimore Sun,* March 3, 1990; USCCR retreat transcript, May 11, 1990 (G Street, box 98, folder 1, 123–318); USCCR meeting minutes, May 11, 1990 (Records of the USCCR); and Wang interview by the author.

18. USCCR meeting transcript, October 27, 1989 (G Street, box 29, folder 2, 507–554); "Saving the Civil Rights Commission" (editorial), *Washington Post*, December 7, 1989; Raul Yzaguirre to Don Edwards, May 15, 1990 (G Street, box 16, folder 1, 1384–1385); Wilfredo J. Gonzalez to USCCR commissioners, January 24, 1991 (G Street, box 62, folder 3, 121–145); USCCR meeting minutes, January 31, 1991 (Records of the USCCR); Fletcher Congressional testimony, June 12, 1991 (G Street, box 15A, folder 2, 667–677); Mary K. Mathews to Gonzalez, June 12, 1991 (G Street, box 111, folder 3, 753–756); USCCR meeting minutes, June 21, 1991 (Records of the USCCR); Fletcher Congressional testimony, July 25, 1991 (G Street, box 85, folder 2, 23–59); "House Extends Civil Rights Panel for Just Two Years," *New York Times*, October 1, 1991; Stephen A. Holmes, "With Glory of Past Only a Memory, Rights Panel Searches for New Role," *New York Times*, October 10, 1991; Wilfredo J. Gonzalez to USCCR commissioners, November 8, 1991 (G Street, box 38, folder 1, 308–329); USCCR meeting minutes, December 6, 1991 (Records of the USCCR); Fletcher Congressional testimony and Edwards to Fletcher, March 19, 1991 (G Street, box 104, folder 6, 222, and box 111, folder 3, 1199–1215); Edwards to Fletcher, May 5, 1992 (G Street, box 104, folder 6, 17); USCCR press release, June 22, and Paul Simon speech, June 26, 1992 (G Street, box 101, folder 6, 366–368); Berry, *And Justice for All*, 250–251; and Wang interview by the author.

19. USCCR retreat transcript, May 11, 1990.

20. *City of Richmond v. J. A. Croson Co.*, 488 US 469 (January 23, 1989); White House press release, January 27, 1989 (G Street, box 116, folder 2, 587); Barry Goldstein, legal analysis, n.d. [February 1989] (G Street, box 18, folder 6, 679–693); *Wards Cove Packing Co. v. Atonio*, 490 US 642 (June 5, 1989); *Martin v. Wilks*, 490 US 755 (June 12, 1989); Donald B. Ayer testimony, February 20, 1990 (G Street, box 68, folder 6, 28); and "Quotas That Never Were" (editorial), *New York Times*, May 22, 1990.

21. White House press release, January 27, 1989; Ann Devroy, "Bush Urged to Support Rights Act: Black Leaders Meet with President Today to Head Off Veto," *Washington Post*, May 14, 1990; R. W. Apple, "Washington Talk; Tiptoeing, Bush Comes to a Fork on Civil Rights," *New York Times*, and Susan Ellicott, "Kinder, Gentler Bush Faces Civil Rights Test," *Times of London*, May 15, 1990.

22. Donald B. Ayer testimony, February 20, 1990; USCCR retreat transcript, May 11, 1990; and Devroy, "Bush Urged to Support Rights Act."

23. US Congress, "Civil Rights Act of 1990," October 20, 1990 (G Street, box 8, folder 5, 604–620).

24. Devroy, "Bush Urged to Support Rights Act"; Paul Craig Roberts, "Maneuvering Us Toward Quotas?," *Washington Times*, May 21, 1990; and "Quotas That Never Were."

25. "Civil Rights Act of 1990."

26. Devroy, "Bush Urged to Support Rights Act"; "Bush Trying to Avoid Vetoing Civil Rights Bill," *CBS Morning News with Charles Osgood* transcript, May 15, 1990; R. W. Apple Jr., "Washington Talk; Tiptoeing, Bush Comes to a Fork on Civil Rights," *New York Times*, May 15, 1990; Frank J. Murray, "Black Leaders Quarrel after Courting Bush on Bill," *Washington Times*, May 15, 1990; Ellicott, "Kinder,

Gentler Bush Faces Civil Rights Test"; Thomas Ferraro, "Bush, Black Leaders Seek 'Common Ground' on Civil Rights Bill," UPI Newswire, May 15, 1990; Devins, "Civil Rights Commission Backslides"; and Bush, *All the Best*, 485.

27. Maureen Dowd, "Trying to Head Off His Own Veto, Bush Holds Meeting on Rights Bill," *New York Times*, May 15, 1990; Ferraro, "Bush, Black Leaders Seek 'Common Ground;'" Ann Devroy, "White House Shifts on Civil Rights Act; Differences with Pending Legislation Described as 'Minimal,'" *Washington Post*, May 15, 1990; "Hiring-Quota Issue Snags Civil Rights Bill," *USA Today*, June 25, 1990; *Meet the Press* transcript, June 24, 1990 (Records of the USCCR); Fletcher, "For Civil Rights, It's Back to the Future," *New York Times*, August 19, 1990.

28. USCCR meeting transcript, June 7, 1990 (G Street, box 103, folder 3, 43–184); USCCR draft press release, June 7, 1990 (Records of the USCCR); Alfred W. Blumrosen to Fletcher, June 20, 1990 (G Street, box 111, folder 3, 91–94); USCCR meeting minutes, June 21, 1990 (Records of the USCCR); *Meet the Press* transcript, June 24, 1990; "Civil Rights Chief: Bush Wary of Bill; Commission Leader Says President Unconvinced Bill Won't Force Quotas," *Associated Press*, June 25, 1990; USCCR press release, June 28, 1990 (G Street, box 105, folder 3, 61–62); and USCCR report, July 1990 (G Street, box 49, folder 1, 17–70).

29. Fletcher draft to Bush, July 7, 1990 (G Street, box 103, folder 3, 380).

30. Ann Devroy, "Administration Renews Threat to Veto Civil Rights Bill if Left Unchanged," *Washington Post*, October 13, 1990; Jessica Lee, "Bush Set to Veto Civil Rights Bill," *USA Today*, October 19, 1990; Alexis Moore, "Sign Major Civil Rights Bill, Marchers in DC Urge Bush," *Miami Herald*, October 20, 1990; and William H. Freivogel, "Civil Rights Showdown Impasse May End in Veto Despite Compromise Effort," *St. Louis Post-Dispatch*, October 21, 1990.

31. Morris B. Abram to Bush, June 7, 1990 (G Street, box 23, folder 3, 104); White House press release and Bush to the Congress, October 20, 1990 (G Street, box 8, folder 5, 630–631); Terrence Hunt, "Bush Vetoes Major Civil Rights Bill," *Associated Press*, October 22, 1990; and Ann Devroy, "Bush Vetoes Civil Rights Bill; Measure Said to Encourage Job Quotas; Women, Minorities Sharply Critical," *Washington Post*, October 23, 1990.

32. Jacqueline Trescott, "Rep. Gary Franks, Unexpected Republican: The Hill's Only Black Conservative, Going His Own Way," *Washington Post*, July 31, 1991; Bush, *All the Best*, 485–486.

33. Michael L. Williams to John Junker, and Department of Education press releases, December 4 and December 16, 1990 (G Street, box 102, folder 4, 1048–1049, 1635–1638); and Anthony Lewis, "Zealotry Gone Mad," *New York Times*, December 17, 1990.

34. James Michael Brodie and Joye Mercer, "U of Louisville, Community Ponder Consequences of Decision to Accept Fiesta Bowl Invitation," *Black Issues in Higher Education*, December 6, 1990; Michael Marriott, "Colleges Basing Aid on Race Risk Loss of Federal Funds," *New York Times*, December 12, 1990; Neil A. Lewis, "Race and College Aid" (editorial), *New York Times*, December 13, 1990; Kenneth J. Cooper, "Scholarships Based on Race Prohibited," and "Designated Scholarships" (editorial), *Washington Post*, December 13, 1990; Carol Innerst and

Carleton R. Bryant, "Colleges Vow to Circumvent Civil Rights Rule," *Washington Times*, December 13, 1990; "Minority Leaders Blast Scholarship Decision," *USA Today*, December 13, 1990; Marriott, "Move against Minority Aid is Debated," Lisa Belkin, "Shock Grips Students Facing Loss of Money," and "Devastating Signal to Minority Students" (editorial), *New York Times*, December 14, 1990; "Virginia: Wilder Asks Bush to Back Scholarships," *Washington Times*, December 14, 1990; Barbara Vobejda, "In the Eye of Racial Controversy: Education Official's Actions Shock Some," Amy Goldstein and Mary Jordan, "'Chilling Effect' Feared," and William Raspberry, "Scholarships and Politics," *Washington Post*, December 14, 1990; and Dennis Kelly, "Schools to Defy Ban on Minority Aid," Richard Benedetto, "Critics Lay Blame at Bush's Feet," and "White House and NAACP respond," *USA Today*," December 14, 1990.

35. Michael K. Frisby, "Black Republicans Assail Bush's Civil Rights Record," *Boston Globe*, December 16, 1990; Lewis, "Zealotry Gone Mad"; and Fletcher to Bush, January 23, 1991 (Bush WHORM SF HU box 11, folder 207503).

36. Carol McCabe Booker to USCCR commissioners, January 11 and January 17, and William Allen to USCCR commissioners, January 23, 1991 (G Street, box 102, folder 4, 1569–1576, 1639–1647); USCCR meeting minutes, January 23, 1991 (Records of the USCCR); and Kenneth J. Cooper, "Rights Commission Asks Bush to Back Minority Scholarships," *Washington Post*, January 26, 1991.

37. Maureen Dowd, "Cavazos Quits as Education Chief Amid Pressure from White House," *New York Times*, and Linda P. Campbell, "Education Chief Quits Amid Rumors of Ouster," *Chicago Tribune*, December 13, 1990; Kenneth J. Cooper and Ann Devroy, "Minority-Scholarship Curb Under Review," and "Accrediting Quotas" (editorial), *Wall Street Journal*, December 14, 1990; Benedetto, "Critics Lay Blame at Bush's Feet"; "White House and NAACP respond"; Ann Devroy and Dan Balz, "Bush Stands Neutral While Aides Debate Scholarship Controversy," *Washington Post*, December 15, 1990; D. S. Onley, David Schumacher, and David Baumann, "President 'Disturbed' by New ED Scholarship Policy," *Education Daily*, December 18, 1990; Tom Wicker, "Who's in Charge?," and Karen De Witt, "Change on Race-Based Scholarship Brings Renewed Criticism," *New York Times*, Kenneth J. Cooper, "Administration Revises Race-Based Grant Rule: President Denies 'Flip-Flop' on Scholarships," and "Turnabout on Scholarships" (editorial), *Washington Post*, Timothy Noah and David Shibman, "White House Drops Ban on Scholarships for Minorities, but Controversy Remains," *Wall Street Journal*, Paul Clancy, "Minority Aid Ban Eased" and "Policymaker Says Decision a Sound One," *USA Today*, Onley and Baumann, "ED Modifies Position on Race-Based Scholarships," *Education Daily*, and Aaron Epstein, "Furor Swells Despite Shift on Minority Stipends," *Philadelphia Inquirer*, December 19, 1990; Andrew Rosenthal, "White House in Disarray: Mishandling of Scholarships for Minorities Reflects Struggle for a Civil Rights Agenda," *New York Times*, Cooper, "Scholarship Policy Called Not Binding: Revision Is 'Personal Opinion' that Lacks Force, Ex-Official Asserts," *Washington Post*, December 20, 1990; Janet Bass, "Official Reverses Scholarship Ban," *Huntingdon Daily News*, December 21, 1990; Alain L. Sanders, "Who's in Charge Here? Embarrassed by a Flip-Flop on Minority Schol-

arships, Bush Chooses a Political Pragmatist as Education Secretary," *Time*, December 31, 1990; and Roger Porter to Fletcher, February 4 and March 1, 1991 (Bush WHORM SF HU box 11, folders 209556CU and 207503).

38. "Some Say King's Warnings, Not Dreams, Are Emerging," *Kansas City Star*, January 21, 1991.

39. White House press release, February 25, 1991 (G Street, box 8, folder 5, 587–590); Carole Ashkinaze, "Civil Rights Chief Is No Lap Dog," *Chicago Sun-Times*, May 2, 1991; Linda Sadler, "Civil Rights Agency Chief Brings Fight to Colorado: Arthur Fletcher Will Direct Efforts to Incorporate Civil Rights Policies into Business," *Rocky Mountain News*, September 10, 1991; Jessica Lee, "A Magnet for Civil Rights Anger," *USA Today*, Ann Devroy, "President Signs Civil Rights Bill; White House Disavows Proposed Directive to End Affirmative Action," *Washington Post*, November 22, 1991; and Berry, *And Justice for All*, 260.

40. Maria Puente, "NAACP Holds Off; Asks for a Meeting," *USA Today*, July 9, 1991; Lynne Duke, "NAACP Defers Decision on Thomas; Group's Board Seeks Meeting with Nominee Before Taking Position," *Washington Post*, July 9, 1991; USCCR meeting minutes, July 15, 1991 (Records of the USCCR); Mathew Cooper, "Washington Whispers: Rights Redux," *US News and World Report*, July 16, 1991; "Rights Activists Research Thomas," *USA Today*, July 16, 1991; Robert Brannum to Fletcher, July 23, 1991 (G Street, box 101, folder 6, 68–69); Michael Frisby, "Rights Chief Supports Thomas Nomination," *Boston Globe*, July 27, 1991; Robert L. Koenig, "Groups to Join Thomas Opposition but Real Test Lies in Civil Rights, Organizations," *St. Louis Post-Dispatch*, July 28, 1991; Ruth Marcus, "Group That Helped Defeat Bork Opposes Thomas; Justice Alliance First of Liberals Expected to Take Position on High Court Nominee This Week," *Washington Post*, July 30, 1991; Marcus, "NAACP Opposes Thomas; AFL-CIO Joins Civil Rights Group," *Washington Post*, August 1, 1991; Roger Wilkins, "Nominee Fails to Understand Race's Struggle," *Atlanta Journal and Constitution*, September 8, 1991; and "About the Court: Frequently Asked Questions," Supreme Court of the United States, https://www.supremecourt.gov/.

41. Ede Holiday to Bush, July 26, 1991 (Bush WHORM SF ME box 5, folder 266648); Sharon LaFraniere, "Civil Rights Official Dismisses His Doubts on Thomas," *Washington Post*, July 27, 1991; Frisby, "Rights Chief Supports Thomas Nomination"; Bush to Fletcher, July 28, 1991 (Bush WHORM SF ME box 5, folder 266648); *Congressional Record-Senate* 137, no. 18 (October 15, 1991): 26354; "What's Ahead for Affirmative Action?," *Jet*, July 10, 1995; and Berry, *And Justice for All*, 261.

42. USCCR meeting minutes, January 31, 1991 (Records of the USCCR); Renata Anderson House to Billyejo Schley, May 15, 1991 (G Street, box 106, folder 4, 71); Christine Spolar, "US Panel Reviewing Complaints of DC Hispanics," *Washington Post*, May 16, 1991; "Civil Rights Commissioner Says USA 'Racist Nation,' Echoes Kerner Report," *Jet*, May 20, 1991; Arthur W. Diggs to Fletcher, May 23, 1991 (G Street, box 101, folder 6, 272–273); Spolar, "Rights Study to Focus on DC Hispanics; Commission to Probe Reasons for Mount Pleasant Disturbance, Abuse Allegations," *Washington Post*, May 29, 1991; James G. Banks to Fletcher, June 25, 1991 (G

Street, box 101, folder 6, 33); Wilfredo J. Gonzalez to USCCR commissioners, July 11, 1991 (G Street, box 102, folder 4, 1075–1077); Cooper, "Washington Whispers"; Fletcher to Bush, July 18, 1991 (Bush WHORM SF PL, folder 255918); USCCR press release, July 22, 1991 (G Street, box 15A, folder 2, 664); "Urban League: No Racial Rhetoric," *USA Today,* July 23, 1991; Cynthia Tucker, "Bush Has Opportunity to Reject Race Politics," *Atlanta Journal and Constitution,* July 24, 1991; Bush to Fletcher, July 24, 1991 (G Street, box 15A, folder 2, 1789); Fletcher to John H. Johnson, August 2, 1991 (G Street, box 101, folder 6, 475–476); Nelson Lund to C. Boyden Gray, August 2, and Gray to Fletcher, August 5, 1991 (Bush WHORM SF PL, folder 255918); Brent Stinski, "Army's Minority Policies Top Other Services,' Chairman Says," *Stars and Stripes,* August 3, 1991; George J. Mitchell to Fletcher, August 8, 1991 (G Street, box 111, folder 3, 1000–1001); Fletcher, "Results of Factfinding from European Trip: A Preliminary Report," August 17, 1991 (Bush WHORM SF HU box 10, folder 278274SS); Jason DeParle, "Bias Is Found at 6 US Bases in Europe," *New York Times,* August 25, 1991; Charles C. Diggs to Fletcher, September 5, 1991 (G Street, box 111, folder 3, 1169); "Fletcher Warns Blacks May Suffer Unfair Portion of US Armed Forces Cutbacks," *Jet,* September 9, 1991; Fletcher to Bush and Bush to Fletcher, September 11, and Phillip D. Brady to Bush, Brady to Patty Presock, and Brady to C. Boyden Gray, September 12, 1991 (Bush WHORM SF HU box 10, folder 278274SS); Carlos Sanchez, "US to Press Mount Pleasant Probe," *Washington Post,* September 12, 1991; Bush to Brady, September 15, and Gray to Bush, September 17, 1991 (Bush WHORM SF HU box 10, folder 278274SS); USCCR meeting minutes, November 15, 1991 (Records of the USCCR); and USCCR press release, January 7, and USCCR hearing schedule, January 29, 1992 (G Street, box 102, folder 4, 1036–1038, 1429).

43. David Lauter, "White House Backs Waivers of Job Bias Suits," *Los Angeles Times,* March 2, 1991; Carol M. Booker to Wilfredo J. Gonzalez, March 25, 1991 (G Street, box 85, folder 2, 1417–1419); William T. Coleman Jr. to Louis W. Sullivan, March 27, 1991 (G Street, box 104, folder 5, 4–5); USCCR meeting minutes, April 5, 1991 (Records of the USCCR); "For the Civil Rights Act of 1991" (editorial), *Chicago Tribune,* April 30, 1991; Robert S. Boyd, "Civil Rights Panel Plans to Ask Politicians Not to Misuse Race in Campaigns," *St. Paul Pioneer Press,* May 4, 1991; Thomas B. Edsall, "Insurance against the Q Word: Democratic Consultants Feel Civil Rights Bill Strategy May Work," *Washington Post,* May 23, 1991; Priscilla Painton, "Quota Quagmire: While Racial Tensions Are Rising in the Country, Washington Politicians are Bogged Down in a Rancorous Dispute over a New Civil Rights Bill," *Time,* May 27, 1991; Joint Center for Political and Economic Studies newsletter, June 1991 (G Street, box 52, folder 1, 7–12; Vernon Jarrett, "Republicans Should Listen to Fletcher," *Chicago Sun-Times,* June 18, 1991; USCCR meeting minutes, October 18, 1991 (Records of the USCCR); Fletcher to Bush, October 21, 1991 (Bush WHORM SF HU box 10, folder 281001); and John F. Kerry to Fletcher, November 21, 1991 (G Street, box 41, folder 2, 766–767).

44. J. Jennings Moss, "Both Parties Claim Victory on Rights Bill," *Washington Times,* October 26, 1991; Jeff Powell, "'Real' Bush Came Through on Rights, Fletcher Says," *Chattanooga News-Free Press,* n.d. [November 1991] (G Street, box

106, folder 2, 8); C. Boyden Gray, "We Won, They Capitulated," *Washington Post,* November 14, 1991; Jessica Lee, "A Magnet for Civil Rights Anger," *USA Today,* November 22, 1991; Ann Devroy, "President Signs Civil Rights Bill; White House Disavows Proposed Directive to End Affirmative Action," *Washington Post,* November 22, 1991; and Margaret Wolf Freivogel, "Uncivil Uproar: Signing of Rights Bill May Not End Debate on Affirmative Action," *St. Louis Post-Dispatch,* November 24, 1991.

45. Kansas City Federal Executive Board conference program, January 10, 1991 (G Street, box 53, folder 1, 894); Kimberley Warden to Fletcher, January 18, 1991 (G Street, box 91, folder 2, 41–42); Anne K. Marshall to Fletcher, January 24, 1991 (G Street, box 101, folder 6, 2–6); Joan R. Flaherty to Fletcher, March 1, 1991 (G Street, box 16, folder 1, 1269–1273); Chuck Morrison to Fletcher, March 4, 1991 (G Street, box 101, folder 1, 39); Lawrence R. Myers to Fletcher, n.d. [April 1991] (G Street, box 101, folder 2, 7); Terri E. Lunine to Fletcher, June 7, Benjamin L. Hooks to Fletcher, June 14, John E. Jacob to Fletcher and W. A. Burnett to Fletcher, June 24, James R. Mapp to Fletcher, July 25, Mike Carroll and Raenell Nagel to Fletcher, July 29, and Albert Shanker to Fletcher, July 31, 1991 (G Street, box 101, folder 6, 83, 89, 119–120, 125–127, 284–286, 289); Betty J. Thompson to Fletcher, August 9, 1991 (G Street, box 101, folder 4, 5–6); Aaron E. Henry to Fletcher, September 10, Marvin R. Adams to Fletcher, September 13, Mary C. Williams to Fletcher, September 23, Rodney J. Long to Fletcher, October 23, and H. Adrian Isabelle to Fletcher, October 29, 1991 (G Street, box 101, folder 6, 85–86, 99, 108–110, 112–113); Anda Cook to Fletcher, November 1, 1991 (G Street, box 105, folder 3, 9); and Linda deLeon to Fletcher, November 14, 1991 (G Street, box 107, folder 5, 458).

46. Daniel L. Ritchie to Fletcher, May 10, 1990 (G Street, box 103, folder 3, 341); Fletcher speech, June 9, 1990 (G Street, box 105, folder 3, 27–36); Jay Grelen, "Grads Told Course for Workforce Uncharted," *Denver Post,* n.d. [June 1990] (G Street, box 49, folder 2, 268; Joseph B. Verengia, "DU Grads Told Civil Rights Vital to US Security," *Rocky Mountain News,* June 9, 1990; Fletcher to Ritchie, July 5, and Wil Alston to Fletcher, August 22, 1990 (G Street, box 103, folder 3, 193–194, 354); Fletcher to R. Bruce Hutton, March 6, and Fletcher to Ritchie, March 7, 1991 (G Street, box 105, folder 3, 57, 40); Janet Day, "Fletcher to Lead DU Program," *Denver Post,* March 26, 1991; University of Denver press release, March 26, 1991 (G Street, box 96, folder 2, 946); Joe Estrella, "Civil Rights Panel Chief Gets DU Job," *Rocky Mountain News,* March 26, 1991; Robert K. Zimmer to Fletcher, April 11, 1991 (G Street, box 72, folder 2, 441); Ritchie to Fletcher, April 12, 1991 (G Street, box 56, folder 3, 664); Alston to Fletcher, May 1, and Thomas L. Watkins to Fletcher, May 6, 1991 (G Street, box 51, folder 2, 105–107); Bush to Fletcher, June 13, 1991 (G Street, box 107, folder 5, 1363); Fletcher to Phil J. Davis, June 14, 1991 (G Street, box 16, folder 2, 56–57); Sadler, "Civil Rights Agency Chief Brings Fight to Colorado"; Steven Sims to Fletcher, September 17, 1991 (G Street, box 85, folder 2, 1078–1081); Barbara Lawson, "The Business of Social Change," *University of Denver Today* (DU newsletter), September 25, 1991 (G Street, box 101, folder 4, 56–57); Hutton to Fletcher, September 30, 1991 (G Street, box 56, folder 3, 670–671); "Civil Rights Chairman to Head Institute for Corporate Social Policy," *CBA Today*

(DU College of Business Administration Newsletter), January 1992 (G Street, box 116, folder 1, 40–43); Janet Swaim to Fletcher, February 4, 1992 (G Street, box 111, folder 3, 894; Robert G, Drummer to Fletcher, February 11, 1992 (G Street, box 146, folder 3, 136); University of Denver College of Business Administration meeting agenda, March 6, 1992 (G Street, box 129, folder 3, 27–28); Fletcher W-2 form from the University of Denver, n.d. [January 1993] (G Street, box 83, folder 3, 3–5); and Berry, *And Justice for All*, 260.

47. Fletcher to William P. Barr, April 30, 1992 (G Street, box 42, folder 7, 104); USCCR press release, April 30, 1992 (G Street, box 101, folder 6, 365); Ann Devroy, "Bush Reaches Out to Activists for Advice; Presidential Leadership, Huge Federal Urban Effort Are Urged," *Washington Post*, May 2, 1992; "Riots Renew Calls for Aid to Big Cities," *St. Petersburg Times*, May 4, 1992; Linda K. Davis to Fletcher, May 20, 1992 (G Street, box 42, folder 7, 103); Carlson, "Man of 'Rage'"; and Robert D. McFadden, "Verdict in Los Angeles; New York Greets Verdicts Quietly," *New York Times*, April 18, 1993.

48. Ann Devroy, "Bush Links Rioting to '60s Policy; In LA, President Tries to Boost Image, Address Urban Ills," *Washington Post*, May 7, 1992; Carlson, "Man of 'Rage.'"

49. "Riots Renew Calls for Aid"; Judy Keen and Jessica Lee, "Bush Moves to Control Damage: President Revives Proposals for Cities," *USA Today*, May 4, 1992.

50. R. W. Apple Jr., "After the Riots: Bush Says Largess Won't Help Cities," *New York Times*, May 7, 1992.

51. "The Peace Dividend, Unredeemed" (editorial), *New York Times*, November 17, 1990; Eric Schmitt, "After the War; Thousands Greet Schwarzkopf's Return," *New York Times*, April 22, 1991; USCCR meeting minutes, May 3, 1991 (Records of the USCCR); Maralee Schwartz and Mark Stence, "Panel Will Ask '92 Campaigns to Avoid Race-Baiting Tactics," *Washington Post*, May 4, 1991; Tom Wicker, "In the Nation; Mr. Bush's Socks," *New York Times*, December 15, 1991; and Leslie H. Gelb, "Foreign Affairs; What Peace Dividend?," *New York Times*, February 21, 1992.

52. David L. Schneier to Fletcher, January 30, 1990 (G Street, box 30, folder 2, 403–404); Fletcher to Amy L. Schwartz, February 22, 1990 (Bush Staff and Office Files, Counsel's Office Appointment File box 1, "Chairman Arthur Allen Fletcher Commission on Civil Rights [OA/ID 20122]" folder); Fletcher to Dole, April 23, 1990 (G Street, box 103, folder 3, 220–223); George Washington University Medical Center to Fletcher, August 24, 1990 (G Street, box 104, folder 5, 24); Fletcher to Blue Cross Insurance, December 26, 1991 (G Street, box 42, folder 4, 72–76); Janet Swaim to Fletcher, February 4, 1992 (G Street, box 111, folder 3, 894); Fletcher to "Collection Agency," November 30 1992; Fletcher to Bernyce Fletcher, May 24, 1993 (G Street, box 48, folder 2, 601–608; Fletcher proposal, n.d. [1994] (G Street, box 16, folder 1, 170–179); Alex Parker to Fletcher, April 23, 1997 (G Street, box 16, folder 2, 1194–1195); and Kathy Keolker interview by and in possession of the author, May 25, 2018. The quotations are from the letter to Bernyce and the Keolker interview, respectively.

53. Fletcher to Bernyce Fletcher, May 24, 1993 (G Street, box 48, folder 2, 601–608); Keolker interview by the author.

54. USCCR report, January, 1993 (G Street, box 47, folder 1, 17–98; Fletcher speech, n.d. [January 1993] (G Street, box 101, folder 6, 426–427); USCCR meeting minutes, January 11, 1993 (Records of the USCCR); Department of Justice press release, January 13, 1993 (G Street, box 139, folder 2, 40); Fletcher notes, February 3, 1993 (G Street, box 95, folder 4, 224–235; box 104, folder 4, 23–24; and box 139, folder 2, 113–131); Gabriel Escobar, "Treatment of DC Latinos Called 'Appalling' by Panel; Study Cites Police Abuse, Denial of Rights," *Washington Post*, February 6, 1993; Mark Mayfield and Tom Watson, "Jail Deaths Spark Call for Probe: Commission Wants Answers in 42 Mississippi Hangings," *USA Today*, February 19, 1993; Jesse Jackson to Fletcher, February 22, 1993 (G Street, box 18, folder 6, 26–34); Leonard Shapiro, "Jackson May Enlist Government Support: 3 Agencies Hear of Sports Racism, Sexism," *Washington Post*, February 28, 1993; James P. Turner to Fletcher, March 5, 1993 (G Street, box 139, folder 2, 39); "Jackson Convenes Commission to Discuss Fairness in Sports," *Jet*, March 22, 1993; Lawrence Glick to Bobby Doctor, March 22, 1993 (G Street, box 106, folder 4, 203–218); Jack A. McDaniel to Fletcher and Wendy C. Dominique to Fletcher, March 26, 1993 (G Street, box 16, folder 1, 1087, and folder 2, 434–443); Barbara Reynolds, "Military Comes Under Fire Amid Charges of Bias," *USA Today*, March 26, 1993; and USCCR meeting minutes, March 26, and USCCR meeting minutes and meeting transcript, May 21, 1993 (Records of the USCCR).

55. Emma Monroig to Wilfredo J. Gonzalez, November 22, 1992 (Bush Staff and Office Files, Personnel Office Katja Bullock Files, "Fletcher, Arthur A.—RACCNR: 12401 FS: A/A [OA/ID 08467]" folder); Fletcher to Bush, December 2, 1992 (G Street, box 15A, folder 2, 1361–1366); Gonzalez to USCCR staff and Gonzalez to Fletcher, January 22, 1993 (G Street, box 102, folder 4, 356, and box 116, folder 2, 575–576); and Berry, *And Justice for All*, 269–271.

56. Fletcher to Bobby Doctor, April 28, 1993 (G Street, box 119, folder 5, 516–517); Russell Redenbaugh to Fletcher, April 29, 1993 (G Street, box 119, folder 1, 41); USCCR meeting minutes and meeting transcript, May 21, and USCCR meeting minutes, September 17, 1993 (Records of the USCCR); USCCR meeting transcript, September 17, 1993 (G Street, box 102, folder 3, 80–279); and Wang interview by the author.

57. Norman D. Tilles to Bruce Lindsey, March 16, 1993 (Clinton Archive Freedom of Information Act request 2016-1160-F [hereafter Clinton], box 1, OA/ID 15700, William J. Clinton Presidential Library, Little Rock, AR); Sandra W. Freedman to Bill Clinton, March 31, 1993 (Clinton box 1, OA/ID 21850); Pete Peterson to Bruce Lindsey, April 5, 1993 (Clinton box 2, OA/ID 43250); David J. Fischer to Clinton, April 13, 1993 (Clinton box 1, OA/ID 21850); Fletcher, Charles Pei Wang, Carl Anderson, Robert George, and Constance Horner to Clinton, June 3, 1993 (G Street, box 51, folder 2, 251); Eleanor Holmes Norton to Clinton, June 16, 1993 (Clinton box 2, OA/ID 12381); James E. Clyburn to Albert J. Gore, June 23, 1993 (Clinton box 1, OA/ID 15700); Thomas A. Shea to Fletcher, July 16, 1993 (G Street, box 101, folder 6, 180–181); Ernest F. Hollings to Clinton, October 5, 1993 (Clinton box 2, OA/ID 43252); H. Martin Lancaster to Clinton, October 13, 1993 (Clinton box 1, OA/ID 15700); Berry, *And Justice for All*, 277–278; and Wang interview by the author.

58. John Conyers Jr. to "CBC Colleagues," June 9, 1993 (G Street, box 102, folder 4, 358); USCCR meeting transcript, November 19, 1993 (G Street, box 90, folder 4, 70–287).

59. USCCR meeting transcript, November 19, 1993; Kevin Merida, "The Firm Founder of Affirmative Action: Arthur Fletcher Isn't Going to Take a Challenge to His Legacy Lying Down," *Washington Post,* June 13, 1995.

60. Don Edwards and Paul Simon to Bruce Lindsey, February 18, 1993 and May 18, 1993 (Clinton box 3, OA/ID 9604, and box 2, OA/ID 12381); Sonya Ross, "NAACP Wants Guinier for Its Staff, Won't Aid Clinton Search," *Associated Press,* June 9, 1993 (Clinton box 3, OA/ID 1906); Raul Yzaguirre to Bruce Lindsey, June 24, 1993 (Clinton box 2, OA/ID 12381); DeWayne Wickham, "While Clinton Fiddles, Rights Commission Burns," *USA Today,* June 28, 1993; Kweise Mfume to Clinton, July 7, 1993 (Clinton box 2, OA/ID 12381); Congressional Hispanic Caucus to Bruce Lindsey, July 15, 1993 (Clinton box 2, OA/ID 12381); and Edwards and Simon to Mack McLarty, July 28, 1993 (Clinton box 3, OA/ID 9604). The quotation is from Ross.

61. DeWayne Wickham, "Clinton Shows Some Muscle on Civil Rights: With Help From Congress, Conservatives' Agenda Is Thwarted," *USA Today,* September 27, 1993; Berry, *And Justice for All,* 278–279.

62. Fletcher to Alexis Herman, October 1, and Fletcher to Mary Frances Berry, October 6, 1993 (G Street, box 102, folder 4, 27–32, 256–258); and Emma Monroig to Bruce Lindsey, October 27, 1993 (G Street, box 116, folder 2, 478).

63. "Edwards's Orthodoxy" (editorial), *Wall Street Journal,* September 23, 1991; "House Extends Civil Rights Panel for Just Two Years"; "One Report, $14 Million" (editorial), *Washington Post,* October 2, 1991; Don Edwards letter to the editor, *Wall Street Journal,* October 3, 1991; Holmes, "With Glory of Past Only a Memory"; and Russell Redenbaugh letter to the editor, *Wall Street Journal,* October 21, 1991; Fletcher to Alexis Herman, October 1, and Fletcher to Mary Frances Berry, October 6, 1993. Berry claims that Fletcher's antipathy to Ishimaru stemmed from anti-Japanese bias over the Pearl Harbor attack. *And Justice for All,* 279.

64. Fletcher to Alexis Herman, October 1, 1993.

65. Jesse L. Jackson to Fletcher, October 28, 1993 (G Street, box 68, folder 6, 268–269).

66. Mary Frances Berry interview, April 13, 2018, by and in possession of the author.

67. Fletcher to Jesse L. Jackson, November 1, 1993 (G Street, box 23, folder 5, 508–509); Al Kamen, "President Proposes; Commission Deposes," *Washington Post,* November 10, 1993; Fletcher to Alexis Herman, November 12, 1993 (G Street, box 48, folder 2, 900–901, continued at box 111, folder 3, 1050); USCCR meeting transcript, November 19, 1993; USCCR press release, November 19, 1993 (G Street, box 102, folder 4, 349); Kamen, "Vote-Flipping Breaks Impasse at Rights Panel," *Washington Post,* November 22, 1993; and Berry, *And Justice for All,* 279.

68. Debra G. Harroun, "Mary Frances Berry," in *Contemporary Black Biography: Profiles from the International Black Community,* ed. Barbara Carlisle Bigelow (Detroit: Gale Research, 1994), 7:11–12; Wang interview by the author.

69. Bobby Doctor to USCCR employees and Constance Horner to Mary Frances Berry, November 23, 1993 (G Street, box 90, folder 3, 79, and box 102, folder 4, 350); Fletcher to USCCR commissioners, November 24, 1993 (G Street, box 90, folder 3, 168); Robert George to Lawrence Glick, November 26, Berry to USCCR staff, November 29, and Glick to USCCR commissioners, November 29, 1993 (G Street, box 102, folder 4, 352–355); USCCR meeting minutes, November 29, 1993 (Records of the USCCR); and USCCR meeting transcript, November 29, 1993 (G Street, box 90, folder 4, 13–69). Berry later asserted that "Doctor didn't act within the bounds of propriety. . . . He went rogue, so to speak." Berry interview by the author.

70. Walter Dellinger to Neil Eggleston, January 13, 1994 (Records of the US-CCR); USCCR meeting transcript, January 14, 1994 (G Street, box 52, folder 1, 170–366); and Berry, *And Justice for All*, 279.

71. Al Kamen, "Chronic Vacancyitis," *Washington Post*, April 8, 1994; Fletcher to Clinton (draft), May 5, 1994 (G Street, box 102, folder 4, 33–36); USCCR meeting transcript and minutes, May 6, and USCCR meeting minutes, June 3, 1994 (Records of the USCCR); J. Veronica Biggins to Clinton, May 18, 1994 (Clinton box 1, OA/ID 21850); Biggins to Berry, May 25, and Berry to Biggins and Biggins to Clinton, May 27, 1993 (Clinton box 1 OA/ID 21850); and Berry, *And Justice for All*, 279–280.

72. Berry interview by the author.

73. Berry, *And Justice for All*, 279–281, 333–334; Wang interview by the author.

74. Wickham, "While Clinton Fiddles, Rights Commission Burns," June 28, 1993; Edwards and Simon to McLarty, July 28, 1993 (Clinton box 3, "Mary Frances Berry OA/ID 9604" folder).

75. "Surf's Up! Republican Waves Are Forming; GOP Ponders What's Left, What's After the Contract," *Seattle Times*, n.d. [February 1995] (G street box 70, folder 3, 144); Major Garrett, "Beyond the Contract," *Mother Jones*, March/April 1995; "Affirmative Action Should Focus on Poor People, Gingrich Says," *New York Times*, June 17, 1995.

76. Charles Krauthammer, "Dodging and Weaving on Affirmative Action," *Washington Post*, March 3, 1995; *Congressional Record-Senate*, March 15, 1995 (G Street, box 87, folder 2, 66–76); Joan Biskupic, "Rights Groups Pay to Settle Bias Case," *Washington Post*, November 22, 1997; and United States Court of Appeals for the Third Circuit opinion 94-5112, August 8, 1996, http://www2.ca3.uscourts .gov/opinarch/96a1395p.txt. Ultimately the white teacher's case was upheld on appeal, and when the Supreme Court agreed to hear the case, the NAACP Legal Defense and Educational Fund and the American Civil Liberties Union helped the school board pay a settlement rather than risk allowing the case to set a negative United States Supreme Court precedent on affirmative action.

77. R. Jeffrey Smith, "GOP Senators Begin Studying Repeal of Affirmative Action," *Washington Post*, February 6, 1995; "Gramm Flays 'Quota' System: As Prez, He'd Nix Affirmative Action," *Philadelphia Daily News*, February 9, 1995; Kendall Wilson, "Affirmative Action in Danger: Uproar Greets Introduction of Harrisburg Bill," *Philadelphia Tribune*, February 24, 1990; Bob Dole press releases, March 15

and March 24, 1995 (Records of Senator Robert J. Dole, "Legislative Relations—Legislative Assistants" series box 84, "5—Labor, Barrata–Stanley–Affirmative Action, 1994–1995" folder); *Congressional Record-Senate*, March 15, 1995; Stephen A. Holmes, "Programs Based on Sex and Race Are Challenged," *New York Times*, and Judi Hasson, "'Race Counting Game Has Gone Too Far,' Dole Says," *USA Today*, March 16, 1995; Kevin Merida, "Dole Takes 180-Degree Turn on Affirmative Action," *Washington Post*, March 17, 1995; James E. Alsbrook, "Affirmative Action Opponents Trying to Pull Up Ladder after They Climbed upon Roof," *Pittsburgh Courier*, March 18, 1995; Holmes, "Past Haunts Republicans on Set-Asides: Dole Defends Stand on Preference Plans," *New York Times*, March 19, 1995; William Raspberry, "The War within Robert Dole," *Washington Post*, March 20, 1995; "For the Record," *Washington Post*, and "The Disappearing Case for Quotas" (editorial), *Washington Times*, March 24, 1995.

78. Ben Wattenberg, "Clinton Plays Slippery Game with Quota Issue," *Newark Star-Ledger*, March 6, 1995; "Negative Reaction: Opposition to Affirmative Action Reaches a Critical Mass" (editorial), *Pittsburgh Post-Gazette*, March 8, 1995; Manning Marable, "Rethinking Affirmative Action," *Philadelphia New Observer*, March 15, 1995; Bob Dole press release and Dole to Charles H. Askew, March 15, 1995 (Records of Senator Robert J. Dole, "Legislative Relations—Legislative Assistants" series box 84, "5—Labor, Barrata–Stanley–Affirmative Action, 1994–1995" folder); Hasson, "'Race Counting Game Has Gone Too Far,' Dole Says"; Merida, "Dole Takes 180-Degree Turn"; Judy Keen, "Issue Lurks as a Politicking Time Bomb," *USA Today*, March 24, 1995; and Howard Fineman, "Race and Rage," *Newsweek*, April 3, 1995.

79. Fletcher to Dole and Fletcher to Gingrich and House Republicans, February 9, 1995 (G Street, box 6, folder 1, 180–181); Angela Cortez, "Delay Affirmative-Action Cut, Rights Chief Says in Denver," *Denver Post*, February 17, 1995; and "Arthur Fletcher Breaks Long Link with Sen. Dole on Affirmative Action," *Jet*, April 10, 1995.

80. Dole to Fletcher, May 8, 1995 (G Street, box 104, folder 1, 50–51).

81. Fletcher notes, n.d. [1995] (G Street, box 17, folder 4, 1008–1009, and box 136, folder 1, 1–6); Fletcher speech, n.d. [July 1995] (G Street, box 91, folder 2, 374–377); and Paul Fletcher conversations with the author.

82. Fletcher press release, April 3, 1995 (G Street, box 112, folder 3, 604–606); "Washington Insight: Affirmative Action Candidate," *Los Angeles Times*, April 20, 1995; Nedra Weaver to Fletcher, June 6, Weaver to Arthur Diggs, June 8, and Weaver to Diggs and Fletcher, June 12, 1995 (G Street, box 30, folder 2, 778, 781, 792); Fletcher to Carl E. Anderson, June 19, 1995 (G Street, box 86, folder 4, 85); Fletcher notes, June 20, 1995 (G Street, box 48, folder 1, 15); Anderson to Charles N. Ofori and Jacqueline M. Waddy to Fletcher, June 24, 1995 (G Street, box 16, folder 2, 1325–1327); Fletcher for President contact information, n.d. [July 1995] (G Street, box 56, folder 1, 10); Curt Anderson, "Rights Official Enters Presidential Race," *Associated Press*, n.d. [July 1995] (G Street, box 17, folder 1, 5); Fletcher press release, July 4, 1995 (G Street, box 48, folder 2, 29–31); Anderson to Fletcher, July 27, 1995 (G Street, box 16, folder 2, 1321–1322); and *MacNeil-Lehrer NewsHour* transcript, October 6, 1995.

83. Dorothy J. Gaiter, "Mr. Fletcher's Plan: Lights, Camera, Affirmative Action! A Republican, He Is Running Uphill Run for President to Save Racial Preferences," *Wall Street Journal*, April 5, 1995; Fletcher itinerary, April 18, 1995 (G Street, box 68, folder 6, 301); Stephen M. Shuster to Fletcher, April 19, 1995 (G Street, box 56, folder 3, 56–57); Jack Nelson, "Arthur Fletcher: Fighting to Stop the GOP's Headlong Plunge to the Right," *Los Angeles Times*, May 7, 1995; Kevin Merida, "The Firm Founder of Affirmative Action: Arthur Fletcher Isn't Going to Take a Challenge to His Legacy Lying Down," *Washington Post*, June 13, 1995; Bob Partlow, "Ex-US Aide: Race Gains in Jeopardy," *Olympian*, June 14, 1995; Tom Webb, "Former Kansan's Fight for Civil Rights Is Not Quite Over," *Wichita Eagle*, July 3, 1995; Ernie Freda, "Washington in Brief," *Atlanta Journal and Constitution*, July 6, 1995; "Arthur Fletcher entered the Republican presidential race yesterday. He said party strategy favors the rich but must embrace minorities and the working class," picture caption, *Philadelphia Inquirer*, "Civil Rights Official Joins GOP Presidential Race," *St. Paul Pioneer Press*, "Black Republican on Rights Panel Seeks Presidency," *San Jose Mercury News*, "Barry Forms in Atlantic," *St. Petersburg Times*, "GOP Presidential Field: Civil Rights Commissioner Running," *St. Louis Post-Dispatch*, Tom Rhodes, "Black Will Enter Republican Race," *Times of London*, and David Broder, "Rights Commissioner Arthur Fletcher Joins GOP Field," *Washington Post*, July 8, 1995; "Civil Rights Official Joins GOP Field for 1996," *New York Times*, July 9, 1995; "GOP Rights Activist Runs for President," *USA Today*, July 10, 1995; "Arthur Fletcher Returns to Political Forefront as a Republican Presidential Candidate," *Jet*, July 31, 1995; and *MacNeil-Lehrer NewsHour*, October 6, 1995.

84. CityVote press release, August 7, and Fletcher to Fletcher for President Steering Committee, August 9, 1995 (G Street, box 93, folder 2, 255–259); Fred Brown, "Preference Poll Striking Out with Big Hitters," *Denver Post*, October 23, 1995; Don Ahern, "Presidential Hopefuls on Ballot Tuesday Despite Little Interest," *St. Paul Pioneer Press*, November 2, 1995; "Caucus Results: Republicans," *Iowa Official Register, 1997–1998*, 399, Iowa Legislature, https://www.legis.iowa .gov/docs/shelves/redbooks/Redbook-1997-1998%20(77GA).pdf; and "Republican Presidential Primary," New Hampshire Office of the Secretary of State, February 28, 1996, http://sos.nh.gov/1996RepPresPrim.aspx.

85. "Oregon Affirmative Action Reinstated in Some Cases," *Wall Street Journal*, June 26, 1995; William J. Clinton speech, July 19, 1995 (G Street, box 109, folder 1, 40–49); Clinton to Fletcher, August 15, 1995 (G Street, box 109, folder 1, 55); "Blacks Told They Need Clinton," *St. Paul Pioneer Press*, September 22, 1995; *MacNeil-Lehrer NewsHour*, October 6, 1995; and Ronald Brownstein, "Affirming Outreach, Not Quotas," *Los Angeles Times*, December 31, 1995.

86. Jim Camden, "Powell Muddles CityVote Results," *Spokane Spokesman-Review*, November 9, 1995; David Hinckley, "Listeners Can Still Dial Up Dems," *New York Daily News*, August 26, 1996; and Fletcher to Simeon Booker, September 11, 1996 (G Street, box 16, folder 1, 217–220).

87. Ayesha Hassan to Sheila Vaden-Williams, August 15, 1995 (G Street, box 68, folder 6, 295); Elaine Martin to Bernyce Fletcher, August 16, 1995 (G Street, box 58, folder 2, 32).

88. State of California high school equivalency certificate for Phillip Fletcher, May 30, 1991, California Medical Center to Phillip Fletcher, August 28, 1991, Phillip Fletcher to Bernyce Fletcher, November 4, 1991, and Phillip Fletcher to unknown, December 23, 1993 (G Street, box 15A, folder 2, 1123–1129, 1149–1150, 1279–1284); Phillip Fletcher to Arthur Fletcher, January 3, 1994 (G Street, box 41, folder 2, 657–658); Daniel C. Bowen to Phillip Fletcher, January 23, 1995 (G Street, box 134, folder 4, 7); Bernyce Fletcher, "Phillip Wayne Fletcher," n.d. [November 1995] (G Street, box 111, folder 3, 1332–1333); Fletcher to Louis J. Boston, November 30, 1995 (G Street, box 16, folder 1, 396–397); Juan-El Fletcher to landlord, December 1, 1995 (G Street, box 93, folder 2, 205); Phyllis Fletcher, "Sweet Phil from Sugar Hill"; Paul Fletcher interviews by the author, September 25, 2010, and April 2, 2011; and Sylvia Fletcher e-mail to and in possession of the author, April 6, 2011.

89. Bernyce Fletcher job application, August 9, 1967 (G Street, box 123, folder 30, 10–11); State of Georgia certificate of marriage for Phyllis Fletcher and Leroy Palmer, July 3, 1969 (G Street, box 6, folder 1, 80); Vera J. Lincoln to Fletcher, February 18, 1970 (G Street, box 78B, folder 18, 175); "Belk Presents Phyllis Palmer," *Greensboro Daily News*, March 26, 1971; Arthur McZier to Fletcher, August 30, 1971 (G Street, box 79, folder 1, 126–127); Grady Memorial Hospital Treatment Record, February 10, 1995 (G Street, box 6, folder 1, 92); Paul Fletcher interviews by the author, July 30, 2010, and April 2, 2011; and Paul and Sylvia Fletcher interview by the author, December 28, 2010. Records do not indicate whether Phyllis Fletcher Palmer received the SBA loan.

90. Fletcher flyer, July 1996 (G Street, box 96, folder 2, 942–943); Fletcher to Booker, September 11, 1996; Harry C. Alford to Board of Directors, National Black Chamber of Commerce, August 19 and September 29, 1997 (G Street, box 41, folder 2, 637–638); Fletcher pamphlet, August 24, 2000 (G Street, box 154, folder 1, 222–227); Fletcher to Roderick Paige, n.d. [2001] (G Street, box 72, folder 2, 24–27); Fletcher, mission statement for Friends of America's Future, December 14, 2001 (G Street, box 85, folder 2, 996); state of Delaware certificate of incorporation for Fletcher's Financial Services, August 12, 2002 (G Street, box 70, folder 2, p.2); Ross Patterson to Fletcher e-mail, July 11, 2005 (G Street, box 61, folder 3, 84–85).

91. University of Washington transcript for Paul Fletcher, n.d. [1970] (G Street, box 13, folder 1, 1–40); Paul Fletcher to Marian Wright-Edelman, March 10, 1993 (G Street, box 102, folder 4, 301); "Paul Fletcher Is Making an Impact on Society: Housing Director Says Community Key to Progress," *Evansville Courier and Press*, July 7, 2001; Paul Fletcher interviews by the author, July 30, 2010, and April 2, 2011; and Paul and Sylvia Fletcher interview by the author, December 28, 2010.

92. Michelle O'Donnell, "Arthur Fletcher, GOP Adviser, Dies at 80," *New York Times*, Andrew Sirocchi, "'Father' of Civil Rights Who Got Start in Pasco Dies," *Tri-City Herald*, Joe Holley, "Affirmative Action Pioneer Advised GOP Presidents," *Washington Post*, "Adviser to 4 Presidents, Arthur Fletcher, Dies," *Deseret Morning News*, and "Civil Rights Pioneer Dies," *New York Times*, July 14, 2005; "Art Fletcher: The Poor Have Lost Their Hero," *Tri-City Herald*, "Arthur Fletcher, Adviser to Presidents," *St. Paul Pioneer Press*, and Chris Moon, "A Beacon of Change," *Topeka*

Capital-Journal, July 15, 2005; "In Our View—Fletcher's Legacy; Black Republican Almost Won in '68," *Vancouver Columbian,* July 16, 2005; Barbara Lee and John F. Kerry, "Honoring Arthur Fletcher," *Congressional Record* 151, no. 100 (July 21, 2005): E1570 and S8661; "Arthur Fletcher, 'The Father of Affirmative Action,' Dies at 80," *Jet,* August 1, 2005; Arthur Fletcher funeral video, in possession of the author; and Paul Fletcher interview, July 30, 2010.

93. Arthur Fletcher funeral video, in possession of the author.

94. Arthur Fletcher funeral video, in possession of the author.

95. Moon, "Beacon of Change."

CONCLUSION. THE CONUNDRUM OF THE BLACK REPUBLICAN

1. Harvey, "Profile of a Bay Area Leader"; "Berkeley Man Wins Washington Race," unknown publication, n.d. (G Street, box 151, folder 1, image 247); Adkins, "Big 'Breakthrough' Man"; and Perlstein, *Before the Storm,* 81–82.

2. "Southern Strategy" (editorial), *New York Times,* August 11, 1988; Graham, *Civil Rights Era,* 303–304, 319.

3. Farrington, *Black Republicans.*

4. Bowen, *Roots of Modern Conservatism,* 6.

5. On the distrust of Black republicans by other Blacks and by other Republicans, see Fields, *Black Elephants.*

6. Rossum, *Understanding Clarence Thomas,* 2–5.

7. Rossum, *Understanding Clarence Thomas,* 4.

8. Rossum, *Understanding Clarence Thomas,* 4–6, 181, 187, 190, 212–213.

9. Farrington, *Black Republicans,* 168; Andrew Young et al., *Andrew Young and the Making of Modern Atlanta* (Macon, GA: Mercer University Press, 2016), 29, 70, 167–169.

10. Thurber, *Republicans and Race.*

11. Brennan, *Turning Right in the Sixties;* Perlstein, *Nixonland* and *Invisible Bridge.*

12. St. George, "Arthur Fletcher."

13. On the origin of the phrase "faithful party service," see Brennan, *Turning Right in the Sixties,* 4. For Eisenhower's use of the idea to achieve party unity, see Bowen, *Roots of Modern Conservatism.* On the new Black conservatives, see Ondaatje, *Black Conservative Intellectuals.*

INDEX

Numbers in italics refer to pages with images.

Herman, Alexis, 266, 277, 372nn62–64, 372n67
Herrington, Kansas, 23, 293n31
Hesburgh, Theodore, 245–246, 247, 269
HEW, 119, 138–139, 145
Hickey, Red, 51–52
Higby, Larry, 176, 342n29
High Commission on Human Rights. *See* United Nations
Higher Horizons, 84–88, 89, 90, 92, 94, 97, 127, 151, 183, 282, 311n47
Hill, Anita, 258
Hill, Betty, 81
Hill, Herbert, 147, 149, 156, 159, 337n78
Hill, Napoleon, 80
Hiltingbury, Hampshire, England, 33
Hines, Earl "Father," 24
Hirsch, Elroy, 53
Hodgkin's disease, 181, 211
Hodgson, James, 128–130, 136, 145–146, 154–155, 159, 160–161, 323n13, 325n25, 333n54, 334n59, 336n66
Holliday, George, 243
Hollywood, California, 212, 216, 230
Holshauser, James, 195
Hometown Plans, 149–153, 155, 156
Honolulu Times, 165
Hooks, Benjamin, 214, 252, 255, 275, 283, 369n45
Horner, Constance, 263–264, 270, 371n57, 373n69
Horton, William "Willie," 238, 240, 253, 271
House of Representatives. *See* US House of Representatives
Houston, Texas, 13–14, 99, 142–143, 200, 213
Howard University, 143, 165, 237, 268
HUD. *See* US Department of Housing and Urban Development
Humphrey, Hubert H., 110, 117, 118, 194, 245
Hussein, Saddam, 254
Hutton, R. Bruce, 260, 369n46
Hyattsville, Maryland, 262

IBM, 222, 232
Ichabods (Washburn University football team), 41, 46–49

Idaho, 202, 241
Illinois, 7, 137, 164, 200, 241, 250
Illinois Department of Transportation, 241
Independence Hall (Philadelphia), 10–11, 273
Independence Mall (Philadelphia), 10–11
Independence Visitor Center (Philadelphia), 10
Indiana, 7, 40–41, 42, 56, 137, 172, 236, 277
Indianapolis, Indiana, 55
Indiana University, 7, 40, 56
Indians (Omaha University football team), 49
Indian Territory, 13, 20
Ingalls Shipbuilding, 128–129
Innis, Roy, 94–95, 119, 160
International Junior Chamber of Commerce, 165–166
Iola Register, 47
Iowa, 81, 198, 212, 234
Ireland, 32
Ishimaru, Stuart, 266–269, 372n63
Israel, 165
Italy, 24, 28, 30, 31, 144

Jackson, Henry M. "Scoop," 143–144, 192, 330n42
Jackson, Jesse, 3, 94, 134, 150–151, 172, 200, 229–230, 235, 236, 248, 253, 255, 263, 267, 275, 278, 279, 334n56, 335n60, 363n14, 371n54, 372n65, 372n67
Jackson, Mississippi, 116
Jackson, Nat, 8, 93, 311n44, 311n47, 315n78, 319n100
Jackson, Samuel C., 50–51, 119–120, 147, 229, 345n62, 350n1, 352n21
Jacob, John, 252, 369n45
Japan, 24, 28, 266, 294n38, 372n63
Javits, Jacob, 137, 141
Jaycees, 165–166
Jayhawk Hotel (Topeka), 43, 59, 62, 103
Jet magazine, 224, 258
Jewish Anti-Defamation League, 254
Jim Crow, 2, 3, 5, 11, 26, 29, 30, 38, 42, 79, 111, 135, 146, 169, 209, 220, 231, 238, 280, 289, 290, 306n6

John Birch Society, 78, 82, 84, 86, 96, 101, 105, 106, 142
John B. Russwurm Award. *See* National Newspapers Association
Johnson, Burnell, 80, 121, 302n54, 306nn8–9
Johnson, Hiram, 81
Johnson, Jack, 18
Johnson, Lyndon, 67, 80, 101, 105, 121, 125–126, 136, 143, 145, 162, 167, 177, 179, 185, 186, 196, 200, 202, 211, 226, 230, 245, 257, 260, 281, 287, 288, 321n3
Jordan, James, 40
Jordan, Vernon E., Jr., 167, 168–169, 172, 173–175, 193, 275, 340n12, 341n24, 346n67
Jordan Patterson Post, American Legion (Topeka), 45
Judiciary Committee. *See* US House of Representatives
Junction City, Kansas, 8, 15, 21, 22, 23, 24, 25, 26, 32, 37, 39–40, 42, 44, 49, 57, 63, 70, 71, 123, 189
Junction City High School, 22, 23, 25, 26, 37
Junction City Ice and Cold Storage Company, 39–40, 57
Junction City *PowWow*, 26–27
Jungle Book, The, 15–16

Kansas, 8, 15, 20, 21, 23, 26, 28, 31, 37, 38, 40–46, 49, 51, 53, 56, 57–67, 68–69, 72, 73, 74, 79, 80, 82, 90, 96–97, 100, 103, 121, 123, 144, 146, 160, 161, 162, 176, 184, 189, 196, 198, 201, 221, 222, 234, 243, 256, 280, 286, 303n68
Kansas City, Missouri, 45–46, 49, 59, 63, 152, 186, 198, 272, 273
Kansas House of Representatives, 67
Kansas State Board Against Discrimination, 62, 302n55
Kansas State Highway Department, 43, 60, 61, 63, 65, 90, 144
Kansas State University, 40, 49
Kemp, Jack, 234, 260–261, 274, 277
Kennedy, Anthony, 251

Kennedy, John F., 69, 78, 80, 125, 174, 226, 244–245, 251
assassination, 77, 125, 245
Kennedy, Robert F., 116
Kennedy, Theodore "Teddy," 137, 192, 251, 253, 256
Kennewick, Washington, 84, 98
Kent, England, 32
Kent State University, 146, 170
Kentucky, 28–29
Kenya, 224
Keolker, Kathy, 8, 116–118, 208–209, 262, 319n97, 319n101, 339n3, 348n90, 349–350nn106–107, 370–371nn52–53
Kerry, John F., 277, 368n43
Keyes, Alan, 273–274
King, Leslie Lynch. *See* Ford, Gerald R.
King, Martin Luther, Jr., 2, 9, 22, 77, 79–80, 93, 94, 95, 101, 116, 132, 134, 150, 151, 158, 159–160, 200, 205, 227, 229, 238, 244, 256, 276, 279, 280, 285, 306n6
King, Rodney, 243–244, 258, 260, 261, 262, 267, 290
King County Council, Washington, 277
King David (biblical), 278
King Solomon (biblical), 278
Kipling, Rudyard, 15–16
Kirk, Russell, 66
Kirkland, Lane, 240
Kirkpatrick, Jeane, 219
KIRO-TV, Seattle, Washington, 114–115
Kissinger, Henry, 193–194, 209, 215–216
Kleppe, Thomas, 181
Knight, Goodwin, 69, 87
Knowland, William F., 66, 69, 87
Koger, John J., 206
Kool & The Gang, 232
KP Services Co., 225
Kramer, A. Ludlow, 98, 100, 108–110, 111, 117, 119, 174, 320n107
Krauthammer, Charles, 271
Ku Klux Klan, 41, 238, 253
Kuwait, 254

Lafontant, Jewel, 219
Laird, Melvin, 218, 226, 352n19, 355n35
Lake Erie, 237

National Youth Administration, 19
Nation of Islam, 22, 206
Neas, Ralph, 252, 279, 283
Nebraska, 41, 47, 49, 231
Negro Leagues, 40
Neshoba County, Mississippi, 217,
    352n18
Nessen, Ronald H. "Ron," 192
Nevada, 198
Newark, New Jersey, 84, 94, 200
Newburgh, New York, 124
New England, 143, 211
New Jersey, 137, 170, 200, 202, 234, 262,
    270
New Mexico, 20
New Orleans, Louisiana, 171, 285
Newport News Shipbuilding and
    Drydock Company, 128–129
New Right Conservatism, 1, 5, 6, 88, 196,
    211, 212, 288
Newton, Huey, 95
New York, New York, 7, 63, 67, 74, 93,
    124, 141, 146, 151, 152, 156, 158,
    159, 164, 168, 170, 173, 175, 190,
    200, 217, 249, 285
New York Amsterdam News, 138
New York Bulldogs, 53, 55
New York Giants, 55
New York Plan, 151–152, 155–156, 159,
    160
New York State, 66, 94, 95, 104, 124, 137,
    157, 162, 168, 175, 190, 200, 234,
    236, 241, 331n43
New York Times, 138, 139, 166–167, 237,
    252–253, 255, 261, 273
New York Yankees (football team), 53
Nigeria, 167, 224
Nixon, Richard M., 6, 69, 94, 106, 109–
    110, 119, 120, 125, 137, 142, 144,
    148, 160, 163, 165–169, 171, 179,
    187, 199, 219, 248, 283, 340n10,
    360n14
  1960 presidential campaign, 72, 286,
    320n104
  1962 California gubernatorial
    campaign, 82–83
  1968 presidential campaign, 67, 105–
    106, 110, 112, 114, 117, 118, 119, 173,
    314n77, 315n79

impeachment and resignation, 142,
    181, 185–186, 340n10, 343n39
  pardon of, 191
  presidential administration and
    reelection campaign, 1–2, 3, 4, 6,
    13, 117–120, 123, 135–138, 140–141,
    142, 145–149, 152–163, 171, 172,
    173, 175, 176, 177, 179–180, 185,
    202, 208, 209, 211, 214, 215, 219,
    221, 226, 227, 229, 231, 235, 239,
    240, 245–246, 250, 251, 252, 254,
    260, 261, 269, 271, 275, 279,
    288, 320n105, 320n107, 320n109,
    323n12, 326n27, 328–329nn37–38,
    330nn42–43, 331n44, 331–
    332nn46–47, 333nn51–52, 333n54,
    336n63, 336n65, 337nn70–72,
    337nn75–77, 337–338nn79–80,
    339n4, 339n9, 341n18, 342n28,
    350n3
  silent majority, 102
  Southern Strategy, 1, 6, 118, 135, 148,
    163, 201, 239, 281
Nofziger, Lyn, 208, 225, 226, 255
Nord-Pas-de-Calais, France, 32
Normandy, France, 32–33
North Carolina, 94–95, 137, 150, 195,
    196, 225, 275, 286
Norton, Eleanor Holmes, 277, 371n57
Notre Dame University, 245

Oakland, California, 69, 73, 83, 88, 95,
    197
Oakland Post, 87
Oakland Tribune, 19, 73
Obama, Barack H., 230, 278, 287, 289,
    331n43
Occidental College, 51
O'Connell, John, 104, 110, 115, 117
O'Connor, Sandra Day, 251
OFCC, 121, 126, 160
Office of Economic Opportunity, 90
Office of Federal Contract Compliance,
    121, 126, 160
Office of Management and Budget
    (White House), 145, 155
Office of Minority Business Enterprise,
    119, 176
Ohio, 66, 146, 147, 162, 282

Plans for Progress, 99, 125

Plaza 50 (New York City residence), 159, 169, 170

Pleasantville, New Jersey, 202, 234, 262

Porter, Roger, 256, 367n37

Powell, Adam Clayton, 93, 196

Powell, Colin, 19, 274, 289

Prairie View, Texas, 13

Prairie View State Teachers College, 13–14

Pratt, Ed, 116

"Presidential Issues Book," 193

President's Commission on Personnel Interchange, 188

President's Committee on Government Contract Compliance, 125

President's Committee on Government Contracts, 82

Princeton, New Jersey, 170

Princeton University, 263

Pritchard, Joel, 110

Progress Plaza (Philadelphia, Pennsylvania), 93

Promoters and Underwriters of Self-Help Enterprises and Related Services, 89

Pucinsky, Roman, 137

Puerto Rico, 230

Puget Sound, 115

PUSHERS Inc., 89

Quayle, J. Danforth, 236

Rainbow/PUSH Coalition, 229

Raleigh, North Carolina, 137, 170

Ramirez, Blandina "Bambi," 246, 249–250, 263

Ramos, Suzanne, 255

Rams (football team), 40, 50–52, 54, 55, 56

Rancho Cordova, California, 70

Rancho Mirage, California, 215

Randolph, A. Philip, 5, 41

Raspberry, William, 207, 230, 235, 239

Ravens (St. Benedict's Men's College football team), 47

Reagan, Nancy, 222, 229, 354n28

Reagan Democrats, 6, 195, 236, 240

Reagan, Ronald W., 1, 2, 3, 6, 70, 87–88, 105, 110, 118, 187, 190, 191, 195, 196, 203, 208, 211, 216, 226, 229, 232, 234, 246, 254, 286, 309n33, 350n2

1976 presidential campaign, 195–198, 215, 225

1980 presidential campaign, 114, 196, 211–218, 219, 225–226, 234, 237, 240, 273, 352n19

presidential administration, 18, 219–222, 225, 226, 228, 229, 230, 234, 239, 241, 245–247, 249, 251, 252, 255, 256, 258, 265, 267, 269, 275, 288, 289, 354n28, 355nn35–36, 357–358nn50–52, 359n55

Reaganism/Reaganites, 3, 4, 118, 237, 246, 247, 254, 255, 258, 263, 265, 269, 270, 273, 287, 288

Reaganomics, 216

Reconstruction, 64, 100, 110, 161

Red Ball Express, 33–34, 143

Redenbaugh, Russell, 249–250, 255, 264, 266, 267, 269, 371n56, 372n63

Redlands University, 51

Redskins (football team), 51–52

Reed, Ishmael, 308n19

Reed, Samuel S., 8, 99–101, 108–110, 116, 118, 121, 313nn63–66, 316n85, 318n92, 319n98, 319n102

refuseniks, 2, 165

Rehnquist, William, 251

Remagen, Germany, 36

Renton Record-Chronicle, 107

Republican National Committee, 106, 142, 144, 145, 147, 152–153, 159, 171–172, 176, 180–182, 185, 189, 201, 203, 207, 209, 210, 211, 212, 214, 216, 219, 222, 226–227, 274, 287, 336n62

Republican Party, 1, 3, 4–6, 18–19, 22, 58–60, 65, 66–67, 69, 85, 87, 100–101, 104, 106, 117–118, 123, 128, 135–136, 142, 146, 148, 161–163, 164, 168, 171, 176, 190, 194–196, 199, 200, 207–210, 211–212, 214, 216, 217, 220, 221, 229–231, 235–236, 238, 243, 252, 261, 270, 272, 278, 279, 281–287, 289–290

Republic of China, 165

Reuters news service, 258
Revised Philadelphia Plan. *See under*
    Philadelphia Plan
Reynolds, Earl Thomas, 60, 61, 301n53
Reynolds, William Bradford, 196, 220–
    221, 246
Reynoso, Cruz, 263–264, 266–267, 269
Rhine River, 36
Rhodes, John, 198
Rich, Spencer, 139
Richard M. Nixon Library, 72
Richland, Washington, 84–86, 91, 167
Richmond, Virginia, 138, 171
Riesel, Victor, 132, 154, 324n19, 324n21,
    336n66
Ritchie, Daniel L., 260, 297n3, 369n46
Riverside, California, 57, 69, 78
Roberts, John, 245
Robertson, Pat, 234
Robeson, Paul, 280
Robinson, Jackie, 18, 30, 50
Robinson, Raymond, 206
Rochester, New York, 84, 94, 200, 241
Rockefeller, Nelson, 95, 104–105, 109,
    116, 157, 162, 173, 190–192, 194,
    196, 198, 209, 211
Rockefeller Fund, 174
Rockets (football team), 50
Rockhurst College (Kansas City), 49
Romney, George, 120, 325n23
Rookard, James, 33–34, 296n62
Rooney, Mickey, 24
Roosevelt, Eleanor, 19
Roosevelt, Franklin Delano, 24, 28, 66,
    124, 135, 280
Roosevelt, Theodore, 20
Rosebush, James, 222, 353n28
Ruble, Web, 98
Rule, Ann, 116
Rumford, William Byron, 81–83, 87, 281
Rumsfeld, Donald, 189, 345n54
Russell, Kansas, 67
Rustin, Bayard, 5
Rutgers University, 128, 222
Rutherford, New Jersey, 170
Rye, Eddie, Jr., 8, 117, 319n101

Sacramento, California, 68–70, 87, 129,
    277

Safire, William, 219, 337n71
Saint-Lô, France, 33
San Antonio, Texas, 52–53, 170
San Diego, California, 105–106, 121, 218
San Francisco, California, 73–74, 83, 124,
    128, 146, 171, 186, 188, 308n19
San Francisco 49ers, 50, 55
San Juan Hill, Battle of, 20
San Quentin (California prison), 18, 27
Santa Ana, California, 51
Santa Fe Railroad, 11, 24, 47, 60, 70
Savannah, Georgia, 284
Scalia, Antonin, 251
Scates, Shelby, 112
Schell, Joe, 82
Schoeppel, Andrew, 42
Schwarzkopf, H. Norman, 262
Schweiker, Richard S., 137, 197–198
Schwerner, Michael, 217
Scotland, 32
Scott, Charles, 45–46
Scott, Elisha, 41–42, 44, 58, 280, 298n16
Scott, John, 45–46
Scott, Stanley, 146, *168, 169,* 176, 188–189,
    192, 337n74, 337n77, 339–340n10
Scranton, William, 188, 344n50, 350n1
Seahawks (defunct football team), 53
Seale, Bobby, 95
Sears, Roebuck and Company, 175, 222
Seattle, Washington, 8, 98, 100–101,
    103–104, 107, 109–112, 115–116,
    132–133, 141, 152, 167, 178, 262,
    275, 277
Seattle Chamber of Commerce, 133
Seattle Port Commission, 110
Seattle Post-Intelligencer, 97, 112
Seattle Public Radio, 275
Seattle-Tacoma Airport, 133
Seattle Urban League, 116
selective patronage, 93–94
self-help (civil rights philosophy), 22, 79,
    80, 85, 88–89, 91, 93–94, 97, 101,
    103–106, 116, 119, 121, 122, 172,
    174, 184, 225, 235, 281, 284
Selma, Alabama, 151, 285
Senate. *See* US Senate
Senegal, 138, 224
Sexton, Edwin T., Jr., 176
Shabazz, Malik. *See* Malcolm X

Shawnee County, Kansas, 62, 65
Shelby, Richard, 283
Shenk, Henry, 23
Shepard, Alan, 164
Sherman, Lewis, 87–88, 309n32
Shultz, George P., 121, 128–130, 137–
    139, 141–142, 145, 155, 158, 159,
    320n109, 323nn13–14, 324n19,
    325nn23–24, 326n26, 326nn28–
    30, 327n31, 327–328nn34–35,
    328–329nn37–38, 331n46, 333n54,
    335n60, 339n7
Sicily, 28, 32
Silberman, Laurence, 128, 131, 138, 140,
    146, 179, 323n17, 328n35
Silent Sell-Out (Arthur Fletcher),
    176–181
Simon, Paul, 250, 266, 270, 364n18,
    372n60, 373n74
Simpson, Alan K., 218, 225–226, 352n19,
    355n33, 355n35, 361n76, 363n14
Sims, Harold R., 167
Skrentny, John David, 136
Small Business Administration, 119, 181,
    189, 222, 223, 225, 228, 233–234,
    242, 251, 275, 354n29, 376n89
Smith, J. Clay, Jr., 219
Smith, Johnny, 52
Smith, Ray, 101, 313n68
Smith, Richard H., 110, 317n88
Smith, Sam, 98
Smith, William A., 42–43, 59, 65,
    302n62
Smithsonian Institution, 219
Snyder, Cameron, 54, 300n36, 301n38
Snyder, Tom, 273
Society for Victorious Living, 181, 263
Soul City, 94–95, 195
South Carolina, 230, 238, 239, 289
Southern Christian Leadership
    Conference, 150, 177
Southern Strategy, 1, 4, 6, 118, 123, 135,
    146, 148, 153, 157, 158, 162, 195,
    196, 201, 239, 281, 288, 326n26
Southwestern College (Kansas), 49–50
Soviet Union, 2, 28, 165, 224, 262, 282
Sowell, Thomas, 220, 279
Spanish–American War, 20
Sparrows Point, 129–130

Spokane County, Washington,
    Republican Convention, 101
Spokane Spokesman-Review, 106
Spottswood, Stephen, 146–149
Sprague, David, 112
Staats, Elmer, 127, 130, 136, 138, 139, 141,
    322n9, 323n17, 326n28, 328n35
State Department, 194
St. Benedict's Men's College, 46–49
Steele, Michael, 278, 287
Steele, Shelby, 220
Steinbeck, John, 68
St. Elizabeth Medical Center (Yakima,
    Washington), 242
Stennis, John, 249
Sterling, Alton, 243
Stevens, John P., 251
St. Louis, Missouri, 48, 171, 178, 296n71
St. Louis Memorial Arch, 124
St. Louis Post-Dispatch, 156
St. Petersburg Times, 261
Strait of Dover, 32
Student Nonviolent Coordinating
    Committee, 95, 205
St. Vith, Belgium, 34
Stydahar, Joe, 52–53
Sugrue, Thomas, 70
Sullivan, Leon, 93–94, 119, 160, 186,
    189, 279
Sullivan, Louis, 257
Summer, Donna, 232
Sumner School (Topeka), 45
Sununu, John, 252–253, 256
Supreme Court. *See* US Supreme Court

Tacoma, Washington, 107, 133
Taft, Robert A., 66, 162, 282
Taft, Robert A., Jr., 147
Tait, Don, 117
Taiwan, 165
Taliaferro, George, 53
Tarzan of the Apes, 15–16
Tasty Baking Company, 93
Taylor, Quintard, 231
Telegraph Avenue (Berkeley), 74
Templar, George, 60
Temple, Shirley, 2, 115
Temple University, 138
Tennessee, 201, 214, 236, 256